Speak for Britain!

*A New History of the
Labour Party*

Electoral Reform in War and Peace 1906–1918

The Making of Modern British Politics 1867–1945

The Tories and the People 1880–1935

Lloyd George

Women and the Women's Movement in Britain 1914–1959

State and Society: British Political and Social History 1870–2007

Storia Della Gran Bretagna 1789–1990
(Britain since 1789: A Concise History)

The March of the Women:
A Revisionist Analysis of the Campaign for Women's Suffrage, 1866–1914

A Companion to Modern European History 1871–1945
(editor)

The Pankhursts:
The History of One Radical Family

'Hurrah for the Blackshirts!':
Fascists and Fascism in Britain between the Wars

'We Danced All Night':
A Social History of Britain between the Wars

Speak for Britain!

A New History of the Labour Party

MARTIN PUGH

THE BODLEY HEAD
LONDON

Published by The Bodley Head 2010

2 4 6 8 10 9 7 5 3 1

Copyright © Martin Pugh 2010

Martin Pugh has asserted his right under the Copyright, Designs
and Patents Act 1988 to be identified as the author of this work

First published in Great Britain in 2010 by
The Bodley Head
Random House, 20 Vauxhall Bridge Road,
London SW1V 2SA

www.rbooks.co.uk

Addresses for companies within the Random House Group Limited can be found at:
www.randomhouse.co.uk/offices.htm

The Random House Group Limited Reg. No. 954009

A CIP catalogue record for this book
is available from the British Library

ISBN 9781847920089

The Random House Group Limited supports The Forest Stewardship
Council (FSC), the leading international forest certification organisation. All our titles that are
printed on Greenpeace approved FSC certified paper carry the FSC logo. Our paper procurement
policy can be found at www.rbooks.co.uk/environment

Mixed Sources
Product group from well-managed
forests and other controlled sources
www.fsc.org Cert no. TT-COC-2139
© 1996 Forest Stewardship Council
FSC

Typeset by Palimpsest Book Production Limited,
Grangemouth, Stirlingshire

Printed and bound in Great Britain by
Clays Ltd, St Ives plc

For
Fran, Hannah and Alastair

Contents

Preface and Acknowledgements   ix

Author's Note   xiii

1   *'The votes of the football crowds'*
Explaining the Rise of the Labour Party   1

2   *'Lily-livered Methodists'*
The Origins of the Labour Party   14

3   *'No bigger than a man's hand'*
The Foundation of the Labour Party   37

4   *'Not a single Socialist speech'*
Labour's Edwardian Breakthrough   60

5   *'Come to your country's aid'*
Labour and the Great War   100

6   *'Dollar Princess'*
The Emergence of a National Party in the 1920s   128

7   *'Aristocratic embrace'*
Labour in Power   164

8   *'Further from Socialism'*
The General Strike and Mass Unemployment, 1925–1931   184

9   *'Reversal of Parts'*
From Crisis to Popular Front, 1932–1939   217

10 *'Speak for England'*
    Labour and the Second World War   257

11 *'We are the masters now'*
    Labour, Consensus and Affluence, 1945–1959   286

12 *'A grand conception'*
    Labour in the Wilson Era, 1960–1976   319

13 *'Forward march halted'*
    Labour in Decline, 1976–1994   353

14 *'She's changed it all'*
    Tony Blair, Lady Thatcher and New Labour, 1994–2007   387

    Notes   415

    Bibliography   437

    Index   453

Preface and Acknowledgements

Readers and reviewers of this book should be aware that it is neither an heroic nor an in-house account; it is not an attempt to debate the current dilemmas of the Labour Party (though it may throw some light on them) or to predict the outcome of the 2010 general election and its consequences; nor is it intended as a history of Labour governments (though it naturally takes account of the activities of governments to the extent that they have impacted on the party). It is an attempt to analyse the evolution of the Labour Party since its origins in the late Victorian period with a view to explaining its development from a modest sectional party to a major national one. Until relatively recently it was difficult to write a rounded history of the party because the primary material was heavily biased towards national politics and national leaders. Now the availability of the records of many constituency Labour parties has corrected the problem and altered the picture. For example, the split between Bevanites and Gaitskellites, which appeared to dominate national politics in the 1950s, was scarcely reflected at local level. The suspension of electoral activity under the party truce during the Second World War, when the Labour leaders became deeply involved in the Churchill coalition government, made only a marginal impact in the constituencies where the party maintained a remarkable level of activity in preparation for its sweeping success in 1945; Labour's parliamentary leaders had so little idea what was happening in the country that their victory took them by surprise.

On the other hand, despite being a history of the party, the book does not neglect or minimise the role of leadership. Indeed, an historical perspective suggests that Labour's perennial problems with leadership have been a significant impediment to its success. Basically the party tends to pick the wrong leaders and, in complete contrast to the Conservatives, tends to retain them when they are well past their sell-by date. Like all political movements Labour celebrates its heroes and demonises its villains, but dispassionate historians are not obliged to follow suit. At the party's conference at Manchester in 2008 delegates were treated to presentations about four famous Labour figures, several of which were grotesque misrepresentations; Fiona McTaggart MP reconstructed Barbara Castle as a feminist pioneer though she devoted most of her long career to avoiding feminism, while David Blunkett claimed that 'Tony Blair and Gordon Brown are both proud to be Bevanites'. The present volume takes a more realistic look at the personalities. This means, for example, that Clement Attlee, who has been given an easy ride by most historians because of his undoubted achievements as prime minister, is exposed as an inadequate party leader who was lucky to be at the top in 1945, largely threw it away by 1951, and hung on until 1955 when he had nothing to contribute. Conversely, while by no means overlooking the shortcomings of the much-reviled Ramsay MacDonald, both as an executive figure and as a party manager, the book recognises his achievement as Labour's outstanding strategist and public voice in the early decades.

Readers who study the notes may be surprised to see that in addition to constituency material, the national party records, party publications and the papers of leading Labour politicians, including recent leaders such as Michael Foot and Neil Kinnock, I have made use of the papers of some non-Labour politicians. The explanation for this is partly that I have indirectly been studying the subject since I researched my PhD thesis nearly forty years ago and have accumulated a wide range of relevant material on modern British political history. But there is a more deliberate calculation too. Many studies suffer from being confined to what appear to be immediately relevant sources, which is understandable as the primary sources for modern history are simply enormous. However, this narrows the perspective, inhibits the range of questions posed and sometimes makes the answers inevitable. Yet it is scarcely possible to understand any one political movement and to explain satisfactorily its failures and successes without understanding its relationship with other contemporary movements and causes. For example, my previous work on the women's suffrage movement reflected its interactions with the political parties and other issues by contrast with narrowly defined studies whose conclusions tend to be limited and predictable. I was more explicit in writing about fascism in interwar Britain. This is a subject traditionally treated as a distinctly self-contained phenomenon, indeed as having little connection with proper British history. But by moving beyond the small fascist organisations to understand how extensively the arguments and personnel of fascism reflected wider political debates and overlapped with other organisations, I was able to place the phenomenon in a wider and more credible perspective. In the same spirit I have deliberately tried to avoid writing a history of the Labour Party in a vacuum. I do not think its long-term evolution, character and success can adequately be explained except by examining the interactions and common ground with other movements, and by this I do not mean the endless friction with the Communists and the ILP in the 1920s and 1930s, but the relationship between Labour and socialist politics, on the one hand, and mainstream Liberalism and mainstream Conservatism, on the other, which has been a central feature from the late Victorian era to the present day. The three parties react to similar trends, exchange personnel and embrace common ideas despite expressing them in different languages. This approach militates against the heroic style of history, but I hope that by taking a different perspective it is possible to offer a more interesting and credible explanation for the remarkable political phenomenon that is the British Labour Party.

To cover Labour's history from Keir Hardie to Tony Blair is an ambitious undertaking and I am obviously indebted to much original research and writing notably by Duncan Tanner, David Howell, Andrew Thorpe, Paul Ward, David Marquand, Patrick Seyd, Paul Whiteley and the late Ben Pimlott as well as younger scholars including Richard Toye, Lewis Mates, Greg Burke and Andrew Walling, though this is not to imply that they would endorse my interpretation of Labour Party history.

I am grateful to Churchill College, Cambridge for permission to use the papers of Neil Kinnock, to Francis Beckett for the John Beckett manuscript autobiography, and to the People's History Museum and Labour History Archive for permission to quote from the Michael Foot Papers and reproduce photographs held in Manchester. The picture of Tony Blair and others during the 1997 election campaign is reproduced courtesy of Getty Images. I would also like to acknowledge the assistance of librarians and archivists at the Labour History Archive in

Manchester, the British Library of Political and Economic Science, Churchill College, Cambridge, the National Archives at Kew, the House of Lords Record Office, Scottish Archives, the Mitchell Library, Glasgow, Birmingham Central Library, Manchester City Library, University of Huddersfield Archives, Kent CRO, West Yorkshire Archives, London Metropolitan Archives, Durham CRO, Newcastle RO, the Borthwick Institute, York University, the British Library Newspaper Library, and the Modern Records Centre at Warwick. In particular I would like to recognise the help given to me by Phil Dunn at the People's History Museum in preparing the photographs, Andrew Riley at Churchill College Archives, the archivists and staff at the British Library of Political and Economic Science who, in my many visits, provided a consistently efficient and friendly service that could not be improved upon, and last, but by no means least, Darren Treadwell at the Labour History Archive in Manchester who was immensely knowledgeable, helpful and good-humoured.

Author's Note

The title of the book is adapted from the famous remark by L.S. Amery in the House of Commons on 2 September 1939. When the prime minister, Neville Chamberlain, sat down after failing to say that Britain would honour her pledge to support the Poles, now being bombed by Hitler, Amery called across the chamber 'Speak of England!' as Arthur Greenwood rose to reply for the Labour Party.

I

'The votes of the football crowds': Explaining the Rise of the Labour Party

On 27 February 1900, 129 delegates gathered at the Farringdon Street Memorial Hall in London, disparagingly described by Robert Blatchford as 'that cathedral of Nonconformity', to establish the Labour Representation Committee. The *Clarion*, reluctant to call it a 'United Labour Party' characterised the LRC as 'a little cloud, no bigger than a man's hand'.[1] Rejecting both socialist efforts to commit the new organisation to the class war and trade unionist proposals designed to leave future Labour MPs 'entirely free on all purely political questions', the meeting managed to agree only on creating 'a distinct Labour group in Parliament, who shall have their own whips and agree upon their own policy'.[2] How, why and when did an organisation founded with such modest aspirations, as an essentially *sectional* party for the small minority of workers who belonged to trade unions, develop into a national party, and become one of the two leading parties of government even to the extent of regarding itself, albeit only occasionally, as the natural party of government?

Over the years writers on the Labour Party have approached the subject in six basic ways: wide-ranging narrative histories of elections and ministries, biographical studies of the heroes and villains of the movement, detailed anatomies of the party's institutions, local studies of the rise of Labour in specific towns and regions, analyses of the movement's ideas and programme, and research into particular stages or problems in the evolution of the party. However, in February 2000 the party's centenary came and went, adding several new volumes to a mountain of scholarship but leaving us without a convincing overall explanation for the evolution of what is a rather unusual political phenomenon. It has always been tempting to measure British Labour by a template developed by social scientists in the context of

Continental socialist parties. On this basis the British Labour Party tends to fall short because it never quite developed the mass membership and comprehensive grass-roots organisation of those parties, and was never as clear ideologically, never wholly agreed about its socialism. This is hardly surprising; the British Liberal and Conservative parties also differ from their Continental equivalents, having evolved in response to different historical and cultural conditions. Much the same is true of Labour. For example, whereas socialists, Radicals and Liberals on the Continent tend to be markedly anticlerical, in Britain left-wing movements have historically embraced the Church in its various forms from Primitive Methodism to Catholicism; even today European socialists find the Labour Party's enthusiasm for involving the churches in education positively bizarre.

It is natural to assume that a party whose origins lay outside the parliamentary system and among people largely excluded from political power would have favoured drastic reform, or even the overthrow, of the existing constitution. Yet the slightest familiarity with British political history after 1918 cannot fail to reveal the absence of the bitter constitutional controversies engendered between Liberals and Conservatives in the Victorian–Edwardian era. Labour not only adapted to the status quo, but leading figures such as Jimmy Thomas and Herbert Morrison rather venerated the British constitution. For most of its life Labour supported the Union with Scotland and Wales and endorsed the electoral system; it quickly dropped its original idea of abolishing the House of Lords; and it was enthusiastic, especially its working-class members, about the monarchy and the empire. Though not widely studied, this habit of accommodation with the system goes a long way to explaining how Labour successfully evolved from its sectional origins into a British national party.

Above all, writing about Labour has been influenced by assumptions about social class. From the outset the party defined itself as the party of the working class – a claim its opponents felt tempted to endorse as it reinforced its reputation for sectionalism and governmental inexperience. Yet the historical record suggests that Labour was always rather less than the party of the working class – but also much more. This is the perspective from which this book is written. To emerge as the working-class party in an industrial, urbanised society, displacing in the process one of the older, bourgeois parties, sounds straightforward enough. Earlier generations of social scientists and historians, influenced by the polarisation of votes between one party based on capital and one party based on labour in the 1950s, assumed that this was a normal condition, perhaps an *inevitable* one; in the elections of 1951 and 1955 over 96 per cent of voters backed the Conservative and Labour parties. Hence the problem resolved itself into an attempt to define and explain at what stage or stages the class consciousness of British workers developed sufficiently to sustain a major political party, perhaps under the influence of industrial strikes or the enfranchisement of the mass of the people.

Yet this approach has always suffered from huge empirical problems. For one thing both the Liberal Party and the Conservative Party proved to be more adaptable and more popular with the mass of the people than this allowed for. It is sobering today to recall that some Victorian observers expected the Conservative Party to disappear after the Parliamentary Reform Acts of 1867 and 1885, which enfranchised only six in ten adult men, along with the other relics of feudalism and the hereditary system. Moreover, the development of a working-class consciousness that could be harnessed for political purposes proved an elusive objective. Some time before the general election of 1945 Hugh Dalton, showing the insight of an ex-Tory, told G. D. H. Cole that Labour would only win power in Britain 'with the votes of the football crowds'; at this, he noted, 'Cole shuddered and turned away'.[3] Dalton grasped that many working men were much less political than socialists assumed and that they were moved by a multitude of social loyalties. Consequently mobilising the workers proved complicated because culturally and politically the British working class constituted several distinct communities, some of which were more susceptible to the appeal of an independent Labour Party than others. As a result Labour's rise proved to be slower in some parts of the country than others and its electoral advance was thus a patchy, regional one rather than a straightforward record of the growth of national class consciousness.

Until comparatively recently historians were reluctant to accept how slow Labour was to benefit from mass participation in the system, even after 1918 and 1928 when all adult men and women finally received the parliamentary vote. It was tempting to assume that before 1914 a large reservoir of natural Labour voters was artificially held back, waiting to be released by parliamentary reform.[4] That this was not so was corroborated by Labour's modest performance after 1918. Between the wars the party's highest share of the vote was 37 per cent in 1929 and 38 per cent in 1935 – an indication that it had not yet won even half of the working-class electors who now constituted around 80 per cent of the population. If politics had polarised neatly along class lines the Conservatives would have been reduced to the status of an almost permanent party of opposition similar to their counterparts in Sweden, whereas in fact they enjoyed power for most of the century because half their vote was working class.

Yet in the 1950s and 1960s historians and political scientists regarded social class as the key to political loyalty and all else as peripheral. Today we are much more sceptical and recognise the 1950s as more like an aberration than the norm. As a result of the apparent disintegration of class-based loyalties since the 1970s academics have become critical of sociologically based explanations that appear to make political loyalty too schematic and artificial. Instead the emphasis has shifted from the general to the particular and to attempts to analyse and explain how political movements articulate their appeal to each section of society and how they build alliances with specific geographical and social communities. From the 1880s onwards the British Conservatives did this through popular organisations like the Primrose League, creating links with workingmen, women and Catholics, integrating them into the system at a time when many did not yet have a vote.[5] In the 1920s Labour extended its reach to middle-class women and Irish voters, a process for which the party's federal structure was well adapted. This approach helps to generate a more credible explanation for the evolution of Labour from a sectional to a national movement not by some sweeping change but by the painstaking construction of alliances and connections.

Finally, the traditional class approach to Labour history has been outflanked by another major development in historical studies. While parliamentary reform created a huge working-class electorate in the interwar period, it also marked the emergence of another majority. By 1928 women had become 52–3 per cent of the British electorate. The gender dimension greatly complicated Labour's advance, but for many years the neglect of women by political scientists meant that the issue barely surfaced in the party's history. The extensive research undertaken by historians into female political activity in recent years has gone a long way to rectifying this weakness, but the extent to which Labour has historically been handicapped and in some ways outflanked by the Conservatives in its approach to women has not been fully appreciated.

A fresh overall explanation for Labour's long-term advance has not only to take account of these new perspectives, but it has also to correct some of the bias encumbering traditional views of the party's history. Labour historiography suffers from a tendency to dwell on the failures, the divisions and the betrayals that have held it back at the expense of the positive reasons for its eventual success. A classic expression of this approach was Ralph Miliband's *Parliamentary Socialism: A Study in the Politics of Labour* (1961) which was undoubtedly stimulating but condemned Labour politicians for compromising with the system and suffering from an innate opportunism. Up to a point Miliband was right, for any appreciation of the party's evolution has to take account of its readiness to work within the British political system rather than trying to overthrow or radically reform it, but this characteristic has to be used positively as part of the explanation, not simply employed polemically to denounce the parliamentarians. One of the themes of the present volume is that we need to go further in correcting the traditional bias by recognising that major aspects of Labour's history that have appeared in a largely negative light really hold a different and more positive significance. For example, assumptions about the negative impact of the General Strike of 1926 still appear to reflect the erroneous contemporary misgivings felt by Ramsay MacDonald who shrank from the crisis for fear that it would damage Labour electorally when it really represented a stage in extending its existing bridgeheads into the working-class community. Similarly the Popular Front campaigns of the 1930s tend to be discussed in the context of the infighting between orthodox Labour and the ILP and Communists, and appear as an heroic but doomed cause characteristic of a movement unable to stem the trend towards appeasement and fascism. This makes the Popular Front unduly narrow and sectarian; from the wider perspective it materially assisted Labour, despite the fears of its leaders at Westminster, in accelerating the shift away from 1920s pacifism, establishing links with the new progressive majority in the country, and articulating its claims to the patriotic high ground, thereby enabling the party to outflank the Tories during the Second World War and at the 1945 election.

Other key aspects of Labour's history have been unaccountably neglected. Take two examples. The negative view of the attitude of the press towards Labour took root in the 1920s when the *Daily Mail* specialised in running scares such as the notorious Zinoviev Letter of 1924, and it has remained lively due to the role of the *Sun* in undermining Neil Kinnock's reputation in the 1992 general election. However, most histories of the party fail to mention the crucial shift of the *Daily Mirror* which abandoned its pro-Conservative stance between 1935 and 1939 to become Britain's leading populist, anti-Establishment, left-leaning, mass-circulation newspaper.[6] In the process the *Mirror* not only added some balance to the national press, but articulated Labour's message among sections of society not usually reached by its semi-official paper, the *Daily Herald*.

In electoral terms Labour's crucial objective lay in extending its appeal into the marginal, socially mixed, suburban constituencies. It is impossible to explain how this was accomplished without considering the dramatic advances that occurred in London where the machine created by Herbert Morrison won a majority on the LCC in 1934 and actually increased it in 1937. However, Morrison's triumphs do not fit comfortably with the conventional picture of the 1930s as a decade of failure by the left and dominance by the National government. Perhaps because of the focus on the divisions and controversies of the 1930s the creation of the Morrison machine has never been the subject of a PhD thesis or monograph and has consequently not generally been recognised as one of the key building blocks on which the Labour landslide of 1945 was founded.

This patchy treatment of Labour history has been repeated in the extensive biographical works. Historians used to experience difficulties in finding adequate sources for books about the Victorian–Edwardian Labour leaders. However, this is far from a complete explanation, especially now that there is a superabundance of material for later generations of Labour politicians. While many biographies are excellent studies in themselves, their cumulative effect has been distorting simply because left-wing individuals have attracted far more attention than right-wingers. Biographies of Stafford Cripps appear at regular intervals. Victor Grayson, who was briefly MP for Colne Valley

(1907–10) and a marginal figure in the party's development, has attracted three biographies, despite the lack of primary sources, because of his reputation as a fascinating failure and as the only true socialist elected to Parliament. Conversely, key figures with a reputation as right-wingers continue to be neglected, notably Jimmy Thomas, a authentic, bucolic, monarchist, imperialist, trade union leader and MP for Derby. Thomas was the subject of a biography as long ago as 1964, but it is widely thought that he left no papers, and few students take the train to Maidstone where the collection is available at Kent County Record Office.[7] An equally central figure, Herbert Morrison, was one of the three men, along with Hugh Dalton and Ernest Bevin, who decisively moulded Labour's fortunes between the wars. Yet although historians commonly criticise the one biography published in 1973, no one seems keen to use the Morrison papers now available in several archives and libraries to write a better one.[8]

Biographical studies of working-class MPs, most of whom emerged via the trade union movement, also contribute to the bias. Historically the role of trade unionists has usually been to enhance the *right-wing* character of the Labour Movement, but this is not always how they emerge from their biographies where their militant and socialist credentials tend to be played up at the expense of their right-wing proclivities. Edwardian and interwar examples include Tom Shaw, Will Thorne, Jack Jones, John Hodge, Will Crooks, James O'Grady and Ben Tillett, all of whom were, to one degree or another, exponents of a Tory-socialist view of politics. Ben Tillett, who managed to combine syndicalism and socialism with a pronounced chauvinism, military conscription and anti-Semitism, might be dismissed as eccentric. But many typical politicians who played a central role in the movement combined left- and right-wing values in a consistent and coherent fashion, championing their class and socialism on the one hand along with class collaboration, patriotism, imperialism and authoritarianism on the other. In fact, this thread runs through Labour history from Edwardians like Will Thorne to interwar figures such as Ernest Bevin, to James Callaghan and George Brown in the post-1945 generation and to more recent leaders including David Blunkett, John Reid and Hazel Blears who have upheld the working-class authoritarian tradition as distinct from the movement's liberal tradition.

Nor has Labour historiography taken full measure of the extent to

which the party became much more than merely a working-class movement by recruiting influential, upper-class men and women, so much
so that it has never really been recognised how much of the Labour
elite emerged from a background in Conservative families. Hugh
Dalton, Stafford Cripps, Hugh Gaitskell, Oswald Mosley and Tony
Blair are famous – or infamous – examples of this phenomenon, but
they represent only the tip of a wider phenomenon.[9] Tribal hostility
towards those such as Ramsay MacDonald, Oswald Mosley and, more
recently, Roy Jenkins and Dr David Owen, who eventually withdrew
from the party, has made it easy to damn *hoc genus omne* as ambitious
careerists who used the movement for personal advance, or even to
write them out of party history altogether. Yet if we are to explain
Labour's evolution into a national party the phenomenon of recruitment has to be seen in a more positive perspective. In 1900 when the
LRC adopted a loose federal structure allowing organisations to affiliate, it created a system well calculated to facilitate the inclusion of
people with varying social backgrounds and ideological perspectives.
Despite the obvious complications arising from Communist entryism,
this was advantageous for a new party that was obliged to foster connections with other political movements from which it would eventually
draw support.

     Unfortunately, the biographers of the middle- and upper-class
recruits have usually passed over the significance of their Conservative
origins and their position within the British Establishment. A succession of biographers of Stafford Cripps have offered little explanation
of his decision to join Labour and found it unnecessary to evaluate
the significance for the Labour Party of the fact that his father, C. A.
Cripps (Lord Parmoor), who was a former Tory MP, joined ten years
earlier; one cheerfully observed 'what finally decided Stafford in favour
of Labour is unknown' and speculated that it was merely a case of
'follow-my-father'.[10] It is as though these recruits do not readily fit the
template implicitly used for depicting Labour leaders and must consequently be seen as marginal or eccentrics rather than as a central
explanatory element in the long-term evolution of the Labour Party.

     Yet the recruitment of supporters from diverse political backgrounds
raises questions about Labour's ideology. How far did the party offer
something distinctive and how far something familiar? Labour history
is often written from the assumption that neither Liberalism nor

Conservatism commanded credibility. However, empirically this does not square with the inability of late Victorian socialism to sustain a major movement. The Edwardian author Robert Tressell depicted the dilemma in his famous novel *The Ragged Trousered Philanthropists* (1911), in which his Hastings painters and decorators debated the merits of the Liberal commitment to free trade and the Conservatives' enthusiasm for tariff reform; for a new party it was difficult to shift the agenda away from these well-worn arguments and tempting to align with one side or the other.

Historians, including the present author, have usually depicted the intellectual and programmatic evolution of the Labour Movement in terms of a synthesis between the Victorian tradition of Radical Liberalism, which Labour effectively inherited following the Liberals' collapse after the First World War, and the socialist-Fabian tradition that emerged during the 1880–1914 period. The synthesis ran strongly though the lives and thought of men such as Keir Hardie and Ramsay MacDonald who plausibly argued that the Radical Liberal tradition was fading as it accomplished its work, leaving Labour to inherit its mantle especially in foreign-imperial affairs, political rights and social reform; they assumed that the steadily gathering crisis of capitalism made this development inevitable. The continuity became obvious in successive generations. William Wedgwood Benn, the father of Tony Benn, sat as a Liberal MP (1906–27) before joining Labour. The Cornish Liberal MP, Isaac Foot, saw two of his sons, Michael and Dingle, join Labour, one in the 1930s, the other in the 1950s.

This explanation of Labour's evolution in terms of a Liberal-socialist synthesis is undoubtedly part of the story. It is sound enough as far as it goes – but it does not take us far enough by any means. For one thing, inheriting the Liberal tradition and the Liberal vote represented at best a limited asset, viable in some regions but inadequate in others. Even in their heyday the Liberals experienced difficulties in carrying some working-class communities, and in major urban-industrial regions including Liverpool–Merseyside, much of Lancashire and Birmingham–West Midlands their support never constituted a sufficient base to enable Labour to overthrow the entrenched populist Toryism.

Moreover, even though socialism imbued many Labour activists with the confidence in the inevitable triumph of their cause, it scarcely offered an electorally popular platform. Accounts of the 'rise of Labour' are often based implicitly, and sometimes explicitly, on the assumption that at some stage the British working class became fully class-conscious and was converted to socialism. Yet it is far from clear that this has ever happened. Why was this so? First, only a modest minority of Victorian workers joined trade unions, and even fewer women; and, despite rapid expansion during the Edwardian period and the Great War, union membership went into a steep decline from 1920 to 1934. The movement represented a vital base for a sectional party but never enough for one that aspired to win a parliamentary majority. Second, because late Victorian socialists struggled to make their creed credible to a community that had good reasons to feel suspicious of the state and apprehensive about all agents of moral improvement. Admittedly, socialism became more tangible and appealing for workers as a result of the state welfare innovations introduced during the Edwardian period and the First World War, but this was a gradual process. In any case, support for a wider role for the state was to some extent undermined by counter-influences, notably by wage inflation that swept millions of manual workers into the income-tax net during the First World War and by the new popularity of home-ownership during the interwar period; even at the height of Labour's post-1945 triumphs the Conservatives had begun to consolidate their alliances with the working-class electorate by low income tax and home-ownership.

The elusiveness of the working-class vote is underlined by the long-term electoral record. Labour's real breakthrough was achieved as late as 1945 with 48 per cent of the popular vote. But its periods in office have sometimes rested on a very slight share: 29 per cent in 1924, 37 per cent in 1929, 37–9 per cent in 1974–9, and 36 per cent in 2005. The party has held power with above 40 per cent only during 1945–51, 1964–70 and 1997–2005. This modest historical record would have astonished Victorian and Edwardian observers.

When the Labour Representation Committee was established in 1900 the working class was far from being a cohesive, class-conscious body. It was divided in a number of ways that inhibited the development of a working-class party in terms of varying skills and wages, 'rough' and 'respectable' lifestyles and values, religious and racial loyalties, local economic interests, and regional political cultures that sometimes sustained right-wing traditions and values well into the twentieth century. Variations in working-class politics made it extremely difficult for a new party to make a clean sweep of even the most industrialised, working-class constituencies. In some, Labour competed with an entrenched Liberal-Nonconformist culture of reform and improvement, but in others it faced a boisterous, bucolic Tory populism. The inevitable result was a patchy geographical advance during Labour's early history and a movement that acquired pronounced local and regional characteristics. The tactics that worked in Lancashire were less relevant in County Durham; Labour was not the same party in London as it was in Yorkshire; its advance in the West Midlands came later than in South Wales. In effect, as a new party Labour was obliged to adapt to the prevailing local or regional culture in its efforts to gain a footing in territory currently occupied by one or other of the older parties. As a result the character of local Labour organisations varied considerably, reflecting their success in mobilising support among trade unionists, Nonconformists, Co-operatives, Catholics, the Irish and women, to take some obvious examples. In effect Labour did not transform working-class political culture so much as adapt to it.

This habit of adaptation and accommodation to existing culture and to the formal institutions of British politics is destructive of the heroic element in explanations for the party's historical rise, but it offers the most realistic means of accounting for Labour's success. We are so familiar with the idea of political parties in perpetual conflict with each other that we often forget how misleading this impression is, partly because party propaganda is designed to represent marginal differences as fundamental, and because historically the parties inter-acted so extensively with one another that they share a good deal of common ground. These relationships inevitably proved to be crucial for Labour as a new party struggling to establish itself in territory occupied by its older rivals. The idea of a common Liberal-socialist tradition commands immediate credibility given that some of the best-known figures in the early Labour Movement, including Keir Hardie, Ramsay MacDonald, Arthur Henderson and Philip Snowden, emerged from this milieu and could have become Liberal MPs; among other things they carried enthusiasm for free trade, temperance, Irish Home Rule, social reform and land reform into the Labour Party.

Historians have also recognised the importance of the Liberal–Conservative relationship, though they have not studied it much. It was, in fact, a vital formative force at several stages in modern British history. After Gladstone's conversion to Home Rule in 1886 a substantial part of Liberal personnel defected to Conservatism as Liberal Unionists. After 1904, when the Conservative Party was being transformed into a party of tariff reform by Joseph Chamberlain, a number of Tories, notably the young Winston Churchill, moved across to the Liberals. During the interwar period the Conservatives capitalised on Liberal decline and anti-socialism to absorb much of middle-class Liberalism, including many Liberal MPs, initially via the Lloyd George coalition and as National Liberals after 1931.

However, the third relationship between the Tory and Labour or socialist traditions has been much less recognised and not always taken seriously. Yet it was – and remains – a crucial phenomenon without which it is impossible to offer a plausible and complete explanation for the rise of Labour over the long term. The significance of the Tory-socialist tradition can be understood at several distinct levels. In the first place it loomed large among the *personnel*, that is, the recruitment of men and women from upper-class, Conservative backgrounds into the party especially between the First World War and the 1930s. Apart from adding enormously to Labour's credibility as a potential governing party, these recruits were, in many cases, intellectually formidable people who played a key role, notably in the Attlee government, so much so that without the ex-Conservatives the socialist element in the party would have been distinctly weaker.

Secondly, the common ground between Toryism and socialism was significant in terms of the *ideas* of the movement. The two traditions embraced a whole range of attitudes towards protectionism, immigration, monarchy, empire, conscription, civil liberties, alcohol, the churches, electoral and constitutional questions, the Union with Scotland and Wales and, later, Europe. Historically, Tories and socialists often found themselves sharing common assumptions in these areas in opposition to the Liberal-Radical tradition.

Thirdly, the tradition had a vital *electoral* dimension in that Labour's patchy advance in some regions and localities is explicable in terms of its capacity to accommodate itself to the prevailing populist Toryism in working-class communities. It is tempting to dismiss this as a

Victorian tradition that simply became anachronistic in the new century, but it proved remarkably durable and remained vigorous right to the end of the twentieth century, though it became less deferential, more secular and issue-oriented in the process. As late as 1997 right-wing working-class voters formed a key part of New Labour's success in overthrowing Thatcherism.

The inevitable consequence of Labour's complex intellectual inheritance has been not only marked regional variations in the movement's character, but also a fluctuating profile at the national level. For example, during the 1920s the strength of the reaction against the Great War and the prominence of Ramsay MacDonald and George Lansbury pushed the Liberal-socialist tradition into prominence. Conversely, during both the First and Second World Wars the national crisis fostered working-class patriotism and the common ground between Labour and Toryism. During the post-1945 period Labour's socialists credentials were more central than at any other time, but in external affairs this period saw the party becoming distinctly right wing and nationalist. Since then the party has fluctuated between periods in office, when the Labour right has largely maintained its dominance, followed by a sharp reassertion of left-wing ideas when in opposition in protest against the leadership's growing tendency to ignore the views of the rank and file as recorded at annual conferences. In this context the phenomenon of Tony Blair and 'New Labour' becomes more comprehensible. For although Blair's capture of the party leadership was an extraordinary coup, when placed in a coherent historical framework his leadership and his ideology seem much less of an aberration than would otherwise be the case. Coming as he did from a Conservative background with almost no political values except those of a typical middle-class, Conservative-leaning family, Blair differed from most earlier recruits in avoiding their conversion to the values of the Labour Movement; but with that qualification he stood squarely in an established tradition of Labour expansion and evolution without which the modest, sectional LRC of 1900 would hardly have grown into a credible, national, governing party.

2

'Lily-livered Methodists':
The Origins of the Labour Party

For British Radicals and socialists the mid-1880s was a stirring time. In 1884 a new Parliamentary Reform Act, designed to extend the vote to several million manual labourers, had been held up by the peers, provoking an agitation for abolition of the House of Lords who eventually backed down. New socialist organisations including the Fabian Society and the Social Democratic Federation were emerging, which, though small, appeared to be pushing at a partly open door. At the 1885 general election one of Gladstone's rising ministers, Joseph Chamberlain, attacked the upper classes as idle parasites – language not used hitherto in such circles – and launched an 'Unauthorised Programme' to reduce the privileges of landowners and the Church and to relieve mass distress by state interventionism. By 1886 this had been overtaken by Gladstone's dramatic conversion to Home Rule for Ireland. But far from being merely a constitutional and strategic question, Home Rule, backed by a mass agitation, was interpreted in England as portending a great social revolution, for the infringements made on private property ownership in Ireland were seen as capable of extension, first to Scotland and then to England. Although Home Rule was frustrated by the House of Lords in 1886, it fostered the conviction that workingmen, however poor and disadvantaged, could seek redress of their grievances, even under an aristocratic and monarchical political system, if they organised themselves.

However, this brief, exhilarating phase turned out to be but an episode in a remarkably protracted struggle for popular political participation that had been going on since the end of the eighteenth century. Although the British system was open to pressure, change proved slow in coming. In 1832 the First Reform Act had consolidated the status quo by incorporating middle-class men as voters by means of a property qualification, but largely excluded the working class. During the 1830s and 1840s the Chartists had waged mass campaigns demanding manhood suffrage and payment of MPs, presented huge petitions to Parliament and staged mock elections to elect their own representatives. Although Chartism petered out as a movement in 1848, its ideas persisted and even began to bear fruit in 1858 when one Chartist demand – the abolition of property qualifications for MPs – became law. In 1866 mass agitation for the vote was revived by the Reform League, and, with Gladstone effectively putting himself at the head of the popular campaign, Parliament enacted a second reform bill in 1867 thereby increasing the number of voters from 1.3 million to 2.4 million. As the new voters were largely working class, this transformed the electorate in some industrial centres; in Newcastle, for example, it increased from 6,000 to 21,000. By 1885 the Third Reform Act had created an electorate of 5.7 million men, and even votes for women was now firmly on the agenda.

In the event, however, no further measures were achieved until 1918. Yet even after 1885 only six in ten adult men were on the electoral register at any one time, mostly as 'household' voters; they were heads of households who had twelve months' continuous residence at a given address, a requirement which effectively excluded many young and unmarried men in all classes who lodged or lived with parents. Admittedly, the extension of elective local government through the creation of school boards, county councils, parish, urban and rural district councils in the later nineteenth century created fresh opportunities for workingmen, especially as the property qualification for councillors was abolished in 1878, though not until 1894 for Poor Law Guardians. However, as a municipal voter had to be a ratepayer *fewer* workingmen qualified for a local government vote than for a parliamentary one. Meanwhile, long working hours handicapped many workingmen; the polls opened at eight when they were already at work and closed at eight in the evening, leaving many of those who had to walk miles to their place of employment perhaps only half an hour to vote. It also proved expensive to stand for election as candidates were required to pay the fees of returning officers; successful candidates spent £1,000 or more on a campaign, and anything from £100 to £300 annually for an agent who kept their supporters' names on the register. Obviously these sums were far beyond the means of the workingman.

Thus, despite the late Victorian reforms, the political system did not yet reflect the huge social changes that had transformed Britain into an industrial and urban society in which around 80 per cent of the population were manual workers. To contemporaries industrialisation seemed to provide ideal conditions for the emergence of a mass organisation of workers. Back in 1852 Karl Marx had forecast that universal suffrage would be a 'socialistic measure' in England: 'its inevitable result, here, is the supremacy of the working class'.[1] Yet not only was a fully democratic franchise slow in coming, but by the 1880s it was evident that the British workers were far from being a monolithic class and not easily organised for common political action. In their divisions lies much of the explanation for the slow emergence of a Labour Party.

We now recognise that an earlier generation of historians exaggerated the impact of the Industrial Revolution on British society. By the late Victorian period much of industry was still small-scale, the average workshop employing twenty-nine men in 1898. As a result the influence of employers remained strong, and many manual workers aspired to set up as small employers themselves. While this did not prevent them developing aspirations to separate class representation, for a long time it compounded their affinity with Liberalism and with Gladstone as a vehicle for their ambitions. In any case, much of society remained in a pre-industrial condition because major sectors, such as the building industry, had not been exposed to the technological innovations affecting manufacturing. Traditional occupations remained very large, notably domestic service which employed nearly two million people by the end of the century, effectively excluding large parts of the working class from independent political organisation. Above all, workers were divided by their skills, or lack of skills, and their incomes varied accordingly.

Working-class communities were also divided between what contemporaries recognised as the 'respectable' and the 'rough'. Working-class respectability was not determined simply or primarily by income and occupation but by a wide range of behaviour and values. The respectable workingman might attend church or chapel, possess a good set of clothes for Sunday wear, manage his wages so as to avoid using pawnbrokers and moneylenders, patronise co-operative societies, savings banks and building societies, contribute to friendly society or insurance policies, pay the rent regularly, abstain from alcohol or at least avoid getting drunk, eschew premarital sex, never swear, gamble or beat his wife, read books, pamphlets and newspapers, frequent libraries, mechanics institutes, concert halls and debating societies, and send his children to school even when it was not compulsory to do so.

The aspiration to live up to these ideals was very widespread in working-class society and it had major political implications. By the 1860s and 1870s respectability was strongly associated with Gladstonian Liberalism because Gladstone championed the right to vote for workers who had shown themselves to be fit to be admitted within 'the pale of the constitution'. He regarded improving workingmen as a vehicle for raising the moral tone of politics and he wanted to exempt them from income tax. Up to 1900 the idea of the small state and low taxation was regarded as a *working-class* interest because by and large government expenditure benefited the higher classes while taxation was drawn disproportionately from taxes on consumption paid by poorer people. Consequently, Gladstonianism was not an anachronism waiting to be swept aside but a popular creed.

On the other hand, working-class respectability proved to be compatible with socialist politics, indeed, it was a key factor in the emergence of the early movement. 'Socialism is not to be found in the slummy and most miserable quarters of towns,' observed Ramsay MacDonald in 1911, 'but in those quarters upon which the sun of prosperity manages to shine. It is the skilled artisan, the trade unionist, the member of the friendly society, the young workman who reads and thinks who are the recruits to the army of Socialism.'[2] Many members of the Independent Labour Party were self-improving workingmen who had elevated themselves to lower-middle-class occupations as clerks, insurance collectors, salesmen, journalists, elementary schoolteachers, telephonists and shop assistants through self-education, thrift and abstention. MacDonald himself, though born into poverty in 1866 as the illegitimate son of a Scottish ploughman and a seamstress, followed a succession of non-manual occupations as a pupil-teacher, secretary, journalist and lecturer.

Consequently, socialists sometimes looked askance at those who neglected respectable standards and aspirations. In 1895 John Bruce Glasier, the party chairman, deplored the decision of Fred Hammill to retire as Independent Labour Party candidate in Newcastle to run

a public house: 'Twill be hard on us if Lab[our] Agitators descend to
the level of prize fighters and footballers.'[3] His remarks reflected the
centrality of alcohol as a symptom of working-class respectability and
of a wider political outlook. It is a mistake to dismiss Victorian temperance campaigns as merely middle-class attempts to reform the workers,
for many Labour politicians, however keen on state intervention,
insisted that the best immediate way for the workingman to improve
his standard of living was to stop drinking. Keir Hardie, Arthur
Henderson, George Lansbury, David Shackleton, Herbert Morrison,
A. J. Cook, John Maclean and Willie Gallagher were prominent
abstainers among the socialist pioneers. Morrison's mother sent him
to the pub as a boy to keep an eye on his father and report back when
he had had enough. Hardie and Lansbury were deeply affected by
their fathers' drinking because it cast the family into poverty and
consigned their mothers to lives of endless struggle. For Hardie, who
took the pledge as an abstainer at seventeen, temperance was his *first*
political cause; he once asked an audience why they 'robbed themselves of their manhood by swilling in a public house'. Alcohol also
helped to make Henderson, Hardie and Lansbury sympathetic to
women's equality and supportive of their claim to the vote. As a
Nonconformist, Sunday-school teacher and abstainer from alcohol,
smoking and gambling, Arthur Henderson travelled his native North-
East, speaking for the North of England Temperance Society, acquiring
in the process a fine training for his subsequent political work.

Unhappily Henderson was just the sort of figure Robert Blatchford
had in mind when he disparaged ILP socialists as 'lily-livered
Methodists'. Today it is easy to overlook the extent to which temperance complicated the appeal of Labour and socialism in many working-
class communities. During the 1870s, when beer consumption reached
its all-time peak in Britain, one building in every seventy-seven in
London was a pub or beer shop – businesses on which the livelihoods
of thousands of people depended, not to mention the pleasures of
many more. It was widely accepted that a manual worker must
consume beer at regular intervals through the working day to maintain his strength, while the teetotaller was regarded as deficient in
masculinity. Consequently, Labour advocates of temperance were easily
dismissed as apologists for middle-class improvers bent on interfering
with the workingman's pleasures.

Not surprisingly, given the centrality of the drinking culture in Britain, there was no shortage of Labour politicians eager to champion the workingman's right to his drink in language recognisable to Tories. 'Beer is our national drink,' insisted Jack Jones, who became Labour MP for Silvertown in 1918. 'Why should any man be in any degree looked down upon because he likes a glass of beer? The public house is the workingman's club – remember that.'[4] Of course, drink was one thing, alcoholism another. Down the decades a succession of promising Labour leaders, including Victor Grayson and Ben Tillett (who started as a teetotaller) before 1914, Jimmy Thomas between the wars, Arthur Greenwood in the 1940s, and George Brown in the 1960s, ruined their careers at least in part by excessive indulgence in alcohol. This was reflected in the spat between Jimmy Thomas, the famously convivial, self-indulgent Labour member for Derby, and Philip Snowden, the first Labour Chancellor of the Exchequer. A devout Wesleyan Methodist from Yorkshire's West Riding, Snowden had contracted a spinal infection that crippled him for life, but he succeeded in becoming a clerk in insurance and the Inland Revenue. Notorious for adopting a high moral tone, Snowden personified the puritanical side of socialism. 'I have calculated that [Thomas] spends three whole weeks each year attending Labour conferences, and one hundred and fifty days attending lunches and dinners of various societies,' he complained. 'I have calculated, too, that he consumes nine gallons of champagne and that his laundry bill for starched shirts amounts to £18 a year.'[5] This was not intended as a joke. Thomas, an ebullient railwayman who relished his role as a minister and a celebrity, remained unrepentant, scornfully replying that Snowden himself had no vices except smoking Turkish cigarettes and consuming ginger pop – 'this horrible drink' – which was promoted by temperance reformers as an alternative to beer.

Their spat signified the extent to which attitudes towards drink, religion and morality reflected the cultural divide within working-class communities – with which a Labour Party had somehow to come to terms. In industries where employment was irregular or casual, wages low and poverty widespread, much of the population remained too absorbed with the daily race to keep ahead of hunger to sponsor friendly societies, trade unions, co-operative societies and the self-help institutions that sustained labour politics. Instead workers became fatalistic, cynical, conservative, and sceptical about the possibility of improvement offered by both Liberals and socialists. As a result they were more susceptible to the patronage and influence of wealthy landlords and employers. Where employment was associated with naval shipbuilding or armaments manufacture the workers embraced an expansionist, imperialist foreign policy and endorsed the patriotic propaganda of Tory politicians. Similarly, if local manufacturing appeared to be threatened by foreign imports they backed the protectionist policy advocated by some late Victorian Conservatives. Wherever such factors were at work socialists found the going hard, however large the working-class population.

In the absence of collective, institutional structures many working-class communities remained fragmented and lacking in class consciousness. Robert Roberts described his neighbours in late Victorian Salford as being acutely aware of differences of *status* among local families, determined by skilled, unskilled or casual employment, by religious or ethnic allegiances, or even by their residence: 'in our community . . . each street had the usual social rating; one side or one end of that street might be classed higher than another'. Similarly, James Sexton, struggling to organise the workers in the Merseyside docks, became frustrated by the fine distinctions he found among the men who insisted on reserving certain jobs for certain groups: 'in those days Liverpool had a caste system quite as powerful as India', he recalled.[6]

Merseyside was an extreme example of the extent to which religion complicated and influenced the emergence of the Labour Movement. But on the positive side, many socialist pioneers in the North of England emerged from a religious background, especially the Nonconformist churches. The Nonconformists' sense of being outside a political system encumbered by the privileges enjoyed by the upper classes, carried over quite naturally into Radical politics as did the belief in brotherhood and sacrifice for others. Edwardian Labour Party meetings often concluded or began with a hymn such as 'When Will Thou Save the People, Lord' or 'England Arise'. In 1890 one socialist speaker in a County Durham mining community, where Primitive Methodism was strong, was advised: 'We want no Karl Marx and surplus values and that sort of stuff . . . Make it plain and simple . . . and then when tha'rt coming t' finishing up, tha' mun put a bit of "Come to Jesus" in.'[7] Philip Snowden's early popularity was built on

his emotional, revivalist oratory, commonly known as 'Philip's Come
to Jesus'. In his most famous lecture, *The Christ that is to be* (1903),
Snowden reminded his audience that 'the only way to regain earthly
paradise is by the old hard road to Calvary – through persecution,
through poverty, through temptation, by the agony and bloody sweat,
by the crown of thorns, by the agonising death'. Ben Tillett, famous
as a leader of the 1889 London dock strike, reached socialism via an
early life as a Congregationalist and church librarian, and never lost
his preaching style as a politician. He took his favourite text from
Matthew Chapter 2: 'Come unto me all ye who labour and are heavily
burdened and I will give you rest.' Victor Grayson, famously known
as the first man to be elected to Parliament as an unqualified socialist
in 1907, had been trained for the Unitarian ministry at the Home
Missionary College in Manchester and routinely addressed audiences
as though they were revivalist church meetings. In his 1907 campaign,
significantly following a period of religious revivalism in Britain, where
he enjoyed the backing of forty local clergymen, Grayson lifted audiences composed of people living humdrum lives on to a higher plane.
'People just went haywire,' said one observer. 'They went mad at his
meetings – he could grip them.'[8]

However, the influence of religion on Labour should not be exaggerated; it was largely a matter of imparting an evangelical style
and a valuable training in platform work. An evangelical tone was
popular in northern England and Wales but less appreciated in London.
By the late nineteenth century many workingmen had come adrift
from Christianity despite the efforts to build new urban churches. Keir
Hardie, for example, once described socialism as 'the embodiment of
Christianity in our industrial system', but he had actually broken with
the Church in 1884, an event regarded as a step on his conversion to
socialism. Moreover, Nonconformity complicated allegiances in that
it helped to integrate workers into Radical Liberal politics and to this
extent it almost certainly slowed down the emergence of independent
Labour politics in areas such as South Wales and Durham, though
after 1918, with the demise of the Liberal Party, it doubtless accelerated Labour's dominance in such communities.

Despite the prominence of respectable workingmen in the Labour
Movement, those whose values reflected the 'beer and Britannia'
lifestyle, like Jimmy Thomas, suffered no apparent handicap. In his

long career as a union leader and a popular MP Thomas cheerfully set an example, confident that his own members aspired to something similar. Those working-class men who deducted money from their wage packets, before handing them over to their wives, to spend on beer, tobacco and gambling, looked askance at a Labour candidate who made temperance too prominent a part of his programme, putting him in the same category as middle-class do-gooders, clergymen and philanthropists. A boisterous proletarian lifestyle dominated by drunkenness, street-fighting, horse racing, boxing and gambling left many men alienated from Nonconformist Liberalism and forged a bond with the populist brand of Toryism which was consolidated by upper-class men, aristocrats and royalty who acted as patrons for gambling, boxing and horse racing. Their social behaviour sustained a hedonist, masculinist, live-for-the-day approach to life which in turn was complemented by Conservative political values and causes: enthusiasm for national institutions, especially the navy, the empire and the monarchy, scepticism towards state intervention, hostility towards immigrants, foreign workers and imported goods, anti-Semitism, and prejudice against the Irish. Late Victorian Conservatives worked hard to maintain these associations through a local infrastructure including employers whose business sustained jobs in their local community, workingmen's clubs that sold cheap beer, and Primrose League habitations designed to unite the classes in social activities. Without these efforts Tory success in elections in industrial regions including Merseyside, Lancashire, Clydeside and Birmingham would hardly have been possible. After 1885 some of the poorest constituencies in London's East End regularly returned Tory MPs including Rotherhithe, Bow and Bromley, Mile End, Limehouse, Stepney, Bethnal Green North East, Walworth and St George's (Tower Hamlets). London was notoriously irreligious, hostile to temperance, deficient in trade unions, subject to casual employment, affected by immigration from eastern Europe, and aroused by great imperial crises; as such it proved difficult for socialists to organise unless they managed to accommodate themselves to the prevailing culture. When Harry Gosling attempted to win a seat on the London County Council at Rotherhithe in 1895, he was financed by his union, the Amalgamated Society of Watermen and Lightermen. But to his dismay his own members brought bundles of Conservative handbills to his meetings which they rolled into balls to pelt at him. 'The exercise of their craft had made them Tory in outlook,' Gosling explained later. 'This strange contradiction runs through the trade union movement still.'[9] After he lost the election his angry supporters retired to the Progressive Club in Bermondsey and from the roof threw fireworks across the road to the Conservative Club.

In this context Ben Tillett's heartfelt complaint – 'I think we Socialists are about the least understood of all people' – is readily understandable.[10] How did the pioneers articulate the idea of socialism among voters for whom it was a novelty at best and a threat at worst? Tillett wanted workingmen to grasp the notion of surplus value – the sum created by a man's labour over and above the cost of materials that was effectively appropriated by the capitalist. But for many this was too abstract. Others attempted to argue from current issues; George Lansbury suggested that if British governments could fix rents, and thus property values, in Ireland they could equally regulate wages and working hours in England. In an address in Bow and Bromley in 1894 he defined the aims of socialism as replacing the present system, based on ruthless competition and production for profit, with a society in which wealth was equally distributed and labour fairly borne by all. 'The cure [for poverty] is in your own hands. You have witnessed a tremendous increase in the wealth of the country, but you have no share in it.'[11]

Yet Lansbury's pre-1914 audiences remained sceptical about his arguments. He enjoyed an early success as a Poor Law Guardian in Poplar because he was able to initiate a series of tangible reforms including better food, cleaning the workhouse, improved clothing for inmates, light employment to relieve the boredom, and the provision of newspapers, dominoes, chess and a weekly ounce of tobacco for men over sixty.[12] This work cast his political creed into a concrete form appreciated by the electors. However, Lansbury's success in Poor Law elections contrasted with his failure in parliamentary elections in the East End. His verbose, unfocused election literature made little impression on voters who doubtless distinguished between the tangible social reforms they understood and theoretical expressions of socialism.

As a result socialist candidates commonly felt obliged to compromise by presenting their socialism as an extension of the more familiar Radical Liberal programme. For example, in 1885 when John Burns, who then belonged to the unequivocally Marxist organisation the Social Democratic Federation, stood at Nottingham, his programme included the standard Radical cries, free education, Irish Home Rule, adult suffrage and abolition of the House of Lords, as well as the eight-hour day and the nationalisation of railways, mines and land.[13] In his first bid for Parliament in 1888 Keir Hardie's main pitch was to promote himself as a workingman deserving of Gladstone's backing and the Liberal nomination; in his election address he reminded voters that Scotland's seventy-two MPs comprised twenty-one lawyers, eighteen landlords, eight merchants, six shipowners, six professors, five army officers, three manufacturers, two doctors, a schoolmaster, a brewer and a newspaper proprietor. With his bearded, rugged appearance and moving, revivalist eloquence, Hardie looked and sounded like an Old Testament figure; he never used notes but relied on the inspiration of the moment to get his message across to the bleak mining communities of the Lanarkshire coalfield. However, he created a confusing impression, claiming to be a good Liberal but warning that the Liberal Party would soon be 'dead and buried'. His aggressive language and his attacks on the upper classes gave him a reputation for extremism that was quite misleading, for he was genuinely committed to constitutional methods.

In any case, Hardie's conversion to socialism was a protracted and incomplete process from the mid-1880s to the early 1890s. Never very familiar with Marxism, his socialism had no real base in economics. Depicting socialism as 'more an affair of the heart than of the intellect' he expressed it in terms of brotherhood and support for the weaker members of the community. Although Hardie appreciated Marx's emphasis on capitalists as a depraved and corrupt class and endorsed his vision of the historical struggle of the workers, he was more influenced by radical propagandists such as Henry George, author of the widely read *Progress and Poverty* (1884), who saw private property in land as the source of economic inequality and injustice. Hardie also endorsed orthodox ideas about running the economy in terms of free trade and paying off the national debt. In common with many late Victorian Radicals he favoured graduated taxation, especially of landed wealth, and compulsory powers to enable the state and municipalities to acquire land. Consequently, his adoption of independent Labour politics during the 1890s reflected frustration with Liberal prevarication over the eight-hour day and his irritation with their local organisations for not conceding more candidacies to men like himself rather than an alternative ideology.

Hardie's foray into parliamentary elections also underlines the regional character of the early Labour Movement. In Scotland the demand for independent labour representation was closely associated with the cause of Scottish Home Rule which was a reflection of its relationship with Scots Liberalism. Yet although Scotland produced many socialist leaders, they found the country unrewarding partly because trade unionism remained weak and because Liberalism was strongly entrenched. Moreover, the Scottish working class suffered acutely from the divisions between alcohol and respectability, and the political rivalry between the Protestant Unionist majority and the Catholic Irish minority, especially in the west of the country. The split was reflected in football teams catering to the two communities – Rangers and Celtic, Hearts and Hibernians. For years Labour found itself handicapped by sectarian divisions; Scots working-class Protestants leant to the Conservative and Unionist Party, Irish Nationalists saw Labour as splitting the Home Rule vote, many Catholics simply disliked socialism, and the unions feared that the collapse of the Irish economy would force more immigrants into Clydeside and Lanarkshire. Thus, even when the Liberals lost ground in Scotland after 1886 as a result of Home Rule, it was the Conservatives who gained. As a result, by 1900 all seven Glasgow seats were Conservative leaving little room for Labour to develop. When Hardie stood at Mid-Lanark in 1888 he won just 600 votes out of 7,000 cast and he did not persist with elections in his native country; other leading Scots including Ramsay MacDonald and John Bruce Glasier never fought Scottish seats.

Yet Hardie's experience was not untypical for pioneering candidates. John Burns polled 700 votes in 11,000 cast at Nottingham in 1885, while George Lansbury won 203 or 3.8 per cent at Walworth in 1895. Such results threw doubt on the readiness of workingmen to vote for men of their own class, and on the viability of socialism as the basis for a mass party. Opponents found it tempting to disparage socialism as irreligious and immoral, as a threat to marriage, as an agent for free love, as a violent, revolutionary movement, and thus as essentially alien and subversive. At the 1900 general election in Blackburn the local Conservatives plastered the town with posters proclaiming:

'DOWN WITH ATHEISM, SOCIALISM AND ANARCHY'.
Jimmy Thomas recalled: 'When I first came amongst you as an engine
driver I had almost to defend my morality. They said such awful things
about me that I had to bring my wife with me, and she had to make
certain that she had her marriage certificate with her [laughter].'[14]

However, crude prejudice was the least of the difficulties, for
socialism remained handicapped by deeper conceptual problems.
Marxist writings were not widely available in Britain, and the politically aware workingman was more likely to be familiar with Radical
ideas drawn from the English Civil War, Chartism and the Victorian
land reformers. Caught in the debates between Liberal advocates of
free trade and cheap food and Tory enthusiasts for tariffs who claimed
that excluding foreign goods would maximise British jobs, socialists
struggled to articulate their alternative. As late as the Edwardian period
Robert Tressell gave a graphic account of this dilemma in his widely
read book, *The Ragged Trousered Philanthropists*. For those for whom
the state was a remote and vaguely oppressive concept it was genuinely
difficult to envisage what a socialist society really meant. Inevitably
people thought of it in terms of familiar institutions: the Poor Law
system, compulsory education, food taxes and the vaccination of their
children, all of which represented attempts to control and regulate
their lives. Socialists therefore laboured, as did reformers of all kinds,
under the cynicism about politics that afflicted many of the poorest
people and led some of them to sell their votes for a few shillings or
some beers at election times.[15] Even after 1900 collectivism gained credibility only slowly through such innovations as the non-contributory
old-age pensions of 1908; pensions came as a revelation to many
recipients, partly because they offered a tangible benefit without a
punitive element, and also because they proved, contrary to popular
assumptions, that a well-run state did not run out of money.[16]

It was to express socialism in less theoretical and more tangible
terms, and to deflect allegations about its alien quality, that Robert
Blatchford wrote arguably the most effective piece of socialist propaganda of the era, *Merrie England*, in 1894. A *Sunday Chronicle* journalist
who had served in the army for seven years, Blatchford was an unapologetic hedonist who despised puritanical socialists like Hardie whom
he called a 'sanctimonious prig'. From 1891 onwards he played a crucial
role in the dissemination of the new thinking when he published the

Clarion, a weekly paper that sold 40,000 copies at one penny each. Its chief rival, Keir Hardie's the *Labour Leader*, was a more sober and political journal but it struggled financially. Almost alone among socialist papers the *Clarion* was viable, so much so that it even paid contributors ten shillings a column. Blatchford promoted his paper by organising a fleet of Clarion Vans to tour the countryside, and a network of Clarion choirs and Clarion clubs for cyclists and ramblers.

The explanation for the *Clarion*'s success is obvious. It included sports reports, especially on great northern football teams like Bolton Wanderers and Preston North End, as well as pages devoted to theatrical productions and items on the activities of members of the royal family and the aristocracy. In short, the *Clarion* offered readers an equivalent to a normal newspaper in which the politics was leavened with entertainment and titillation. Blatchford understood that his readers enjoyed hearing about the lives of the rich while condemning their wealth at the same time. In 1895 he famously reported on an ostentatious ball held at Warwick Castle for Frances, Countess of Warwick, cheerfully denouncing her annual income of £30,000 at a time when people were starving. To his astonishment the countess turned up at his office where an argument ensued. But Frances purchased £10 worth of books about socialism, joined the Labour Party in 1904 and became a major donor during the 1920s.[17]

In his determination to promote independent representation for labour Blatchford provoked more than just countesses. He tried to prise workingmen away from their Liberal loyalties by giving prominence to issues like the eight-hour day.[18] At the election of 1892 when many Labour men were still angling for Liberal backing to get into Parliament, he announced that 'Labour will rejoice to see Liberals beaten'.[19] Nor was he afraid of criticising the trade unions for aspiring, as he put it, 'to get within the pale of respectability'; and he poured scorn on the tactics of the Fabians for 'the hopeless, spiritless, unclean abortion which they call permeation'.[20] For Blatchford the unions were deluded if they believed they were strong enough to protect the rights of the workers: 'the most that Trade Unionism has secured, or can ever hope to secure, for the workers, is a comfortable subsistence wage'.[21] A strike, he argued, was 'at best a bitter, a painful and a costly thing' and no substitute for political action. He challenged workingmen with their inconsistent behaviour: 'you never ask an employer to lead you during a strike', but during elections 'when you ought to stand by your class, the whole body of Trade Union workers form into blacklegs, and fight for the capitalist'.[22]

However, Blatchford's chief contribution lay in expressing the case for socialism in a digestible form. In *Merrie England*, which sold 700,000 copies at one penny each in the first year and 25,000 in the one-shilling version, he employed a direct, conversational style. The book stood in a tradition of patriotic socialist literature, rooted in the belief that 'at present Britain does not belong to the British: it belongs to a few of the British'. The historical theory behind this varied. Blatchford favoured the view that everything had gone downhill with the Norman Conquest when the land was stolen from the people. Conversely, socialists like William Morris and Henry Hyndman depicted a golden age for labour in the fourteenth and fifteenth centuries. But all agreed that since the late eighteenth century capitalism had diverted the course of British history, destroying a more prosperous and humane society in the process.

Blatchford took as his immediate opponent the 'Manchester School' – code for Victorian economic Liberalism – whose thinking fostered the belief that British prosperity depended on free trade, buying in the cheapest markets, maximising world trade, and investment abroad. Arguing instead for an autarkic economy, Blatchford suggested that competition was wasteful and unnecessary since Britain could produce the food she required at home. Free trade and manufacturing industry, he claimed, had damaged the environment through overproduction and urbanisation; he singled out 'the unhealthy and hideous country like Wigan or Cradley [Heath]' in the Black Country, suggesting that people preferred to live in 'a healthy and beautiful county like Surrey'.[23] Here Blatchford struck a chord with those who believed that Britons had been happier in their pre-industrial past when society was less dynamic but more cohesive because it was based on mutual support rather than on competitiveness and individualism. This placed socialism in a traditional *English* context and distanced it from its alien associations. Conversely, by attacking free trade Blatchford put himself at odds with typical working-class opinion that saw it as a guarantee of cheap food and rising prosperity. The 'Free Breakfast Table', that is, the removal of all duties on basic food items, was a popular Liberal cry and it continued to figure in Labour propaganda up to 1931.

However, during the depression of the 1890s some Conservatives revived protectionism. Edwardian socialists, including Will Thorne and Herbert Morrison, shared their doubts about free trade, recognising the force of Tory criticism that British industries were suffering from foreign competition and that the erection of tariff barriers might boost the domestic market and thus safeguard employment. It was no accident that Thorne and Morrison took their socialism more seriously than most Labour politicians, frankly recognising that control over imports represented a more logical policy for a socialist government than free trade.

Blatchford also tried to defuse hostile propaganda by reminding readers that Britain had already embarked on the route to socialism via legislation that infringed the rights of property owners, the Factory Acts, compulsory education, municipal gas and water works, and, above all, the Post Office which he cited as evidence of the practicability of socialism: 'it is standing proof that a vast and intricate business may be managed by the state without any spur of opposition or profit'.[24] The state simply had to go further down this road by instituting employment schemes for agricultural and general labourers, house-building and acquiring the ownership of land, mines and railways. Although radical for the 1890s this was not wildly adrift from contemporary thinking.

Much of Blatchford's writing also appealed to Tory sentiment, not least his hostility to industry and the 'Manchester School' and his 'Britain for the British' economic strategy. Repudiating Liberal internationalism, Blatchford articulated the strategic aspect of socialist-Tory thinking by arguing that in wartime Britain would be vulnerable to enemy attack on food imports: 'if we destroy our agriculture [i.e. by free trade] we destroy our independence at a blow and become a defenceless nation'.[25] At a time when agriculturists were complaining about the effect of cheap food imports this was a shrewd line to take. Blatchford's warnings about wartime also reflected current fears about naval-building in France and Germany and the threat of an invasion launched from the Continent. In this way he articulated the patriotic element in socialism and opened channels to Conservative workingmen. Scorning working-class individualism, he portrayed socialism as a co-operative, communal system epitomised by the family and the nation. He had no hesitation in defending drink as a necessary resort

by those who endured dull lives, excessive work and squalid surroundings: 'Give the people healthy homes, human lives, due leisure and
amusement and pure meat and drink, and drunkenness will soon
disappear.'[26]

In this way Blatchford articulated a coherent synthesis of socialism
and Toryism during the 1890s, also favoured by Henry Hyndman and
H. H. Champion of the Social Democratic Federation and by trade
union leaders such as Will Thorne and Ben Tillett. The synthesis
united domestic interventionism with a patriotic and imperial bias
manifested in support for the Boer War, compulsory military training
and restrictions on immigration. In the context of the British tradition
of voluntary recruiting the idea of conscription appears eccentric, but
the Napoleonic concept of a Citizen Army was perfectly compatible
with left-wing politics. As a young man the ILP chairman, John Bruce
Glasier, had volunteered to fight the Russians: 'Why should not every
British youth be prepared to defend the glorious privileges of his
country? . . . Shall it never be written in history that Britons lost their
rights and liberties so dearly purchased by the blood of their fathers,
through negligence and weakness.'[27] During the 1890s and 1900s the
sense of a growing threat from Russia, France and Germany made
the idea of a socialist Citizen Army increasingly fashionable, though
it did not become central until the Great War.

Yet Blatchford's propagandist skill was never replicated by the organisation with which he was most closely associated, the Social
Democratic Federation, originally founded in 1881. Notable for its intelligent but argumentative members, including Henry Hyndman, H. H.
Champion, William Morris and John Burns, the early SDF devoted
much of its energy to ideological disputes and personality clashes. Its
founder, Hyndman, was an improbable, even bizarre, leader for a
socialist organisation. Born into a wealthy family, a graduate of Trinity
College, Cambridge, and a staunch Tory until 1880, he was probably
the only Marxist to have played county cricket (for Sussex). He stood
for Parliament five times, but was thought to alienate voters by quoting
Virgil at them – in Latin. Although Hyndman's money subsidised the
SDF's journal, *Justice*, there was always something implausible about
an anti-capitalist organisation whose finances fluctuated according to
how Hyndman was doing in his speculations on the Stock Exchange.
The SDF became discredited as early as 1885 when Hyndman and

Champion apparently sanctioned a scheme to fund two candidates in London by accepting £340 from another Tory, one Maltman Barry. Backed by their 'Tory Gold' the two candidates, who polled a derisory twenty-seven and thirty-two votes, were denounced as stooges designed to split the anti-Conservative vote. As a result the SDF lost members. 'If [socialists] are to be unscrupulous', complained Ramsay MacDonald, 'where are we to look for scruples?'[28] For some years afterwards this episode was used to discredit all attempts to persuade the TUC to promote independent Labour candidates and to cast suspicion on advocates of independent Labour as agents of Toryism in the eyes of Liberal-leaning unions. Even Keir Hardie was dogged by questions about who financed his campaigns which he never fully answered. Yet the connection between the SDF and Toryism was more than financial, for the organisation strongly endorsed Blatchford's view that socialism, far from being alien, represented the continuation of a British Radical tradition determined by race and climate. As Hyndman put it 'the men of our race have so far been able to work out political problems without that dangerous element that has attended the endeavour to solve them elsewhere'.[29] In short, British socialism had nothing to do with the anarchism and violence associated with Continental movements.

For a time the SDF managed to combine direct action with a parliamentary strategy on the pattern currently used with some success by the Irish Nationalists. During 1886 and 1887 it capitalised on the growth of unemployment by organising demonstrations in Trafalgar Square demanding the institution of public works schemes. The arrest of several SDF leaders gave the movement huge publicity, though it frightened off some supporters. However, as the agitation died down, it seemed difficult to implement the other half of the strategy. As Champion admitted, 'I find that Home Rule is practical politics because the Irish vote counts, and that the Labour problem is not practical politics because the Labour vote is not effectively organised.'[30] By the end of the 1880s the SDF had only around 1,000 members, and its claim to have 10,000 by 1900 is regarded as a great exaggeration; it made only modest inroads into working-class communities partly because its strict ideological approach alienated trade unionists and because of its association with Conservatism. Although the organisation maintained its connections to the extent of affiliating to the Labour Representation Committee in 1900, it withdrew in 1902.

The SDF also lost its most impressive leader, John Burns, a South London engineer and a fiery orator who had been imprisoned for six weeks following the 1887 demonstrations. In contrast to his colleagues Burns was rooted in the working class and took a realistic view of elections. But his poor performance as an SDF candidate convinced him that a Marxist movement was not viable, and in 1889 he got elected for Battersea to the new London County Council by co-operating with the Progressives, becoming the MP in 1892. Keir Hardie liked to scoff at Burns for 'playing to get the vote of the mere Liberals' and for being measured up for his frock coat on entering Parliament, though the distinction between them was slight as Hardie, too, angled for Liberal votes while maintaining his formal independence. As Burns succeeded in retaining his seat and cultivated relations with the Liberal Party, he eventually became a Cabinet minister in Campbell-Bannerman's government in December 1905. Burns was one of Labour's 'lost leaders', arguably the most significant, and his early abandonment of independent Labour politics indicates that there was nothing inevitable about the emergence of the new party in 1900.

Admittedly in the 1880s the SDF loomed large in public perceptions, despite its minimal membership, because it was part of a wider socialist revival that included, among others, the Fabian Society, founded in 1884. As a result of its association with prominent figures including Beatrice and Sidney Webb, G. B. Shaw, Edward Pease, Hubert Bland, Annie Besant and H. G. Wells, and the prolific writings of its members, the Fabian Society was once thought to occupy a major role in the emergence of the Labour Party. By 1906 it had published 129 *Fabian Tracts* and *Fabian Essays in Socialism* (1889). This reputation now seems greatly exaggerated. The strength of Fabianism lay in its skill in tapping into a wider *fin de siècle* mood reflecting the relative decline of British industry, the loss of competitiveness and the revelations about the extent of poverty, ill health and poor training among the urban population. In the 1850s similar alarming studies of poverty had been met with the assumption that as industry continued to expand it would eventually absorb everyone who wanted to work and extend prosperity throughout society; but by the 1890s this had plainly not happened. As Britain began to be overtaken by rivals such as Germany and the United States complacency gave way to a fear of 'National Decadence' for which the fashionable remedy lay in 'National Efficiency'. Fabian socialism spoke eloquently to this concern, for many Liberals, not to mention Conservatives, including A. J. Balfour, Lord Milner, Lord Curzon and Joseph Chamberlain, accepted that state intervention was a necessary element in improving the nation's efficiency and virility. The Fabian view that society could achieve an incremental advance towards socialism under cover of collectivist policies softened the anti-capitalist rhetoric associated with the SDF. Fabians proceeded by means of detailed studies into social conditions, collaboration with Liberal and Conservative politicians, and involvement in local government where they promoted municipal ownership of utilities, such as gas and water supplies, and direct labour departments that accepted 'fair wage' clauses in their contracts. Sidney Webb famously ridiculed anti-socialists in his *Socialism in England* (1889): 'The Individualist Town Councillor will walk along the municipal pavement, lit by municipal gas and cleansed by municipal brooms with municipal water, and, seeing by the municipal clock in the municipal market that he is too early to meet his children coming from the municipal school hard by the county lunatic asylum and municipal hospital, will use the national telegraph system to tell them not to walk through the municipal park but to come by the municipal tramway to meet him in the municipal reading-room by the municipal art gallery, museum and library . . . "Socialism, sir," he will say, "don't waste the time of practical man by your fantastic absurdities. Self-help, sir . . . that's what's made our city what it is."'[31] Today it is forgotten that socialist candidates often argued for municipalisation on the grounds of *efficiency*, for it enabled local councils to run utilities at lower cost to ratepayers and avoid the wastefulness and high costs involved in supply through private companies. Public enterprise was seen as 'the work done by the community as a kind of joint-stock company with a view to affording an efficient and economic supply to the consumer as a body or individually'.[32] In this view the council's electors were comparable to shareholders in private companies.

On the other hand, the Fabians' permeation tactics inevitably gave them more influence among the higher social classes than among the workers. Their membership remained very small and metropolitan, they never aspired to become a popular movement and they especially disparaged the union leaders for lacking any grasp of socialism. In 1896

when Ramsay MacDonald suggested using the society's funds to establish provincial branches he was squashed from a great height by the
supercilious Beatrice Webb who asked: 'Do we want to organise
unthinking persons into Socialistic Societies, or to make the thinking
persons Socialistic? We believe in the latter process.'[33] As a result, despite
affiliating to the LRC in 1900 Fabians did not yet regard an independent
Labour Party as a priority. 'The nature of an Englishman seems to be
suited only to a political fight between two parties – the party of order
and the party of progress,' as Sidney Webb put it in 1891. Not until the
First World War did they revise this view.

As the Webbs suggested, the final stumbling block for late Victorian
socialism lay in its relations with what was much the largest working-
class organisation – the trade union movement. As yet, however, even
the unions were not the key for they represented only a minority of
the working class. From 600,000 members in the later 1880s they grew
to 1.5 million in the 1890s, representing one worker in every seven; by
1900 there were around two million and the expansion of the
Edwardian period took the total to 4.1 million by 1914. A product of
the mid-Victorian era, trade unionism comprised many small unions
based on skilled trades and two larger semi-skilled groups in mining
and textiles. For skilled workers the mass of unskilled men represented
a perennial threat as they undermined wages by migrating into towns
or were imported by employers as blacklegs, leading the unions to
promote emigration to reduce the surplus of labour and enhance their
bargaining powers. As a result, though the unions were proudly
working-class institutions, they were regarded as lacking proper class
consciousness by socialists.

Conscious that the strikes designed to prevent wage cuts during
times of economic depression invariably failed because the employers
simply locked the men out, union leaders tried to prevent unofficial
action and to time strikes for periods when the owners were willing
to make concessions. They accepted that in industries dependent on
exports, such as coal, their members' wages would fluctuate according
to the price commanded by their product in world markets, which
inevitably exposed them to criticism during depressions. They were
also constrained by the fear of dissipating union funds in futile strikes,
for one of the major attractions of membership of the craft unions
lay in their role as friendly societies offering benefits against sickness,

accident and death, and contracts with doctors to treat their members in return for small weekly contributions. Between 1898 and 1905 the one hundred leading unions spent 27s. 10d. per member annually of which only 3s. 3d. went on strike pay compared with 5s. 8d. on sickness and accident benefits, 6s. 3d. on unemployment, 2s. 8d. on funerals and 3s. 8d. on pensions.[34]

Prudent management of union funds won approval from contemporary politicians but attracted criticism from some socialists who felt they were too keen on respectability and neglectful of the wider interest of the working class. This was unfair since the Victorian trade unions effectively pioneered a political role for workingmen. Established in 1868 the TUC acted as a pressure group by means of its Parliamentary Committee, which monitored legislation affecting the legal status of unions, promoted new bills for employers' liability for accidents and supported working-class candidates through its Labour Electoral Association.

But was this sufficiently ambitious? After the redistribution of 1885 some eighty-five seats, represented by ninety-five MPs, were reckoned to be dominated by working-class voters. This appeared to offer the basis for a substantial Labour Party comparable to the Irish Nationalists who had managed to win eighty to eighty-five of the 103 seats in Ireland and thus to hold the balance in the House of Commons on several occasions. Ostensibly the unions possessed the resources to do this, for their accumulated funds stood at £4 million by 1900. Yet the TUC felt bound to be cautious about introducing political divisions, recognising that many members were loyal Gladstonian Liberals while others were Tories, especially in the textile districts of Lancashire. They felt incurably suspicious about overtures made by small, unrepresentative socialist societies anxious to milk their funds to promote hopeless candidatures.

This reluctance was compounded by the success of individual unions in developing an alternative to independent labour representation. In 1874 two manual workers had been elected to Parliament with the backing of local Liberal Associations, Thomas Burt at Morpeth and Alexander MacDonald at Stafford. Known as 'Lib-Labs' because they took the Liberal whip, these members numbered twenty-four by 1906, including Henry Broadhurst, a stonemason, and Joseph Arch, an agricultural labourer; but most were miners representing their own coalfields notably William Abraham (South Wales), Charles Fenwick (Northumberland), John Wilson (Durham) and Ben Pickard (Yorkshire). Underestimated by later generations, including historians who have given much more attention to their critics, the Lib-Labs were formidable figures in their frock coats and watch chains and commanded enormous prestige in working-class communities up to 1914. Broadhurst served both as TUC president and also as a junior minister in Gladstone's 1886 government.

However, for advocates of independent labour representation the Lib-Labs presented a roadblock in the path of progress; 'a kind of deadly stupor covered them' as Tom Mann put it. In 1887 Hardie began to undermine them at the TUC conference in Swansea with a blistering attack on Broadhust as one of the 'dumb dogs who dare not bark' for his refusal to support legislation for an eight-hour day in Parliament. Not surprisingly his proposal to promote independent labour representation was heavily defeated in 1888. The next year Hardie criticised Broadhurst personally for owning shares in Brunner and Mond, the chemical manufacturers.[35] By 1890 Congress had adopted the eight-hour day and Broadhurst resigned as secretary. The first generation of working-class MPs was a little complacent and too loyal to orthodox Gladstonianism. They made little intellectual contribution to the 'New Liberalism' that was developing among middle-class Liberals during the 1890s or to the post-1906 social welfare reforms. Above all, while Lib-Lab representation flattered the miners, the experiment was not easily capable of extension to other workers who were too scattered to dominate a constituency and therefore lacked the miners' advantages in bargaining with Liberal Associations. Consequently the Lib-Labs were eventually discredited by the advocates of independent representation for labour.

3

'No bigger than a man's hand': The Foundation of the Labour Party

In January 1893 120 delegates met at the Labour Institute in Peckover Street in Bradford to found the Independent Labour Party. According to the *Bradford Observer* 'the large number of Socialists among them was apparent from the large proportion of wideawakes [stand-up collars], red ties, and shirts with flannel collars which were worn'.[1] They included Keir Hardie, Ben Tillett, Robert Blatchford and George Bernard Shaw whose credentials were challenged on the grounds that as a Fabian he had no intention of joining. The gathering was the culmination of several spontaneous initiatives between 1888 and 1892, taken largely out of frustration with the refusal of the unions to promote independent labour representation; these included the Scottish Labour Party in Glasgow, the Bradford Labour Union, the Colne Valley Labour League (later Union) in the West Riding of Yorkshire, the Labour Electoral Association in Salford and an Independent Labour Party in Manchester. As they were all seeking the same goal it seemed logical to concert their efforts in the shape of an Independent Labour Party. The timing appeared highly opportune because at the recent general election in 1892 three workingmen had been returned to Parliament: Keir Hardie, John Burns and Havelock Wilson.

However, the meeting engendered much disagreement over what to call the new party. Some favoured the 'Socialist Labour Party', but 'the great mass of British workmen . . . do not understand Socialism and have rather a prejudice against it'.[2] Ben Tillett threatened that 'if the Labour Party was to be called the Socialist Party he would repudiate it (cheers)'. Tillett invited his listeners to consider the textile operatives in neighbouring Lancashire under their Tory leaders: 'for great, vital, effective work there was not a Socialist Party in the whole world who could show such an effective organisation as those men could (cheers)'.[3] The inaugural debate is thus a caution against the usual view of the ILP as simply the left-wing conscience of the Labour Movement; its provincial roots, especially in Lancashire, meant that it incorporated right-wing working-class opinion too. The deliberate inclusion of the word 'Independent' indicated the new party's intention to outflank the Lib-Lab members who took the Liberal whip. On the other hand, by excluding the word 'Socialist' from its title the ILP served notice of its flexible, all-embracing attitude; as it aspired to harness the resources of the unions there was no sense in frightening them away at the start.

Accordingly the ILP put together a programme comprising a vague commitment to nationalisation, interventionist social reforms such as pensions, free education, land reform and the eight-hour day, plus the standard Radical political causes. This was calculated to be sufficiently socialist to appeal to the activists but not too extreme to offend the unions. In practice ILP ideology varied from one branch to another. In Lancashire branches recruited working-class Conservatives, but in Finsbury Central, for example, membership was open to anyone over the age of sixteen who declared themselves to be socialists. Members were asked to pay one and a half pence per week and one penny a month to the party's ruling body, the National Advisory Committee.[4] This meant that money was always short, so the ILP made a virtue of necessity by organising members to speak at regular outdoor Sunday morning meetings and often on street corners during the week. Apart from spreading the message cheaply, this offered members an excellent apprenticeship in political campaigning at an early age. Looking back fondly to 'the days of soap-box and street-corner oratory' Ben Turner of Batley recalled: 'There was no pay for the job. Many of us have travelled many miles, spoken at a Sunday morning meeting, had a snack meal in a coffee house, gone to an afternoon meeting, had tea with a comrade, done another meeting at night and gone home poorer and prouder for our task.'[5]

The ILP was also distinctive for focusing on municipal elections which were held every November and thus offered regular practice in organising campaigns at a time when general elections could be seven years apart. Admittedly, a workingman had to get time off to attend council meetings at a time when no expenses were paid; in the late

1890s the Labour members of the London County Council were supported by 'wages funds' raised in their constituencies.[6] But the abolition of property qualifications for Poor Law Guardians in 1894 enabled workingmen to be elected to the boards where they succeeded in highlighting the need not only to improve conditions inside the workhouse but to grant outdoor relief to workers who became temporarily unemployed in periods of economic depression. They also attempted to extend the Guardians' role by funding local schemes to create employment during slumps or wintertime. In January 1895 Emmeline Pankhurst, who had been elected to the Chorlton Board of Guardians in Manchester, upbraided her colleagues for 'a tendency to put the present state of affairs down to the depraved character of the people themselves [but] these poor people could not make employ-ment'. The other Guardians insisted it was their job to relieve the unemployed not create jobs, but her husband, Dr Richard Pankhurst, and other ILP leaders led delegations of the unemployed to the boards at Manchester, Salford and Chorlton. Amid what the press called 'Lively Scenes at Chorlton Guardians' the board reluctantly agreed to receive the deputation, but suggested only that Manchester City Council should start public works schemes and that men should not be dis-enfranchised for receiving Poor Law relief. Eventually Dr Pankhurst marched the men back to Manchester for a distribution of free soup.[7]

Although inadequate resources from the rates put severe limits on what could be achieved, these controversies over unemployment gave credence to the ILP's critique of capitalism and convinced many that social problems would eventually have to be tackled at national level. Socialists argued that the state must ultimately accept responsibility either to provide employment or to ensure relief for the unemployed. Despite this, any conspicuous success for Labour and socialist groups was limited to places such as Bradford and West Ham where Labour won a majority in 1898 and initiated a minimum wage and an eight-hour day for council employees, and two weeks' annual holiday. Although the majority was swept away two years later, such successes gave Labour a pronounced municipal character and demonstrated how municipal work could reinforce parliamentary campaigns.

Meanwhile, it seemed for a time as though a real breakthrough had been achieved at the parliamentary level at the election of 1892. However, of the three MPs, J. Havelock Wilson, leader of the Seamen's

Union, at Middlesbrough, was not really part of the independent
Labour Movement at all. At Battersea John Burns won, ostensibly as
an independent Labour candidate, but was in fact working closely
with the Liberals. This left only Keir Hardie's historic victory at West
Ham South, a working-class suburb dominated by soap and chemical
works, docks and engineering at the Great Eastern Railway and Thames
Ironworks. His campaign benefited from municipal election organisation and the recent success of Will Thorne in mobilising semi-skilled
workers in his new Gasworkers Union. But there was also an element
of luck. Shortly before the poll the Liberal candidate died and could
not be replaced; helped by the general swing in the Liberals' favour
Hardie succeeded in uniting the votes of trade unionists, Radicals and
the local Irish community, who normally backed the Liberals over Home
Rule, to defeat the Tory.

Initially Hardie brilliantly dramatised the breakthrough for independent labour representation. In this he was assisted by a hostile
press that unwittingly portrayed his arrival at Westminster as an
alarming turning point. On 3 August his constituents hired a wagonette
to drive him to Westminster accompanied by a trumpeter who played
the 'Marseillaise'. The newspapers printed fictional accounts of an
East End rabble with brass bands carrying the Red Flag into the House
of Commons, though Hardie actually entered the House alone. But
he raised eyebrows by refusing to conform to the usual members'
dress, a black frock coat, silk top hat and starched wing collar.
Descriptions of his attire vary widely. Burns claimed he wore 'knickers
of check . . . you could have played draughts on'. He was variously
thought to have worn a red tie, a red handkerchief and a 'home-made
purple comforter' round his neck, and on his head a workman's peaked
cap, a soft cap, a blue scotch cap and a deerstalker. It seems likely that
he stuck to the tweed suit and deerstalker he had used in West Ham
which were certainly outlandish enough to cause comment.

Hardie devoted his maiden speech to unemployment in the form
of an amendment to the Queen's Speech prepared by the new Gladstone
government. This was usually the prerogative of the official Opposition,
but Hardie brushed this aside: 'I am told my amendment will be a vote
of censure . . . It is meant for a vote of censure.'[8] John Burns stayed
away but 109 Tory members supported him. Hardie's speaking style
was not really suited to the Commons, and he irritated the honourable

members by referring to them as 'men'. However, he wisely made use of parliamentary questions to put specific cases of working-class grievances to ministers. Unfortunately Hardie suffered from an inability to co-operate with potential supporters; instead of putting together an alliance of workingmen he soon became isolated in the House, having alienated Burns, Havelock Wilson and all the Lib-Lab members. Nor could he resist the temptation to shock his colleagues. His criticisms of the state pensions paid to peers hit the target, but he rashly included the royal family in his strictures even though he was not a republican. In 1893 he objected when the House sent congratulations to the Duke of York on his marriage, and next year he said they should be discussing a mining disaster in South Wales not congratulating the Yorks on their new baby. Demanding to know 'what particular blessing the Royal Family has conferred on the nation that we should be asked to spend a whole day on this issue', he attacked the Prince of Wales for his £60,000 income drawn from slum property.[9] All this caused scandal in the Commons as MPs tried to howl him down, and Hardie failed to understand that the royal family was immensely popular at this time especially among his working-class constituents.

He was also dogged by financial problems. It emerged that he had accepted £100 from Andrew Carnegie and another £100 from H. H. Champion, supposedly originating with a Tory soap-manufacturer, to fight the election. After the election a friend, Frank Smith, offered him board and lodging in London; but he still had to budget carefully, for every day spent in Parliament deprived him of a day as an itinerant lecturer for which he usually charged three guineas.

In the event, 1892 proved to be a false dawn for independent labour representation, and Hardie lost his seat in 1895. Some light is thrown on the difficulties of sustaining an effective grass-roots movement by the records of socialists in Colne Valley during the 1890s. It was in July 1891 that twenty members, all men, gathered to form the Colne Valley Labour Union.[10] The constituency comprised a collection of small towns and industrial villages dependent on textiles scattered across the moorlands between Huddersfield and Oldham. Industry was small-scale, relationships often paternalistic, and trade unions comparatively weak, with around 1,500 members in all. Consequently the new committee quickly decided that 'the best way [to create an organisation] will be by establishing Labour clubs'.[11] In Meltham the new Labour Club rented rooms for 2s. 3d. a week, opened from eight in the morning to ten at night or eleven on Saturdays, and accepted members aged sixteen years and upwards at twopence a week. The moralistic and individualist style of local socialism was evident from the outset for the club purchased coal and aerated water but no alcohol, and resolved: 'No gambling, profane or obscene language be allowed in the Club rooms.'[12] Based on respectable, upwardly mobile work-ingmen, the Colne Valley organisation included small employers who were themselves skilled manual workers, such as minor mill-owners, tailors, bootmakers and farmers, as well as lower-middle-class employees such as insurance agents. Such men traditionally formed the basis for local Radical Liberal politics throughout Victorian England, and in the case of Colne Valley many of these individuals crossed back and forth between Liberal and Labour organisations, standing as candidates for each party.[13] Another sign of respectability was the separate organisation of women in most of the districts, and the maintenance of links with church and chapel. The new committee decided to print 4,000 sheets of hymns and to organise a music committee which engaged a brass band.[14]

Yet although the Colne Valley Labour Union was firmly rooted in the local political culture, it struggled to establish itself. As early as October 1891 the organisers contemplated contesting the imminent general election and repeatedly invited Tom Mann, now famous for his role in the London dock strike of 1889, to become the candidate. Mann, however, prevaricated and no one stood in the 1892 election. Like most ILP groups, Colne Valley was badly handicapped by money. In negotiations with Mann the committee pledged itself to 'fulfil [his] conditions in respect to finance and Trade Union organisations' which meant not only raising his election expenses but establishing a fund to maintain him if elected.[15] However, with a membership of a little over 200 in 1892, reaching 300 by 1898, paying sixpence a quarter, this was ambitious.[16] In order to reap even this meagre harvest from subscriptions each Labour club appointed a collector, enabling the League to start a fund and to finance Mann's parliamentary campaign in 1895. But in the absence of trade union subsidies the organisation existed on painfully small resources; its annual expenditure during the three years from 1912 to 1914 was £102, £68 and £85.[17] Moreover, after 1895 the organisation appears to have gone into a decline until rescued by the revival of the early 1900s, so that it failed to contest the general elections in 1900 and 1906. Thus, while the experience of Colne Valley suggests that a Labour organisation was viable, even in the absence of union backing, it casts doubt on assumptions about the steady rise of the movement before 1914. The Colne Valley socialists also failed to find a comfortable place in the wider movement. They affiliated to the ILP but not, apparently, to the Labour Representation Committee or the Labour Party; discussions on whether to join in 1904 and 1908 failed to reach a decision.[18] The organisation changed its name to the Colne Valley Socialist League (previously Labour League) and affiliated to the British Socialist Party, in effect moving away from the mainstream of the Labour Movement.

This experience underlines the significance of Colne Valley in demonstrating the obstacles to a decisive breakthrough by the ILP in parliamentary elections. In 1895, the first general election for the new party, the ILP ran twenty-eight candidates none of whom was elected and most of whom obtained only a modest vote. Even Keir Hardie suffered defeat at West Ham, despite enjoying a straight fight with a Conservative, largely through his own incompetence. He had neglected his organisation and gone out of his way to alienate the Irish voters by backtracking over Home Rule, promoted proposals to shut down the local liquor trade, and continued to insult the Liberals on whose votes he depended. Consequently, although the victorious Conservative increased his vote only slightly, Hardie lost a quarter of his original vote.

In any case, London was far from being Hardie's natural habitat. Its labour force was concentrated in traditional crafts and trades, there were few large-scale trade unions, and many workers remained trapped in casual and unskilled employment. Working-class communities here were notably irreligious and failed to sustain the kind of Nonconformist socialist leaders typical of northern England. A high proportion of families moved house every year in a desperate bid to avoid paying rent, which meant a high level of disenfranchisement. Everything militated against the development of an organised, institutional framework of the kind that was sustained in the more stable working-class communities of the North. As late as 1899 the ILP was thought to have only 500 members in the whole of the capital, and not until 1914 was the London Labour Party established. Although the decline of

London's Radical clubs in the 1890s created opportunities for socialism by weakening the Liberal Party, the main beneficiaries were the Conservatives who cultivated the xenophobic susceptibilities of a population influenced by immigration, anti-Semitism and imperialism. After 1892 there were to be no more Labour parliamentary victories in London until 1903. Meanwhile, Labour organisations varied in character according to the local leaders and conditions. In Bow and Bromley George Lansbury struggled for years to promote a Progressive, pacifist, temperance-style socialism that went against the grain for much of the population. In the face of an entrenched Conservatism Lansbury never won the seat during the pre-1914 period except briefly from 1910 to 1912. By contrast, in working-class suburbs such as Woolwich and Deptford where the labour force was more stable, skilled and better organised in unions and co-operative societies, a socialist organisation became feasible. But even here successful Labour campaigns were necessarily founded on a right-wing appeal calculated to challenge the prevailing Conservatism centred around the Woolwich Arsenal.

The setbacks faced by Keir Hardie, George Lansbury and others reflected the ILP's tendency to misread working-class communities not only in London but in the northern strongholds. When Tom Mann contested Colne Valley in 1895, winning only 13 per cent, he appeared to take votes almost as much from the Tories as from the Liberals. The constituency, straddling the Yorkshire–Lancashire border, encapsulated the divergent different political cultures of the two counties. Towards the Lancashire end the ILP and the Liberals often co-operated, whereas on the Yorkshire side the ILP was hostile towards Liberal employers and prised working-class support away from the Conservatives.[19] By the 1880s Lancashire's politics were becoming dominated by ethnic and religious divisions stemming from extensive Irish immigration; as a result denominational education promoted by both Catholics and Anglicans became a major issue. This fostered working-class Conservatism which was already expressed in trade union membership and reinforced by Conservatives' defence of the sport-and-drink culture and philanthropic activity by local employers. Conservatism thus became very strong especially in the west of the county, in textile towns such as Preston and Blackburn, in the Manchester–Salford conurbation, in areas of heavy industry including

Wigan and St Helens, and on Merseyside where xenophobia generated by the Irish reached its peak. In Liverpool the Irish question
became institutionalised by the Orange Lodges which allied with the
Conservatives for election purposes. As a result Liberalism became
moribund in some towns, leaving scope for intervention by socialist
candidates. Yet the ILP, which had thirty-eight branches by 1899, also
struggled. In Lancashire it was not sufficient to mop up Liberal votes
for the party could win only by chipping away at the Tory working
class too. This dual strategy was adopted in 1895 by James Tattersall,
the ILP's candidate at Preston, where the combination of Conservative
workingmen's clubs, voluntary Church schools and Irish issues made
things tough for a socialist. Tattersall made concessions to Tory opinion
by backing rate aid to voluntary schools, opposing Church disestablishment, and supporting compensation for publicans who lost their
licences. Though accused of trimming, he polled strongly at the election. These tactics were taken even further in a rather different
constituency, East Bristol, where a by-election occurred in March 1895.
This was a working-class seat held by the Liberals, but the ILP candidate, Hugh Holmes Gore, enjoyed a straight fight with them. Gore
was frank about his tactics. 'If I were to stand', he told Keir Hardie,
'I should stand as a Unionist Socialist'.[20] In his campaign he opposed
Liberal policies, including Home Rule and disestablishment, but
supported the Church schools and the drink trade and opposed Sunday
closing and graduated income tax. As a result Gore mopped up the
Conservative vote and came within a whisker of winning the seat.
This was an extreme case, but it offered emphatic evidence for the
electoral viability of the Tory-socialist strategy.

    Conversely, ILP candidates who felt less inclined to compromise with
Toryism in areas such as Lancashire were invariably doomed to disappointment. One of the ablest of the party's leaders at this time was
Dr. Richard Pankhurst who made three unsuccessful attempts to get
into Parliament. A lawyer of impeccable Radical views, Pankhurst
supported republicanism, women's suffrage and secular education, and
opposed imperial expansion. With his high-pitched voice, pointed red
beard and penchant for going over the top he often came across as a
high-minded fanatic to his audiences. In 1885 he had been frustrated
by working-class Conservatism at Rotherhithe in London, but his
prospects appeared better in 1895 when he stood as ILP candidate at

Gorton, a wholly industrial constituency adjacent to Manchester dominated by coal mines, hat-making and railway rolling-stock works, and
where his wife, Emmeline, was well known as a Poor Law Guardian.
But although Gorton had been Liberal in 1885, it gave steadily higher
votes to the Conservatives who were frustrated only by the opposition
of Irish voters. In 1895 when the Liberal MP withdrew, the Liberals
delayed over a replacement, allowing Pankhurst to step in and enjoy a
straight fight with the Conservative. His programme included the eight-
hour day, old-age pensions, nationalisation of land, mines and railways,
abolition of the House of Lords, Home Rule, Church disestablishment
and the 'local veto' which was designed to allow each community to
suppress publicans' licences. This classic Liberal-socialist formula made
no concessions to right-wing opinion. Pankhurst almost certainly lost
votes through his temperance views and the refusal of the Irish
Nationalist leader, T. P. O'Connor, to endorse his candidature in view
of 'the people he is mixed up with', a comment that reflected Catholic
disapproval of ILP socialism and a general dislike of independent Labour
for splitting the anti-Conservative vote.[21] As a result the Conservatives
achieved a large swing in their favour and won the seat by a margin
of fifty-eight to forty-two. Although Pankhurst blamed the Liberals for
his defeat, he was refusing to recognise the unpopularity of ILP views
among large sections of the working class.

Yorkshire's political culture not only differed from that of Lancashire
but varied within the county. As a result independent Labour was
comparatively weak in the mining districts of the south but strong in
the woollen textile towns around Bradford, Halifax, Huddersfield,
Keighley and Dewsbury. Encouraged by a Chartist tradition and
provoked by major Liberal employers including Sir James Kitson in
Colne Valley and Alfred Illingworth in Bradford, the idea of independent Labour emerged early here and the ILP and the Liberals were
often at daggers drawn. With the woollen industry in decline, profits
were squeezed and wages subject to cuts, making for militancy among
the labour force. As the Irish question was less relevant in Yorkshire
the ILP was able to fight on Radical ground and pay less attention to
Conservatism than in Lancashire. Even so, versatile ILP candidates
did best as was evident when Ben Tillett fought Bradford West in 1892.
Like Mann, Tillett had acquired a great reputation from the London
dockers' strike, but his brand of Labour politics was complex.

Originally a respectable Lib-Lab figure, he became fiercely anti-Liberal, authoritarian, patriotic and imperialistic; he was also a socialist, used revolutionary language and enjoyed attacking the employers. One of Tillett's techniques to attract the support of Tory trade unionists involved disparaging foreign socialists; speaking at Bradford in 1893 he insisted 'he would sooner have the solid, progressive, matter of fact, fighting trades unionism of England than all the hare-brained chatterers and magpies of Continental revolutionists', provoking one ILP-er to enquire 'whether Mr Tillett means to say that Karl Marx was a chatterer and blatherer'.[22] Though his views were increasingly erratic and unstable, Tillett was far from untypical. J. R. Clynes expressed similar prejudices in 1893 when attending an international congress of socialists at Zurich: 'It was difficult to co-ordinate the statements of the stolid British delegates, abhorring armed violence, as much as the mock heroics, with the inflammatory verbal orgies of the representatives of certain of the Latin and Slavonic races.'[23]

Tillett certainly showed himself adept at reaching the different working-class communities. The choice of Bradford West was interesting as it was the least working class of the town's three constituencies. However, it had been the scene of the bitter Manningham Mills dispute in 1890–1 which began with an attempt to reduce wages by 30 per cent and led to a strike and a lockout. This inevitably exacerbated friction between middle and working classes and made the sitting Liberal MP, Alfred Illingworth, who was a major mill-owner himself, vulnerable. 'Liberals joined hands with Tories to bring soldiers and police to Bradford to intimidate the workpeople of Manningham and cause riots,' in Tillett's words.[24] Despite this the Bradford Labour Union managed to persuade the local trades council to approve an independent Labour candidate by only forty-seven to thirty-three. This was too even a split to be comfortable and one TC member warned: 'May I assure Mr Tillett that his candidature has driven a knife into every labour organisation in town.'[25] But this was a necessary part of the process of prising trades councils away from their Lib-Lab loyalties. It also seemed justified by Tillett's excellent result. 'It was a thrilling experience', recalled Snowden. 'Workers thronged to his meetings in their thousands, and they came away having seen the vision of a new Earth.'[26] Although third, he polled 30 per cent, by attracting Conservative as well as Liberal voters. By contrast, when Keir Hardie fought a by-election in Bradford East in 1896 he did much less well than Tillett because, though overwhelmingly working class, the East was a *poorer* area and the Tory vote correspondingly stronger and resistant to his appeal. The importance of tapping the Labour–Conservative electorate was underlined in nearby Halifax, a double-member borough where electors could use two votes if they wished. In 1895 an ILP candidate won 20 per cent of the vote, a third of which came from electors who had 'split', that is used one vote for the ILP and one for the Conservative.[27]

On the other hand, in the absence of a notorious employer or a recent strike to stimulate the campaign, the ILP was less successful in Yorkshire. In Barnsley where a by-election took place in 1897, the Liberal candidate was a mine-owner who supported the eight-hour day. The ILP's Pete Curran, who suffered the indignity of being chased out of some pit villages, won only 1,000 votes compared with 3,400 for the Tory and 6,700 for the Liberal. The cause of independent labour representation was slow to take light throughout the coalfields of South Yorkshire and even in Sheffield itself partly because the Liberals benefited from progressive candidates and local Nonconformist support among both middle and working classes. Moreover, Sheffield's economy relied heavily on small-scale, labour-intensive light-metal trades and increasingly on larger steel and engineering works. Both were dependent on exports and increasingly vulnerable to foreign competition. This gave a big boost to Conservative advocates of tariffs designed to protect the domestic market and maintain local employment. Consequently when Liberal workingmen became disgruntled they migrated towards the Conservatives, who held three of Sheffield's five seats, rather than to the ILP.

In 1894 the ILP staked its claim to representation by fighting a by-election in one of Sheffield's Liberal seats, Attercliffe. However, the local trades council endorsed their choice by only forty-three to thirty-eight votes, leaving it too divided to be able to play a major role in the campaign. Matters were not helped because the candidate, Frank Smith, was a Londoner and the speakers imported to back him were regarded as strangers to Sheffield.[28] Given their support among local miners, the Liberals felt no great pressure to make concessions to the ILP, but the by-election caused friction between the two parties. One by-product of Attercliffe was that Ramsay MacDonald finally committed himself to the ILP. During 1894 he focused on Southampton where he attempted to persuade the local Liberals to adopt him as a joint candidate with the sitting Liberal MP for the two-member seat. Angry at being rejected, MacDonald complained that the Association had 'cast themselves adrift from the forward movement in politics'. Yet as an outsider in Southampton he had few claims and was not even a trade unionist as critics on the local trades council pointedly observed. At the 1895 election the Liberals shrewdly selected H. H. Wilson, who was president of the trades council, to run with the sitting member; 'Mr Wilson is a bona fide workingman', commented the local newspaper.[29] MacDonald stood for the ILP, polling a mere 7 per cent but just enough to cause the defeat of the sitting Liberal by the two victorious Conservatives.

After the failures of 1895 the ILP cast around rather inconclusively for a fresh strategy. By 1898 membership stood at only 9,000 falling to around 6,000 by 1900; the party really amounted to a loose collection of branches concentrated in the North rather than a genuinely national movement. In 1897 a debate took place over amalgamation with the SDF, but although thought to be widely favoured by members, the proposal was rejected by many branches.[30] In any case amalgamation was seen by Hardie, Glasier and the other leaders as likely to be fatal to their chances of enlisting the trade unions to the cause of independent labour representation. Although tempted to fight the next election on a wide front to maximise the vote, the leaders eventually decided to contest only twenty-five seats in the hope of getting a few members elected; but the logic of this approach implied co-operation with the Liberals. The ambiguity was reflected in an article by Hardie and MacDonald in the *Nineteenth Century* in which they reiterated the standard argument that 'The Liberal Party has done its work . . . It was evolved to meet the needs of past generations', and suggested that 'Socialism is to inspire the progressive forces of the twentieth century as Individualism inspired those of the Nineteenth.'[31] However, they carefully made overtures to the Liberal Party. Arguing that as the ILP was 'in the apostolic succession' from Liberalism and 'has never been averse to alliances', they suggested that 'it is wise to work with those who are willing to go a long way with us'.[32] This coded bid for Liberal neutrality in the twenty-five constituencies selected for the next election can be seen as a prelude to the electoral pact negotiated by MacDonald in 1903.

In effect the ILP had become the victim of wider currents in British politics, for its early life coincided with a phase of Conservative and Unionist domination triggered by the reaction against Irish Home Rule. Under Lord Salisbury the Conservatives rallied to the defence not only of the Union but of private property. They also derived some advantage from a succession of imperial crises with France and Russia, culminating in the Boer War in 1899–1902, and a growing perception of external threats in the shape of immigration from eastern Europe, invasion scares and naval-building programmes by France and Germany. The Irish issue in particular had split the Liberals, alienated some of their wealthier supporters, and helped the Conservatives to win elections in 1886, 1895 and 1900 thereby dominating government up to December 1905. One important indirect consequence of the Home Rule split was the loss of funds by local Liberal Associations which made them more reliant on businessmen who contributed to their election costs and reluctant to adopt workingmen who usually had to be financed by the party.

Yet the ILP was not simply the victim of circumstances, for it had made mistakes. In the early years its candidatures had too often been essentially *propagandist*, designed to ventilate the need for independent labour representation rather than trying to get candidates elected. Richard Pankhurst's campaigns were classic examples. Even Ben Tillett insisted on fighting the least working-class seat, Bradford West, in 1892 although the Liberals offered him a straight fight with the Conservatives in the more winnable Bradford East. Hardie's bid at Mid-Lanark had also been propagandist; he thoughtlessly got himself into debt and had no means of supporting himself had he been elected, but cheerfully insisted he had had 'more fun that I had ever enjoyed before or since'. Several leading candidates were actually chary about serving as MPs. Tillett had warned his supporters in Bradford that they were not giving him enough funding: 'if he represented them they would have to do their share of the work or he would chuck it . . . if his part were working, speaking and travelling, it was their part to contribute the means for his doing so'.[33] It was symptomatic of this detachment that ILP candidates, even when authentic workingmen, often appeared as *outsiders*, easily accused of introducing divisions into the constituencies they contested. Prominent figures were often para-chuted into constituencies with which they had no real connection, including Mann (Colne Valley), Tillett (Bradford), MacDonald (Southampton), Curran (Barnsley), Keir Hardie (West Ham, Bradford East, Preston, Merthyr Tydfil), H. H. Champion (Aberdeen), Frank Smith (Sheffield) and Tom McCarthy (Hull). Facing entrenched local employers and established trades council and union leaders, they were denounced for interfering in the local community's affairs.

The ILP also suffered defects in its conduct of election campaigns, not entirely due to a shortage of funds. It made a virtue of necessity by training enthusiastic recruits to speak on the stump at street corners and relying on inspirational public rallies at elections. At a time when public meetings were widely regarded as a form of free entertainment this was an ideal way of spreading the message. During the 1890s Will Crooks spoke every Sunday at the East India Dock gates in London, a tradition that became known as 'Crooks' College'. Keir Hardie's campaign at West Ham in 1892 chiefly relied on endless speeches at dock gates, street corners and even in fields. However, inspirational rallies were often misleading as a guide to voting. Many of those who attended did not actually possess a vote, while others turned up to hear *all* the candidates' speeches, and were equally moved by them. But getting one's supporters to the poll called for more mundane techniques. The doorstep canvass, once regarded as a dubious means for landlords and employers to exercise undue influence, was becoming accepted practice as a result of the huge expansion in the number of voters. However, in the Labour Movement the traditional suspicion lingered, understandably, for many years. In 1889 the TUC's Parliamentary Committee approved a proposal to prohibit canvassing by law, while Philip Snowden boasted that 'I have never in all the elections I have fought, ever made a personal appeal to a voter to give me his vote'.[34] As late as 1924 Arthur Henderson felt obliged to press the case for canvassing because 'the objection is often raised that it is undignified to canvass for votes and that the electors ought not to be worried into doing anything that is inconsistent with the spirit of the [Secret] Ballot Act'.[35]

A meticulous canvass went hand in hand with the annual registration of electors commonly undertaken by professional agents employed by the parties. As household electors lost their place on the register if they moved during the twelve-month period of residence there was a substantial turnover of voters each year. The point of the agents' work was to ensure that their own supporters were registered and to lay objections to the names of known opponents. In this way the party agents played a considerable role in determining who actually had a vote. Where the miners, for example, nominated 'Lib-Lab' candidates, they usually benefited from the registration work done by the Liberal Association; but otherwise Labour organisations were unlikely to be able to afford to compete.

By the late 1890s the ILP felt obliged to launch a fresh attempt to find a viable form of independent labour politics for fear of gradually losing its most able and ambitious figures. Several of the leaders could have followed John Burns on the route to full incorporation into the Liberal Party, for there were no fundamental ideological obstacles. Ramsay MacDonald, Arthur Henderson and George Lansbury, for example, were employed by Liberal MPs as secretaries and agents, and a high proportion of leading socialists had been offered Liberal candidacies at some point. However, they had sometimes been frustrated by local Liberal Associations. The classic case was Henderson who was approved as a candidate in Newcastle, another marginal two-member borough where the Liberals needed a 'Labour' candidate, but was subsequently turned down on financial grounds. MacDonald, who retained his Liberal sympathies longest, did not even join the ILP until 1894 and continued to associate with Liberals in pressure groups such as the Rainbow Circle. However, the frustration of their ambitions eventually made them lose patience. Nor could they be uninfluenced by the knowledge that the defeat of Gladstone's second Home Rule Bill by the peers in 1893, followed by the ignominious collapse of Lord Rosebery's brief Liberal government in 1895, had created a sense that the Liberal Party might be in permanent decline, or at least increasingly susceptible to pressure; in the circumstances the bid for a fully independent strategy seemed less risky.

These calculations coincided with some modifications in the tactics of the trade unions. By the late 1890s their political strategy and their reliance on traditional self-help expedients seemed increasingly inadequate. The value of 'friendly society' benefits for members was increasingly dubious as the societies operated on a financial basis that was no longer viable. In addition, many of their skilled and well-paid members were becoming exposed to higher unemployment as a result of the depression of the 1890s, especially shipwrights, iron-founders, steel smelters and blast-furnacemen. Some employers tried to take advantage of the weaker bargaining position of the men by inflicting lockouts of boot and shoe operatives and engineers. The Shipping Federation, always an aggressive body of employers, tried to curtail union activity, and the railway companies simply refused to recognise the Amalgamated Society of Railway Servants. A series of legal cases also undermined the legal status the unions thought had been settled and infringed their rights to peaceful picketing. In short, everything seemed to underline the need for extra representation to put the workers on a more equal footing with their employers in Parliament.

The pressure for such a change was strengthened by qualitative changes in the movement ushered in by the 'new unions'. For once London led the way. In June 1889 Will Thorne seized an opportunity to sweep aside the apathy of the gasworkers at the Old Kent Road and Becton in West Ham with a strike designed to stop the employers extending the working day. His timing proved to be excellent because a temporary boom had created full employment and an expanding gas industry. Keen to meet the demand and to avoid irritating the public by an interruption in supply, the employers were willing to bargain. In just two weeks Thorne's success attracted 3,000 members to his new National Union of Gasworkers and General Labourers; six months later he had 20,000, and by 1891 45,000. Men could join up for one shilling and pay only twopence a week. This was less than the older unions charged, but the benefits were inferior. Thorne insisted: 'I do not believe in having sick pay, out of work pay, and a number of other pays.'[36] Similar initiatives in 1889 resulted in a famous strike among the London dockers led by Tom Mann and Ben Tillett who won the 'docker's tanner' and established another new union, the Dock, Wharf, Riverside and General Labourers Union. Encouraged by these victories new unions also sprang up in Liverpool, Newcastle, Glasgow and Hull.

This development represented more than a numerical expansion of trade unionism. Mann, Tillett and Thorne were more inclined to socialism than most traditional union leaders, more alienated from Liberalism, and, partly because of the relative weakness of their unions, keener on political action. A member of the SDF, Thorne was very militant but, like Blatchford, he felt convinced that industrial pressure must be complemented by a political strategy. He urged his members to recognise that 'in a strike there are no Tories or Liberals amongst the strikers, they are all workers. At Election times there are no Tory or Liberal Capitalists, and all of them are friends of the workers.' In 1891 Thorne was elected to West Ham Council along with two other gasworkers, Jack Jones and Arthur Hayday, and he stood there in the general election of 1900. By 1914 four gasworkers – Thorne, J. R. Clynes, James Parker and Pete Curran – became Labour MPs.

However, the influence of the new unionism as symptomatic of a new class consciousness and as the catalyst for the foundation of the Labour Representation Committee in 1900 is easily exaggerated. Once the boom of 1889–91 had collapsed the new unions went on to the defensive, being forced into several unwinnable strikes as a result of which they lost members; the gasworkers, for example, lost £20,000 over a strike and by 1896 their membership had dwindled to 24,000. Consequently, by 1900 the new unions represented around 100,000 in a total of a million men affiliated to the TUC and were never strong enough by themselves to determine the overall strategy of the trade union movement.

On the other hand, their industrial weakness strengthened the leaders' desire for an effective *political* strategy for labour. Moreover, their votes helped to tip the balance in favour of a fresh initiative. Meeting at Plymouth in September 1899 TUC delegates approved a resolution drafted by the Doncaster branch of the Railway Servants Union to establish a new and independent political organisation by 546,000 to 434,000. As this was a fairly narrow margin the support of the new unions was crucial. The chief proponents were the railway workers, dockers, gasworkers, printers, and boot and shoe operatives and notably excluded the miners and textile workers whose members were more strongly committed to the existing political parties. This vote led to the gathering of 129 delegates at the Farringdon Street Memorial Hall in London on 27–28 February 1900 where the Labour Representation Committee – subsequently known as the Labour Party – was born.

Despite the general agreement about the need for more represen-tation, it was not an easy task to define the aims and methods of the new party. Reflecting the anti-socialist view, George Barnes of the engineers proposed that it should accept candidates representing any constitutional organisations: 'He was getting tired of working-class boots, working-class trains, working-class housing, working-class margarine. He believed the time had arrived . . . when they should not be prisoners to class prejudice but should consider parties and policies apart from all class organisations.'[37] At the opposite extreme the SDF tried to commit the organisation to being 'separate from the capitalist parties, based upon a recognition of the class war, and having for its ultimate object the Socialisation of the means of production, distribution and exchange'. For their part Hardie and MacDonald recognised that as it was essential to tap the resources of the trade unions, which the ILP had failed to do, they must compromise on programme and on organisation; this ruled out any unequivocal commitment to socialism. Also, while wanting the party to be independent, they wished to leave the relationship with Liberalism slightly obscure at this stage. This called for a delicate balancing act which they achieved by means of an ILP motion proposed by Hardie to establish 'a distinct Labour Group in Parliament, who shall have their own whips, and agree upon their policy which must embrace a readiness to co-operate with any party which for the time being may be engaged in promoting legislation in the direct interest of labour'.[38] John Burns objected that a distinct Labour group already existed: 'They had not called themselves independent, they had not worn trilby hats and red ties, but they had done the work.'[39] However, the ILP's compromise offered enough to appease the Lib-Lab sentiments of the unions while giving socialists a commitment to an independent party.

The same logic required that the Labour Representation Committee should have a loose federal structure with no leader but a national executive committee comprising seven union representatives, two from the ILP, two from the SDF, one Fabian, and an unpaid secretary in the shape of Ramsay MacDonald. The affiliated societies were entitled to send one delegate for every 2,000 members to the annual conference where voting was to be by card, that is, one card for every 1,000 members. Financial demands upon the constituent members were kept to an absolute minimum for fear of frightening the unions away; each organisation was to pay ten shillings in respect of every 1,000 members it affiliated. As Blatchford put it: 'At last there is a United Labour Party, or perhaps it would be safe to say, a little cloud, no bigger than a man's hand, which may grow into a United Labour Party.'[40] Yet seven months later, when the LRC was plunged into a general election held in the midst of the disastrous war in South Africa, only 312,000 members had been affiliated and its resources were meagre. Although the election stimulated sufficient interest to boost affiliations to 376,000 by the end of the first year this was well short of the 546,000 votes cast for establishing the new party in 1899.

The 'Khaki' Election of 1900 took place against a background of imperial crises and controversies arising out of the fact that the world was running out of territory for the European empires to grab. Britain's high commissioner in South Africa, Lord Milner, collaborated with the Colonial Secretary, Joseph Chamberlain, to force the Boer settlers into war in 1899 on the assumption that, after an easy victory, Britain would be able to incorporate all the territories into a single South Africa under her control. This proved to be a reckless miscalculation, for within weeks British forces were on the retreat and besieged at Ladysmith, Kimberley and Mafeking. Salisbury's government attempted to capitalise on the situation by holding an election designed to exploit the patriotism engendered by its incompetence in mismanaging the war.

For many socialists the South African War confirmed their Gladstonian instincts: the war was an unnecessary expense for a country whose prosperity required trade not conquest. They considered that Britain had been manipulated by foreign and Jewish investors and speculators seeking the gold and diamond resources believed to exist in the Boer territories. However, the war exposed acute divisions within the Labour and socialist movement. The ILP's NAC condemned the war as an act of aggression on Britain's part. But the Fabian Society reacted to an anti-war resolution by deciding not to adopt a formal position, leading to the resignation of a number of members including Ramsay MacDonald. Subsequently George Bernard Shaw drafted a document, *Fabians and the Empire,* justifying Britain's imperial role on the basis that responsible powers must play their part in ruling Asia and Africa for the time being. The Fabians' enthusiasm for promoting efficiency through colonial administration gave them a common bond with the Tory imperialists. The SDF was also split with Hyndman attacking the Jews, advocating a socialist patriotism and urging British victory in South Africa. Blatchford reflected working-class Conservative sentiment when he reminded readers that 'I am an old soldier and I love Tommy Atkins. England's enemies are my enemies . . . when

England is at war I'm English. I have no politics and no party.'[41] For him, too, socialism and patriotism simply went together; though he accepted that Britain's original acquisitions in Asia and Africa had been unjustified, he felt that she could not back down now because the challenge to her position in South Africa was a threat to the empire everywhere.

Historians have sometimes attempted to dismiss working-class imperialism, or to argue that manifestations of jingoism were not really proletarian but expressions of lower-middle-class sentiment. This is an absurd misrepresentation. For the generation that had grown up at a time of popular celebrations of colonial expansion and monarchy, reinforced by racism and a sense of external threat, it was difficult not to be carried away by events like the Boer War and the First World War; to contemporaries the very fact that other nations envied the British Empire appeared to confirm that it was worth having. Anxious to avoid provoking a split between activists and rank and file, the new Labour Representation Committee simply ducked the issue of the South African War at the 1900 election. It issued a brief manifesto comprising commitments likely to reassure the widest possible range of supporters: old-age pensions and work schemes for the unemployed to appeal to social reformers, adult suffrage and payment of members for Radicals, nationalisation of land and railways (but not mines) for socialists, rejection of compulsory vaccination for working-class individualists and a Citizen Army for patriots and the SDF. Opponents of the current war found themselves condemned as unpatriotic or even as traitors. In Bow and Bromley Lansbury ignored the war in his election address, focusing instead on threats to the unions, Poor Law work, pensions and landlords.[42] In boisterous, patriotic Blackburn Philip Snowden stood against a popular local employer and benefactor who, according to Tory propaganda, had 'a greater claim upon the town than any foreigner that comes here'.[43] He polled well but only because no Liberal stood. Just two of the fifteen LRC candidates were elected: Keir Hardie at Merthyr Tydfil and Richard Bell at Derby.

Hardie's experience was the most revealing for he actually contested *two* seats, Preston and Merthyr Tydfil. Merthyr, a two-member constituency in South Wales dominated by coal and loyal to Liberalism, gave him a surprise victory. Although the desire for independent labour representation was not strong, an opportunity arose due to dissatisfaction with one of the sitting Liberal members who supported the current war. As a result the local trades councils, though not the miners, took the initiative and invited Hardie to stand. Although he agreed, he was unwilling to spend much time at Merthyr because he thought his chances were better at Preston. This turned out to be another misjudgement. At Merthyr the other Liberal opposed the war, allowing himself and Hardie to appear as acceptable candidates to the orthodox Liberal majority; they were both elected as, in effect, sound Radicals despite Hardie's fierce commitment to the cause of independent labour.

Meanwhile Hardie spent more of his time campaigning at Preston. As the Conservatives won on average 58 per cent of the vote in Preston from 1885 to 1910, and 65 per cent in 1900, the attraction the town exercised for Labour is perplexing, even allowing for the fact that Liberal weakness created an opportunity. An industrial town, Preston's main industries were cotton and engineering. As a result of its large Catholic population there was strong support for voluntary, that is religious, schools.[44] The local Conservatives were well attuned to a working-class culture based on religion, imperialism and the public house. Yet Hardie, misreading the constituency, devoted considerable attention to the temperance question which 'did not produce the anticipated result' as the local newspaper observed.[45] He was also advised *not* to give his views on the South African War but ignored it. This was magnificent but it was not electioneering.

In a constituency with Preston's traditions, accentuated by war fever, Hardie's moralistic, principled pacifism was never likely to be popular. In the absence of a Liberal candidate he managed to poll 4,835 votes to 8,944 and 8,067 for the two Tories. But he remained alarmingly out of touch with the more hedonistic and frivolous aspects of working-class life. He was known to support the boarding up of the back entrances of public houses and refusing them licences for dancing because if drinking and dancing took place 'immorality was apt to be great'.[46] Colleagues recalled that 'a smutty story made him leave a railway carriage', and on one occasion in Manchester when Blatchford invited him to a club attached to a theatre Hardie was reportedly so shocked at seeing a woman sitting on a man's lap that he pulled out his watch and left at once. He regarded pubs, theatres and music halls as degenerate and it was only later in life when Sylvia Pankhurst took him to such places that he relaxed his attitude a little.

The election of 1900 thus underlined the complexities involved in adapting Labour's appeal to the political culture of the different regions of Britain. In Derby Richard Bell had won as, in effect, a Lib-Lab trade unionist leader and Hardie had been accepted for his Radical Liberal credentials rather than for his socialism. Consequently, the idea that their success marked the triumph of the ILP must be heavily qualified. Nor did the election of Hardie and Bell indicate the demise of the Tory-socialist school. Although the leading exponents of Tory-socialism, Hyndman, Champion and Blatchford, did become marginalised after 1900 as a result of the revival of free trade, their views continued to enjoy support among the working-class rank and file. In some respects the movement grew closer to Tory-socialism during the Edwardian period, and at the grass roots the ILP itself turned out to be much less left wing than its national leaders, though this was not apparent until 1914. Moreover, the election of trade unionist Labour MPs in 1906, especially in Lancashire, brought into Parliament many men who leant towards Liberalism at national level but felt obliged to compromise with Toryism locally. There was, as yet, no obvious, single strategy for the new party.

4

'Not a single Socialist speech': Labour's Edwardian Breakthrough

The wave of jingoism generated by the Boer War conspired to throw beleaguered anti-war Liberals and socialists together in common defence of the Gladstonian tradition in foreign affairs. However, as the war dragged on until 1902 it caused acute tensions within the Conservative government, now under A. J. Balfour, because of the need to raise taxes, thereby undermining the popularity of imperialism. In 1903 Joseph Chamberlain attempted to break out of the financial impasse by launching a campaign for tariff reform in a speech at Birmingham. Although Chamberlain succeeded in converting a majority of Tories, he left the party badly divided, forcing many free-trade Tories to join the Liberals. When the next election came in 1906 a huge popular reaction in support of free trade and cheap food helped create a landslide victory for the Liberals. This new agenda inevitably pushed the LRC towards the Liberals because, despite scepticism about free trade among some socialists, cheap food was very popular among working-class voters.

Even so, there was nothing inevitable about Labour's Edwardian breakthrough, not least because the new organisation lacked adequate resources and neither of the MPs provided effective leadership. Hardie remained too hostile towards the Liberals to capitalise on the new situation and he continued to be uncomfortable in Parliament: 'I feel like a bird with its wings clipped when I am there.' Conversely, Richard Bell rapidly emerged as more loyal to the Liberals than to the LRC, under whose auspices he had been elected at Derby, and showed no interest in developing Labour's independent role.

However, although the leader-in-waiting, Ramsay MacDonald, did not enter Parliament until 1906, as secretary he put the fledgling party on to a firm footing and enabled the LRC to bargain both with its own constituent elements and with the Liberals. Originally the LRC had been an expedient by the ILP to harness the resources of the unions, but under MacDonald it began to look the other way round: socialism was being marginalised. However, this was partly obscured by MacDonald's intellectual command and his power base in the ILP. In a series of books, *Socialism and Society* (1905), *Socialism and Government* (1909), and *The Socialist Movement* (1911) he sketched a theoretical framework for the party, a useful tactic at a time when its short-term programme was hard to distinguish from that of the Liberals. MacDonald sounded sufficiently like a socialist to satisfy the ILP-ers but reassured the unions by using language that suggested continuity with Radicalism.

Even so, the SDF quickly became so disillusioned with the LRC that it withdrew its affiliation in 1902. This explains the frosty response MacDonald gave to Lady Warwick in 1905 when she invited him to a dinner at Warwick House for Labour candidates and their wives 'to talk over mutual interests'. Aware that Lady Warwick had joined the SDF, he dismissed her scathingly: 'You have very suddenly come amongst us from totally different circumstances and have taken sides instantly . . . I have doubts as to the permanent good which can be done to a democratic movement by the exploitation of an aristocratic convert.'[1] Prickly and sensitive about the new organisation being used or bought by wealthy people, MacDonald had not yet evolved into the urbane politician who happily cultivated Lady Londonderry in the 1930s.

MacDonald's paranoia was justified, for the LRC's loose federal structure evidently left it open to penetration by SDF members at the local level where the National Executive Committee's writ did not run. As the local LRCs themselves comprised affiliations by trade union and socialist society branches, the SDF retained its footing despite the prohibition at national level. In Bethnal Green, for example, when the LRC invited nominations for municipal elections the local SDF promoted three 'Socialist and Labour' candidates.[2] As late as 1909 this branch managed to function under LRC auspices, presumably because from the local perspective it seemed wiser to co-operate with fellow socialists rather than to exclude them.

In putting the LRC on to a stronger foundation MacDonald bene-fited greatly from the notorious Taff Vale Judgement of 1901, a legal ruling that made the Society of Railway Servants in South Wales liable for the costs of a strike involving the Taff Vale Railway Company. As the unions had enjoyed immunity for thirty years this came as a stunning blow, lending unexpected urgency to the claim that labour needed extra parliamentary representation. As a result affiliations to the LRC increased from 376,000 in 1900 to 861,000 in 1903 and to 921,000 by 1906; at that stage 158 trade unions and seventy-three trades councils had joined along with 16,000 socialist society members.[3] While gaining extra members the NEC also raised the level of fees payable to a penny per member affiliated, generating an annual income of £3,000 for 700,000 members. The additional funds enabled the NEC to offer a £200 salary to MPs elected under its auspices, thereby strengthening its control over candidates; this was a key step in transforming Labour into a conventional political party. Despite this the party clearly operated on exiguous finances. MacDonald had been appointed secretary partly because he could afford to do the job unpaid because his wife, Margaret, had inherited settlements of £460 per annum and capital of £5,000.[4] MacDonald received nothing from the LRC until January 1901, when it gave him just twenty guineas, though from 1904 he was paid a salary of £150. Lacking even an office, the committee met in a backroom of the MacDonalds' flat in Lincoln's Inn Fields at this stage.

Meanwhile MacDonald quietly pursued his wider electoral strategy by bargaining with the Liberal chief whip, Herbert Gladstone. Sympathetic to the idea of labour representation, Gladstone was inclined to see the Labour MPs as the working-class wing of Liberalism. After the friction of the 1890s, there had been signs of greater warmth between the two parties even in Yorkshire. In two-member Halifax the Liberal MP was keen to accept James Parker, a moderate ILP-er, as joint candidate, while in Bradford West the Liberals stood down for the ILP's Fred Jowett who almost took the seat from the Conservatives in 1900. When Bruce Glasier visited Bradford he was kept in the background: 'They don't want me just now. Quite right perhaps. They expect Liberal support.'[5]

This conciliatory mood made possible several dramatic Labour gains in by-elections. In August 1902 a vacancy in Clitheroe, a cotton-textile constituency in Lancashire, was won by David Shackleton, president of the Accrington Weavers Association. Wholly acceptable to the Liberals and indistinguishable from the Lib-Labs, Shackleton was returned unopposed. Shackleton's election made it easier for Gladstone to conciliate Labour in subsequent by-elections. In March 1903 when a Tory seat fell vacant at Woolwich, where the Liberals were weak, they stood aside for Labour. Will Crooks, a trade unionist noted for his Cockney humour, was already a member of Poplar council and board of Guardians; he received backing from the London Liberal Federation and the Liberal *Daily News* which collected £844 towards his election costs. But the key to Crooks' success was his ability to appeal beyond conventional Radical and unionist opinion to populist Toryism.[6] With the reaction against the Tory government in full flood he won comfortably because, in this Conservative-leaning constituency he had attracted more votes than a conventional Liberal was likely to do. Contemporaries interpreted his victory as evidence that the LRC represented a viable asset in the coming struggle to oust the Balfour government.

Meanwhile, the death in July 1903 of Sir Joseph Pease, Liberal member for Barnard Castle in County Durham, caused an unusual opportunity for Labour. Pease had employed as his agent Arthur Henderson, a North-East trade unionist and workingman of impeccable Liberal credentials, who now stood for the LRC. By adopting a candidate who was hostile to free trade the local Liberals played into Henderson's hands, making him, in effect, the best available Liberal. With the support of many local Liberals he won by just forty-seven votes.

The three by-elections demonstrated the viability of Liberal–Labour co-operation but did not show how strong Labour was vis-à-vis the Liberals. Any hopes of an independent breakthrough were dispelled by Labour interventions against Liberals at Dewsbury and Norwich where its candidates polled poorly and the Liberals emerged at the head of the poll. Another Labour campaign in a by-election at Preston in May 1903 also proved disappointing though it was significant as an indication of the party's capacity for adapting to Lancashire politics. This time Labour adopted a very different candidate, John Hodge of the Steel Smelters Association. Hodge, who combined an ebullient patriotism with the trade union programme, was much more attuned to Preston politics than Hardie had been. He actually dispatched a telegram to Hardie *discouraging* him from coming to speak at Preston: 'I think it unwise to overload the platform from our side,' he said.[7]

This was his way of saying that Hardie would only deter the Tory workingmen whose votes Labour had to win for victory. To this end Hodge secured the support of the leader of the Preston spinners who resigned from the local Conservative Club. Hoping to make it easier for local Tories to support him, Labour claimed it 'has dissociated itself absolutely from either Liberal or Conservative and has fixed on Labour alone as its exclusive programme, leaving the candidate open, if returned, to exercise his judgement on all other questions in the House of Commons'.[8] Hodge increased Labour's vote by 1,600, attracting some Tory workingmen in the view of the local press, but as this only cut the Conservative majority by half he felt disappointed. He blamed the Catholics for sticking with the Tories, but the *Preston Guardian* commented that 'the workingmen of Preston have shown that they do not trust the trades union leaders'.[9]

The combination of setbacks at Preston, Norwich and Dewsbury with Labour's three by-election gains fortified MacDonald in his view that an accommodation with the Liberals offered the best prospects at the forthcoming general election. Aware that the Liberals were anxious to return to power and were fearful of splitting the anti-Conservative vote, he made overtures to Herbert Gladstone via his secretary, Jesse Herbert, who reported to the chief whip: 'The LRC can directly influence the votes of nearly a million men . . . mainly men who have hitherto voted for the Liberal Party.'[10] This was an exaggeration, but as Herbert and Gladstone were sympathetic they accepted the claim. Equally exaggerated but more telling was MacDonald's claim that the LRC enjoyed a fighting fund of £100,000; from Gladstone's point of view it would be enormously advantageous if Labour shouldered the cost of fighting seats in which the Liberals were weak especially in the West Midlands and Lancashire. By September they had settled the details and Herbert travelled to Leicester, where the TUC conference was meeting, to confirm the agreement with MacDonald.

Both men denied the existence of any formal pact. MacDonald naturally feared antagonising the socialists on the one hand and offending working-class Tories on the other. However, his subsequent denials were rather disingenuous. For his part Gladstone quietly put pressure on some Liberal Associations to allow Labour a free run, while MacDonald exerted himself to kill burgeoning Labour candidatures

in certain Liberal seats; indeed this activity occupied a high proportion of NEC time right up to 1914.[11] While MacDonald could hardly
control local socialist societies, he could emasculate their efforts by
denying them the official LRC nomination – effective because it warned
local trade unions that a rebel candidate was a socialist.

As a result of the Gladstone–MacDonald Pact fifty LRC candidates
stood in 1906 of whom thirty-one had no Liberal opponent. Of the
twenty-nine Labour MPs elected no fewer than twenty-four had enjoyed
Liberal backing. On this limited scale the pact proved surprisingly
uncontroversial. Mostly 'sober, earnest Liberals' as MacDonald himself
put it, the LRC candidates were largely acceptable to the Liberal Party.
Some stood in single-member constituencies where the Liberals' own
chances were not good. But many victories were won in two-member
boroughs, where Labour and Liberal ran jointly, including Bolton,
Blackburn, Halifax, Preston, Derby, Newcastle, Sunderland and
Portsmouth. These were mostly marginal or Conservative constituencies where the Liberals usually struggled to take both seats but where
Labour could help by splitting the Tory working-class vote. The strategy
worked very well in 1906 because the leading issues drew the two
parties together in defence of free trade, to repeal the Taff Vale
Judgement, introduce welfare reforms such as pensions, and condemn
the Tories for importing 'Chinese Slavery', that is indentured labourers,
into the South African mines, thereby filling the jobs they had promised to British workers. The LRC's manifesto largely ignored a 1905
conference resolution in favour of replacing capitalism with public
ownership, and endorsed the Liberal line.

The effect of these issues in encouraging voters to see the two
parties as an alliance, is corroborated by the voting in the two-member
boroughs. For example, in Halifax Labour's James Parker received 8,937
votes of which 8,573 were from electors who had used their other vote
for the Liberal; in Leicester MacDonald won with 12,998 votes including
12,316 'splits' with his Liberal colleague. The pact had worked extremely
well by minimising losses to the Conservatives. There were only
seventeen three-cornered contests in the entire country so that
although the Conservative poll was actually quite high at 43.6 per cent,
they won only 157 seats.

With twenty-nine MPs Labour had achieved a major breakthrough
and a substantial footing in Parliament at last. But the party spent the

next eight years arguing over the question: should the pact be maintained or was it safe to venture beyond it? This was complicated by
the fact that the electoral arrangement had imparted a distinct regional
bias to Labour representation. The party had returned only one
member in Wales, one in the Midlands, two in Scotland, three in
Yorkshire, three in the North-East, and three in London. In Scotland,
where the pact had not been operative at all, eleven LRC candidates
stood, all in three-cornered fights; according to the Scottish Liberals
nine or ten of them were confirmed socialists, denounced by Winston
Churchill, then a Liberal, as 'an obscure gang of malignant wire-
pullers'.[12] One consequence, in the Liberal view, was that the
Conservatives had lost 'fully as many votes to the Labour Party as the
Liberals did', enabling George Barnes to capture the Tory seat of
Glasgow Blackfriars.[13]

Consequently, Labour was poorly represented in some of its
strongest areas because the Liberals retained strength there too.
Conversely, no fewer than thirteen of the twenty-nine MPs sat for
Lancashire–Cheshire seats because the Liberals had found it easier to
make concessions there. In the process Labour had demonstrated its
capacity to win votes from entrenched Conservatism and had already
begun to compromise with the local political agenda by supporting
voluntary schools, opposing Church disestablishment and approving
compensation for publicans whose licences were suppressed – all issues
that separated Labour from orthodox Liberalism. But as many ILP
members had been recruited from Conservatives this was not problematical. In Preston where the textile industry made free trade popular,
Tory workers deserted their old party, but they went more heavily to
the Labour candidate, who topped the poll, than to the Liberal. At
Blackburn Philip Snowden ran comfortably ahead of his Liberal
colleague because, as he said, 'the Labour Party had drawn its support
very largely from conservative working men'.[14] In St Helens, a town
that returned a Tory member despite an economy based on glass,
chemicals and mining, the result was felt to turn on the behaviour of
the large Catholic population. The local clergy met and declared the
views of the Labour candidate, Thomas Glover, a local mining official, to be satisfactory.[15] Glover also made it easy for Tories to switch
to him by casting himself expressly as an independent, that is, not
associated with either of the big parties.[16] In Manchester Gorton, John

Hodge dislodged the Conservatives by bidding for the patriotic vote: 'I do not know why the Tory Party should have a monopoly of the Union Jack. They have not honoured it. We will have the British flag too – but with no slavery under it [loud cheers].'[17] Focusing on the Boer War, Hodge demanded that Britain 'stop the landing of any more Chinese in South Africa' and he questioned the high rate of casualties suffered: 'For what? To enrich a small body of foreign financiers whose names could only be pronounced by saying anything and sneezing thrice.'[18] Though not the language usually associated with Labour candidates, Hodge's boisterous, left-wing expression of nationalism was another harbinger of Labour's adaptation to the politics of the North-West.

Whatever the regional variations, however, MacDonald's strategy seemed to have been fully justified by the results. 'It is not too much to say, after two months' experience, that the independence of Labour in the House of Commons has proved a triumphant success,' commented the *Jarrow Labour Herald*. 'The LRC men sitting in a body on the Opposition benches below the gangway have a tactical advantage which is quite out of proportion to their numbers . . . the same numbers of men, in the leading strings of the Liberal Party, would be comparatively powerless.'[19] In the context of 401 Liberals, this was an exaggerated assessment of the role of the twenty-nine Labour members. However, it made sense during 1906–8 when Labour often made the running by pushing successfully for legislation to reverse the Taff Vale Judgement and introduce free school meals, while pressing for the introduction of old-age pensions and measures to reduce unemployment through the 'Right to Work' Bill.

On the other hand, the euphoria of 1906 generated high expectations that quickly created strains between the national leadership and rank-and-file members who felt MacDonald was slipping too easily into the role of a client of the Liberal government. 'Not a single Socialist speech has been delivered in the English Popular Assembly,' complained Hyndman in December 1906.[20] His view was corroborated by the social reformers on the Liberal side who were very appreciative of the Labour members because their pressure encouraged the government in the direction they wanted to it go. Charles Masterman saw the party as 'a mixture of old-fashioned Trades Unionists, with a sprinkling of well-behaved and pleasant Socialists' who were 'eager in making a bargain with the Government'.[21] H. W. Massingham argued the Liberals need not worry about Keir Hardie's attacks: 'it is notorious that he does not really get his way in his own party, and . . . he is not so sedulous a Parliamentarian as Mr Shackleton or Mr MacDonald'.[22] For his part Ramsay MacDonald frankly accepted that as the two parties had to co-operate in Parliament to force progressive legislation through in the face of hostility from the House of Lords, it was logical to maintain co-operation in the constituencies; he scorned 'this false idea of independence, that only Labour or Socialist votes should be given to Labour or Socialist candidates. It is humbug.'[23]

But did this oblige Labour to stick strictly to the terms of the pact negotiated in 1903? The frustration of much government legislation by the peers between 1906 and 1908 made the Liberals vulnerable – and thus tempted ILP activists to take advantage by intervening in by-elections. In August 1906 the party stood in a by-election at Cockermouth where the candidate polled badly but split the Liberal vote sufficiently to give the Conservatives victory. Under pressure the ILP agreed to refrain from promoting new candidatures, but so many by-elections occurred that this self-denying ordinance proved impossible to maintain, especially in July 1907 when two Liberal members died: Sir Charles Mark Palmer at Jarrow and Sir James Kitson at Colne Valley. In 1906 Pete Curran of the Gasworkers Union had contested Jarrow and spent three years working the constituency where he enjoyed the backing of several ILP branches in the mining communities and published the *Jarrow Labour Herald*. The journal's advertisements provide evidence that Labour could tap a wide range of small businesses in the constituency including a chimney sweep, a boot repairer, a tailor, 'The People's Chemist', a hatter, a coal merchant, a metal, rag and bone merchant, a furniture merchant, a maker of wreaths and crosses and a dealer in cage birds. Faced with an entrenched Liberal employer whose shipyards guaranteed employment for Jarrow, Curran carefully attacked landowners who, he said, did the workers of Jarrow 'the great honour of robbing them every year, in strictly legal fashion, of many thousands of pounds in the way of ground rents'.[24]

Clearly Curran's candidacy was more than propagandist, though his victory in 1907 was attributable to several accidents. The local Irish, who had consistently backed Palmer, decided to step up the pressure on the government for a Home Rule Bill by running a Nationalist candidate, while the Conservatives, who had not stood in 1906, now intervened. As a result the Liberal vote was split three ways and Curran won even though his own vote had fallen since 1906. But although Curran was an official Labour candidate, he was also an unapologetic socialist which made his victory awkward for the parliamentary leaders in the light of the more dramatic events unfolding in Colne Valley.

Labour had not fought Colne Valley in 1906 and consequently the adoption of a pronounced socialist, Victor Grayson, represented a challenge to the NEC. As Colne Valley was not affiliated to the LRC Grayson could not be a Labour candidate, but he was not even on the list of ILP candidates and his adoption was completely irregular. However, the national party was presented with a fait accompli.[25] 'If we are going to have a dozen Colne Valleys', complained MacDonald, 'we might just as well shut up shop altogether, more particularly as it comes after Jarrow.'[26] Grayson responded: 'I think most sincerely this cleavage has to come sometime, and nothing will be lost by precipitating it.'[27] So determined were the Labour leaders to maintain their strategy that they refused to support Grayson's campaign, though this was partly because they disliked him personally. 'I don't care for Grayson, he is a young, cheap orator, not at all the type we wish to get into Parliament,' commented Bruce Glasier. Even Keir Hardie lamented that 'men who have grown grey in the movement should not feel that they were put aside to make room for younger men'.[28] As most of the Labour MPs were middle-aged union officials they resented the rise of a twenty-five-year-old who evidently held their achievements in contempt.

As a result only Philip Snowden assisted at the by-election. Grayson, however, benefited from the fact that the Liberals, who had been unopposed in 1906, had allowed their organisation to deteriorate and were made vulnerable by the unpopularity of the government. The charismatic Grayson stirred the constituency and he was followed everywhere by admiring crowds especially of young mill girls. Conscious of his charms, the candidate interrupted his own speech at Marsden to say: 'I've changed my hair-style, ladies. Do you like it ?'[29] In a desperately close contest he won by 153 votes.

Down the decades Victor Grayson's fraught relations with the

Labour Party over socialism and youth were to be regularly replicated. Despite being repudiated by the party he had been conciliatory towards the Labour MPs and his election address followed the orthodox party line, including the 'Right to Work' Bill, old-age pensions, votes for women, land taxation, state land purchase, free trade, school meals, graduated income tax, payment of MPs, abolition of the House of Lords, railway nationalisation and the eight-hour day.[30] However, the parliamentary leaders, exaggerating Grayson's extremism, failed to see that, properly used, he was an asset to the movement. He himself allowed his language to run away with him in the aftermath of his victory, boasting that 'This epoch-making victory has been won for pure revolutionary Socialism . . . We have not trimmed our sails to get a half-hearted vote.'[31] This dig at the other Labour members only compounded his unpopularity and the isolation that was to be his undoing over the next three years.

Inevitably Grayson overplayed his hand and embarrassed the Labour leaders so much that even the ILP played down his success, arguing, 'We must not overstrain the Colne Valley victory as a Socialist victory.'[32] But the critics now felt emboldened to challenge MacDonald's caution. In a notorious pamphlet, *Is the Parliamentary Labour Party a Failure?* (1908), Ben Tillett claimed that the party in the country had nothing but contempt for its parliamentary representatives: 'The Lion has no teeth or claws, and is losing its growl too.' He regarded it as futile for the MPs to strive to support Liberal legislation, that was in any case being mangled by the peers, when they should be concentrating on unemployment. Before long MacDonald recognised that the rebels were jeopardising his electoral strategy and threatening his power base in the ILP. In 1908 several ILP branches supported an SDF candidate in a by-election at Newcastle, a two-member seat held jointly by Labour and the Liberals. This proved enough to split the Liberal vote and lose the seat to the Tories thereby creating a crisis in the ILP. Consequently, when Tillett stood as an unofficial candidate against the Liberal, Sir Alfred Mond, in a by-election at Swansea, MacDonald intervened publicly to announce: 'Had I a vote at Swansea it would not be given for Mr Tillett.'

The attacks of Tillett and Grayson had exposed the flaw at the heart of the Edwardian Labour Party. For although the 1906 election appeared to mark the success of the ILP's strategy of harnessing trade union resources to the cause of independent labour representation, the electoral success had tipped the balance of the party against the socialists. Only six of the MPs were ILP-ers: MacDonald, Hardie, Snowden, J. R. Clynes, Fred Jowett and James Parker. Most members were union officials, some of whom could not easily be distinguished from the Lib-Labs, while several combined pronounced right-wing opinions with their socialism. Dissatisfaction reached a head at the 1909 ILP conference where the rank and file made it clear that they wanted local branches to be free to run candidates regardless of national policy, thereby provoking MacDonald, Snowden, Bruce Glasier and Hardie to threaten to resign from the party. The conference was so shocked by this that it backed down, agreeing to abide by Labour policy – but only by 244 votes to 146. As a result MacDonald declined to attend the conference for the next five years. The withdrawal of the ILP from the Labour Party was already in prospect.

Moreover, the party continued to find itself caught between Liberal-socialist politics on the one hand and Tory-socialism on the other. This divide had been obscured in 1906 by the prominence of such issues as free trade and 'Chinese Slavery' that united Labour with Liberalism. However, during 1907–8 fresh controversies erupted that exposed the ideological and cultural divisions within the movement. In deference to their Nonconformist supporters' hostility towards Balfour's 1902 Education Act, which had abolished elected school boards, the new Liberal government tackled education. It thereby provoked opposition from Catholics who wanted state support for their schools but insisted on keeping control, avoiding inspection and imposing religious tests on teachers. MacDonald, who agreed with the Nonconformists that state-subsidised schools should offer non-denominational or 'secular' religious teaching, backed the Liberals in Parliament, as did most of his colleagues. However, Labour could not expect to be immune to the controversy because Catholics loomed large in many northern industrial constituencies. James Sexton, who had almost been elected in Liverpool, and James O'Grady, who represented Leeds East, fought strongly against secular teaching in schools and for subsidised Catholic education. Both men were Catholics themselves working in constituencies with large Catholic communities. In Jarrow, where Labour's Pete Curran was also a Catholic, the party was troubled by the need to conciliate divergent opinions. Catholic Labour supporters, protesting at attempts to 'drive the Priest out of the school', asked: 'What right have you to interfere with our schools? It was the money of Catholics that paid for them and the Catholics of Jarrow pay to keep them going.'[33] Getting on the wrong side of Catholic opinion proved costly for Labour in the 1908 municipal elections when the party attributed setbacks in towns such as Leeds, Manchester, Wigan, Clitheroe and Hartlepool to a shift of angry Catholics to the Conservatives.[34]

Thus, while most MPs backed the Liberal line at Westminster, locally Labour increasingly compromised with the immediate pressures and interests facing it. In Lancashire the recognition that socialism was not a great asset to the party inevitably provoked a schism between ILP and SDF activists on the one hand and Labour pragmatists and trade unionists on the other. The disagreement seriously handicapped the party in the textile areas such as Bury, Burnley, Eccles, Hyde, Oldham and Stockport where the strength of local Liberalism dictated the politics of the pact and left the ILP increasingly marginalised.[35] Conversely, outside the spinning and weaving districts Labour lost support if it resisted the Tory causes. Hence, in Merseyside, Preston, Wigan, St Helens, Manchester, Salford and throughout the heavy industrial areas of western Lancashire the party began to distance itself from Liberal Nonconformism, especially where religion and education were concerned. In Blackburn Labour simply abandoned its support for non-sectarian schooling, which was not too difficult as 40 per cent of ILP members there were former Conservatives; but in Burnley the LRC collapsed because it could not agree what line to adopt.[36] The process was accelerated in constituencies where Labour aspired to fill the vacuum left by a weak Liberalism. Thus in Salford and Manchester the party prospered in the poorest Tory-leaning wards, while in Liverpool James Sexton adopted Tory tactics by exploiting the threat posed by Jewish and Chinese labour and by campaigning on material issues such as the housing shortage. This enabled Labour to cultivate communities that divided along sectarian lines and were gripped by poverty and apathy, but it also meant ditching moralistic socialism for a more hard-headed and right-wing approach.

In Birmingham and the adjacent West Midlands constituencies including Handsworth, Wednesbury, West Bromwich and Wolverhampton, the Conservative and Liberal Unionist alliance enjoyed such wide support in both affluent and depressed areas that

Labour struggled to establish itself. As the Liberals were traditionally weak they willingly stood aside for Labour in several seats, but the party was divided between socialists and trade unionists. In the event Labour made advances in municipal elections in Smethwick, Birmingham East and Wolverhampton West – all Tory seats – by focusing on house-building and municipal tramways. As a result the party began to establish itself as the alternative to the Conservatives thereby laying the foundation for several surprise victories in the West Midlands in 1918.

In London the situation was complicated by the concentration of Progressive Liberal MPs whose advocacy of interventionist social policies largely satisfied working-class demands. As a result, where Labour scored victories in West Ham, Bow and Bromley, Woolwich and Deptford it was essential to mobilise Liberal support but when this was repudiated, as at Bow in 1912, the seat was lost. By comparison with the North of England support was difficult to mobilise in London because of the casual employment, desperate poverty, low unionisation, weak Nonconformity and protectionist sentiment. Like the Liberals, Labour depended on middle-class leaders to organise and subsidise the machine: Dr Alfred Salter in Bermondsey, R. C. K. Ensor in Poplar and Clement Attlee in Stepney. In Labour seats such as Woolwich and Deptford the Conservatives were also strong, so much so that they recaptured Woolwich from Will Crooks in January 1910. Charles Bowerman held on to Deptford, an impoverished constituency with naval and military traditions, by appealing to the local Tory culture; he was linked to the Club and Institute Union and defended working-class recreations such as gambling. In contrast to the East End Labour managed to win Woolwich and Deptford by creating a trade union party capable of attracting Tory votes, but as a result the ILP socialists felt themselves increasingly redundant by 1914.

Labour was also troubled by the renewed controversy over alcohol. Although the 1906 conference approved a resolution in favour of the 'local veto' on licensed premises, some delegates condemned attempts to reduce the number of public houses as a futile method for stopping drunkenness. One delegate pointedly suggested 'they could serve the cause of Labour better than by tinkering with the worn-out pledges of the Liberal Party'.[37] Yet in 1908 when the government introduced a Licensing Bill it was loyally backed by Labour MPs, including

Henderson, Snowden, Shackleton, MacDonald and Hardie, who were denounced by Ben Tillett as 'the Temperance bleating martyrs' for their pains; 'what a mockery it was, and merely a waste of time', a reference to the mangling of the bill in the House of Lords. Tillett saw drink as only one symptom of a wider gulf within the movement: 'If the Labour Party could select a King,' he complained, 'he would be a Feminist, a Temperance crank, a Nonconformist charlatan . . . an anti-sport, an anti-jollity advocate, a teetotaller, as well as a general wet blanket . . . Horse-racing would vanish [and] as for music halls, they would be anathema!'[38]

Yet there was a third way. In his 1907 campaign Victor Grayson had advocated public control of the drink trade. In a 200-page analysis, *Socialism and the Drink Question* (1908), Philip Snowden condemned the trade as a prime example of capitalist exploitation of workingmen designed to keep them in their present station in society. But he dismissed prohibition as a proven failure and argued that local option had failed to reduce consumption in New Zealand, Australia and Canada. Despite his disapproval of drinking he accepted that governments must 'provide for the satisfaction of a reasonable indulgence in drink, but [should] prevent the abuse of it'.[39] His solution involved eliminating the private profit motive, which boosted consumption, by adopting municipal control of the trade. Municipalisation offered a satisfying means of reconciling a socialistic policy with toleration of working-class drinking, but it effectively aligned Labour with the Tory rather than the Liberal side in the debate.

This was the direction in which the movement was moving at the grass roots. Originally few Labour clubs had sold alcohol, 'which is more than can be said for our Liberal and Tory opponents' as one activist put it. But this was impossibly idealistic especially in areas where Conservatives championed the workers' beer. During the late 1890s Labour had started to distance itself from the temperance controversy in municipal elections by aligning itself with the growing number of workingmen's clubs; even the ILP had formed an Independent Labour Club which affiliated to the Club and Institute Union (CIU). Working through local clubs to promote sports on the one hand and relief for the unemployed on the other, it offered socialists an excellent means of engaging with workingmen and establishing themselves as a non-party force distinct from both Liberal temperance fanatics and Tory brewers. In Wolverhampton they even formed 'Non-political Workingmen's Clubs' which were in fact used as a base for local election campaigns.[40]

In effect each LRC coped with the issue in the light of local conditions. For example, in Jarrow the party attracted criticism from its own members for holding a smoking concert in a public house on the grounds that Labour should not associate with 'the monopolists of the Liquor Trade'.[41] But although 'it was painful . . . to watch a crowd of strong, intelligent young fellows indulging freely in stuff which could do them no good', the critics admitted that public houses offered the most comfortable rooms for Labour meetings. Consequently the Jarrow party compromised with the workers' appetite for alcohol regardless of national policy pronouncements.

The cultural divide was also exposed by the running debate about national defence, especially the German naval-building programme which the Conservative press exploited by launching scares about an invasion of the British Isles. Lord Roberts of Kandahar had launched a campaign for universal military training to put Britain on a more equal footing with her Continental rivals, but although many Tories sympathised, they were afraid to adopt it as party policy in view of the traditional pride in voluntary recruiting. Although the majority of Labour politicians appear to have shared the Liberal belief in voluntarism, a vociferous, patriotic school of socialists associated with the SDF saw the issue in terms of the link between citizenship and military service. Ben Tillett argued that an army of conscripts was not likely to be employed to break strikes, a relevant consideration in the context of the current industrial turmoil.[42] In 1908 Will Thorne introduced a Citizen Army Bill, involving a form of compulsory annual military training for those aged between eighteen and twenty-nine; they would then enter the reserves and elect their own officers. The force was to be used in cases of civil emergency or foreign invasion. Thorne justified the Citizen Army as 'a guarantee of individual liberty, of social freedom and of national independence'. However, these sentiments were anathema to most of the Liberal–Labour leaders; the ILP condemned Thorne for trying to 'unbag his little abortion to the public gaze'.[43] But among the rank and file, where national defence ranked higher than individual liberty, his ideas were much more acceptable, as became clear during the First World War.

The attacks launched by Grayson, Tillett and others on the party leadership gained force during 1907–8 because of the optimism generated by the by-elections and disillusionment with the government. However, this phase came to an abrupt end in 1908 when the Liberals recovered the initiative. This was the result of several innovations including the introduction of non-contributory old-age pensions and Lloyd George's 'People's Budget' in 1909 which imposed higher taxes on unearned income and motor-car taxes paid by a wealthy minority, and raised the prospect of effective taxation of landed wealth following a comprehensive valuation of land ownership. The rejection of his Budget by the peers provoked a major constitutional crisis leading to two general elections in 1910, culminating in the curtailment of the powers of the House of Lords in 1911. In the process Labour became marginalised in the sense that it had no option but to back Liberal social and financial reforms and welcome the attempt to clip the peers' wings. For a time these issues polarised politics, making it almost inevitable that Labour would stick to the electoral pact as being even more necessary than it had been in 1906. Moreover, earlier assumptions that that the Liberal Party would become obsolete were now largely discredited partly because there was so much life in Victorian issues such as free trade, education and constitutional reform, but also because the Liberal programme had been redefined in terms of collectivist measures designed to raise working-class standards of living.

In addition, the relationship between the Labour Movement and the Liberal government went beyond electoral and parliamentary collaboration. As a result of the extensive programme of state social welfare reforms, a number of new state organisations were established beginning with labour exchanges in 1908. The authorities were keen to employ workingmen and trade unionists in the local exchanges to help reassure clients that they would not be pressed into accepting employment below union rates, and that there would be no attempt to supply blackleg labour as had happened in privately organised bureaux in the past. In 1910 Richard Bell, the member for Derby, accepted a post in the labour-exchange department of the Board of Trade at an annual salary of £400. In 1913 The Times claimed that 374 known socialist and Labour activists were employed in government departments, notably at the National Insurance Board, the Board of Trade and the Home Office. The best known of these was David

Shackleton MP who became an adviser to Winston Churchill at the Board of Trade. Shackleton had been instrumental in preparing the legislation that reversed the Taff Vale Judgement in 1906 and in negotiating over the labour-exchanges scheme in 1908. In 1910 he became senior labour adviser to the Home Office and in 1911 a commissioner at the National Health Insurance Commission, moving on in 1916 to become permanent secretary of the newly formed Ministry of Labour. This pattern of integration into the official system complemented Labour's political alliance and it underlined the gradual marginalisation of the left-wing critics of party strategy.

The task of keeping the party united was not made easier by Grayson's erratic behaviour after entering Parliament. As he had no means of support, the Colne Valley party considered how to find him a salary. Eventually the ILP offered 200 guineas annually but only on condition that Grayson accepted party policy and abstained from criticism.[44] However, as he refused to sign the Labour Party constitution he was not granted the Labour whip and would not receive funding once the ILP's money ran out. Instead of conciliating the movement, Grayson seemed bent on exacerbating divisions between socialists and trade unionists. He denounced unionism on the grounds that 'its economic theory is hopelessly insufficient, and also because its political practice [is] childishly innocent', and even attacked the railway union MP, G. H. Wardle, in Stockport, his own constituency.[45] Grayson also offended colleagues by his poor attendance in the Commons and his increasingly anti-parliamentary tone. They especially deplored his drinking habits; in 1908 he tried to insist that the Commons debate unemployment but was suspended from the House when 'obviously under the influence of alcohol' according to Fenner Brockway. 'Grayson is making an utter fool of himself,' observed MacDonald. At the party conference in Portsmouth in January 1909 he was kidnapped by local Conservatives who drove him into the countryside where they plied him with alcohol – as was obvious on his return to the conference.[46] It was at Portsmouth that a motion forbidding any Labour MP from appearing to support any measures on Liberal or Conservative platforms was debated and rejected by 788,000 to 113,000, a clear repudiation of Grayson's views.

As a result, by 1910 Grayson had become a discredited figure. At the January election he boasted 'I have not been a nerveless automaton worked by Party Whips', but he was pushed into third place in Colne Valley.[47] Increasingly marginalised, he joined the British Socialist Party which was formed at Bradford in September 1911, an amalgamation of seventy-seven SDF branches, thirty Clarion clubs and thirty-six ILP branches. Though indicative of the disillusionment among some rank-and-file socialists, the BSP represented no great threat to Labour and was too weak to mount an electoral campaign. In the end Grayson had helped to bury the challenge to MacDonald rather than to exploit it.

Meanwhile Asquith's government decided to hold a general election in January 1910 so as to overrule the peers' rejection of the Budget, but before proceeding to reform the House of Lords – which required the creation of hundreds of extra Liberal peers – the king insisted that they win a second election which took place in December. The two elections virtually became referenda, one on the Budget and the other on reform of the Lords, which polarised the country and left Labour with little room for manoeuvre. Although MacDonald fairly argued that his pact with the Liberals did not amount to an alliance, over time it certainly acquired the characteristics of an alliance, a process accelerated by the controversies of 1910 which left Labour even more closely implicated in the Liberal cause than in 1906.

In this situation the NEC had little patience with demands by a handful of local enthusiasts to run new campaigns without having the resources and organisation to support them. As late as 1913 only 143 constituency organisations had affiliated to the Labour Party, and of these seventy-three were actually trades councils rather than LRCs. Although a trades council could become the base for a parliamentary campaign, many of them did not consider themselves as having a party political function which they saw as a distraction from their proper industrial role. Consequently, Labour scarcely had, as yet, the organisational base necessary to conduct a genuine national campaign. In December 1909 the NEC, looking at thirty-three constituencies where a three-cornered contest was in prospect, agreed to reconsider many of them 'with a view to minimising the number of probably unsuccessful contests'.[48] As a result, although 110 candidatures had been under consideration in the autumn of 1909, Labour fought seventy-eight seats in January, an increase on 1906 but a modest one. After the first election the party's national agent urged the NEC to reduce the list: 'I do not think that the vote at Crewe under present circumstance justifies our continuing to contest it. The same is true of Holmfirth, Middlesbrough, Wakefield and [Liverpool] West Toxteth. Nor do I think a further contest at Portsmouth or Leith would be of any value.' He advised 'a much shorter list of candidates than we had last January with a much bigger proportion of wins'.[49] Consequently only fifty-six candidates stood in December, compared with fifty in 1906.

The outcome of the 1910 elections is not easy to assess. At the dissolution Labour technically had forty-five MPs as a result of the decision of the Miners Federation to affiliate to the party in 1908 which brought fifteen miners' MPs – formerly Lib-Labs – and 550,000 affiliated members into the party. However, this created a confusing situation in that a number of the miners' members including Thomas Burt (Morpeth), John Wilson (Wansbeck), Charles Fenwick (Mid-Durham) and William Abraham (Rhondda) refused to stop appearing on Liberal platforms or even to sign the Labour constitution in some cases. In the January election Labour lost eight seats and gained three, giving a new total of forty. This rose to forty-two in December. Taking the two elections together Labour won seventy-seven of the ninety-two straight contests with Conservatives, but only two of thirty-eight contests where Liberals were involved. In the thirty-five three-cornered contests the party came third in twenty-nine and second in six. In effect, the pact had worked very well, arguably better than in 1906. Labour had done well within its confines but poorly when it ventured outside it. The Liberals recovered Colne Valley and Jarrow and Labour candidates dropped into third place in both cases. In those seats where the original pact collapsed the results were dire. At Gateshead, where Labour had won comfortably in a straight fight with the Conservatives in 1906, the Liberals intervened and recaptured the seat, pushing Labour into third place; in December Labour did not even contest Gateshead.

As very few constituencies enjoyed a run of three-cornered contests it is difficult to measure the level of Labour support over time. One exception was Huddersfield where all three parties fought strongly and Labour's share of the poll fluctuated from 33.8 per cent in 1906 to 31.6 in January 1910 and 29 in December. This suggests that after a surge around 1903–6, Labour support had fallen back a little and then stabilised. There was thus no basis for thinking that the party could risk a major breakthrough especially as it lacked the organisation and the financial resources to do so. This was the thinking behind the NEC's determination to maintain the pact – negotiation left a little scope for additional Labour contests, but not much.

Yet although theses tactics appeared justified by the overall increase in party representation, they inevitably exacerbated the discontent among some activists. After the January election the ILP's East Ham branch unanimously carried a resolution expressing its 'indignation at the deplorable weakness of the action of the Labour Party group now being pursued in the House of Commons and calls on it for a more independent and fighting policy'. Two weeks later the branch declared 'the time has arrived to declare for a straight Socialist policy, believing alliances with any other Party to be detrimental to the objects of Socialism'.[50] Yet the leaders recognised that, quite apart from safeguarding the party's own electoral interests, the pact made complete sense from the national perspective. The Conservatives, who had pushed their share of the vote to over 46 per cent, would have won an overall majority of seats if Labour and the Liberals had not severely restricted the number of three-cornered contests. As a minority government the Liberals were now dependent on the votes of the forty-two Labour members to enact reforming legislation especially as the eighty Irish were not always reliable.

This situation was far from unwelcome to Ramsay MacDonald, for not only did he and his colleagues endorse controversial Liberal proposals, including Irish Home Rule, but he also appreciated that the situation gave Labour more scope for bargaining. For example, the introduction of payment of members in 1911, at an annual salary of £400, was an innovation greatly in Labour's interest. That MacDonald accepted the logic of the new situation is underlined by his private correspondence with his fellow Scot, Alexander Murray, the Liberal chief whip, which shows how harmoniously they worked together. During 1911 MacDonald promised to keep the Labour members up to the mark in supporting the government's National Insurance Bill – to which many Labour MPs objected because of the compulsory contributions extracted from the insured employees – and he offered Murray support for 'any reasonable application of the closure' to speed the legislation through the House.[51] Macdonald enjoyed friendly relationships with Murray and other leading Liberals as is indicated by invitations he issued to come and play golf at Lossiemouth: 'let us discuss together whether you could not be induced to lead the House of Lords as a member of a Labour Ministry'.[52] As Murray was not much of a socialist this may have been a joke. However, the remarks must be seen in context; in 1912 Murray wrote 'men like yourself cannot for long be outside a British cabinet'; and Lloyd George began to float the idea of including MacDonald in a Liberal government. A skilful short-term tactician, the Labour leader also thought ahead, and his mind had begun to run on the possibility of incorporating progressive Liberals into a Labour ministry as eventually happened in 1924. In short, he was not going to be diverted from his collaboration with the Liberals.

Inevitably, however, these developments left Ramsay MacDonald even more detached from the ILP, though he had consolidated his position in the Labour Party itself. Strictly speaking the party had no leader at this stage, only a chairman of the parliamentary party. After 1906 this role had been filled by Hardie, followed by Henderson in 1908 and George Barnes in 1910. None of these appointments commanded general satisfaction; the unions disliked Hardie, while the socialists regarded Henderson as too pro-Liberal. Yet MacDonald had felt reluctant to give up the secretaryship because of the influence it gave him. However, in 1911 he passed it over to Henderson and became chairman. On both counts this was the right choice. Although stubborn and intolerant of criticism, and therefore not adept at managing colleagues, MacDonald had quickly emerged as the party's outstanding parliamentarian. He never succumbed to the temptation to make a protest or a scene in the Commons like Hardie and Grayson, but he learned how to intervene effectively in debates. 'Governments are not afraid of Socialist speeches,' he observed, 'they are very much afraid of successful criticism in detail.'[53] As the comments of Lloyd George and Murray suggest, his talent had been recognised outside the party.

Nonetheless, the undercurrent of criticism persisted because the critics had exposed Labour's basic dilemma: for how long could a party designed to be genuinely independent allow itself to be confined to the status of client to a larger party? Throughout the period up to the outbreak of war socialist activists argued that the time had come for Labour to emancipate itself from this role. Yet as long as the political agenda was dominated by Liberal initiatives including Home Rule, health and unemployment insurance, and Lloyd George's campaign for land reform, house-building and minimum wages, it proved difficult for Labour to offer a distinctive programme. It could not outflank the Liberals because socialism was insufficiently popular, but it could not beat them on their own ground either. There were, however, two chinks in the Liberals' armour. One was votes for women, a cause Labour belatedly adopted in 1912, thereby highlighting the illiberalism of Asquith's government. The other, more potent in the end, was foreign and defence policy which involved not only massive expenditure on an arms race with Germany, but a drift into a virtual alliance with France and Russia. As all this was repugnant to many Radical Liberals, it allowed Labour scope to seize some of the high ground of Liberalism and thus accelerate the disintegration of the Liberal Party which MacDonald always believed must come eventually.

There was, however, an alternative route out of Labour's electoral impasse. Standard accounts of Labour's history have not recognised the extent to which the party became consumed by a debate over reform of the electoral system during the Edwardian period. After all, the rationale for the pact, which now appeared to be holding the party back, lay in the fact that Britain's first-past-the-post system threatened to return Conservative governments on a minority vote. Since the mid-1880s some Liberals had campaigned for proportional representation using a transferable vote in multi-member constituencies. This would have enabled the Liberal and Labour parties to run candidates against each other throughout the country if they wished, without splitting the anti-Conservative vote, and thus allow Labour to extend its electoral front in line with its local organisation and resources. As W. C. Anderson, MP for Fife West, observed, every socialist and Labour party in Europe at that time favoured proportional representation. Along with Philip Snowden and G. H. Roberts, Anderson was among its most prominent Labour promoters. There was wide support for both PR and the Alternative Vote among the MPs and in the wider movement. In 1911 the TUC conference voted for PR by a three-to-one margin, in 1912 the NUR and the National Union of Clerks adopted it for internal elections, and in 1913 the ILP conference demanded its introduction. According to Snowden PR would have given Labour a hundred MPs which 'it cannot get for a generation under the present system'.[54] As the election of a member could be secured on the basis of a quota of votes this meant that with 9 per cent in a ten-member Liverpool seat or 8 per cent in an eleven-member Birmingham seat

Labour could anticipate representation in places where it currently found the going hard.[55] This prospect would naturally have given a spur to constituency organisation and removed the friction between local activists and the NEC over new candidates. As things stood the party's national agent found himself in the embarrassing position of urging the creation of local organisations but postponing the adoption of candidates to an indefinite point in the future.[56] According to supporters of PR the system would relieve Labour candidates from the need to trim for Liberal votes and promote 'a closer political relationship' between elected members and their supporters. As a result, by 1914 with Labour's representation apparently stagnant, the case for reform seemed compelling.

Despite this, the movement remained unconvinced. To some extent this reflected the attitude of the rank and file who were, as one put it, 'always suspicious of anything that came from the middle-class [that is, socialist] movement'.[57] But above all, Ramsay MacDonald was antagonistic to the whole idea because, like Gladstone back in the 1880s, he perceived the issue primarily in terms of party management. In multi-member constituencies it would have been comparatively easy to elect uncompromising socialists to Parliament, but from MacDonald's perspective this meant multiplying his existing problems with the Tilletts and the Graysons, not to mention preserving the Lib-Lab elements, and thus exacerbating the schismatic propensities of his party. In any case, MacDonald felt content to take a long-term view of electoral reform as something Labour would eventually be able to manage without. He claimed that PR would confine Labour to a fixed number of seats which was, in fact, the situation the party currently found itself in. Above all, he argued there was no point in electing Labour MPs independently of Liberals since they had to combine in Parliament: 'Our political fights at present have to be conducted in such a way as to compel people to face actual parliamentary conditions, whereas under Proportional Representation fights are more or less in the air.'[58]

Electoral reform came to a head at the Lambeth conference in January 1913 where the rival proposals for PR and the Alternative Vote were remitted to the Electoral Reform Subcommittee which failed to agree and merely issued reports of the members' views.[59] These were published by the NEC and raised at the Glasgow conference in

January 1914. As a result PR was rejected by 1,387,000 to 704,000 votes, and the Alternative Vote by a similar margin despite MacDonald's support, leaving the party in the uncomfortable position of accepting the status quo while being dissatisfied with it.[60]

An even more tempting means of enabling Labour to outflank the Liberals was to push for a wider franchise designed to incorporate more working-class men into the electoral registers; after all, the 7.9 million parliamentary electorate represented only around six in ten adult British men at this time. It was natural to assume, as some contemporaries did, that Labour was really stronger than it appeared to be on the basis of the Edwardian elections – an interpretation later endorsed by some historians. However, if a large reservoir of Labour support existed among the unenfranchised, why did contemporary Labour politicians fail to see it? For although the party favoured adult suffrage in principle, it never made it a priority issue. Arthur Henderson became involved with the People's Suffrage Federation and Margaret Bondfield with the Adult Suffrage Society, but both were small organisations lacking the resources necessary to sustain a major campaign.[61]

In fact, while a democratic franchise appears in retrospect the key to Labour success, this was far from obvious before 1914. The theory rests on the assumption that the non-voters were different from the voters – and thus more likely to support Labour. Yet this is not plausible partly because few of those not currently on the lists suffered from *permanent* disfranchisement. Men actually passed back and forth into and out of the electoral registers according to changes in their circumstances, usually their place of residence, which interrupted the twelve-month residence requirement for household voters. Nor are there good grounds for assuming that the existing system discriminated heavily against *working-class* men. They constituted approximately 70 per cent of the electorate as opposed to forming around 80 per cent of the population. The qualifications for household and lodger voters made it comparatively easy for slightly older, married men who had set up a separate household to register for a vote. Conversely, they discriminated against younger and unmarried men in *all* social classes because they were usually not heads of a household but lived with their parents or moved around renting accommodation near to their place of work. This affected middle-class men, who were inclined to delay marriage more than those lower down the scale, as much as working class. This helps to explain the lack of strong pressure for reform amongst men who largely accepted that when they married and became householders they would acquire a vote. The only quali-fication to this is that younger men may have been more disposed to support independent labour representation than their fathers. There is impressionistic evidence for this in some coalfields such as South Wales where the 55 per cent of miners who had the vote were largely Liberal whereas younger men were apparently more hostile to their employers, more militant and more pro-socialist.

Moreover, the distinctive social characteristics of permanently disen-franchised men were not of a kind that predisposed them to support for the Labour Party. Some, for example, were employed as domestic servants or as soldiers, others were so poor that they depended on poor relief which was a disqualification before 1918. In the pre-1914 era such people were much more likely to be Liberal or even Conservative supporters due to their dependence on employers or their deference, and were largely isolated from the conditions and institutions that fostered Labour voting. It was in the stable and comparatively prosperous working-class communities of workers who were skilled, politically aware and participated in an institutional network of self-help bodies that the early socialist and Labour organ-isations could best be sustained. Consequently, at this stage in Labour's development, it focused not on the entire working class, but on those sections of the working class that could be mobilised in the cause of independent labour representation. Eventually full adult suffrage helped the movement, but not until well after the First World War.

The Edwardian debates over electoral and franchise reform were symptomatic of a widespread feeling that although the strategy of harnessing trade union resources to the socialist societies had yielded results, it had only worked up to a point. The resources of the unions had by no means been fully tapped and many prominent trade union-ists continued to pay lip service to the idea of independent labour representation. This was frustrating since a wave of successful strikes during the Edwardian economic boom helped to boost union member-ship from two to over four million by 1914 by which time 2.6 million members were affiliated to the Labour Party. However, this growing strength was not yet fully reflected in the political wing of the move-ment because many members continued to regard Labour simply as an ally of Liberalism. And not without reason. In 1906 the Trades Disputes Act overthrew the Taff Vale Judgement, restoring the immunity from prosecution for the costs of strike action. Although the unions criticised some aspects of Liberal legislation, notably the National Insurance Act, they were largely supportive. Most unions were content to fund their own officials as MPs taking the Labour whip because they saw no fundamental distinction between them and the Lib-Labs who still took the Liberal whip. Meanwhile the majority of rank-and-file members continued to vote Liberal and Conservative. In 1909 this inconsistency was exposed by one W. V. Osborne, a Liberal who was also secretary of the Walthamstow branch of the General Railway Workers Union. Osborne challenged his union's right to use its funds for political purposes. This resulted in a legal ruling that upheld his complaint, thereby reducing union funding for the Labour Party by £27,000–28,000 between 1909 and 1914.

Eventually, however, the party negotiated an agreement with the government leading to a new Trade Union Act in 1913 which allowed the unions to collect a political levy from members provided that they had the right to opt out. However, before the levy could be collected each union was obliged to hold a ballot to enable members to ratify the creation of a political fund. Voting in these ballots varied a good deal. Some unions actually refused to hold one despite requests by Arthur Henderson. Others revealed a high level of opposition, notably the Northern Counties Weavers who approved the fund by 98,000 to 76,000, reflecting the Conservatism among the rank and file, the carpenters and joiners who approved it by 13,000 to 11,000, and the miners who approved it by 261,000 to 195,000, reflecting their rank-and-file Liberalism. Some results were close, including the boilermakers who backed the fund by 4,752 to 4,404.[62] Conversely, the original pioneers of independent labour representation gave emphatic support: the gasworkers by 28,000 to 4,000, the railway clerks by 15,000 to 1,000, the NUR by 102,000 to 35,000. However, interpretation of the voting is also complicated by the wide variations in turnout, only 14 per cent among the boilermakers, 22 among gasworkers and 25 among engineers, for example; but where the opposition to the fund was much stronger it reached 81 per cent of miners and 85 per cent of weavers. The weavers had organised a secret ballot in members' homes which probably boosted the hostile vote. Among the cotton spinners' operatives sixteen of the sixty-one districts showed a hostile majority, but even among them turnout ranged from 20 per cent in Oldham to 59 per cent at Bolton.[63] It seems likely that as Bolton had had a Labour MP, A. H. Gill, for eight years, who was elected under the pact with a Liberal, union members who were Liberals were content to support the fund. This was not generally the case in the mining areas which enjoyed single-member seats and thus more scope for friction between Liberal and Labour workers.

However, when all the qualifications are made, the significance of the 1913 ballots is that all except for three of sixty-three unions approved the proposal. In the long run the Trade Union Act proved to be a huge advantage for Labour. Whereas previously money spent to support candidates and elections had been taken from the general funds, and thus competed with other needs, now each union had a discrete fund devoted entirely to political purposes. The question in future would not be whether to subsidise candidates but how many and which individuals should be supported. As this coincided with a major increase in union membership before 1914 and during the war, it greatly enhanced the resources at the party's disposal. Although the new funds did not become available before the war, they became an important factor in promoting hundreds of extra candidates in 1918.

This pattern of endorsement of the parliamentary process by the trade unions has received much less attention in traditional accounts of the Edwardian Labour Movement than the extensive industrial militancy and the eruption of syndicalism. It is, however, a corrective to assumptions that the organised working class was becoming detached from the political system. On the whole the unions were ready to make what use they could of the system through electoral participation and through the employment of their members in official schemes. This stance was not inconsistent with the use of industrial pressure when opportunity arose. The number of annual stoppages rose from 300–400 during 1902–6 to 800–900 during 1911–14, the peak being in 1913 when there were 1,459 separate strikes, though most working days were lost in 1912 – forty-one million – when the miners were on strike. The chief motivation behind the Edwardian strikes was not political but material; after a period of inflation generated by the South African War when real wages had fallen back, the men were trying to recover lost ground. There was, however, a novel quality to the industrial

action of these years in that some leaders attempted to organise sympathetic strikes. In 1911 Ben Tillett re-emerged in his industrial role by
co-ordinating action among the seamen to create the National
Transport Federation, and in 1912 he led the London dock strike in
opposition of the use of non-union labour by the Port of London
Authority. These initiatives culminated in the formation of the 'Triple
Alliance' of miners, railwaymen and transport workers in 1914 whose
action threatened to paralyse the whole economy.

Sympathetic strikes were a crucial element in the syndicalist strategy
advocated by a handful of leaders, notably Tom Mann. Syndicalism
was intended to culminate in a general strike that would overthrow
the parliamentary system and replace it with industrial democracy or
workers' control. The idea aroused some sympathy in South Wales
during 1910 when feelings were inflamed by the shooting at Ton-y-
Pandy of two miners by troops called out by the Home Secretary,
Churchill, to restore order. In *The Miners' Next Step* (1912) Mann
proposed the creation of one huge national union and political action
by the miners on the basis of 'hostility to all capitalist parties with an
avowed policy of wresting whatever advantage it can for the working
class'. In that year he was prosecuted for urging troops not to fire on
men engaged in strikes in an 'Open Letter to British Soldiers', and in
1913 Jim Larkin of the Irish Transport Workers received a seven-month
sentence for sedition during the strike in Dublin.

What was the political significance of this militant phase? For the
government it was undoubtedly embarrassing to have two union
leaders in gaol. However, militancy caused much more trouble for the
Labour Party whose parliamentary representatives showed absolutely
no sympathy for Mann, Larkin, Tillett and their syndicalist supporters.
They resented the threat posed to their own authority as union leaders
and the damage they expected to suffered as MPs. Union officials
considered the syndicalist leaders irresponsible and were pleased when
the Dublin strike collapsed in January 1914. Thus, although Mann and
Larkin had gained a temporary prominence from the dramatic strikes,
they enjoyed little popular following and were marginalised within the
movement.

Indeed, though distracted by industrial militancy during these years,
the Labour leaders remained largely preoccupied with maintaining
their electoral strategy in the face of claims that the party's position

in the country had become strong enough to justify fighting on a wider front. As the Asquith government became embroiled in a series of controversies over Home Rule, National Insurance, suffragette militancy and strikes, the strains within the Labour Movement inevitably intensified and the pact between the two parties was breached so often between 1911 and 1914 as to raise doubts as to whether it could be extended through a fourth general election in 1915, especially as the Liberals were now reluctant to make further concessions.

Officially there was no change as the NEC did its best to smother new Labour candidatures. In the absence of a viable constituency organisation it regarded local initiatives as frivolous and unjustified. According to Arthur Peters, the national agent, organisation came first: 'The moment a local Labour Party produced satisfactory evidence that a creditable organisation has been set up the question of a candidature is comparatively an easy matter.'[64] Peters, whose commitment to electoral expansion was in doubt, was on strong ground because comparatively few constituency LRCs were affiliated: seventy-seven in 1904, ninety-two by 1908 and 155 in 1909. The number then fell back to 142 in 1914, representing fewer than a quarter of the constituencies. Headquarters was handicapped because, following the failure of Henderson's attempt to start a scheme for individual party membership in 1912 the party relied largely on the ILP to recruit individual members who were inclined to demand new contests. Where a strong ILP branch existed the NEC could not always control the situation. A revealing report on the situation in Sunderland summed up the difficulty: 'The Trades Council is a one-man show. The ILP is a collection of Victor Graysons and the Labour Party is too slow. All are jealous of one another and working for a fall as far as Parliamentary Representation is concerned.'[65] The result was a series of damaging by-elections starting in November 1911 when Labour stood in Liberal-held Oldham and the seat fell to the Conservatives. The Liberals retaliated and as a result three Labour and six Liberal seats were lost up to 1914 – proof of the dangers of allowing the pact to lapse at a general election.

Conversely, the NEC's hand was strengthened by the dismal performances of Labour candidates in this period. There was no repetition of the triumphs of 1907. Labour defended four seats and lost every one. Of these, Bow and Bromley was a special case arising

out of George Lansbury's rash decision to resign his seat to seek a
mandate on women's suffrage. Having won it in a straight contest
with a Tory in December 1910 he was defeated by a Tory anti-suffragist.
Bow and Bromley did not involve breaking the pact, but it suggested
that Labour support was now in decline. In July 1912 the Liberals broke
the pact by intervening in a by-election at Hanley in the Potteries with
the result that they regained the seat and pushed Labour into a humiliating third place with 12 per cent. MacDonald appeared to be resigned
to further sacrifices of Labour-held seats: 'In places like the Potteries
where poverty and degradation is of the blackest kind, the Labour
Party is bound to be weak.'[66] Two more Midlands seats were lost at
Chesterfield and North-West Derbyshire in three-cornered contests,
reflecting the enduring strength of Liberalism among the miners of
the region and the fragility of Labour's original advance in 1906. These
setbacks reduced the party's total to thirty-eight MPs.

Despite these discouraging performances there were signs of
progress in local government where it was easier for rebel candidates
to defy the strategy determined in London. As municipal elections
occurred annually in November it was possible for Labour to raise its
profile by concentrating on one constituency, force withdrawals by
the Liberals and establish itself as the alternative to the Conservatives.
Although pacts sometimes operated at municipal level, relations
between the parties varied widely. Sometimes Labour and the Liberals
co-operated against the Tories, but in the North where socialists
enjoyed more success it proved tempting for Liberals and Conservatives
to stand down in one another's favour to check further Labour
advances. For example, in the 1908 municipal elections Labour candidates enjoyed straight fights with Conservatives in 255 wards (46 per
cent) and with Liberals in 189 wards (34 per cent), and in 1911 with
Conservatives in 222 wards (45 per cent) and with Liberals in 180 wards
(36 per cent).[67] Some activists were content to weather short-term
losses provoked by collaboration between the two other parties because
'the moral effect of having forced the enemy openly into one camp
will be of more help to us here in the future than if we had returned
a man under different and more favourable circumstance'.[68] This observation came from Wakefield where Labour organisers claimed that
Liberals and Conservatives issued joint poll-cards in two-member wards
and even used the same committee rooms. In effect, two inconsistent

strategies were being followed; in the long run Labour and the Liberals could not be allies in parliamentary elections and opponents in local government.

However, the pronounced regional distribution of Labour's municipal campaigns suggests that expansion involved less than a complete overthrow of national policy. Candidates were heavily concentrated in Lancashire, Yorkshire and northern England: 69 per cent of the total in 1909 and 67 per cent in 1912, for example. In any case municipal campaigns were not likely to disrupt national co-operation unless the party did so well as to provoke the Liberals into retaliation. In fact, Labour and socialist candidates fought on a narrow and fairly stable front: a total of 374 wards in 1906, 313 in 1908, 312 in 1911 and 442 in 1913.[69] Considering that at least 6,000 seats were vacant this represented a very modest campaign.

Nor was the party's performance in these local elections consistent with claims of a significant upward trend in support before 1914. In view of the unpopularity suffered by the Liberals as the incumbent party nationally, their opponents enjoyed excellent opportunities in local elections, but it was the Conservatives who benefited rather than Labour. Between 1905 and 1913 the number of Labour and socialist councillors elected annually fluctuated within a fairly narrow range: 136, 91, 86, 109, 122, 113, 142, 58, 184, 78.[70] In most years the party recorded a modest net gain in seats from ten in 1907 to thirty-three in 1910, thirty-nine in 1912 and eighty in 1914. In effect Labour's footing in local government was smaller than its parliamentary representation. The party enjoyed concentrations of support but even these were modest; in Bradford, for example, Labour had thirteen councillors in 1907, a good year, alongside forty Tories and thirty Liberals.

However, useful lessons were drawn from the municipal contests. In 1908 when Labour suffered a net loss of thirty-three seats, reports from towns including Oldham, Stockport, Norwich and Manchester attributed the results partly to Liberal–Conservative collaboration and also to voters' reaction against socialism triggered by the prominence attained by Victor Grayson. In Birmingham where Labour suffered heavy defeats in straight fights with Conservatives, 'We have to fight on the Socialist issue whether we want to or not, as a Labour man who does not call himself a Socialist is only supposed to be "dodging" by the public, and loses influence in consequence.'[71] However, this

problem may have been exacerbated where the SDF ran its own candidates. In Newcastle where the party was defeated in five out of six
contests in 1908, local activists blamed the result on reactions to the
parliamentary by-election where Labour had intervened despite the
pact, provoking Liberal retaliation in the subsequent municipal elections: 'I hope we will be wiser from the lesson.'[72] These mixed results
and reactions make generalisation difficult but they suggest that even
at local level there were obstacles to the abandonment of the pact,
and that Labour's municipal performance was broadly consistent with
its parliamentary in showing that there was no significant take-off
by 1914.

It was not until 1912 that the party embarked on what, on the face
of it, represented a flagrant breach of its relations with Liberalism by
negotiating an electoral pact with the National Union of Women's
Suffrage Societies explicitly directed against the Liberals. The route to
this deal was a tortuous one. In retrospect it seems surprising that
Labour was slow to adopt the cause of votes for women, though the
explanation is fairly clear. In the early days of the LRC female suffrage
seemed entirely peripheral to its chief aims. Trade unionists were often
suspicious of female participation in politics as a threat to their status,
while socialists felt inclined to dismiss women's suffrage as irrelevant
or merely as something that would follow the establishment of a
socialist society but would not help to bring it about. Back in 1889
Beatrice Webb had signed an anti-suffragist petition though by 1906
she had recanted. Many Labour politicians shared the unease of the
Liberals about bills designed to enfranchise a small number of single
women who were heads of households on the assumption that they
were disproportionately middle class and would thus increase the
pro-Conservative bias in the system.

Despite this fear, the ILP recruited some prominent female suffragists including Charlotte Despard and Isabella Ford, not to mention
Richard Pankhurst whose wife, Emmeline, and daughter, Christabel,
had originally been active in socialist politics in Manchester. However,
although most Labour MPs supported the principle of women's
suffrage they refused to treat it as a priority and many of the prickly,
insecure characters in the ILP resented pressure from assertive
middle-class women such as Emmeline and Christabel. 'Really the pair
are not seeking democratic freedom,' complained Bruce Glasier.

'Christabel paints her eyebrows grossly and looks selfish, lazy and wilful. They want to be ladies not workers, and lack the humility of real heroism.'[73] By 1906 Labour had become largely alienated by the change of tactics by the Women's Social and Political Union. Concluding that co-operation with Labour was a waste of time, Christabel classed the party as the enemy, along with its Liberal allies, as became obvious in the 1906 by-election at Cockermouth where she invited electors, in effect, to vote Conservative.[74]

As a result many Labour members regarded the Pankhursts as Tory stooges, and found the dedicated support given to them by Keir Hardie and George Lansbury bewildering. A long-standing friend of the Pankhurst family, Hardie was deeply moved by suffragette hunger strikes and he became emotionally involved with Sylvia Pankhurst. In 1907 Hardie was so angered when the party conference rejected proposals to enfranchise single women in favour of adult suffrage that he astonished his colleagues by issuing a statement to the effect that he would have to consider 'whether he could remain a member of the parliamentary party'. An irritated Bruce Glasier archly described Mrs Pankhurst as 'the Delilah who has cut our Samson's locks'. Not given to compromise, Hardie had always been a Victorian Radical at heart, that is, a man of *causes*; his principled stand for women's suffrage was admirable but went a long way to discrediting him with his party and minimising his influence.

In 1912 his colleague, George Lansbury, seemed determined to repeat Hardie's sacrifice. By this time suffragette militancy was reaching its peak in the shape of arson and window-breaking, tactics that antagonised most MPs. 'I have the very strongest objection to childishness masquerading as revolution,' commented MacDonald who dismissed the suffragettes as 'pettifogging middle-class damsels'.[75] Lansbury, by contrast, was so outraged by the forcible feeding of suffragettes in prison that at one point he crossed the floor of the Commons, shook his fist in the prime minister's face and shouted 'You are beneath contempt . . . You will go down in history as the man who tortured innocent women!' This episode earned him masses of congratulatory correspondence: 'You are splendid,' wrote one admirer. 'It brightens life to know there is one decent man left in England.'[76]

This response may have encouraged Lansbury to push Labour further than it wished to go. Attempting to rouse the constituency parties into backing the women's legislation in October 1912, he was frustrated by the NEC and responded by resigning his seat to fight a by-election in order to obtain a mandate for women's suffrage.[77] This unnecessary by-election was naturally resented in the party especially as his upper-class suffragette supporters showed little sympathy for working-class causes and toured Bow and Bromley telling voters of their opposition to socialism. 'Frankly . . . they are using you as a tool,' one supporter told Lansbury. Another reminded him that his voters 'sent you to the House to advocate the interest of the workers – and not to advocate votes for women who [are] rich, well-placed individuals'.[78] Lansbury himself only made matters worse by emphasising his dispute with the Labour Party and his opposition to the Liberal government despite his dependence on Liberal votes. He also went out of his way to justify window-breaking and other suffragette tactics which offended some of the respectable working-class voters on whom he relied; Lansbury was not as well attuned to working-class sensibilities as he, and his admirers, then and now, believed.

As a result, in another straight fight with a Conservative anti-suffragist he was defeated. Not surprisingly, many in the party concluded that votes for women was not popular and that Lansbury had made a fool of himself. In his critics' eyes he compounded his error by advocating militant methods in a speech at the Albert Hall in August 1913, for which he was charged under an obsolete medieval statute with disturbing the peace and inciting others. After refusing to be bound over Lansbury was imprisoned at Pentonville where he undertook a hunger strike and was released after four days on account of a heart condition.

Lansbury's actions seemed especially perverse in the light of the new initiative Labour had taken to promote the women's cause. Events earlier in 1912 had brought the whole issue to a head when the non-militant Nation Union of Women's Suffrage Societies had become completely alienated by Asquith's obstruction of suffrage bills and was impressed when Labour's conference at Birmingham resolved by 919,000 votes to 686,000 – for the first time – that no suffrage legislation would be acceptable that did not include women. In April the NUWSS president, Millicent Fawcett, floated the idea that the time had come to work with Labour. Her colleague Eleanor Acland commented: 'I am more and more convinced that our movement has got to be linked to democracy rather than pure feminism. People are *bored* with feminism and the militants have given it a bad name.'[79] Although the Labour MPs were too few to be decisive, contemporaries felt that their unqualified commitment would have a crucial moral effect. As Snowden put it: 'If the Labour Party would, they could force this question. They have only to say . . . No Home Rule unless Votes for Women . . . and the thing would be done.'[80]

By May 1912 the NUWSS had agreed to establish an election fighting fund to be used to promote Labour candidates in constituencies chosen with a view to defeating anti-suffragist Liberals and to send volunteers to assist their campaigns.[81] This initiative was calculated to redress Labour's lack of the large female membership that would have enabled it to compete with the two other parties on a more equal footing. To this end the Women's Labour League had been started in 1906 to help 'break down the prejudice which prevails even in our own ranks', as Margaret MacDonald put it.[82] But by 1913 the WLL had only 4,000 members and 122 branches.[83] The very idea was barely tolerated among some working-class and socialist activists, as Mrs Sims learned when trying to recruit in Gateshead: 'I found some of the old trade unionists afraid we should spoil their homes by taking women out to meetings!!!'[84] In this situation a dramatic rapprochement between the two movements was expected to yield dividends. The journalist Henry Brailsford assured MacDonald and Henderson that the female activists 'can be won for Socialism almost insensibly' and that 'in the course of a fighting alliance most of them would end up becoming decided permanent adherents of the Labour Party'.[85]

Despite this encouragement the party failed to make up its mind until July 1912. Though more comfortable with the non-militants, Labour found it difficult to establish working relations with women's organisations. MacDonald remained sensitive to feminist criticism and especially resented any implication that the party could be bought or used to serve a purpose other than that for which it had been founded.[86] Above all he appreciated the danger that the suffragists might draw Labour into wholesale conflict with the Liberals, putting Labour seats at risk in the process. However, after prevaricating for some months the NEC accepted the proposal, seeing, no doubt, the tactical advantage of outflanking Asquith by seizing a classic Liberal cause.

In the event the extent of collaboration was largely determined by

by-election vacancies. During the next two and a half years the suffragists campaigned for Labour at Holmfirth, Hanley, Crewe, Midlothian,
Houghton-le-Spring, Lanark South, Durham North-West and Leith.
As the NUWSS tactfully employed women who were already
sympathetic to Labour, the alliance worked very well and the party
recognised that they had raised its vote considerably. On the other
hand, Labour scored no victories in this period. Henderson also with-
stood pressure to oppose anti-suffragist Liberals at several by-elections
including Ilkeston, Bolton, Manchester North-West and Carmarthen
East, and also left Whitechapel, Leicester, Reading and West Lothian
uncontested.[87] Thinking ahead to a general election, the suffragists
targeted the seats of four Cabinet ministers at Rotherham, Rossendale,
Bristol East and Monmouth North, and others at Accrington, Bishop
Auckland and Gateshead, but Labour refused to be hustled into such
commitments.

　　The reason for caution is clear. The by-elections of 1911–14 occurred
in some strongly working-class and unionised constituencies including
Holmfirth, Houghton-le-Spring, Keighley and Durham North-West
where the government was supposed to be vulnerable. Labour fought
them because it wanted to, not through pressure from the suffragists.
Yet although Labour polled well, its candidates were consistently third
and the Liberals retained their seats. In effect these results indicated
that Labour lacked the momentum to justify a wider challenge to the
Liberals in a general election. MacDonald wanted to extend Labour's
campaign in the mining constituencies but was frustrated because Lib-
Lab sentiment proved to be strong. During the summer of 1914
organisers toured the Derbyshire and South Yorkshire coalfields but
dispatched dismal reports on them. From Belper W. S. Holmes advised:
'The work here will be exceedingly difficult as I do not yet see much
desire on the part of the rank and file for LP organisation.'[88] J. S.
Middleton replied: 'You are practically starting at rock-bottom . . . it
looks as though we are going to lose all these seats one by one, and
in every case the loss will be chiefly due to the sheer neglect on the
part of the Mining Associations concerned.'[89]

　　In this context MacDonald's determination to retain control of electoral strategy during the last two years of peacetime is understandable.
With Labour down to thirty-eight MPs he had no wish to provoke
further Liberal retaliation. He was tested severely in 1913 when the

Liberal member in Leicester, with whom he had been jointly elected, died. As some local activists insisted on contesting the by-election the NEC dispatched Henderson and G. H. Roberts to Leicester where they were 'subjected to many angry interruptions' by members who wanted to demonstrate that MacDonald had not been elected by Liberal votes: 'The Labour Movement throughout the country was becoming disheartened because of a fear that Labour policy was too much influenced by consideration for the Liberal government, and a fight at Leicester under present circumstances was calculated to remove that fear.'[90] Despite this the NEC refused to sanction a candidate although a rebel socialist stood instead. MacDonald even threatened to withdraw as Labour candidate at Leicester, a sanction that was publicised by the Liberals and may have helped them retain the seat.[91]

However, the controversy at Leicester did not prevent the NEC putting judicious pressure on the Liberals to concede a few more contests at the next election. By June 1914 the party had adopted candidates in just thirty-six Labour-held constituencies; the NEC had sanctioned candidates in eighteen others, candidates had been selected locally, but not granted NEC approval, in twenty-two cases, and a further forty seats were ranked as 'uncertain'.[92] However, assumptions that Labour was set to contest all 117 of these seats or even more are unfounded. As the NEC records show, local organisation was chronically weak in many cases and it was revealing that the 'uncertain' category included places such as Colne Valley, Hanley, Chesterfield and Chester-le-Street that had actually elected a Labour MP at some stage but now lacked the local organisation required for a serious contest. Ultimately the total of 117 was too large to be consistent with maintenance of the pact, and as in 1909–10 the number would have been trimmed back as the election approached. MacDonald's intention was obvious in March 1914 when he met with Lloyd George to negotiate the mutual withdrawal of candidates and renew the pact.[93] As late as 1915, with an election assumed to be imminent, only sixty-five candidates had been sanctioned by the NEC.

Yet despite these internal controversies, by 1914 Labour had established itself as a substantial parliamentary party with thirty-eight MPs and an affiliated membership of 1,858,000 workers in 130 trade unions. Whether it enjoyed the popular momentum, the programmatic appeal, or the organisational strength to advance significantly beyond the bridgeheads won by 1910, let alone to displace the Liberals as the leading progressive party, seems very doubtful. The breakdown of the electoral pact would probably have removed the Liberals from office, but it would also have resulted in the defeat of many Labour members. As always, the movement was inhibited by the attitude of the organised working class. Although the unions had given their support to the party it remained conditional as is indicated by the refusal of several nominally 'Labour' MPs in mining districts to accept the Labour whip. As late as 1913 W. Johnson (Nuneaton) and W. E. Harvey (North-East Derbyshire) were reported for continuing to flout proscriptions against appearing on Liberal platforms.[94] As Beatrice Webb observed, 'The solid phalanx of miners and textiles don't want the Labour members to cut loose from the Liberal Party, and MacDonald knows it.'[95] Despite the new funding arrangements, the unions seemed surprisingly reluctant to finance an anti-Liberal election campaign in 1914–15. Following the union ballots many members showed themselves unwilling to pay the levy; in some unions half the members contracted out and several held dangerously close ballots on proposals to disaffiliate from the Labour Party.[96] Far from promoting extra candidates, members of the ASE and the Miners Federation rejected proposals to sponsor them and by 1914 the trade unions as a whole were backing *fewer* candidates than in the 1910 elections despite the availability of political funds. Their pragmatic view of their role and that of the Labour Party dictated that they should continue to enjoy the advantages of having a Liberal government and refuse to risk the return of the Tories by splitting the vote.

Trade union obstructionism could not be ignored because, despite the crucial role of socialists in creating the new party in 1900, socialism had not emerged as a major factor in undermining the Liberals; indeed it continued to be regarded as more of a handicap. Only a handful of the parliamentary leaders were drawn from the ILP, most of whom adopted a pragmatic rather than an ideological approach to strategy, while Keir Hardie had become marginalised by 1914. In the context of the 1.8 million union members the socialist societies affiliated only 31,000, a much wider disparity between the two elements than there had been in 1900. As a result, not only was Edwardian Labour basically a trade union party, but the more it mobilised the working class the less left wing it became. Consequently some socialists, not only in the SDF but even in the ILP, had already quit in favour of the BSP and there was a threat of others following them. In East Ham, where the ILP was down to thirty-three members by 1914, the branch was suffering from 'chronic inertia' according to the secretary. 'Our connection with the LRC tends to limit our activities and I think the time is coming when the ILP in East Ham, if it is to keep in existence, will have to leave off trying to push the Trades Unionists into activity. We shall have to lead and let them follow.'[97] By 1914 disillusionment in the ILP in the face of union assertiveness raised the danger that the party might revert to its original constituent parts. That it avoided this is attributable partly to the dominance acquired by MacDonald and his colleagues who maintained a footing in both camps, but also to accident; the outbreak of war in 1914 offered a welcome release by distracting the movement from immediate controversies and, eventually, enabling the dissident elements to reunite under more propitious circumstances.

5

'Come to your country's aid':
Labour and the Great War

The outbreak of the Great War in August 1914 proved to be a crucial, arguably *the* crucial, turning point in Labour's fortunes. Yet at the time this was far from apparent. For like the Liberals, Labour found itself divided by the decision to enter the war between an anti-war minority and a pro-war majority. Crucially, however, this division, ultimately ruinous for the Liberals, proved manageable, and even advantageous, for Labour. Why was this so?

On 29 July Keir Hardie represented British labour at Brussels where the International Socialist Bureau gathered with a view to throwing the weight of organised labour against the war machine now palpably cranking into action in Vienna, Berlin, St Petersburg, Paris and Belgrade. But within days everything fell apart. On returning to Paris the French socialist, Jean Jaurès, was immediately assassinated in a café. In London Hardie and Arthur Henderson led the British section of the ISB in organising a peace demonstration in Trafalgar Square. There, on Sunday 2 August, along with George Lansbury and Will Thorne, they addressed the crowds in the pouring rain as the jingoes heckled from the sidelines. Next day, a bank holiday, holidaymakers came out in droves to enjoy the returning sunshine, while Germany declared war on France and her troops marched through Luxembourg heading for Belgium.

Meanwhile, in the House of Commons the Foreign Secretary, Sir Edward Grey, explained that Britain was committed to France because her own strategic and imperial interests dictated that she could not allow her to be occupied by Germany. All the party leaders, including the Irish Nationalists, accepted his rationale for British participation except Ramsay MacDonald who insisted: 'He has not persuaded me.' Pointing out that national honour had been invoked to justify previous wars in the Crimea and South Africa, MacDonald showed a flash of insight in his moment of despair: 'I have been through this before [a reference to the Boer War], and 1906 came as part recompense,' he reminded the members. 'It will come again.'¹ Although MacDonald's prophesy proved correct, the reaction against British involvement was not to come for five or six years. More immediately the critics of the war were swamped by a wave of nationalist paranoia. Writing in the *Labour Leader*, Fenner Brockway argued: 'Workers of Great Britain, you have no quarrel with the workers of Europe . . . The quarrel is between the ruling classes of Europe.'² But when Brockway addressed public meetings the crowds, who had been 'silent and wondering' in July, swiftly turned hostile and violent. At Marple in Cheshire he 'tried in vain to speak to a howling mob for two hours' before quitting the platform under police protection from patriots determined to throw the speakers into the canal.³

Suddenly opponents of the war felt terribly isolated even within the Labour Movement. Will Crooks had led the Commons in singing the national anthem to mark Britain's entry into war. When the party's executive met on 5 August, the majority, led by Arthur Henderson and J. R. Clynes, who had opposed war only a few days earlier, criticised government diplomacy but were adamant about backing the war effort: 'Having got to a stage where our protests could not keep England out of a war which was already in existence, we could serve her better by unswerving, if protesting, loyalty.' MacDonald, who, along with Philip Snowden and Fred Jowett, led the dissenting minority, at once resigned as chairman of the Parliamentary Labour Party, confessing in his diary: 'The Chairmanship was impossible . . . it was sad, but [I was] glad to get out of harness.'⁴ The NEC's decision left the Labour Party officially pledged to back the war though the ILP remained opposed. The value of Labour's federal structure now became evident, for it managed to accommodate these differences right up to 1918. Wisely no attempts were made to expel or punish the rebels who retained their places on the NEC and other party committees. Herbert Morrison, for example, refused to undertake military service but continued as an employee of the London Labour Party. Like many Labour opponents of war, Morrison was not a pacifist, but he objected to Britain fighting in alliance with the detested tsarist regime.

For its part the ILP was obliged to tread carefully not least because, despite its reputation for pacifism, much of the rank and file actually supported the war, especially in Lancashire. This prevented the party from disciplining two ILP MPs, James Parker and J. R. Clynes, who became prominent supporters of the war. As Clynes reminded them, the ILP branches in his Manchester constituency took the same view as he did; he argued that his stance was 'consistent with the actions of a Socialist when the choice is no longer between peace and war, but between peace and submission to the warmaker'. Other ILP branches adopted a more cautious stance; in East Ham, for example, members agreed that 'whilst attacking "war in general" the platform should not be used to condemn or otherwise the present war but to centre on socialist work'.[5] Germany's dramatic march through Belgium into France had genuinely shocked British opinion, but Clynes himself admitted that if the Germans had been held up in the early stages opposition in the Labour Movement to British participation would have been much stronger. His experience was replicated in most of the working-class constituencies held by Labour and Liberal MPs. Where an MP opposed the war his local supporters repudiated him, sometimes to the extent to refusing to nominate him again. The real-isation that all over Europe the workers were rallying to the support of their countries and refusing to see the conflict as either a class struggle or as a crisis of capitalism came as a demoralising blow to some on the left. Ernest Bevin spoke for many trade union patriots when he derided the ILP's opposition to war as 'fatuous' and demanded to know whether the German Social Democrats were going to strike to stop it. Keir Hardie, now fifty-eight, was, according to observers, broken by the war. 'I can't fight this war like I fought the Boer War,' he admitted.[6] After attempting to organise anti-war strikes and protests he became withdrawn and 'shrank into a travesty of his former self'. After Hardie's death the resulting by-election took place in Merthyr Tydfil in November 1915 where the official Labour candidate, James Winstone, president of the South Wales Miners Federation, was opposed by C. B. Stanton, the runner-up in the miners' ballot, who stood as a pro-war Independent Labour candidate. The voters repu-diated the Hardie tradition and elected Stanton by a comfortable margin. As the parties observed a truce during wartime, which prevented them from intervening in each other's seats, the only other by-election evidence of Labour opinion came at Salford in November 1917 when Ben Tillett gained a seat, again standing as Independent Labour on a militantly pro-war platform.

For a time the hostile climate effectively drove the scattered critics of war off the public platforms. MacDonald received letters headed 'Herr Ramsay MacDonald', he was expelled from the Lossiemouth golf club, *The Times*, a scurrilous newspaper for all its pretensions, alleged that 'no paid agent of Germany had served her better', and the *Spectator* asked why he was receiving an MP's salary. But the nastiest blow was struck by *John Bull* which printed his birth certificate in September 1914 showing that he was 'the illegitimate son of a Scotch servant girl' and had been registered as 'James MacDonald Ramsay'.[7]

In this situation only the ILP offered a sympathetic refuge. Several Liberal rebels, including E. D. Morel and Charles Trevelyan, joined it, but not until 1918. Meanwhile, there was an urgent need for a separate organisation with an agreed view on the war. This was met by the Union of Democratic Control, a new pressure group which demanded more control for Parliament over foreign policy, the abandonment of secret diplomacy, a peace settlement that did not humiliate the defeated side, frontiers that were not to be drawn artificially to appease the victors and no transfers of territory without plebiscites. In future, the UDC argued, British policy should pay less attention to the balance of power and rely more on international councils to settle disputes; it should abandon the arms race that was increasingly blamed for the current war, reduce armaments, nationalise the arms industry and impose controls on the export of arms. During the 1920s much of this was to become mainstream Labour thinking on foreign affairs. However, in the immediate circumstances these ideas were championed by a courageous handful including MacDonald, Snowden and several Liberal MPs, notably Trevelyan, Morel and Arthur Ponsonby. They were joined by Norman Angell, the author of *The Great Illusion*, a book in which he had warned that the economic consequences of a European war would be as damaging to the victors as to the vanquished.

However, for several years these critics were isolated because Labour had no policy beyond backing the war effort and the fight-to-a-finish strategy; as late as January 1917 the annual conference rejected proposals for a negotiated peace with Germany. Not until the autumn of 1917 did the party sit down to draft a fresh statement of international policy. At that stage, seeking to draw a line between current discontents and a better future, it drew upon the ideas of the UDC and ILP.

Yet although it was a small and beleaguered organisation, the UDC acquired considerable significance for its role in easing the transition of rebel Liberals to Labour. Like the Boer War, the First World War united Radical Liberals and socialists against the Establishment. Initially MacDonald anticipated that the war would form a brief but decisive interlude in domestic politics leading to a rapid transformation of Labour fortunes. He appreciated that the war would accelerate the disillusionment among Liberals over the naval arms race and the ententes with France and especially with tsarist Russia. By dissociating himself from this MacDonald effectively articulated what Liberals regarded as the Liberal tradition in foreign affairs. Consequently, when the reaction against the war came in the 1920s MacDonald's personal stand gave him immense prestige as an idealist who had suffered for his principles. Hence the appreciation for him among liberal writers and intellectuals including Bertrand Russell, Arnold Rowntree, Leonard Courtney, G. Lowes Dickinson, J. A. Hobson, Charles Buxton, C. P. Scott, Philip Morrell and Graham Wallas. Not all of them abandoned their former allegiance, but for many the UDC, and later the ILP, offered bridges by which they could cross over to Labour, giving it thereby the cachet of intellectual and literary circles during the 1920s and 1930s.

This process was accelerated by Asquith's decision to form a coalition government including the Conservatives in May 1915. 'No one on earth can pretend that we were elected to support this Government,' complained one Liberal MP, Richard Denman, who subsequently joined Labour.[8] Left-wing Liberals became increasingly disillusioned by the adoption of military conscription in 1916, the formation of a more right-wing coalition under Lloyd George in December 1916, and by his decision to fight the general election of 1918 in alliance with the Conservatives.

On the other hand, the restoration of MacDonald's reputation and the credibility of the anti-war critique in the 1920s could not obscure the extent to which his thinking was untypical of working-class opinion during wartime when the bulk of the Labour Movement became vociferously patriotic. Will Crooks, for example, travelled 50,000 miles during the first fifteen months of war to speak on recruiting platforms. Even Victor Grayson shocked his admirers by insisting on the compatibility of war and socialism. 'War', he declared, 'has made us what we have never been before – a nation.' He even praised the peers for their patriotism, luridly reminding audiences that 178 peers were serving in the forces in January 1915: 'the soil of France is already coloured with their blue blood'.[9] Consequently, any explanation of Labour's evolution has to take account of the extent to which the patriotism of men like Grayson, Crooks, Blatchford and Hyndman who threw themselves into recruiting campaigns, was, in fact, integral to their socialism. Tory-socialists responded instinctively to the crisis posed by war and the threat of invasion, seeing it as a positive force uniting the community.

More typical were the trade union MPs, old-fashioned patriots, monarchists and imperialists, who felt the appeal of the call to fight for king and country and to preserve the empire against Britain's enemies. Jimmy Thomas argued that Germany had made the mistake of thinking that she could take advantage of domestic controversies over strikes and Home Rule, but the English recognised that the interests of the nation were greater than those of any one section. 'If you believe, as I believe, if you love liberty as I love liberty,' he told an audience at Blackheath, 'and if you respect freedom as I respect freedom, then it is your duty immediately to come to your country's aid.'[10] Taking a more extreme line John Hodge flatly denied that Britain bore any blame for the outbreak of war: 'I have never believed in any claim for an appeal to what was called the German moral conscience. You have got to stop German militarism – this is Labour's war aim.'[11] James O'Grady, a Leeds Labour MP, recognising that workingmen had become belligerently patriotic all over Europe, admitted he had previously under-estimated the force of nationalism: 'my assertion is that the Socialist ideal is not in any sense anti-national'. O'Grady argued that the establishment of a socialist or co-operative commonwealth would go hand in hand with nationalism.[12] This theme was picked up by Thomas in speaking of his pride in the 'spiritual revival' engendered by the war: 'In the dark period of 1914–18 this great Empire of ours . . . was defended and preserved by the men from the slums as well as the men from the palace, recognising a common duty and a common obligation.'[13]

Such contemporary comment underlines the impact of war in enhancing and focusing the patriotic, monarchist and imperial sentiment that existed within the Labour Movement. It also prefigured the language adopted by Labour at the end of the Second World War when the rapprochement between socialism and patriotism became more explicit and realised more tangible political dividends than in 1918. But even at this early stage a belligerently nationalist Labour Party was struggling to assert itself.

Admittedly, some mainstream Labour politicians like Arthur Henderson were reluctant supporters of war, accepting it as a regrettable necessity and recognising the immediate need to keep the movement together despite its divisions. Several socialists, including Sidney Webb and G. D. H. Cole, had taken a pragmatic attitude from the outset, arguing that, as there was little Labour could do about the war, it would be wise to avoid pursuing fruitless internal controversies or discrediting itself by association with the anti-war camp. This was an easy option for those who expected a short war. But even after four years many Labour supporters managed to see the issue from this perspective when the election came. For example, in November 1918 the ILP in Preston admitted that it did not agree with the pro-war stance adopted by Tom Shaw, the Labour candidate, but it 'recognised that the war was only a phase'.[14]

This realistic approach to the war enabled the Labour Movement to focus on its common aims during the four-year conflict. By contrast, the war had the effect of demoralising many Liberals because it derailed their domestic reform agenda and destroyed their successful Edwardian government. The Conservatives, rallying to the patriotic cause, gained a badly needed sense of purpose from the war and returned to office after losing three elections during the Edwardian period. Labour, too, derived a renewed sense of its role and purpose but in a different way. The war was widely expected to disrupt British trade, thereby causing mass unemployment and social distress. Although the booming economy and the huge demand for labour meant that this dismal scenario failed to materialise, wartime nonetheless generated all kinds of material grievances: high food prices, profiteering, rising rents, state direction of labour, threats to the status of skilled men. Such issues reinforced the conviction of the movement that it must concentrate on using its influence to defend the living and working conditions of the British working class, a task that was seen as perfectly consistent with support for the war effort.

As a result, although the British Establishment feared the pressure exerted by organised labour, it was immensely relieved at the determination of patriotic union leaders to rally to the national cause. After reaching a peak around 1911–13 strikes suddenly dwindled, partly because of patriotism but also because thousands of manual workers had joined the armed forces. However, the pattern was significant; from 1,459 strikes in 1913 the annual total fell to 927 in 1914 and 672 in 1915, but thereafter the number rose again to 730 in 1917 and 1,165 in 1918. Patriotism clearly had its limits; as the conflict wore on workers grew restless about profiteering and questioned whether the sacrifice could be equal when the employers were making fat profits from generous government contracts. As a result the anxiety of the three wartime governments to control labour, and thus maximise the output of munitions, was tempered by a readiness to make concessions in terms of rent restrictions, wage rises, food rationing and, in 1918, the extension of the parliamentary vote to all men over twenty-one. Broadly speaking this strategy worked. Britain achieved a mass army, initially by volunteering, then by conscription, achieved huge increases in the supply of munitions and largely avoided the serious food shortages that demoralised civilians in other countries and provoked mutinies in their armies. This allowed Britain to bring her industrial might gradually to bear on the war and thus sustain the Allied armies to their eventual victory in 1918.

Clearly the three wartime governments were alive to the concerns of labour and willing to incorporate it into the war effort, but it is easily forgotten that the strategy worked because organised labour was largely willing to be incorporated. At the centre the vehicle for collaboration was the War Emergency Workers National Committee, a mundane-sounding body that had originally been intended as a peace committee, but rapidly reoriented itself. In effect the WEWNC constituted itself as the representative of the working class, pressurising ministers and civil servants on a range of issues including rent controls, food prices, benefits for servicemen and their families. Its links with Labour's grass roots gave the committee credibility when negotiating with the national authorities. Under Jim Middleton, assistant secretary to the Labour Party, the committee expanded to include some forty members stretching across the spectrum from patriotic union leaders like Will Thorne, Ben Tillett and Havelock Wilson, to right-wing MPs including James O'Grady, C. W. Bowerman, John Hodge and J. A. Seddon, moderates such as Arthur Henderson and Fred Bramley, and war critics like Bob Smillie, Fred Jowett, W. C. Anderson and Ramsay MacDonald. In this way the committee helped to keep together the leading personnel of the Labour Movement, united by positive action for the workers, at a time when they were otherwise divided over the war.

The work of the WEWNC complemented the local activities of trades councils and hundreds of individuals. War generated a multitude of local bodies on which working-class representation was deemed to be essential including relief committees, Belgian refugee committees, committees to administer allowances for war widows and dependants, employment committees, food committees, profiteering committees to punish errant shopkeepers, and tribunals to administer a new scheme on recruiting. Admittedly disputes frequently arose because municipal councillors feared that trades council nominees would be too left wing, but they usually had to put up with it.[15] This work offered a useful safety valve for many socialist and union activists; at a time when they were poorly represented on municipal councils, it gave them a personal sense of involvement in the national cause and enabled them to win concessions for fellow workers. This participation had a knock-on effect in the post-war period especially in focusing Labour representatives on tackling the housing shortage. The rent strikes of 1915 forced drastic concessions in the form of controls on rents, an interference with the rights of private property owners that was almost unprecedented and was never entirely abandoned between the wars despite the vicissitudes of party politics. The combination of controversy over rents and the new opportunities to build council houses under Christopher Addison's 1919 Housing Act offered a huge incentive to Labour in local elections during the 1920s and 1930s; the implementation of the council-house programme not only became a central task for municipal authorities but it also symbolised continuity as Labour inherited the social reform tradition from Edwardian Liberalism at a time when many Liberals were drifting away from it.

Meanwhile in May 1915 Labour dramatically raised its status by joining the Cabinet for the first time. Inevitably the movement felt equivocal about this. Although participation in a coalition followed logically from Labour's pre-war alliance with the Liberals, long-term considerations pointed to cutting loose and exploiting the Liberals' difficulties. Initially the MPs voted by nine to eight against accepting Asquith's invitation, but on 19 May the NEC came down in favour by nine to three, and at a joint meeting with the parliamentary party it was agreed by seventeen to eleven to join.[16] Henderson served as president of the Board of Education and later as Paymaster General, though his real role was to act as mediator between government and the unions. William Brace and George Roberts were appointed junior ministers. Other senior Labour figures were already filling official roles for the government,

Hyndman on the Consumers Council and Clynes on the Munitions Workers Health Committee dealing with exposure to picric acid which caused yellowing of the skin. Jimmy Thomas declined a ministry on the grounds that he had more to offer by using his influence to check outbreaks of strikes, especially during the railway disputes in 1917 and 1918. In 1917 the Cabinet sent him to the United States to advise American industry on wartime industrial problems in the light of British experience, for which he was made a privy councillor on his return. In 1916 Labour's new role was endorsed by a vote of 1.5 million to 600,000 at a party meeting at Bristol at which seventy-three unions, thirty-nine trades councils and forty-one Labour parties were represented.

More surprising was the party's willingness to serve in the more Tory-dominated Lloyd George coalition that succeeded Asquith's in December 1916 which was boycotted by the majority of Liberals. An angry MacDonald mocked Henderson for joining Lloyd George after he had declared that Asquith was indispensable: 'He reminded me of the story of the virgin nuns who kept Satan behind them until someone suggested spiritual service, and thereafter kissing and holiness were combined.'[17] But once again party conference in 1917 endorsed Labour's participation by a six-to-one margin. So emphatic a decision was indicative both of rank-and-file patriotism and of the growing instinct that it served Labour's interests to keep a hand on the levers of power. Henderson joined Lloyd George's five-man War Cabinet, John Hodge became Minister for Labour (a new department), succeeded by George Roberts, and George Barnes became Minister for Pensions (also a new department), while junior posts went to Stephen Walsh, William Brace, George Wardle and James Parker. J. R. Clynes, who had been a critic of food policy, was appointed parliamentary secretary to the new Food Control Ministry under Lord Rhondda and succeeded him in 1918. Rebutting ILP criticism for accepting this role Clynes insisted he had wide backing from trade unions and party members.[18] Aware that imports had become highly vulnerable to submarine attacks on merchant shipping, Clynes and Rhondda took the risk of imposing a comprehensive food rationing policy, a step that presaged the more sweeping socialistic measures adopted during the Second World War.[19] More immediately this work enhanced the prestige of the Labour leaders and fostered their sense of involvement in the national cause. After 1918 their wartime experience left them more confident of their ability to use the machinery of state, and fortified them in resisting the attractions of 'direct action' urged by local 'Soviets' and the new British Communist Party. Among the interwar generation of Labour politicians this appreciation of the system mitigated any feeling that the British constitution was in need of radical reform.

As the example of food rationing suggests, participation in government also raised wider questions about ideology and policy. By placing conventional economic thinking under strain, the wartime crisis forced politicians in all parties towards interventionism in the economy and elevated the principle of collective action and community interest above private enterprise and individualism, at least temporarily. But did it put socialism on the agenda? The Webbs certainly thought so. 'It is useless for Lord Kitchener to think he can repel the invader if the working class is starving behind his line of troops,' commented Beatrice. Certainly by 1918 the state loomed larger in people's lives through the Defence of the Realm Act (DORA) and higher taxation; it ran the railways, operated and even owned hundreds of mines and munitions factories, directed labour, bought most of the food consumed and regulated prices.

However, these innovations, dramatic as they were, complicated the road to socialism inasmuch as they grew from a series of ad hoc expedients to meet crises rather than a considered overall policy. They also proved vulnerable to a sharp reaction against interventionism after 1918, leading to the dismantling of most wartime controls in the early 1920s. This was probably inevitable as wartime collectivism provoked varied reactions in each party. Progressive Liberals welcomed the expansion of state resources as a means of extending Edwardian social reforms, but were antagonised by authoritarian wartime policies especially DORA, conscription and censorship, as a threat to individual liberty. Most Conservatives had reservations about higher taxation and the takeovers of private business but recognised the limitations of the market in the face of the wartime crisis and welcomed the restrictions on strikes, guaranteed profits for industry and the exclusion of German imports as a step towards protectionism.

Labour and socialist responses also varied widely. As a Guild Socialist G. D. H. Cole felt sceptical about the wartime role of the state as a premature expression of socialism that effectively sheltered capitalists from the pressure of the workers and created a formidable official machine designed to control the unions. Cole was dismayed to see how readily the union leaders signed up to the new corporate enterprise. But at the other end of the spectrum the Webbs found pragmatic wartime state interventionism congenial; it demonstrated the feasibility of advancing towards a collective state step by step under cover of the national interest without provoking too much controversy. The Webbs' *de haut en bas* approach left no room for the workers' participation favoured by Cole and R. H. Tawney, and when the party devised its new constitution in 1918 it was the Webbs' approach that was incorporated in the celebrated Clause IV that committed Labour to: 'secure for the producers by hand or by brain the full fruits of their industry, and the most equitable distribution thereof that may be possible upon the basis of the common ownership of the means of production'. Historians have been sceptical about the significance of Clause IV because during the 1920s Labour's policy development scarcely got to grips with its practical implementation. Yet Clause IV had a *symbolic* value as part of a wider strategy of offering a distinctive appeal and emancipating Labour from its client relationship with the Liberal Party.

Above all, the union leaders, whose influence was consolidated in the new constitution, showed little grasp of or support for a socialist policy. Jimmy Thomas, for example, never really became a socialist. He saw no general implications for peacetime policy in the wartime industrial controls, regarding them as matters of expediency rather than principle: 'It is foolish to boast of the nationalisation of English industries as a victory for Socialism.'[20] But this did not mean ignoring the lessons of wartime. Thomas expected, as did politicians of other parties, that the railways, which had been operated by the state under legislation dating back to 1870, would not be returned to private control: 'If the government ownership of railways is so successful during the war,' he commented, 'why couldn't it be the best economical arrangement in normal times?'[21] Yet Thomas failed to see coal in the same perspective, arguing that as it was an export industry it would not be appropriate for nationalisation. By contrast the miners' leaders recognised that wartime intervention had brought gains for the workers, notably in the form of national wage settlements, as opposed to pit-by-pit agreements, and judged that the best way of preserving them lay in nationalisation. However, few in the movement approached the question in terms of a wider theory about how best to run the economy; the ad hoc approach left Labour with a formal socialist commitment but without a considered economic rationale or a detailed plan for implementing state ownership of industry.

Indeed, socialism was only one, and arguably not the most significant, of the ideological factors influencing the movement at this time. It is easy to overlook the extent to which war revived and consolidated the common ground between Labour and *Conservatism* that proved to be of crucial electoral importance in helping the party to adapt to the patriotism, monarchism and imperialism in the working-class community. For Labour politicians such as O'Grady and Thomas such sentiments were clearly relevant to socialism in so far as they fostered a positive view of the state. In particular it was the issue of military conscription that crystallised the thinking of the Tory-socialists during wartime. Hitherto Britain's liberal tradition based on voluntary recruiting cast compulsion in an authoritarian light as something suited to Continental societies and therefore un-British. However, during 1914–15 voluntarism was tested to destruction by the profligate offensives on the Western Front. Eventually, as the supply of willing men began to dwindle and the generals demanded still more recruits, Liberals argued that if too many men were taken industrial output would suffer and thus hamper the war effort. Many also thought it *morally* wrong for the state to impose its will over the consciences of individuals, and, as a result, when conscription was introduced in 1916 provision was made for conscientious objectors to appeal to tribunals for exemption from military service.

The Liberals counted on organised labour to resist military conscription on the grounds that it would lead inexorably to *industrial* conscription. However, Labour reactions proved surprisingly mixed. When the Conscription Bill came before Parliament thirteen Labour members opposed it but eight supported it: George Barnes, C. W. Bowerman, Charles Duncan, John Hodge, S. Galbraith, D. B. Foster, Robert Toothill and Alex Wilkie. Even Jimmy Thomas, a critic of the bill, refused to adopt the Liberal view that conscription represented a threat to civil liberties; as a trade unionist he approached it pragmatically, fearing that it might antagonise the workers and play into the hands of revolutionary agitators.[22] Along with most Labour leaders, Thomas had thrown himself into the recruiting campaign, hoping that it would work so well that compulsion would never be necessary, but he shared with the Labour pro-conscriptionists a gut feeling that every man had an obligation to join up. The Leeds socialist, D. B. Foster, argued that it was not primarily a matter of individual conscience: 'people should be self-sacrificing for the community'; the future MP, John Beckett, who enlisted in August 1914, admitted, 'I have never been able to overcome the repugnance which pacifism and conscientious objection in particular arouses in me.'[23] The Socialist National Defence Committee effectively drew a line between Liberalism and socialism, arguing that: 'Socialism is not a system of go as you please. Socialism is not Anarchism.' It even suggested that in wartime conscientious objectors were comparable with blacklegs during a strike.[24] James O'Grady professed himself simply unable to comprehend the attitude of conscientious objectors because 'he was a Socialist, and he had a conception of what the state is, and he averred that he could not live apart from the state. The state had a right to call upon him for service, even for his life.'[25] In this way the issue split the political class down the middle with many Liberals and some Labour figures on one side and the Conservatives and much of the Labour Movement on the other. Conscription had demonstrated the effect of war in crystallising the common elements in the Tory and socialist outlook.

The positive view of the state was also reflected in domestic issues such as the consumption of alcohol. For temperance reformers the crisis of wartime offered their best opportunity for imposing restrictions on the country's drinking habits by means of shorter licensed hours, reductions in alcoholic strength, and higher taxes on beer and spirits. Ministers believed that if the workers drank less they would turn up more regularly on Mondays and produce more munitions; there would also be less pressure on scarce supplies of grain by the brewing industry. Meanwhile, in America pressure built up to put an end to brewing altogether, a demand that culminated in 1919 in the disastrous experiment with Prohibition. The issue revealed Labour, once again, as two parties, one leaning towards respectability and temperance, the other towards the masculinist, Tory support for alcohol. As Food Controller, Clynes repeatedly came to the defence of the brewing and drinking classes, arguing that 'to the workingman beer is food, drink and recreation'.[26] His Conservative colleague, Sir Arthur Steel-Maitland, was prepared to impose full state control on the industry and thus guarantee the workers a supply of beer – an indication of the lengths to which some Tories were ready to go towards intervention at the expense of private owners. This is not to imply that Tories and socialists shared identical views, rather that war brought out the common elements in their thinking that separated them from the Liberal tradition.

Steel-Maitland's interventionist line on brewing was by no means eccentric in the context of the earlier enthusiasm for National Efficiency among Conservatives who recognised the need to extend the role of the state in both imperial and domestic contexts. Lord Milner, now a member of the War Cabinet, freely condemned laissez-faire economics, which he blamed for unemployment, and was ready to adopt nationalisation of key industries such as coal. In this Milner reflected a Bismarckian sense of the state as a positive good, capable of regenerating a complacent society shaken by the challenges of wartime. Milner's thinking was complemented by other leading Tories including Lord Selborne, Lord Salisbury and Steel-Maitland who were deeply affected by the patriotism shown by the working classes and believed that 'the fellowship of the trenches would be a bond between Englishmen of the most varied classes in the future'.[27] As a result they concluded that it would now be safe and even desirable to extend the vote to all men. In 1916 Selborne privately explained his change of view in terms of the need to 'secure the votes of the men who have fought as a deliverance from the domination of the Trade Union influence . . . I think these men will be an immense support to us for years to come against radical and Liberal insanity in the matter of foreign policy, navy etc.'[28] This comment reflected widespread Tory outrage that the Liberals, whom they regarded as cosmopolitans and traitors, had been in power in August 1914; consequently they were all the more relieved to find that their own values were widely shared among the working classes.

This sense of common ground formed the seed-bed for the reassertion of a Tory-socialist programme during the war and, more surprisingly, an organisation designed to put it onto a lasting basis for electoral purposes. Informal attempts were made to bring Conservative and Labour politicians together 'with a view to discovery of a common basis for a patriotic and national policy', and in November 1917 a group comprising Milner and four Tory MPs, Steel-Maitland, L. S. Amery,

Edward Wood (later Lord Halifax) and Sir Laming Worthington-Evans, drafted a comprehensive statement of the Tory-socialist peacetime programme.[29] In this document the MPs recognised the principle of state intervention in industries of national importance, especially railways and those threatened by imports or goods made by sweated labour and subsidies. They advocated imposing tariffs to defend British jobs and industry, the adoption of minimum wages, limitations on profits, public acquisition of canals, afforestation, regulation of milk and coal supplies, regular military training, and housing reforms. In effect they sought a triangular partnership between the state, labour and capital to promote the national interest.

The organisation behind this scheme had begun to take shape as early as the spring of 1915 when Victor Fisher, a member of the Social Democratic Federation, the Fabian Society and later the British Socialist Party, arranged a meeting of the Socialist National Defence Committee. It had a dual aim: to promote socialist measures in order to help the war effort, and 'to counteract the peace at any price policy of the anti-national elements in the Socialist and Labour movements'. In addition to Fisher the committee included Robert Blatchford and A. M. Thompson, editor of the *Clarion*, and was supported by Ben Tillett, John Hodge, George Roberts and Henry Hyndman at a rally at the Queen's Hall in July 1915. It backed C. B. Stanton, the pro-war victor at the Merthyr Tydfil by-election. In 1916, with subsidies from Milner, the SNDC was put on to a permanent footing as the British Workers League. The SNDC defined its aims as 'the maintenance of national rights, the consolidation of all the states of the British Empire into a democratic federation . . . to put an end to the laissez-faire policy which would mean the ruin of England and to bring about a reversal of the Little England Cobdenite doctrine of the Radical Party'.[30] Militantly hostile to Asquithian Liberalism, conscientious objectors and German imports, the BWL aligned itself with the fight-to-a-finish school. As membership of the league was compatible with membership of the Labour Party at this time it enrolled several parliamentary backers including one former MP, J. A. Seddon, and current MPs Stephen Walsh, Robert Toothill, John Wadsworth, William Abraham and James O'Grady.

However, relations became complicated in 1917 when the league announced the adoption of parliamentary candidates including J. A. Seddon at Hanley, which was represented by an anti-war Liberal, and

J. F. Green at Leicester, which was MacDonald's constituency. Fisher claimed that the only purpose was to 'challenge the re-election of the Pacifist members of the Labour Party, notably Mr Ramsay MacDonald, Mr Philip Snowden, Mr Jowett and others'.[31] By way of justification the pro-war George Barnes argued that the ILP had already adopted a candidate to oppose him in his Glasgow constituency. As Labour's long-term strategy and policy remained uncertain at the start of 1917, these initiatives threatened to dissolve the party into its constituent elements under the strain of war; indeed the league attempted to persuade the TUC to establish a 'Trade Union Labour Party'.

At this stage the parliamentary party consisted of thirty-eight MPs of whom no fewer than eleven joined the BWL.[32] Although several subsequently withdrew, the effect of the interaction with Tory politicians was to help consolidate the Labour right and, as it turned out, to enable the party to win certain seats in the 1918 election. Things came to a head in 1918 because Lloyd George, now contemplating a wartime election, was ready to accommodate working-class patriotism by giving a free run to some BWL candidates. By the time of the election in December the league, now renamed the National Democratic Party, ran twenty-eight candidates of whom twenty enjoyed the official backing of the Lloyd George–Conservative coalition and ten were elected. However, as the ten were mostly elderly trade unionists who retired in 1922 their long-term impact was minimal.

These manoeuvres drew attention to the fact that Labour Party strategy had remained unchanged since the outbreak of war. In 1914 the electoral pact with the Liberals was still officially intact and the party expected to fight the general election, due in 1915, under its auspices though with a few adjustments and extra candidacies. By continuing to hold annual conferences the party kept in touch with its activists more effectively than the other parties. Early in 1915 Labour was quietly preparing for an election; the NEC approved a new candidate in Accrington and appointed a subcommittee to deal with registration of voters;[33] Herbert Morrison was employed as secretary to the London Labour Party; and two national organisers, S. Higginbotham and W. Holmes, were sent on regional tours to help identify which seats should be contested.[34] However, by April 1915 registration work had been suspended because the mass movement of voters into munitions factories and the forces had reduced the electoral register to chaos. The formation of a coalition in May appeared to make an election unnecessary and Parliament passed legislation to postpone it at intervals throughout the war. As a result, the electoral pact was left to wither though it was not repudiated. By 1917, with the Liberals increasingly split between the followers of Asquith and Lloyd George, it had become uncertain on what basis they would fight an election, and the pact with Labour simply lapsed. Eventually it was overtaken by Lloyd George's decision to fight the election as leader of the coalition in alliance with the Conservatives.

The postponement of the election enabled Labour to focus on the more distant question of reform of the electoral system. For although the war had initially swept reform, including the vexed issue of women's suffrage, off the agenda, it subsequently revived it. The explanation lay in the drastic reduction in the number of men registered to vote as a result of migration by male workers who interrupted the twelve-month residence requirement for household voters. All parties agreed it would be intolerable to hold an election from which patriotic war workers and servicemen were excluded. In March 1916 the NEC's Electoral Reform Subcommittee pronounced: 'In view of the fact that the electoral machinery throughout the country has broken down and the electors scattered, no election should take place until a new scheme of franchise reform (including women's suffrage), Registration and Redistribution [of constituencies] has been effected.'[35] Henderson was instructed to put this before the Cabinet. Reminding his colleagues that they had accepted the principle of enfranchising munitions workers and troops, he argued that if this were done as a reward for patriotic service it would hardly be possible to exclude men withheld from the army in reserved occupations, volunteers rejected on medical grounds, and women.[36]

The Cabinet, convinced that it would be impossible to devise an agreement acceptable to all parties, eventually decided to pass the whole question of electoral reform over to an all-party committee chaired by the Speaker which began sitting in October 1916.[37] The three Labour members of the thirty-two-man Speaker's Conference were co-operative, pro-government figures; indeed Stephen Walsh and G. J. Wardle served in Lloyd George's coalition. Labour's aims, which largely coincided with those of the Liberals, were adult suffrage based on a short residential qualification instead of the existing twelve months, simultaneous elections on a single day (instead of spreading them over several weeks), extended polling hours which would make it easier for workingmen to vote, restrictions on expenditure by the candidates, and the introduction of the Alternative Vote.[38]

To general surprise the Speaker's Conference reached a comprehensive agreement and delivered its recommendations to Lloyd George at the end of January 1917. Meeting in March, Labour's annual conference instructed Labour MPs to support the Speaker's proposals 'as a minimum' and to secure 'the inclusion of women on the broadest possible basis, and especially to ensure that the bulk of the wage-earning women are not excluded'.[39] The Speaker's proposals included a franchise for female local government voters and for wives of local government voters subject to a thirty-year age requirement thereby creating no fewer than 8.4 million women electors which satisfied Liberal and Labour opinion. Overall, the reform package, amounting to a new electorate of twenty-one million dominated by working-class men over the age of twenty-one, appeared to contain major advantages for Labour and offered further proof of the wisdom of working within the system.

By the summer of 1917 the concatenation of electoral reform, trade union expansion and Liberal divisions seemed to point to a fresh initiative by Labour. However, the party remained so far a loyal, if minor, element in the Lloyd George coalition and the eventual breakaway was largely a contingency rather than a matter of deliberate judgement. At fifty-four Arthur Henderson was now Labour's pre-eminent leader. As long as he felt content to work in the War Cabinet any change of course would have been difficult, and so far he had resisted pressure to change the party's constitution, strategy and programme. However, Lloyd George made the mistake of taking Henderson for granted. In June 1917 he rejected his request to have control over the reconstruction issues that affected labour including demobilisation and industrial reorganisation. The mistake was compounded by the outcome of Henderson's visit to Russia in June 1917. The British government sent him because it was concerned about the ability of the new Provisional government under Alexander Kerensky, that had succeeded the tsar, to keep Russia in the war. Deteriorating conditions and the alarming evidence of Bolshevik activity convinced Henderson that some hope of peace must be held out to the Russian people. One immediate means of doing this lay in participation in a conference being organised at Stockholm by European socialists to relaunch the demand for a negotiated settlement with Germany. Previously Henderson had steered the NEC away from participation in this conference, to the irritation of MacDonald who complained: 'the stupidity of some of its members is painful'.[40] However Henderson now changed his mind with the result that on 25 July members voted five to two to sanction Labour representation at Stockholm, a decision ratified by three to one by a special conference. Although a Labour delegation would have been embarrassing for the government, Henderson argued that he was acting in his party capacity not as a member of the Cabinet. However, at its next meeting the War Cabinet decided against British representation at Stockholm, and humiliated Henderson by keeping him waiting outside the door for an hour before demanding his resignation.

Although George Barnes replaced Henderson and Labour remained officially part of the coalition, a turning point had been reached almost unintentionally. Lloyd George had blundered in his treatment of Henderson who proceeded to embark on a completely new course that had not previously been in prospect. According to Clynes, Henderson's resignation came as 'a bombshell to all the Labour members'. Thomas responded in language that seemed to herald the Second World War: 'This is a people's war. The people must have a voice in the settlement. Labour has already shown its value in the success of the Allied cause. Labour must also speak by its influence and power and declare that a lasting peace is necessary.'[41] Coming from the patriotic Thomas this signified a new assertiveness in Labour's ranks.

Henderson's unexpected release from Cabinet made it easier for him to collaborate with MacDonald, the Webbs and others to initiate a redefinition of Labour's aims, structure and organisation during the autumn of 1917, a critical stage as things turned out. Hitherto the Webbs had devoted their efforts to influencing Liberal and Conservative politicians, regarding Labour as unlikely to attain power. But by 1917 they had readjusted their attitude, calculating that investment in Labour would yield greater dividends. The first initiative was a fresh statement of 'War and Peace Aims' written largely by MacDonald, Henderson and the Webbs in October 1917. In effect the controversy

over Stockholm had forced Labour to assert itself as against the coalition and to contrive a rapprochement between the patriots and war
critics within the movement by focusing on future policies on which
everyone could agree. This was followed by a new domestic
programme, entitled 'Labour and the New Social Order', ratified at
a special conference in September 1918.

Another major step involved drafting a new party constitution.
Although the 1918 constitution became famous for Clause IV, its
importance lay in the fact that it entrenched the role of the unions
and opened the party up to wider participation. The NEC was expanded
from sixteen to twenty-three members including eleven union representatives, two for the socialist societies, five from the constituency
parties and four women. But whereas under the original constitution
they had been chosen by each affiliated society, now they were to be
selected by conference as a whole – effectively giving power to the
unions. MacDonald resisted this, complaining 'the tyranny of the vote
of the big TUs has become intolerable', but he was outvoted.[42] On
this basis the union leaders, who remained very suspicious of the ILP
and even toyed with the idea of seceding from the party, allowed themselves to be persuaded to accept Clause IV by Henderson; as they
would control policy the socialist commitment hardly seemed to
matter.

At the same time the decision was taken to create a local Labour
Party in every constituency and to develop an individual party membership. Individual membership undermined the role hitherto played by
the ILP, indeed it threatened to make it superfluous, and was also
important in encouraging women, few of whom were likely to join
via trade unions, into the party. Since April 1917 a subcommittee of
the Women's Labour League under Dr Marion Phillips had been
considering recommendations to the NEC about organising women
in anticipation of an extension of the vote. The enfranchisement of
8.4 million women made this an urgent necessity. However, the reforms
aroused controversy because the female subscription was set at
sixpence, compared with one shilling for men; this was justified on
the grounds of female poverty but it provided an excuse to deny them
equal rights and effectively make them second-class members.[43] A
separate hierarchy was created for women involving women's sections
in the constituencies, women's advisory councils in each region, an

annual conference whose resolutions could reach the party conference only through the NEC, and a women's department headed by Phillips as chief woman officer and eight organisers. The rationale for separate organisation, a principle also adopted by the Conservatives, was that as women were less experienced in political work they would feel more comfortable in female-only organisations.[44] Although this innovation caused discontent between the wars, in 1918 it seemed a timely advance as women were about to become 40 per cent of the electorate.

The final arm of Henderson's new course was an ambitious strategy to contest the general election, now expected to be held during wartime, on a wide front. This crucial breakthrough occurred surprisingly late in the war. Up to 1914 only 179 local parties had been affiliated; the total stagnated at 177 in 1915, rising slightly to 199 in 1916 and 239 in 1917, followed by a major rise to 389 in 1918, a total very close to the actual number of seats contested. During 1917 the NEC accelerated the work of its travelling organisers who visited seventy-nine districts in that year.[45] The number of election agents also increased from seventeen in 1912 to eighty by 1918.

The explanation for this breakthrough is not hard to find. The disarray in the Liberal ranks was an open invitation for Labour to declare its independence. This appeared to be the ideal moment to tap a whole new reservoir of Labour support in the new electorate, up from 7.9 million to 21.4 million. The resources available to the party had also increased partly because union membership had grown from 4.1 million to 6.5 million during wartime, with affiliated membership up from 2.6 million to 5.2 million, and partly because the funds collected under the 1913 Trade Union Act had accumulated, making it feasible to sponsor many more candidates. Finally, after his visit to Russia Henderson had become impressed by the prospect that post-war society might see social upheaval and political extremism and he believed that Labour, with its war record and new authority, must resist the anti-parliamentary elements by putting itself at the head of the men returning from the forces.

One further factor contributed to Labour's broad-front strategy in 1918. Before 1914 Labour had never fought more than seventy-eight seats at a single election, partly for lack of resources and partly for fear that three-cornered contests were guaranteed to deliver Liberal and Labour seats to the Tories on a minority vote. Yet by October 1917 Henderson evidently contemplated running 200 candidates and even spoke of 500 at one point. Even the actual total – 388 – was incompatible with an electoral pact and threatened a disastrous split in the non-Conservative vote. Crucially, however, the danger appeared to have been obviated by the Representation of the People Bill which included provisions for the Alternative Vote system in single-member seats and Single Transferable Vote in major cities. However, although the Conservatives recognised that STV would assure them minority representation in big cities, they expected to lose from the Alternative Vote. Conversely, the Liberals and Labour calculated on the basis of Edwardian experience that the Alternative Vote would meet their needs.[46] Henderson, clearly assuming that some form of proportional representation would remain in the legislation, told C. P. Scott in December 1917 that Labour might run 500 candidates and explained that he would rely on 'the Alternative Vote and on a friendly under-standing between Liberalism and Labour to give each other their second choice'.[47] It was not until February 1918, after the bill had shut-tled back and forth between the Lords and the Commons, that the Alternative Vote was finally dropped from the bill, as was STV.[48] Immediately the NEC met to reconsider its candidates and to 'review the whole political situation'. However, recognising that by this time it was too late to reverse the process, the NEC decided to give the activists their head and to fight 'wherever the local parties desire'.[49] As a result Labour contested 388 seats, a majority, for the first time in its history, though the figure would probably have been lower but for the expectations engendered by the Alternative Vote. In the long run the consequences of this narrowly missed opportunity were to prove serious for both Labour and the Liberals.

After the high hopes aroused by the new electorate the outcome of the 1918 election proved to be an anticlimax. Lloyd George fought in alliance with the Conservatives, some Liberals and the NDP to most of whom he and Bonar Law, the Tory Leader, issued a 'Coupon' or letter of approval. Although Clynes and most of the parliamentary party had wanted to remain in the coalition until the peace treaty had been signed, they were overruled by the NEC. When the Armistice was unexpectedly announced in November Lloyd George immediately decided to seek a mandate as 'The Man Who Won The War' while his prestige was at its height. Consequently, the election was held while wartime emotions and anti-German hysteria were still high and easily exploited by coalition candidates who freely cast aspersions on the patriotism of their opponents. Some newspapers dispatched telegrams to candidates demanding: 'For the guidance of your constituency will you kindly state whether, if elected, you will support the following: 1. Punishment of the Kaiser 2. Full payment for the war by Germany 3. The expulsion from the British Isles of all Enemy Aliens.' Candidates increasingly pandered to the mood by claiming that vast sums could be extracted from the defeated powers in reparations. Not surprisingly the coalition forces won 54 per cent of the vote and a massive 74 per cent of the seats.

Despite its new foreign policy statement Labour entered the Coupon Election virtually as three parties: the anti-war rebels, the belligerent patriots, and the mainstream who attempted to adopt a patriotic but moderate line. Opponents of the war were overwhelmingly rejected, MacDonald obtaining only 23 per cent in a straight fight in Leicester West, and Snowden 19 per cent in a three-cornered contest at Blackburn. Some Labour candidates publicly repudiated them. When heckled in Birmingham, one speaker protested: 'Whatever Ramsay MacDonald and Snowden have been on the war I am not responsible for. Because they are pacifists I can't help that.'[50] Conversely, some Labour candidates competed effectively with the Tories. George Barnes advocated hanging the kaiser and John Hodge declared that 'the guilty must pay the penalty'.[51] Caught between the extremes was Arthur Henderson who had unwisely abandoned his County Durham seat to stand at East Ham South where, despite his wartime service, he was attacked by a former Labour MP, J. A. Seddon: 'Mr Henderson was very sore because he was being labelled a pacifist. He might not be a pacifist but he had his foot on the slippery slope.'[52]

Labour's performance is not easy to interpret. The 22 per cent share of the vote undoubtedly marked a breakthrough. The fifty-seven MPs, or sixty-one if Independent Labour MPs are included, made Labour the largest Opposition party, since the seventy-three Sinn Fein members refused to attend Westminster and the Asquithian Liberals had only twenty-eight. Consequently Labour, with some hesitation, occupied the Opposition front bench, a symbolic step towards its new status as the government-in-waiting.

On the other hand, fifty-seven MPs represented a very modest improvement on the forty-two elected in December 1910. Moreover, as thirty-three of the victories occurred in mining seats this hardly looked like a breakthrough so much as a consolidation of the existing bridgeheads in the coalfields of South Wales, Yorkshire, Durham and Lancashire. In the process the party had also shifted markedly to the right. Only three of those elected were ILP nominees and even they rejected ILP views on the war. No fewer than fifty-one of the MPs were union nominees including twenty-five from the Miners Federation. Viewed from a social-geographical perspective Labour's real breakthrough was postponed until later in the 1920s.

Nor do sociological explanations for Labour's performance help. One major factor that was expected to help the party – the huge new working-class electorate – failed to make an impact; the performance in working-class areas was far too patchy. There was no positive relationship between the increase in the Labour vote and rise in the proportion of new voters in a constituency.[53] Even allowing for the pro-Conservative bias of the female voters and the fact that only 900,000 of the 3.9 million service electors actually voted, the results cast serious doubts on the idea that the new electorate was distinctively pro-Labour. However, any assessment must be qualified by the unusually low turnout in 1918 – 57 per cent – largely because few of the four million servicemen voted. There is plenty of impressionistic evidence of the differences between soldiers and civilians in 1918. Those who had remained at home during the war wanted to strike a vicarious blow against the enemy by backing patriotic candidates. In Manchester Sir Arthur Haworth complained that 'the working-class vote and especially the women among them, have all been out for the Kaiser's head'. By contrast contemporaries believed that the troops were more sympathetic to Labour, even to anti-war candidates, because they felt detached from the shallow jingoism they heard at home and were often alienated by patriotic rhetoric. By 1917 there was evidence of the radicalising effect of military service as men began to voice their discontent over poor pay and uncertainty about what they were fighting for. However, when the election came most soldiers failed to use the postal and proxy votes to which they were entitled and as a result the political impact of the mass army was delayed until the election of 1922.

But why did Labour win in certain districts? The explanation lay less in structural changes than in the character of the political appeal made by some candidates in 1918. At Derby Jimmy Thomas emerged top of the poll in a two-member seat. He faced his electors flourishing letters of congratulation from assorted luminaries including Field Marshal Sir William Robertson, Field Marshal Sir Douglas Haig, Andrew Bonar Law and J. L. Garvin, editor of the *Observer*, for his role in keeping the railways running during the war. Unusually for a Labour candidate he was endorsed by the local newspaper and even the Derby Tories thought he deserved to be included in the Cabinet![54] But apart from his personal attributes, Thomas understood the tactical need to appropriate the war from the Tories: 'I say that Labour has won the war.'[55] Other successful candidates saw how to turn the patriotic argument to Labour's advantage and thereby to justify the party's social policy. John Hodge argued that 'if Britain could spend so much to destroy life she could now spend to make life worth living'; capital and labour, he said, should co-operate to promote reconstruction at home.[56] In Silvertown Jack Jones made the class appeal even more bluntly: 'We had won the war and no section had done so much to win it as the section to which they belonged [Hear, hear]. When they counted the dead and the widows and orphans they found that 80 per cent of them were those who had no property to fight for but simply fought from a patriotic sense of duty [Applause]. The nation must not forget the widows and the orphans.'[57]

In this way some Labour candidates managed to advance beyond the party's existing territory by making a populist appeal to working-class patriots. In Lancashire Labour won several Tory working-class strongholds such as Wigan and Preston. Tom Shaw, Labour's candidate in Preston, was not liked by local left-wingers on account of his enthusiasm for the war, but he was a bluff, sporting, John Bull figure whose blend of Toryism and socialism suited the constituency. Shaw claimed that 'the Germans deliberately provoked the war and that they carried it on in a way that was monstrous . . . Germany must pay the bill.' His patriotic credentials enabled him to take the offensive over social policy and advocate socialism from a position of strength. He advocated 'national ownership' of railways, mines and canals and focused his campaign on the treatment of the ex-soldiers, arguing that they had a right to a wage rather than a pension: 'as a debt that the nation owed them and a debt that the nation ought to be proud to honour'.[58]

More surprising was Labour's breakthrough in six constituencies in the West Midlands, another traditional Tory region in which they had hitherto been unrepresented: Smethwick, Burslem, Wednesbury, West Bromwich, Leek and Kingswinford. In West Bromwich the Labour victor, F. O. Roberts, was one of the three surviving ILP MPs but like the others he was pro-war. Roberts brought a combination of political and cultural qualifications, being a printer chosen by the Typographical Association but also vice-chairman of West Bromwich Football Club; a JP, he was closely involved with the local community and the war effort through his role in the Allied War Fund, the Local Tribunal, the East Midlands Committee for War Pensions and many other organisations.[59]

Labour scored an even more notable victory over the coalition at Smethwick, a new seat carved out of Handsworth, a traditional Tory stronghold despite being dominated by heavy industry. Lloyd George and Bonar Law had granted the Coupon to Christabel Pankhurst who had established ferociously right-wing credentials during the war by her campaigns against strikes and violent attacks on Bolsheviks. Condemning the Labour candidate as unpatriotic, she proclaimed that 'the fight today is between the Red Flag and the Union Jack'. These tactics worked in most places in 1918, but not in Smethwick where J. E. Davison, an experienced union official and organiser for the Ironfounders Society, stood for Labour. Davison had played a consistent role in promoting recruitment and working on wartime government committees. He deflated Christabel's rhetoric by arguing that men and women had won both the war and the vote through their sacrifices for their country. He also advocated the nationalisation of 'key industries' as a natural development from wartime.[60] Davison's victory, based on patriotism and socialism, was rather exceptional in 1918 but significant because it carried overtones of Labour's appeal in the landslide of 1945.

The third important advance in 1918 was in London, another area of very limited Labour success. In London Labour was starkly polarised between Bow and Bromley where George Lansbury struggled to champion the Radical Liberal-socialist tradition against the Tories in a desperately poor constituency, and a clutch of near-jingoes in the working-class suburbs. In between, Arthur Henderson, who unwisely abandoned his County Durham seat for something more convenient, stood in East Ham South where he came third behind NDP and Conservatives. While Lansbury lost to a Tory in Bow, four Labour members were elected, all voluble supporters of the war. Will Crooks and Will Thorne were returned unopposed at Woolwich East and Plaistow respectively, C. W. Bowerman increased his majority at Deptford, and Jack Jones won in the Silvertown division of West Ham. Initially there had been some doubt as to whether Will Thorne and Jack Jones would stand for Labour or the NDP. Thorne explained that 'if he ran as the local Labour Party candidate, he would be called upon to stand on the platform of pacifism, and that he was not prepared to do'.[61] But he managed to square his anti-capitalist and pro-nationalist politics with the orthodox ticket. Jack Jones, a docker and builder's labourer, had risen through the General Workers Union. He championed the right of the workingman to his beer, was keen on outdoor sports, and used coarse language that would have made many Labour candidates blush; but these qualities were tempered by his reverential monarchism and belligerent patriotism. As he said himself, 'he was no half-hearted supporter of England'.[62] Jones emerged as the most authentic representative of the working-class Tory-socialism of London's East End. After comfortably winning Silvertown in a three-cornered contest in 1918, he retained the seat for Labour until his death in 1940. Though figures like Jones can be dismissed as eccentrics or as characters, his irreverent, populist brand of politics was to become an integral part of Labour's appeal to the next generation as voiced by the *Daily Mirror* in its heyday during the 1940s and 1950s. However, it was to take another world war to bring this expression of Labour politics to its peak.

6

'Dollar Princess': The Emergence of a National Party in the 1920s

In January 1919 Labour's fifty-seven MPs seemed rather surprised to find themselves occupying the Opposition front bench. Widely regarded as an uninspiring bunch of elderly trade union officials, they included forty-nine union men of whom twenty-five were miners; though more working class, the parliamentary party had become more conventional and right wing in character. From 1919 to 1920 it was led by William Adamson, whom Beatrice Webb dismissed as 'dull-witted', and from 1921 to 1922 by J. R. Clynes who had wanted to remain in the coalition in 1918. 'They have tasted the flesh pots,' Ramsay MacDonald wrote bitterly in his diary as he contemplated the new leadership from his lonely position outside Parliament.[1] The parliamentary party undoubtedly missed the tactical sense and forensic skills of MacDonald and Snowden. Despite its status as the official Opposition, Labour was slow to behave like a government-in-waiting, and, as the reaction against the war and the Lloyd George coalition began to gather force, critics questioned its reluctance to offer serious opposition to the government; for example, the peace settlement negotiated at Versailles was allowed to pass with only one Labour MP voting against. Admittedly, the opposition parties felt dwarfed by the coalition's 478 MPs, memorably described by the Tory Stanley Baldwin as 'hard-faced men who looked as though they had done well out of the war'.

In this situation the activists, regarding the parliamentary party as marginal, increasingly turned to local campaigns as a better means of challenging a government ensconced in power for five years. Hence the upsurge of enthusiasm for 'direct action'. Several million demobilised soldiers, aggrieved at missing the full employment and high wages of wartime, were keen to make up lost ground and were angry about wartime profiteering by employers feather-bedded by generous government contracts. During the brief boom of 1919–20, fuelled by rash investment in textiles and other products previously in short supply, this dissatisfaction generated a mood of rising expectations in working-class communities and an aggressive tone in the Labour Movement. 'The master class have reaped a golden harvest from the shambles of Europe, and their ill-gotten gains, in the shape of watered stock and over-capitalisation, is one of the principal reasons why wages must come down to pay interest on their investments,' commented Birmingham Labour Party in 1920.[2] Reflecting the gathering reaction against war, Birmingham condemned 'the infamous terms of the Peace Treaty [which] strangle European trade . . . War is a game in which the worker never wins.' By 1920 the boom was collapsing, in the process pushing unemployment from 3.9 to 16.9 per cent in a single year and galvanising the trade unions whose membership now exceeded eight million. In February 1919 the miners had voted six to one for strike action designed to secure better pay and coal nationalisation. During that year there were 1,352 stoppages and thirty-five million lost working days, followed by 1,607 strikes and twenty-six million lost days in 1920. In this militant atmosphere support for syndicalism revived, notably in the shape of the pre-war Triple Alliance of miners, railwaymen and transport workers. The vision of a general strike was most closely realised in Glasgow where wartime rent strikes and threats to the status of skilled workers had had a radicalising effect. Fearful that their wartime gains were about to disappear, thousands of workers joined a forty-hour strike in January 1919 aiming to stop the abolition of rent controls and to reduce unemployment by shortening the working week. The strike culminated in a demonstration of 100,000 people in St George's Square denounced absurdly by the Scottish Secretary as a 'Bolshevist Rising'. In London ministers overreacted, mobilising 12,000 troops and six tanks and setting up machine guns on hotel rooftops in the city, making Glasgow feel like a city under foreign occupation. Afraid to use local troops from the Maryhill barracks, the authorities allowed the police to draw their batons and charge the crowds, resulting in a riot on 'Bloody Friday', as the events became known.

Meanwhile, the Labour parliamentarians and union leaders, sensing a threat to their authority, attempted to stem the tide of direct action.

Towards the end of 1918 an exasperated Arthur Henderson had declared: 'If you want me to lead the Labour Movement as a Bolshevist I give you notice I am done with the job. Would to God some of our people who are espousing the Bolshevik cause knew what it was.'[3] At the party's annual conference in 1919 the chairman, J. McGurk, deployed the classic case against the use of strikes for political purposes: 'If we are constitutionalists, if we believe in the efficacy of the political weapon (and we do, or why do we have a Labour Party?) then it is both unwise and undemocratic because we fail to get a majority at the polls to turn round and demand that we should substitute industrial action.'[4] However, the rank and file were so dismayed by the performance of the MPs that they simply wanted to take on the coalition government, and conference voted in favour of direct action by 1.8 million to 900,000.

In the event, however, the discontent focused around an issue more acceptable to the leadership – the danger of British interference in support of the counter-revolutionary forces in the civil war in Russia. In fact, by January 1920 British troops had withdrawn from Russia and the Cabinet decided to stay neutral and avoid supporting the Poles against the Bolsheviks, but in view of the pronounced anti-Bolshevik opinions of Winston Churchill, Secretary of State for War, socialists suspected the authorities were turning a blind eye to counter-revolutionary activity. 'The Russian people should be left free to work out their own salvation,' as Lansbury put it. In April when the Poles resumed their offensive, he launched a 'Hands Off Russia' campaign in the *Daily Herald*, and Tom Mann and Harry Pollitt agitated among the London dockers to refuse to load the *Jolly George* with arms for Poland. In June Labour's annual conference voted for direct action to stop the sending of munitions. By July, with the Polish forces now in retreat, the Lloyd George coalition appeared to contemplate intervention to support Polish independence. This provoked the formation of the Council of Action by the TUC and the Labour Party, pledged to using industrial power, including a general strike, to prevent another war, a decision that attracted the backing of most of the movement including Clynes, Thomas, Adamson and MacDonald.

These events created a compelling myth to the effect that the organised working class had saved Britain from another war: 'it taught me how powerful we were, if we were united,' wrote Arthur Horner.[5] Nor was the danger entirely imaginary, for Lloyd George's gung-ho proclivities were still apparent in September 1922 when he came within a whisker of embarking on war with Turkey. Interestingly, the intelligence services advised the government in 1919 that working-class hostility to intervention against the Soviet regime was not a reflection of pro-Bolshevism so much as opposition to war and to the extension of conscription.[6] However, conventional politicians went in fear of Communist subversion in post-war Britain. The overthrow of the tsarist regime in 1917 had been greeted with delight, and many socialists welcomed the subsequent Bolshevik Revolution as signalling the end of capitalism. A convention at Leeds in June 1917 had attracted 1,150 delegates including Labour MPs, unions, local parties, women's and peace organisations, to discuss the organisation of workers' soviets in Britain. It is difficult now to appreciate the optimism engendered by the revolution. By 1920 British socialists like Lansbury had begun to visit Russia to see a socialist government at work. 'I expect the Revolution soon, don't you?' wrote Sylvia Pankhurst in a letter intercepted by Special Branch. 'Parliament is a decaying institution; it will pass away with the capitalist system.'[7] The intelligence services were well aware that she and other socialists travelled to the Continent to collect subsidies to promote left-wing newspapers and organisations from exotically named agents such as the 'Eye of Moscow' at this time. By the summer of 1920 the Russians were impatient for the small and scattered British Marxist groups to co-ordinate their work. As a result a Unity Convention, dominated by members of the British Socialist Party, was held in July to found the British Communist Party. However, Special Branch cheerfully reported that the new organisation was irretrievably split over both tactics and personalities.[8] A minority rejected the idea that socialism could be attained through parliamentary action and denounced the Labour Party as 'Opportunists', but others regarded parliamentary activity as 'a means of propaganda and agitation towards the Revolution', and a majority voted to seek affiliation with the Labour Party.

Yet despite the excitement engendered by direct action there was never much doubt about the movement's response to Communist overtures. At the 1921 party conference Communist affiliation was massively rejected by 4.1 million to 220,000, a verdict repeated over the next four years. In 1925 conference accepted Henderson's proposals to ban Communists from becoming Labour candidates, members or trade

union delegates to the party. 'The only road to progress and the salvation of the country was the constitutional one through Parliament,' as
Clynes put it. According to Will Thorne, 'To every form of anarchism,
whether it were called by its real name or were disguised as Bolshevism
or "direct action", they as Socialists were resolutely opposed!'[9]
Consequently the parliamentary party rebuffed requests to receive the
Labour whip by two Communist MPs, Walton Newbold and Shapurgi
Saklatvala, in 1922 and 1924.[10] At local level Herbert Morrison earned
himself the title 'our chief witchfinder' for his efforts in rooting out
Communists in the London Labour Party. Morrison argued that the
Communists' resort to physical force was incompatible with Labour's
vision of the peaceful social transformation of society, and that, in
seeking election, Communists were loyal neither to the party nor to
the political system: 'The Communist . . . like the militarist, is not
working for constructive social reorganisation but merely for "a bloody
mess" in the hope that he can seize power in the middle of it.' Morrison
sometimes persuaded Communists who wanted to leave their party to
stay and report to him on their plans.[11] In the North the 1920s saw
regular disputes in union lodges where Communists demanded that
ballot boxes be 'peeped' or checked before voting started to ensure the
officials had not rigged the result.[12]

However, Labour's loose federal structure made the enforcement
of national policy difficult. Between 1926 and 1929 twenty-seven
constituency parties were disbanded for ignoring the ban on
Communist members. In Battersea five councillors enjoyed membership of both parties, and Saklatvala stood for Labour in 1922 and 1923,
but as a Communist, unopposed by Labour, in 1924, effectively representing both parties. Despite being officially proscribed, Communists
were widely seen as 'an integral part of the working-class movement',
as Harry Pollitt put it. According to Lansbury, whose son and daughter
were for a time Communist members but became Labour councillors, 'the Communists are not our enemies but our friends because
they agreed on replacing capitalism'.[13] In Barrow-in-Furness the Labour
Party allowed the Young Communist League to use a room 'on usual
terms'. In Salford a resolution protesting against the official ban on
Communists acting as party officers was lost by only twenty-one to
twenty, an indication of the different perspectives of individual
members and the union-dominated annual conferences; local parties

simply regarded Communists as good voluntary workers. At Morden, in South London, where the ward committee agreed *not* to expel Communists, it transpired that their secretary was a Communist; he was asked to resign from the Communist Party but 'could not see his way to do this' and quit as secretary.[14] Nor did official policy stop a Communist member, J. T. Murphy, applying to become Labour candidate at Tottenham South in 1927 where he promised financial assistance from the Communist Party.[15] More awkward to handle was the case of Dr. Robert Dunstan who stood at Birmingham West in 1924 as a Communist but with the support of several local Labour parties; this provoked a two-year controversy as he enjoyed wide Labour sympathy.[16]

Yet despite the complications, the emergence of the Communist Party proved useful to Labour's leaders because it helped them draw a line between constitutionalism and direct action. The turning point came in April 1921 when the Triple Alliance collapsed as several key union leaders, including Ernest Bevin and Jimmy Thomas, withdrew from strike action leaving the miners in the lurch. As the number of strikes now began to diminish the parliamentary leaders felt that they had weathered the challenge of direct action and could safely repudiate the idea of the class war as a Continental aberration. 'Nowadays', Clynes was to write later, 'I think the most loyal class is the working class. As the Labour Party has grown in power, the menace of revolution has dwindled.'[17] By 1921 the realisation that Lloyd George's coalition was disintegrating in Parliament and losing support in the country helped them to regain the initiative. The Conservatives had adopted Lloyd George in 1918 as a necessary bulwark against the rise of Labour; but as Labour began to gain popularity the prime minister increasingly appeared as a liability. Up to 1922 Labour made thirteen by-election gains including Spen Valley, Bothwell and Widnes in 1919, Dartford and South Norfolk in 1920, Southwark, Dudley, Kirkcaldy, Penistone and Heywood and Radclyffe in 1921, and Manchester Clayton, Camberwell North, Leicester East and Pontypridd in 1922. The party's vote rose from 29 per cent to 50 per cent at Dartford and from 27 per cent to 57 per cent at Southwark.

Progress in parliamentary elections was, however, overshadowed by dramatic gains in local government. While the 1918 election had caught the anti-German hysteria, by November 1919, when municipal elections took place, the electorate had focused on domestic issues again. Housing shortages, food prices and profiteering now dominated the agenda to Labour's advantage. In 1919 the party gained 400 seats outside London, winning majorities in County Durham, Glamorgan, Monmouth and Bradford. The foundations for eventual success were also laid in places such as Birmingham, hitherto a backward area, where Labour had twenty-nine councillors by 1921. In 1922 the party's candidates polled 48,000 votes in the city compared with 49,000 for the Conservatives, and though the vote fell back to 42,000 in 1923, Labour was beginning to pose an effective challenge to the traditional Tory dominance. But the biggest breakthrough came in London where Labour won 572 seats out of 1,362 in 1919, including thirty-nine out of forty-two seats fought in Poplar, forty out of sixty fought in Stepney, and twenty-four out of twenty-eight fought in Bethnal Green. As a result Labour mayors took office: Herbert Morrison in Hackney, Clement Attlee in Stepney, and George Lansbury in Poplar. These gains were on an altogether greater scale than anything achieved in the Edwardian period. In London much ground was won at the expense of the Liberals whose candidates steadily dwindled in number even when their party enjoyed a revival at the parliamentary level. By 1922 Labour had become the majority or the leading party in Battersea, Bermondsey, Bethnal Green, Camberwell, Deptford, Fulham, Greenwich, Hackney, St Pancras, Shoreditch, Southwark, Stepney and Woolwich, leaving only nine other London boroughs.[18]

Municipal politics proved to be a major formative force in Labour's evolution, partly because local elections were much more vigorously and frequently contested than they are today. Herbert Morrison, who built his reputation on municipal success, got elected to the NEC in 1922. He believed that Labour must first demonstrate competence in local government before the electorate would willingly entrust the party with national power. 'A small, unprepossessing-looking man with an almost blind eye and queer expression of furtive pugnacity mainly engendered by a stubborn jaw and an unruly forelock', Morrison was the son of a Tory policeman. 'I see you've got that bloody rag round your neck again,' he used to say as the young Herbert donned his red tie to attend socialist meetings. As secretary of the London Labour Party Morrison drove himself, his staff and his volunteers hard: 'He was insensitive to people,' as one contemporary put it. 'He was dedicated to Labour and politics; that was his life.'[19] Recognising that London, with its sixty-one MPs, expanding suburbs and relatively weak trade union movement, required novel methods Morrison developed an organisation more comparable to that of the Conservatives by fostering social activities. 'The new school of Labour politics is a scientific school,' he boasted. 'It knows that noisy tub-thumping does not make up for careful organisation.'[20] In his own constituency, Hackney South, a mixed suburban district where he won in 1923, 1929 and 1935, Morrison appreciated that he could not rely on union organisation or funds. Women were therefore a crucial element both as doorstep canvassers and as fund-raisers. He held regular ward parties and dances as well as parties attended by several hundred children who enjoyed tea and entertainment in the form of conjurors, comedians, singing and sketches.[21] Morrison always turned up and danced with everyone though he never drank and never felt comfortable on the dance floor.

To organise this key battleground the London Labour Party established its headquarters above a Lyons tea shop in Westminster Bridge Road from which Morrison could walk to the House of Commons, Transport House and County Hall. He concentrated his resources in a central fund supported by the Royal Arsenal Co-operative Society and 24,000 affiliated Transport and General Workers Union members. As secretary he was paid £5 a week initially, rising to £8 in 1920, supported only by a full-time organiser and a Woman Officer. He wrote the copy for the *London Labour Chronicle*, later *London Labour News*, single-handedly and never asked for a higher salary. By 1930 the London constituencies boasted an individual membership of 45,000. But Morrison recognised that Labour needed something equivalent to the German Social Democratic Party's machine, capable of creating an entire social and cultural life for its members by engaging whole families in political work. This involved running speakers' classes, a legal advice bureau staffed by sympathetic lawyers to help with housing, rents and pensions, a Young People's Advisory Committee, a Labour Choir backed by local choirs to perform at meetings, a Dramatic Federation, a London Labour Symphony Orchestra, an Annual Labour Fair, a Festival of Labour at the Crystal Palace, an LLP Sports Association, and an annual reunion each January. Although not all these initiatives flourished, they enabled the LLP to go well beyond the limited machine typical of the trade union-dominated constituencies.

Municipal campaigns were, arguably, more effective than parliamentary work in defining Labour's programme and its overall sense
of purpose during the interwar period. Labour councillors focused on
building council houses, implementing the 1918 Maternity and Child
Welfare Act by establishing local clinics for mothers, providing baths
and wash houses, maintaining the unemployed, improving municipal
tramways, and extending the electricity supply. Housing, the one aspect
of social welfare neglected in the Edwardian period, assumed huge
importance for Labour councillors. Although the 1919 Act fell victim
to expenditure cuts, it was effectively revived by John Wheatley in the
1924 Labour government and by Arthur Greenwood in the 1929 government. The result was a transformation of housing tenure in Britain,
for between the wars 31 per cent of all new houses were in the public
sector, and as much as 70 per cent in Scotland, compared with virtually nothing before 1914. As a result of wartime rent controls the private
rented sector, which accounted for 90 per cent of all housing before
1914, went into a steep decline.

As municipal councillors and Poor Law Guardians Labour representatives were also in the forefront of the debate over unemployment
and the extent to which the unemployed should enjoy maintenance
from public funds. Despite the extension of unemployment insurance
to twenty million workers in 1920, the onset of long-term unemployment meant that thousands ceased to qualify for benefits, thus forcing
them to apply to the Poor Law Guardians. This caused a protracted
struggle between Conservative ministers in London and locally elected
Guardians who often paid at higher rates than was approved.
Unemployment also highlighted socialist claims that the free-enterprise
system had failed. In the early 1920s most economists, bankers and
businessmen expected a return to pre-1914 conditions, and thus to full
employment, but as the depression lengthened the view of capitalism
as doomed gained credibility and endowed socialists with a sense of
their inevitable triumph. In 1923 Philip Snowden highlighted the issue
by initiating a parliamentary debate over the failure of the capitalist
system, arguing for its gradual supercession by 'public ownership and
democratic control of the instruments of production and distribution'.[22]
Although Labour had no precise idea how to advance from capitalism
to socialism, the debate served some purpose for Snowden was opposed
by Sir Alfred Mond for the Liberals and by Sir Philip Lloyd-Graeme

for the Conservatives, thereby helping to polarise politics to Labour's advantage. Meanwhile, as a Labour government appeared to be a distant goal, municipal government offered a more realistic and immediate means of making socialism tangible. In London Morrison took the initiative by advocating public ownership of the generation and distribution of electricity supply. As Britain conspicuously lagged behind other western states and the electricity system was handicapped by a multiplicity of small, inefficient, privately owned companies whose charges to consumers varied widely, the case was compelling. As Morrison argued, the existing companies could be purchased at a fair price under legislation dating back to 1888.[23]

However, in the early 1920s more controversy was aroused by the Labour councillors in Poplar. Under Lansbury Poplar embarked on a programme of house-building, a £4 minimum wage and equal pay for women. The idea was that the council, as a major employer, could exert some influence on the wider labour market by instituting high standards, in effect working towards a socialistic society in the face of the prevailing economic system and a hostile central government. However, by 1921 when Poplar had 15,574 men unemployed, this had become financially unsupportable because a one-penny rate in Poplar yielded only £3,200 compared with £29,000 in Westminster.

As a result the long-standing campaign to equalise the London rates came to a head in 1921 when Poplar faced a 28 per cent rate rise and the councillors refused to levy the 'precept' required by the London County Council. On 29 July Lansbury led twenty-nine Labour councillors, backed by brass bands and 2,000 supporters, on a five-mile march from Poplar to the law courts. In September the councillors were arrested, the men being given six-week sentences in Pentonville, while Susan Lawrence, Minnie Lansbury, Julia Scurr and Mrs Cresswell, who was pregnant, were incarcerated in Holloway. As the government feared that other boroughs were about to emulate Poplar, the minister employed Harry Gosling to act as a go-between, negotiating with the councillors in prison. As a result they were discharged on the basis that a conference would be held to consider rate equalisation, and Poplar won an extra £400,000 in poor relief.[24] This famous victory gave Labour the moral high ground and offered further proof of the power of the workers if well organised.

However, Poplar was an unusual council with a high level of popular participation and a sense of ideology more akin to socialist movements on the Continent than in Britain. Significantly, few Labour councils were keen to follow its example, though later in the 1920s councillors at West Ham, Chester-le-Street and Bedwellty were suspended by Neville Chamberlain in disputes over poor relief. The party leaders frankly regarded Lansbury as a liability likely only to undermine their reputation as men fit to hold office. Morrison criticised Lansbury's tactics for putting excessive burdens on the ratepayers.[25] He also argued that if Labour adopted illegal methods it would play into the hands of its opponents who would feel tempted to do the same when the party came to power nationally. By and large the new Labour councillors were law-abiding and anxious to conform in all respects. In Hackney Morrison worked closely with his officials, showed no suspicion about their political views, and refused to regard them as class enemies.[26] Whereas Lansbury as mayor had declined to use the symbols of his authority – robes, mace and cocked hat – Morrison retained his trademark red tie, brown tweed suit and brogues, but also donned the mayoral robes and regalia because they helped confer prestige and legitimacy on him and the party. He also conformed by unveiling war memorials, attending public functions and meeting royalty. For him, Labour's route to government lay through discrediting propaganda about extremism by accepting convention and using the Establishment.

On the other hand the municipal dimension exaggerates the extent of Labour's advance during the 1920s. The party's share of the national vote rose from 22 per cent in 1918 to 29.5 in 1922, to 30.5 in 1923, to 33 in 1924 and to 37 in 1929. This was the basis for contemporary confidence in Labour's inexorable rise. However, closer inspection suggests this was steady rather than dramatic. As a result of the 1918 franchise reforms working-class voters comprised around 80 per cent of the electorate, enabling Labour to form a majority government if it had been capable of winning even a bare majority of working-class support; but its modest share of the vote suggests that this remained an elusive goal. What the voting figures reflected was the steady expansion in constituency Labour parties (CLPs) and thus in the number of candidates fielded rather than the sudden creation of a new constituency. Under Arthur Henderson as secretary and Egerton Wake as national agent, the affiliated constituency Labour parties increased from 397 in 1918 to 626 in 1924 – more than the 615 constituencies because of some double affiliations. Whereas in 1921 140 constituencies lacked a CLP, by 1924 only nineteen did. The number of candidates rose from 388 in 1918 to 411 in 1922, 422 in 1923, 512 in 1924 and 571 in 1929 when the party fought on virtually as wide a front as the Conservatives.

There are two broad explanations for Labour's rise in popularity during the 1920s: on the one hand favourable contingencies, issues and accidents including the timing of general elections, and, on the other, the development of the party machine in the form of a series of building blocks – institutional, social, intellectual – that gradually transformed Labour from a sectional party to a national one by 1945. Among these building blocks the trade unions were clearly crucial. Their membership rose to a peak of 8.4 million in 1920 before commencing a steady decline to 1934 as a result of long-term unemployment. But the relevant factor was the *affiliated* union membership, based approximately on those who paid the political levy, which stood at 3.5 million in the early 1920s and fell to just over two million by 1928. The unions formed the steel frame of many constituency Labour parties through the affiliation of local union branches and their financial resources. Unions offered subsidies to CLPs for adopting their representatives as candidates which resulted in the safer Labour seats being held by middle-aged or elderly union officials; after the 1922 election, for example, eighty-five of the 142 MPs were union-sponsored.

Unfortunately, the reliance on affiliated union members proved a mixed blessing for it inhibited the attainment of the mass party membership that had been provided for in the 1918 party constitution. Figures were not published until 1928 when 215,000 individual members were recorded; however, as each constituency was assumed to have not less than 240 members this must be regarded as an exaggeration. Where local parties enjoyed plenty of union affiliations they often neglected recruitment of individual members. As MP for Bishop Auckland, a constituency run by the Durham Miners Association, Hugh Dalton cynically commended *inactive* parties: 'Too many members might upset the apple cart and bring in the militants.' In Wansbeck, a Northumberland mining seat, the CLP had 13,828 affiliated members by 1925 while the individual membership stood at just 195 men and 661 women.[27] Neglect of individual membership was understandable as members paid in small instalments which involved repeated and laborious collections. In 1927 the Barrow-in-Furness party, for example, adopted a much-favoured system using a collector in each ward whose remuneration was 20 per cent of the money collected; they were required to live in the ward and restrict collections to that ward.[28]

Conversely, the indirect, affiliated membership, however large, was less useful in electoral terms because many paid the levy without realising it; also the numbers were sometimes rather arbitrary and inflated because they earned each union conference delegates. In any case union membership was a dwindling asset from 1921 down to 1934 as a result of the depression. Above all, reliance on the unions meant that Labour's resources were invariably concentrated in its safest seats, ensuring a substantial bloc of MPs but only a minority. It was necessary to win the socially mixed, industrial-residential constituencies, but for a long time the maldistribution of resources put this beyond reach. As general secretary Henderson was keen to transfer union money to marginal seats, but in face of their inflexibility he only managed to persuade conference to raise the political levy from twopence to threepence in 1920, which yielded an extra £40,000–50,000 per annum. In 1923 he resurrected the fighting fund to assist impecunious CLPs which had been abolished in 1919. It spent £20,000 in 1924 though this fell well short of Henderson's goal of equalising the expenditure of the richest and poorest parties; constituencies fought by miners' candidates, for example, spent 50 per cent more than the average, though they could have managed on less. In 1933 the annual conference at last agreed to place limits on the financial dependence of CLPs on unions. In future local parties were required to find 20 per cent of election expenses and affiliated organisations to donate up to £150 in boroughs and £200 in county seats each year.[29]

Yet struggling CLPs naturally found it hard to resist a trade union subsidy which typically included the cost of a full-time agent and contributions to general-election expenses. In 1918 agents were being offered £200 per annum, though the Labour Registered Agents Association officially recommended £337. In 1921 the Barrow party accepted this figure but was unable to afford it and agreed to treat the balance as a debt.[30] Prior to the 1922 election Barrow considered the claims of John Bromley, who was backed by several unions offering £350 for an agent plus election contributions, and Charles Duncan on whose behalf the Workers Union offered 80 per cent of the agent's salary and 80 per cent of expenses.[31] Although Duncan had represented Barrow before the war and been narrowly defeated in 1918, the party chose Bromley, perhaps influenced by his superior resources.

An insight into the local parties' dilemma is offered by Tottenham South, a London suburban constituency won by Labour in 1923 and 1929. In the absence of outside backing the income for 1921 was a meagre £81. As Tottenham South was a marginal seat with little union presence the CLP adopted a succession of middle-class candidates, presumably on the basis that it had to attract a wider vote: Sir Leo Money (1918), R. H. Tawney (1922), Percy Alden (1923 and 1924) and F. Messer (1929).[32] Money and Alden were former Liberal MPs. When a new candidate was sought in 1925 the party attracted eleven applications. At one extreme were two women who offered no money at all. At the opposite end were B. E. Goldstone of the NUT, who brought all expenses and an agent, and J. J. Mallon from the Postal Workers Union which agreed to fund a full-time agent plus 80 per cent expenses. In between them came a lawyer, J. B. Melville, who assured the committee 'while not being prepared to "buy" the constituency, [he] is willing if necessary to render considerable financial assistance to the Party – at a General Election £150 deposit, plus £300 and a fairly substantial subscription'. Although the officers clearly examined the financial credentials of the applicants, they warned: 'The Committee trusts, however, that this question will not be given too great a prominence in the final selection, feeling that with the right type of candidate financial support would be forthcoming.'[33]

There is plenty of evidence that well-endowed candidates were not always the key to victory. In Gateshead, where the strength of Liberalism as well as Conservatism made things difficult, Labour was defeated at the 1923 election despite having spent a generous £800. Yet in 1924 the party won despite spending only £322 against £799 for the Conservatives and £973 for the Liberals.[34] The key to success lay in a different candidate and a high level of participation by local members. Gateshead had adopted John Beckett, a twenty-nine-year-old not backed by a union. Previously chosen to fight Uxbridge, Beckett found 'I could not pay my own expenses and had little faith in the ability of the local people to raise the money'. He complained that 'where a local party had been pampered by a wealthy candidate or union, its independence and vitality took some time to return'.[35] In 1923 he was

persuaded to fight the hopeless seat of Newcastle North where he
found things similar to Uxbridge. According to one local activist 'the
Labour Movement in Newcastle, except for [Sir Charles] Trevelyan,
was dead from the neck up'.[36] As Newcastle lacked ILP branches,
Beckett was attracted to neighbouring Gateshead where a strong ILP
branch had about 150 members of whom only eighty were in employment; working from a corner shop these volunteers ran a 'dry canteen',
an office, a hall, regular Sunday meetings at the town hall, an amateur
orchestra, whist drives, a choir and a dramatic society. 'From these
figures', observed Beckett, 'something of the greatness of their
achievement may be understood.'[37] The ILP branch warmed to
Beckett's stirring socialist oratory, adopted him as candidate and put
his name forward to Gateshead Labour Party: 'and then the difficulties began'. As the agent was currently funded by the AEU the local
unionists wanted a union official for the subsidies he would bring.
Despite this Beckett was accepted and, against the national trend,
gained the seat by a 9,000 margin in a three-cornered contest in 1924.

Alternatively, in the absence of union subsidies some CLPs simply
relied on well-off middle-class candidates. A classic example was the
Limehouse division of Stepney which had been won by the coalition
in 1918 but fell to Clement Attlee in 1922. Though well known for his
philanthropic work among boys' clubs and as a local councillor and
mayor, Attlee was an improbable parliamentary candidate and never
became an orator. A forty-year-old bachelor who lived with his batman,
'Attlee needed careful nursing. His strongest cards were his erudition
and wit,' recalled John Beckett, 'both of which were over the heads
of a Limehouse audience which needed crude fireworks.'[38] But Attlee
compensated by employing the extrovert Beckett as an agent-secretary
at a generous £6 a week and he gave the ground floor of his large
house for the use of the local party. As Limehouse was not only a
poor area but was divided into two 'Irish' wards and two 'Jewish'
wards, Beckett felt he 'had no hope of building an orthodox party
machine or raising any substantial amount of money by party effort'.
The solution lay in building up Attlee as a source of free help and
advice to anyone in difficulties. Each day Beckett drove Attlee around
in an old two-seater motor car with a few helpers clinging on as best
they could. They would pull up in a street, making as much commo-
tion as possible, and knock on doors. When a sufficient audience had

gathered Beckett delivered a speech introducing Attlee who, 'looking extremely unhappy, would answer questions and exchange friendly greetings before we drove to the next street'.[39]

This old-fashioned, personalised style of campaigning, reminiscent of Conservative and Liberal methods, represents a corrective to the assumption that Labour pioneered a modernised approach to organisation and electioneering after 1918. Herbert Morrison's methods in the London Labour Party were the exception at this time; generally the party was eclipsed by the Conservatives in mobilising the mass electorate. One symptom of this weakness was the deficiency of professional agents; the party employed 112 in 1921 and 133 in 1922, but the total fell back to 113 in 1924. In addition the Miners Federation employed twenty to thirty agents. By 1929 there were still only 169 agents, concentrated in the safe seats, though Labour needed at least 300 to compete effectively with the Conservatives.

Labour also continued to rely on the Victorian Radical technique of big, inspirational rallies and whistle-stop tours to mobilise its support, which placed a heavy burden on MacDonald, Henderson and a handful of leaders. Even this was not professionally organised. While MacDonald was undoubtedly an inspiring platform performer, he proved difficult to manage because he was incapable of delivering a short stump speech, always becoming involved in a lengthy oration; at the 1924 election he embarked on a seven-day speaking tour unaccompanied even by a secretary. During the 1920s platform oratory gradually became redundant due to the use of the 'wireless' broadcast, but Lloyd George continued to deliver speeches at the microphone at full blast as though outdoors, while MacDonald initially used live platform speeches for his broadcasts which meant that as he bobbed about his voice was alternately loud and lost by the microphone. Baldwin, by contrast, undertook to be coached in the new technique and treated his broadcasts more as conversation pieces. The Conservatives, as Morrison was well aware, were quicker to adjust to the diminishing importance of public meetings and put more emphasis on the quieter techniques of doorstep canvassing, transport to the poll, and organising postal votes, methods that were better calculated to mobilise support amongst an enlarged electorate that now included many comparatively uncommitted voters not susceptible to Radical revivalism. Henderson strove to remind his colleagues that 'public meetings do not win an election. It is important that our people recognise that seats are often won or lost by voters who never enter the doors of any public hall to listen to the speeches of any parliamentary candidate.'[40] He also urged the party to overcome its suspicion of canvassing, especially as voters were increasingly dispersed to large housing estates which lacked the community infrastructure that promoted political involvement.

On the other hand, Labour recognised the importance of the national press at a time when newspapers were largely in the hands of its enemies. It was for this reason that the party had founded the *Daily Citizen* edited by Clifford Allen. The better-known *Daily Herald* originated in 1911 as a temporary strike newspaper of the London Society of Compositors, but it was revived in April 1912 by a committee of London trade unionists who invited Lansbury to become editor. This proved to be good timing as it coincided with the *Titanic* disaster, allowing the paper to condemn the discrimination against the poorer steerage-class passengers on board. Meanwhile, the *Daily Citizen*, which was too bland and pro-leadership, lasted only three years, while the *Herald*'s attacking line appealed more to readers. Lansbury printed opinions of all kinds and attracted some distinguished contributors including Siegfried Sassoon, Hilaire Belloc, G. K. Chesterton, Rebecca West, H. G. Wells, G. B. Shaw, Osbert Sitwell, Aldous Huxley and Robert Graves. But the paper's star was Will Dyson, the Australian cartoonist, who, for only £5 a week, delighted readers with his caricatures of 'Fat', an obese, cigar-smoking businessman.

After the war the *Herald* extended its circulation to 400,000 despite raising its price to two pence at a time when one penny was the norm. It survived on minimal resources and struggled in a competitive market against the *Mail*, *Express*, *Graphic*, *News*, *Chronicle* and *Mirror*. Never a great commercial success, the *Herald* enjoyed a hand-to-mouth existence, relying on the generosity of Mr Drewe, the manager of Victoria House Printing Company, who printed the paper even when Lansbury was unable to pay his bills. It also drew heavily on Lansbury's battalion of wealthy sympathisers, notably Joseph Fels, an American industrialist, Henry Harben, the heir to the Prudential Insurance Company, Muriel, Countess De La Warr, who became a *very* close friend, and the ex-Tory lawyer, Major Graham David Pole, who bought shares in Victoria House, supported *Lansbury's Labour Weekly*, and helped raise the

£100,000 required to turn the *Herald* into a daily paper.[41] In 1922 the *Herald* was taken over by a combine of the TUC and the Labour Party, followed in 1930 by Odhams Press in combination with the TUC. During the 1920s the paper changed character becoming more of a loyal party organ. Although Labour clearly needed such a paper, in the long run this limited the *Herald*'s value to the cause. It became too heavily political, too sober and too partisan to reach far beyond the party's committed supporters.

Meanwhile another building block fell into place in the shape of the alliance between Labour and the Co-operative Society which had five million members by 1925. The Co-operatives began to become politicised around 1917 as a result of government interference with food supplies; they felt their profits were being taxed too heavily, they were denied a fair share of food supplies, and consumers' interests were being ignored. As the movement had been a major expression of Victorian Liberalism, its loyalties were for some time contested between the Liberal and Labour parties, so much so that as late as 1921 the Co-operative Congress narrowly rejected a proposal to affiliate to the Labour Party. Liberal propaganda characterised Co-operative thinking in terms of self-help as 'strictly individualistic', but this was countered by A. V. Alexander who described it as 'a direct challenge to, and an alternative system to, the capitalist system'.[42] This was true up to a point. The Co-op was socialistic in that it distributed profits to members and dealt in goods produced under union-approved conditions. However, many members saw it as distinct from socialism on the grounds that consumption, not labour and production, was the basis for a new society and that it empowered women rather than men.[43] As Co-operators were keen to retain freedom from the state and refused to accept socialist support for a state monopoly on food importation, there was always some tension between the two movements and socialist intellectuals like Harold Laski were inclined to be patronising towards the society. Nonetheless, Labour eventually became the leading spokesman for the movement largely as a result of the role played by A. V. Alexander, who was full-time secretary from 1920 onwards and became elected MP for Sheffield Hillsborough in 1922. A staunch free-trader, patriot and former West Country Liberal, Alexander wore a starched 'Come to Jesus' collar and reinforced the party's conventional approach to both policy and methods. An indefatigable orator, he once delivered such a forceful speech that his false teeth flew from his mouth, but 'catching them with the agility of a Yorkshire slip fielder, he returned them to their proper place without interrupting his peroration'! [44]

Part of the Co-operative movement's significance lay in its mobil-isation of women through the Women's Co-operative Guild with 67,000 members by 1931. The guild aimed to change the political agenda by raising the profile of issues affecting ordinary married women including subsidies for maternity clinics, women's health, especially the maternal mortality rate, home helps for pregnant women, food prices and profiteering. Clearly much of this represented common ground with Labour. However, as the WCG had a history going back to 1883 it refused to be manipulated by male organisations. While Labour largely treated women in terms of their domestic interests, the WCG went further in several ways. Its members engaged in peace propaganda, selling white poppies and wreaths, peace handkerchiefs and tablecloths in protest against the official, triumphalist Armistice Day celebrations. It also had a feminist agenda incorporating family allowances, equal divorce law, birth control and legalised abortion which antagonised much of the party including the trade unions. Hence a certain amount of friction arose when the WCG tried to promote its leaders as Labour candidates. The general secretary, Eleanor Barton, contested Birmingham King's Norton for Labour in 1922 and 1923 but complained of receiving inadequate support from the local Labour Party. Subsequently Mrs Barton was outbid by trade union nominees and never became an MP, a failure that rankled with the WCG throughout the 1920s and 1930s. [45]

Yet it was dangerous to offend the WCG because it symbolised the wider role and aspirations of women in the post-war world. As the reforms of 1918 made women 39.6 per cent of voters, and around 43 per cent by 1924 when the new system had settled down, each party was anxious to organise them. Labour had a lot of ground to make up. Some middle-class suffragists gravitated towards Labour via the League of Nations Union and other pro-peace movements while Mary Macarthur and Margaret Bondfield, who were gaining prominence in the trade unions, also emerged as aspiring Labour MPs in the 1920s. Labour's 1918 constitution made it easy for women to join as indi-vidual members paying a lower fee than men. As a result female membership increased rapidly from 70,000 in 1921, to 150,000 in 1924 and 250,000 by 1928, though these figures are only estimates. By 1928 some 1,845 women's sections were in existence, each represented on the local CLP executive.

However, feminists had reservations about the separate organisation. One former suffragette, Hannah Mitchell, scornfully dismissed the sections as 'official cake-makers to the Labour Party'. But Dr Marion Phillips, the chief woman officer, argued that as women were largely inexperienced in political work they required their own organisation in which to develop the necessary confidence and skills, though studies of local parties, for example in Manchester, indicate a good deal of friction between the men and the women's sections.[46] Conflict was mitigated, however, where individual membership involved *couples* so that wives sometimes attended their section in the afternoon and accompanied their husbands to the constituency party meeting in the evening. When Tottenham North's West Ward found they had more female than male members they organised a husbands' party to which women were admitted only with a husband in tow, and produced twenty-three new members! [47] The 1918 constitution also provided for the election of four women to the twenty-strong NEC, the first being Ethel Snowden, Dr Ethel Bentham, Susan Lawrence and Mrs Harrison Bell who was replaced by Mary Macarthur in 1919. However, as they were effectively chosen by the union majority this generated friction in the long run as only the most orthodox and loyal women emerged while troublesome feminists were excluded. At the time, however, it appeared that a balance had been struck between the needs of the party and the aspirations of women.

In view of the maldistribution of the party's resources, women were potentially the key to electoral expansion in that their voluntary work could enable Labour to compete with the superior Conservative machine and extend its range beyond the trade union strongholds. However, most women's sections operated on a very modest basis. Monthly meetings of the Bishop Auckland women's section in County Durham, for example, attracted around twenty members who sang 'The Red Flag' and 'England Arise' and held collections that usually raised two shillings.[48] Meetings featured talks on 'current events', whist drives, refreshments served by 'tea hostesses', summer outings, and an 'Exhibition of Homecrafts'; they regularly held competitions to win 'The Surprise' donated by one member. In the 1930s the section knitted garments to send to the Republicans in Spain, heard talks on air-raid precautions, and lost some members to ARP work.[49] This mixture of social and political activities suggests a pattern similar to that used by the Women's Institutes between the wars. This may even have been deliberate since the WIs were rivals for membership and Labour loyalists regarded them as agents of bourgeois feminism.

Although the female membership recruited during the 1920s represented a huge advance, it is put into perspective by the Conservatives who had four times as many. Also, Labour's membership appears to have reached a peak around 1928–9 and then stagnated. Why was this? Despite Labour's pretensions as the women's party, its appeal was limited to social welfare and standards of living. 'Women were going to be very conservative', as Mary Macarthur put it in 1918. 'Women were going to bring a new idea into politics – the idea of the family.'[50] In effect Labour addressed women almost entirely in terms of their domestic role: free trade and food prices, reductions in duties on food imports, improved milk supply, better-designed housing, maternity clinics and widows' pensions. According to Henderson: there was 'no fundamental difference between men and women on political issues or any conflict of ideas in the field of social reform'.[51]

However, this was more an expression of hope than a statement of fact. Although the women's conference could forward policy resolutions to the party conference, they were debated only if accepted by the NEC, so that in practice anything controversial was frustrated. Labour proved reluctant to come to terms with questions such as equal pay and family allowances, which were regarded as a threat by trade unionists, not to mention birth-control information which offended Catholics. Nor were leading Labour women such as Phillips and Bondfield willing to put feminist causes before loyalty to the party.

The movement's conventional thinking also restricted the progress of Labour women as parliamentary candidates. In six general elections from 1922 to 1935 Labour women stood on ninety-two occasions altogether, more than double the Conservatives' total. However, 80 per cent of these occurred in seats safely held by another party and the best the women could expect was a tough three-cornered contest.[52] An angry Ellen Wilkinson noted the mindset of one senior party organiser: 'There is about a hundred-to-one chance in that division, but it might be won.

It is just the sort of seat a woman ought to fight.'[53] Female candidates were disadvantaged by their lack of trade union subsidies and by assumptions that they had too many domestic ties – hence the early Labour women MPs were unmarried. As a result the other parties managed to send women to Parliament first: Nancy Astor (Conservative) in 1919 and Margaret Wintringham (Liberal) in 1921. No Labour women were elected until 1923 when Susan Lawrence won at East Ham North, Margaret Bondfield at Northampton and Dorothy Jewson at Norwich. However, all three lost in 1924, leaving Ellen Wilkinson, newly elected at Middlesbrough East, as the only women MP until 1926 when Lawrence and Bondfield were returned at by-elections.

Ellen Wilkinson's status as the highest-profile woman MP partly reflected journalists' habit of trivialising her by reporting extensively on her dress, her red hair, her habit of crashing her motor car, and her diminutive size; just under five feet, she used a case as a footstool in the Commons. But Wilkinson, who was an exception among Labour women in refusing to hide her feminism, used the press effectively. When adopting the new fashion for short hair, she wrote an article on 'Why I Shingled', arguing that for a working woman shingles saved time and, like short frocks and comfortable shoes, freed women from convention.[54] As a driver, a spinster and a career woman she epitomised the 1920s notion of the 'emancipated girl'. In 'Why I Am Not Married' she argued that there was so much prejudice against female employment that an independent woman was often obliged to turn her job into her life's work.[55] In short, Wilkinson succeeded better than her contemporaries in retaining her feminism while occupying the mainstream in Labour politics. Before 1914 she had been an active suffragist and continued to work with the National Union of Societies for Equal Citizenship which other Labour women avoided. But she had also been an organiser for the National Union of Distributive and Allied Workers, joined the Communist Party for a time, and toured America raising funds for the miners after the General Strike. Nor, despite her lively platform performances, was Ellen Wilkinson merely a rabble-rouser. In the Commons she delivered concise, effective speeches, introduced bills and sometimes shamed the government into legislating. It was, however, a comment on the contemporary party leadership that it preferred to promote the loyalist Bondfield who never showed Wilkinson's independence of mind.

Another building block that loomed large, at least for a time, in each party's calculations was the ex-soldiers returning from the war in search of civilian employment. Several attempts were made to mobilise them, starting with the Comrades of the Great War, led by Tory politicians and financed by big business who hoped to counter industrial militancy in the forces. It was rivalled by the Soldiers, Sailors and Airmen's Union, formed to try to recruit former servicemen for the Labour Party, and by the National Union of Ex-Servicemen which apparently received Communist funding.[56] Eventually, however, these organisations merged into the British Legion, a relatively non-political organisation. Labour candidates in the 1920s included several ex-soldiers such as Major Clement Attlee, Major Graham David Pole, and General Christopher Birdwood Thomson, as well as John Beckett and Jim Simmons, a Birmingham councillor and MP, who both worked for the National Union of Ex-Servicemen for a time.

Yet although there is evidence of widespread discontent among the troops by 1918, few seem to have become politicised. At the Coupon Election some soldiers openly supported anti-war Labour candidates and observers at the poll noticed that a high proportion of absent votes were cast for Labour; sometimes soldiers expressed their discontent by writing 'demobilise first' on their ballot papers.[57] This sentiment was a harbinger of the army's pro-Labour vote in 1945. However, few Labour candidates turned their military experience to political effect. It gave Beckett the confidence to take on right-wing candidates: 'I have always refused to allow a monopoly of patriotism to my Conservative opponents,' he wrote; indeed in 1924 the Gateshead Tories accused him of fighting under the Union Jack![58] By contrast, Jim Simmons, who had exposed the field punishments inflicted on the British troops and the use of the death penalty on shell-shocked men, had received a three-month prison sentence.[59] Three times wounded, Simmons lost a leg in the war, became a pacifist, returned home to join the ILP and championed the interests of the former soldiers from a pacifist perspective. From 1919 onwards he contested municipal and parliamentary elections by appealing for the servicemen's vote. When attacked by the Tories he responded: 'The Young Man Who FOUGHT replies to the cowardly attack by the Old man who stopped at home.' His military record gave credibility to his pacifist stance. However, the examples of Simmons and Beckett were exceptional. As a party Labour made no attempt, after the 1918 election, to treat ex-soldiers as a distinct group, believing that the huge conscriptionist army was a temporary phenomenon. The party shrank from organising men as soldiers because, in Morrison's words, they 'objected to anything that would lead to the army being looked upon as a respectable profession'.[60] This was understandable in the context of disarmament and the reaction against Edwardian policies, though it did leave the field to the Conservatives.

After the war Labour also made strides in harnessing two important overlapping communities: the Irish and the Catholics. It is tempting to assume that as Irishmen were mostly manual labourers they were inexorably absorbed into the Labour Movement due to the growth of class consciousness, union organisation and the appeal of socialism, not to mention the increasing irrelevance of religion. This would be erroneous, however, for the interwar Irish community, fortified by an expanding and politically aggressive Catholic Church, continued to be distinctive especially where it was concentrated in Lancashire, Yorkshire, Tyneside, Clydeside and Birmingham. Sectarian divisions remained surprisingly lively in Scotland and Merseyside, so much so that the Catholic hierarchy showed some interest in forming a separate party for their community.

Consequently Labour found itself obliged to *adapt* to Catholic sensibilities rather than sweep them aside, as John Wheatley found in Glasgow where he struggled to convince his co-religionists that he could be a good Catholic *and* a socialist. Adaptation was best attained at the local level where Labour strove to find a formula that would reconcile socialism with religion. In Limehouse, for example, the CLP was the product of the unification of the Irish Nationalists and the local ILP in 1918, while in Stepney the party made a pact with the United Irish League in 1919 with the result that twelve of Labour's forty-three councillors were Irish. A similar alliance was achieved in Gateshead in 1919 where the party welcomed the local branch of the Irish Labour Party as an affiliated organisation and attributed its gains in municipal elections to the unification of Irish workers with the rest of the movement. 'We are not anti-Catholic nor are we pro-Catholic,' insisted the party's newspaper. 'Neither are we anti-Protestant nor pro-Protestant. But the Labour Party has its ideals. It believes the Fatherhood of God and the Brotherhood of Man are not empty phrases. That among other things they imply equality of opportunity for all the human family.'[61] It may be significant that Labour obtained by far its biggest majority in Gateshead in 1929 when its candidate, J. B. Melville, was a Catholic. In effect Labour found itself obliged to function as several distinct parties reflecting the local working-class culture of communities like Gateshead, Limehouse and Stepney.

However, the Bolshevik Revolution greatly complicated relations as the Church regarded socialism with horror. This made it more urgent for Labour to distance itself from the Communist Party which launched vitriolic attacks on the Catholic Church during the 1920s, rudely denouncing the Pope as 'His Oiliness'. Labour's refusal to accept Communist affiliations made it easier for the Catholic hierarchy to believe that it was not really a socialist party at all. In any case, the Catholic clergy felt obliged to be cautious about condemning Labour for fear of antagonising their own followers, not all of whom were willing to follow the Church's lead.[62]

After 1918 Labour found it easier to mobilise the Irish community because the Liberals had undermined their loyalty as a result of Asquith's heavy-handed response to the Easter Rebellion in 1916 and Lloyd George's use of the Black and Tans. In any case, the settlement of the Home Rule issue in 1920–1 largely removed the previous constraints on Labour voting. On the other hand, relations were not greatly helped by the 1924 Labour government which was rather too anxious to conform to the attitudes of its Conservative predecessor towards Ireland. The Cabinet resisted an independent role for the Irish Free State at the League of Nations and upheld British opposition to the issuing of passports unless they included the words 'British Subject'.[63]

However, national policies probably mattered little at local level where the Labour Movement found ways of overcoming the sectarian divide. The task proved relatively easy in Glasgow partly because the Catholic and Protestant communities were less segregated by residence than elsewhere, and because Catholics were concentrated in unskilled occupations and Protestants in skilled employment. With less conflict between the communities Labour found it easier to attract people of both denominations on the basis of its ideological stance. The process gained force from the abandonment of the party's temperance policies in the early 1920s especially in Glasgow where the Irish organisations were dominated by publicans. However, even in Glasgow there were limits to Labour's advance as the Conservative and Unionist cause continued to mobilise much of the Protestant working-class vote while Labour gathered the Catholic Irish support; as a result the Conservatives retained six of Glasgow's fifteen seats during the 1920s.

This is an indication that the emergence of a homogeneous working class was a slow process, so much so that in some areas Labour developed largely as a Catholic party in deference to local loyalties. In Liverpool before 1914 Labour had been squeezed between the Catholic wards, dominated by the Irish Nationalist organisation, and the Protestant wards, controlled by the Conservative, Unionist and Orange Order machine under Alderman Archibald Salvidge. After 1918 Liverpool Labour continued to lag behind the party elsewhere partly because the voluntary schools kept sectarian loyalties alive, especially in municipal elections.[64] Even at general elections Labour performed poorly, winning only one of Liverpool's eleven seats in 1923, two in 1924 and four in 1929. However, after the war the loyalties of the Catholics wards shifted in Labour's favour as the party, in effect, acquired the mantle of Nationalism. Labour's achievement was symbolised by the by-election following the death of the veteran Irish Nationalist MP, T. P. O'Connor, in 1929. His Liverpool Scotland seat was inherited, without opposition, by Labour's David Logan, who had been a local Nationalist councillor, but converted to Labour in 1924. However, the preservation of the Victorian sectarian character of Liverpool politics enabled the Tories to retain a majority of the city's constituencies even in 1929, though closely challenged by Labour in several of them.[65]

Yet despite successes with the Catholic community in places such as Liverpool, the alliance was always unstable. Labour could not take the Catholic vote for granted because of the eruption of a series of awkward issues including the cultivation of relations with Soviet Russia by Labour governments, the General Strike of 1926, state policy towards voluntary schools, divorce reform and birth control. In 1924 MacDonald helped to defuse Catholic suspicions by appointing the Clydeside Catholic, John Wheatley, as Minister for Health in which capacity he maintained the ban on the provision of advice on birth control by local authority maternity clinics. The NEC, fearful of alienating

Catholic support, evaded the issue by arguing that birth control was not a party political question but a matter of individual conscience. Such careful tactics helped to keep the Labour–Catholic alliance intact but the result was the emergence of some socially conservative Labour parties in parts of Scotland and Merseyside, radically different in character from the more liberal, feminist constituency parties more typical of Labour in suburban London and South-East England.

Much less complicated were Labour's relations with Nonconformity. Despite the settlement of the last great Nonconformist grievance, the disestablishment of the Church in Wales, in 1920, such loyalties did not suddenly become irrelevant after 1918. Although many middle-class Nonconformists remained loyal to Liberalism, some had followed their anti-war principles into the ILP, and by 1924 forty-five Nonconformists sat as Labour MPs. Studies of voters who had reached voting age by 1914 suggest that working-class Anglicans divided evenly between Conservative and non-Conservative voting, whereas working-class Nonconformists were anti-Conservative by four to one.[66] In areas like Durham where many workingmen had been Primitive Methodists this made for a smooth transition from Liberal to Labour loyalties during the 1920s.

Nonconformity also continued to exercise some influence over the character of the movement in ways that made it compatible with socialism. While alcohol ceased to provoke the controversy it had aroused before 1914, its place was to some extent taken by gambling. Since the Street Betting Act of 1906 it had been illegal to place cash bets outside racecourses. However, by 1924 the three-party consensus had broken down as the Baldwin government proposed effectively to recognise cash betting by taxing it. Led by MacDonald, Henderson and Snowden, many Labour MPs condemned this as a step towards legalisation. According to Snowden gambling was 'the second greatest curse of the country' and in 1926 eighty-eight Labour members voted against a bill to legalise street betting. For them Nonconformist Puritanism pointed the same way as socialist anti-capitalism in disapproving of easy gains made by speculation rather than by honest work.[67] However, Labour MPs, including Jimmy Thomas, Hugh Dalton, James Sexton, Jack Jones, Charles Bowerman, George Buchanan and Ernest Thurtle, sympathised with working-class hedonism and reflected the culture of 'rough' working-class communities rather than

Nonconformist respectability. Sexton cheerfully recorded backing the winner of the Grand National in 1921 and watching the race with King George V and the Prince of Wales in 1922.[68] They argued that the 1906 law discriminated against workingmen and disparaged opponents of gambling as puritanical hypocrites. Just as in the 1890s, the movement still struggled to straddle the divide within the working-class community.

Perhaps the most striking indication that Labour was becoming a national party rather than a sectional one was its advance up the social scale during the 1920s. Among the Labour MPs returned at the election of 1922 were nine public school boys, twenty-one university graduates and twenty-six professionals – harbingers of another crucial formative phase in the party's evolution. Middle- and upper-class recruits usually found the Fabians and the ILP the most convenient means of joining their new party. Their prominence provoked the more reactionary Tories into betraying their patronising view of working-class people. Lord Londonderry, the Durham coal-owner, derided Sidney Webb, who became the member for Seaham, as 'a fetish with the Labour Party and with ignorant people who thought that in the doctrines he expounded, and which he made as ambiguous and obscure as possible, there was something which they ought to follow'.[69] The entry of the 'intellectuals', as they were widely known, caused a culture shock on both sides. When Susan Lawrence first addressed meetings in the East End the combination of her monocle, cropped hair, severe dress and strangulated upper-class vowel sounds provoked fits of laughter in her audiences as though witnessing a music-hall turn. In 1922 when Fenner Brockway contested Lancaster for Labour he produced George Bernard Shaw who subjected one meeting to a rambling, ninety-minute speech. Concluding, Shaw assured his restive audience: 'Ladies and gentlemen, you will at least be able to inform your incredulous grandchildren that you heard Bernard Shaw when he was dull!'[70]

However, this recruitment involved more than a change in social composition for the movement, for it largely involved men and women drawn from the other political parties. The detachment of Liberals that had begun during the war was accelerated as careers were wrecked in the 1918 election and as loyalties became strained by the prolonged civil war between followers of Asquith and Lloyd George. Prominent former Liberal MPs included Charles Trevelyan, Arthur Ponsonby, Percy Alden, Sydney Arnold, Charles Buxton, Noel Buxton, Joseph King, E. D. Morel, Philip Noel-Baker and H. B. Lees-Smith. As with most shifts of allegiance their move involved elements of conviction and opportunism. These men had been alienated by pre-war mandarin diplomacy, the arms race, wartime conscription and the post-war peace settlement. But other Liberal recruits, including Dr Christopher Addison, Sir Leo Money, Richard Haldane, William Wedgwood Benn, R. L. Outhwaite, Edward Hemmerde, Josiah Wedgwood, Richard Denman, and Alexander MacCallum Scott, were influenced less by the war than by social and economic issues. Hemmerde, Outhwaite and Wedgwood, for example, were keen land taxers. Haldane betrayed an almost Fabian enthusiasm for improving legislation designed by an expert, metropolitan elite. Addison, who had played a key role in social reform under Lloyd George and pioneered the municipal housing scheme in 1919, expressed his thinking as 'Practical Socialism'. These recruits saw their move essentially in terms of *continuity* for Labour and upheld the classic Liberal causes including free trade, Home Rule and state social welfare. 'All social reformers are bound to gravitate, as I have done, to Labour,' as Trevelyan put it.[71] The Liberal migration largely occurred between 1918 and 1924, though Wedgwood Benn was a late convert in 1927, partly because he had managed to hold his seat at Leith, but was finally alienated by Lloyd George's takeover of the party leadership in 1926.

For Ramsay MacDonald these Liberal recruits offered proof that he had been correct in arguing that Labour would eventually inherit the mantle of Radical Liberalism. As experienced MPs and ministers they strengthened Labour's appeal in the country, especially as candidates for difficult constituencies. Noel Buxton, for example. won North Norfolk for Labour having once represented it as a Liberal. Trevelyan spearheaded the party's campaign in Newcastle. Egerton Wake, the national agent, carefully placed Addison in Swindon: 'It will require a special type of candidate, as the ordinary industrial nominee will never lift it.'[72] Alone among the Liberal recruits, Wedgwood Benn was nominated for an existing Labour seat at Aberdeen North in 1928.

Much more intriguing, and certainly disconcerting for contemporaries, was the readiness of a number of Conservatives to join Labour; it was one thing to leave the Liberal Party's sinking ship but quite another to quit the party that held office for almost the entire interwar period. Several Tories, including Susan Lawrence, Hugh Dalton and Clement Attlee, had already joined Labour before 1914, but the majority came over in the 1920s, the later converts being Stafford Cripps in 1929 and the twenty-eight-year-old Earl of Kinnoull in 1930.[73] While reactions against the war are associated with rebel Liberals, it is often forgotten that similar considerations motivated some Conservatives including Lord Parmoor, formerly the Tory MP Charles Alfred Cripps, Oliver Baldwin, son of the Tory leader, who had been traumatised by military experience in Russia and Turkey, the young Earl 'Buck' De La Warr who was a conscientious objector, and William Arnold-Forster who joined the UDC. Others were influenced by social and economic issues especially those who had experience of local government such as Susan Lawrence who had once attacked the 'wicked Socialists' on the London County Council. In 1912 her faith collapsed when she realised what low wages were paid to charwomen: 'What she learned shocked her and she moved from right to left overnight, changing not only her politics but her dress and her way of life.'[74] The young Viscount Ennismore, heir to the Earl of Listowel, who joined Labour in 1924, recalled: 'My reason was simply that I regarded the Labour Party as representing the underdog.'[75]

Some of the most influential ex-Conservatives were affected by the economic backwash from the war, notably John Sankey, who chaired the 1919 Royal Commission on coal and backed nationalisation, and John Strachey, son of the owner of the *Spectator*. By November 1923 Strachey's articles in the pro-Conservative *Spectator* acquired an unexpected tone as he began to focus on economic issues, concluding that socialism offered a rational and equal way of distributing resources and generating sufficient demand in the economy. The recruits also included successful businessmen such as Arthur Strauss, a former Tory MP and wealthy metal merchant, and his son George, William Stapleton Royce, an entrepreneur who built bridges and railways, and Valentine Crittall, the mass-manufacturer of metal window frames for interwar houses at Maldon in Essex.

Perhaps the biggest shock was the conversion of Sir Oswald Mosley, who joined Labour in 1924 aged twenty-eight. Since being elected as a coalitionist in 1918 he had consistently advocated an interventionist policy for unemployment. Mosley epitomised the feeling of the ex-Tories that the war had proved the case for a more positive role for the state but rapidly became disillusioned as the older generation imposed their grip on politics and betrayed the young men who had fought. As Godfrey Elton put it in language more usually associated with 1945: 'the principle of national control . . . had saved us from losing the war. I saw no reason why, after the war, these inspiring characteristics should not be reproduced in a nation organised for peace.'[76] The impact was all the greater because with Mosley came his wife, Lady Cynthia, the daughter of Lord Curzon, a former Indian viceroy and Foreign Secretary. In view of his later trajectory to fascism Mosley has effectively been written out of Labour's history, but in the 1920s he was an immensely popular figure. Seventy CLPs invited him to become their candidate and female members of his audiences were known to swoon 'Oh Valentino!' Far from being immune to the aristocratic appeal, even the egalitarian *Daily Herald* could not resist referring proudly to Mosley as 'Son-in-law of Lord Curzon'. One amazed contemporary witnessed the two Mosleys' arrival at a Labour meeting in 1924 where an excited steward explained: '"Lady Cynthia Mosley" . . . and later, as though thinking that he had not sufficiently impressed me, he added "Lord Curzon's daughter". His whole face beamed proudly.'[77]

It is tempting to assume that in repudiating their family traditions the former Conservatives were eccentrics or misfits, alienated from the British Establishment. Naturally their defection caused some friction. The eighteen-year-old Viscount Ennismore was thrown out of his London home by his father, and the Baldwins suffered a bitter and emotional estrangement with Oliver.[78] However, this is easily exaggerated. Hugh Dalton enjoyed cultivating a misleading reputation as a rebel, while John Strachey liked to joke that he had become a socialist 'from chagrin at not getting into the Eton cricket eleven'![79] It is significant that in several cases *two* generations defected from the same family: the Strausses, the De La Warrs and the Crippses, for example. Moreover, thoughtful Conservatives, far from damning the defectors as class traitors, frankly recognised Labour's appeal. L. S. Amery told Stanley Baldwin in 1923 that 'the real, healthy and natural division of parties in this country is between constructive Conservatism on the one side . . . and on the other hand, Labour Socialism. Both these views stand for something real and living for which people can work and fight.'[80]

In fact, far from being alienated from the Establishment, the Tory recruits were securely placed within it. Many of them were closely connected with the Church of England by career, by family, or by conviction: John Sankey, Susan Lawrence, Lord Parmoor, Clifford Allen, Grace Colman, William Temple, Archbishop of Canterbury, and Hugh Dalton, whose father was canon at St George's, Windsor Castle. Several of them had actively defended the Anglican Church against Liberal threats of disestablishment, and, as Labour did not make disestablishment an issue in the 1920s, they saw no inhibition about backing the party. Devotion to the national Church made these Conservatives more comfortable about the state than many of their erstwhile colleagues, a mindset that was further reinforced by their legal affiliations. A high proportion were lawyers and judges, some of whom had represented trade unions seeking compensation for injuries to workers, including Parmoor, Cripps, Sankey, J. A. Lovat Fraser, Graham David Pole and Hugh Macmillan. Not part of the individualistic, entrepreneurial, buccaneering side of Conservatism, these men emerged from families and schools that fostered a high-minded sense of public service and collective duty rather than pursuit of the profit motive. Cripps told his fellow lawyer, Hugh Macmillan, that he had been influenced by his readiness to serve in the 1924 Labour government: 'I then felt that I must really make up my mind to do my share of work besides earn money.'[81] Experience at public school was formative for Parmoor, Hugh Gaitskell, Arnold-Forster and Lord Chelmsford, all products of Winchester, and for Attlee, educated at Haileybury, for these schools inculcated the ideal of public service at home, in India and the colonies among their boys. Several joined Labour while at university including Dalton (1907), Temple (1905), Strachey (1923), Colman (1916) and Gaitskell (1924). Their migration to Labour via the Fabians was promoted informally by senior left-wing figures including George Lansbury (De La Warr and Graham Pole), Herbert Morrison (Strauss), Harold Laski (Sankey), J. L. and Barbara Hammond (Elton), and G. D. H. Cole, who taught Gaitskell history at Oxford.

The significance of these Conservative recruits tends to be grossly neglected in traditional accounts of the evolution of the Labour Party, though, not surprisingly, it made a considerable impact at the time. In 1923 when Oliver Baldwin delivered his first speech from a Labour platform he received 'a mass of correspondence, most of it abusive and some of it indecent'.[82] The right-wing press professed to be highly amused by John Strachey for addressing his Birmingham constituents as 'Ladies and gentlemen', not 'Comrades', and signing himself 'Your obedient servant'. At twenty-three he had only recently left Oxford where he led a typical, decadent student life, rising at twelve noon to consume a breakfast consisting of chocolate cake and crème de menthe! The newspapers hoped to discredit the defectors by drawing attention to their wealth. The *Mail* and the *Express* habitually disparaged Strachey and George Strauss as 'rich theorists', dubbing Strauss as 'The Capitalist Who Could Buy Up The Socialist Party'.[83] The press routinely pilloried the Mosleys for their luxurious lifestyle and grand connections. 'A droller choice as Labour candidate for an industrial constituency than this debonair young sprig of the aristocracy [Oswald] could scarcely be conceived,' scoffed the *Birmingham Mail*.[84] Lady Cynthia, who was fashionably attired in fox furs and enjoyed an annual income of £30,000 from investments as the heiress to the American Leiter family, was derided as 'The Dollar Princess'. However, Lady Cynthia riposted that she took all the money she could get hold of from America and either invested it in Britain or gave it to the Labour Party. 'I am one of the most lucky ones in the country and I am not satisfied with things as they are. Surely to goodness if I am not satisfied, then the millions who live in squalid and miserable conditions are not.'[85]

In fact, the Tory press missed the point. Many working-class people felt flattered by the attentions of upper-class candidates, reasoning that they were too wealthy to be in politics for the money. Women also loved the glamour surrounding titled candidates. Nancy, Viscountess Astor, had successfully exploited this at Plymouth as a Conservative and Lady Cynthia did the same in her 1929 election at Stoke.[86] A link with powerful, wealthy and glamorous men and women appealed strongly to those who endured humdrum and deprived lives. Even more than the ex-Liberals, the former Tories helped Labour to gain otherwise unwinnable constituencies such as Valentine Crittall at Maldon and William Royce at Holland-with-Boston. Mosley himself formed the cutting edge of Labour's attack on the West Midlands by taking on Neville Chamberlain in Birmingham Ladywood in 1924. Cripps alone received a safe seat at Bristol East in 1930.

Nor was this the only advantage for Labour. The Mosleys, Strauss and De La Warr made donations and the Countess of Warwick also offered her Essex home, Easton Lodge, as a conference centre for the parliamentary party in 1923. Benefiting from private incomes, candidates such as Charles Trevelyan and Noel Buxton spent several thousand pounds on an election campaign, while Susan Lawrence and George Strauss were able to devote themselves as full-time party workers to their constituencies. The formidable appeal of a former Tory was evident in South Derbyshire where Major Graham Pole, a war hero who had been invalided out of the army in 1916, won in 1929. Nattily attired in wing collar, striped trousers, cravat, watch chain and waistcoat, Pole looked the conventional upper-class MP but with a common touch as he invited groups of constituents to visit him at Westminster. On becoming candidate in 1925 he financed election expenses, annual subscriptions, a constituency office and an agent's salary as well as donating to local causes. Like Attlee, Pole took up many personal cases especially with the ministries of Health, Pensions, Labour and Transport, which he publicised in reports to his constituents three times a year, appeared frequently in the local press and delivered dozens of speeches.[87]

The relationship between Birmingham and Mosley is equally revealing. After standing at Ladywood in 1924, where he came within a handful of votes of unseating Neville Chamberlain who immediately fled to a safer constituency, Mosley switched to Smethwick in 1926 following the death of the sitting Labour member. The local party adopted him without going through the proper procedure, perhaps in its anxiety to gain access to his resources. When the NEC intervened Mosley airily declared he had no confidence in Head Office.[88] However, Mosley not only paid £337 for his agent's salary in Smethwick, but also continued to finance Ladywood. Between March 1926 and January 1927 he contributed sums totalling £1,700 which funded the agent's salary at £350, a Labour hall, and even municipal election expenses.[89] The new Ladywood candidate, Wilfrid Whiteley, who had been his agent in 1924, continued to pester Mosley to give £450 towards the annual costs of £600.[90] But by 1928 Mosley was running out of patience partly because 'I can see no record of money having been raised locally during the last two years', and in 1929 he declined to pay Whiteley's election expenses in Ladywood.[91] He also reminded

Whiteley that he could not increase his £450 contribution as 'I have given an undertaking to the National Executive not to make any fresh expenditure on politics without their permission . . . urgent demands for assistance are coming in daily from all over the country' – a claim that is corroborated by the NEC minutes.[92] The correspondence suggests that Labour was effectively exploiting Mosley during the 1920s.

As peers, MPs, ministers and colonial governors, the recruits from both other parties helped to deflate Conservative charges that Labour would lack the competence to form a government. 'No one could pretend that a Cabinet containing Haldane, Parmoor or Chelmsford was either contemptible or likely to ruin the empire,' as Sidney Webb put it.[93] When he formed the first Labour administration in 1924 MacDonald was, at least in part, fortified by the realisation that he could call upon this wider range of talent and experience. But, while the recruits made the party a more credible force, was there any ideological significance to their role? The Liberal recruits regarded Labour in terms of continuity with Liberal tradition in both domestic and foreign policy and thus betrayed no sudden conversion to socialism; rather they accepted the commitment like many party members without taking it too literally. In the 1920s they reinforced the movement's pacifist and free-trade leanings, and they included some vociferous advocates of land taxation and the capital levy. In 'A Levy On Capital' Trevelyan argued that a charge on the accumulated wealth of 300,000 people would enable the government to pay the interest on the national debt, thereby saving £100 million in taxation.[94] However, by 1923 Snowden and MacDonald had abandoned the capital levy, and land taxation was never seriously attempted. Only a few were influenced primarily by economic questions, notably Leo Money, who withdrew from the coalition in protest at the decontrol of industry, and William Wedgwood Benn who explained: 'For some time I have questioned the truth of an economic outlook based upon the theory of private enterprise and free competition.'[95]

By contrast the ex-Conservatives were of some ideological significance. Many of them were intellectually formidable figures, notably Strachey, Dalton and Lawrence, who made important contributions to Labour's thinking on economics. As the defection from their old party involved a sharper ideological break than that experienced by the Liberals, they found it necessary to face up to the moral challenge posed by socialism and to recognise the failure of private enterprise to generate the investment and the rational allocation of resources the national interest demanded. Many ex-Tories strongly believed that since the 1890s unregulated private enterprise had let the nation down and that interventionism had proved its value during the war. It would thus be mistaken to assume that the Tory recruits diluted or impeded the adoption of a left-wing policy. Paradoxical as it may seem, during the 1920s they criticised their new party for failing to take its commitment to socialism seriously enough! Strachey evidently regarded it as his responsibility to convert the 1924 Labour government to socialism. In collaboration with Mosley, Strachey argued that the Victorian free-trade doctrine and the restoration of international markets offered no solution to the problem of unemployment, and he began to develop a strategy based on central economic planning and Keynesian management techniques. After the debacle of 1931 Strachey wrote extensively about socialism during the 1930s and, along with Dalton, Cripps and Strauss, played a major role in economic policy after 1945. In this way the recruits left their mark on Labour for some decades to come.

7

'Aristocratic embrace':
Labour in Power

On Sunday 20 November 1922 a huge, exuberant crowd of supporters packed into St Enoch's Square in Glasgow, singing 'Jerusalem' and the 'Internationale', to speed the newly elected Labour MPs off to London. 'When we come back,' David Kirkwood told them, 'this station, this railway, will belong to the people.' His hyperbole was understandable, for Glasgow alone had returned ten Labour members, compared with just one in 1918. As the Labour vote was sorted in Bridgeton, Jimmy Maxton had reportedly commented: 'Hardly worth counting them all up, let's just weigh them.'[1] Of the 142 Labour members thirty came from Scotland; this alone made the parliamentary party more socialist and it gave Scotland a prominence in the party that it retained for many years. Yet despite this success no one seriously expected Labour to gain office just over a year later as a result of a series of contingencies, accidents and misjudgements that accelerated the party's growth in the early 1920s.

The first step in the process was the rebuilding of Ramsay MacDonald's political career. In 1918, aged fifty-two, he had been understandably depressed by his defeat and frustrated by the inept leadership of the party. But the gloom soon lifted. 1918–22 was a good Parliament to miss, and defeat released MacDonald to argue Labour's case in the country while the MPs toiled fruitlessly at Westminster. Not that recovery was easy. The resignation of Will Crooks in February 1921 created a by-election in Woolwich East in which MacDonald stood. But Crooks had been elected as a pro-war candidate in a constituency containing a large ex-servicemen's vote and no ILP organisation. The Conservatives nominated a decorated soldier, Captain Robert Gee, who waged a scurrilous campaign, accusing MacDonald of being an atheist, a revolutionary and a traitor who was opposed to marriage and to pensions for soldiers. MacDonald lost by 600 votes.

However, the defeat proved less of a bar to MacDonald's career than it appeared at the time, for in 1922 he was adopted by the miners and steelworkers of Aberavon in South Wales where the ILP had a branch 1,000 strong. Events moved rapidly when the Conservative MPs, meeting at the Carlton Club on 19 October, killed the coalition by voting to fight the next election independently of Lloyd George. The prime minister promptly resigned and the Conservatives chose a new leader, Andrew Bonar Law, who took office but immediately called a general election which was held in mid-November.

In South Wales MacDonald's moving exposition of socialism went down well. He advocated a levy on fortunes over £5,000 to pay off the national debt, the implementation of Sankey's report on coal nationalisation, and the maintenance of free trade, and he condemned the reckless foreign policy that had recently brought the country close to war with Turkey.[2] While the Conservatives returned with 347 members, Labour won 142, comfortably ahead of the more-or-less reunited Liberals with 117. The return of thirty-two ILP nominees shifted the composition of the parliamentary party leftwards. In addition to MacDonald several experienced figures including Snowden and Lansbury returned to Parliament, joined by new members such as Sidney Webb, Clement Attlee and Emmanuel Shinwell, a formidable group of Clydesiders among whom Jimmy Maxton, John Wheatley and David Kirkwood were the best known, and the Liberal recruits Charles Trevelyan, Arthur Ponsonby, Noel Buxton and E. D. Morel. After a tussle with the Speaker it was agreed that Labour would have three of the four Supply days in the Commons and that in debates precedence would be granted to its leader. However, Clynes was denied his demand for exclusive use of the Opposition front bench, a failure that may have damaged him in the subsequent election for leader in which MacDonald beat him narrowly by sixty-one votes to fifty-six.[3]

Even at this stage not everyone was convinced by Ramsay MacDonald. In 1922, when the Clydesiders and the ILP gave him the crucial votes he needed, Henderson presciently warned Kirkwood, 'It will be only a few years before you will be trying to put him out.'[4] But MacDonald undoubtedly looked the part – an important consideration for a party that was officially the government-in-waiting but hesitant about assuming the role. 'His head was a thing of beauty', wrote Kirkwood. 'Black hair waved and rolled over a fine brow . . . his voice was ragged but soft, and, as he spoke, there came into it a throb . . . Standing upright he was a splendid figure of a man, and his appearance of height and strength was increased by his habit of rising on his toes and throwing back his head.' According to John Beckett 'the handsome face behind the heavy black moustache, the organ-like voice and the graceful gestures seemed too good to be true'.[5] With hindsight the flaws are obvious, but in the 1920s MacDonald represented a huge asset to Labour: a striking, romantic figure, capable of charming with his soft, musical Highland Scots voice and of dominating the platform with his forceful, emotional oratory. His command of foreign policy, increasingly important as the reaction against war gathered pace, enhanced Labour's new status as a party looking for office. For once Labour had managed to choose the right leader. For MacDonald was a unifying force for the disparate movement, comparable to Gladstone's role among the Liberals in the late Victorian period. His ambiguous rhetoric satisfied all sections and conveyed a compelling sense of moral purpose. Though he took a dim view of the trade union leaders, he commanded their support for his moderation, his constitutionalism and opposition to the class war. He spoke sufficiently fluently about socialism to reassure the left, though his recent role as a critic of the war made him appear more anti-Establishment than he was. But MacDonald's principled stand over British entry into the war endowed him with huge moral authority in the 1920s; he was the man who had made sacrifices for his beliefs and been proved to have been right. As it became fashionable to attack the Treaty of Versailles MacDonald proved attractive to disillusioned Liberals as a man upholding the best traditions of Liberal foreign policy, and, as he had always envisaged Labour as a classless party, he now appealed to the ex-Conservatives who warmed to his vision of Labour as a *national* party. 'Had it not been for [MacDonald]', wrote John Sankey, 'I think our Party would have remained a Labour party and would never have become a Socialist one. A mere Labour Party would never obtain real power in England, nor would it deserve it. It is a class party just as much as the right wing of the Conservatives is a class party. The Socialist Party, on the other hand, is a National party in which all classes can find a home.'[6]

It was around this time that Labour MPs began to be noticeable attending society and royal functions. With the benefit of hindsight this habit became damned as the 'aristocratic embrace' – an all-purpose explanation for failings in office and in particular for MacDonald's 'betrayal' of the movement in 1931. MacDonald first met Edith, Lady Londonderry, at Buckingham Palace in February 1924 and thereafter regularly met her and other aristocratic figures on social occasions. But well before then the arrival of Labour MPs in London brought them into contact with wider social circles. Inevitably, as Labour acquired professionals and landowners like Trevelyan and Buxton, it behaved more like the older parties. But how far were workingmen and women to go in accommodating themselves?

At one extreme stood Ethel Snowden who became notorious as a social climber in the 1920s. More typical was Jimmy Thomas, a convivial figure who enjoyed moving in society circles while remaining authentically working class. Conversely the ILP members scorned the cosy, cross-party life of Westminster, believing that they had come to London to fight the Establishment not socialise with it. 'We were all puritans. We were all abstainers. Most of us did not smoke. We were the stuff of which reform is made,' wrote Kirkwood. In Glasgow they had held a Service of Dedication at which a declaration was read announcing the principles of the new MPs: 'In all things they will abjure vanity and self-aggrandisement, recognising that they are the honoured servants of the people.' They published a manifesto pledging themselves not to attend social functions at the homes of their opponents.[7] In practice most Labour MPs avoided the London clubs, though they had their own modest 1917 Club. But in 1921 Beatrice Webb bought a flat for the use of the parliamentary party and founded the Half-Circle Club where she organised lunches with a view to bringing together the wives of Labour members, freeing them from social isolation and instructing them in the etiquette appropriate to their status.[8] It flattered Beatrice to be able to fill this role. Though her gatherings were modest beside the grand parties organised by Lady Londonderry for the Conservatives, the Labour wives, who were less likely to attend conferences and mostly lived in the provinces, had as great a need for social events. However, Beatrice's object was in part to *protect* them from falling into the embrace of society by offering an alternative. Not that all of them stood in need of protection. Herbert Morrison's wife entirely avoided political functions even though she lived in London. John Wheatley explained that his wife would not even come to London as 'she is a very quiet,

168 SPEAK FOR BRITAIN!

domesticated, working-class woman, and I doubt whether she will feel equal to social life in London'.[9]

In any case, the significance of the 'aristocratic embrace' is easily exaggerated. Whatever effect it may have had later on, in the early 1920s it was, on balance, a helpful factor for the party in defusing the sense of crisis and subversion engendered by Labour's approach to power. Once firmly entrenched as the official Opposition Labour was forced to focus more sharply on its underlying political purpose: how far, as a party founded by forces outside Parliament and designed to break the upper-class monopoly on power through the entry of the working class into office, must it reconstruct the British political system and how far simply accommodate itself to conventional practice? Labour's response to this question was of immense importance for British politics during the 1920s and 1930s.

Inevitably the response was ambiguous. In 1922 the party had almost no representation in the House of Lords and was officially committed to abolishing the hereditary peerage. In 1923 Arthur Ponsonby introduced a bill to abolish hereditary titles altogether. But already signs of compromise with the system had become evident. While Tory propaganda strove to depict Labour as subversive and anti-Establishment, leading politicians were busily defusing the charge. In 1922 when Clynes and other Labour figures attended the wedding of George V's daughter, Princess Mary, he explained: 'I felt that the vast majority of Labour voters throughout the country would like to be represented at a wedding to which they obviously offered their good wishes.'[10] In March 1923 several MPs., including Jimmy Thomas, James Sexton, Arthur Henderson, Charles Bowerman, D. Adams, C. G. Ammon, T. Gavan-Duffy and T. Greenall, along with their wives, attended Buckingham Palace garden parties and even dined with the king. The criticism they attracted was firmly rebuffed by Thomas who argued it was pointless to place an embargo on people of a different class if that meant 'ignoring many in our own ranks whose brains and sacrifice are a great asset to our party'.[11] When the parliamentary party discussed whether members should accept invitations to Windsor and the palace, members voted thirty-eight to thirty-seven in favour of acceptance; the question was then referred to the NEC who simply decided to leave it to individual discretion.[12]

In effect, the movement's disdain for and suspicion of snobbery and

Establishment influence was balanced by the reassuring evidence that Labour was being taken seriously as the government-in-waiting. Among other things this implied accepting honours. The trade unionists had led the movement into compromising with the system in 1917 when David Shackleton accepted a knighthood, though there was a long gap until 1931 when two more union leaders, Ben Turner and James Sexton, did the same, as did Walter Citrine in 1936. The OBE, created in 1917 specifically to honour civilians for their contribution to the war effort, was also bestowed on labour leaders for recruiting and other work, though it was somewhat discredited by the honours scandals after 1918. Moreover, the need for Labour to be represented in the Upper House led to the award of peerages to several middle-class recruits: C. B. Thomson, Sydney Arnold and Sydney Olivier in 1924, and to John Sankey, Sidney Webb, Noel Buxton, Arthur Ponsonby and William Mackenzie Amulree in 1929. Harry Snell became the first working-class peer in 1931. As a result of these interwar precedents there was little controversy over the mass creation of Labour peers after 1945.

Pressure to observe the conventions also became irresistible in the Commons where the leaders frowned upon members who broke the rules by causing scenes. In June 1923 several Clydesiders including Maxton, Wheatley, Campbell Stephen and George Buchanan were suspended for describing a reactionary Tory, Sir Frederick Banbury, as a murderer. Significantly, although half the Labour MPs voted against their suspension, a parliamentary party meeting issued a call for self-restraint on the basis that 'when a Labour government arrives it will be greatly hampered if, in the meantime, Parliamentary Government has been destroyed'.[13] MacDonald regarded the Clydesiders' protests as an irrelevant distraction from the party's advance to power; with some reason he felt that they were not revolutionaries at all but merely agitators whose activities achieved nothing except to play into the hands of their enemies.

By 1923 Conservative propaganda had raised fears that if Labour were called upon to govern they would be obstructed, and that George V would feel reluctant even to invite them to form a Cabinet. In fact, despite his pronounced right-wing opinions, the king was acutely aware of the importance of conciliating Labour so as to avoid embroiling the Crown in controversy. But this reflected a mutual interest, for the more Labour was accepted by the Establishment the more the right-wing propaganda lost credibility. In the event the problem failed to materialise because George V had become such a popular figure by the 1920s that Labour monarchists such as Jimmy Thomas confidently dismissed all reservations about him. 'The workers are even more conservative than the Conservatives,' he claimed. 'No question of Republicanism as a serious proposition ever finds a place in Labour discussions.'[14] Thomas played a key role in reassuring the Establishment about the prospect of a Labour government. At the 1923 party conference, when Ernest Thurtle moved a resolution that 'the Royal Family is no longer necessary as part of the British Constitution', delegates spent just fifteen minutes in debate before rejecting it by 3.69 million votes to 380,000. 'If Labour came to power tomorrow,' declared Thomas, 'they would find the King prepared to accept their advice as readily as that of the Liberal or Tory parties.'[15] When he made this claim Thomas was unaware how soon his words were to be put to the test.

Despite an improved performance in the election of November 1922, a Labour government scarcely appeared to be imminent. With their comfortable majority the new Conservative government seemed secure for five years. However, the situation was rapidly transformed by several accidents. In May Bonar Law retired for health reasons bringing Stanley Baldwin unexpectedly to the premiership. Baldwin's career proved to be relevant to Labour in two main ways. Unusually for a leading Conservative, he frankly accepted that a Labour government was an inevitability not a national disaster. By contrast Neville Chamberlain referred so sarcastically to the Labour members that they hissed him in the Commons; when Baldwin urged him not to treat Labour as dirt, Chamberlain replied, 'The fact is that intellectually, with a few exceptions, they are dirt.'[16] Conciliatory towards working-class interests, Baldwin even advised his own party to emulate Labour by widening the social range from which it drew candidates and offering opportunities to men to rise from humble beginnings. In so doing he helped undermine his own party's anti-Labour propaganda and prepared the way for cross-party co-operation later in the 1930s.

More immediately, Baldwin transformed politics by seeking a wholly unnecessary dissolution of Parliament and an election in November 1923. This decision has never been satisfactorily explained. Ostensibly

Baldwin wanted to obtain a mandate to introduce tariffs as the only way of tackling unemployment, but this explanation was scarcely plausible. Though high, unemployment did not represent the kind of crisis sufficient to justify risking a five-year term of office. In any case, most Conservatives had already spent the recent election seeking a mandate for protectionism from the voters. The alternative explanation was that Baldwin was playing a deeper game, hoping that by polarising politics over free-trade and tariffs he would force the coalitionist Tories to part company with Lloyd George and rejoin official Conservatism. To a considerable extent he succeeded in this aim. However, the election proved to be a serious miscalculation because, although few votes changed hands, in a tight three-way split even small shifts of votes produced exaggerated changes in seats. The Conservatives' total fell from 347 to 258, while Labour won 191 and the Liberals 159. As no party had a majority it was uncertain for several weeks who would form the new government. The confusion began to clear when Baldwin waited to meet the new Parliament and resigned when Labour and the Liberals voted him out.

In this situation there were four options facing Labour. One, advocated by Jimmy Maxton and some socialists, was that Labour should take office and immediately introduce a full socialist programme which would inevitably be rejected; they would then go to the country again, politicising the workers by rousing them for a real socialist mandate. There was no likelihood that this would be attempted. Labour had no socialist programme at this stage, and MacDonald was anxious to disperse any sense of crisis surrounding the first Labour government rather than to accentuate it. He intended his administration to reflect *continuity* and thus legitimise Labour rule. A second option urged by Lansbury, Kirkwood and Bob Smillie was that Labour must refuse to take office as a minority because it would be unable to achieve anything. There was a stronger case for this, not least because the party had no popular mandate. Despite gaining fifty seats, Labour had polled only 120,000 extra votes and its poll share rose from 29.5 per cent to 30.5 per cent. On the other hand, to decline office would have looked like running away from the responsibility and corroborating claims that the party was unfit to govern. Worse, a refusal could well have resulted in Asquith forming a Liberal government, the Tories then occupying the Opposition front bench and Labour being relegated to third place.

The third possibility involved MacDonald forming a coalition with the Liberals which would have enjoyed a majority in the Commons. Many accounts of Labour's history assume that there was a deal with the Liberals which subsequently made it impossible for the first Labour government to introduce radical measures. Such accounts are not only incorrect, but betray a basic misunderstanding of the strategy MacDonald was pursuing. He remained absolutely opposed to any coalition or agreement with the Liberals. His whole policy was founded on the need to exclude the Liberals from power and elevate Labour as the only realistic alternative to the Conservatives. This was threatened by the revival the Liberals had enjoyed in 1923, raising their popular vote to 29.6 per cent, only fractionally below Labour's at 30.5 per cent. Hindsight makes Liberal decline seem inevitable, but at the time no one could be sure they would not continue to recover and overtake Labour.

This left a fourth option: Labour should form a minority administration, without deals, in the knowledge that it would only last a short time, in order to demonstrate its competence as a governing party. This would represent an investment in the future. 'I want to gain the confidence of the country and shall suit my policy accordingly,' MacDonald told Lord Parmoor. Reflecting the pressure of Tory propaganda, Snowden insisted 'We must show the country that we [are] not under the domination of the wild men.'[17] In his determination to follow this course MacDonald enjoyed the support of the NEC and the TUC.

Meanwhile, the prospect of a MacDonald government generated excitement bordering on panic in some quarters. As historians have generally depicted the first Labour government as a damp squib it is difficult to appreciate the shock waves it sent through British society in 1924. Winston Churchill, as if to prove that his rhetoric was superior to his political judgement, described the prospect as 'a national misfortune such as has usually befallen a great state only on the morrow of defeat in war'. Politicians even further to the right drew upon the example of Russia to warn that the arrival of a moderately subversive government was the prelude to chaos and bloody revolution. Sir Frederick Banbury MP assured a public meeting of his readiness to lead a battalion of the Coldstream Guards into the chamber of the House of Commons in order to save the British constitution![18] These bizarre antics were symptomatic of the post-war mood created by fears about the threat of revolution and the consequent admiration for Mussolini who was thought to have checked the advance of Communism in Italy; as a result ministers turned a blind eye to military drilling by the British fascists.[19] In this situation the Labour Movement wisely refused to overreact. The *Daily Herald* professed itself amused by 'the cajolery and threats being resorted to by the Rothermere press as a frantic attempt to induce Mr Asquith to combine with the Tories to prevent a Labour Government assuming office'. Clynes, noting the attempts in the City to raise scares about national bankruptcy, observed: 'Our enemies are not afraid we shall fail in relation to them. They are afraid that we shall succed.'[20]

In fact, behind the noisy headlines in the Rothermere press, a different tune was being played. In December Earl De La Warr had admitted to MacDonald that he was not a wholehearted supporter of any party 'but my sympathies are all with yours . . . I fully realise . . . that the Labour Party will need support in the next Parliament, and I shall gladly help, by constant attendance and vote whenever possible.'[21] Lord Bledisloe assured him that many moderates in and out of Parliament 'are determined that panicky prejudice against the extremists shall not, if they can help it, stand in the way of any constructive and much-needed measures which you may put in hand for the public good'.[22] This attitude was especially evident among lawyers such as Lord Muir Mackenzie, Hugh Macmillan and J. C. Fenton who agreed to act, respectively, as Lord-in-Waiting, Scottish Lord Advocate and Solicitor General for Scotland under MacDonald despite having been previously adopted as Conservative candidates. Macmillan's appointment was evidently endorsed by Baldwin who saw it as his duty to assist the new prime minister on the understanding that it was 'on a basis entirely non-political'.[23] As lawyers they strongly believed in the need for continuity of administration rather than obstructionism when Labour took office. Above all, the king himself lost little time in summoning MacDonald to the palace and inviting him to form a ministry without making conditions, despite the precarious nature of a government backed by only 191 MPs, thereby cutting the ground from beneath the anti-Labour propagandists in the press and the Conservative Party. Given the intensely monarchical mood of 1920s Britain, George V's show of confidence represented an important means of legitimising the first Labour government.

MacDonald, who spent Christmas at Lossiemouth mulling over his new appointments, was not, apparently, challenged by his colleagues over his selection, perhaps because they felt so delighted at the prospect of forming a government. In fact MacDonald consulted almost no one except the ex-Liberal, Richard Haldane, who told his sister: 'My relations with Ramsay are wonderful. I think he has opened the whole of his mind to me. He has consulted me about every appointment.'[24] The two men spent long periods together and MacDonald used Haldane as his go-between with ministers drawn from outside the Labour ranks.[25] The new premier was concerned both about the confidence inspired by his ministers and about their capacity to handle Whitehall. 'We shall have to put into some of the offices men who are not only untried, but whose capacity to face the permanent officials is very doubtful,' he told Henderson.[26] As a result he included several right-wing trade unionists such as Tom Shaw (Labour), Vernon Hartshorn (Postmaster General), Stephen Walsh (War) and William Adamson (Scotland), but excluded Lansbury, who might have exposed the government to attack, and appointed only two left-wingers, John Wheatley (Health) and Fred Jowett (Works). Fitting in the leading personalities proved difficult; MacDonald took the Foreign Office himself, making Snowden Chancellor of the Exchequer, Clynes Lord Privy Seal, Henderson Home Secretary, Thomas Colonial Secretary and Webb President of the Board of Trade. Former Liberal appointments included Haldane (Lord Chancellor), Trevelyan (Education), and Noel Buxton (Agriculture). Peerages were created for Sydney Olivier (India Office) and MacDonald's golfing partner, C. B. Thomson (Air Ministry). Although Sankey was not included, two ex-Conservatives were appointed: Parmoor (Lord President) and Viscount Chelmsford (Admiralty).

The appointment of Chelmsford, a peer of no particular distinction who had been Indian viceroy, 1916–21, came as a bombshell. When the *Daily Herald* sent a reporter to seek an explanation Chelmsford disarmingly admitted he was as surprised as anyone: 'I enquired, naturally, when the offer was made, as to what the Labour policy was likely to be in the immediate future . . . I had to satisfy myself that that policy, so far as disclosed to me, was such as I could reasonably help to promote.'[27] Given this less than ecstatic endorsement of a party to which he did not even belong it was hardly surprising that, in Webb's words, 'the Labour Party growled'. Webb, however, suggested that Chelmsford was a progressive Tory after his period on the LCC and, as governor of New South Wales, had worked well with an Australian Labor government in 1910. Webb concluded that the party was 'so pleased at all difficulties being surmounted that it did not kick'.[28]

However, the PLP felt sufficiently shocked by these dubious appointments to debate a motion that it was 'contrary to the best interests of the Movement to have in a Labour cabinet two peers whose policies have always been identified with the Tory Party, and requests the Prime Minister to ask Lords Parmoor and Chelmsford to resign from the cabinet.'[29] This was withdrawn in favour of a decision to invite the peers to attend party meetings even if they were not party members.[30]

The explanation appears to be that MacDonald, who had been afraid of offending the armed services, especially the admirals, calculated that a figure like Chelmsford would pre-empt resignations and ensure continuity. This was presumably why he put General Thomson at the Air Ministry and the arch-patriot, Shaw, at the War Office. MacDonald had some reason for concern since the admirals were in a sensitive state in the 1920s as the role of the Royal Navy as Britain's crucial defence was being subordinated to that of the RAF. Certainly MacDonald's tactics worked. Writing from Bengal Lord Lytton privately congratulated him for showing 'a discrimination amounting to genius' and reported that the composition of the Cabinet 'has caused great relief out here'.[31] A month later one Liberal MP noted: 'The Labour Government's main weakness is vanity; they are all . . . delighted with the good impression they are making on the middle class.'[32]

Inside the government, however, things were less happy. Trevelyan's opinion of MacDonald deteriorated as soon as he saw him in office. Although he had displayed an acute understanding of the strategy necessary to win power, he had less idea about using it effectively. Insecure and introspective, MacDonald entered office in a surprisingly gloomy frame of mind, already showing signs of giving way to the melancholy and self-pity that characterised his later years. After becoming leader in 1922 he had confided to his diary: 'The work is prodigiously heavy but I flourish under it. I am lonely though . . . The victory comes when there is no one to cheer' – a reference to the deaths of his wife and mother.[33] As a result MacDonald was unable to confide in colleagues, refused to delegate and soon got out of touch. He never used the official machine available to him, even trying to open all his mail initially, and he soon tired himself through overwork. He lacked confidence in the trade unionists and was suspicious of socialists like Wheatley whom he had been reluctant to appoint. 'Wheatley finally fixed,' he wrote in his diary. 'Necessary to bring Clyde in. Will he play straight?'[34] So grudging a view of, arguably, his most able and successful minister was an indication of his poor judgement. His choices had been made for their political utility rather than for executive competence.

Outside the Cabinet, however, things went as smoothly as MacDonald had intended. 'King plays the game straight, though I feel he is apprehensive,' noted MacDonald on 22 January. 'It would be a miracle if he were not.'[35] Earlier that day when ministers had been sworn in the king had grumbled about Labour MPs singing 'The Red Flag' at an Albert Hall rally; but the prime minister explained that a riot would have ensued if he had tried to stop them. Clynes, admitting they were 'somewhat embarrassed' at first meeting the king, recalled: 'the quiet little man . . . swiftly put us at our ease . . . I had expected to find him unbending; instead he was kindness and sympathy itself. Before he gave us leave to go he made an appeal that I have never forgotten: "The immediate future of my people, their whole happiness, is in your hands, gentlemen. They depend upon your prudence and sagacity."'[36] George V liked his new premier very much, perhaps because he chose to regard the Highland Scot as a gentleman of sorts despite his illegitimate birth. 'The King has been most friendly and appreciative,' MacDonald wrote after a week in office. Reassured by royal favour, he soon felt at home at Windsor and Buckingham Palace where, he suggested, rather improbably: 'the kindly homeliness was that of a cottage'.[37]

As a result there was scant indication that a new era had begun even though the prime minister's groceries arrived at Downing Street in a Co-op van, and when the Cabinet met on 23 January Jimmy Thomas broke with convention by sauntering in puffing at his cigar. But the challenge to convention stopped there. Richard Haldane explained the etiquette to the new ministers including the need to wear court dress when receiving the seals of office. As George V was completely obsessive about dress and ceremonial, his secretary, Lord Stamfordham, wrote to say that ministers could obtain a set of clothes from Moss Bros for only £30! MacDonald professed to see no problem in conforming: 'These braids and uniforms are but part of an official pageantry . . . a gold coat means nothing to me but a form of dress to be worn or rejected as a hat would be.'[38] In fact he enjoyed the dressing up, and it was in any case consistent with his tactics to do so. However, not all ministers acquired court dress, but it seems to have been agreed that people could share or simply wear black evening dress and knee breeches at court. At the king's first levee at St James's Palace in March, Webb, Buxton, Hartshorn, Clynes and MacDonald were in attendance but only the latter two wore full levee dress while the others used a modified form, according to *The Times* which took their photographs.[39]

Not everyone, however, took the royal charades so seriously. The Tottenham North MP, R. C. Morrison, reported that a West End fashion agency, reminding him he would be unable to attend court functions without proper dress, was offering a complete set for £57 'including nine guineas for the regulation sword'. Morrison reported that at the levee he saw men bedecked in medals who had never served in the armed forces: 'If I had known that such gorgeous dresses would be worn [I] would have gone to Tottenham Fire Brigade and borrowed a helmet and tunic for the occasion.'[40] However, other members adopted a more critical attitude, arguing that the conformity was more than symbolic, suggesting a betrayal of the principles of the Labour Movement. Lansbury doubted whether 'the Labour Party fulfils its mission by proving how adaptable we are and how nicely we can dress and behave when we are in official, royal or upper-class circles'. In the Commons John Maclean protested that ministers were unable to tackle unemployment 'but have plenty of time to go to flunkey banquets in full dress', and he warned that 'sooner or later there will have to be a stop to these functions'. Correspondents in the *Daily Herald* complained about those who 'take an especial delight in donning the apparel and copying the ideas of the class of society who are keeping us in the conditions in which we live today'. Another observed, reasonably enough, that while Labour must conform by placing

representatives in the Lords, 'there really seems no necessity for knight-
hoods for the Attorney and Solicitor Generals'; Labour, he argued,
'had always denounced the absurdity of titles except of real merit
(which are usually refused)'.[41]

· Nonetheless, the movement largely swallowed its misgivings
because members felt so pleased that Labour had assumed office
without provoking the anticipated crisis. This was especially the
achievement of Philip Snowden at the Exchequer. He had the delicate task of speaking for a party committed to achieving socialism
while continuing to administer a free-enterprise economy. For the nine
months of the government's life Snowden managed to reassure
opponents and delight his supporters by sounding like an orthodox
chancellor. He and MacDonald had prepared the way by abandoning
the capital levy which might have provoked a reaction from the
business community. Having fought the election on the basis that
unemployment could be reduced by restoring British export markets
and maintaining free trade, Snowden went on to introduce a model
Gladstonian Budget. He reduced direct taxes by £14 million and indirect taxes on tea, sugar, cocoa and coffee by £29 million. This was
well received on the Labour and Liberal benches, though Snowden's
caution about unemployment rang alarm bells in some quarters. He
funded a token programme of relief schemes which made little impact,
though unemployment did fall from 11.7 per cent in 1923 to 10.3 per
cent in 1924.

Economics was closely linked to foreign policy because of the
assumption that the best solution to unemployment lay in a restoration of international relations. MacDonald was a closer student of
foreign affairs than his Conservative counterparts and spoke with
greater authority. Under his guidance Britain recognised the Soviet
Union for the first time with a view to promoting British manufacturing exports and food imports. He was also instrumental in some
delicate negotiations with the French who were persuaded to abandon
their occupation of the Ruhr, to accept a more realistic level of reparations from Germany and to adopt disarmament; he achieved this by
reassuring them of British support against aggression. For the Labour
Movement MacDonald's work was a great morale booster, offering
proof that the party could more than match the grand panjandrums
of the Tory Party in managing Britain's interests abroad.

The movement was also enthusiastic about John Wheatley's role at Health where he reintroduced Addison's policy by offering councils a subsidy of £9 per house, resulting in the construction of 520,000 new homes. On the other hand, the government missed the opportunity to tackle popular policies for women such as equal franchise and widows' pensions; this legislation was within reach of a minority government as neither the peers nor the other parties could risk outright opposition. Baldwin took up both issues on returning to office. More troubling for party supporters was the friction with trade unions during the nine months of the ministry's life. In February the Cabinet demonstrated its orthodox approach by threatening to invoke a state of emergency against a dock strike under the 1920 Emergency Powers Act. This meant using the Supply and Transport Committee to keep essential supplies moving during a strike. The dispute was no sooner resolved by arbitration than another conflict arose in March with the Transport and General Workers Union over a London tram-workers strike. Urging higher pay and a state takeover of public transport, the TUC's General Committee and the NEC warned the Cabinet against invoking the Emergency Powers Act. But the Cabinet rejected this, proposing to keep the trams running and provide protection by mobilising special constables and employing naval ratings to operate the power stations. 'I wish it had been a Tory government,' growled Ernest Bevin. 'We would not have been so frightened by their threats.'[42] Eventually a face-saving formula was found by proposing a bill to reorganise London transport, which was supported by the Conservatives, and to offer a modified wage settlement.

During its nine months of life the government's precarious parliamentary existence was fortified by the maintenance of its popular support. Labour won two by-elections, one at Burnley, retained by Henderson with a greatly increased majority, and Liverpool West Toxteth, a gain from the Conservatives. Subsequently the movement created a myth that the first Labour government had been destroyed by plots organised by the Opposition. This was far from being the case for Baldwin, who needed some time to restore his leadership and the party's morale, and went off to tour the country. Meanwhile, in Parliament the Tories held their hand. For example, in March when forty-five Labour MPs abstained on the government's Trade Facilities Bill, Conservative and Liberal members gave their support. If the two

Opposition parties had wanted to gang up to overthrow the government they could easily have done so. In fact the Liberals naïvely assumed that having won the election over free trade they would be able to co-operate with Labour. But the Liberals' hopes were dashed. It would have made sense for MacDonald to conciliate them thereby obtaining control over the parliamentary timetable and facilitating official business; and, as the Liberals had no desire to upset the government and cause another general election, he could have used them to maintain himself in office much longer. But he was too sensitive towards Asquith and Lloyd George and allowed his opportunity to slip.

By September the prime minister had exhausted himself and taken his eye off the domestic situation. Though adept at diplomacy he was less skilful in managing domestic complications. His most embarrassing error was the so-called 'Biscuit Affair' that arose out of an attempt by Alexander Grant, the proprietor of the Scottish biscuit manufacturers, McVitie & Price, to redress the disadvantage MacDonald suffered as a poor man coping with the expenses involved in being prime minister. Grant gave him the use of a Daimler and the interest on £40,000 worth of capital strictly during his period in office. However, in April 1924 Grant received a baronetcy. MacDonald, who had been shocked by the sale of honours under Lloyd George, had blundered into a scandal perhaps through the arrogance or innocence that made him assume he was above suspicion. On September 11 the *Mail* reported on the McVitie & Price shares, leading the Westminster wags to quip: 'Every man has his price, but not every man has his McVitie & Price.'

Eventually the Opposition parties decided, separately, to challenge Labour policies. The Liberals took up the treaties agreed with Russia on the basis that Britain had given the Russians what they wanted without resolving the claims of British bondholders who had suffered in the revolution. MacDonald reacted peevishly to this, accusing them of being unscrupulous and dishonest. Meanwhile the Conservatives focused on the editor of a Communist journal, John Campbell, who had called upon British soldiers to refuse to fire on workers. Sir Patrick Hastings, the Attorney General, proposed to prosecute him for incitement to mutiny but Maxton and others protested, arguing that Campbell's views had been widely expressed at party conferences. MacDonald sympathised with this view and, after a confused discussion at Cabinet, Hastings withdrew the prosecution in August on the implausible grounds that it might fail. Questioned about whether he had instructed the Attorney General to withdraw, MacDonald became rattled and gave misleading explanations. The result was a second censure motion against the government.

The prime minister's reactions to these challenges betrayed his state of mind. 'I am inclined to give the Liberals an election . . . if they force it,' he wrote. 'The conditions of office perhaps bribe me to take this chance of ending the present regime.'[43] Far from being driven from office, he seemed almost to be looking for a way out. As the crisis surrounding his government deepened he became strangely cheerful, and when both Liberals and Conservatives tabled their motions he wrote: 'I am living in rare air tonight; the end is definitely in sight.'[44] After nine months he was evidently tired and dispirited. With Labour backbenchers adopting an increasingly critical attitude over unemployment it became tempting to find a way out under cover of a defence of sound left-wing causes. Thus, although the Liberals were ready to compromise by appointing an inquiry, MacDonald insisted on treating their motion as one of confidence on which he was bound to be defeated. He duly lost by 364 to 198 votes. He then had a friendly interview with the king who made no objection about granting a third general election in three years to suit his prime minister's convenience.

For MacDonald the 1924 election campaign took the form of a triumphal tour. He addressed huge and ecstatic meetings of 3,000 people at Edinburgh, 4,000 at Newcastle, where a further 12,000 waited outside the town hall, 6,000 at Leeds, a reported 20,000 at Huddersfield, and 15,000 at Birmingham. However, the voting in Newcastle and Birmingham suggested that the rallies told a misleading story. Labour tradition holds that the party was manoeuvred out of office in 1924 by a reactionary conspiracy designed to frighten the voters. Certainly the mood in right-wing circles was very peculiar. Candidates became the target of bizarre propaganda warnings that the Communists would come to power and that Communist spies were operating as health visitors. In Whitechapel Harry Gosling's campaign acquired the character of a John Buchan novel. Among his weird correspondence was a warning from 'The Red Hand of Ulster': 'Take grim note of what we have to say. It's a matter of Life and Death to you! . . . we give you the sporting offer of either withdrawing your candidacy even now, or voting with us on the Irish question – if you are returned Bolshie Candidate for Whitechapel and St George's.'[45]

However, the outcome of the election reflected poor tactics by Labour. The party was not sure what line to adopt apart from claiming that Labour's competence in managing the economy and foreign affairs had been proved. MacDonald spent the entire first week focusing on the Russian Treaty and the Campbell case, thereby playing into Conservative hands by keeping the idea of Bolshevik subversion alive. Many candidates took the line used by Herbert Morrison who protested that 'The Election is not of our seeking. It is obvious that as a minority Government it was impossible for us to carry in the House our programme as submitted at the last General Election.'[46] In marginal Southampton Reginald Sorensen insisted: 'Long ago the Liberals and Conservatives decided, because the Labour Government was getting on too well, that they must go to their doom.'[47] As Sorensen needed Liberal votes it was a mistake to polarise the debate in this way. Labour's aim should have been to separate the two parties rather than push them together.

The climax came on Saturday 25 October. Jimmy Thomas woke Snowden with the words 'Get up you lazy devil! We're bunkered.'[48] An hysterical headline in that morning's *Daily Mail* proclaimed: 'CIVIL WAR PLOT BY SOCIALISTS: MOSCOW ORDER TO OUR REDS: GREAT PLOT DISCLOSED YESTERDAY'. A letter by one Grigori Zinoviev, president of the Communist International, dated 15 September, ordering the unleashing of the class war in Britain, had fallen into the *Mail*'s hands. The letter was a forgery by some White Russian émigrés planted in the Foreign Office by British Intelligence and Conservative Central Office and released four days before polling for maximum effect. But in the excitable mood created by the Campbell case it carried plausibility. 'Now we can see why Mr MacDonald has done obeisance throughout the campaign to the Red Flag with its associations of murder and crime,' pontificated the *Mail*. 'He is a stalking horse for the Reds as Kerensky was . . . Everything is to be made ready for a great outbreak of the abominable "class war" which is civil war of the most savage kind.'[49] Unfortunately MacDonald gave some credence to the *Mail*'s effusions by keeping silent for twenty-four hours and then publishing the letter as though he regarded it as genuine.

In retrospect the Zinoviev Letter assumed huge significance in the Labour Movement as proof of the tricks played by reactionary forces to exclude the party from power. This idea helped MacDonald by giving him some cover as a victim of right-wing conspiracies and thereby diverting attention from the shortcomings of his administration. But this probably exaggerates its impact. Working-class voters were little worried by the scare, though it may have had more influence among the middle classes and helped the Conservatives to bring erstwhile Liberals, who had few candidates to vote for, into their camp. However, now that they had dropped protectionism the Conservatives were bound to win anyway.

With 48 per cent of the votes and 412 seats the Conservatives did indeed win overwhelmingly. Yet for Labour 1924 was far from a disaster. The party's vote increased to 33 per cent, the highest to date, or from 4.4 to 5.4 million. But it also became a victim of the electoral system as its higher vote resulted in a net *loss* of forty-two seats. With sixty-four losses and twenty-two gains the party returned 151 members.[50] The national agent took defeat calmly, attributing it to a rise in the Conservative vote due to a transfer of Liberal support, but he noted that in most places Labour's vote had improved.[51] The Liberals with only 17.6 per cent of the vote and forty-two seats were the real losers. MacDonald's strategy of squeezing the Liberals so that they were no longer seen as a viable alternative to the Conservatives had paid off. After a period of three-party politics the country was now moving back towards two-party competition. In this sense the experiment with government had consolidated Labour's status and left the movement largely content despite the reservations over MacDonald's policies.

8

'Further from Socialism':
The General Strike and Mass
Unemployment, 1925–1931

Not everyone regretted the early demise of the first Labour government. According to David Kirkwood it had 'accomplished nothing and challenged nothing', while Jimmy Maxton insisted that 'every day they were in led us further from Socialism'. The perspicacious John Wheatley commented: 'If the Tories were an intelligent Party, they would make [MacDonald] their leader.' One Birmingham ILP-er complained 'Amid banquets and garden parties . . . we played at being imperial statesmen and gentlemen . . . Labour had literally been knocked into a cocked hat.'[1] The critics had a point: on the evidence of the nine months in office socialism was unlikely to be attained through gradualism as MacDonald had claimed. In December 1924 Maxton tried to persuade Lansbury to challenge MacDonald for the leadership and at the 1925 party conference Ernest Bevin condemned his conduct as prime minister by proposing a motion designed to commit Labour to refusing to take office as a minority again. But despite TGWU backing, this was rejected by 2.5 million votes to 500,000. The vote was an indication not only that the movement was still delighted at Labour's sudden elevation as a party of government, but also that the failings of Cabinet had been obscured by the manner of its departure from office. The idea of a conspiracy of Tories, Liberals and the reactionary Rothermere press designed to evict Labour from power and then to frighten the voters was a myth, but a powerful one that helped MacDonald by creating an alibi for his shortcomings, thereby enabling him to fend off his left-wing critics during the rest of the 1920s.

Even so, he could not entirely escape a debate about party strategy and in particular whether the next government should attempt something bolder on the economic front. The ILP forced the pace in this debate. During the post-war years its role as the source of individual members for the party was declining, so much so that some of its members opted to join their local CLPs, leaving the ILP looking increasingly like a refuge for left-wing militants and troublemakers. Yet the ILP remained a force to be reckoned with. Its membership had reached 35,000 by 1921, fell back to 30,000 by 1925 but rose to 38,000 by the later 1920s. These were the years in which the ILP made its final effort to commit the Labour Party to a socialist programme – and in its failure was clearly written the painful decision to disaffiliate after the crisis of 1931.

Yet perceptions of socialism were now complicated by the Bolshevik Revolution and its aftermath. Although the Labour leaders looked askance at the Russian regime because the Tories used it as a stick with which to beat them, they could not ignore the positive influence it exercised; in a period of failing capitalism, the Soviet Union offered a tangible example of the planned economy. Most socialists assumed that Britain would attain this objective, not by a sudden revolutionary change, but by a gradual and inexorable progression involving a series of modest reforms. Indeed, it was arguable that Britain had already embarked on such a transition, for even Conservative governments were extending state planning and intervention by means of such innovations as the Forestry Commission (1920) and the Electricity Generating Board (1926). As a result socialists were not looking for the dramatic collapse of capitalism, in which the workers suffered most, but for an interim strategy for managing the free-enterprise system en route to socialism. The longer the depression lingered the more confident they felt that the replacement of capitalism by socialism was inevitable. However, in the interim this placed Labour governments in an awkward position. As unemployment increased from 10 per cent in 1924 to 12 per cent in 1926 they accepted the obligation to provide the unemployed with maintenance; but at a time when a high proportion of state revenue already disappeared into servicing the national debt and the balance of payments was moving deeper into deficit this was financially embarrassing.

In this situation Labour's approach suffered from two flaws – the lack of a medium-term strategy for managing the economy in a period of depression and the failure to develop a widely accepted system of values capable of sustaining the socialist society. Socialist intellectuals such as R. H. Tawney, G. D. H. Cole and Harold Laski were very aware that no socialist revolution could be secure without democratic support, but once the working-class movement embraced anti-capitalist values a socialist state would be widely welcomed as a moral advance, not as an imposition. The public ownership of industry would be more acceptable in the context of a participatory democracy in industry. Conversely, if the state merely replaced private ownership but otherwise perpetuated the old system the change would not be secure or even desirable; indeed after the war Cole and others appreciated that in the hands of capitalists the state could become a formidable weapon for use against the workers.

However it was far from clear that such an evolution of thought was in progress. Wartime experiments in state intervention had convinced the Webbs that socialism could be instituted by means of a skilled, central bureaucracy, and in so far as plans for public ownership were developed in the 1920s they discounted industrial democracy and relied on small boards of experts and businessmen. Crucially, the trade unions themselves showed little sympathy for workers' participation and as a result interest in the idea dwindled even among socialist intellectuals as the 1920s wore on.

Meanwhile, the confidence of socialists in the inevitable discrediting of capitalism proved to be optimistic despite the prevalence of mass unemployment. It is often forgotten today that Britain's slump was much less severe than that of Germany and the United States; the depression was far from continuous and even included periods of marked growth; moreover, because of the dramatic fall in prices, most employed people enjoyed rising real wages. This made possible an improvement in food consumption, a huge expansion of luxury goods including cigarettes, football pools, cosmetics and clothes, and the growth of the leisure industry in cinemas, dances and holidays. Politically the most significant symptom of consumerism was the emergence of the British obsession with housing and especially with home-ownership. It has often been assumed, erroneously, that the marked trend towards home-ownership between the wars was not a working-class phenomenon because so many council houses were being constructed. In fact, by the late 1920s three-quarters of building-society loans were for sums of £500 or less and by 1938 37 per cent of Abbey Road borrowers were described as 'wage earners'; by 1936 a semi-detached house could be purchased for £450 with a £25 deposit and weekly payments of around thirteen shillings, putting home-ownership within reach of thousands of working-class families.

This development had major long-term political implications. For those Conservatives who recognised the moral charge of socialism, home-ownership offered a means of giving ordinary people a stake in property and thus building bulwarks for capitalism. It was the Tory MP Noel Skelton who coined the phrase 'the property-owning democracy' in this period. Yet this trend was not incompatible with the rise of Labour. Home-ownership went hand in hand with socialist aspirations as several leading Labour politicians recognised. Ramsay MacDonald pointed out that there could be no ethical objection to investment in building societies as it gave workers an incentive to save and help their fellow men at the same time. Jimmy Thomas commended the building-society movement as a triumph for working-class organisation: 'It's an escape from the ruinous cost of renting and from [the] dependency and insecurity of the landlord system. It promotes the formation of a body of independent, thrifty and law-abiding citizens.'[2] On the other hand, Labour's determination to build council houses, sometimes in the face of obstructionism by Conservative governments, did begin to undermine its enthusiasm for home-ownership and over time allowed their rivals to pander to working-class aspirations to improved housing and the status that went with it. Consequently the steady rise of housing as a political issue set limits to the spread of the socialist values on which Tawney had set such store.

In the 1920s, however, attention focused much more on the problems entailed in managing the economy during the depression. After 1924 two of the former Tories, Mosley and Strachey, concerned about their new party's lack of preparation, devised an economic strategy, published by Strachey as *Revolution By Reason* in 1925. Like Cole, Strachey dismissed the Fabian penchant for piecemeal nationalisation; there was no point in taking over industries that had become obsolete or unprofitable, leaving private enterprise to enjoy easy profits. Strachey and Mosley took a strategic view, advocating state control of the banking system with a view to providing the necessary investment, and management of the economy along Keynesian lines by boosting working-class incomes through family allowances and increases in pensions.[3] However, even though MacDonald was much more susceptible to Mosley's influence than to that of the ILP, he resisted the pressure to adopt such a policy. This was partly because he felt reluctant to be committed to precise policies of any sort, preferring to take refuge in general statements of principle and aim, as well as because of the resistance to such advice from upholders of orthodox thinking such as Snowden.

Nor could MacDonald fail to see that there was a good deal of common ground between the Mosley–Strachey strategy and the ILP programme. Dismayed by the performance of the party in office and keen to fill the gap in policy, the ILP appointed several commissions in 1925 to give a cutting edge to future policy, of which one, comprising J. A. Hobson, H. N. Brailsford, E. F. Wise and Arthur Creech Jones, produced *The Living Wage*. This document was adopted by the ILP conference in 1926 and published as *Socialism in Our Time*. Influenced by Hobson's underconsumptionist thinking, the programme incorporated the idea of a compulsory minimum wage, nationalisation of recalcitrant businesses, family allowances and redistributive taxation, combined with control of the banks and credit.

However, *Socialism in Our Time* was rejected at the 1926 Labour conference. There were several reasons for this. The trade unions remained instinctively suspicious of any interference with wage levels by the state. MacDonald, who shrank from any strategy that threatened to provoke a crisis, correctly interpreted the document as an alternative to gradualism. The fact that Jimmy Maxton had become ILP chairman in April 1926 also damaged *Socialism in Our Time* since he was so unremittingly hostile to MacDonald. Finally, the left-wing critics were inclined to take refuge in the claim that the programmes of the ILP and Mosley–Strachey represented compromises rather than wholesale socialism, implying acceptance of a free-enterprise economy for some time to come. This was perverse since official policy reflected exactly that assumption, but until the 1930s it prevailed. The campaign led by Maxton and A. J. Cook to force a socialist agenda on the party during 1928–9 made the battle lines increasingly rigid and MacDonald, personalising the issue as always, regarded their efforts as a threat to his authority. Snowden left the ILP in 1927 and MacDonald himself was rejected in his attempt to become its treasurer.

Official Labour thinking about managing the economy during a depression reflected a basic divide, not between socialism and capitalism, but between Victorian-internationalist solutions and domestic-Keynesian ones. Labour shared with the Conservative governments of the period a commitment to maintaining sterling as the major international currency, restoring the pre-war level of world trade, and thus recovering the export markets for British industry and reducing unemployment. This complemented Labour's political view: the condemnation of the Treaty of Versailles, the disruption of trade by protectionism, the imposition of reparations on Germany and the reluctance to trade with Russia. Conversely, the sceptics, from the ILP to Mosley, Keynes and Lloyd George, considered internationalism unrealistic partly because Britain no longer enjoyed the power to influence world trade and partly because supporting sterling implied keeping interest rates high and restricted government spending; for them the only solution to unemployment lay in the *domestic* sphere by boosting the demand for British goods by raising real wages.

This conventional stance was somewhat obscured by Labour's rhetoric that condemned free enterprise for creating trusts and monopolies and focused on a distant future in which many industries would come under the control of the state. MacDonald was content to accept the Fabian view that wartime experiments had demonstrated the viability of interventionism but he saw no need to go much beyond general and even utopian proposals. He left short-term economic management to Snowden who dazzled the movement with his grasp but whose rigid economic orthodoxy was somewhat at odds with his vitriolic condemnation of capitalism. In practice Snowden intended to emulate Conservative governments in balancing the budget, avoiding inflation and defending the value of sterling by keeping interest rates high. This led to some inconsistency in the statement eventually produced in 1928, *Labour and the Nation*, on which the party fought the general election of 1929. This wordy and vague document caused concern well beyond the ILP. Bevin recognised its flaws but, as an opponent of the ILP, he failed to co-operate with the left to force the leadership into some clearer or more precise thinking. *Labour and the Nation* advocated the nationalisation of 'Foundation Industries' such as land, coal, power, transport and credit, though without indicating how. It proposed some redistributive measures by higher death duties, graduated taxes on incomes over £500 and tax on rents from urban land. It suggested a living wage to be achieved via extended trade boards. But the section dealing with unemployment referred vaguely to developing national resources by using scientific knowledge. Some interpreted this as a resort to underconsumptionist techniques although counter-cyclical policy was increasingly out of favour and the party was not keen on using taxation to redistribute income and boost purchasing power; the Webbs simply disparaged 'schemes of work' as mere palliatives. As a result Labour lacked an interim strategy for running the economy and detailed proposals for tackling unemployment; after 1929 this was to leave the Cabinet caught between pressure to maintain the unemployed and an orthodox approach to the national finances.

Meanwhile the economic orthodoxy was being vigorously implemented by the Baldwin government. In 1925 when the chancellor, Winston Churchill, returned Britain to the gold standard, in effect revaluing the pound, he forced manufacturers to find ways of reducing their costs for fear of pricing British goods out of foreign markets. As a result it became common ground among businessmen, economists and politicians that there must be a *general* reduction in wages. This was the underlying cause of the General Strike of 1926. However, the proximate cause lay in the coal industry where the owners argued that, as wages represented 70 per cent of their costs, they must abandon the national wage agreements that had been adopted during wartime. As some coalfields were more profitable than others this implied not only lower wages but varying cuts in wages around the country.

The miners were led by their president, Herbert Smith, a patriotic Yorkshireman, and their secretary, A. J. Cook, a syndicalist from South Wales who had briefly joined the Communist Party. After the miners' experience with the Triple Alliance in 1921 Smith and Cook believed that they must carry the rest of the movement with them in any future industrial action. To this end they persuaded the TUC to take the lead in concerted action – in effect a general strike. This historic commitment had been undertaken during the absence of several of the moderate leaders in the Labour government, so that by 1925 Margaret Bondfield, Ernest Bevin, Arthur Pugh and others found themselves with responsibility for leading a strategy in which they did not really believe. They hoped that the mere threat of a general strike would suffice to force the government to find a compromise. But the pace was forced in June 1925 when the coal-owners announced the end of national wage settlements. Cook and Smith thereupon appealed to the TUC for support to place an embargo on movements of coal. This was not an unselfish action on the part of the other union leaders who had good grounds for assuming that the struggle in the coal industry was the prelude to *general* reductions in wages for their members. Consequently, co-ordinated action made sense. The General Strike was thus a defensive move by a movement that was losing members to resist cuts in wages; it was not motivated by ideological considerations. On the other hand, the TUC expected that the loss of industrial output would be so serious that the government would be obliged to call a general election at some point, and to that extent the General Strike had major political implications.

For a time it appeared that the TUC's calculations were correct, for Baldwin offered a temporary subsidy to maintain wages pending an investigation chaired by Sir Herbert Samuel. 'Thank God!' wrote the king on hearing the news. 'There will be no strike now.'[4] 'Red Friday', as the Cabinet climbdown became known, confirmed the union leaders in their belief that they would not have to go through with their threat. However, although the prime minister was genuinely anxious to avoid a general strike, he had limited room for manoeuvre especially as his party and Cabinet regarded the subsidy as a humiliation. In March 1926 Samuel's report offered nothing sufficiently attractive to either side. By this time the subsidy had cost £23 million and Baldwin's options had narrowed as his colleagues blocked any further retreat. In the intervening period the Home Secretary had resuscitated the official machine comprising eleven regional commissioners who would run the country during a general strike, and announced a semi-official body, the Organisation for the Maintenance of Supplies, which would appeal for volunteers to keep essential services running. With every-thing in place a further compromise became more difficult. On 6 April the TUC General Council decided to initiate its plans, such as they were, for implementing a general strike. Their bluff was called when, on 3 May, compositors working on the *Daily Mail* refused to set a hostile editorial and stopped work. The Cabinet withdrew from talks and the strike began on 4 May.

Labour responses to the General Strike underlined the gulf developing between the parliamentary party and the trade unions.

MacDonald felt humiliated by the offer of a subsidy because the Cabinet had conceded to union pressure what it had already refused to the Labour leaders. This compounded his dim view of the union leaders whom he saw as rigid and ineffectual negotiators. The 1924 Labour government had done very little for the unions, only six unionists had been represented in the cabinet and, as the party expanded, they seemed to become increasingly marginal. When negotiating over German reparations to the detriment of British coal exports in 1924, MacDonald had noticeably failed to consult the miners. While Arthur Henderson remained sensitive to union concerns and conscious of the need to keep the two wings of the movement together, MacDonald had become dangerously detached. In March 1926 he told Walter Citrine, the TUC secretary, that he 'would be glad to keep away from the whole business [i.e. the strike] because it was going to be very difficult. The Miners Federation had always told the political party to keep off, while at the same time expecting the politicians to pull them out of their difficulty when they finally got into a mess.'[5] Considering that two mining constituencies had rescued his parliamentary career this was ungenerous. After 1924 MacDonald ditched Aberavon in favour of Seaham in County Durham because it promised to make almost no demands on him; he need visit the constituency only once a year and pay no subscriptions. 'We ought to be able to do our work', the local agent assured him, 'and allow you to do yours on larger issues.'[6] Not surprisingly the miners felt they were being taken for granted; in 1925 they affiliated 800,000 members to the party and sponsored forty MPs. Herbert Smith complained that they contributed 26 per cent of Labour's income but received twenty-five minutes' time at the annual conference.[7]

Personalising the issue as usual, Macdonald disparaged A. J. Cook as a threat to his entire strategy of building Labour into a respectable party of government. Two days before the strike began he wrote in his diary: 'It really tonight looks as though there [is] to be a General Strike to save Mr Cook's face. Ignorant man! . . . The election of this fool as miners' secretary looks as though it [will] be the most calamitous thing that ever happened to the Trade Union movement.'[8] However, MacDonald ignored the fact that support for the strike ran strongly throughout the movement due to fears about general wage cuts rather than the influence of syndicalism. Admittedly he had some grounds for fearing that a general strike would play into Conservative hands by damaging Labour's electoral prospects. The authorities were endeavouring to rekindle the mood associated with the Zinoviev Letter. In October 1925 twelve leading Communists who had been prosecuted for seditious libel and incitement to mutiny were sentenced to between six and twelve months. The Duke of Northumberland, a fascist sympathiser, argued that the miners were merely pawns in a wider game: 'The Third International plans to organise a revolution in Britain by getting control of the trade unions and manipulating the mass of workers. The role of the Parliamentary Labour Party is to camouflage this design until the time is ripe for action for a revolutionary strike on a gigantic scale.'[9] Without actually endorsing such wild theories, some politicians accepted that Britain had become the target of a conspiracy financed by the transfer of funds from the Soviet Union via the Narodny Bank where they were held in special accounts before being passed to the Communist Party.[10]

Such interpretations were not merely the delusions of the far right but were partially endorsed by some of the Labour leaders who feared that the Communists wanted to discredit Labour after its nine months in office leading to a rejection of parliamentary methods by the workers. As a result most Labour MPs gave little support to the General Strike and professed to regard it as doomed. John Beckett turned up at TUC headquarters to help but found 'I need not have hurried. The General Council's offices were in wild confusion, and it was impossible to see anyone with authority, or obtain information or permission to do anything.'[11] Beckett then left London for Gateshead by car, making supportive speeches on the way. But others kept their distance.

In the immediate aftermath the Labour leaders described the strike as 'bungled', 'a dreadful debacle', and an inevitable failure because it provoked the full resources of the state. By contrast Ernest Bevin recognised it as 'a wonderful exhibition of solidarity' and raised the prospect of a repeat unless there were changes in industrial policy.[12] The pessimistic view of contemporary politicians has largely been reflected in the historiography of the General Strike which portrays it as a failure, an anticlimax and as an aberrant example of direct action by men devoted to constitutional methods. Yet it is a misunderstood episode and one of greater significance in the history of the Labour Movement than the received view suggests. In narrowly industrial terms the

General Strike did indeed prove to be anticlimactic. Although the union leaders became targets of criticism from Communists as 'sham Leftists' for their inept leadership, they retained their control. Union membership fell after 1926, but this was little more than a continuation of the trend prevailing since 1920 and continuing down to 1934 when the economy picked up again. Above all, the general wage cuts so widely predicted failed to materialise; indeed in the later 1920s and even early 1930s prices fell faster than money wages. Admittedly the miners suffered not only from lower wages but also from a split caused by the breakaway union led by George Spencer in the Midlands and South Yorkshire coalfields. But they were the exception.

On the other hand, while the industrial effects were modest, the political ramifications of the General Strike proved to be significant. Why was this? In the first place, although the strike itself had lasted for only nine days, the miners stayed out for a further six months – which largely altered public perceptions. During the crisis Oliver Baldwin shrewdly reminded MacDonald that 'the majority of people are in favour of the miners' claims but against the general strike', and therefore recommended that calling off the General Strike and putting support behind the miners would achieve the desired results from a political point of view because 'the mass of the people would be with us'.[13] In effect this is what happened. During the six months of the coal strike local Disputes Committees continued to operate and, along with local Labour parties, helped miners' families by organising collections in cinemas and other places of entertainment, distributing food tickets, holding supportive demonstrations and appealing for donations of clothing, boots and vegetables from allotments.[14] When the miners were eventually driven back to work on the owners' terms they aroused widespread public sympathy, thereby going some way to erasing memories of the General Strike itself.

This was compounded by the punitive response of the Cabinet and its supporters. According to Lord Londonderry, the reactionary coalowner, 'The miners have sacrificed £600,000 in wages over seven months. A. J. Cook has used the miners as pawns in his game.'[15] Before 1926 Baldwin had resisted pressure within his own party to legislate to curtail the use of the political levy by the unions. But as the initial euphoria at the end of the strike gave way to criticism, he backed down and introduced the 1927 Trades Disputes and Trade Union Act.

This measure made sympathetic strike action illegal, excluded civil servants from trade unions affiliated to the TUC, and replaced the practice of contracting out of the political levy with contracting in which had the immediate effect of reducing Labour Party income, £66,800 in 1926, by about a third.[16] On average Labour candidates spent £452 at the 1929 election compared with £905 for the Conservatives. However, this disparity was not new, and the significance of the legislation was more symbolic in that it gave the movement a sense of grievance and a focus for united political action. CLPs mobilised support by portraying the 1927 Act as a deliberate attempt to retard the growth of the unions. 'Workers, you now have a splendid opportunity of replying to Mr Baldwin for his dastardly treatment of you during the 1926 coal lockout by signing the "Contracting–In" Form as supplied by your local Unions.' Taking the moral high ground, the Seaham party in County Durham argued, 'The Labour Party depends upon the pence of the workers which provides an honourable way to accumulate funds as contrasted against the ignoble and dishonourable methods adopted by the Liberals and Tories in the sale of honours.'[17] Admittedly Bevin took umbrage at the way MacDonald had distanced himself from the strike, accusing him of being 'wantonly guilty of stabbing us in the back at the moment when we had the whole force of capital unleashed against us'.[18] However, this reaction was not typical even among the miners. Herbert Smith's loyalty to the party remained undimmed; one South Wales miner, Vernon Hartshorn, hailed MacDonald as 'the greatest political leader in the world', and another miner claimed 'for the time being our salvation lies in the leadership of Mr MacDonald'.[19] In effect the unions closed ranks in order to focus on winning the next election and thus repealing the legislation.

Moreover, the strike made a major impact on the general public by detracting from Baldwin's attempts to be seen as even-handed and by undermining the Conservatives in industrial constituencies. Defeated candidates at by-elections in 1927 privately reported that the other parties had used the Trades Disputes Act to damage them and that it was regarded as 'a capitalist attack on the Trade Unions'.[20] In Sheffield one activist reported, 'Electors who have been known to be strong Conservatives have left the defence of their policy severely alone, and do not attempt to even discuss in public as they previously did. There does seem to be a definite wave against Baldwin and his party.'[21] The explanation is that support for the General Strike had been very solid in working-class communities. This was confirmed by the reports issued by the eleven regional commissioners who found little evidence that men were returning to work; the strikers and their families believed that they were in the right and were winning, so much so that many who had not been called out wanted to join the strike.

Consequently its political significance is not to be understood in the light of the official congratulations or the propaganda in the *Daily Mail*. In the mid-1920s large numbers of working-class people continued to vote Conservative and Liberal; but the strike had polarised opinion, leaving many of them uncomfortable about supporting grasping employers and a vindictive government. During the strike a parlia- mentary by-election was being conducted at Hammersmith North, a Conservative seat that Labour gained comfortably, and in July 1926 Labour's majority at Wallsend rose from 1,600 to over 9,000. In each case Labour's *vote*, not just its share, rose sharply, suggesting that MacDonald's misgivings about the electoral impact of the strike had been misplaced. The strike also coincided with an intriguing munic- ipal by-election in the Ladywood ward of Birmingham, a large part of the Ladywood constituency that was still held by Neville Chamberlain for the Conservatives despite being very working class. So strong was the reaction of local residents against the government that Conservatives were deterred from campaigning; one Conservative activist admitted that 'owing to the violent Labour opposition, it was . . . more prof- itable to leave leaflets at the houses and not to attempt canvassing'; they lost the ward to Labour by a large margin.[22] In the Erdington constituency of the city the Conservatives abandoned their usual open- air meetings in the summer because of local anger provoked by the suffering of the miners. In September Labour gained another ward adjacent to Ladywood and went on to take the parliamentary seat in the 1929 general election. This was followed by extensive Labour gains in the national municipal elections from 1926 to 1929.

Only a week after the General Strike Oswald Mosley, more in touch than his party's leaders, addressed a large Labour demonstration in Birmingham's Summerfield Park where he proclaimed the strike a 'glorious triumph' for the unions who 'had beaten the boss class'. He asked: 'Who would doubt after this that Birmingham at length had reverted to its great tradition of progress? The Chamberlain tradition was dead. Today the workers dominated Birmingham, and would sweep it from end to end for Labour next time.'[24] If Mosley's rhetoric was over the top, he had seen something the Labour leaders, nervously entrenched in London, had largely missed.

The impact of the General Strike in Birmingham and the West Midlands reinforced significant changes in the perception of Labour that began around 1924. Up to that point Labour had made only modest progress in both municipal and parliamentary elections. Although the city had a large working-class population, the slum areas were well mixed with more prosperous residential districts which enabled the Conservative machine to mobilise both classes.[25] Their candidates included workingmen who were popular representatives of the local community and complemented the prestige of the Chamberlain family. Their large female membership helped to maintain an extensive programme of social activities that extended the Conservative appeal beyond the narrowly political.[26] In view of the reluctance of local trade unions to fund Labour the party found it difficult to compete with the Tories. Consequently, wealthy patrons like Mosley, who donated money to the Ladywood, Erdington and Sparkbrook divisions, began to put the party on a more equal footing.[27] In 1924 Labour attacked Neville Chamberlain as the minister responsible for the Rent Restriction Act which allowed landlords to raise rents after relaxing the wartime controls.[28] When Mosley squeezed his majority to a mere seventy-seven votes and Labour made its first gain in the King's Norton seat, a turning point had been reached: Chamberlain decided to move to the safer Edgbaston. With some justice Mosley claimed that he 'undertook to go [to Ladywood] to break the Chamberlain tradition. When Chamberlain ran away that tradition was broken.'[29] Mosley stayed in the West Midlands, becoming adopted for Smethwick in December 1926, following the death of the Labour member, where he raised the majority from 1,253 to 6,582. In the by-election his colleagues made the most of his upper-class origins. 'What has Mr Mosley to gain?' asked Arthur Ponsonby. 'There was no fortune to be gained by joining the Labour Party.' As he was rich, declared John Wheatley, he was beyond corruption.[30] During the later 1920s Mosley spearheaded Labour's advance in the West Midlands where he was joined by other upper-class ex-Tories including Lady Cynthia Mosley (Stoke), Oliver Baldwin (Dudley), John Strachey (Birmingham Aston) and J. A. Lovat Fraser (Stafford). For voters accustomed to respecting their social superiors and the national traditions and institutions associated with them, this was an intriguing challenge. The upper-class candidates felt no inhibitions about combining claims to patriotism with a radical domestic stance. Strachey, for example, scorned his opponents for talking about patriotism: 'He wanted a patriotism that could not rest while one British worker was housed in the conditions in which many in that very district were housed.'[31] Baldwin freely attacked the Tories for 'working in the interests of the rich' and he revived the coal controversy. 'Did God . . . put the mineral in the ground for the benefit of one class? The mineral was put there for the good of all the people.' He suggested that 'Forty-two-and-a-half million people in the country were working and striving so that two-and-a-half million could live in comfort. The Duke of Hamilton received thirteen pounds per hour just because he happened to own land under which coal was found.'[32] This was language not used since Lloyd George's 'People's Budget' campaign of 1909–10 and stood in contrast to the cautious approach of most Labour candidates. By raising the stakes and forcing the coal strike on to the agenda, rather than trying to avoid it, these Labour candidates put the Conservatives on to the defensive in 1929. The Minister for Labour, Sir Arthur Steel-Maitland, who sat for Birmingham Erdington, attracted so much anger that he was obliged to abandon meetings in his constituency, and became one of the surprising casualties of the 1929 election.[33] Even after Mosley had left the party the Labour agent for Erdington gave him full credit for the party's six gains in Birmingham in 1929 and for the near defeat of both Austen and Neville Chamberlain.[34]

However, while Labour was making inroads into the working-class majority during the later 1920s, its relationship with the female majority continued to be complicated. In 1929 the total electorate expanded to 28.8 million, from 21.7 million in 1924, following the Equal Franchise Act of 1928 which added 3.29 million women under thirty years as well as 1.95 million women over thirty to the registers. As a result women constituted almost 53 per cent of the British electorate. But the implications were by no means clear. The Conservatives had widely attributed their 1923 defeat to the votes of housewives fearful of dearer food following the introduction of tariffs. In 1927 Baldwin's announcement of the Equal Franchise Bill provoked an hysterical campaign in the *Daily Mail*: 'WHY SOCIALISTS WANT VOTES FOR FLAPPERS'. Impressionable young females, so the argument ran, would easily be manipulated by the Labour Party.[35] Yet the Conservative MPs ignored the *Mail*'s ranting and passed the bill into law. Historians have never discovered any basis for contemporary claims about the left-wing proclivities of the female voters, rather the contrary. Labour had not apparently gained from the new women's vote in 1918, 1922, 1923 or 1924, and attempts to correlate changes in the share of the female electorate with changes in the Labour share of the poll in 1929 suggest the 1928 reform made no significant difference.[36] Another source of evidence is provided by a comparison between nine by-elections fought during January–March 1929 on the *old* register and the same seats in the May general election with the new female voters. In these three-cornered contests Labour's share of the vote *fell* by an average of 2.9 per cent at the general election while the Liberals, who had already done well in the by-elections, further improved by 1.5 per cent and the Conservatives by 3.7 per cent.[37]

Why was this? It is possible that as women as a whole were older than men they reflected the loyalties of the pre-war generations before Labour had become a major factor. Another possibility lay in the greater religiosity of the female population which fostered their adherence to the Conservatives as the party of the Established Church. But above all women were less likely to enjoy the workplace experience and trade union membership that promoted Labour support among men. By 1918, as a result of the war, there were 1.2 million female union members compared with 5.3 million males; but their numbers fell faster, declining to 800,000 compared to 4.6 million men by 1925. Women often found membership dispiriting because most unions were not bothered about them. 'When I said to one man why don't you ask us if we are [union] members, he said "Well, women don't count very much."'[38] This experience of a woman in an East End clothing workshop underlines the extent to which women missed the sense of class unity and the politicisation fostered by workplace experience. Hence the importance of finding alternative methods for mobilising them.

Unfortunately many constituencies merely paid lip service to the party's 1918 constitution because their organisation was so firmly oriented around male concerns. Where women loomed large in the

local labour force the men often felt threatened, a prejudice exacerbated by the entry of women into male jobs during the war. In Preston,
for example, it was expected that Labour would back the implementation of the commitment to restore 'pre-war practices', that is, eliminate
women, in the textile industry.[39] On this basis Labour support improved
in Preston in the early 1920s as unemployment increased. The Preston
party's organisation continued to be based on the trades council and
not until 1924 did it even agree to establish women's sections for fear
that this would 'divide the sexes and create a sex war'.[40] Throughout
the interwar period unemployment reinforced assumptions that a
woman's role lay in domesticity and that employment was essentially
a male concern. As late as 1935 one female delegate at the women's
conference asserted that the employment of married women was
'definitely opposed to the principle of the Labour movement'.[41]
However, as the Preston party discovered, this attitude handicapped
them, contributing to losses in municipal elections. Yet despite attempts
to mobilise women, there was no significant change. Although Preston
was a two-member seat Labour never risked more than one, male,
candidate from 1918 to 1929 and its share of the vote, which had been
25.8 per cent in 1918, had risen only to 29.5 per cent by 1929, way
behind the general advance.

   Nationally Labour had been outflanked by the Conservatives who
had granted widows pensions in 1925 and equal franchise in 1928, and
enjoyed a huge female membership of between 700,000 and 900,000
by the late 1920s. Yet contemporary Labour opinion suggests complacency towards the female electorate. One member later claimed, 'There
has never been any difference between men and women in the Labour
Party.'[42] In fact, although the party absorbed middle- and upper-class
male recruits, its relations with middle-class female activists proved
uncomfortable because it associated them with feminism which was
taken to be an essentially bourgeois cause. Labour women of the
Edwardian generation, such as Margaret Bondfield and Susan Lawrence,
scarred by earlier conflicts with the Pankhursts and instinctively hostile
to feminist organisations, reflected the wider retreat from feminism
after 1918. Even Jennie Lee was heard to complain that feminist groups
always ended up discussing the problem of finding servants![43] In effect
the feminist organisations were seen as competitors for the loyalty of
working-class women, so much so that in 1925 the party only narrowly

rejected a proposal to ban Labour women from being members of the Women's Citizens Association and the National Union of Societies for Equal Citizenship – the body with which Labour had had an electoral alliance in 1912. To this extent Labour actually distanced itself from the women's movement after 1918.

All this made life awkward for middle-class Labour feminists such as Dorothy Jewson, Edith Picton-Turbervill, Monica Whately and Barbara Ayrton-Gould, who remained members of the NUSEC because they believed that women should retain independent organisations for fear of being absorbed and exploited by male-dominated parties. They reflected the attitudes and experience of the Edwardian generation of suffragists. By contrast, the younger, post-suffrage generation posed a less obvious problem for Labour. Jennie Lee, who became an MP in 1929 when still in her twenties, and Barbara Castle, who became a candidate later in the 1930s, had no history in the women's campaigns and consequently regarded Labour's separate women's sections as a cul-de-sac. Content with the women's reforms already achieved and confident of their personal ability to compete with men, they preferred to work in the mainstream of the party; if they were elected as women's representatives to the NEC they felt they would be marginalised as merely spokeswomen for female interests.[44] As a result Labour relied on dutiful loyalists who ran the women's organisation, on the one hand, and ambitious women who failed to give a lead to women in the wider world, on the other.

During the 1920s, however, many feminists still considered it worthwhile to campaign within the Labour Movement. Their interest in social welfare and housing offended no one, but the party reacted against anything that smacked of feminism by infringing male interests. Eleanor Rathbone's campaign for the 'Endowment of Motherhood', better known as family allowances, proved surprisingly controversial. As it was tantamount to offering a wage for motherhood and housework, the unions felt it conflicted with their commitment to the 'family wage'; it was crucial to male pride to be able to maintain a family without the necessity for the wife to go out to work. In 1930 one union delegate warned that instead of workingmen collecting their wages at the factory office their wives would draw their wages at the post office. A Labour MP, Somerville Hastings, remarked insultingly that family allowances were a bad idea because working-class women lacked the necessary skill to spend the money in the best way.[45] Even Marion Phillips, the party's chief woman officer, refused to support the reform. As a result, by 1929 family allowances had simply dropped off the agenda, a singular symptom of a movement obsessively focused on masculine sensitivities.

Less surprising but even more divisive was the controversy over birth control. The publication of Marie Stopes' book *Married Love* in 1918 went a long way to making the spread of information about birth-control respectable, and the appalling effects of repeated childbirth were recognised as a major cause of bad health and high mortality among poor women; the Women's Co-operative Guild had highlighted the problem by publishing dozens of horrendous case studies in *Maternity: Letters from Working Women* (1915). Yet Labour politicians proved unable to take the issue on board. This reflected the social conservatism of the working class, the party's fear of antagonising the Catholic Church, and even embarrassment, for in the 1920s people were still being prosecuted for obscenity for printing birth-control material. One exceptional Labour MP, Ernest Thurtle, introduced legislation to allow the provision of birth-control information by the local authority clinics, but this was pronounced to be an illegal use of ratepayers' money by John Wheatley and Arthur Greenwood as Ministers for Health. Marion Phillips deployed the party loyalty argument to thwart the reformers, reminding feminists they were 'bound in our loyalty to the common cause of labour not to force them to separate themselves from us on an issue that is not a political one but in a very special sense a matter of private conviction'.[46] She also claimed that if they waited for socialism there would be no need to limit family size on economic grounds – the argument once used by socialists to oppose the women's vote. Despite this, the Labour women's conference voted for birth control four years in a row, but the NEC simply refused to allow a debate at party conference on the grounds that it was not a party question. Labour, according to Henderson, could not 'legislate in advance of public opinion'. In fact, as Catholic women were adopting birth-control in the 1920s, the party was probably exaggerating the electoral dangers. In 1930 Greenwood finally admitted that it was permissible for local authorities to fund birth control information, though it remained optional to do so.

During the 1920s these controversies divided and to some extent demoralised the Labour women's movement at a time when the party should have been extending its reach in the female community. Although women had proved their competence in local government for several decades before 1914 the male dominance of the organisation after 1918 was such that the party failed to make further advances. Constituency parties often ignored women as a source of municipal candidates, even when the women's sections put names forward, or simply failed to notify them when the candidates were being selected.[47] This had important knock-on effects because, in the absence of trade union experience, local government service was a vital means for a woman to prove her credentials, and the fewer women who had a municipal record the fewer appeared as credible aspirants for parliamentary candidacies. As a result women found it difficult to overcome male control of the CLPs and some drew the conclusion that the party's constitution needed modification. As the women appointed to the NEC were not representative of the rank and file, they proposed in 1929 to allow women's sections to elect them directly; this was rejected by the NEC though women's representation was increased from four to five. Even worse, the original provision allowing CLPs to send a second, that is female, delegate to annual conference for 500 individual members was increased to 2,500. As few parties had such a large membership, this change, supported by Susan Lawrence, effectively put an end to the second delegates and thus to female representation. Labour conferences became largely all-male affairs at a time when at Conservative conferences women comprised 36 per cent (1927) and 38 per cent (1930).[48] As a result, by the 1930s gender issues had become marginalised in the Labour Movement and women were largely treated as hewers of wood and drawers of water for the party.

At the time, however, it was not so obvious that Labour had largely missed its opportunity. Although the other parties returned women to Parliament earlier, Labour appeared to catch up in the elections of 1923 and 1929. Women, were, of course, handicapped as aspiring candidates by the lack of union funding and by the need to demonstrate a record of loyalty to the movement. Some, however, managed to work the system. As an official of the General and Municipal Workers Union Margaret Bondfield did obtain official backing. Accustomed to working with men, she was not regarded by them as a threat because she avoided women's issues and cultivated a very maternal image – during

General Strike meetings she placidly continued her knitting – despite being unmarried. Yet Bondfield struggled to get into Parliament by fighting a tough three-way marginal at Northampton which she narrowly won in 1923 and lost in 1924 before being re-elected at Wallsend in 1926. Few women enjoyed even these advantages. Leah Manning won the backing of the National Union of Teachers and a safe seat at Bristol East in 1929, only to be ordered to vacate it at the last minute for Stafford Cripps. [49] The alternative was available only to women like Susan Lawrence who was sufficiently wealthy to offer herself as a full-time candidate and party worker to a constituency otherwise strapped for money. Lawrence fought East Ham in 1922, won in 1923 with only 36 per cent, lost in 1924, was returned at a by-election in 1926 and re-elected in 1929, still with only 42 per cent; after her defeat in 1931 she never returned to Parliament – a disappointing record for such an able woman.

Jennie Lee managed to get adopted for Lanark North despite being an ILP-er, a schoolteacher and only twenty-three. But she admitted 'I came from the right stable', a reference to her father, a miner, and her grandfather, an official in the Fife Miners Union.[50] Even so, the local miners resented her not least because she brought no resources to the organisation. This was a handicap for all ILP candidates who were also increasingly suspected of harbouring left-wing views. Some female aspirants, including Selina Cooper and Hannah Mitchell, failed to become candidates at all largely because they were seen as too radical or too feminist by a movement that placed high importance on discipline.[51] A notable exception to this rule was Ellen Wilkinson who suffered from being both a former Communist and a feminist sympathiser with a pre-war record of suffragist activity. But she managed to get backing from the NUDAW and contested Ashton-under-Lyne in 1923 before winning the highly marginal Middlesbrough East in 1924 with just 38.5 per cent of the vote. Wilkinson was constantly under pressure to play down her feminist loyalties and toe the party line if she wanted to emerge as Labour's leading female politician. Like most of the Labour women she felt she suffered the practical drawback of being unmarried. Hence her heartfelt cry: 'What I need is a wife.' Jennie Lee managed by importing her parents from Scotland to keep house for her and Nye Bevan. Several women emulated Conservative practice by contesting their husbands' constituencies in their absence – proof of wifely loyalty. Lady Noel-Buxton sat for North Norfolk when her husband became a peer in 1930, and for three months in 1929 Ruth Dalton kept Bishop Auckland warm for Hugh who had arranged a transfer from Peckham.

These expedients contributed to a modest tally of nine women MPs in 1929, though only thirty female candidates stood: Cynthia Mosley, Ellen Wilkinson, Jennie Lee, Margaret Bondfield, Susan Lawrence, Marion Phillips, Mary Agnes Hamilton, Dr Ethel Bentham and Edith Picton-Turbervill. Six of the nine were middle or upper class, a sign that the party was making effective, if limited, use of such women to tackle otherwise difficult constituencies. The potential was dramatically demonstrated at Stoke-on-Trent where Cynthia Mosley overturned an 8,000 majority and doubled the Labour vote from 13,000 to 26,000.[52] Edith Picton-Turbervill, a middle-class Churchwoman with no base in the Labour Movement, was selected for The Wrekin in preference to a trade unionist; by extending Labour's appeal to an agricultural and an ex-Liberal electorate she also pulled off a victory. However, like other women Picton-Turbervill found parliamentary life unrewarding. After accepting an invitation to lunch at Downing Street with the other women members she emerged disappointed as Ramsay MacDonald was reluctant even to discuss politics with women, preferring to confine the conversation to trivialities – the weather and his silver collection.[53]

Labour did, however, recognise how much women could strengthen the party ticket in the double-member boroughs. Although these constituencies contained a good deal of industry it usually proved difficult to win both seats and in places such as Preston Labour ran only single candidates in the five elections from 1918 to 1929. However, the party attempted to extend its appeal among voters by combining a standard male trade unionist with a middle-class woman in Norwich (Dorothy Jewson), Blackburn (Mary Agnes Hamilton), Sunderland (Marion Phillips) and Brighton (Mrs. R. Moore).[54] This was a deliberate tactic that Labour repeated subsequently in Sunderland (Leah Manning, 1935), Norwich (Lady Noel-Buxton, 1945) and Blackburn (Barbara Castle, 1945). In Blackburn, where the Weavers Union gave Labour 90 per cent of its money, no demands were made on Mrs Hamilton who was paired with T. H. Gill, president of the National Railway Clerks Association.[55] She ran ahead of Gill in three elections,

1924, 1929 and 1931, polling 1,500 more than him in 1929 because she won more split votes with Liberal and Conservative candidates. In Norwich Dorothy Jewson stood with W. R. Smith, an official of the Boot and Shoe Operatives. Both won in 1923, both lost in 1924 and Smith won in 1929 when he obtained more split votes than she did. The explanation may be that Jewson was by this time seen as a pronounced feminist who had promoted birth control and may have alienated some working-class voters.

The Sunderland experiment was the result of irritation among the women's sections throughout County Durham where the party's representation was virtually monopolised by the miners. They pushed for a female candidate in Sunderland though they could not offer more than £70 a year to support her. Marion Phillips donated another £50 towards the agent's salary. Since 1918 Labour had never won in Sunderland, but carried both seats in 1929 with Phillips 700 ahead of her male colleague. There was a move to extend the Durham scheme but in 1927–8 the party decided to impose financial quotas on all women's sections to support candidates, thereby effectively sidelining the idea.[56] As a result the party failed to make the most of its female candidates and, with the exception of Ellen Wilkinson, none of the leading women in the party were keen to take up the issue.

After 1926 the inability of the Baldwin government to reduce unemployment raised expectations about Labour's return to office. The prospects were complicated, however, by the prominence of Lloyd George who, after becoming Liberal leader in October 1926, embarked on collaborative work with J. M. Keynes, William Beveridge, B. S. Rowntree and Walter Layton to devise an impressive strategy for getting the unemployed back to work. This rendered the other parties' claims about the choice between capitalism and socialism redundant. The resulting report, Britain's Industrial Future, otherwise known as the Liberal Yellow Book, showed some common ground with the ILP but was unusually detailed and precise, involving state investment of £250 million in specified sectors of the economy; it was an altogether superior prospectus to Labour and the Nation. In an abbreviated version for the 1929 election, We can Conquer Unemployment, Lloyd George promised to cut unemployment by half a million within a year. As the Liberals gained a string of by-election victories at Conservative expense it began to look as though they were attracting the Tory defectors Labour needed.

Embarrassed by this, Labour offered an inconsistent response to Lloyd George. Some socialists simply dismissed his solutions as palliatives designed to shore up a failing system. But others complained that his schemes had been 'stolen without acknowledgement from Labour'. In the 1929 election the party took refuge in orthodox Treasury-style arguments to the effect that it was 'madcap finance' and would never work, while MacDonald ridiculed the campaign as stunts; one Birmingham candidate, Fred Londgen, reminded voters that 'the promise was like that of hanging the Kaiser, making the Germans squeal, and the statement about a country fit for heroes to live in'.[57] Despite this, many Labour supporters evidently assumed that their party would implement Lloyd George's policy if elected.

Labour emerged from the May 1929 election with 288 MPs, not far short of an overall majority, and with a much more diverse parliamentary party reflecting the new personnel; 172 of the new members had *not* been sponsored by trade unions compared with only ninety among the 191 elected in 1923, for example. Where did the extra 137 Labour members come from? For the first time the party's modern urban strongholds emerged clearly in the shape of five of the seven seats in Sheffield, four of four in Bradford, and four of five in Bristol, while a breakthrough was achieved in several hitherto backward cities, notably Liverpool with five victories in eleven seats and in Birmingham with six in thirteen. Labour also gained a footing in several mixed rural-industrial constituencies including South-West Norfolk, The Wrekin, Brecon and Radnor, Carmarthen and Frome. Regionally there were net gains of sixteen in Yorkshire, twenty-seven in the North-West, six in the North East, fourteen in the West Midlands, nine in Wales, ten in Scotland, eleven in the East Midlands, three in East Anglia, eight in the South, and six in the South-West. Above all, London produced twenty-six net gains including not only inner-city suburbs in Islington, St Pancras, Lambeth and Hammersmith, but also residential suburbs around the periphery such as Acton, Enfield, Leyton East and West, Walthamstow East and West, Hackney Central and South, Greenwich, Fulham West, Battersea North and South, Wandsworth Central and Tottenham South.

This regional spread left Labour looking like a national party for the first time. It had benefited from the backlash against the Conservatives' handling of the General Strike. Also, in the context of a government failing to manage the depression Labour was the chief beneficiary of Lloyd George's unemployment campaign because voters saw it as the most viable alternative. And now that the reaction against the Treaty of Versailles and the arms race was in full spate, Labour's commitment to disarmament and the League of Nations made it appealing to voters who had not supported it before. On the other hand, despite these advantages, Labour had still fallen short of a majority. Moreover, the electoral system had flattered the party, for it had won twenty-six more seats than the Conservatives despite winning just 37 per cent of the vote to their 38 per cent. Many narrow gains had been made in tight three-cornered contests on a minority of the vote. Why had Labour not done better? The underlying, structural reason lay in the major change in the composition of the electorate which worked to Labour's disadvantage; given the large number of close results, the female voters enabled the Conservatives to retain many marginal seats. The second explanation involves the circumstances of the election itself. Historians, following contemporary comment, have often assumed that the extra Liberal contests damaged the Conservatives. However, it was more complicated than this, for Lloyd George's compelling message about unemployment diverted some of those voters, disillusioned with Baldwin, who would otherwise have opted for Labour. The result was a Liberal poll of five million votes to eight million for each of the other two parties – a return to three-party politics. This was exactly what MacDonald had been keen to avoid, and in 1929 there could be no certainty that it would be temporary.

On 31 May MacDonald left Seaham, arriving at King's Cross to find a cheering crowd of 11,000 people who 'literally swept him off his feet'. But the triumph had left the prime minister as prickly as ever and his mood increasingly fatalistic. He found the business of forming a Cabinet more painful and exhausting than in 1924, complaining that 'one [colleague] all but fainted when I told him he could not get what he expected'. Personal relations between MacDonald, Henderson and Snowden were now extremely poor, and things did not improve when several senior figures insisted that it was impossible for MacDonald to combine the Foreign Office with the premiership as in 1924. Eventually Henderson became Foreign Secretary, Snowden chancellor, Clynes Home Secretary, Thomas Lord Privy Seal, Webb Colonial

Secretary, Bondfield Minister for Labour and the patriotic A. V. Alexander was judged sound enough to go to the Admiralty. As MacDonald refused to appoint Wheatley on account of his links with Maxton he reluctantly put Lansbury at Works as the token left-winger. The ex-Conservatives were represented by Sankey as Lord Chancellor and Parmoor as Lord President, while the former Liberals, Trevelyan, Noel Buxton and Wedgwood Benn took Education, Agriculture and the India Office respectively.

Apologists for the 1929 administration claimed that its room for manoeuvre was hopelessly restricted by the economic problems gathering around it. This, however, is debateable for Britain was far less affected by the depression than Germany and the United States in terms of unemployment or loss of industrial output. In June, when the new government took office, unemployment stood at 1.1 million: a problem but hardly a crisis. The crisis only developed as the unemployment figures rose inexorably to 1.5 million by January 1930, 1.9 million by June and 2.7 million by December, accompanied by bankruptcies and falling output. In this situation Labour supporters argued that capitalism was clearly doomed but that socialism was not attainable in the short term. However, between these two assumptions no way forward was found during the entire two and a half years of the government's life. Snowden simply ruled out every constructive option, arguing that major economic innovation and reconstruction was an unaffordable luxury. As things deteriorated it became clear that the prime minister had become too detached and was leaving Snowden to determine policy. In February 1930 he recognised this to the extent of establishing an Economic Advisory Council but it only offered another talking shop for experts.

The council was itself evidence of the original flaw in MacDonald's appointments. Unemployment became the responsibility of Jimmy Thomas as Lord Privy Seal, assisted by three junior ministers, Oswald Mosley, George Lansbury and Tom Johnston. Yet his department had no powers or resources, and Thomas, out of his depth in economics, proved ineffective. Relying heavily on his permanent secretary, Sir Horace Wilson, Thomas invariably dismissed suggestions with: 'I agree with 'Orace 'ere.' He resorted to the Victorian remedy for poverty by proposing emigration to the colonies and wasted time in Canada attempting to drum up interest in buying British exports. This proved to be a futile exercise not least because Canada and the other colonies were suffering too serious a collapse of their own industrial and agricultural economies to be able to bail Britain out; indeed by the 1930s more people were returning to Britain than emigrating.

Consequently, while Thomas and colleagues fiddled ineffectually and the costs of supporting the unemployed mounted inexorably, official policy became almost paralysed by the authority enjoyed by the Chancellor of the Exchequer. Caught in a Victorian time warp, Snowden insisted on balancing the budget, using any surplus to pay off the national debt, maintaining the currency and trying to promote world trade. He believed that questions such as credit and currency were far beyond the understanding and competence of Parliament, and few Labour MPs and ministers seemed disposed to challenge his judgement. Their deference towards orthodoxy was so great that in 1931 when the Cabinet was desperately wrestling with proposals to balance the budget by reducing expenditure, Snowden devoted £60 million to paying off the national debt. His retrenchment policy was designed to maintain confidence in the currency and thus avoid a devaluation of the pound, yet when a new government took office in 1931 Britain simply went off the gold standard and the pound was drastically devalued: 'no one told us we could do that', commented one disconsolate Labour minister.

Yet as the situation deteriorated, several political and economic options remained open to the Cabinet. As in 1924 there was no Liberal alliance but Lloyd George persistently negotiated with a view to offering the government a secure parliamentary majority in return for bold measures to tackle the depression. MacDonald's correspondence suggests that he played the Liberal leader shrewdly but cynically, keeping him engaged in negotiations without reaching conclusions so as to minimise the damage the Liberals could do. Throughout 1930 and 1931 he encouraged Vernon Hartshorn to involve the Liberals in talks about housing, agriculture and unemployment. 'The great thing is to keep in touch with them and so humour them,' he told Tom Johnston.[58] He was even prepared to appease the Liberals' desire for electoral reform by appointing a Speaker's Conference in 1930. MacDonald evidently contemplated countenancing the Alternative Vote for he considered an analysis by Labour's national agent on the likely effects of this reform. On the assumption that a third of voters

'Socialism: a system of government that will make poverty impossible':
a horse-drawn *Clarion* van, 1890s.

The Council of the Independent Labour Party, 1899: Ramsay MacDonald (*back left*), John Bruce Glasier (*front left*), Keir Hardie (*front second from left*) and Philip Snowden wearing 'wideawakes' (*front right*).

A rare photograph showing the slightly intimidating atmosphere in an Edwardian polling booth as a workingman is about to cast his vote.

Breakthrough: newly elected Labour MPs outside the House of Commons, 1906. (*Front from left*) Arthur Henderson, Ramsay MacDonald, Keir Hardie and David Shackleton.

Keir Hardie addresses
a suffragette rally
with Emmeline
Pankhurst under the
lions of Trafalgar
Square, May 1906.

George Lansbury
with constituents in
Bow and Bromley,
c.1910.

Ben Tillett, pre-war Labour MP for Salford, visits troops on the Western Front, 1917.

New recruit: Sir Oswald Mosley, Labour MP for Smethwick, poses at the annual conference in Brighton, September 1929.

Looking the part: the second Labour Government, 1929. (*Front from left*) Jimmy Thomas, Ramsay MacDonald, Arthur Henderson and (*back*) J.R. Clynes.

Cheerful delegates at the Labour Women's Conference at Swansea, 1936.

Ellen Wilkinson
MP relaxes with
constituents
on the Jarrow
March, 1936.

PARLIAMENTARY DIVISION OF DUDLEY

GENERAL ELECTION, 1945.

POLLING DAY, THURSDAY, 5TH JULY, 1945.

THE LABOUR CANDIDATE, Addresses

Lieut.-Col. George Wigg

Stands for:—

Beating the Japs

Work for all

Homes for the People

Social Security

A Square Deal for Children

A Sound Health Policy

A Solid and Enduring Peace

BRIEF BIOGRAPHY

Served in the last war as a volunteer. Joined the Regular Army as a Private in 1919, and served continuously until 1937. Rejoined the Army in 1940, and now holds the rank of Lieut.-Colonel. I have held several Staff appointments in A.A. and other Commands, and during my Army career have served in Turkey, Egypt, India, Iraq and Palestine. Recently I have served, in a specialist capacity, in East and West Africa. Won a scholarship from an elementary school to a Secondary School, and received further education in Oxford University Tutorial Classes. I have done extensive pioneer work in social reform and popular education (including Army Education), and know what it is to climb the educational ladder. I am an active Trade Unionist, having joined the National Union of Clerks' and Administrative Workers' in 1937, on leaving the Army.

YOUR EFFORTS WON THE WAR.
VOTE FOR WIGG TO WIN THE PEACE.

The election address of George Wigg at Dudley captures the essence of Labour's appeal at the end of the Second World War.

Labour volunteers at Ernest Bevin's campaign headquarters in Wandsworth, 1945.

Herbert Morrison meets employees at the London Passenger Transport Board in East Lewisham, 1945.

Clement Atlee with voters in Walthamstow in the 1951 general election.

Left-wing rebels elected to the National Executive Committee at the 1951 annual conference: (*from left*) Nye Bevan, Ian Mikardo, Tom Driberg and Barbara Castle.

At the famous Scarborough conference in 1960 an obviously depressed Hugh Gaitskell (*in glasses*) watches as Frank Cousins of the Transport and General Workers Union opposes official party policy on nuclear disarmament.

Michael Foot, Neil Kinnock and Tony Benn watch the crowds at the
Centenary Durham Miners Gala, 1983.

Planning the 1997 general election campaign: (*from left to right*) Peter Mandelson,
Margaret Beckett, Alastair Campbell, Tony Blair and Gordon Brown.

would not use their second preferences and that of the rest Conservatives would divide 60–40 for Liberal and Labour, Labour would divide 75–25 for Liberal and Conservative, and Liberals would divide 60–40 for Labour and Conservatives, the results in the 313 seats where no candidate had won a majority in 1929 would be modified; Labour would increase from 120 to 135, the Liberals from 41 to 88, and the Conservatives would fall from 152 to 67.[59] While this modest rise would have put Labour within reach of an overall majority, it would also have consolidated the Liberal position and possibly boosted their first preference votes. Fred Pethick-Lawrence advised that the Alternative Vote would 'encourage weak-kneed electors who are anti-Conservative (and today vote Labour because they see the Liberals have no chance) to give first choice to Liberals and second to Labour'.[60] The prime minister accepted this logic, preferring to continue to allow the single-member system to squeeze the Liberal vote. The consolidation of Lloyd George's advance in 1929 might have put an independent Labour majority beyond reach and ensured that a progressive majority 'would always have to be . . . a Coalition with a sharing of offices, or a Government such as we have at the present moment depending upon the support of the Liberals'.[61] MacDonald was therefore content for the bill incorporating the Alternative Vote to become bogged down in the House of Lords where the Tories could be relied upon to emasculate it.

While these private talks proceeded MacDonald's colleagues grew increasingly restive. In January 1930 Oswald Mosley had brought things to a head by presenting the Cabinet with a memorandum of proposals designed to reduce unemployment by focusing on the domestic market rather than exports, promoting self-sufficiency by imposing tariffs, raising the level of purchasing power by £200 million investment in road-building and other projects, and establishing a state finance corporation to invest and restructure industry; the strategy was to be managed by a small War Cabinet under the prime minister. This met with total obstruction from the Treasury as well as from the transport minister, Herbert Morrison, who had his own road programme and declined to be pushed faster. 'Clearly Mosley suffers somewhat from Lloyd George's complaint: the road complex . . . road work can assist but it cannot possibly be a principle [sic] cure of unemployment,' he wrote.[62] In any case Snowden already thought Morrison was spending too

much money although only £10 million of the £95 million allocated
for public works schemes had been spent.

Yet although MacDonald had begun to lose confidence in Snowden,
he was not ready to risk overruling him, and in May the cabinet
predictably rejected Mosley's memorandum whereupon he resigned;
though Lansbury and Johnston agreed with him they declined to follow
him. Most MPs and trade unionists, though increasingly despondent,
felt unable to offer an intellectual challenge to Treasury orthodoxy.
Many reassured themselves with the belief that schemes like Mosley's
would only prolong the life of capitalism which must be drawing to
its close. 'It is not Socialism that is on trial,' as Walton Newbold put
it. 'It is Capitalism.'[63] As a result Mosley won just twenty-nine votes
against 210 at a meeting of the parliamentary party on 22 May.

However, by the summer of 1930 party morale was beginning to
disintegrate both in Parliament and in the constituencies. Labour lost
seats in by-elections at Fulham West, Shipley, Sunderland and Ashton-
under-Lyne; at Gateshead a Labour majority of 16,700 was slashed to
just 1,400. Labour's share of the vote in municipal elections in twelve
Yorkshire boroughs dropped from 50 per cent in 1929 to 41 per cent
in 1930. These are indications that it was the party's performance in
office after 1929 rather than simply the 'betrayal' of MacDonald in
1931 that eventually produced a collapse of popular support.[64]
Meanwhile, in April 1930 the ILP members asserted their independence from the PLP when their conference decided that its MPs must
accept ILP policy; only candidates who agreed to this would be
nominated in future. Although only eighteen MPs accepted this ruling,
the decision was another step towards severance from the Labour
Party.

Despite this discontent, MacDonald saw off his critics at the party
conference at Llandudno in October by resorting to the familiar line
of argument: 'So, my friends, we are not on trial; it is the system
under which we live. It has broken down . . . it has broken down everywhere, as it was bound to break down.' This was sufficient to defeat
a motion of censure on the government by Maxton, but after a debate
on inviting the NEC to examine Mosley's memorandum the proposal
was only narrowly rejected by 1.25 million to 1.04 million. The delegates also signified their dissatisfaction by voting Mosley on to the
NEC for the constituency section. If Mosley had been patient he would

have been in an immensely strong position after the collapse of the government in 1931, but he was now becoming convinced that neither Conservative nor Labour parties had the competence or grip to cope with the depression, and in February 1931 he impetuously resigned from the party along with several other MPs, Cynthia Mosley, John Strachey, W. J. Brown, Robert Forgan and Oliver Baldwin, who formed the New Party. In March another minister, Trevelyan, resigned, attacking MacDonald for his failures. By the summer, even Snowden, aware that proposals were being mooted to elevate him to the House of Lords, was contemplating resignation.

However, during July rebels and loyalists alike were overtaken by the gathering financial crisis. The projected deficit in government spending had swollen to £120 million, so large that financiers, fearing a devaluation of the currency, were withdrawing funds from sterling. In this situation the Cabinet set itself to reassure the Bank of England and the foreign holders of sterling by finding enough cuts to eliminate the deficit; a total of £78 million was found including reductions in unemployment benefit and transitional benefit. Initially ministers seemed willing to swallow this, but on 20 August a TUC subcommittee comprising Ernest Bevin, Arthur Hayday, Walter Citrine, Arthur Pugh and A. G. Walkden met MacDonald, Snowden, Henderson, Thomas and Graham. Flatly refusing to accept cuts in unemployment benefits, they argued that reduced wages for teachers and police 'would be the signal for a wage-cutting campaign in trades and industries generally'.[65] They questioned Snowden's insistence on devoting £60 million to paying off the national debt and rejected the endless and demoralising policy of deflation. Challenged by Thomas as to what they would do in the crisis, Citrine replied that they were not convinced the situation was 'quite as desperate as was alleged'. Influenced by this reaction the Cabinet again voted in favour of the cuts on 23 August but by a perilously narrow margin of twelve to nine. The pivotal player in this was Henderson who had originally sided with Snowden but realised how badly TUC opposition would divide and damage the movement. As on other critical occasions in 1914 and 1917 Henderson showed himself much more alive to the unity and morale of the movement than his leader. MacDonald regarded the unions merely as a sectional interest whose influence ought never to be allowed to jeopardise Labour's role as a national party. But by this stage his relations with Henderson were so bad that he found it impossible to recognise his concerns, dismissing him as cowardly and opportunistic in giving way to pressure.

Yet as MacDonald recognised that a twelve–nine split was too even to be sustainable, he offered the king his resignation, expecting to go into opposition. However, the king did not take the natural step of inviting his alternative prime minister to form a government. As Baldwin was abroad at the crucial moment he first saw Herbert Samuel, the acting Liberal leader, who urged the formation of a temporary National government. In a remarkable exercise of royal power George V, who liked MacDonald, thereupon invited him to continue as prime minister with a three-party National government. This was naturally flattering to a prime minister increasingly irritated by and isolated from his colleagues. But in agreeing to join a coalition MacDonald completely mismanaged his party. The decision was bound to come as a shock, but if presented as a purely temporary expedient prior to a new election it need not have been wholly damaging. David Kirkwood, no friend of the prime minister, admitted that MacDonald still retained the loyalty of the MPs and if he had taken the trouble to consult the party about the new government, rather than present it with a fait accompli, 'most of them would have agreed'. Instead, he dispatched Lord Sankey, who, as a relatively recent recruit, knew little of the movement. 'He made a poor show, talking to us like a benevolent old gentleman who carried peppermints in his pocket to give to the poor workers.'[66] It was the blunder of an arrogant leader who had lost touch with his party.

MacDonald was clearly surprised at the extent of his failure to carry his colleagues with him. He tried to emasculate Henderson, his likely successor as party leader, by offering him a peerage, but was rebuffed. He attempted to persuade several junior ministers including Shinwell, Cripps and Morrison, to join the National government, disingenuously assuring Shinwell that 'the Government that has been formed is not a Coalition but a co-operation between individuals who are banded together to avoid the disaster. No parties are involved in it, and as soon as the country gets on an even keel again the Government will cease to exist.' But he spoilt the effect by his patronising remark: 'I know it is hard to understand this.'[67] Much to his annoyance they turned him down. Only four ministers, including Snowden, Thomas and Sankey, agreed to serve in the National government along with thirteen Labour backbenchers. Despite soothing reassurances by Henderson to the effect that the party was 'ready to receive Mr MacDonald back again' he had been decisively rejected.[68] The party chose Henderson as the new leader and in September the NEC ruled that all members of the National government 'automatically ceased to be members of the Labour Party'. All over the country Labour supporters turned MacDonald's photograph to the wall or ripped it into pieces. Even in Seaham the constituency party asked him to resign as MP which he angrily refused to do; he insisted he had not left the party, but that his colleagues had deserted him.

Before long MacDonald's reassuring words proved to be hollow. The National government had ostensibly been formed on the basis that it would last a few weeks to take emergency measures to defend the pound before splitting up to allow the parties to fight an election separately. None of this materialised. Britain went off the gold standard and the pound was devalued. The new ministers began to fear the consequences of taking unpopular decisions. In particular the Conservatives saw an opportunity to introduce protectionism but, fearing another electoral rejection, decided it would be wiser to get an election out of the way first. Thus, by the autumn opinion had crystallised around an early election which was held on 14 October.

In the circumstances a Conservative victory was inevitable with or without a National government, but the scale of Labour's defeat astounded contemporaries. The party found itself in disarray especially in view of Henderson's inept leadership. As he had originally supported the measures now taken by the National government he could not put together a credible rationale for his opposition to it at the election. Labour candidates endeavoured to treat the crisis that had engulfed them as 'evidence of decaying capitalism' rather than government incompetence. In Leyton Reginald Sorensen used what became a popular argument: 'Bankers dictated to the Government of this country as to how its people should live.'[69] But with government propagandists asking 'Will you trust the Quitters?' the party could not shake off the charge that it had run away from the crisis. Labour's claims were blown away by its own former leaders, notably Snowden who, in a radio broadcast, denounced the Labour programme as fantastic and impracticable: 'This is not Socialism. It is Bolshevism run

mad.' Most damagingly he warned that a Labour government would
raid voters' personal savings. 'He has done so much to win us the
election,' admitted Chamberlain. Along with the Liberals, Labour
hoped that they would minimise any electoral damage by playing the
free-trade card, but for the first time it failed to work.

In the aftermath of the election a myth arose to the effect that
Labour support had held firm in 1931 and that it had been defeated
by tricks or by a conspiracy of the capitalist parties. In 1929 four in
every ten Labour seats had been won on a minority vote, whereas in
1931 most contests involved only two candidates; the number of Liberals
fell from 513 to 173 and three-fifths of the former Liberal vote went to
the National government. But this does not fully account for the result;
only fifty-two Labour members survived, including five ILP-ers, and
all Cabinet ministers except Lansbury lost their seats. The party polled
30.5 per cent of the vote reflecting the loss of two million votes, a
huge withdrawal of support. In forty-nine comparable Labour–
Conservative contests Labour's vote fell by a quarter between 1929
and 1931. The disaster was almost uniform across the country even
in heavily working-class regions; in Durham–Tyneside, for example,
fourteen of Labour's sixteen seats were lost. The only significant
concentration of Labour victories occurred in South Wales where
eleven seats were retained, many by large majorities. Facing 556
National government MPs the party appeared to be back to the
position it had occupied in 1918.

9

'Reversal of Parts': From Crisis to Popular Front, 1932–1939

In the conventional historiography the 1930s – the decade dominated by National governments, mass unemployment, appeasement and the descent into fascism – represents the nadir of Labour's history. The emphasis has been on MacDonald's betrayal, controversies with the Communists and the ILP, tactical errors and the fruitless pursuit of noble, but doomed, causes like the Popular Front. From this dismal catalogue the movement was decisively rescued by the Second World War. In fact, the 1930s proved to be a crucial formative phase in which the foundations for the post-1945 success were laid as Labour evolved from the original sectional pressure group into a national force, and belatedly found its voice as the British national party. This positive view has not generally been recognised partly because the underlying advances have been interpreted as failures or simply been overlooked, but also because the movement's evolution was not consistently in one direction; for example, while Labour defined its left-wing thinking more clearly, it also consolidated its right-wing tendencies, achieving in the process a synthesis that was to underpin its success in the second half of the century. While the Second World War undoubtedly accentuated the advance, it was not the origins of it.

Inevitably the collapse of MacDonald's government in 1931 provoked a reaction, leaving the movement suspicious of dominant leaders and of anyone likely to manipulate it for personal aggrandisement. Unfortunately, this enhanced tribalism was profoundly unhelpful for it militated against the logic that required Labour to keep reaching beyond its heartlands into wider society. The loose federal structure that was admirably designed to incorporate new supporters into the system now appeared as a source of weakness. During the 1920s Labour had steadily been evolving into a national party but at the 1931 election it seemed

to have shrunk back to its origins as a trade union party limited to a
handful of industrial regions. The combination of electoral failure and
an uninspired right-leaning parliamentary party inevitably generated
friction with the left over socialism, parliamentary methods and the
movement for a United Front and a Popular Front. More immediately,
the deteriorating relations with the ILP swiftly reached a climax. Five
ILP MPs, Jimmy Maxton, George Buchanan, John McGovern, David
Kirkwood and Dick Wallhead, had survived the electoral catastrophe
in 1931, but already the ILP had become a party within a party by
requiring candidates to sign a pledge of loyalty to its policy and to defy
the Labour whips if elected. At a special conference at Bradford in July
1932 a proposal to disaffiliate from the Labour Party was carried by 241
to 142. This decision proved to be less significant than it would have
been a decade earlier because Labour relied much less on the ILP for
individual members. Of the 653 ILP branches, 203 collapsed during 1932
alone, and membership fell from 16,773 in 1932 to 7,166 by 1934, many
having simply joined the Labour Party.

Nonetheless the schism was damaging not just because of the
infighting and diversion of effort it generated. The ILP had traditionally offered an apprenticeship in street-corner campaigning to young
men and women that was not as easily available through the senior
party. By the 1930s the movement had become encumbered by a huge
bureaucracy at local level often comprising the constituency party, ward
committees, women's sections, miners' lodges, union branches and
trades councils. Activists, for whom an official position in one of these
bodies represented a lifetime's achievement, devoted themselves to
collecting minutes, amending and enforcing rules, nominating delegates, and above all to retaining control of the machine on which their
authority and status depended. Many middle-aged men remained
entrenched as minor office-holders until removed by infirmity or death.
As a result, though only thirty years old, Labour was already becoming
an old man's party. In this context young activists often looked like
trouble because they were left-wing firebrands or simply rivals for office.
The fact that they enjoyed greater scope in smaller and newer organisations partly explains the appeal of the Communist Party whose
membership increased from 2,300 in 1930 to 9,000 by 1932. It then fell
back before growing again to 11,500 in 1936 and to 18,000 in 1938.[1] This
was still modest but it included many activists.

Suspicion towards the Communists and the ILP also inhibited Labour from putting itself at the head of the interwar protest movements. From 1922 onwards a series of hunger marches were organised and new organisations including the National Unemployed Workers Movement sprang up to mobilise men outside the trade unions. But the Labour leaders kept them at arm's length in the belief that they represented anti-parliamentary, and thus anti-Labour, organisations. This conceded scope to Communists to lead the protests but whether the rank and file were really subversive is doubtful. One contemporary observer of the local contingent in Blackburn as they prepared to march in October 1932 described them as 'a good-natured, law-abiding lot. I doubt there was a revolutionary among them.' He recorded one explaining: 'We're going off to tell t'King that we need work and food. Once 'e knows it will be put right, there's no doubt about it.'[2] The famous Jarrow March of 1936 was notable more for its respectability than its subversiveness. Alcohol was banned, half the marchers were ex-servicemen, many wore their British Legion badges, and 80 per cent were married men; Special Branch failed to find any Communists among them, the one known Communist having been excluded by the organisers.[3] But the Labour leaders did their best to deter CLPs from assisting the marchers and when they arrived at Westminster they sent them off on a Thames steamboat while the petition was being presented in order to avoid risking a scene in the Commons. As a result the Jarrow March was a non-political affair – that was the flaw. Labour never really gave leadership to such movements or tried to use them to mobilise a wider coalition against the National government.

Labour also suffered from the less conspicuous drain of activists to the *right* in the aftermath of 1931. Two Labour MPs, Dr Robert Forgan and John Beckett, actually joined Mosley in the British Union of Fascists in 1932. They were less eccentric than they might seem. Former ILP-ers such as John Scanlon and W. J. Leaper also participated in the BUF. Moreover, studies of rank-and-file fascists have revealed that many came from a background in the Labour Party, the ILP, the Communist Party, the National Unemployed Workers Movement, or the trade unions.[4] One Lancashire fascist explained: 'Ex-Communists made the best active members. They were not nervous of street work, or of opposition. It was not unusual for Communists to come to our meetings with the intention of causing a riot, and then to stay behind to fill in an enrolment form of BU membership.'[5] This offers a corrective to the common assumption that fascism was unable to expand because the working class was already absorbed into the Labour Movement. On the contrary, the huge fall in union membership since 1920 had left most of the working class outside its organisational framework, and the increase in the number of BUF branches to 500 in 1934 created plenty of scope for ambitious young men to assume leadership roles.

There is also a credible ideological explanation for migration into right-wing organisations. Working-class fascists explained the attraction of fascism in terms of the combination of 'Socialism plus Patriotism' it offered them. 'I suppose it would have been easy to have joined the Communist Party,' admitted one East End fascist. 'But I found that the more patriotic party had a lot more appeal to me . . . You could have gone one way or the other.'[6] By the 1930s such men had become disillusioned with Labour, feeling that it offered no effective defence against the ravages of capitalism or prospect of radical social change. By contrast Mosley offered a compelling interventionist strategy for tackling the depression along with a bracing defence of empire, monarchy and nationalism. The popular appeal of a socialism-plus-patriotism formula should not be in doubt as a variation on the theme eventually became central to Labour's own success during and after the Second World War.

Meanwhile, in the aftermath of the 1931 split the Parliamentary Labour Party had little by way of inspiring leadership to offer the movement. With almost all senior figures swept away in the election, the party resorted to the seventy-two-year-old George Lansbury as leader with Clement Attlee as his deputy. Along with Stafford Cripps, the only other surviving minister, this triumvirate did its best to represent Labour views on every topic from the Opposition front bench. They co-operated well and had a reassuring effect on the party. Lansbury enjoyed considerable popularity as a man with no obvious political ambition or interest in social climbing who had always been devoted to the movement, but, as a rebel himself, was tolerant towards dissent. On the other hand the triumvirate was short of ideas and less effective in reaching out to the wider public. By 1935 Lansbury's attachment to old-fashioned, Nonconformist-pacifist thinking had begun to marginalise him as the party responded to the burgeoning problems of appeasement and rearmament. In any case, while the triumvirate largely kept things together, it proved to be of far less significance than three other leaders, none currently in Parliament – Herbert Morrison, Ernest Bevin and Hugh Dalton – who were to be instrumental in repositioning Labour during the 1930s and determining its role after 1945.

Gradually the victims of 1931 made their way back. Arthur Greenwood was elected at Wakefield in 1932, though his predilection for drink undermined his effectiveness. Henderson returned at Clay Cross in 1933 though he was now discredited and out of touch. Not until the 1935 general election did Morrison (Hackney South), Dalton (Bishop Auckland) and A. V. Alexander (Sheffield Attercliffe) recapture their seats. Among the younger men, Aneurin Bevan had retained Ebbw Vale in 1931 and Jim Griffiths won Llanelli in 1936. A few women were also elected: Ellen Wilkinson at Jarrow in 1935, Agnes Hardie at Glasgow Springburn in 1937, Dr Edith Summerskill at Fulham West in 1938, and Jennie Adamson at Dartford in 1938. But it proved a slow process and inevitably the parliamentary party appeared a marginal element for several years after 1931. It also had to resolve some awkward questions about the relationship between the industrial and political wings of the movement. In a speech in 1932 Walter Citrine reflected the irritation among the unions that they had lost influence since 1918 both in government and at party conferences; lack of consultation by the Cabinet in both 1924 and 1929–31 had been 'accentuated by the personal prejudices of the late Labour Prime Minister'.[7] Citrine insisted that the unions could not be confined to industrial issues and excluded from broader political ones. The best means of conciliating them lay in improving coordination through the National Joint Council which comprised the NEC, the PLP and the TUC. Its monthly meetings under alternating chairmen kept the three elements in touch and allowed the appointment of subcommittees focusing on specific policy areas.[8] In 1934 this body was renamed the National Council of Labour. It played a useful role especially in reassuring the unions whose leaders had become frustrated by what they saw as the party's vague, unfocused policy.

The unions were also crucial in countering the wider response to the events of 1931 which could easily have triggered a reaction against conventional parliamentary methods for achieving socialism. In some quarters dire implications were indeed drawn. According to Stafford Cripps the collapse of MacDonald's Cabinet offered 'the clearest demonstration of the power of capitalism to overthrow a properly elected Government by extra-Parliamentary means'. It was argued that even if Labour won an outright majority the bankers would gang up to destabilise a future Labour government. Cripps therefore roused party conferences by proposing that the immediate act of the next government should be to take emergency powers to overcome the resistance of the House of Lords and the Civil Service. Harold Laski, a professor at the London School of Economics who got elected to the NEC in 1937, warned that democracy had been allowed to develop while capitalism was expanding and successful, but now that the system was in decline capitalists were ready to extinguish it in favour of fascism.

However, few saw things in such apocalyptic terms. Cripps' oratory was a useful safety valve for conference delegates but he failed to detach the movement from its commitment to parliamentary methods. Ernest Bevin regarded Cripps and Laski with contempt as typical middle-class intellectuals, unbalanced and unreliable. 'The difference between the intellectuals and the trade unions', he told G. D. H. Cole, 'is this: You have no responsibility, you can fly off at a tangent as the wind takes you. We, however, must be consistent and we have a great amount of responsibility.' Bevin's remarks seem restrained by comparison with Dalton who robustly dismissed his fellow intellectuals, notably Laski, Cole and the historian A. L. Rowse, as 'these semi-crocks, diabetics and undersized Semites'.[9]

In this light Labour's remarkable failure to adopt a radical, or even a reformist, stance towards constitutional questions during the 1930s becomes explicable. Some slight claims for the party's reformism have been advanced on the strength of the minor innovations implemented by Morrison after 1945.[10] However, such evidence only corroborates the wider point about the marginal role of reform in the party's history, for Morrison's measures were simply designed to improve the efficiency with which a legislative programme could be implemented – not to change the system. Indeed, Morrison's own book *Government and Parliament* (1954) was redolent with conservatism and complacency about the British system, though even he was not as fulsome as Jimmy Thomas who expressed his 'gratitude that the constitution enables the engine cleaner of yesterday to be the minister of today. That constitution, so broad, so wide, so democratic, must be preserved, and the Empire which provides it must be maintained.'[11] What requires explanation is why radical reform did not become a priority for Labour even after 1931. Despite paying lip service to the idea of a bankers' ramp, leading politicians and trade unionists recognised that both Labour governments had been casualties of their own defects rather than victims of the system or of reactionary forces. Given a parliamentary majority and a clear set of policies, a Labour government was viable. Even Laski accepted that the British system of government, characterised by centralisation, a strong executive and traditions of secrecy, was especially well suited to the implementation of a programme by a government that knew its mind; this is why Fabians had always regarded it with such confidence.

In fact, in some ways, Labour became *more* orthodox and conservative in its attitude towards existing institutions during the 1930s rather than less. For example, confidence in the electoral system, which grossly under-represented the party in 1931, and even in the 1935 election, was not shaken. Indeed, electoral reform died for several decades to come. Another striking symptom was the gradual demise of the sympathy for Scottish and Welsh parliaments that had been evident up to the early 1920s. Its champions had been the Clydesiders who subscribed to traditional Radical ideas about London as the seat of wealth and conservatism; they were as much anti-English as anti-capitalist. However, as the ILP-ers became more marginal so did devolutionism. Devolutionists such as Roland Muirhead had already left Labour, harbingers of the later drift to the Scottish National Party. Even the economic depression, which hit Wales and Scotland very hard, failed to generate support for local parliaments. On the contrary, socialists considered them an obstacle to the implementation of a socialist programme, preferring central direction and planning from London. Some of the Welsh MPs elected later in the 1930s, including Jim Griffiths and David Grenfell, supported devolution or at least a Secretary of State for Wales. However, Welsh Labour had reservations about national sentiment as backward and reactionary, especially younger socialists such as Aneurin Bevan. Though notably Welsh in English eyes, Bevan was a distinctly cosmopolitan figure who lacked sympathy with Welsh identity and separatist thinking and scorned local nationalism as a divisive force that would merely isolate the people from the mainstream of British life; he believed that the economic problems afflicting Wales were exactly the same as those in the rest of Britain.[12] As a result, advocacy of parliaments for Scotland and Wales dwindled during the 1930s leaving Labour a predominantly

Unionist party, at least as much as the Conservatives. Indeed, in Scotland, where the Conservatives absorbed much of Liberalism, they were arguably more sympathetic to devolution than Labour.

There was also a tacit agreement between the two parties to avoid controversy over the House of Lords in this period. On the one hand the Tory leaders reneged on their promise, given in 1911, to reform the House by restoring its powers. On the other hand, Labour dropped its pledge to abolish the upper chamber in 1928. Although critics such as Laski continued to denounce the House of Lords as 'an indefensible anachronism' and argued 'its ending is alone compatible with the objective of Socialism', the party was inexorably accommodating itself to the status quo.[13] Elderly Labour politicians viewed the hereditary element pragmatically on the basis that in the short term the party must be represented there and in the longer term they could retire there. Consequently, when party conference debated the upper chamber in 1935 it failed to call for abolition but 'deprecates the acceptance by members of the Party of titles or honours other than those which a Labour Government finds necessary for the furtherment of its own business in Parliament'.[14] Even delegates who argued that 'You are in the Labour Movement because you believe in the ultimate classless society', recognised this view was not consistent with the honours system. They attempted to make the NEC responsible for setting rules governing how far Labour should accept honours from capitalist governments and participate in ceremonial functions. But the NEC disparaged their concern as a 'footling business' not worthy of its time; the main object was for Labour to accept its duty to the electorate and be properly represented in all institutions. As prime minister after 1945 Attlee created no fewer than eighty-two hereditary peerages as well as eight promotions in the peerage, and he symbolised Labour's stance by taking the customary earldom himself.[15]

To ignore this trend in Labour's treatment of constitutional issues is to misrepresent both the party and the period. Had Labour adopted a radical approach, British domestic history would have been quite different in the post-1918 era; it would have resembled the late Victorian and Edwardian period when controversies involving constitutional issues formed a staple element in Liberal–Conservative rivalry. It is no accident that the demise after the war of the Liberals, for whom political reform was a congenital interest, effectively ended this tradition for some decades. Neither Labour nor the Conservatives treated constitutional matters as a priority, preferring to accept the status quo if it generated the desired results.

The consensus between the two parties was most strikingly demonstrated during the crisis surrounding the abdication of Edward VIII in December 1936. Faced with a request from the king to introduce legislation to grant him a morganatic marriage designed to allow him to marry Mrs Simpson without making her queen, the prime minister, Stanley Baldwin, adamantly refused. But he boxed the king in by taking care to consult Attlee as Leader of the Opposition. Attlee and his colleagues adopted the conventional view that a royal marriage was not a private and personal matter but a public and political one on which the king must accept the advice of his ministers. Consequently Labour indicated it would refuse to form an alternative ministry if Edward dismissed Baldwin. 'Mrs Simpson was out of the question,' commented Attlee, closely reflecting the British Establishment mentality. 'And I was sure the Commonwealth would take the same view.'[16] Hugh Dalton expressed the typical upper-class moral view that the king should simply make a conventional marriage while maintaining Mrs Simpson as his mistress, but he took it for granted that the relationship would not be tolerated by ordinary people; Baldwin, he thought, would be backed by 'the formidable and pervasive Puritanism of the electorate'. We now know that Dalton and Attlee were as out of touch with public opinion as Baldwin. Angry letters poured in to the *News Chronicle*, the *Daily Mirror*, the *Daily Mail* and the *Daily Express* supporting the royal marriage on the grounds that Edward VIII was a modern monarch who was trying to do the decent thing by marrying his 'sweetheart' rather than importing a foreign princess. As a result the dutiful *Daily Herald* was the only popular newspaper to back Baldwin over the abdication. In the process Labour threw away its best opportunity for splitting the National government and outflanking it in the country, for Baldwin could hardly have avoided resignation if the king had stood firm. The whole episode was a signal indication of Labour's orthodoxy in the 1930s.

An equally striking symptom of the consensus between Labour and the Conservatives between the wars lay in imperial questions. This is not surprising since all middle-aged politicians had grown up in an era when the popularity of monarchy, patriotism and empire had been at its height, while Attlee and the upper-class recruits had been educated at schools such as Haileybury and Winchester that promoted imperial service as a noble ideal. However, the idea seems inconsistent with received assumptions about Labour as essentially anti-imperial and about the working class as being less enthusiastic about empire than the middle and upper classes.[17] No doubt the movement contained some voluble critics of empire, notably Keir Hardie whose visits to India before 1914 had embarrassed the government, and George Lansbury, Reginald Sorensen, Arthur Creech Jones and Fenner Brockway who saw British rule as exploitative and advocated self-determination for subject peoples. However, they represented an articulate minority, not the mainstream. This was certainly the interpretation of interwar *Conservative* leaders who had been impressed by the patriotism and imperialism shown by British workingmen during the war. After 1918 Baldwin concluded that there was no need to engage Labour in controversies over imperial issues of the sort that had dominated pre-1914 debates with the Liberals, for broad agreement was now possible.

It is usually forgotten that Labour's attitude to empire reflected the perspective adopted by contemporaries. Whereas later generations saw empire in terms of race and nationalism, the late Victorian, Edwardian and interwar movement was much less preoccupied with the problems of alien rule over Asian and African people because it thought of the British Empire predominantly in terms of the colonies of white settlement. Most pre-war Labour politicians who had visited Australia, New Zealand, Canada and South Africa believed the colonies had a lot to offer Britain through commercial development and as an inspiration for the domestic labour movement. British socialists admired the white Australian labour movement, appreciated the support sometimes given by its trade unionists to British strikers, and saw it as a model as early as 1907 when the Australian Labor Party formed a government in Western Australia. William Pember Reeves, a minister in New Zealand, actively propagated the idea that his country offered European workers a model for a progressive social policy. New Zealand pioneered state old-age pensions and compulsory arbitration procedures in industrial disputes in the 1890s, while the Australian state of Victoria adopted wages boards and minimum wages before 1914.[18]

Consequently it would be erroneous to assume that in the 1920s Labour simply inherited the anti-imperial stance of Radical Liberalism.

In effect there was a convergence of views among former Tories with imperial experience, including William Stapleton Royce MP, Major Graham David Pole MP, and Lord Chelmsford, and pragmatic, patriotic working-class leaders such as Ernest Bevin, A. V. Alexander and Jimmy Thomas who regarded the colonies as an essential source of food supplies, raw materials, exports and employment for British workers. When Alexander visited Canada as part of the Empire Parliamentary Association in 1926 he sought to promote British exports, and studied Canadian attempts to outlaw combines and price-fixing: 'In the light of this legislation and administrative example from a young and virile Dominion, ought we not to be buckling on our political armour to secure similar powers in the British Parliament?'[19] Such thinking had led Jimmy Thomas to Canada in 1929–31 seeking emigration opportunities to relieve unemployment. The election of a Labour government in New Zealand in 1937 offered a morale boost to British CLPs who catalogued its achievements under such headlines as 'How Labour Rules': minimum wages, public works, a forty-hour week, nationalisation of the Reserve Bank, guaranteed prices for dairy farmers, rent controls and free daily milk for schoolchildren.[20]

This hard-headed, materialistic approach was not inconsistent with some of the idealistic official statements of Labour policy. In 1920 the annual conference adopted resolutions favouring democratic self-determination for Egypt and India, and in 1921 it endorsed an ILP resolution to the effect that imperialism 'tends to perpetuate the reign of capitalism, not only by increasing the power of wealth, but by neglecting the needs of the Home market, and leaving the natural resources of our own country undeveloped'.[21] Yet even Lansbury accepted that 'there is no reason for breaking up the British Empire any more than there is a reason for smashing our national institutions'.[22] The party also drew a distinction between Indians, who had a well-developed nationalist movement, and Africans, who were not considered fit for self-government in the foreseeable future; as Colonial Secretary, Sidney Webb thought Kenya, for example, would take a hundred years to prepare for self-government. As a result, during the 1930s Labour adopted a paternalistic 'Trusteeship' philosophy towards Africa designed to prevent capitalism from exploiting vulnerable people and to ensure that Britain acted as a guardian of native rights rather than handing them over to white minorities.[23]

The element of consensus was strikingly manifested in connection with India. In 1929 the Conservative viceroy, Lord Irwin, announced that it was Britain's aim to grant India dominion status, and to this end a commission under Sir John Simon and later a Round Table Conference were appointed to consider the extension of democratic rights to Indians. MacDonald and his Secretary of State, William Wedgwood Benn, endorsed this strategy. Commenting on the Round Table Conference in 1931 Graham Pole commended the Indian princes, whose assent the authorities were keen to win, and pointedly ignored Gandhi and the Congress who were refusing to participate.[24] Subsequently the National government pressed ahead with sweeping reforms, designed to give Indians full self-government at provincial level, which finally became law in 1935. This reform policy generated a bitter controversy – but the debate was conducted within the Conservative Party, between Churchill and the leadership, not between Labour and the Conservatives. In effect Labour had become part of the consensus that led by successive instalments of reforms to Indian independence in 1947.

Constitutional and imperial issues were significant indicators of Labour's role in the political spectrum, but for the time being they assumed marginal importance beside economics. The failures of 1929–31 had decisively discredited MacDonald's faith in a gradualist approach to socialism, but what was to put be in its place? At the party conference in October 1932 Charles Trevelyan carried a familiar motion instructing a future Labour government to promulgate socialist legislation immediately on taking office and to stand or fall by its principles. But the leaders accepted that something more tangible and substantial was now required. Recognising the need to convert the public to socialism, left-wing authors published a series of books and tracts on the subject. John Strachey, author of *The Coming Struggle for Power* (1932), *The Nature of Capitalist Crisis* (1935) and *The Theory and Practice of Socialism* (1936) was rightly regarded as the most effective populariser of socialism. His 1938 pamphlet *Why You Should Be A Socialist* sold 250,000 copies at threepence a time. Strachey's style was so readable and jargon-free that his publications were reputedly read by middle-class ladies under the hairdryer! Although Strachey's critique was seen as Marxist it actually contained a large measure of Keynesianism. As capitalism was afflicted by inadequate demand arising from the impoverishment of labour and the counterproductive attempt to boost profits by reducing wages, Strachey advocated redistributive measures to increase the income of those who had a high marginal propensity to consume and to use the banks to promote investment without damaging the profit rate.

Yet despite his role as a propagandist, Strachey had only a marginal impact on Labour's policy. This was partly because his writing remained at a general level, and also because from 1932 onwards he was a Communist and a Left Book Club author, though the Communist Party rejected his application for membership. However, Labour now enjoyed an immense range of resources in mapping out its economic strategy. A battalion of academic economists, including Douglas Jay, Hugh Gaitskell, Evan Durbin, Barbara Wootton, James Meade, Colin Clark and Hugh Dalton, contributed to this work. 1931 saw the formation of the New Fabian Research Bureau, including Gaitskell, Meade, Durbin and Clark, and the Society for Socialist Inquiry and Propaganda, including G. D. H. Cole, Frank Wise and H. N. Brailsford, which aimed to improve the socialist element in party policy. In January 1932 a number of City financiers who were sympathetic to Labour established the XYZ Club to advise the party on finance, and in the same year a number of former ILP-ers set up the Socialist League. Equally influential were trade unionists such as Bevin and Citrine acting through the TUC's Economic Committee (1932). Finally, the NEC itself appointed several influential sub-committees, notably the Finance and Trade Committee, in which Hugh Dalton and Herbert Morrison were key figures, to conflate the output of the other bodies and reach an agreed programme.

During 1931–3, as the National government failed to defend the pound and unemployment rose still further, socialists continued to take comfort from the inevitable collapse of the existing system. However, 1934 brought evidence of a recovery as unemployment fell and low interest rates boosted the boom in house-building and consumer-goods industries. In these circumstances it became increasingly unrealistic to assume that the demise of capitalism would usher in the socialist society. Although the election of 1931 had taken place in extraordinary circumstances, it seemed unlikely that Labour could simply rely on a swing of the pendulum to restore it to power, a conclusion amply borne out by the 1935 election. If the party was to restore its credibility it had to recognise that in 1924 and 1931 it had been the victim of its own failure to work out what exactly it wanted in terms of socialism and how to achieve it. Paradoxically, the departure of those in the ILP, who had complained so strongly about the neglect of socialism, eased this task in so far as the parliamentary leadership had hitherto been incapable of judging ILP economic proposals on their merits because they interpreted them as a challenge to their authority.

To some degree all Labour's advisers were impressed by the idea of economic planning as manifested by the five-year economic plan launched by Stalin in 1928. Naïve visitors to Russia such as the Webbs fed the movement with heart-warming accounts of the improvements enjoyed by the Russian people brought about by the professional expertise of the Communist bureaucracy. Planning was seen as the means of introducing order and stability in place of the insecurity and anarchy inflicted on the British people since 1920. For its most devoted advocates the planning of output, wages, prices and the location of industry was essentially a technical question, not one for amateur politicians and parliaments. However, although planning became a fashionable notion, Labour's conception of planning was subject to severe limitations from the start. Durbin, Meade and other academic economists insisted that the market mechanism would continue to play a key role even under a socialist system. Nor would there be any fundamental change in the relations between the state and the economic system; in particular the financial system based on the City of London would remain intact. In effect, Labour would leave existing institutions in place but inject elements of rationalisation and reorganisation via a central planning body. As a result Labour's proposed Supreme Economic Authority sounded more socialist than it was, consisting of a bureau responsible for collecting statistics, making forecasts and undertaking analyses rather than exercising direct control over the economy. Hence the importance placed by Douglas Jay on employing Keynesian techniques for managing the economy in his 1936 book *The Socialist Case*.

It was universally accepted on the left that a drastic extension of state ownership offered the obvious means of rationalising resources and promoting economic efficiency. Nationalisation had become less contentious as a result of a series of ad hoc collectivist measures taken, often by Conservative governments, since 1918: the formation of the Forestry Commission in 1920, the rationalisation of the railway companies into four groups, the creation of the Central Electricity Generating Board in 1926, and the London Passenger Transport Board which was planned by Morrison in 1930–1 but was implemented by the National government. These measures reflected the rationale for state control: many British industries were too handicapped by fragmented, small-scale companies to be capable of attaining efficiency through mass production, and private enterprise had largely failed to generate the investment required if British industry was to become competitive. However, when the annual conference voted to nationalise the banks in 1932, Dalton and his colleagues resisted the idea partly because of the electoral unpopularity and because they regarded it as unnecessary; it would be sufficient to nationalise the Bank of England and create a National Investment Board. A 1933 report, 'Socialism and the Condition of the People', envisaged state ownership of coal, railways, gas, electricity, water, iron and steel, shipping, shipbuilding, engineering, textiles, chemicals, insurance, and credit which was officially adopted in 1934. In addition the 1935 manifesto included armaments and cotton to the list.

As this catalogue suggests, the debate on nationalisation ran more widely than simply the strategic industries that were taken to underpin economic planning. Since the war, when profiteering in scarce commodities had caused controversy, there had been an alternative argument for state control based on sectors where combines and monopolies exploited consumers by extracting huge profits. This involved consumer-goods industries including cotton, food distribution, brewing and motor cars. In the 1920s, for example, Labour sponsored a campaign to extend wartime interventionism by taking over the brewing industry. To this end deputations from constituency parties visited the state-owned pubs at Carlisle. The Gateshead party, which included some abstainers, concluded: 'We sincerely think that the state owned and controlled public houses are a step in the direction of better social surroundings for those who believe in beer as a "national beverage".'[25] However, at a time when drinkers and publicans were still suffering from wartime restrictions and taxes the political risks seemed too great, and the issue subsided along with temperance. As the cotton textile industry suffered from a multitude of small firms badly in need of investment, the party agreed to nationalise it in 1935 but jettisoned the idea in 1937.[26] The case for taking over motor cars was less obvious because the industry had greatly expanded its output. However, British manufacturers suffered from poor productivity because they failed to reap the advantages of large-scale production and were undercapitalised by comparison with

American competitors, partly because too high a proportion of the
profits disappeared as dividends. The more successful companies kept
taking over the less profitable ones but failed to rationalise the industry.
Eventually, however, Labour backed off because a state motor-car
industry would have been too big a burden and rationalisation would
have led to further unemployment.[27] Party members were most keen
on state control of the wholesale food distribution industry because
some sectors were dominated by scores of inefficient middlemen, while
others were succumbing to huge combines and monopolies that extorted
high profits from consumers; the Vestey Meat Trust, United Dairies and
Tate & Lyle were among the worst offenders. The 1929–31 government
had tried to tackle this by creating agricultural co-operatives to benefit
farmers as well as consumers, but they were frustrated and eventually
Labour concluded that the policy was impractical and the vested interests too strong.[28]

As a result of Morrison's earlier development of the concept of the
public corporation the party now had a clear idea of how to proceed
with nationalisation. His insistence on paying compensation to the
former owners was attacked by Cripps at conference, but Morrison,
who dismissed Cripps' approach to socialism as 'romantic nonsense',
argued that without compensation nationalisation would amount to
confiscation which would alienate the managers and professionals
Labour wanted to convert. He also renewed his debate with Bevin
over workers' participation. The promise in the 1918 manifesto about
democratic control of nationalised industries was ridiculed by the
Webbs who believed that Britain should follow the Soviet example by
relying on experts and bureaucrats to run industry. Morrison himself
argued that 'the majority of workmen are . . . more interested in the
organisation, conditions and life of their own workshop than in those
finer balances of financial and commercial policy which are discussed
in the Board room'. As his colleagues largely agreed, the party accepted
that nationalised industries would be run by small boards of experts
and businessmen largely free from interference by workers or control
by Parliament.

Yet even Labour's extensive programme of nationalisation and planning left the economy effectively in private hands and thus reliant on
the market for the allocation of resources. However, the socialist
aspects of the strategy were complemented by a large element of

Keynesianism. During the 1920s MacDonald had been so keen to make Labour respectable that he had shied away from anything as unconventional as Keynesianism, and Henderson recalled that when he quoted Keynes in Cabinet, 'Snowden said he was a fool!'[29] Even in the 1930s several of the academic economists, including Gaitskell, Dalton and Durbin, who retained their orthodox outlook, were slow to be converted; preferring balanced budgets, they feared that Keynesian methods for stimulating the economy would cause inflation. Others on the left felt inclined to dismiss Keynesianism as a distraction from socialism because it merely aimed to revive a failing system. Nor did Keynes himself go out of his way to cultivate the Labour Movement; Beatrice Webb complained he was 'contemptuous of common men, especially when gathered together in herds', a surprising comment for her to make!

On the other hand, Labour's inheritance of pre-war underconsumptionist ideas predisposed it to Keynes' methods, a tradition reinforced by the post-war Liberal recruits. In effect, Labour politicians adopted what they liked in Keynes' writing, such as his attack on the return to the gold standard in 1925, and ignored other aspects. During the 1930s the leading advocates of Keynesianism were Douglas Jay, Ernest Bevin and John Strachey. Essentially a pragmatist, Bevin appreciated Keynes on common-sense grounds. Since 1930, when he had sat on the Macmillan Committee on finance and industry, he had grasped Keynes' analysis of the breakdown of the financial system and the effect of Britain's adherence to the gold standard in condemning workers to prolonged unemployment; this experience gave him the confidence to defy MacDonald's Cabinet over its pursuit of economic orthodoxy in 1931.[30] Moreover, as the 1930s wore on Bevin and other trade unionists were impressed by the impact of the New Deal in America following F. D. Roosevelt's election in 1932. Given that the depression was far worse in America than in Britain, the massive deployment of the resources of the state to reduce unemployment was impressive. Arguing that socialists could not sit around waiting for the final collapse of capitalism, Bevin saw no inconsistency between Labour's socialist proposals and deficit finance along New Deal lines. As a result, in 1933 the TUC commended the New Deal as a strategy worthy of emulation in Britain, advocating a combination of public works programmes financed by national credit, a maximum forty-hour

week, and raising the school-leaving age to sixteen. This was spelt out
in Labour's official policy in 1934 in terms of state investment in the
electrification of railways, the building of houses, schools and hospitals, land drainage, afforestation, road-building and improved water
supplies. As a result, when Keynes published *The General Theory of
Employment, Interest and Money* in 1936, Labour politicians commonly
accepted it as offering a reputable intellectual rationale for Labour
policy; Barbara Castle, for example, claimed that she 'instinctively
believed that Socialism meant using expenditure on public works to
set men and women producing goods and services people were crying
out for'.[31] In this way, by the later 1930s Labour had abandoned Fabian
gradualism in favour of a decisive mobilisation of the economic power
of the state by means of Keynesian management; the party now had
a much clearer idea of the extent of the state's proper role in the
economy and of the means by which it was to be exercised by a future
Labour government.

On the other hand, as these advances yielded scant gains in the
1930s it became clear that Labour's recovery as a credible party of
government would be a long-term process. After the electoral nadir
of 1931 there were abundant signs of revival but their significance is
not easy to interpret. On the positive side the party's machine remained
intact, if weakened, and ready to capitalise on any failings of the
National government. This was especially true since the only alternative, the Liberal Party, had been led into the National government
by Sir Herbert Samuel in 1931 and then out of it in 1932, resulting in
a further split with the National Liberals under Sir John Simon who
remained in the government. These misjudgements left the Liberals
further diminished and too associated with the right to be able to
regain popular momentum. Not until Sir Archibald Sinclair became
leader in 1935 did they seize the high ground by attacking appeasement, but by then the party was down to twenty MPs and was very
short of resources.

Meanwhile, the fall in unemployment around 1934 led to an increase
in trade union membership at last, with knock-on effects for Labour
in the form of affiliated membership rising from 1.85 million in 1934
to 2.2 million by 1939. In 1932 the NEC launched a new drive for individual members; from a low of 297,000 in 1931 membership increased
to 372,000 in 1932, 418,000 in 1935 and a peak of 447,000 in 1937.

Admittedly, these figures are very unreliable, especially as, since 1928, all constituency parties had been affiliated on the assumption that they had a minimum of 240 members. Also, the gains were not uniform geographically, being concentrated in the suburbs of the South, especially in areas such as Middlesex and Surrey, while little changed in the North, Wales and Scotland. While some parties co-operated with central recruiting initiatives, others ignored them; in 1932 the Wrexham CLP, for example, admitted 'a tremendous apathy and indifference existed almost everywhere in connection with this work'.[32]

London was the major exception. Even in 1931 the London Labour Party had launched an individual membership campaign with a trophy for the most successful CLP.[33] Following the collapse of MacDonald's Cabinet Morrison resumed his secretaryship of the LLP at £500 per annum.[34] Despite the demoralisation at national level the local party demonstrated its resilience and organisation by maintaining its Sports Association, annual reunion, Choral Society, Youth Advisory Group, speakers' classes and women's sections; indeed the LLP checked regularly to identify any constituencies lacking active women's sections. By 1932 the LLP had begun endorsing its candidates for the 1934 LCC elections. London membership increased from 42,863 in 1931 to 70,108 in 1937, an annual rise except for 1933; by comparison, membership in Scotland, with ten more MPs, was 22,784 in 1934 and 27,458 in 1935.[35] The spread of new housing estates in and around London between the wars underlined the necessity for a machine capable of undertaking a doorstep canvass and weekly collections; this was laborious but effective in raising funds and keeping members in touch. One Merton and Morden activist recalled: 'The growth of the LCC Estates of course drove everybody into a positive frenzy of canvassing . . . innumerable people from all ends of London thrown into a community on the outposts of civilisation.'[36] In Mile End, which boosted its individual membership from 1,083 to 2,626 by 1939, the seventy-three collectors brought in £363 a year: 'each one is a propagandist keeping contact with the members who are the solid core of election success'.[37] Major membership gains were made in suburban seats including Lewisham West, up from 944 to 2,128, and Fulham East, up from 632 to 1,784. By 1939 the West Bermondsey party boasted 3,156 members in an electorate of only 30,800. As a result the best-organised parties had memberships comparable with the strongest Conservative seats: Woolwich with 5,032 and Deptford with 4,155.

The downside to this expansion was a growing resentment, especially in the Home Counties, over the lack of influence for constituency parties at conferences and on the NEC. As a result, a campaign was initiated by Ben Greene between 1932 and 1937, known as the Constituency Parties Movement, to reform the system. For several years the NEC turned its face against the campaign, regarding it as evidence of left-wing subversion, but by 1937, faced with an effective rebellion by local parties, it retracted to the extent of agreeing to increase constituency representation on the NEC from five to seven and to allow direct and separate election.[38]

It is, however, striking that the Constituency Parties Movement failed to make common cause with the women's sections whose numbers steadily sank from a peak of 1,845 in 1928 to 1,580 by 1935, though some women now preferred to join their CLP, not the women's sections.[39] During the 1930s Labour women became increasingly marginalised. The women's sections stopped pushing for improvements in their role in the party and few appeared at the annual conferences by contrast with the Conservatives.[40] The explanation is that, as the movement became preoccupied with unemployment, the threat of fascism and the prospect of war, women's issues were neglected. No one seemed willing to recognise the extent to which the treatment of women by the 1929–31 government had alienated them. Margaret Bondfield's notorious Anomalies Act of 1931 had targeted married women's claims to unemployment benefit on the assumption that they did not intend to return to work; its immediate effect was to deprive nearly 80 per cent of married women of their benefits. Unfortunately the employment of married women ran so counter to the masculinist culture of the movement that not even Labour women such as Susan Lawrence were prepared to criticise Bondfield's legislation.[41]

Female candidates also continued to experience difficulty winning Labour nominations partly because of the complications in attracting Catholic voters. Although the party had compromised over the education question, it became embroiled in two fresh controversies in the 1930s. Some Catholics were offended by Labour sympathy for the Republican cause in Spain because of the treatment of Catholic clergy and churches there. However, reactions are easily exaggerated, for in places like Jarrow and Gateshead the large Catholic population seems to have accepted the Aid Spain campaigns.[42] More problematical was birth control. In Liverpool Labour's Catholic MP, David Logan, a father of ten, condemned not only birth control but divorce as threats to the family, an attitude that was light years removed from middle-class Labour women. In Sunderland Leah Manning attributed her defeat in 1935 to last-minute scares designed to highlight her views on sex which alienated Catholics. When Edith Summerskill, a doctor and staunch advocate of birth control, stood in Bury in 1935 the Catholic priests presented her with an ultimatum: they would advise Catholics to vote against her unless she agreed to desist from giving birth-control advice to her patients.[43] Summerskill, who had not even raised the issue, refused and was heavily defeated. However, such examples underline the wide variations in local political culture, for in London, where Summerskill subsequently won a seat, she appears not to have been handicapped by such prejudice.

For those constituencies hampered by a lack of union sponsorship – the ones Labour had to win – fund-raising continued to pose a problem that was best resolved by retaining a large membership through an elaborate programme of social events. In Lambeth North this included dances, whist drives, children's teas, and football and cricket teams. Subscriptions were laboriously gathered by collectors who kept threepence in every shilling while another penny went to the secretary for each new member.[44] Even so, the Lambeth party relied on contributions from the Royal Arsenal Co-operative Society and occasionally from the candidate, George Strauss, to make up the arrears in its agent's salary.[45] That a comparatively well-organised constituency experienced difficulty paying an agent explains why the total number of Labour agents remained almost static at 131 in 1932 and 136 in 1935.

Increasingly in the 1930s local parties resorted to an alternative means of raising money: lotteries. This was an innovation for a movement still influenced by the Puritanical traditions of Nonconformity which disapproved of all forms of gambling. In 1936, when football pools were pioneered, George Lansbury voted to ban them. However, in view of the working-class fondness for betting on horses and the popularity of the newly built greyhound tracks, he and the other traditionalists were rowing against the tide. Moreover, Labour MPs became increasingly antagonised by the class bias in the 1906 law that had made cash betting – the only method open to most workingmen – illegal away from racecourses. 'The evils of gambling are only discovered when workingmen start gambling,' complained Jack Jones MP.[46] However, in 1934 the law was modified to permit private sweepstakes, lotteries and tombolas run by voluntary organisations, and although the NEC advised constituency parties *not* to take advantage of this, the instruction was widely ignored.[47] Admittedly, as it took time for prejudices to disappear, it was not until the post-1945 period that lotteries became a standard fund-raising technique.

As most parliamentary seats were now held by the National government, by-elections offered ample scope for promoting Labour's recovery. The party made gains at Wakefield and Wednesbury in 1932, Rotherham and Fulham East in 1933, Hammersmith North, Upton (West Ham), Lambeth North and Swindon in 1934, and two Liverpool seats at Wavertree and West Toxteth in 1935. However, in a total of forty by-elections this was not very impressive, and the results were not a good indicator for the general election. They loomed large, however, because of the dramatic result at Fulham East where a 10,000 Tory majority was converted to a 5,000 Labour one. Yet the significance of this unexpectedly large victory is unclear. The National government leaders claimed, retrospectively, that it was a vote against rearmament. Ostensibly Labour's commitment to disarmament constituted an asset because the by-election took place while the disarmament convention at Geneva was at a critical stage. However, the Labour candidate, John Wilmot, actually made no mention of the issue in his election address, concentrating on the government's domestic failings over rising food prices, housing and unemployment.[48] Although the Tory candidate favoured a bigger navy and air force, the government had not yet adopted rearmament; and in any case Conservatives did very well at by-elections at Basingstoke and Aberdeen, for example, where their candidates advocated rearmament. Wilmot's large majority reflected a high turnout, his ability to appeal to the Liberal vote in the absence of a Liberal candidate, and the appearance of the former Liberal candidate on Labour's platform.[49] In effect, Fulham East was not so much a disarmament by-election as a 'Popular Front' one, for although it pre-dated the Popular Front by several years it reflected the rationale behind that strategy by showing that Labour's route to recovery lay through reaching out to Liberals and non-voters to outflank the National government.

Labour also made progress in municipal elections, gaining 458 seats in 1932, for example. But the most signal indication of the party's future success lay in the London County Council election of 1934 when it won a majority for the first time, winning sixty-nine seats to fifty-five for Municipal Reform. Under Morrison's leadership Labour approached the election with an unapologetically socialist programme involving the public ownership of utilities, and it accused the Conservatives of maintaining private ownership to protect the profiteers. Labour also advocated strategic powers designed to create a green belt around London and argued for improvements in housing, education and health provision even at the cost of higher rates; according to Morrison economies were often false because in the long run the council ended up spending more money.[50] Morrison improved on the victory in the next LCC election in 1937 when Labour won seventy-five seats to forty-nine for its opponents, foreshadowing the sweeping triumph of 1945.

Despite these advances the by-elections proved to be a poor guide to the general election that took place in October 1935. Since 1931 the situation had changed in ways that helped the government: the salary cuts imposed in 1931 were being reversed, tax reliefs were introduced, interest rates had fallen, and cheap mortgages were fuelling a building boom, with the result that the country seemed to be emerging from the worst of the depression. However, as recovery was not yet secure enough to be taken for granted, voters were easily deterred from supporting Labour for fear that its return would bring the crisis in its train; Conservatives again warned voters that savings in building societies would be at risk. The rise of fascist regimes on one side and Stalinism on the other enabled Baldwin to characterise the National government as a bulwark of moderation and to condemn Labour as extremist. During the summer of 1935 he also derived some indirect benefit from the patriotic mood engendered by the celebrations for George V's Silver Jubilee with the result that Labour's performance in by-elections had already subsided.

Labour also faced an unexpected dilemma over the party leadership. During 1934 when Dalton and the NEC had committed the annual conference to a shift of foreign policy based on supporting collective security against aggressor powers, Lansbury had been confined to hospital. However, at the 1935 conference the extent of Lansbury's detachment from the new line could not be concealed and, faced with a resolution supporting sanctions against Mussolini, he protested that he could not adopt a 'Jekyll and Hyde position'. An angry Bevin followed Lansbury to the platform, complaining: 'It is placing the Executive and the Movement in an absolutely wrong position to be hawking your conscience round from body to body asking to be told what to do with it.'[51] As a good trade unionist Bevin had read the mood of the movement correctly: everyone must respect collective decisions, and socialists like Lansbury, Cripps and Trevelyan should not intrude their individual consciences too often. Bevin revelled in his role. 'I say the nasty things, while others get the credit,' he complained. 'Lansbury's been dressed in saint's clothes for years waiting for martyrdom. All I did was set fire to the faggots.' A week later Lansbury resigned and Baldwin announced the election. As deputy Clement Attlee assumed the leadership for the campaign but he was largely unknown in the country and made little impression.

In the event Labour achieved a limited recovery over 1931, pushing the vote from 6.6 to 8.3 million or 38 per cent, slightly ahead of 1929. This produced a net gain of ninety-four seats giving a total of 154 in addition to four ILP members, but the National government with 54 per cent retained 435 members. At Seaham Emmanuel Shinwell ousted MacDonald by 20,000 votes, but in the North and Scotland generally things improved only slightly. The highest swing to Labour occurred in London, despite the economic growth in the region, but it was below average in the equally prosperous West Midlands. In 1929, with almost the same vote, Labour had won 288 seats, nearly twice as many as in 1935. In forty constituencies which had straight Labour–Conservative contests in the three successive elections, Labour had recovered only two-thirds of the support lost in 1931. The party had won six of twelve seats in Birmingham in 1929 but none in 1935, three of three in Salford in 1929 but none in 1935, two of four in Newcastle but none in 1935, five of eleven in Liverpool but only three in 1935. This was a measure of the failure even in industrial centres.

In the aftermath of the general election Labour returned to the leadership question. Despite the sense of loyalty towards Attlee he won only fifty-eight votes in the first ballot compared with forty-four for Morrison and thirty-three for Greenwood. With his superior skills as an organiser, tactician, policymaker and orator, Morrison was the outstanding candidate. However, he suffered from his association with London in the eyes of some northern MPs, was thought to be too accommodating to business and the middle class by others, and fell victim to Labour's fear of having another dominant leader; the party felt comfortable with the unassuming Attlee who said too little to offend anyone. As a result, on the second ballot Attlee won by eighty-eight to forty-eight votes. In this way the party chose a mediocrity in preference to the talented Morrison, though the consequences of this error were not to be fully apparent until 1950. During the next four years Labour chalked up more by-election gains at Derby and Peckham in 1936, at Wandsworth Central and Islington North in 1937, at Ipswich, Fulham West, Lichfield and Dartford in 1938, and at Kennington, Southwark North and Brecon and Radnor in 1939. Despite this tally, however, most contemporaries doubted that the party would be able to win the next election.

At the time this gloomy mood obscured a number of developments that were beginning to work to Labour's advantage. Already a change of political generations that is usually associated with the 1945 election was beginning to make itself felt. For example, in 1935 45 per cent of those who voted for the first time supported Labour, a proportion markedly ahead of the party's overall share.[52] This was an early symptom of the reaction of younger voters who felt the brunt of unemployment and a herald of their politicisation during the Second World War.

A second important shift occurred in Labour's relations with the media. In the 1930s the cinema newsreels and the BBC were biased against the party in that they gave far more generous treatment to National government ministers, to the spreading of good news and to the promotion of a mood of patriotism and national well-being; they played down anything controversial or divisive that could destabilise the government.[53] In 1935 all the Sunday newspapers except *Reynolds News* had been anti-Labour, as were all the national dailies except the *Daily Herald* and the *Daily Worker*. Admittedly, not all newspapers felt enthusiastic about the National government but they largely rallied to it. However, 1935 was the last occasion on which Labour was so disadvantaged.

Although the role of the *Daily Mirror* as a pro-Labour newspaper after 1945 is well known, it has been strikingly absent from analyses of the party's rise to power. Established in 1903 by Alfred Harmsworth, who sold it to his brother, Lord Rothermere, the *Mirror* began life as a picture-paper for ladies, with a middle-class readership and politics to match. However, by the 1930s the middlebrow market was over-crowded and the *Mirror* opted for a bold new direction under Harry Guy Bartholomew, editorial director from 1934, Cecil King, a director from 1929, Hugh Cudlipp, features editor from 1935, and William O'Connor who became the political columnist 'Cassandra'. These men were Radicals rather than socialists. Taking the *New York Daily News* as their model, they transformed the paper, adopting an aggressive style with huge front-page headlines focusing on a single story, a language designed to attract more working-class men, and a left-wing political stance. In 1935 the *Mirror* began to attack the National govern-ment over its handling of the Abyssinian crisis, the inadequacy of Britain's air defences and appeasement generally. During the next four years it increasingly urged Labour to embrace the Popular Front as the only means of winning an election and saving democracy from fascism.[54] At the time such a robust attitude offended the incorrigibly cautious Labour leaders who, in any case, found it difficult to warm to the new *Mirror*. Middle-class parliamentarians regarded it with mingled disdain and hostility as a lightweight paper whose expansion was likely to be at the expense of the *Daily Herald*. Attlee and his colleagues shared with Baldwin a prejudice against press proprietors as irresponsible and regarded mass newspapers as 'a danger to demo-cracy and a menace to public life'.[55] Even Nye Bevan dismissed the *Mirror*, saying, 'If the paper depended on my purchasing it, it would never be sold.'[56] These reactions underlined the extent to which Labour politicians were remote from the working-class culture to which the *Mirror* appealed so successfully. Morrison, who wrote for the paper in the 1930s, was probably closest.

Despite this the *Mirror* was of huge significance for Labour. Between 1936 and 1939 it subjected the policies of Baldwin and Neville Chamberlain to ridicule, and cultivated a rapprochement with Labour based upon the revision of its entire foreign and defence policy. Meanwhile the *Daily Herald* dutifully reproduced the official party line. Many party activists had been unhappy when Odhams Press took a

51 per cent holding in the *Herald*, because they felt it passed into capitalist hands and neglected socialist and trade union propaganda.[57] In fact, many readers disliked the *Herald* precisely because it was boring and had too high a political content; although promotional campaigns managed to raise circulation to around two million by 1933, this was its ceiling. Most working-class readers wanted a less sober paper that gave more space to crime, sport, sensation and gambling.[58] As a result, although the *Herald* kept Labour in touch with its core support, it failed to reach more widely to women, to the young, to the non-political and to working-class communities outside the trade union sphere. The *Daily Mirror* neatly complemented the sober *Herald* by offering personalities, entertainment, sensation, fashion and sport; it was considered 'easy to read' and ideal 'if you haven't much time to read a paper properly'.[59] Irreverent and anti-Establishment, it also expressed working-class monarchism and patriotism in a way its rival could not. Consequently, although the *Mirror*'s circulation had not yet reached its peak, it enabled Labour to reach sections of British society that had so far eluded its influence, though this only become clear during the Second World War.

The *Daily Mirror*'s reaction against the National government was symptomatic of a wider concern about fascism and appeasement during the later 1930s that eventually altered the whole configuration of British politics. As the newspaper regularly complained, Labour was in some ways hesitant about taking advantage of the shifting mood, though by 1939 it had effected a radical change in policy. Throughout the 1920s the party had benefited from its repudiation of the pre-war arms race and secret diplomacy and from the work of MacDonald and Henderson in promoting disarmament. This appeared consistent with the public mood, especially in the late 1920s and early 1930s when a series of books by Robert Graves, Siegfried Sassoon and Vera Brittain, among others, focused attention on the 'Lost Generation' and the follies of trench warfare. This was compounded by alarmist publicity about a future war, now expected to commence with heavy bombing raids on Britain's vulnerable cities. It was calculated that every ton of bombs dropped would result in fifty deaths, and, extrapolating from this, that Britain would suffer 83,000 casualties during the first week alone. Hitler's withdrawal from the disarmament convention at Geneva and the League of Nations in 1933 only heightened these fears.

However, the public appeared more pacifist than it was because the opponents of war were more vociferous in making their case, and the same was true of the Labour Party. At the 1933 annual conference at Hastings delegates endorsed a resolution proposed by Trevelyan committing the party to resist any future war by calling a general strike. But trade unionists, recalling the collapse of similar ideas in 1914, were sceptical about this. 'Who and what is there to oppose?' demanded Bevin, increasingly conscious that one of the earliest actions of fascist regimes was the abolition of trade unions. By 1934 the party leadership was anxious to detach itself from pacifism and to invoke the principle of 'collective security' under the League of Nations to resist aggression by the dictators. As a result delegates at the Southport conference adopted a new document on collective security, 'For Socialism and Peace', agreed by the NEC, TUC and PLP. This represented a major change since the 1920s when Labour had regarded the League as the creature of the victorious powers, designed to maintain an unjust peace settlement. Consequently, Hugh Dalton, the chief architect of the new policy, felt obliged to introduce it by stages between 1934 and 1937. Meanwhile, Labour MPs routinely voted against the military estimates, and for several years the party adopted an inconsistent position, favouring sanctions against the aggressors while resisting the rearmament necessary to implement such a policy. As a result, to the general public there was, as yet, no very clear difference between the two main parties, both claiming to support the League while being cautious about rearmament.

However, in 1935 opinions began to polarise as a result of the crisis over Abyssinia. Both parties had entered the election pledging support to the League against Mussolini's imminent plan to invade that country, but shortly afterwards the National government's deception was exposed when the Foreign Secretary, Sir Samuel Hoare, floated a deal to give the Italians most of what they wanted. From this point onwards ministers' readiness to ditch the League and their determination to cultivate Mussolini, Hitler and, later, Franco, undermined their credibility and opened a major opportunity for Labour to emerge as the spokesman for British national interests. In this sense the period from 1935 to 1939 formed a turning point in British politics that was to leave its mark up to the 1950s.

Nonetheless, as yet there was enough ambiguity in Labour's

position to reassure the rank-and-file members for whom it remained an article of faith that the National government could not be trusted with rearmament. The adoption of a rearmament programme in 1935 provoked this reaction by Gateshead CLP: 'Workers of this country, as of almost all countries, are strongly pacifist in feeling; whoever gains by war, the workers of all nations always lose!'[60] In 1936 the local party claimed that the government was 'frightened by the spread of pacifist feeling as manifested in the "Peace Ballot"'.[61] This was an interesting but typical misrepresentation of the ballot which was organised by supporters of the League of Nations in 1935. In the ballot eleven million people voted by three to one in favour of applying sanctions, even military ones, against aggressor states. The misnamed 'Peace Ballot' was thus significant as a symptom of the country's emergence from its anti-war phase and its readiness to face the prospect of another war, however reluctantly.

1936 brought the Labour Movement into line with the popular mood owing to the outbreak of the civil war in Spain. With France becoming surrounded by fascist regimes on three sides it began to look as though the democracies would be obliged to resist the tide now sweeping across Europe. By rejecting the election of a left-wing, Popular Front government in Spain, the Nationalists and Falangists forced British democrats to accept that some wars were just. Initially, however, Labour showed its confusion when the 1936 conference endorsed an official resolution proposed by Arthur Greenwood supporting the National government's non-intervention policy in Spain as the only practical option. As so often the issue was clouded by infighting and fraught personal relations within the movement. Dalton, Bevin and Morrison were incurably suspicious when they saw Cripps and Trevelyan, recent pacifists whose judgement they wholly distrusted, suddenly adopting an interventionist line.

Despite this initial stumble, over the next few years the movement continued to reorientate itself to the prospect of war. In April 1937 the TUC and party conference adopted a 5,000-word document based on the assumption that as a Labour government must be able to handle the fascist powers and play a full role in collective security, 'it would be unable to reverse the present programme of rearmament'.[62] From 1937 onwards the Labour MPs voted *for* the military estimates. In that year conference also reversed its previous position by rejecting non-intervention in Spain and subsequently a 'Labour Party Spain Committee' began to work for the Republican cause. Its work was, however, overshadowed by extensive 'Aid Spain' campaigns by local parties involving concerts, jumble sales and other efforts to raise funds to send huge convoys of food and medical supplies. The non-partisan character of this activity was demonstrated by work in Gateshead in the summer of 1937 where a town meeting under the auspices of the mayor appealed for funds and members participated in a 'Tyneside Spain Week'. Although much of this effort was humanitarian, as opposed to ideologically anti-fascist in character, this in no way detracted from its wider significance.[63] If anything, it enhanced it partly because humanitarian work mitigated the divisions between the activists and the national party, and also because it attracted men and women who wanted to help but were otherwise put off by sectarian arguments. For a party that had to extend its reach this was the way forward.

On the other hand, Labour responses to Spain were greatly compli-cated by its association with the wider idea of a United Front, Popular Front and People's Front against fascism abroad and at home. The significance of the Popular Front in Labour history has been misunder-stood because it has largely been seen in the context of the fraught relations between Labour on the one hand and the ILP and Communists on the other. In fact, the idea for a People's Front emerged in 1936 in articles by G. D. H. Cole and Hugh Dalton, inspired by the triumphant election of Popular Front governments in France and Spain which offered a contrast to Labour's dismal showing in the 1935 election.[64] Cole argued that, as Labour was unlikely to win the next election, or even the one after that, the cause of democracy could not be left to the mercies of pro-fascist governments; progressive forces must therefore concert action to resist the threat. Seen in the context of the party's electoral weakness, the rationale for a Popular Front lay in mobilising the support of Liberals, non-voters, the uncommitted and even some Tories who had not responded to a one-party appeal. From this perspective attempts to promote unity with the Communists were irrelevant as they commanded insignificant electoral support: 'The game is not worth the candle,' according to A. L. Rowse, Labour's candidate in Penryn and Falmouth.[65]

However, this notion was blown off course in January 1937 when

Cripps launched the United Front campaign on behalf of the Socialist League with a view to incorporating the ILP and the Communists into a joint effort with Labour. Already advanced by Harry Pollitt, secretary of the Communist Party, the United Front was condemned by the NEC, though it commanded formidable support. In October Cripps was re-elected to the NEC by the individual members where he formed a left-wing bloc with Ellen Wilkinson, Harold Laski and D. N. Pritt. He and George Strauss also financed a new journal, *Tribune*, to create an additional platform for their views.

Against the background of MacDonald's betrayal in joining the National Government in 1931, the movement was understandably suspicious about external forces trying to manipulate Labour for their own purposes, a fear accentuated by the prominence of upper-class recruits such as Cripps, Trevelyan and Strauss among the Popular Fronters. Admittedly, in time the NEC recognised that it should not put Communists and Liberals in the same category, but meanwhile it expended much time and energy trying to impose its line on the rank and file. In fact, the records of constituency parties now available show that, however strict its official pronouncements, the NEC's writ did not always run at local level. At one end of the spectrum the loyalist party at Frome in Somerset rejected local ILP pressure to join the United Front in 1937, and in 1938 decided against a Popular Front because 'the Party could not afford to place reliance in the Liberal Party who were in reality using the situation to revive the Liberal Party'.[66] In 1939 it reaffirmed this view but regretted the NEC's decision to expel Cripps. In London Morrison energetically suppressed signs of cross-party co-operation but with mixed success. In Hendon the party favoured co-operation between Labour, the ILP and Communists to find 'a common front against the capitalist parties'; however, when the parliamentary candidate tried to take them further into involvement with the Popular Front and the Left Book Club, they fell out and he eventually resigned.[67] In Merton and Morden the CLP responded to an NEC interdict on the Popular Front by agreeing it was 'not in favour of cooperating with any Capitalistic Party', though its loyalties were strained: 'While we condemn the opportunistic Popular Front policy advocated by Sir Stafford Cripps, we strongly protest against the action of the Executive in expelling him as bureaucratic and against the interests of free speech'.[68] In Lambeth North George Strauss disobeyed central instructions by accepting Communist help at elections, supporting multi-party campaigns to organise aid for the Spanish Republicans, and signing the United Manifesto in 1937. As Strauss was 'Mr Morrison's protégé' and right-hand man at County Hall, this proved so embarrassing that Morrison sacked him from his LCC committee chairmanship in April. However, the North Lambeth party organised a mass meeting to back him at which he was supported by his agent, George Lansbury and Aneurin Bevan. Subsequently the North Lambeth party was suspended.[69]

In Birmingham where the party had previously been pacifist, involvement with the Spanish Republican cause and the recruitment of volunteers to fight in the civil war seems to have promoted Popular Front sympathies, much accentuated by the close identification of the local MP, Neville Chamberlain, with appeasement. Complaining that the government stood by while British ships were bombed by fascist aeroplanes, the party observed: 'The strangest thing in politics today [is] a complete metamorphosis of the traditional true-blue Toryism.'[70] The Bishop Auckland party followed a shrewdly inconsistent line by agreeing to endorse the action of its own MP, Dalton, in expelling Cripps while refusing to take action against local members who supported Cripps. Two months later it did expel two members but in one case the expelled husband left his wife to continue promoting the Popular Front and raising funds for the International Brigade within the party![71] Arthur Woodburn, secretary of the Scottish Labour Party, struggled to prevent Labour involvement in Popular Front meetings, usually under the aegis of trades council activity, all over the country from Lanarkshire to Orkney and Shetland; in the latter he reported the party had been 'considerably affected by the Left Book Club and Popular Front activities and that in Shetland especially the majority of the Party were openly opposed to the Labour Party'.[72]

Despite national disapproval there was nothing to stop Labour Party members volunteering to fight in Spain – and returning as heroes. In 1936 the formerly pacifist Gateshead CLP celebrated the Popular Front victory in France which 'should be a lesson to us all to close our ranks in the face of a common enemy'. The Gateshead Labour Herald carried propaganda on 'The Need for a People's Front' as 'the only defence against Fascism, against war and against the increasing attacks of capitalism'.[73] It also published articles and photographs of North-East volunteers in the International Brigade including Wilf Jobling who died in Spain: 'Our regret is tempered with a sense of pride and real comradeship in the thought that Wilf Jobling belonged to our great movement.'[74] Jobling was actually secretary of the Chopwell Communist Party. As late as 1939 members of both parties participated in rallies and marches on Tyneside to honour the volunteers, lay wreaths and erect memorials.[75] It was almost impossible for London to prevent participation by individuals in these joint activities with members of other parties. The ultimate sanction against constituency parties – disaffiliation – was sometimes invoked, but there were obviously limits to its use especially at a time when local parties felt their voice was insufficiently heard at national level.

In this context the conclusions of Herbert Morrison's biographers that he helped to keep Labour 'on the path of sanity' by his resolute opposition to the Popular Front and Communism were both erroneous and beside the point. They reflect the conventional appreciation of the Popular Front movement as, at best, an unrealistic and idealistic effort doomed to failure. However, this narrowly bureaucratic perspective misses the wider significance of the campaigns for Labour. The effort devoted to excluding infiltrators and to disciplining party members absorbed a lot of time and served little purpose. For, as Cole, Rowse and others saw at the time, the Communists were largely irrelevant; the question was how far Labour could realise the real rationale for a Popular Front by extending its appeal beyond the party faithful.

Admittedly, an electoral deal bristled with difficulties. In France the Popular Front had been easier because the socialists, Radicals and Liberals enjoyed roughly equal support and the second ballot system enabled them to combine their votes in the second round of voting. Also, the French Radicals were disciplined whereas it was not certain the British Liberals could deliver their votes.[76] However, this question could only be resolved by an active joint campaign. Labour's underlying fear was really that a successful Popular Front campaign would boost the Liberals at a time when they appeared likely to disappear altogether. Against this, Labour Popular Fronters pointed out that the party needed a fresh initiative because it was now handicapped by the electoral system; in 1935 the Opposition parties had won 46 per cent of the votes but only 30 per cent of the seats; turnout had dropped by 7 per cent in 1935, evidence that while voters felt disillusioned with the National government they were not being mobilised by Labour.

What made the strategy feasible was enthusiastic support from such Liberal MPs as Wilfrid Roberts, Richard Acland, Megan Lloyd George, Geoffrey Mander and Isaac Foot, and increasingly the leader, Sir Archibald Sinclair, who was outraged by the National government's betrayal of the League and its cultivation of the fascist regimes.[77] From 1936 onwards the cause was consistently promoted by the News Chronicle – significantly a Liberal newspaper read by many Labour supporters – its editor, A. J. Cummings, and its diplomatic correspondent, Vernon Bartlett. 'The present Government totters, without falling, from one shock to another,' Cummings wrote, 'largely because of a general disbelief in the ability of the Labour Opposition to provide a more efficient alternative'.[78]

Collaboration was clearly feasible, the question was how. Cummings quickly recognised that the route lay, not in challenging the national parties, but through local action in by-elections where the two sides were willing. Although only two famous by-elections at Oxford and Bridgwater in 1938 have usually been recognised as Popular Front campaigns, they were, in fact, part of a much wider movement between 1936 and 1939. Co-operation began with the resignation of Jimmy Thomas, the National Labour member for Derby, in May 1936. As Labour had trailed Thomas by 12,500 votes in 1935 a major effort was required if the National government candidate was to be defeated. It was a sign of sympathy for a Popular Front that the NEC quickly lost the initiative at Derby. Labour's candidate, Philip Noel-Baker, received strong backing from the News Chronicle, Wilfrid Roberts and the local Liberals who organised meetings for him, and Lloyd George who turned up to support him.[79] Although the NEC put its foot down by insisting that Lloyd George must not appear on a Labour platform, it was unable to prevent Noel-Baker's campaign assuming the character of a Popular Front. Labour's subsequent victory gave momentum to the strategy despite attempts by Attlee to pour cold water on it. The lesson was rubbed in two weeks later at Balham and Tooting where Labour met with the usual failure; Popular Fronters argued that in the absence of a joint campaign to overcome voter apathy the Balham turnout was only 49 per cent compared with 65 per cent at Derby.

During 1937 the case for a Popular Front gained strength from the replacement of Baldwin as prime minister by Neville Chamberlain, whose rigid pursuit of appeasement polarised politics. In this situation many Labour and Liberal activists took initiatives by organising joint meetings and even adopting joint candidates.[80] The *News Chronicle* urged Liberals to support Labour in all the 1937 by-elections, and at St Ives, where Isaac Foot stood as a Liberal against the National government, his nomination papers were signed by Labour members and he was backed by the former local Labour candidate, William Arnold-Forster.[81] Labour also stood down for the Liberals in North Dorset who then reciprocated at Plymouth Drake, where Lloyd George and John Foot spoke for the Labour candidate.

1938 brought further successes, notably at Fulham West, a marginal seat where the *News Chronicle* repeatedly urged Liberals to vote for Dr Edith Summerskill and Lloyd George organised a Council for Action rally on her behalf.[82] Summerskill's victory was followed by further Labour gains at Ipswich and Lichfield also in the context of active Liberal support. After this the Popular Front was adopted by *Reynolds News*, the Co-operative newspaper, and endorsed by the Home Counties Labour Association, the Labour Spain Committee and the Provisional Committee of London Labour Parties.[83] By this stage it seemed clear that Labour had much to gain and little to lose from collaboration. Despite this, in April the NEC issued another circular proscribing the Popular Front.[84] However, rank-and-file supporters continued to ignore these injunctions. At the by-election at Aylesbury in May an official Labour candidate stood but only in the face of public opposition from the local party; several officers resigned, other Buckinghamshire branches openly declared for the Popular Front, and hundreds of members, including many women, actively worked for the Liberal.[85] The Liberals, who were angry that the NEC had insisted on running a candidate, retaliated by withholding support at the Stafford by-election where the small Conservative majority should have given Labour an easy gain; Labour was shocked when the Conservatives retained the seat by a larger majority.

Under these pressures the national party gradually softened its stance. In May 1938, though voting sixteen to four against the Popular Front, the NEC recognised that rank-and-file Liberals were not trying to manipulate Labour like the Communists.[86] The NEC was also frustrated by a major flaw in its strategy in the shape of the Left Book

Club which had been founded by Victor Gollancz in 1936 to promote a Popular Front. A Communist, Gollancz had been a Liberal until 1929 and he attracted Liberals such as Acland, Roberts and Bartlett into the LBC. Although he never succeeded in forcing Labour into a Popular Front, the LBC enrolled 57,000 members by 1939 and circulated two million books. The NEC tried to counter Gollancz with a less successful Labour Book Club, and instructed constituency parties that the LBC could not affiliate as it included 'members of various political opinions'; joint activities should therefore be avoided.[87] Yet it had no means of preventing individual Labour members participating in local LBC groups. Gollancz reported: 'We are receiving a great number of applications from members who are handing on to their friends the enrolment cards contained in each Club choice.' In the South-West, where Popular Front sentiment was strong, the party's organiser appealed to Labour women to concentrate on their own work, but she admitted, 'It is difficult to say that they ought not to have joined the Left Book Club.'[88] One women's section in Yorkshire thought it 'deplorable and undemocratic that Labour women should be instructed what and what not to read', and although one loyalist later reported 'you will be glad to know that we have no left-wing elements in the section now', this was simply because members had left in disgust.[89] In effect the LBC met such a widely felt need that efforts to proscribe it were largely counterproductive. George Strauss warned the NEC not to 'waste their energies in nosing about the local Labour parties up and down the country to try to find something active and militant, and then calling it Communist and setting upon it'.[90]

Rank-and-file feeling reached a peak during 1938 owing to the crisis that culminated in the Munich Settlement. Wilfrid Roberts appealed to Attlee to put himself at the head of the anti-appeasement movement, arguing that 'we may very shortly be faced with an election in which Chamberlain will seek to capitalise the national relief to his own political advantage'.[91] But Attlee remained so cautious that he was known to leave a platform if he saw any danger of being in the company of a Popular Fronter. The price he paid was to allow Sinclair, the Liberal leader, to champion the anti-appeasement cause, leaving Bevin to complain, 'The Party's got no leadership.'

Evidence of the extent to which the leadership was losing control came in the by-election at Oxford in October 1938, a seat where Labour's candidate, Patrick Gordon-Walker, had enjoyed a straight fight with the Conservatives in 1935 and naturally felt reluctant to withdraw for a Popular Front nominee. However, the Oxford academic community included keen Popular Fronters, G. D. H. Cole, Gilbert Murray, A. L. Rowse and Richard Crossman, who promoted A. D. Lindsay, the Master of Balliol, as an Independent Progressive backed by Labour and the Liberals. During October a struggle ensued in which deputations from Oxford waited upon Attlee and the national agent while an increasingly angry Gordon-Walker smeared Lindsay's Labour supporters as tools of the Communists and as representing 'an hysterical middle-class element which was scared by the crisis'.[92] Initially Transport House instructed Gordon-Walker to continue as candidate, but after another deputation on 13 October the NEC agreed not to insist on a contest.[93] A meeting of local Labour members voted 109–30 to withdraw the candidate, a decision subsequently ratified by Oxford's General Council by 48–12.[94] However, Gordon-Walker sabotaged Lindsay's campaign by insisting 'I am not standing down, the local Labour Party is withdrawing the Labour candidate', and he wrote to the press to emphasise that his withdrawal 'in no way indicates positive approval for Mr Lindsay's candidature . . . On the contrary I regard the decision of my local party as highly ill-advised and short-sighted.'[95] The national agent rapped Richard Crossman and Frank Pakenham over the knuckles for their role in the by-election, warning that the NEC 'would have to take very serious notice indeed' if repeated.[96] Candidates throughout Oxfordshire, Berkshire and Buckinghamshire were summoned to meetings to stop the movement spreading: 'Remember, the General Election is not far off and a stop must be put to this LIB-LAB movement.'[97]

Yet despite these injunctions headquarters was forced into a second retreat in November over the dramatic by-election in Bridgwater. As at Oxford the Liberal and Labour parties withdrew in favour of an Independent Progressive, Vernon Bartlett, of the *News Chronicle*. The local organisation had already been softened up by Richard Acland who had been using LBC groups to form new Labour branches in the constituency.[98] As Labour was in third place in Bridgwater, the NEC allowed it to endorse Bartlett. Demonstrating a shrewd appreciation of left-wing influence, Bartlett and Acland rejected an offer to speak from Cripps. They really wanted the two party leaders, but while Sinclair was willing, Attlee kept himself aloof. In the event Bartlett captured the seat by overthrowing a Tory majority of 10,500; he had mobilised both the Liberal and Labour vote and pulled in thousands of non-voters to achieve an 82 per cent turnout. Faced with so compelling a vindication of the Popular Front rationale the *Daily Herald* buried the news in an obscure corner of the paper, while Attlee floated the idea of disciplining the thirty-nine Labour MPs who had supported Bartlett. This was mere foolishness for it would hardly have been feasible to discipline a quarter of the PLP.

Soon after Bridgwater the Popular Front movement gained a fresh dimension from a split among the Conservatives in Kinross and West Perthshire where the MP, the Duchess of Atholl, had made a habit of appearing on left-wing platforms to attack government policy over Spain and appeasement. Provoked by her deselection as Tory candidate, she resigned her seat to fight a by-election in December 1938, thereby raising the prospect that progressive Tory MPs, including Sir Anthony Eden, Harold Macmillan and Vyvyan Adams, who had supported Lindsay at Oxford, could be prised away from Chamberlain. Hugh Dalton, who had been sceptical about a Popular Front, believed a *Conservative* split would make the strategy viable, and he negotiated privately with rebel Tories, including Macmillan, with a view to forming a parliamentary committee, though he privately considered them 'gentlemanly wishy-washies' and preferred Churchill: 'He is a real tough and at the moment talking our language.'[99] By February 1939 even an official party statement recognised that a Popular Front could succeed if Tory MPs joined the movement.[100] The Scottish Labour Party decided against fighting the by-election in Kinross and West Perthshire, though the putative candidate ruefully observed, 'I don't know why all these Labour people are so keen to support a Conservative duchess.'[101] The Liberal withdrawal effectively made the duchess a Popular Front candidate who received support from twenty-one Labour MPs.[102] However, as she narrowly failed to retain the seat the Conservative anti-appeasers remained cautious about rebelling, though collaboration eventually bore fruit in the overthrow of Chamberlain in May 1940.

This formed the immediate background to the dramatic events of January 1939 when Cripps' latest proposal for a National Petition Campaign was rejected by the NEC by seventeen to three and he responded by immediately sending a mass mailing to Labour MPs and party organisations to seek support. 'The man has the political judgement of a flea,' complained an exasperated Dalton.[103] Even so, Dalton felt doubtful about the wisdom of expelling Cripps because of the extra publicity and sympathy expulsion would give him; it would also lead to other expulsions and might tempt Chamberlain to take advantage of Labour divisions by calling a snap election.[104] Such was the irritation, however, that the NEC decided to expel him from the party by eighteen to one, followed by Trevelyan and Strauss in February.[105] The members especially objected to his memorandum on the grounds that it was too defeatist and assumed another Labour failure at the next election.

Consequently, when the annual conference met at Southport in May it was inevitably dominated by a debate over whether to refer back the NEC's decision. The occasion was notable for the emergence of a voluble young delegate from St Albans, George Brown, who argued, 'It is time somebody pricked this bubble once and for all.' Employing the tactics Bevin had used against Lansbury, Brown dwelt on the need for loyalty among members: 'We are entitled to expect the same from Sir Stafford Cripps, lawyer or no lawyer.' He appealed to the activists who were Cripps' sympathisers by reminding them that in St Albans they had built a large membership 'but we have spent nine blasted months in a pre-election year just doing nothing else but argue the toss about Cripps!'[106] Delegates appreciated this and endorsed the expulsion by 2.1 million to 400,000. Brown was correct that Cripps had become a distraction both for the party and the Popular Front. His new challenge simply fortified the NEC in its determination not to be driven off course. It underlined this by resisting pressure to withdraw in favour of the Liberals at the Holderness by-election despite the wish of the local Labour officers to do so.[107] However, in July Labour backed the Liberal candidate in the North Cornwall by-election who won with an increased majority and a 79 per cent turnout; this was the last Popular Front campaign before the outbreak of war.

Defending the expulsion of Cripps for breaches of discipline over several years, Morrison derided 'Mr Acland's recipe for corpse revival' and argued that Labour could win an election by itself 'if the split-ters and superior people will hold off'; he cited the increase in Labour MPs in London to twenty-eight as proof.[108] However, Morrison conveniently ignored the fact that several of the London gains had occurred in the context of joint campaigns with the Liberals and that in other

regions Labour was not doing as well. Although the national leadership had managed to fend off pressure for a Popular Front it had not
checked the sentiment behind it. At a peacetime election in 1939–40
a de facto Popular Front would have operated in areas such as the
South-West where it enjoyed the support of both parties, and local
pacts would have been implemented elsewhere. In January, Philip Noel-
Baker privately advised Dalton that Labour had reached the point
where it must adjust to face a general election; this meant ignoring
the Communists and avoiding terms like United Front and Popular
Front, but agreeing with the Liberals to minimise the number of three-
cornered contests.[109] Dalton himself had come to recognise the
advantage of co-operation in some regions, though 'the scope of such
arrangements is very limited', and he and Morrison advocated 'greater
elasticity' in handling such cases. But as they felt such plans had to be
implemented quietly 'the possibility of doing anything at all of this
kind is ruined by such moves as Cripps's'.[110] By 1939 it was clear that
resistance to co-operation had been unwise, for Labour had gained
much more than the Liberals in the by-elections and its interest now
lay in placing itself at the head of a broad anti-appeasement movement. In effect this was happening locally despite the caution of the
national leaders especially in places such as Birmingham where the
prominence of Chamberlain offered Labour an irresistible target.[111] In
the process the party had begun to adopt the language of patriotism
at a time when its opponents were neglecting it. As the *Daily Mirror*
observed, the logic of Labour's reorientation implied making a bold
appeal to national sentiment: 'One of the oddest political twists of
our time is indeed this – The old pacifists have become warlike. The
True Blue Tory warmongers now coo like doves. Who knows what
the effect of that reversal of parts will be upon the voters at the next
election?'[112] By the outbreak of war Labour had effectively repositioned
itself, almost in spite of the parliamentary leaders, and to this extent
the conditions that were to generate a landslide in 1945 pre-dated the
Second World War.

'Speak for England': Labour and the Second World War

The Second World War proved to be a crucial watershed in British politics; it dissolved the mood of apathy that had sustained the National government for so long, it accelerated trends in the Labour Party that had been developing since 1931, it enabled Labour to resurrect the national voice it had briefly found in 1918, and it generated a progressive consensus that lasted for several decades.

Yet when Neville Chamberlain reluctantly took Britain to war in September 1939 expectations among Labour's leaders were low despite their public expressions of confidence. Although the credibility of Chamberlain's government had dwindled since Munich and began to collapse when Hitler marched into Czechoslovakia in March 1939, contemporaries assumed that he would be difficult to dislodge in a normal election. They discounted the new Gallup polls published by the *News Chronicle* since 1937 because they could not accept that a small sample accurately reflected public opinion. Throughout the war politicians preferred to rely on their instincts and on precedent which indicated that, as in 1900 and 1918, war generated emotions advantageous to the Conservatives. As a result, the Labour leaders spent the war cocooned in ministerial office and out of touch with trends in the country, unwilling, right to the end, to recognise the electoral earthquake that was moving beneath their feet.

Despite these shortcomings they played a skilful game, though they were helped by the ineptitude of Chamberlain. When German troops crossed into Poland on 1 September, activating the British guarantee, politicians and the public expected to hear a prompt declaration of war. But for two days none came. When Chamberlain notoriously failed to make the announcement in the House of Commons on 2 September he was received in ominous silence by his own members,

and L. S. Amery shouted 'Speak for England!' across the chamber to
Arthur Greenwood who was to reply for Labour. The episode crystallised the entire experience of the Second World War. In contrast to
the reaction in August 1914 the Labour Movement showed little
hesitation about British entry into war and Attlee and Dalton had been
irritated on a recent visit to Paris to find the French socialists 'either
pacifist or defeatist'.[1] 'Thank God,' Dalton told Lord Halifax on hearing
that Britain was at last to declare war on Germany. Labour promptly
announced its backing for British entry subject only to insistence on
maintaining its right to criticise and its refusal to join any coalition led
by Chamberlain. The only fear was that some colleagues might be
tempted by offers of jobs by the prime minister. However, Dalton
stamped on this idea at a shadow Cabinet meeting, citing the experience of Henderson in the First World War: 'it is not as though our
present leaders were supermen capable of exercising vast influence
though in a tiny minority'.[2] Reinforced by the PLP, this closed the door
to any deal designed to bolster Chamberlain's failing premiership during
the nine months of the 'Phoney War'. Meanwhile Dalton made effective use of his links with a civil servant, Hugh Gaitskell, now promoted
as head of Intelligence for Enemy Countries, who leaked secrets and
advised him on the best questions to put to ministers![3]

   Who was responsible for eventually bringing down Chamberlain's
regime? Though Dalton's biographers claim the credit for him, at least
three individuals brought the Opposition together early in 1940. The
Liberal, Clement Davies, organised a cross-party ginger-group of anti-
appeasers, Lord Salisbury formed a Watching Committee of Tory
rebels, and Dalton cultivated his contacts with such Tories as Harold
Macmillan, Robert Boothby, Anthony Eden and L. S. Amery whom
he had always regarded as the key to the destruction of Chamberlain.
Their opportunity came on 7 May with the parliamentary debate over
the fiasco of the Norwegian Campaign. Initially Labour feared that if
a motion of no confidence produced only a small Tory rebellion, the
prime minister might feel tempted to risk a snap election or, as was
strongly rumoured, try to inveigle Alexander and Greenwood to join
his Cabinet. But it was Morrison who seized the initiative at the NEC,
committing it to forcing a division over Norway: 'Herbert was the
active Leader and he saw the chance to destroy the government,' as
James Griffiths put it.[4] Dalton then briefed Macmillan that the PLP

would treat the matter as one of confidence so that he in turn could prime the anti-Chamberlainites. The bold approach proved justified during the debate in which Chamberlain was provoked by an attack by Amery: 'I appeal to my friends – and I still have some friends in this house – to support the Government tonight.' This made the issue sound petty and personal. Some MPs returned from the forces aware of how badly prepared the army had been, or heard a similar message from their constituents. In the division forty-one government supporters opposed Chamberlain and sixty-five abstained, giving him a nominal victory by 281 to 200. Struggling to avoid resignation, Chamberlain invited Attlee to join the government, but on meeting him at Downing Street at 6.30 on the evening of 9 May the Labour leader flatly refused: 'Our party won't have you and I think I am right in saying the country won't have you either.'[5]

Attlee, however, agreed to Chamberlain's request to consult the party, now assembling for its annual conference at Bournemouth. The sudden German invasion of Holland and Belgium on 10 May created a fresh crisis that appeared to make it awkward for Labour to with-hold its co-operation. Meeting at the Highcliffe Hotel the NEC agreed by seventeen to one that it would join any government except one led by Chamberlain. This finally forced 'the old limpet' out. Attlee and Greenwood thereupon left for London where they met the new prime minister, Churchill, and agreed on posts for the new Labour ministers. According to Attlee he did not bargain: 'I was resolved that I would not, by haggling, be responsible for any failure to act promptly.'[6] However, when the conference formally opened the reactions were distinctly mixed. Given his history in handling strikes Churchill scarcely seemed an appealing choice for Labour members, and some delegates argued against participating in another imperialist war while others felt reluctant about accepting the electoral truce that a coalition entailed.[7] But Dalton, who rather liked Churchill, had no patience with the critics whom he derided as 'a lot of freaks talking pathetic rubbish'. In fact the decision was hardly in doubt; delegates endorsed the decision to join by 2.45 million to 170,000.

The formation of the coalition government in May 1940 proved crucial for Labour's fortunes in two main ways. First, it restored Labour as a party of government thereby eventually obliterating memories of the 1929–31 administration. The effect was compounded by the ministers' prominence in the war effort. Attlee and Greenwood joined Churchill's five-man War Cabinet without departmental duties; Morrison became Minister for Supply, Bevin Minister for Labour and National Service, Dalton Minister for Economic Warfare and Alexander First Lord of the Admiralty. Labour also filled eight junior posts rising to seventeen by 1945. In the process Bevin and Morrison became so closely associated in the public's mind with Britain's victorious war effort that they enhanced the party's credibility. Second, as a party Labour coped with the strains of participation in government in a way that the Conservatives largely failed to do. Initially Churchill's position was similar to that of Lloyd George in 1916 in that he had displaced a premier of his own party but was not himself a party leader. Although the Tory members were not invited to choose Chamberlain's successor, contemporaries believed they would have preferred Lord Halifax. Chamberlain remained in the Cabinet and, like Asquith in 1916, remained party leader until his death when the MPs accepted Churchill in his place. But they felt understandably reluctant, for Churchill had been a consistent rebel and troublemaker throughout the 1930s. As a result he was a somewhat nominal leader. As he regarded the party machine as his enemy and was in any case distracted by the war, he largely neglected party interests until the end of the coalition. Although it was not apparent at the time, this was greatly to Labour's advantage when the time came to emerge from the constraints of wartime politics.

For Labour the great danger lay in the prospect that the longer the coalition government lasted, the more the movement in the country would become detached from the parliamentary leaders and lose its sense of purpose. However, the danger was mitigated initially by the sheer enthusiasm for the war effort among the rank and file, in particular for Germany's unconditional surrender and the eradication of the fascist regimes.[8] Conventional accounts, dominated by Churchill's wartime rhetoric, tend to neglect the extent to which Labour indulged in similar language. In a 1940 broadcast, A. V. Alexander, a classic working-class patriot and imperialist, asked: 'Does anyone imagine the English-speaking races of the world are going under? . . . There can be no turning back . . . No half measures are possible; one must give all, dare all, ensure all or lose all. Let nobody imagine peace terms or negotiations are possible with Hitler.'[9]

Churchill had no monopoly on Churchillian prose and his party no monopoly on patriotic activity. Since 1938 local Labour parties had become involved in war work, including ARP organisation, evacuation and civil defence arrangements.[10] In Merton and Morden, for example, the CLP organised shows, entertainments, lunches and teas for wounded soldiers financed by party members.[11] In Birmingham the declaration of war saw the formation of a joint committee of the trades council, Labour Party and the Co-operative Party to obtain representation on the new Area Councils set up by the Ministry of Supply, and on all other committees with a view to protecting workers' interests – much as had happened in the previous war.[12] The London Labour Party took up a succession of issues with government ministries and quickly adapted to the official system via London mayors, whips and constituency officials who participated in local Food Control and Ministry of Information committees.[13]

Moreover, in contrast to practice in the First World War, the constituency organisations maintained much of their regular activity in terms of socials and fund-raising events, not least because throughout the Phoney War period and even in 1940 they expected to have to fight a general election. Some constituencies were still selecting parliamentary candidates in the autumn of 1940.[14] The London Labour Party reduced its staff, but otherwise sustained a routine hum of work including publishing *London News*, and holding conferences and reunions. As a minister Herbert Morrison was granted leave of absence but managed to attend LLP executive meetings and to address annual conferences. It was not until 1941–2 that the diversion of personnel by war work seriously disrupted normal activity.[15]

Yet as in the previous war the party found itself restricted by an electoral pact to abstain from contesting vacancies in seats held by other parties. This naturally proved irksome at local level. Aneurin Bevan consistently argued that the party was throwing away an opportunity to wage war on Toryism and promote a social revolution. Yet Bevan largely failed to persuade the constituency parties, partly because of their enthusiasm for the war but also because of the latitude they enjoyed. Labour made a distinction between an electoral truce and a *political* truce which had never been part of the deal. Whenever subjected to criticism about the truce, Attlee reminded his supporters that 'there is no obligation whatever on members of the Party to abstain from advocating party policy'. This left CLPs free to organise meetings and disseminate propaganda. In 1941, for example, constituency parties promoted Labour's 'Help Russia Fund', organising door-to-door and street collections for aid for Britain's new ally. The publication of the Beveridge Report in December 1942 'gave us another opportunity to break out of the purdah of the party truce', as Ian Mikardo recalled of wartime campaigns in Reading.[16] Even the Bishop Auckland party held a discussion, accepted 'without reservation the principles embodied in the Beveridge Report Plan', urged the appointment of a minister to implement it, and dispatched resolutions to Churchill and their MP, Dalton.[17] By 1943–4 local parties were holding regular meetings to discuss Beveridge, post-war employment, pensions and women's role in industry. Overall, the constituency records suggest that members managed to combine support for the war effort with a measure of normal political activity.

This pattern throws some light on the claim that Labour weathered the war years far better than their Conservative rivals. There is a good deal of validity in this in the sense that Labour retained a strong and even enhanced sense of its purpose while its rival became disorientated and lost the patriotic high ground over the inadequate preparation for the war. 'Our Party has not lost its identity. In the main it still speaks in the House as a Party,' as the conference chairman put it in 1942.[18] In fact, Labour drew together after the controversies of the later 1930s, following the readmission of rebels such as George Strauss as early as March 1940, followed by Trevelyan, Bevan and Cripps.[19]

On the other hand, retaining party membership and agents proved more complicated. Certainly Labour continued to hold annual conferences, unlike the Conservatives, and used the Area Organisers to keep constituencies in touch with headquarters. Trade union membership remained steady at around 2.2 million, reflecting losses to the forces balanced by gains as industry expanded and incorporated new workers. Inevitably individual membership proved harder to maintain, declining from 239,000 in 1939 to 175,000 in 1940 and 129,000 in 1941 before rising again to 134,000 by 1943 and 153,000 in 1944. Over the five years of war the extensive movements into the forces and new employment, combined with bombing of industrial areas, disrupted recruitment even in the best-organised parties. By 1944 Merton and Morden admitted 'many rank-and-file members were not fully paid up because collectors had been unable to call'.[20] Hendon's membership fell from 2,247 to 1,102 between 1940 and 1944. In Woolwich where the 5,032 of 1937 had dwindled to a still impressive 3,108 by 1941, the organisers recorded losing 1,318 by death and removals, 301 who were called up or evacuated, 313 who had been bombed out of their homes, and ninety-nine new members by 1942.[21] At the opposite extreme Bishop Auckland's individual membership languished at seventy-one (1941), sixty-seven (1942) and seventy-three (1943); a membership drive pushed this to eighty-two in 1944 but it slipped to seventy-eight in 1945.[22] Here at least the war made little or no difference, and it is worth noting that at the 1945 election Labour's majority in Bishop Auckland increased by less than 800, a very poor performance in the circumstances and probably symptomatic of the neglect of individual membership in such constituencies.

In the aftermath of the 1945 election the Conservatives attributed their defeat to inferior organisation on the grounds that many more of their agents had been lost to the war effort. However, such claims must be treated with caution, partly because the swing of opinion was so emphatic that organisation cannot have been more than a marginal factor, and, in any case, the Conservatives' traditional advantage in paid agents was not lost so much as narrowed by 1945.[23] In the late 1930s they had 352 agents compared with 115 for Labour, and although both parties urged local organisations to retain their agents many left because they wanted to serve in the forces, undertake other forms of war work, or lost their posts through lack of funds. By 1940 193 Tory agents had been lost. Petrol rationing severely hampered their efforts to keep in touch with branches especially after July 1942 when the basic petrol ration was withdrawn from private motorists. In Frome, a winnable Somerset seat, the Labour Party levied special contributions to retain the agent and received £25 from headquarters towards his salary; but by August 1940 he had been replaced with a secretary at £1 a week.[24] Although the total number of Labour agents remained steady at 117 in 1940, and 103 in 1941, it had fallen to sixty-two by 1942 and fifty-eight by 1943, recovering slightly to sixty-four by May 1945.[25] During 1944, as thoughts turned to the post-war election, pressure was exerted on ministers to secure the release of agents from the forces. However, although many Conservative agents were released in the spring of 1945 this was probably too late to make a significant impact on the election, and the relative shortage simply provided a convenient excuse for the disaster rather than the cause. Although Labour fought the 1945 campaign with fewer agents than at any time since 1918, the party suffered less than its rivals because it was accustomed to relying on unpaid, part-time and amateur agents.

By far the greatest period of frustration for rank-and-file members came during 1942–3 when the price paid for the electoral truce became apparent as Independents and candidates of the Common Wealth Party, founded in 1942, captured Conservative seats in by-elections. 'Having spent half a century on educating the people of Britain to Socialism,' grumbled Bevan, 'the Labour Party has maladroitly manoeuvred itself into a state in which it cannot take advantage of it.'[26] At the 1942 conference Bevan's resolution to terminate the truce was only narrowly defeated by 1.275 million to 1.209 million votes. When he tried again in 1943 and was heavily beaten he angrily complained of the 'bovine, inert and irresponsible' bloc vote of the unions. 'The trade unions are no longer paying affiliation fees to the Labour Party,' he protested. 'They are paying its burial expenses.'[27] But although Bevan recognised more clearly than the parliamentary leaders the groundswell of opinion for radical social policies, he was mistaken in fearing that Labour had thrown away its advantage by committing itself to the coalition. In effect, the party won a double dividend by gaining credit for its patriotism and effectiveness in office while also maintaining its distinct political profile as an alternative to the Conservatives.

Bevan was also frustrated at the conferences by the safety valve that drew the pressure from rank-and-file discontent. Of the 161 parliamentary seats vacant during the war, sixty-six were filled unopposed but seventy-five were contested by Independent or Commonwealth candidates, many of whom were actually Labour proxies. Several Common Wealth candidates, including Richard Acland, Elaine Burton, Desmond Donnelly and George Wigg, subsequently became Labour MPs. Moreover, existing Labour figures masqueraded as Independents including W. J. Brown, a former Labour MP who won Rugby, Jennie Lee, also a former MP, at Bristol Central, and Tom Driberg who overturned a Conservative majority of 8,000 at Maldon in Essex when the coalition was at its most unpopular following the fall of Tobruk in June 1942. Although Attlee instructed the local parties to support the incumbent government candidate and party headquarters dispatched speakers to Maldon to this end, local members and officers commonly ignored the official injunctions. Many wrote in to protest, some citing the narrow vote at the 1942 conference as justification: 'I think the conference released us from the Truce, for a majority of 66,000 out of two-and-a-half million is really no majority,' as one put it.[28] In effect, while headquarters upheld the truce to the extent of expelling some members and disbanding several CLPs, it was largely unable to control individual members; despite the embarrassment when Conservatives were defeated, there were limits on how far they could go.

In any case, by the start of 1944 the worst period had been weathered as the grass-roots activists began to focus on the anticipated general election. Some were well advanced; Birmingham, for example, had begun preparations during 1943 and had selected all thirteen candidates by the end of 1944.[29] In Gloucester the party resumed public meetings in 1943 and printed regular articles by the candidate in the *Gloucester Labour News* including attacks on the sitting MP for voting in favour of Mussolini's takeover of Abyssinia, the Munich Settlement and Chamberlain in the Norway debate.[30] In London some 450 delegates attended a special conference in June to consider local organisation, the redistribution of seats and other election preparations.[31] In Frome the Labour candidate, who had been adopted in 1943, spent the spring of 1944 touring the constituency; in January 1945 the CLP sought a new paid agent, and by May the organisation of the election campaign was in full swing with sixty-five meetings arranged for a two-week period alone.[32] Of course, not all areas were as far advanced as London, Birmingham, Frome and Gloucester, but in these areas where Labour expected to make gains it enjoyed a head start over the Conservatives. Against this background of rising activity in 1943–4, the constituency parties began to pressurise the NEC to insist on abandoning the truce in the spring of 1944, a view it endorsed in October.

Meanwhile at Westminster Labour performed an uncomfortable balancing act throughout the war, forming a key part of the coalition government and accepting responsibility for its shortcomings while also constituting the parliamentary Opposition. Inevitably some ministers got out of touch, resented criticism and saw the Commons as a diversion from their work, especially those of an autocratic temperament.

'Why don't you shut up this bloody monkey-house, or at any rate only
open it one day a week?' an exasperated Dalton asked the Tory chief
whip a few days after the formation of the coalition.[33] Dalton found
the tea-room plotting with Tory MPs far more congenial than long-
winded meetings of the Parliamentary Labour Party. Yet most Labour
leaders made a point of attending the annual conferences, the PLP and
the NEC to defend their policy and to conciliate members. The diary
kept by one junior minister, James Chuter Ede, underlined the extent
to which they were called to account and the value of the confronta-
tions as a safety valve. Labour ministers were vulnerable to the charge
of having sold themselves too cheaply in May 1940, but despite some
lively meetings, the decisions of the NEC fully conformed to the leaders'
wishes; in the worst period of the war it rejected a proposal to ditch
the electoral truce by a comfortable seventeen-to-seven margin. By
contrast Conservative discontent was largely left to fester, according to
R. A. Butler, who noted: 'Members had no contact with Ministers but
spent their time in the Smoke Room consuming expensive drinks but
also intriguing.'[34]

Labour's Opposition was led by Harold Laski, Aneurin Bevan and
Emmanuel Shinwell. As chairman of the NEC Laski proved to be an
especial irritation not least because he was determined to destroy the
truce and schemed to replace Attlee as leader with Bevin or Dalton.
Though only a backbencher, Bevan elevated himself into a major
figure during the war, partly by his venomous attacks on Churchill
whom he mocked as 'the spokesman of his order and of his class, and
that class and that order is dying'.[35] Churchill returned the compli-
ment by describing him as 'a squalid nuisance'. Bevan also subjected
Attlee to some devastating criticism for his failure to give leadership,
referring to him on one occasion as 'yet another Socialist passing into
the limbo of collaboration'. On the other hand, Bevan's rhetoric was
much appreciated by the movement and arguably helped to maintain
morale at a time when Labour's sense of identity might have been
lost in coalition and consensus. In the Commons, Shinwell, who had
declined a junior post in 1940 and nursed his grievances, effectively
acted as Leader of the Opposition. Dalton liked to deride him as
'Shinbad the Tailor'. But to the general surprise Shinwell co-operated
with Liberal and Tory rebels, notably an extreme right-winger, Earl
Winterton, the pair earning the epithet 'Arsenic and Old Lace'.

However, as both Shinwell and Bevan were keen to promote the war effort, the Labour rebels never collaborated with the pacifist minority. Nor did they work with the one politician capable of up-setting party strategy: Sir Stafford Cripps. After being sent to Moscow as special ambassador, Cripps' career enjoyed a dramatic resurrection for he was widely, if implausibly, credited with bringing Russia into the war at a stage when Britain desperately needed an ally. On his return in May 1942 Cripps enjoyed a level of popular acclaim only a little less than Churchill's and was widely regarded as an alternative prime minister. Churchill wisely offered him a post as Minister for Supply which, ominously, he rejected. But Cripps was too dangerous to both Attlee and Churchill to be left at large, and he subsequently became Leader of the Commons, a role to which he was not obvi-ously suited though it put him in the position of having to defend the government.

Shinwell and Bevan challenged the leadership over a number of military issues, social and economic grievances and the treatment of Labour interests by the coalition. Serious rebellion began in December 1941 when thirty-five Labour members voted for an amendment to the Manpower Bill designed to nationalise transport, coal and muni-tions. In July 1942 Bevan, capitalising on reactions to the fall of Tobruk, led an attack on military strategy with a great speech in which he complained that the Allies had been culpably slow to relieve Russia by launching a second front, but he attracted only twenty-five votes despite enjoying wide sympathy on the Labour benches. Churchill conciliated the party in his 1942 reshuffle by appointing Cripps and by elevating Attlee as deputy prime minister, but also antagonised members by sacking Greenwood who had become an alcoholic by this time: 'the poor old chap couldn't even sign his name after midday', noted Dalton.[36]

Much the biggest rebellion was provoked by the Cabinet's grudging response to the Beveridge Report which was debated in February 1943 when ninety-seven Labour MPs defied the whips to vote for early legislation; only two MPs outside the government had backed the leadership. When challenged over the report at a PLP meeting, Bevin, always intolerant of criticism, lost his temper and threatened to resign, leaving Morrison to save the party from an even worse split by an eloquent appeal for support. It was a sign of the importance Beveridge was now assuming that in a debate on the subject at the 1943 party conference the thirty-two-year-old Barbara Betts (later Castle) made her reputation by complaining they were always offered 'Jam yesterday, and jam tomorrow, but never jam today!' The friction would have been even worse had members appreciated the extent to which the Labour leaders shared Churchill's fears that to raise expectations about implementing the report would dangerously undermine the public's willingness to endure further hardship; Attlee, who became irritated by Beveridge's arrogance, commented that he 'seemed to think the war ought to stop while his plan was put into effect'.[37] Fortunately for party unity, Churchill and his chancellor, Kingsley Wood, attracted most of the criticism for obstructing the report on financial grounds, but the episode compounded feelings that Labour should quit the coalition as soon as possible.

However, 1943 brought further controversy, notably in April, when sixty-one Labour members voted for an increase in pensions, and in October over the decision to release the fascist leader, Oswald Mosley, from internment. As Home Secretary Morrison bore the brunt of the protests in the shape of hostile demonstrations, bottles labelled 'Rat Poison' that arrived by post, and an angry deputation of Labour MPs sixty-two of whom voted against the government on the issue; at a meeting of the PLP members backed Morrison by just fifty-one to forty-three. During 1944 ministers continued to show their deter-mination not to give way to rank-and-file pressure by their reactions to a surprise amendment to R. A. Butler's Education Bill to give equal pay to women teachers. Churchill demanded a vote of confidence in his government and Bevin actually threatened to resign if the offending clause were not dropped.[38] In April Bevin again provoked anger by imposing a penalty of five years in prison on anyone who participated in unofficial strikes. In a savage attack Bevan condemned this as typical of a corporate state, and fifteen Labour MPs voted with him while seventy-three abstained. By this time Bevan had emerged as a popular figure, winning election to the NEC which gave him even more scope for criticism. His next opportunity was provided by the row over government policy in Greece in December. Labour members felt outraged by Britain's desire to disarm and crush the Communist resist-ance movement that had led the fight against the Germans, and were appalled at the Labour leaders for letting them get away with it;

following the release of Mosley the policy raised doubts about Britain's commitment to waging a war on fascism. The parliamentary rebels received widespread backing from constituency parties who adopted resolutions condemning official policy. Yet once again Attlee and his colleagues entirely agreed with the Conservative ministers, foreshadowing post-war Labour divisions over foreign policy. Bevan, conscious that rank-and-file anger was now putting the coalition in jeopardy, insisted that ministers must either 'exercise a more decisive influence upon the conduct of our affairs or else leave the Tories to do their own dirty work themselves'.[39] Despite the critics' inability to alter the policy, their protest over Greece left the leaders in no doubt that they could not disregard Labour principles much longer and that the party would have to leave the coalition soon.

However, this catalogue of controversy must be seen in perspective. Close examination of Labour's wartime experience creates an exaggerated impression of dissent and division because the plentiful source material is biased towards the views of the critics. The question has to be asked: why, despite so much disagreement, was there no breakdown between the parliamentary leaders and the party in the country? There are three main explanations. First, the party's democratic structure allowed critics to call their leaders to account through the PLP, the NEC and annual conferences, in contrast to the position among Conservatives who were largely denied such outlets. Second, members' dissent was mitigated by feelings of patriotism, pride that Labour had rescued the government in dire circumstances and an awareness that, for all its shortcomings, the coalition was susceptible to Labour pressure; it was not, in fact, Labour that was losing the debate but the Conservatives. Bevin had increased wages for low-paid workers, Morrison had nationalised the fire service, food rationing had established the principle of shared sacrifice, and extensive plans for reconstruction were underway. Several Labour ministers even appreciated the value of Labour pressure in helping them to win arguments within the government. Dalton's technique involved writing a policy document, getting the NEC to approve it, and then putting it into the official machine as Labour policy that could not easily be rejected.[40] Chuter Ede, though only a junior education minister under R. A. Butler, successfully insisted on an education reform bill because 'the Labour Party wanted something on account and we were most easily able to provide it'.[41] The third factor was electoral constraint. Although discontent reached a peak during 1942–3 due to the clamour to create a second front and by-election defeats for the Conservatives, Labour remained fearful about the consequences of pushing revolt too far. It was assumed that if Labour split the Cabinet or left the coalition too soon, it would give Churchill an excuse to hold a wartime election in which Labour might be reduced to as few as thirty seats.[42] Though this seems preposterous with benefit of hindsight, such expectations acted as a powerful deterrent, at least until 1944.

Of course, the discontent at local level reflected the much greater awareness about changes in public opinion among ordinary members than among ministers. There are good grounds for thinking that the Second World War formed a watershed in shifting opinion to the left and ushering in a prolonged period of consensus. The availability of Gallup polls, Mass Observation reports and Ministry of Information surveys gives us a much better picture of wartime attitudes than exists for the First World War. By the end of 1942 40 per cent of people told Mass Observation that their political views had changed.[43] What seems remarkable in retrospect is that such findings were not taken seriously by most of the politicians even as late as 1945. Establishment figures were dismissive of the popular expressions of radicalism and scepticism that manifested themselves early in the war and underpinned Labour's eventual triumph. The tone was set by the popularity and prestige enjoyed by the two newspapers, the *Daily Mirror* and the *News Chronicle*, that had consistently attacked appeasement, fascism and Chamberlain in the 1930s; by comparison the rest of the press had become discredited for the unending apologia it had offered for failed policies. In July 1940 the publication of *Guilty Men*, an attack on the leading appeasers, Chamberlain, Hoare and Simon, by three authors including the young Michael Foot, caught the angry mood generated by the fiasco of Dunkirk, and the book went through ten impressions in July alone. The cartoonist David Low helped propagate the idea that the country was being run by reactionary and out-of-date incompetents through his famous character Colonel Blimp. To the consternation of Churchill the BBC ran what he regarded as subversive programmes including the *Brains Trust*, which featured left-wingers like Julian Huxley and C. M. Joad, and *Postscripts*, a broadcast by J. B. Priestley that went out on Sunday evenings after the news. After the pro-Establishment role played by the broadcasters under Sir John Reith's leadership this was a shock and was probably the origin of post-1945 Conservative views of the BBC as a purveyor of left-wing propaganda; following Conservative protests Priestley was taken off the air.[44]

Authority was even more concerned about the armed forces. A strong tradition developed, supported by some impressionistic though compelling evidence, that in 1945 servicemen voted Labour. When Churchill casually observed to Air Chief Marshal Harris 'I suppose that, when the election comes, I can count on the votes of most of the men in the Air Force?' he was shocked by the reply: 'No sir, eighty per cent of them will vote Labour.'[45] This was corroborated by Labour candidates such as Leah Manning who was trailing at her count at Epping until the ballot boxes containing the forces' votes were opened and put her ahead. At Reading Ian Mikardo noticed that he could 'see the outcome in the overwhelmingly Labour majority in the separately counted forces vote'.[46]

But what is the explanation for such claims? Contemporaries complained that the men had been brainwashed by the Army Bureau of Current Affairs. The origins of this organisation lay back in 1920 when the Army Education Corps had been formed to teach citizenship. After being abandoned following the outbreak of war it was revived as the Army Bureau of Current Affairs as a result of concern about morale and boredom among the troops during the Phoney War period. The authorities were conscious that the new recruits were much less enthusiastic and more critical than the naïve patriots who had volunteered in 1914. It seemed appropriate to offer them lectures and discussions about current affairs generally, and Britain's war aims in particular, though Churchill had grave reservations about the whole idea: 'Will not such discussions only provide opportunities for the professional grouser and agitator with a glib tongue?' he demanded.[47] His fears appeared justified in 1943 when the troops started discussing the Beveridge Report. 'Whoever dreamed up the ABCA at the War Office was in part responsible for Labour's landslide victory in 1945,' claimed Woodrow Wyatt who was elected for Birmingham Aston in the election.[48] However, such comment almost certainly exaggerates its influence. The men in the forces were predisposed to support Labour partly because they felt dissatisfied over poor pay and allowances, and had experienced at first hand the inadequacy of the preparations for war. And like other first-time voters they leaned heavily towards Labour.[49] Moreover, by 1941 30 per cent of the troops read the *Daily Mirror*, a newspaper that encouraged them to ventilate their grievances in its columns. Two *Mirror* journalists, Garry Allighan, subsequently Labour MP for Gravesend, and Barbara Betts, subsequently Labour MP for Blackburn, edited 'Question Time in the Mess' which offered troops advice on welfare, rights and even court martial procedure. All this greatly antagonised Churchill and provoked Harold Nicolson to complain that the *Mirror* had 'pandered to the men in the ranks and given them a general distrust of authority'.[50] In the light of such impressions it certainly seems probable that servicemen leant further to Labour than the rest of society by 1945, though the significance must not be exaggerated. Of the 4.5 million service personnel, 2.9 million applied to become voters by post or by proxy, of whom 1.7 million actually voted in 1945, not a decisive element among the twenty-five million electors.

Some contemporaries also believed that Labour gained an advantage from the spread of a spirit of egalitarianism and a weakening of class prejudices during wartime, triggered by fears of an invasion in the summer of 1940 and a resulting sense that everyone must shoulder the sacrifices in the national interest. Throughout the war the *Daily Mirror* fostered egalitarianism, criticising teachers, for example, for being slow to tackle class distinctions: 'During the war, many members of the diverse social groups have been thrown together in the Services, in factories, and in evacuation centres. Learning to appreciate one another, they have made the happy discovery that, in all things that really matter, they are alike . . . We may all be equal in death. But many thousands of Britons have given everything in this war in order that we might be equal in life too.'[51] By linking egalitarianism with patriotism the *Mirror* found a more effective way of attacking upper-class privilege than pre-war socialists.

On the other hand, wartime egalitarianism was something of a passing phase, sustained by Dunkirk and the Blitz. Expressions of egalitarianism such as food and petrol rationing commanded popular support, but in time public tolerance for them dwindled especially once victory began to be taken for granted. In 1943 Labour pounced on Nancy Astor MP who was fined £50 for contravening the rationing ordinance by obtaining a fur jacket, silk stockings, gloves, shoes and an evening gown from America.[52] But it was easy to misjudge the mood. Dalton, for example, decided to save resources by banning the manufacture of umbrellas and turn-ups on trousers, saying, 'There can be no equality of sacrifice in this war. Some must lose lives and limbs, others only the turn-ups on their trousers.' In 1943 he pledged not to buy a new suit of clothes until the war was over.[53] But although this earned Dalton credit within the movement, it exposed him to ridicule outside it as only the well-off could afford suits that lasted for years. Amid these ephemeral symptoms it is hard to find evidence that the fundamentals of a class-divided society really changed.

However, other currents of opinion helped the Labour Party in less complicated ways, as Bevan recognised at the outset. 'War opens minds that were sealed, stimulates dormant intelligence and recruits into political controversy thousands who would otherwise remain in the political hinterland.'[54] The Conservatives never recovered from the disgrace of association with the leading appeasers, one of whom, Samuel Hoare, was dispatched to Madrid as ambassador, while Chamberlain and Simon remained in office for some months. They were embarrassed by revelations about MPs' links with fascist organisations before the war and by the defeatism that led Tory peers, including the Duke of Hamilton, Lord Brocket, the Duke of Buccleuch, the Marquis of Tavistock, Lord Londonderry and the Earl of Mar, to pressurise the government to make peace with Germany during the Phoney War. Sir Thomas Moore MP, who was derided as 'Hitler's friend' by the *Sunday Pictorial*, was called to task by his Ayr party, while the Bristol Conservatives deselected their MP, Cyril Culverwell, for pro-Nazi activity. Captain A. H. M. Ramsay, MP for Peebles and founder of the notorious Right Club, was arrested and interned in May 1940. Lord Erskine, a member of the January Club, a British Union of Fascists front organisation, actually became MP for Brighton in 1940 but suddenly resigned without explanation in 1941.[55] While the accusation levelled by Konni Zilliacus that 'most Tories have never regarded Fascism as an enemy' was absurd, there was sufficient evidence of pro-fascist and pro-appeasement sympathies to keep the party on the defensive up to the election in 1945.[56]

Whether this negative reaction was complemented by a more positive leftward trend in opinion is less obvious. Did socialism become more acceptable in Britain as a result of the extraordinary popularity enjoyed by the Soviet Union following Germany's invasion of Russia in June 1941? Although the authorities were nervous about symptoms of enthusiasm for the Soviet Union, it seems improbable that this was translated into support for a Communist system. It is more relevant that 'expert' military predictions about the Soviet Army rapidly proved baseless. The Red Army coped better with the Germans than expected and the Soviet system proved to be more resilient and efficient. By extension, state control and planning might not be such a disaster as had been believed before the war, and Conservatives recognised that they could not expect to win elections on a simple anti-socialist cry in the future. As Sarah Churchill told her father in June 1945: 'Socialism as practised in the war did no one any harm, and quite a lot of people good.' By 1945 this presentation of socialism as something reassuringly familiar that had worked during the war, rather than an imported novelty, became the hallmark of Labour propaganda. As Arthur Greenwood put it, as controls had proved their value in wartime they would be necessary in peacetime: 'I make a present of that to the Tory Party.'[57] A. V. Alexander chose to defuse public fears about state control by pointing to the shipbuilding industry which 'was left in chaos after the Great War' but had been revived: 'What a difference a plan can make. Without a plan we would never have won the war.'[58]

Despite this tactical advantage, the parliamentary leaders continued to feel nervous about propagating an unqualified socialist programme. During 1944 post-war economic policy was being carefully devised by Dalton and the NEC's subcommittees to be published as *Full Employment and Financial Policy*. However, as the ambitions and expectations on the left of the movement raced ahead, official party policy struggled to keep pace. One symptom of this mood was the widespread criticism even of the Beveridge Report during 1942–3. Zilliacus approved of Beveridge merely as a stepping stone to socialism, Shinwell disparaged the report as 'no more than ambulance work intended to conceal the more hideous features of the existing society', and the eloquent Bevan claimed that 'Sir William has described the conditions in which the tears might be taken out of capitalism.'[59] In the face of this rising tide Morrison, who was drafting the party's manifesto for the post-war election, sought to put limits on Labour's commitment to nationalisation; but at the conference in December 1944 things got out of hand. 'I cannot for the life of me understand how we are going to fight a general election when we are in practically complete agreement with the Conservative Party,' objected Bessie Braddock, soon to be elected for Liverpool Exchange.[60] The chairman, Noel-Baker, attempted to have a resolution calling for sweeping public ownership withdrawn, but its proposer, Ian Mikardo, a delegate from Reading, refused and it was subsequently carried on a show of hands. On his way out the triumphant Mikardo was waylaid by Herbert Morrison who told him: 'Young man, you did very well this morning . . . but you realise, don't you, that you've lost us the general election.'[61] In the event the official manifesto ignored Mikardo's resolution, but in any case the politicians were obsessing over details; what counted with voters by 1945 was the broad impression that wartime 'Socialism' had done its job and held no great terrors.

Or did it? In recent years some historians have attempted to cast doubt on the extent of popular radicalism during the war and to suggest that far from wanting a Labour victory people had simply become apathetic and cynical about politics.[62] This, however, is a classic case of academics misunderstanding popular politics by adopting a *de haut en bas* view of it. The negative view is quite inconsistent with the basic facts of the 1945 election. At 73 per cent, turnout was actually higher than in 1935 (71 per cent), let alone the 59 per cent recorded at the more comparable 1918 election. On this showing apathy had actually *declined*. Many voters were rejecting a party and a government they disliked as much as endorsing one they liked, but that is true of all elections and there are no grounds for thinking it was more true in 1945. Indeed, there is evidence that prior to the election voters had become unusually politicised and that Beveridge, in particular, had crystallised a positive view about post-war policies. That voters were more assertive and less deferential is more obvious by comparison with the impact of the First World War. The Second World War saw nothing comparable to the patriotic interlude of 1914–16 on the industrial front. The number of strikes actually increased in 1939 and continued to do so up to 1945 because workers were determined not to lose the gains to be made from a booming economy. Mass Observation surveys regularly revealed that the public was sceptical towards authority and official propaganda about food economy and warnings about discussing the war in public. But far from alienating them from politics this mood translated into a clear idea of political priorities in terms of house-building and full employment after the war.

The final element in the popular radicalism of wartime was the *Daily Mirror*. Attempts have been made to minimise its significance by suggesting it did not explicitly back Labour until late in the election campaign.[63] This, however, is to misunderstand its role. The *Mirror* did not offer an unqualified endorsement of Labour like the *Daily Herald* nor proclaim full-blooded socialism. Its role lay in explaining Labour's socialism to voters not accustomed to support the party. It had prepared the ground by destroying the credibility of Chamberlain following the collapse of appeasement and the failures of the Phoney War period. Referring to the Norwegian Campaign the paper editorialised: 'The prime minister is an expert at this art of explaining away failure. He gets so much practice in it.'[64] The *Mirror* also gave prominence to Morrison, Bevin and Cripps as key men in the war effort, and quoted extensively from patriotic comments by Attlee and others at Labour's wartime conferences, recasting the party as the epitome of the British national cause.[65] Taken with the paper's enthusiasm for the wartime role of the king and queen, the pro-Labour material merged into a daily diet of patriotism and egalitarianism that was radical and reassuring at the same time. 'There must be something seriously wrong with a political and economic system which brought us so near to disaster,' argued the *Mirror* in January 1945. 'That something was the fact that no real fusion existed between public and private interests.'[66] This was the route that led the paper to a socialistic stance without actually talking explicitly about socialism. It presented Labour's programme in almost non-ideological terms on the basis that it encouraged private enterprise but was underpinned by state intervention and nationalisation of those industries that had been allowed by their owners to become inefficient.[67] 'It is true that there is no new idea in [Labour's] statement of policy,' the *Mirror* wrote in April 1945. 'No revolutionary proposals [but] ideas and proposals which have survived many tests of practical experience have been welded into a considered, cohesive plan to serve the public interest. Labour's Declaration offers a typically British solution for British problems.'[68] This approach neatly defused voters' fears, detached party policy from extremism, and linked socialistic ideas firmly to the national cause.

The scene was set for the general election by the decision of the NEC on 7 October 1944 that Labour should fight as an independent party, a view compounded by anger over the coalition's policy in Greece. When Germany surrendered in May 1945 there followed two weeks of uncertainty because of the possibility that the coalition might continue until Japan had been defeated. Several Labour ministers, including Attlee, Bevin and Dalton, favoured extending its life into peacetime. However, when the NEC met at Blackpool for the conference on 19 May it followed Morrison's lead, effectively overruling Attlee by voting to withdraw from the government. The conference was such a triumph for Morrison that it engendered a new move to push Attlee aside and make him Leader. By 1945 the party displayed little enthusiasm for Attlee largely because few were able to appreciate his work behind the scenes in innumerable government committees. However, the critics failed to agree on an alternative candidate. After the conference the irrepressible Laski wrote to Attlee advising him of the general view that 'the continuance of your leadership is a grave handicap to our hopes of victory in the coming election'. With a serenity he can hardly have felt, Attlee replied: 'Thank you for your letter, contents of which have been noted'!

Meanwhile Labour's withdrawal from the coalition resulted in a temporary Conservative administration and further manoeuvring by the parties over the date of an election now five years overdue. Labour argued that it should not be held until the autumn, allowing time to prepare an accurate register including the servicemen. But Churchill insisted on either an immediate election or a continuation of the coalition until the defeat of Japan. For Labour the object of a delay was to allow voters the opportunity to focus on peacetime issues once again. Their thoughts were dominated by memories of the Coupon Election of 1918 which had been held in December following hot on the heels of the Armistice in November, when anti-German emotions had been high. They also assumed that Lloyd George's victory as the man who won the war offered a sure precedent for Churchill whose prestige was naturally very high. Even as shrewd an electioneer as Morrison considered it 'suicide' for Labour to fight the election close to the defeat of Germany. 'The electors would rally behind Churchill in the coming election and the Labour Party would be cast into the wilderness for another generation,' warned Dalton.[69] Most observers agreed with Churchill in expecting a Conservative majority of around thirty.

Why were these contemporary predictions so completely wrong? In the first place because the politicians preferred to trust their instincts rather than scientific evidence. Since July 1943 the Gallup polls had given Labour a consistent lead of 12 per cent or more over the Tories; but few believed that a small sample could be an accurate reflection of opinion. In February 1944 a remarkable by-election had taken place in the safe Conservative seat at West Derbyshire which fell to Charlie White, a local Labour Party member who stood as Independent Labour. In some ways the by-election presaged the general election; White won applause when he commended Churchill's war record but even more when he insisted that this did not justify a post-war vote for him. However, Attlee, writing to Bevin, dismissed White's victory on the grounds that voters had been tempted to express their passing irritation with the government and that, as the result could not affect the coalition, the vote could not be taken as signifying support for an alternative government. As late as July 1945 Attlee complained: 'The chief difficulty of this election is to credit the optimism of all our people.'[70]

The second explanation is that 1918 was not a sound precedent for 1945 despite the similarities. In 1918 a military victory had not been anticipated and so the public was still in belligerent wartime mode, whereas in the Second World War it had been assumed from 1943 onwards that the Allies were bound to win; consequently, there had been ample opportunity to refocus on peacetime issues as local Labour parties had clearly been doing. In fact, several years of full employment and higher wages had generated a mood of rising expectations by 1945, accentuated by an understandable fear that the workers' gains might be snatched away from them in the aftermath of victory. Given their post-1918 record in office, the Conservatives appeared more suspect in this respect.

The third explanation is that Churchill was never quite the asset Lloyd George had been as war leader, partly because his party was so vulnerable and because his own relations with it were so complicated. The Conservatives felt uncertain how to fight the campaign as they were outflanked by Labour on the domestic front and had already forfeited their traditional authority in external affairs. By default they relied on Churchill's prestige, many candidates putting his photograph on their election addresses with a frank plea to vote for *him*. However, Churchill's own grasp of the situation was faulty. Resorting to the scaremongering tactics that had been employed to frighten voters away from Labour in the 1930s, he quickly abandoned his status as a national leader for the role of a partisan. In his first broadcast Churchill alleged that a Labour government 'would have to fall back on some kind of Gestapo, no doubt very humanely directed in the first instance'. The next night Attlee responded in a dignified way: 'When I listened to the Prime Minister's speech last night . . . I realised at once what was his object. He wanted the electors to understand how great was the difference between Winston Churchill the great war leader . . . and Mr Churchill the Party Leader of the Conservatives. He feared lest those who had accepted his leadership in war might be tempted out of gratitude to follow him further.' How much impact this made is unclear. Mass Observation reported that the speech 'is generally felt for a man of Churchill's prestige to be a very poor effort and a cheaply electioneering speech', and some correspondents reported that Conservatives had been alienated by it.[71] Certainly Labour exploited it; in Reading Ian Mikardo instructed his chairman to introduce him at meetings as '"Obergruppenfuhrer Ian Mikardo, prospective Gauleiter of Berkshire, Buckinghamshire and Oxfordshire". That always got us off to a good start.'[72]

Even so, Labour's tacticians felt they must defuse Churchill's appeal by exposing the divisions between him and his party. In his radio broadcast A. V. Alexander quoted extensively from Churchill's speeches attacking the Tories over inadequate national defence, and suggested he was merely a stalking horse: 'As soon as Mr Churchill has served his purpose the Tories will elbow him out just as they dispensed with Lloyd George once he had served his purpose by winning the Khaki Election for privilege.'[73] However, it would be rash to assume that these efforts entirely succeeded, for Churchill embarked on a 1,000-mile tour where he was usually received with acclaim by huge crowds. Morgan Phillips, Labour's general secretary, protested to the Newsreel Association for sending a large staff of photographers on his tours without giving Labour similar treatment. But to no avail. 'The Prime Minister's tour . . . is considered to be of news interest, apart from any political interest, and the Newsreel Companies are at liberty to film it,' came the reply.[74] Phillips was right to be concerned, for Labour's advantage in the polls had dwindled from 18 per cent in February 1945 to 8 per cent by July. The only explanation for this recovery is Churchill's popularity. Yet the pattern suggests that his personal standing was insufficient to obliterate the reputation of his party; the campaign was not crucial as the result had been determined long in advance of the election. Labour candidates exploited the gap between Churchill and his party by targeting individual Tory MPs handicapped by a record as Chamberlainites and by connections with pro-Nazi organisations including The Link, the Anglo-German Fellowship, the Right Club and the British Union of Fascists. As Harold Macmillan commented later, 'It was not Churchill who lost the 1945 election; it was the ghost of Neville Chamberlain.'[75]

On the positive side Labour seized the patriotic high ground on the basis of its wartime record and its insistence that the leading Nazis must be brought to trial; consequently there was no possibility of their rivals using 'Hang the Kaiser' tactics as in 1918. This is especially evident in the broadcasts delivered by Bevin, Dalton, Alexander and Morrison who argued: 'Now this election is about whether we are going to be a great people or a small one – leader or hanger-on – a nation rich by our own efforts, or a seedy nation, living on the memories of past greatness.'[76] For patriotic chutzpah Morrison's language matched the Conservatives and was, moreover, a pointer to the Labour government's stance in external affairs after the war. In effect by 1945 the party had resurrected the patriotism-plus-socialism formula that some of its candidates had used successfully in the 1918 election. An equally important means of putting the Conservatives on the defensive lay in relentlessly reminding voters what had happened on the domestic front after the last war using the slogan: 'Ask Your Father'. The success of Bevan's book *Why Not Trust the Tories?*, which sold 80,000 copies in 1944, indicated that the public was receptive to this line. In May, as soon as it was clear that the election would take place sooner rather than later, the leaders began to exploit concerns about the transition from war to peace. Bevin, for example, demanded: 'Come out into the open. Is it your intention to take off control of food and let prices rise?'[77]

The national campaign was run from Transport House by Morgan Phillips, and G. R. Shepherd, the national agent. Labour's improved presentation and literature reflected the input of professionals from the *Daily Mirror*, including Ted Castle, Garry Allighan and Philip Zec, the cartoonist. They co-ordinated ten radio broadcasts addressed by Attlee, Bevin, Morrison, Cripps, Alexander, Ellen Wilkinson, James Griffiths, Philip Noel-Baker, Tom Johnston and George Tomlinson. Correspondence received at headquarters suggested that they went down well though some showed a lack of professionalism: 'Mr Attlee's delivery was a little monotonous at times', wrote one, 'and we could hear the crackle of his papers.'[78] The Labour leader embarked on a tour in the family's modest car driven by his wife, Violet, that took him to the West Midlands, Lancashire, Newcastle, Yorkshire, East Anglia and back to London. His seventy extempore speeches were well received and contrasted with the exuberance attending Churchill's meetings.

For the first time Labour enjoyed virtual parity of readership with the Tories in terms of national daily newspapers, its chief backers being the *Daily Herald*, the *Daily Mirror* and the Liberal *News Chronicle*. With its brash, risqué style the *Mirror* ruffled feathers in Labour's puritanical heartlands. In Sheffield the twelve-year-old Roy Hattersley distributed Labour leaflets that included the *Mirror*'s famous strip cartoon character, Jane, who exposed much of her body. But the agent, Councillor Ballard, who considered this pornography, quickly intervened: 'holding the leaflet at arm's length between thumb and forefinger [he said] it would be quite wrong for a boy of my age to handle such material'.[79] More importantly, the *Daily Mirror*'s propaganda complemented that of the party machine during May, June and July by running scare stories warning voters about factories already closing down as evidence of the threat to employment after demobilisation. It also ran the 'Vote for Him' campaign involving a concerted effort to mobilise women, many of whom had proxy votes for 1.873 million servicemen as well as their own, by reminding them: 'You know what way your man would march.'[80] It scarcely mattered that Labour was not mentioned, for by this stage the paper's meaning was clear.

The only minor complication in this campaign lay in occasional interventions by the Labour left, still angry over the treatment of Greece. 'A silly speech by someone like Aneurin Bevan might be used to stampede the electors from Labour,' warned Attlee.[81] But the main offender was Laski who took the opportunity of Attlee's visit to the conference at Potsdam to remind the world that he would attend only as an observer. This was seized upon by the Conservatives as evidence that the party's leaders were merely tools manipulated by extremists behind the scenes. Churchill and Attlee engaged in an exchange of letters in which the latter endeavoured to explain that neither the party conference nor the NEC enjoyed the right to determine the policy of the parliamentary party. Although the correspondence petered out shortly before polling day, Laski continued to commit such indiscretions over foreign policy, eventually provoking another memorably restrained dismissal from Attlee: 'A period of silence on your part would be welcome.'

However, even a well-run national campaign could not entirely supersede the local struggles to fill 640 seats, up from 615 in 1935 as a result of a redistribution. At their best, local Labour campaigns eclipsed those of their rivals. In Frome, for example, the campaign included an agent, twelve sub-agents (some of whom were paid), fifty-seven committee rooms covering 102 of the 109 polling stations, 1,500 posters, 53,000 leaflets, 4,000 pamphlets, one hundred public meetings of which thirty-four were held indoors, a visit by Bevin and forty-six supporting speakers, and the use of 123 motor cars.[82]

Morgan Phillips' advice about what to include in local literature was widely followed.[83] Consequently many candidates put 'The complete defeat of Japan' at the top of a list of pledges, presumably to defuse any accusations of lack of patriotism. Britain 'must remain on a war footing until a decisive victory has been won over Japanese barbarism', wrote Richard Sargood in Bermondsey West.[84] Only a handful of candidates risked offending patriotic sentiment. Bevan's address made almost no reference to the war or its relevance to the election; while in Leyton the Reverend Sorensen declared 'I have a lifelong religious conviction that cannot be reconciled with capitalism and war'.[85] More typically, however, Labour candidates pictured themselves in military uniform – at least sixty-four were serving in the forces – and made explicit appeals to servicemen. 'If you are in the Forces,' wrote John Diamond (Manchester Blackley), 'I ask you to realise that only Socialism provides the opportunity of continuing that same comradeship which you have experienced and enjoyed, whereas capitalism means every man for himself, a scramble for jobs, and the survival of the slickest.'[86]

Some candidates were aware that their Tory opponents were vulnerable through their fascist sympathies. Sir Thomas Moore (Ayr) was candid enough to admit to membership of The Link and the Anglo-German Fellowship, but he buried his 1934 *Daily Mail* articles praising the British Union of Fascists.[87] At Devonport Michael Foot attacked Leslie Hore-Belisha for making favourable comments about Mussolini, and in Deptford Labour's John Wilmot printed photographs of Neville Chamberlain happily greeting Mussolini and Hitler.[88] 'Let us remember', urged Roy Jenkins (Solihull), 'that hiding behind Mr Churchill's war record are hundreds of Tory members of parliament, men who sought to buy off Nazism and Fascism with loans and friendship.'[89] In East Ham South, Alfred Barnes tried to outmanoeuvre his Tory opponent by claiming: 'I supported the views of Mr Churchill towards Nazi Germany before 1939 when the Conservative MPs derided and scorned him.'[90]

Despite these skirmishes, however, most candidates focused on how Labour would handle the economy in the aftermath of war. Their first tactic was to remind voters about 1918. 'You remember how the soldiers came back to find not "Homes for Heroes" but chronic unemployment and soaring prices,' warned Richard Crossman (Coventry). 'For the sake of the soldiers this must not happen again.'[91] The second tactic involved an appeal to fairness. 'This has been, and is, a people's war,' commented J. E. Whittaker (Heywood and Radcliffe). 'We of the Labour Party intend that a people's peace shall follow.' Only occasionally did candidates allow passion to show through, as at Holborn where Irene Marcouse asked: 'Who is going to win the Peace? Are you – the ordinary citizens of Holborn and Britain? Or are THEY – the privileged few who have always cheated you and the peace and plenty you have earned?'[92] More positively candidates expressed Labour's policy as 'Controls versus Chaos', as Major R. N. Hales (Galloway) put it. Socialism was firmly placed in the context of wartime. 'We know from our experience in two wars', wrote Stafford Cripps (Bristol East), 'that if the Government plans and controls our resources we can rid ourselves of unemployment and produce vast quantities of all those things that are needed by the people. The Conservative alternative is a return to the chaos of private enterprise, and control in the hands of those few who hold the economic power.'[93]

Beyond appeals to servicemen, Labour candidates rarely addressed themselves to specific sections of society. Morrison was exceptional in referring to 'large numbers of professional, technical and administrative workers' in his Lewisham East constituency. He also quoted letters written by former Conservatives endorsing Labour's policy.[94] On the other hand most candidates avoided any explicitly proletarian appeal by eschewing 'Comrades' in preference for 'Ladies and gentlemen' or 'Sir and madam' in their addresses. Appeals to female voters were also noticeably absent in 1945 except in so far as some candidates included messages from their wives. In this respect Labour had not changed. However, women were almost certainly more receptive partly because during wartime they had been more depressed by the blackout, food queues, poor housing and the disruption of family life, leaving them dissatisfied with the status quo. Polls suggested that voters generally, and women in particular, were most concerned about housing, health, the Beveridge Report and unemployment, the issues on which Labour seemed more trustworthy. Subsequently Gallup polls showed that in 1945 the Conservatives lost their usual advantage among female voters who now favoured Labour by 45–43 per cent, whereas among men the party enjoyed a 54–35 per cent lead. Labour also enjoyed an advantage among young voters in 1945. Although there had been no reforms the electorate had changed significantly since 1935 in that an unusually large number of people, around a fifth, were voting for the first time. Of these, no fewer than 61 per cent backed Labour according to later studies. This generation had grown up in an era of mass unemployment, had been radicalised by wartime experiences, and was now anxious not to lose the gains generated by a booming economy.

When the poll closed the ballot boxes were sealed for three weeks to allow time for servicemen's votes to be returned for the count on 26 July. The first indication of a landslide came with the result at Manchester Exchange, a consistently Conservative seat where Labour's poll rose from 28 per cent to 55 per cent. Soon afterwards, the first ministerial defeat was announced – Harold Macmillan at Stockton. With almost twelve million votes Labour had 47.8 per cent of the vote to 39.8 per cent for the Conservatives. This produced 393 seats to 213 Tories including 179 gains, seventy-nine of which had never been won by Labour before. For the first time the party dominated all the country's urban-industrial regions, taking ten seats of thirteen in

Birmingham, twelve of thirteen in Manchester and Salford, and eight of eleven in Liverpool, for example. But the greatest victory was in London where Labour enjoyed a 17 per cent swing, compared with 12 per cent nationally, giving the party 57 per cent of the poll and forty-eight of the sixty-two constituencies. This reflected huge advances in some suburban and middle-class seats such as Lewisham East where Morrison overthrew a 6,500 Tory majority to be elected by a margin of 15,200 votes. It was a similar story in the suburban districts around London, notably in Middlesex where Labour won Acton, Brentwood and Chiswick, Heston and Isleworth, Spelthorne, Uxbridge and Ealing North. The Hertfordshire and Essex suburbs yielded further victories at Enfield, Edmonton, Hendon North, Harrow East, and Ilford North and South. In Kent, traditionally a staunch Conservative county, Labour gained Faversham, Dartford, Chiselhurst, Gravesend, Chatham, Bexley and Dover. Thus, in both social and geographical terms the 1945 election marked the party's emergence as a genuinely national movement; 'we are a cross-section of the national life, and this is something that has never happened before', as Arthur Greenwood summed up Labour's achievement.

II

'We are the masters now':
Labour, Consensus and Affluence,
1945–1959

'The new Party is a great change from the old,' noted Chuter Ede when Parliament assembled after the election. 'It teems with bright, vivacious servicemen. The superannuated Trade Union official seems hardly to be noticeable in the ranks.' 1945 proved to be a turning point comparable with 1906 in that 327 MPs were new to Parliament, and of the 393 Labour members two-thirds had never sat before. They included far fewer from working-class backgrounds and many more professionals and university-educated men. With apparent satisfaction the new prime minister noted that he had appointed no fewer than twenty-eight public school boys, including seven Etonians, five Haileyburians and four Winchester men, to his government.[1] The newly elected members included the men and women who became the public face of Labour for the next forty years: Harold Wilson (Huyton), Jim Callaghan (Cardiff), Michael Foot (Devonport), Hugh Gaitskell (Leeds South), Barbara Castle (Blackburn), George Brown (Belper), Ian Mikardo (Reading) and Anthony Crosland (South Gloucestershire); they were joined by Roy Jenkins (Stechford) in 1950 and Denis Healey (Leeds East) in 1952. In his talented, but weathered, Cabinet Attlee managed to include two of the party's young stars, Wilson and Gaitskell. But most of the new members played a modest role. According to Jean Mann the MPs were instructed to 'avoid private members' bills, to keep quiet and vote the government's legislation through'.[2] Herbert Morrison wisely created a constructive role for the backbenchers by appointing seventeen policy committees to keep them in touch with ministers and avoid the breakdown in relations that had occurred in previous Labour governments. By and large they were content, for Attlee's administration soon came to be seen as the most successful of the entire post-war era; in 1945–6 alone, seventy-five pieces of legislation were enacted, the government brought a fifth of the economy under state control, introduced the welfare state, maintained full employment, kept inflation low and generated an export-led boom – all under the enormously difficult conditions inherited from wartime.

Of the three Labour chancellors Hugh Dalton initially bore the brunt of the crisis created by the Americans who abruptly ended the lend-lease arrangements on which Britain had been relying; as a result of the diversion of resources to war production exports stood at just 46 per cent of pre-war levels, and £1 billion of investments had been sold, resulting in a balance of payments deficit. J. M. Keynes was hastily dispatched to America to raise a large dollar loan which came at a high price but created a breathing space for the implementation of long-awaited social reforms including family allowances, National Insurance and the National Health Service. Contrary to later propaganda the cost of the welfare state was not excessive – spending on social services rose from 34 per cent of central expenditure in 1937 to 40 per cent by 1950. Dalton, Cripps and Gaitskell kept a very tight rein on expenditure and, in any case, Beveridge had based the whole idea on the assumption that the scheme would be viable provided that unemployment did not exceed 8 per cent; in effect the beneficiaries to a large extent paid for their own benefits through income tax and National Insurance. By 1947 unemployment was a mere 1.6 per cent and rarely exceeded 2 per cent in the post-war era. Government controls and food subsidies helped to keep inflation down to 3.3 per cent until 1948 and only 2 per cent from 1949. This enabled ministers to exercise enough moral-political influence to restrain demands for higher wages which rose by only 2.8 per cent annually up to 1949. In this way Attlee's ministers achieved a politically and economically viable combination of full employment, low inflation, modest wage settlements, welfare benefits and a limited redistribution of resources, until, that is, they were derailed by miscalculations resulting from external events.

In retrospect the post-1945 government attracted criticism from the left for falling some way short of the planned economy that had been widely heralded at the end of the war. Post-war planning consisted of restrictions on imports designed to check the shortage of dollars, controls on prices, food subsidies, nationalisation of the Bank of England, civil aviation, cable and wireless, coal, railways, electricity, gas, long-distance transport and steel, and investment to promote regional development. As a result 51 per cent of new factories during 1945–51 were sited in the 'Development Areas'; and, by focusing resources on manufacturing, rather than on consumer goods and housing, the government managed to stimulate a much-needed boom in exports.

Nonetheless this impressive strategy suffered from several obvious limitations. Of the ministers responsible for economic affairs Cripps showed by far the most single-minded grasp of the planning of scarce resources. Although nationalisation put a fifth of the economy in the state sphere, in the absence of a central body the use of separate boards for each industry frustrated any co-ordination between them. Ironically it was the inability to control labour by overcoming the resistance of the unions that represented the greatest single flaw in planning, hence the reliance on moral-political pressure. Moreover, because of the lack of involvement by the employees, there was little grass-roots support for extending nationalisation into other industries; in fact workers were more likely to be marginalised under national-isation because negotiations became concentrated at national level. As a result, by 1951 Labour had settled for a mixed economy with little idea about taking socialism further. By 1949 the president of the Board of Trade, Harold Wilson, had already signalled the retreat from wartime policy with his 'bonfire of controls'.

In any case, though Keynes himself died in 1946, Labour ministers increasingly invoked 'Keynesian' thinking to justify their strategy, even though their interpretation of it was very much their own.[3] Dalton and Cripps deliberately used Keynesian techniques to regulate demand in the economy and to restrain inflation where necessary by running a budget surplus. This remained central to Labour thinking even after 1951. As Anthony Crosland put it in 1956, liberal-minded people who thought of themselves as 'socialists' 'have now concluded that Keynes-plus-modified-capitalism-plus-welfare-state works perfectly well'.[4] For most Labour politicians Keynesianism represented the best practical means of advancing in the direction of socialism.

The successful achievement of such an extensive social and economic programme inevitably reinforced the movement's existing confidence in the British political system. As Lord President of the Council Morrison implemented some minor adjustments to ease the passage of legislation; the House of Lords' delaying powers were curtailed from two years to one; and Attlee created over eighty Labour peers to help Christopher Addison, Labour's leader there, to promote government business. Morrison subsequently recorded his admiration for the system in *Government and Parliament* (1954), while Attlee adopted a classic Whig view when he claimed that the constitution was 'responsive to the need for change [and] alterations due to changed conditions or shiftings of political power. It is precisely this which has for so long kept this country free from violent revolution.'[5] Consequently pressure to reform the upper chamber largely evaporated. The only other innovations were the end of plural voting, a minor element since 1918, and the abolition of the twelve university seats. The local government vote, still restricted to ratepayers and wives, was extended to include all adults. On the other hand, the Attlee government showed little respect for Labour's municipal traditions; although four in ten Labour members had local government experience they allowed the government to remove control over hospitals, gas and electricity from elected councils, and require all their loans to be approved by the Treasury. An expression of the centralising philosophy that now made devolved institutions seem irrelevant, these measures proved to be the start of a long-term process of concentrating power nationally at the expense of elective local authorities.

As Labour leader and prime minister, Attlee has traditionally enjoyed uncritical acclaim among historians and party activists. But his strength in war and peace lay largely in his ability to manage committees within the official machine; relaxed about delegating, he was prepared to appoint strong ministers and trust them to run their departments. These qualities, combined with a large majority and a clear set of priorities, enabled him to preside over a remarkable achievement. On the other hand, after only six years Labour's landslide majority was swept aside. This is a reminder that Attlee's reputation reflects his conduct of government rather than his wider role as party leader or as political tactician in which he suffered from some crippling defects. He became too absorbed by government and too detached from the rank and file, including the parliamentary party, so much so that as early as 1947 George Brown started canvassing the Commons on behalf of an 'Attlee Must Go' campaign. Although this collapsed for lack of alternatives, it was symptomatic of how quickly the prime minister had become isolated. Bevin urged him to familiarise himself with the backbenchers by visiting the Tea Room and the Smoking Room. As a result MPs were astonished, one day, to see Attlee hesitating at the door. According to Ian Mikardo, 'He looked around the room, blinking helplessly like an owl in sunlight, till I called out to him, "Clem, come and have a drink."' The prime minister shuffled over but the conversation sank like a stone until one member asked him about the Worcester–Yorkshire cricket match: 'In an instant his eyes lit up.'[6] However, Attlee only ventured into the Tea Room twice: 'He just couldn't mix.'

At the time most members were tolerant of Attlee's myopic approach to party leadership because they assumed that Labour had established itself as the natural party of government. In 1945 one of the new members, Patrick Gordon-Walker, had confided to his diary: 'I think we're going to be in for 20 years of power ahead of us.'[7] More famously, the Attorney General, Sir Hartley Shawcross, told the Commons in April 1946: 'We are the masters at the moment, and not only at the moment, but for a very long time to come.' Although some left-wingers expressed misgivings about the cautious approach to economic planning, the unduly tough treatment of workers' pay, and the rapid abandonment of the wartime alliance with Russia, the party generally recognised the record of solid achievement and expected to remain in power for many years.

This optimism reflected confidence in the strength of the wartime consensus and in the expansion of the resources that sustained the party after 1945. One of the first acts of the new administration was to repeal the 1927 trade union legislation; as a result an additional two million union members paid the political levy so that union political funds increased from £200,000 in 1945 to £800,000 in 1958. By 1950 the party's individual membership was recorded at 908,000 and, boosted by two elections, at 1,014,000 in 1952. However, the official figures painted a wildly optimistic picture of the movement for CLPs were required to affiliate for a minimum of 800 members in 1958 and 1,000 in 1963. Despite Labour's success in 1945 the party never quite managed to transform itself into a mass party or to overcome its suspicion that the rank and file posed a threat to the national leadership.

This is underlined by the moribund condition of some local parties during the 1950s. At one end of the spectrum the Glamorgan constituency of Pontypridd had given Labour 68 per cent of the vote in 1945. There the constituency party busied itself in parochial, almost non-political, activity, discussing local telephone booths, ambulance services, the provision of public conveniences, broken fences, straying horses and wandering sheep; its agenda had more in common with a parish council or a Women's Institute. When a general election approached in 1950 the party wondered whether to make some plans – 'a door-to-door canvass might be conducted' – but decided it was not essential![8] Labour's post-war story is even more eloquently told by Swansea whose the two constituencies were represented by union-sponsored members, each endowed with £300–350 annually, and were run by Percy Morris who was both an alderman and MP for Swansea West. The business of the local party was dominated by the affairs of Swansea town council which remained in Labour control for many years; seven councillors sat for the entire 1941–64 period and some trade unions regarded the representation of certain wards as almost a hereditary right.[9] However, by the later 1950s the neglect of the organisation left the two constituency organisations with scarcely 500 members each. On the assumption that both seats were safe for Labour the local party ignored pressure from the Welsh Regional Council of Labour to renew the organisation, although Swansea West became increasingly marginal with Labour's share of the poll dwindling from 58 per cent in 1945 to 53 (1950), 52 (1951), 51 (1955) and 49 (1959). Despite its rudimentary organisation Labour largely managed to hold its vote together, but the loss of Swansea West to the Conservatives by 400 votes in 1959 underlined how disastrous neglect of local organisation could be.

At the opposite end of the spectrum superior Labour organisations in London and Birmingham managed to slow the decline in the face of competition from a formidable opposition. With some reason Herbert Morrison characterised his own South Lewisham as 'a model of what a constituency Labour party ought to be'. In the 1950s its steel frame comprised the constituency executive, the ward committees, and polling district committees each with two to six polling district officers, along with up to four women's sections and four branches of the Labour League of Youth. With 7,200 in 1952 and 7,674 in 1953, South Lewisham boasted the largest individual membership in the country. Thirty collectors gathered £1,500 in subscriptions annually, in addition to donations of £850.[10] They were remunerated on a 33 per cent basis: 'This seems to be the most satisfactory arrangement and collectors are encouraged to take this commission, although some pay it back into their ward funds.'[11] Collectors called once a month with a newsletter, headquarters leaflets and information about social events: dances, bazaars, teas and outings. The party also maintained a central canvassing corps of thirty-five which was capable of recruiting an extra 845 members from May to June 1952, for example.[12] At elections the party paid anything from £1 to £3 for the use of each committee room and a guinea each to clerks or tellers at polling stations. Canvass returns were kept and routinely marked up on each new electoral register with checks for any changes in voting.[13] Not surprisingly the London district organiser concluded that 'there is no aspect of the work of the Party which is not done well'.[14]

In Birmingham, too, the party was obliged to keep on its toes because Conservatism remained a formidable force capable of engineering a recovery from the defeat of 1945. Labour treated the annual local elections as a proxy for the general election, routinely comparing the municipal votes with parliamentary ones in each constituency. As a result the Birmingham party was more politically aware than many CLPs and quick to criticise the Cabinet for failing to keep local organisations informed about the reasons for its policies. For example, in 1947 it attributed eight losses in the municipal elections, which left the city poised between sixty-eight Labour, sixty-five Conservative and three Independent councillors, to poorly timed government cuts in the bacon and petrol rations.[15] In 1946 it expressed its view on a wide range of issues including conscription, rationing and Indian independence; in 1948 it demanded a more socialist approach to the distribution of goods, minimum wages, profits limitation and the promotion of trade with the Soviet Union: 'Without such agreement Britain is in danger of becoming politically and economically dependent on the USA and the development of Socialism is impossible.'[16] In 1949 the party began cautioning the Cabinet against placing any new charges on NHS prescriptions because 'the burden of this measure will weigh heaviest on sections of the community least able to stand the expense'.[17]

This political awareness was reflected in keen attention to organisational strength in Birmingham. Lacking substantial trade union funding, the central party ran a Unity Labour Supporters Pool, which had around 29,000–30,000 members during the 1950s, offering an easy means of raising money by tapping into local enthusiasm for football.[18] Consequently, in 1949, when the party identified signs of organisational decline, it decided to employ three extra agents to counter the large staff used by the Birmingham Tories. By January 1950 Birmingham had been preparing for a general election for six months and it retained nine of the thirteen constituencies in both the 1950 and 1951 elections, the same proportion as in 1945.

If constituency parties generally had been as effective as Birmingham, Labour would have retained office during the 1950s. As it was, the party's setbacks in 1950 and 1951 were received at the time as something less than a real defeat – partly for the very good reason that they did not reflect any significant withdrawal of popular support. Labour lost office less because of any underlying shifts of opinion than because of a series of misjudgements on the part of its national leaders, shrewd tactics by the Opposition, and the effects of the electoral system.

Critics in the constituency parties had some grounds for attributing their difficulties to errors made at national level, notably the foreign and defence policies that blew the Attlee administration off course and generated misgivings among backbenchers including Richard Crossman, Michael Foot, Ian Mikardo and Barbara Castle who formed the 'Keep Left Group' in 1947. The disintegration of the wartime alliance between Britain, America and the Soviet Union, the drift towards the Cold War and, in particular, the outbreak of the Korean War in June 1950 were the critical developments. As early as 1946 the Foreign Secretary, Ernest Bevin, an instinctive anti-Communist, had concluded that the Soviets, not the Germans, now represented the main threat and he enthusiastically involved Britain in a close alliance with the United States. This came at a high price in the shape of a British Army comprising no fewer than 900,000 men and defence expenditure that rose from £2.3 billion to £4.7 billion, or a massive 14 per cent of GNP, by 1951. Admittedly, this was consistent with the broad view of Attlee and Bevin who were determined that Britain should retain her status as a great power, develop atomic weapons and retain her empire despite the concession of independence to India in 1947. Although Attlee realised that Bevin's excessive backing for America was encumbering Britain with damaging costs, he failed to restrain his policy.

For Labour both the immediate and the long-term ramifications of Cold War strategy proved to be crucial. The Americans, though ostensibly anti-imperialist, encouraged Britain to retain her colonies because they provided bases from which the West might contain the growth of Soviet influence; hence the start of a series of counter-insurgency actions with the war in Malaya against left-wing nationalists. Bevin, who reportedly declared 'there'll be no messing about with the British Empire' on entering the Foreign Office, retained an old-fashioned belief in empire as a necessary source of food supplies and employment for Britain; he believed that Britain should exploit her resources in Africa more vigorously, betraying a mindset similar to that of L. S. Amery who had attempted the same strategy as long ago as the 1920s. This dedication to empire and great-power status had the further consequence of inhibiting any reappraisal of Britain's role in the world generally and in relation to Europe in particular. When Jean Monnet, one of the pioneers of the early initiatives for the creation of a Common Market, visited Britain in 1949 he found Labour unresponsive. 'If you open that Pandora's box you never know what Trojan 'orses will jump out,' Bevin reportedly told his officials.

More immediately the costs of Cold War defence began to undermine Britain's economic recovery. By 1948 the recession in America had effectively reduced Britain's dollar earnings, undermined the balance of payments and thus led to speculation against sterling. In this situation the appropriate response was to boost the manufacturing industries by a devaluation of the pound. However, most ministers, still in thrall to interwar conservatism, shrank from the prospect, though eventually Hugh Gaitskell, Douglas Jay and Harold Wilson took the decision to devalue from $4.03 to $2.90 in 1949. An entirely rational act of economic management, devaluation proved advantageous in improving the balance of payments and, in the longer term, creating a beneficial balance between the dollar economy and the non-dollar world. However, in the short term Attlee's ministers allowed themselves to be trapped by the conventional wisdom that regarded the currency as a symbol of national virility, and devaluation as a defeat. They thereby set themselves on a course that culminated in loss of office in 1951.

The political logic of devaluation required either an immediate election or a period of deflation and delay while the benefits in terms of improved exports and economic growth accrued. However, Attlee, never an inspired tactician, failed to recognise the need to delay a general election for as long as possible. His cavalier approach to the date is explicable in that like most ministers he evidently expected to win a majority of seventy to a hundred, though as the parties were neck and neck in February 1950 the basis for their confidence is obscure. Attlee, apparently contemplating either February or June 1950, allowed himself to be influenced by the chancellor, Cripps, who, astonishing as it now seems, considered it would be improper to introduce a spring Budget shortly before an election. Cripps, who had evidently been somewhat unhinged by the devaluation crisis, was suffering from poor health and 'determined to give up office in any event'.[19] Attlee ignored the views of the one minister with a grip on the situation, Morrison, who advised against February. Nor did he take notice of Morgan Phillips, the general secretary, who complained that the Labour Movement 'has not been geared to the possibility of an early general election'. This was an understatement. Labour was actually preparing to celebrate its fiftieth anniversary on 2–5 February 1950, but the arrangements had to be ditched at the last minute because activists could hardly travel to London for four or five days at a critical point in an election campaign.[20]

Ill-prepared organisationally, the party approached the election uncertain about how it wanted to extend its achievements. At Dudley George Wigg employed a typical line by emphasising Labour's social reforms and full employment and resurrecting 1945 warnings about the dangers of returning to pre-war conditions.[21] By comparison the Conservatives had been preparing themselves for a campaign focused on high taxation, shortages, food rationing and the alleged failure to build houses. Throughout 1949 they had kept the government on the defensive with a professional campaign against the nationalisation of sugar, generously funded by Tate & Lyle and Aims of Industry, an organisation founded in 1942 for 'the defence of free-enterprise and to promote a free-market economy', which enabled the Conservatives to evade legal restrictions on election expenditure. The campaign was fronted by an endearing cartoon character, Mr Cube, who was depicted as the little man pitched against the socialist leviathan. For a nation with the world's highest sugar consumption, still suffering from short-ages, and fretting under a failed attempt by the minister, John Strachey, to de-ration sugar, this was shrewdly chosen. By entering the election campaign promising 'Labour intends to transfer to public ownership all sugar manufacturing and refining concerns' the party played to Tory demands that the state should keep its hands off the people's sugar.

Mr Cube proved to be of wider significance in highlighting the unpopularity of more nationalisation among the working class and the uncertainty in the Cabinet about where to go next; in 1950, even among Labour supporters, only 38 per cent backed sugar nationalisation and 45 per cent iron and steel nationalisation, while only 21 per cent considered the existing nationalisation a success.[22] Sugar also helped to focus the wider discontent over rationing and complemented the Conservatives' campaign among housewives. Inevitably, once the war was out of mind voters grew resentful about controls, rationing, queues and food shortages. For the Conservatives campaigns over 'austerity' dramatised the claim that economic planning was ineffective and endowed their programme with an ideological edge that obscured the large area of consensus between them and the Attlee government. The groundwork had been laid since 1945 by the Housewives League, now energetically backed by national newspapers such as the *Daily Mail* which had denounced the introduction of bread rationing in July 1946 as 'the most hated measure ever to have been presented to the people of this country'.[23] By 1947 a Conservative revival in by-elections left ministers rattled by the apparent success of these tactics.

Despite these weaknesses, Labour support rallied and the 1950 election found the parties neck and neck. On polling day, 23 February, it poured with rain but the turnout rose to an impressive 84 per cent. Labour's share fell modestly by 2.7 per cent to 46.1, while the Conservatives' increased to 43.5 per cent. However, the turnover of seats was much greater, Labour returning 315 members, a loss of seventy-eight, to the Conservatives' 298, leaving Attlee an overall majority of only six. Much of the explanation for this outcome, as Morgan Phillips pointed out, lay in the redrawing of constituency boundaries which gave the Conservatives a gain of thirty by eliminating Labour seats in the inner cities in favour of new suburban seats.[24] Britain had divided along regional-class lines. Although the average national swing was 2.9 per cent, it was twice this in the ninety-two

constituencies in middle-class districts of the Home Counties, encom-
passing swings of 8 per cent in outer Essex and Middlesex, which had
the effect of reducing Labour representation in the five counties
bordering London from fifty-three to twenty-eight. By contrast, the
swing was only 2–3 per cent in Birmingham, Liverpool, Manchester
and Sheffield, 1.5 per cent in South Wales, 1 per cent on Clydeside and
0.5 per cent in Durham–Teesside.[25] There were even swings in Labour's
favour in Scotland, Wales and the North-East. Analysing the results
Labour sources accepted that the Conservatives had recovered a good
deal of middle-class support especially in suburban constituencies
around London antagonised by high taxation. In 1945 Dalton had
reduced wartime standard tax rate – but only from ten to nine shillings
in the pound. Anthony Crosland thought taxation 'the most important single issue which caused these people to swing Tory'. The NEC
concluded that 'the weight of taxation appears to have been overwhelmingly felt among the lower and middle ranks of the salaried
and professional groups, especially the teachers who are aggrieved by
the salary question'.[26] Cripps, having refused to introduce a pre-election
Budget, subsequently corroborated this view by cutting taxes, though
this did nothing to help the lowest paid and also put limits on resources
for food subsidies.

In retrospect historians have identified fluctuations among female
voters as the key to Labour's poor result in 1950. However, this is an
exaggeration for the movement was slight; Labour's two-point advantage among women in 1945 had given way to a modest two-point
Conservative advantage (45–43). This suggests that if some housewives
had been moved by austerity campaigns others had been influenced
by food subsidies in keeping down the cost of living. In fact, men had
shown themselves *more* volatile than women, for whereas in 1945
Labour enjoyed a 54–35 advantage among male voters, this had
narrowed to 46–41 in 1950. On the other hand, Labour's standing
amongst women continued to represent an underlying weakness in
that 52.5 per cent of working-class men voted Labour compared with
only 44.5 per cent of working-class women, an 8 per cent gap representing about a million voters. 'It is easy to picture the happy results
that would follow if workingmen could only persuade their women-
folk to share their opinions,' as an internal Labour memorandum
expressed it.[27]

As this comment suggests, there are grounds for thinking that the party's interpretation of the 1950 results was a little complacent. Though fully aware of the evidence for the loss of male working-class votes the official analysis concluded that men could be won back quite easily for 'it is quite possible that the Tory effort of the last few years has already done its worst among such people'.[28] Yet 29 per cent of working-class electors had voted Conservative, comprising no less than 54 per cent of that party's total vote. In this sense, even the landslide of 1945 had failed to destroy the existing configuration of British elections; the traditional Tory populism had been trimmed back but by no means destroyed. This was obvious in the perennial marginal constituency of Preston, where Labour had struggled since the 1890s and which it captured in 1945; but in the 1950s Preston once again returned two Tory MPs, a tribute to the remarkable continuity of British political culture.

Labour's verdict on 1950 also missed the significance of the age composition of its vote. The party's analysis correctly noted that Labour's support was highest among the youngest and the oldest groups.[29] However, this was to miss the point. Of those who had not been eligible to vote in 1945 only 43 per cent were now voting Labour, by comparison with 61 per cent of the first-time voters in 1945. Though not apparent at this early stage, the slippage of support among the young was to become a crucial feature of Labour's steadily declining electoral position throughout the 1950s.

With a majority of six, Attlee's government struggled on, though not for as long as it could have done. In October when Cripps retired through ill health Attlee replaced him with Hugh Gaitskell, a rising star of the Cabinet whose appointment was calculated to inject some life into the fading administration. Unfortunately Attlee mismanaged his promotion by offending Aneurin Bevan who, as a conspicuous ministerial success and an outstanding performer in Parliament where he regularly routed Churchill in debate, had every right to expect a leading post but was sidelined as Minister for Labour. Attlee repeated his mistake in April 1951, following Ernest Bevin's resignation as Foreign Secretary, when Bevan was again denied promotion and correctly felt that he was being marginalised.

Hugh Gaitskell was one of those able but flawed men who only occasionally rise to the top in British politics. Like Sir Robert Peel and

Edward Heath, he possessed the qualities of a first-rate civil servant, which he had been during the war, but was hampered by defects of temperament and was especially miscast as a party manager and party leader. Elected in 1945, Gaitskell had spent only one year as a back-bench MP before becoming a minister, an experience that played to his weakness. As a recruit to Labour from middle-class Tory circles Gaitskell was an outsider, an intellectual and an elitist who found it hard to understand the movement he had joined. He exacerbated this failing by promoting a vendetta with Bevan which was to have long-term effects on the party.

Admittedly, as chancellor Gaitskell inherited an awkward situation in the shape of the huge rearmament programme. Even so, his 1951 Budget proved to be a complete disaster partly because he seemed determined to use it to advance political-personal aims by courting a breach with Bevan. Included in the tax increases and expenditure cuts were new NHS charges levied on false teeth and spectacles which were almost calculated to provoke Bevan. There was, in fact, nothing inevitable about Bevan's resignation, which he postponed several times, and, as the charges raised a mere £13 million they were not worth the controversy they caused. However, Gaitskell adopted a rigid attitude as though he saw the issue as a personal struggle between the two of them, while Bevan allowed himself to be provoked by hecklers at a by-election in Bermondsey into declaring, 'I will not be a member of a Government which imposes charges on the patient.' Dalton, contemplating another election in late summer or early autumn, tried to persuade Bevan to stay: 'to resign on this would be thought by most people to be a gesture out of proportion to its pretext'.[30] However, Attlee failed to intervene and the dispute eventually resulted in the resignation of three ministers, Bevan, Harold Wilson and John Freeman.

Gaitskell's miscalculated Budget thus split the Cabinet, blew the government off course in terms of the economic revival, and set Labour up for another ill-timed election. 'The Labour Party is in danger of losing the next election,' complained the Birmingham party, 'as on present showing it has no Policy upon which it could win this vital contest.'[31] Rank-and-file dissatisfaction centred on Gaitskell's Budget, pensions, the Korean War and recent NHS charges. One ward party, supporting Bevan's resignation, argued: 'Charges on teeth and spectacles supplied by the

Health Service hits at the workingman's pockets and defiles one of the proudest achievements of the Labour government.'[32] Yet Attlee opted to go to the country in October 1951 rather than delay, apparently on the grounds that King George VI intended to embark on a six-month tour of Australia and New Zealand early in 1952 and it would be unwise to risk a political crisis at home during that period.[33] This concern for the king's convenience was symptomatic of Attlee's conventional mode of thought, but while giving priority to royal comfort he had, once again, given no consideration to the needs of his party. By holding an election in October he disrupted the annual conference which had to be short-ened so that MPs could return to Westminster for the recall of Parliament on 4 October. Morrison, reminding him he had opposed the timing of the 1950 election, warned: 'I don't want us to make another mistake.'[34] But Attlee, who was losing his grip by this time, declined to wait until later in 1952 when the king had returned and the economic situation eased; the fact that the new Conservative government managed to reduce the punitive defence spending and cut taxes in 1952 indicates the extent to which the prime minister was throwing away Labour's chances by another premature rush to the polls.

That Attlee had ignored the question of party morale was under-lined by the reaction in Birmingham where the announcement of an election 'came somewhat as a shock to many of our Constituency Parties'.[35] Not surprisingly, the campaign began rather quietly and 'for the first 8 to 10 days agents were alarmed at the response of their appeals for workers'.[36] For a second time Labour candidates found themselves on the defensive and uncertain what to say about a future Labour programme. In his marginal Devonport constituency Michael Foot resorted to the old tactics by comparing Labour's post-1945 achievements with the Tories' post-1918 record as he had done in 1950: 'Do you want to plunge back into the industrial chaos and mass unem-ployment before the war?'[37] The only new issues were the danger of war if the Tories were elected and the prospect of rising food prices, neither of which seemed especially helpful for Labour. The Conservatives, meanwhile, renewed their claim that the economic crisis was the result of socialist controls, and used the recent reductions in the meat ration caused by a dispute with Argentina to appeal to housewives. Attlee evidently saw no need to alter his usual routine for the election – a series of provincial speeches delivered without notes.

A *Daily Mirror* journalist reported his campaign: 'While his wife drives, Mr Attlee puts on his glasses, rests on a brown-green folk-weave cushion, and does newspaper crossword puzzles. Occasionally when they are driving he unwraps a mint . . . and pops one into his wife's mouth. If their car is held up at a level crossing Mrs Attlee gets out her knitting – a pair of grey socks.'[38] This charming domestic vignette underlined the amateurishness of Labour's campaign at a crucial election in which the Tories were deploying sophisticated PR techniques.

A drastic fall in the number of Liberal candidates from 475 to 109 boosted both main parties' share of the vote in 1951, but Labour remained ahead with 48.8 to 48 per cent. However, with more votes the party emerged with *fewer* seats – 295 to the Conservatives' 321; it had lost twenty-two to the Tories but gained two from the Liberals. The result had been distorted by the electoral system in that the Conservative vote was better distributed, yielding many suburban seats with small majorities while Labour piled up large majorities in its northern strongholds. At the time it proved tempting to attribute the result to ex-Liberal votes, but this is not entirely plausible for Labour's share had risen by 2.7 per cent and the Tories by 3.5 per cent; in 1950 the party had recognised that a high proportion of existing Liberal voters were working-class and susceptible to Labour's appeal. This time the volatile element was the female electorate. Whereas among male voters Labour enjoyed a 51–46 advantage, the same majority as in 1950, among women the Conservatives now led by 54–42.[39] The gender gap, previously just 2 per cent, had widened to 12 per cent. On the basis that women constituted 53.8 per cent of all electors this gap represented potentially 1.2 million votes in an election where only 230,000 separated the parties; women, in short, had been crucial to the outcome in 1951.

In retrospect 1951 was a critical defeat because it put the Conservatives into office at the start of the prosperity and consumerism of the 1950s. At the time, however, this was far from obvious. 'The Party is in good fettle,' reported the general secretary.[40] Labour's support was at an historically high level and its policies reflected a consensus respected by its rivals for years to come. It was common in the party to refer to Churchill's 'stopgap administration' and the Conservatives themselves shared Labour's expectations that it would probably return to office before long. Yet this comforting perspective on the defeat left the movement reluctant to adjust, to reconsider its ideas or to reform its organisation. At the 1952 women's conference a resolution attributing the defeat to failures in education and propaganda in countering the Tory appeal to housewives was repudiated by the loyalist majority as being 'unfairly critical'.[41] Activists often implicitly assumed that as Labour constituted the natural majority the objective of a campaign was to mobilise the party's core vote and avoid stirring up the opposition. Ian Mikardo reflected this thinking in his 'Reading system' which used carbon copies of canvass returns to help knocking up firm Labour voters before the poll closed.[42] However, this was a misconception for roughly half of all voters failed to identify strongly with any party, making it essential for Labour to extend its reach to the relatively uncommitted as the Conservatives did.

Yet there was nothing inevitable about Labour's gradual decline during the 1950s. Following the fashion of the period, observers have traditionally seen the party as the victim of social change, especially its inability to adapt to an increasingly affluent working class. However, the electoral shifts were comparatively slight and the extent of social change has been exaggerated. The alternative explanation sees Labour's fortunes as determined more by *contingencies*: the extent to which the party was handicapped by poor leadership, by internal divisions and by the tactics of its opponents. Too much of the party's energies were absorbed by internal controversy following the resignations of April 1951 which led to the emergence of a 'Bevanite' group of forty-seven members in 1952 among whom Harold Wilson, Barbara Castle, Ian Mikardo, Richard Crossman, Michael Foot and Tom Driberg were prominent. Ideologically their disagreement was fairly narrowly based on foreign and defence policy, especially Britain's reliance on NATO and nuclear weapons. There was a taste of things to come at the 1951 conference when Mikardo and Castle were elected to the NEC, in the process pushing out the veteran Emmanuel Shinwell who was reportedly so angry he took the first train back to London. In March 1952 fifty-seven MPs rebelled against the party line by voting against the government's support for German rearmament, a prelude to a bad-tempered party conference at Morecambe where the right-wing chairman, Sir Will Lawther, attempted vainly to control the delegates by shouting 'shut yer gob' at them. Bevan and Wilson scored a notable success at Morecambe by getting elected to the NEC at the expense

WE ARE THE MASTERS NOW'

of Dalton and Morrison. But instead of accepting the decision, the party Establishment created a furore with speeches and articles in the *Daily Herald* and *News Chronicle*. Autocratic union leaders including Will Lawther and Arthur Deakin made the split seem worse than it was by launching public attacks on the left. Gaitskell protested: 'It is time to end the attempt to mob rule by a group of journalists . . . and restore the authority and leadership of the sensible majority'; while Attlee complained, 'What is quite intolerable is the existence of a party within a party.'[43] Considering that by 1954 just six of the twenty-eight NEC members were Bevanites this was an absurd overreaction. Gaitskell's intemperate language was an ominous sign of the poor judgement he was to bring to the party leadership. Although both Gaitskell and Bevan subsequently protested that the party was largely united, the exchanges created a lasting impression of division.[44] In October the PLP followed the suggestion of Morgan Phillips by demanding the disbanding of the Bevanite group.

Subsequently the controversy subsided until 1954 when the split resurfaced in a Bevanite revolt over German rearmament which led Bevan to resign from the shadow Cabinet. He was also heavily defeated by Gaitskell in the election for party treasurer. In March 1955 Bevan intervened in the Commons to repudiate Attlee for supporting the prime minister over American policy in South East Asia, and sixty-three Labour members abstained in a Commons vote in defiance of Attlee's support for the government's decision to build a British hydrogen bomb. As a result the PLP voted by 141 to 112 to withdraw the whip from Bevan.[45]

This was a dangerously even division of opinion, but it underlined the extent to which the dispute was not ideological but a personal struggle between Bevan and Gaitskell. Bevan himself, who contemptuously disparaged his rival as 'nothing, nothing, nothing', professed to regard Gaitskell as a 'desiccated calculating machine', and his acolytes, Patrick Gordon-Walker and Roy Jenkins, as a mere elite, detached from the soul of the movement and confined to clandestine gatherings at their leader's home in Frognal Gardens, Hampstead. For their part the Gaitskellites saw their rivals as doctrinaires, extremists, class warriors and pro-Soviets who were damaging the party in the country.

Despite their alarmism the Labour right dominated the annual conferences through three union leaders, Arthur Deakin of the TGWU, Tom Williamson of the GMWU and Will Lawther of the mineworkers, and controlled the central party machine through the national agent who maintained dossiers on left-wingers such as Konni Zilliacus with a view to withdrawing their candidatures.[46] Conversely the left benefited from the 'meteoric rise of Bevanism amongst the Party membership', according to Mikardo's account.[47] Bevan certainly enjoyed wide sympathy. The Birmingham party, for example, voted by 104–50 to condemn the withdrawal of the whip in 1955: 'The action is completely unjustified and will only assist the enemies of the party.'[48] However, the extent of Bevanite popularity has been much exaggerated, partly as a result of the romantic biography of Bevan by Michael Foot. For example, female NEC members were invariably chosen from right-wing loyalists such as Bessie Braddock, Alice Bacon, Edith Summerskill and Jean Mann. According to a 1952 Gallup poll 51 per cent of party members were for Bevan and 44 per cent against, but among union members he had only 41 per cent support to 52, and among Labour supporters only 33 per cent to 55.[49] Although Bevan himself attracted huge and enthusiastic audiences and his colleagues ran popular 'brains trusts' in the provinces, his supporters never organised themselves properly; though Mikardo tried, he complained that the public school boys were too individualistic to accept unofficial whipping.[50] Consequently, the group was never remotely comparable to the ILP. The Bevanites simply held discussions in Parliament and published *Tribune* under Foot's editorship, thereby creating a misleading impression of being 'a party within a party'; their real weakness was, in fact, that they were never sufficiently well organised.

Moreover, the records of constituency parties suggest that grass-roots Bevanism was something of a myth because most members felt detached from national controversies and took little interest in ideological questions. In Salford, for example, ostensibly 'Bevanite' because its two MPs, Stan Orme and Frank Allaun, aligned with the group, the local members remained unaffected by ideological divisions, preferring to maintain their focus on tangible local issues such as housing which united left and right; for them the council's direct works department was the real expression of socialism. Similarly, South Lewisham's huge membership identified socialism with local causes, not with support for Bevan.[51] Even South Wales failed to become a stronghold of Bevanism. The explanation is partly that, for all his Welshness, Bevan himself operated largely in metropolitan circles and never cultivated a provincial following. Both the Gaitskellites and the Bevanites were essentially elites rather than popular movements.

However, while internal factionalism was a distraction for Labour during the 1950s, it was of marginal significance in the context of the new political configuration. It was in this period that Labour became the *victim* of the political consensus that had sustained it in 1945. The importance of consensus has been lost sight of amid detailed academic research designed to attack the idea by demonstrating that minor differences between the main parties remained lively. Contemporary activists, as we have seen, often felt that Labour was failing to distinguish itself sufficiently from its rivals. But it is important not to neglect the wider significance of the *Conservatives'* tactics and the dilemma they created for Labour.

Although the wartime consensus included full employment, the welfare state and the mixed economy, it subsequently extended to foreign, imperial and defence policy. Conservatives could scarcely object to Labour's determination to maintain Britain as a great power, support the Americans against Communism, develop the atomic bomb and slow the trend towards decolonisation; after 1951 they simply reduced spending on the armed forces thereby relieving the pressure that had been so destructive for Labour. They also calculated that electoral survival required them to uphold the domestic consensus because they were vulnerable to Labour warnings that their return to office would see a higher cost of living, mass unemployment and attacks on the welfare state. Significantly, however, this nightmare vision failed to materialise, for although Churchill had returned to office amid some stirring rhetoric about 'setting the people free' and giving them 'good red meat' after the years of socialist austerity, this was mostly propaganda designed to arouse Conservative activists. Churchill had not spent nineteen years as a Liberal (1904–23) at a time of interventionist state welfare and higher taxation of wealth for nothing; moreover, by 1951 he was anxious to end his career as a unifying figure not as a divisive one. In any case the Conservatives' precarious electoral position dictated respect for Labour's achievements. Thus, despite some modest tax cuts, an end to rationing and the abolition of controls already begun by Harold Wilson, the new government upheld the

fundamentals of the consensus. Far from dismantling the welfare state
Churchill increased the real value of pensions and other benefits. He
and his successors, Eden and Macmillan, were determined to maintain full employment. He was also content to operate a mixed economy
subject to denationalising steel and road haulage about which Labour
had also entertained doubts.

In addition the Conservatives began to outmanoeuvre Labour in
appealing to manual workers. The effect of introducing PAYE during
the war had been to draw many workingmen into the tax net. 'Income
tax is now paid by such a large group of the population that it will
not be wise politically for the Labour Party always to oppose indirect
and favour direct taxation,' as Gaitskell observed in 1943.[52] As a result
Labour began to distance itself from its Edwardian preference for
reducing indirect taxes on the basis that they were paid disproportionately by the poor and became increasingly sensitive to higher-paid
workers who paid income tax. By 1948 PAYE yielded only £197 million
a year compared with £139 million on purchase tax and a massive £767
million on beer and tobacco duties. The new Conservative chancellor,
R. A. Butler, capitalised on this in 1952 when he cut income tax,
increased tax reliefs, raised family allowances and lifted two million
earners out of income tax. In effect Butler was outflanking Labour
by appealing to certain sections of working-class opinion, especially
the better paid, calculating that they would appreciate lower direct
taxes and rely on bargaining for higher wages to counter any increases
in the cost of living.

This was consistent with Churchill's concern to avoid conflict with
the trade unions. After the election he had summoned Walter
Monckton to Downing Street with the greeting: 'Oh my dear . . . I
have the worst job in Cabinet for you!'[53] As Minister for Labour,
Monckton's conciliatory handling of the unions attracted condemnation from a later generation of Thatcherite Conservatives, but in 1951
his was a shrewd and successful appointment. Monckton upheld
wartime practice by consulting the union leaders, abstained from
legislation, refused to interfere with the closed shop, and concentrated
on settling industrial disputes by informal negotiations with the two
sides; as inflation rose, higher wage settlements seemed fair and
inevitable.[54] In this way Monckton kept the peace, won golden opinions from the union leaders and generally deprived workers of any

sense of having been badly treated under the Conservatives. The conciliation of labour was a critical element in Conservative electoral strategy. By 1955 the cumulative effect, along with tax and welfare policy, was to make it hard for Labour to argue with any credibility that its achievements had been threatened, and as a result Labour candidates found it difficult to know what line to take at the election; even an internal party report of 1955 identified 'the absence of clearly defined differences between the parties' as a cause of Labour's defeat.[55]

Yet this dilemma had scarcely been apparent to the Labour MPs who felt they had done well in attacking the new government during the 1951–5 Parliament, especially Gaitskell who subjected Butler's irresponsible Budgets to critical scrutiny. Clearly things did not appear in the same light among the constituency parties who felt the parliamentarians never really grasped the initiative: 'If we are honest, we have to acknowledge that the work of the Parliamentary Labour Party . . . has been dull and uninspiring and lacking in drive if compared with the work put in by the Conservative Party from 1947 to 1950.'[56] The Birmingham party concluded, in retrospect, that 'Labour's programme was indistinguishable in broad outline from that of the Tories'.[57]

During 1952 the Gallup polls had put Labour ahead of the Tories and the party made substantial gains in local elections in 1952, 1953 and 1954. However, they slipped behind after the 1953 budget when Butler took sixpence off income tax, and in May Labour lost a by-election at Sunderland South, the first occasion since 1924 when a government had gained a seat at a by-election; thereafter the two were level-pegging until the spring of 1955. At this stage Churchill's long-awaited retirement came as a relief and the new premier, Sir Anthony Eden, capitalised on the mood by announcing that a general election would be held in May. Once again Butler ignored inflation and resorted to an electioneering Budget that cut income tax and lifted 2.5 million people out of income tax. Handicapped by lack of ideas and forced on to the defensive, Labour fought a backward-looking campaign. In Leyton, for example, Reginald Sorensen offered a thin election address with no new ideas and largely failed even to attack the Tories; his main theme was the promotion of peace and the need to stop experiments with the hydrogen bomb. In Devonport Michael Foot, perhaps influenced by his own role as a rebel, delivered an abstract message about freedom and independent-minded MPs, dwelling on peace, the bomb and attempts to end the Cold War.[58] Like many candidates, Foot, who lost his seat, was not really engaging with the voters and found it hard to recapture the focus and aggression of 1945.

Campaigners received little leadership from Attlee who delivered a detached and defensive election broadcast; he had simply run out of ideas, energy and enthusiasm. Admittedly the absence of Churchill, on whom Labour usually relied, made it difficult to generate serious controversy in 1955; he was 'something to get our teeth into', as Emmanuel Shinwell put it. 'But this time we are fighting Snow White and the Seven Dwarfs.'[59] In effect Labour struggled to find compelling reasons to reject the government. Tranquillity suited the Conservatives who increased their majority from seventeen to fifty-eight seats. The turnout fell sharply to 76.8 per cent, Labour's share slipping to 46.4 per cent and the Conservatives rising to 49.7 per cent.

The defeat of 1955 underlined the folly of continuing to rely on the formula that had triumphed in 1945. Admittedly, there had been some attempt at rethinking Labour's programme and philosophy. Bevan had published *In Place of Fear* in 1952, but apart from urging an element of democratic accountability in the nationalised industries, he had little to say. Richard Crossman had edited *New Fabian Essays* which included chapters by Crosland, Jenkins and Healey but failed to launch a new debate. The outstanding contribution did not appear until 1956 in the shape of Anthony Crosland's *The Future of Socialism* which frankly proposed to redefine socialism in the light of what Labour had accomplished since 1945. Crosland argued that as the state had acquired adequate means of controlling the economy there was no need to provoke controversy about the ownership of industry or to extend nationalisation. Instead socialists should focus on *ends* rather than means, recognising that the priority lay in promoting welfare and equality, ending class antagonism, redistributing the resources of society, and opening access to the underprivileged through education. This diagnosis was certainly in tune with a society now enjoying economic growth and increasingly dedicated to consumerism. But although widely read and admired, *The Future of Socialism* was one of those influential books that never quite enjoyed the influence it deserved. This was partly because the able and articulate Crosland was a middle-class politician who never cultivated a following in the movement. By the standards of the 1950s his attitudes marked him as distinctly liberal, a herald of the 'permissive society' of the 1960s. Crosland derided Labour's austere Fabian traditions, arguing that 'total abstinence and a good filing system are not now the right signposts to the socialist Utopia'.[60] However, in a movement that remained socially conservative, even puritanical, those politicians who enjoyed the metropolitan lifestyle took care to confine it to London. Ultimately Crosland's influence was limited by his reputation as a revisionist. Though not originally part of the Gaitskellite circle he became associated with it because to be detached was to be isolated; as a result he and his ideas became a victim of the Bevanite–Gaitskellite split. Yet Crosland had a better grasp of socialism and how to implement it than many notional Bevanites such as Harold Wilson, and in the long run his detachment proved to be unfortunate for the party and for Labour governments.

Meanwhile the way ahead seemed to lie through adopting a fresh leader rather than a reconsideration of socialism. By 1955 Attlee was seventy-two, tired and bereft if ideas; he had clung on as leader far too long, largely because he wanted to stop Morrison, who was only five years younger, from succeeding him. The party, always indulgent towards leaders who were past their sell-by date, made no move, but eventually, in December 1955, he resigned, calculating that Gaitskell was now strong enough to defeat his rivals. In the ensuing contest Gaitskell obtained an overall majority with 157 votes to seventy for Bevan and forty for Morrison. The prognostications for the new leadership were not good, for Gaitskell had built himself up by making bitter attacks on Communist influence in the party, tactics that won him the backing of a phalanx of right-wing union leaders but did nothing to promote party unity. In the event, though not a natural conciliator, he showed himself sensitive towards the left and keen to promote unity. He made no attempt to force his views on his colleagues and made a point of appointing Harold Wilson as shadow chancellor and Bevan first as Colonial Secretary and later as Foreign Secretary. As a result the party leadership was younger and more vigorous in the later 1950s than it had been for years.

In the aftermath of the election the best way forward appeared to lie through tackling the less divisive question of organisational reform, thereby sidestepping ideological disputes and the reformulation of policy. To this end Harold Wilson chaired an investigation into the party organisation, a role that helped him to emancipate himself from his reputation as a left-winger and emerge more as a pragmatic moderniser acceptable to people on all sides of the movement. Wilson's review concluded: 'our surprise is not that the General Election was lost but that we won as many seats as we did'; the national agent listed thirty-five seats that could have been won with improved organisation.[61] Inevitably the inquiry focused on the need to recruit more individual members. While the Conservatives officially claimed 2.8 million members, of whom about half were women, Labour's membership had dwindled to 843,000 by 1955. Unfortunately the resolution of this problem encountered local resistance both because of the time and trouble involved in recruiting new members and because entrenched constituency officers sometimes regarded recruitment campaigns initiated by headquarters as a threat to their position and status; one ward party in Salford was thought to be 'largely made up of old-age pensioners'.[62] As a result, by the 1950s many constituency parties had developed into rigid, bureaucratic organisations of elderly men who controlled both the party and municipal authorities through caucuses of loyalists but made minimal contact with the wider community. Even the MPs themselves often adopted an attitude of lordly neglect towards their local constituency despite the fact that they had been entitled to free rail travel from London since 1924. Members of Attlee's generation considered it beneath them to turn up for regular weekend constituency surgeries, though younger men often adopted them during the 1950s. In Sheffield Hillsborough, a strong Labour seat, A. V. Alexander was considered an unusually good MP in that he visited Sheffield once a month to hold a surgery, though as he crammed six speeches into the weekend visits he cannot have had much time to see constituents personally. Even Alexander's successor, George Darling, agreed to visit the constituency just once every three months on a Saturday and be available to see constituents.[63]

Wilson's report also identified the need to transfer election workers from safe seats to marginal ones as the Conservatives did, but he admitted that 'full employment and the widespread employment of married women affected not only political attitudes, but also the numbers of voluntary workers willing and able to carry on election activities'.[64] In addition Wilson recommended the appointment of more professional agents and efforts to concentrate them in marginal constituencies; in practice, however, Labour seats often relied on a senior alderman to act as an unpaid agent though he performed only at election times. Finally Wilson looked for greater efficiency at party headquarters, implicitly criticising the general secretary, Morgan Phillips, and the national agent, Len Williams.

However, local constituency records suggest that Wilson's report made little impact. In 1956 the Newcastle West CLP noted that head-quarters had issued them with a target of 750 *new* members by 1957; early in 1957 they discussed the Wilson Report with the other Newcastle parties but no action followed.[65] The only obvious advance came in September 1955 when Gaitskell persuaded the unions to increase affili-ation fees from sixpence to ninepence a head, thereby boosting party income by 50 per cent. But it is not clear that this was used to remedy the organisational deficiencies at headquarters. Even Wilson's report accepted that Labour could not copy the Tories in creating a profes-sional machine: 'it would be offensive alike to our traditions and our principles'.[66] To some extent the leadership bypassed headquarters staff by spending union funds on professional advice about advertising and television rather than on employing local agents. But the main theme was continuity; Phillips remained in post to be succeeded by Williams on his retirement and individual membership continued its steady decline, dwindling to 750,000 by 1961.

Significantly, Wilson's investigations failed to focus on the party's continuing problems in mobilising the female vote. Between 1945 and 1959 twenty-nine women were elected as Labour MPs including recruits such as Elaine Burton and Eirene White (1950) Harriet Slater and Lena Jeger (1953), Joyce Butler (1955) and Judith Hart (1959). Women achieved a higher profile after 1945 in that several enjoyed long parliamentary careers: Jennie Lee, Alice Bacon, Bessie Braddock and Margaret Herbison sat for twenty-five years, Judith Hart for twenty-eight and Barbara Castle for thirty-four; Ellen Wilkinson, Alice Bacon, Edith Summerskill, Margaret Herbison and Barbara Castle also served as party chairwomen and all but Wilkinson acted as NEC chairwoman.[67]

Yet despite this, women remained marginal within the party. As female candidates still found it almost impossible to win union spon-sorship most women stood in hopeless constituencies.[68] Combining socialism with feminism proved as difficult as ever for the few who attempted it. Monica Whately, who contested several seats, complained: 'I have over and over again been threatened with excommunication owing to my fight for the complete emancipation of women.'[69] Whately insisted on maintaining her role in the independent women's organisations, but mainstream Labour could not rid itself of suspicions that they were vehicles for middle-class feminism. As a result, the female Labour MPs never formed a women's group to press their causes, remaining split between left and right, and between the loyalist majority and the feminist minority. In 1950 when Eirene White won fifth place in the members' ballot she adopted a bill to liberalise the divorce laws but immediately came under pressure from party leaders to drop it for fear of antagonising Catholic voters. Significantly White's bill was not even supported by the Labour Women's Organisation and was eventually sidetracked by the appointment of a Royal Commission. Most of the women calculated that such causes simply marginalised female MPs. 'I have never had any conscious determination not to take up women's issues,' admitted Barbara Castle, 'I have just not been particularly interested in them. I always thought of myself as an MP not as a woman MP.'[70] In fact, the tactics adopted by Castle, Jennie Lee and Judith Hart, for example, were more deliberate than this implies. They sought election to the NEC as constituency representatives in competition with men, not as women's representatives; all three interested themselves in defence and colonial questions, not simply in 'domestic' ones. Party loyalists like Alice Bacon frankly disparaged women's politics and women's rights, preferring to concentrate on traditional domestic issues where female experience could be seen as relevant – the very rationale that had been employed in the late Victorian era to justify women's role in local government.[71] However, the long-term effect of Bacon's approach was to promote a women's organisation that remained completely loyal but deteriorated into a dull annual gathering of about 500 delegates who heard perfunctory addresses by party leaders. Few of the women MPs bothered to attend or speak in its debates.

As a result little challenge was offered to the dominant masculine culture of the Labour Movement. In its propaganda the party identified women essentially as housewives and mothers, a perception reflected strongly in the welfare-state schemes that rewarded women in so far as they were married but not if they were single. 'Nature itself made the first and greatest division of labour and no arguments by superior intellectual women can cancel that out,' insisted Arthur Woodburn, Secretary of State for Scotland 1947–50. This conservatism towards women was striking because the party was far from wholly immune to social change. All but four of the twenty-nine women MPs in this period were married, in contrast to those of the interwar era, among whom Castle, Hart, Braddock and Summerskill had husbands who were supportive of their political careers. Moreover, several Labour couples, including Jennie Lee and Nye Bevan, and Barbara and Ted Castle, had no children, presumably practised birth control, and enjoyed distinctly liberated lifestyles that left room for relationships outside marriage. However, during the 1950s all this remained below the parapet in a movement still ostensibly true to its puritanical traditions. Consequently, when the new movement for women's liberation emerged in the 1960s it largely took Labour by surprise.

On the face of it Labour's neglect of women should not have been a great handicap, for the Conservatives, with only fifteen women MPs between 1945 and 1959, were hardly at the forefront of feminism either. Yet they managed to outflank Labour partly by identifying themselves with affluence and consumerism and also by undertaking a few judicious reforms for women. Although Labour's annual conference had voted for equal pay in 1947 the issue was ignored by the NEC and rejected by successive chancellors, Dalton, Cripps and Gaitskell, on the grounds that it would be inflationary. Mary Sutherland, the woman's officer, supported their view.[72] Attlee refused even to meet deputations from the Equal Pay Campaign Committee although it included several Labour MPs – Edith Summerskill, Leah Manning, Barbara Gould, Elaine Burton and Eirene White. During the 1950s economic growth gradually weakened the economic case against equal pay, and, by focusing on teachers and civil servants, the EPCC attracted support from members such as Douglas Houghton who introduced motions and bills on the subject. The Conservatives, conscious of the tight electoral arithmetic after 1951, granted equal pay to teachers and civil servants in 1954 and extended it to employees in gas, electricity and the NHS in 1956. Although this was the extent of Conservative feminism, at the time it was enough to retain the advantage.

However, in the later 1950s these underlying weaknesses appeared to be insignificant as Labour's position noticeably strengthened.

Internal controversies petered out in a mood of co-operation; Bevan returned to the shadow Cabinet, became party treasurer in 1956, and was appointed shadow Foreign Secretary, the post he coveted. At the 1957 Brighton conference he famously shocked his left-wing followers with an attack on unilateral disarmament as 'an emotional spasm', warning that Britain could not send her Foreign Secretary 'naked into the conference chamber . . . to preach sermons'. He also distanced himself from socialist proposals for more nationalisation, saying, 'Candidly I doubt whether the public ownership plan is a positive and saleable proposition.' Always less of a rebel than he appeared, Bevan now shared Gaitskell's anxiety to avoid leading Labour into a third electoral defeat, and he was ready to settle for a new Labour government even of a revisionist character.

While Labour benefited from the new Bevan–Gaitskell axis, the Conservative government lost credibility through its mismanagement of the economy and the Suez invasion of 1956. Initially Suez placed Gaitskell in an awkward position, caught between the pro-Nasser opinions voiced at the party conference in October and patriotism in the country. Eventually, however, when it became clear that Sir Anthony Eden had deceived the country, Gaitskell delivered a courageous denunciation of his policy in a television broadcast. Despite this, the long-term political impact of the Suez fiasco was limited. The deep disillusionment it caused among many educated people gave momentum to the Liberal revival under Jo Grimond in the late 1950s. But as Eden's successor, Harold Macmillan, restored British relations with the United States, the sense of crisis soon passed and most voters remained unconcerned about the immorality and ineptitude of government policy.

Up until the spring of 1959 Gaitskell expected to win the next election, though by the autumn Labour had fallen behind in the polls. At first the Conservatives were thought to be losing the election campaign as Labour fought far more effectively and aggressively than in 1955 and offered a clearer alternative programme including the repeal of the Rent Act, an increase in old-age pensions, and the abolition of the eleven-plus examination. Labour observers thought that the turning point came when Gaitskell delivered a speech at Newcastle on 28 September in which he tried to spike any Conservative scare about higher taxes under Labour by announcing that there would be no increase in income tax. When Macmillan challenged Gaitskell to extend this promise to indirect taxes, Labour's position began to lose credibility. According to Mikardo, who lost his seat at Reading, this 'foolish and gratuitous undertaking' had an immediate effect on the doorstep as voters voiced their scepticism.[73] Yet although the Conservatives drew ahead in the latter stages of the campaign the swing against Labour was only 1 per cent. The Conservatives gained twenty-eight seats but lost six, including five to Labour in Scotland and Lancashire where unemployment was high. Labour won votes among the middle class and especially among electors over sixty-five; but young and working-class voters, influenced by the prevailing prosperity, moved towards the Conservatives.

In the aftermath of the 1959 election Morgan Phillips reported – not for the first time – that the party enjoyed excellent morale and that it generally recognised that Gaitskell had fought an excellent campaign. Outside the movement, however, this third successive defeat was widely interpreted as evidence that Labour had become the victim of underlying social and political change, a mood captured by Mark Abrams and Richard Rose in *Must Labour Lose?*(1960). The thesis was somewhat exaggerated in that at 43.8 per cent Labour's support was only 4 per cent below that of 1945, and the fall in 1959 was partly a statistical consequence of the doubling in the number of Liberal candidates. Nonetheless, Labour appeared to be suffering from a steadily shrinking base as the number of manual workers had diminished by half a million between 1951 and 1959 while an extra million became white-collar employees and thus occupationally middle class. As 87 per cent of the party's vote was working class the prospects seemed poor.

For a time it was fashionable to assume that the key to shifts in allegiance lay in affluence. During the 1950s British economic growth was boosted by the 1947 devaluation, the General Agreement on Tariffs and Trade, the shift of the terms of trade in Britain's favour, the reduction of defence spending after the Korean War, and the housing boom. Keynesian economic management enabled British workers to enjoy a golden age of full employment which, combined with a more relaxed attitude towards working mothers, led to the spread of the two-income family. Inflation was around 4 per cent, money wages rose from an average of £8 a week in 1951 to £15 by 1961, home-ownership spread from 35 per cent in 1939 to 47 per cent by 1966, and the relaxation of credit controls boosted the demand for consumer goods.

But how exactly did these trends impact on the Labour Party? As the decade wore on even the most efficient local parties found their efforts handicapped by affluence. In South Lewisham the organisers reported that attendances at the women's sections were dwindling especially in the absence of good local leaders. 'This is not easy,' they admitted, 'owing to the fact that most first-class women are doing a job these days, either full-time or part-time.'[74] Although membership remained high in Lewisham the pattern was for members to drop out but then 'just rejoin to get rid of the canvassers'.[75] Employment patterns undermined voluntary organisations of all kinds, but the expansion of jobs for working-class wives clearly hit Labour relatively hard. By the mid-1950s attendance at ward meetings was low and declining which was seen partly as a reflection of 'the general apathy which has descended on the Party as a whole', but the Lewisham agent also recognised 'the difficulty of canvassing very much during the evenings, owing to the viewing of television'.[76] He tried to get round this by visiting on Sunday mornings but this did not allow enough time given the number of homes to be reached.

However, some contemporaries believed that affluence affected voters in more profound ways in that it led manual workers to adopt some of the values and aspirations usually associated with middle-class people – in effect a process of *embourgeoisement*. One 1959 study of 500 working-class voters found that 40 per cent of them actually described themselves as middle class; they were potentially subject to cross-pressures, finding it difficult to reconcile their traditional Labour allegiance with their current affiliation with Conservative values.[77] However, this thesis was undermined by empirical studies of working-class *embourgeoisement* in towns such as Luton, typical of the expanding, affluent communities. Won comfortably by Labour in 1945, Luton had been narrowly lost in 1950 and recorded a 5,000 Conservative majority in 1959. Yet researchers found no indication that the Luton workers had become less attached to trade unions or aspired to a middle-class lifestyle.[78]

The real flaw in the affluence thesis was that it reflected the obses-sion of 1950s social science with social class and neglected other relevant features, notably generation and gender. In 1959 Labour still

led the Conservatives among men by 48–45 but trailed among women
by 51–43; the gender gap had narrowed only because the Conservatives
had lost some female support to the Liberals. After 1945 Labour did
not win a majority among women voters again until the election of
1966. Moreover, it is now recognised that the social-science explanations
took the relationship between voting and social categories as unduly
passive; the connections only work when political parties make
deliberate efforts to mobilise support and build alliances with specific
sections of society. After 1951 the Conservatives devoted a great deal
of attention to affluent workers by promoting home-ownership, by
introducing premium bonds in 1956, by repeatedly easing restrictions
on credit, by reducing income tax, and by leaving trade unions free
to capitalise on full employment by bargaining for higher wages.

Conversely, Labour was never sure how to respond to affluence
especially as manifested in hire purchase, commercial television, advertising and the new youth culture which was symptomatic of
consumerism. Many socialists interpreted all this as evidence of the
penetration of Americanism in British society and as proof that big
business was manipulating working people. Several left-wingers
adopted an uncompromising stance. Richard Crossman argued in 1960
that Labour should 'refuse in any way to come to terms with the
affluent society', while Bevan famously denounced it: 'This so-called
affluent society is an ugly society. It is a vulgar society. It is a mere-
tricious society. It is a society in which priorities have gone all wrong.'[79]
Disapproval of gambling and indebtedness reflected the movement's
Nonconformist roots, and attacks on business recalled Edwardian criticism of the brewers for exploiting workingmen. To this extent Labour
disparagement of Tory chancellors for financial recklessness was deeply
rooted in the party's history.

On the other hand, alongside its puritan tradition the movement
had always encompassed an indulgent, bucolic, live-for-the-day culture
that was ostensibly consistent with 1950s working-class consumerism.
Up to the 1920s Labour leaders had been enthusiastic advocates of
home-ownership, a characteristic feature of the affluent society.
However, over time the cultural-political meaning of home-ownership
had changed; once associated with thrift and sobriety it increasingly
signalled self-indulgence and speculation. This was far from inevitable,
but the Labour leaders had gradually allowed themselves to become

detached from the idea of home-ownership while their rivals had stren-
uously appropriated it as integral to Conservatism. At a personal level
puritanism was a wholly unnatural creed for socialists such as Bevan,
Gaitskell and Crosland whose private lives were characterised by indulgence and hedonism. Crosland, who recognised early on that it was a
mistake for Labour to be seen as hostile to affluence, wished to recast
socialism in more egalitarian and libertarian terms: 'Abstinence is not
a good foundation for socialism.'[80] However, Crosland was too bourgeois to carry much influence. Bevan, on the other hand, had rapidly
abandoned his early puritanism with his arrival in London and his
marriage to Jennie Lee. Their indulgence in good food, quality wine,
fine cigars, first-class tickets on Cunard and taxis to Harrods meant
that they spent beyond their income. But Bevan felt no embarrassment
about this, even when disparaged as a 'Bollinger Bolshevik', arguing
that whatever was good enough for the higher classes was fine for
the workers.[81] Consequently, as an authentic working-class socialist-
cum-hedonist Bevan was perfectly placed to articulate Labour's case in
an era of affluence. Yet this was the one service he signally failed to
perform for his party, perhaps because he appreciated that he had made
himself vulnerable by cultivating upper-class habits and by failing to
respect the Labour preference for keeping to one's place and one's
roots. As a result the Conservatives were allowed to consolidate their
links with affluence largely unchallenged until the early 1960s when
the collapse of the boom eventually deflated working-class confidence
in consumerism and restored Labour's electoral prospects. The electoral consequences were thus more the result of misjudgement rather
than sociological inevitability.

'A grand conception': Labour in the Wilson Era, 1960–1976

'If there is anything that the 1959 general election shows,' observed Hugh Gaitskell, 'it is surely that unity is not enough.'[1] Unfortunately this insight led him into a hasty misinterpretation of Labour's three defeats. Within days of the election the Gaitskellites, in conclave at Frognal Gardens, concluded that they had lost because the party was too old-fashioned, steeped in class war, and wedded to nationalisation. Douglas Jay even proposed that Labour should change its name. However, when Roy Jenkins and Christopher Mayhew put these ideas before the PLP they attracted little sympathy: 'we reached the end of the week with the Hampstead poodles in complete rout', as Richard Crossman cheerfully recorded.[2] Undeterred, Gaitskell surprised even his own followers by proposing to remove Clause IV, the socialist commitment, from the party's constitution. Even Jenkins and Crosland considered this tactically unwise. Harold Wilson, who had emerged as an effective shadow chancellor, thought Gaitskell was being absurd: 'We were being asked to take Genesis out of the Bible.'[3] Clause IV had never been interpreted literally at any time since 1918, but for party members it meant something that Gaitskell failed to grasp; not surprisingly his proposal was rejected at the annual conference at Blackpool. In effect Gaitskell had drawn attention to Labour's commitment to nationalisation when he really wanted to minimise it.

Unhappily the debate over Clause IV proved to be only the prelude to two years of controversy over defence which further undermined Gaitskell's credibility as leader. In the early 1960s he became apprehensive about the spread of pacifist sentiment among the unions and about the success of the Campaign for Nuclear Disarmament in winning converts among CLPs which seemed certain to revive the influence of the Bevanites. This triggered an argument among the

Gaitskellites who feared that their leader was overreacting with his talk about returning to the back benches with a hundred members if he failed to get his way. 'I begin to fear that Gaitskell has the seeds of destruction in him,' wrote Patrick Gordon-Walker, 'he wants to take up absolute and categorical positions and is becoming distrustful of his friends.'[4] Colleagues also realised that despite his integrity and formidable intellectual talents, Gaitskell was inadequately organised for his role. 'Your leadership still lacks a proper system of intelligence and Forward Planning,' as Crosland daringly told him.[5] According to Crosland, Gaitskell was too slow to see 'how rapidly opinion was changing on the H-bomb'; he urged him to hold regular consultations with union leaders and loyal MPs and, most of all, to appoint a full-time staff to meet daily and advise him.

However, Gaitskell, who was not an easy man to advise, ignored the criticisms.[6] His followers spent an uncomfortable few months in 1960 trying to persuade him to adopt a realistic formula on defence, but 'Gaitskell says anyone who disagrees with him is a fudger'.[7] In a glum mood the Gaitskellites prepared for the annual conference at Scarborough with their leader 'rather spoiling for a showdown between the Parliamentary Party and the Conference', in Gordon-Walker's words. Gaitskell believed passionately that Britain must retain her role in NATO and that unilateral nuclear disarmament would make Labour look like a mere party of protest. However, a combination of unions and CLPs adopted a resolution supporting unilateralism, thereby placing the parliamentary leadership in the embarrassing position of being dictated to by the conference. In response Gaitskell famously declared his intention to 'fight, fight and fight again to save the party we love', while Jenkins wrote that unilateralism would 'destroy the hopes of a Labour Government for generations'.[9]

As so often this overreaction only exacerbated the sense of crisis, and Gaitskell's divisive rhetoric demonstrated his poor grasp of tactics. It required only a limited shift of union votes to reverse the 1960 decision – the TGWU alone could do it. Meanwhile, the women's conference, held shortly after Scarborough, endorsed Gaitskell's view by three to one. However, the controversy inspired the Labour right to organise itself by creating the Campaign for Democratic Socialism under the chairmanship of William Rodgers which issued a manifesto under the names of Dick Taverne, Brian Walden, Bryan Magee and other right-wingers. Insisting 'We are convinced that our Movement cannot afford another Scarborough', the signatories hoped to 'reassert the views of the great mass of Labour supporters against those of doctrinaire pressure groups'.[10] In particular the CDS aimed to persuade two or three unions to switch allegiance on unilateralism, reverse the 1960 vote on defence, strengthen Gaitskell's position, vote more 'moderates' on to the NEC and, with the help of the general secretary and the national agent, prevent the adoption of left-wing candidates in Labour seats.

By 1961 the CDS felt it was winning. Meeting at Blackpool the annual conference rejected unilateralism thanks to a change by the TGWU and USDAW. Meanwhile plans were afoot to expel twenty-five to thirty MPs, among whom the CDS identified fourteen 'Communists' and 'two or three madmen', including Tom Driberg, Frank Allaun, S. O. Davies and Konni Zilliacus.[11] However, while this forced the left on to the defensive it was only a recipe for prolonged infighting. In any case, the CDS admitted that there was no evidence that Labour's popularity had improved, indeed the polls suggested a decline in Gaitskell's standing, no doubt because he had focused attention on the party's extremism and on himself as a divisive figure.[12]

Indeed, Gaitskell's aggressive tactics precipitated a formal challenge to his leadership in October 1960 by the shadow chancellor, Harold Wilson. Though emerging from a modest provincial background in Huddersfield, Wilson had comparatively shallow roots in the Labour Movement. At Oxford he had joined the Liberal Club, alienated by the posh socialists; he acquired a fellowship in applied economics and worked as a research statistician during the war. But Wilson 'wore his roots like a badge', maintaining his Yorkshire accent and cultivating his reputation as a hard-working provincial. Despite having no experience in the movement he managed to win the nomination for Ormskirk, straight from the Civil Service, and was swept into Parliament on the 1945 landslide. In an elderly Cabinet the thirty-one-year-old Wilson stood out as president of the Board of Trade and became one of the government's successes. Yet colleagues felt he lacked strong opinions, and his decision to join Bevan by resigning in 1951 was regarded by left-wingers less as a matter of principle than as a marker for the future; he shared their dislike for Gaitskell but was not otherwise left wing. However, Wilson shrewdly consolidated his standing as chairman of the 1955 inquiry into party organisation which enabled him to develop contacts with CLPs all over the country, an asset for a man with no base in the movement, and reinvented himself as a moderniser uncontaminated by the fractious disputes between Bevanites and Gaitskellites.[13]

After the death of Bevan in 1960 Wilson emerged as the leading figure on the left, if not actually its leader, and came under intense pressure to launch a challenge for the leadership. Gaitskell's folly in exacerbating controversy over Clause IV and defence had created an opportunity for Wilson to stand as the 'unity' candidate. However much he was disparaged privately by his colleagues, his claims were credible for he campaigned for compromise on defence, argued that all official pronouncements should follow collective agreement by the NEC and the PLP, and insisted on abandoning attempts to rewrite the constitution. This enabled him to gather support from left, right and centre of the party. Anthony Wedgwood Benn, who had worked closely with Gaitskell and stood on the right at this time, refused to vote for Gaitskell: 'It's hard to believe that he really wanted the Clause IV thing to go through smoothly.'[14] In the event Gaitskell did slightly better than expected, winning 166 votes to Wilson's eighty-one, though according to Benn many members who voted for him 'have told me quite frankly that they don't believe it is possible for him to last'.[15] The victory did Gaitskell little good as he had been rejected by a third of the PLP and Wilson had established himself as principal candidate for the succession despite losing the election for deputy leadership to George Brown by 133 to 103.

Meanwhile Gaitskell's fragile leadership had developed yet another fracture. In July 1960 Roy Jenkins resigned from the front bench to be free to promote the case for British membership of the Common Market.[16] The issue moved up the agenda in 1961 when the prime minister, Harold Macmillan, initiated Britain's first application to join, in the process triggering a whole series of damaging splits in both main parties. While many Conservatives disliked Europe as a means of extending socialism, many Labour members saw it as a club for capitalists. For Jenkins it offered a realistic way of enabling Britain to recreate her role in a post-imperial world. Gaitskell, however, adopted a characteristically inflexible and conservative view culminating in a notorious speech to the 1961 conference: 'What does a federal Europe mean?' he demanded. 'It means the end of a thousand years of history.'

However, as all his followers were enthusiastic Europeans, Gaitskell had again isolated himself and put in doubt his ability to work with them in the long term.

Yet while Gaitskell's leadership looked increasingly precarious, Macmillan's government was also becoming vulnerable over its management of the economy, now suffering from a balance of payments deficit, speculation against sterling, poor economic growth and rising unemployment. In July 1961 Selwyn Lloyd raised bank rates to 7 per cent, inflicted expenditure cuts and introduced a pay pause. The collapse of Conservative support became apparent at the Blackpool North by-election in March 1962 when the Liberals reduced a 16,000 majority to 900. Hard on its heels came Orpington where the Liberals gained the seat by nearly 8,000 votes and Labour lost its deposit. Although the Liberal revival lost momentum during 1963 and 1964, it proved to be the first in a series of revivals heralding the return to multi-party politics in Britain. Although Labour gained three by-election seats in 1963, it found itself in competition for floating voters with the Liberal leader, Jo Grimond, who attracted Conservatives but was also radical enough to win over activists who might otherwise have worked for Labour. The Liberal revival underlined that however much Gaitskell impressed his circle of acolytes, he had a limited appeal among the wider electorate. In view of the desperately close result of the election in 1964, when Labour fought under a more skilful successor, the conclusion is inescapable that Gaitskell would have led Labour to a fourth successive defeat. In the event his sudden death in January 1963 made the question academic.

This unexpected turn of events largely killed the CDS counter-offensive because the Labour right now lacked a credible leader. The abler figures such as Jenkins and Crosland were too junior and had no standing in the party. The obvious right-wing candidate was George Brown, an authentic working-class conservative who had risen through the trade unions and held office under the Attlee government. However, though articulate, passionate and energetic, Brown was seriously flawed. Regarded even in the unions as a loud-mouthed upstart, he was temperamentally unstable and followed a long line of Labour politicians in his growing propensity for alcohol. In May 1960 Brown had fallen down at the House of Commons and been taken to hospital with a suspected skull fracture: 'George was very drunk,' explained Gordon-Walker.[17] As deputy leader Brown was so confident of victory that he failed to see how his support was dwindling. 'Are we going to be led by a neurotic drunk?' asked Anthony Crosland, one right-winger who voted for James Callaghan and then for Wilson in the run-off.[18]

Although Wilson stood ostensibly as the candidate of the left, this was purely nominal for he had steadily distanced himself from his colleagues' views during the 1950s despite retaining personal links with Barbara Castle and Richard Crossman. He had co-operated with the right over reversing the vote for unilateral disarmament, in the process enhancing his reputation for opportunism. 'If we are to die in the last ditch,' commented Brown, 'Harold won't be there. He will have scrambled out.'[19] However, his ministerial experience, competence as shadow chancellor and image as a contemporary, classless figure made him reassuring. On the first ballot he won 115 votes, to eighty-eight for Brown and forty-one for Callaghan who withdrew leaving Wilson to win by 144 to 103.

For once the party had made a shrewd choice. Brown would have damaged Labour by his personal failings and he lacked an appeal to the middle-class electors now disillusioned with the Conservatives. Wilson, by contrast, was ideally placed to outflank the Liberals and capitalise on the weaknesses of the Macmillan government. During 1963–4 he proved to be an outstanding Leader of the Opposition. Wilson immediately impressed his colleagues by his openness and accessibility; whereas Gaitskell had been inclined to lecture, he was conciliatory, respected the ordinary party members and seemed to appreciate their socialist values. William Rodgers gathered a handful of Gaitskellite *enragés* for annual dinners of the '1963 Club', but sensible right-wingers, recognising the new leader as a moderate and a revisionist, saw that they had nothing to fear. As Ian Mikardo pointed out, Wilson's election had been no more than a negative victory for the left because it was a defeat for the right.

Indeed, in a shadow Cabinet dominated by right-wingers in which only one member, apart from himself, had voted for him, Wilson looked slightly beleaguered. 'I am running a Bolshevik Revolution with a Tsarist Shadow Cabinet,' he liked to tell left-wing supporters.[20] Essentially a lonely figure, and increasingly insecure as time passed, he relied heavily on a small circle of confidants, notably Marcia Williams, his personal political secretary who had worked at Transport House and reacted against its right-wing bias. A forthright and loyal character, Williams gave Wilson frank advice and controlled access to his office, though in time she became obsessive about rivals to her authority. The lawyer, Arnold Goodman, who saw him each week, could also be relied on for neutral advice and legal opinion. But Wilson's most singular adviser was Colonel George Wigg, member for Dudley since 1945, who boasted an army career and a talent for tipping horses. Unusually for a Labour politician Wigg relished the clandestine world of the security services and the armed forces; he gathered 'intelligence', briefed Wilson on parliamentary gossip, offered advice about honours, and kept files on the activities of his colleagues including Marcia Williams. According to Crossman, who was also close to Wilson, Wigg saw him 'four or five times a day and is virtually living with him'.[21] Eventually, though, Wigg's influence became unhealthy as he fed the prime minister's paranoia about plots against him.

Yet the new leader's dependence on Wigg was established at the outset through his role in exploiting the Profumo scandal. The affair followed the recent defection of Kim Philby to the Soviet Union and the disgrace of William Vassall, an Admiralty clerk who was blackmailed and convicted of spying. It was this context that gave the comparatively trivial facts of the Profumo scandal their significance among contemporaries – but only with the skilful manipulation of it by Wigg and Wilson. Macmillan's war minister, John Profumo, was discovered in a relationship with one Christine Keeler, not something that would normally have aroused much political interest except for the fact that as Keeler's clients included a Captain Ivanov, a naval attaché at the Soviet embassy, it involved a possible threat to national security. Wigg first alerted Wilson to the scandal in autumn 1962 but the Labour leader, not wishing to be seen exploiting the issue, left it to him to raise the matter in the Commons. Wigg gathered evidence from participants including Dr Stephen Ward which Wilson passed on to the prime minister who appeared to take no action. In this way the noose was gradually tightened around Macmillan's neck; when it emerged that Profumo had lied to Parliament Macmillan began to look evasive and out of touch. The appointment of a judicial inquiry into the affair under Lord Denning found nothing significant but served to keep the whole issue alive and to lend it importance. Wilson's handling of the affair was masterly in that he had not overplayed his hand, steered clear of the moral aspects and focused on national security; he kept the government on the defensive for many months, succeeding in fixing an indelible impression of Macmillan's regime as

a survival from a lackadaisical, Edwardian era. The political signifi-
cance was underlined by the admiring correspondence attracted by
Wigg – filed as 'Profumo Fan Mail' – which included letters from
Conservatives angered by Macmillan's incompetence.[22]

Profumo represented the negative side of Wilson's strategy as Leader
of the Opposition, complementing his efforts to present Labour in terms
of modernism, efficiency, science and technology in contrast to the
blinkered traditionalism of his opponents. As a highly educated, classless politician, Wilson was especially well placed for this and he devoted
his speech to the annual conference in 1963 to the theme of reinvigor-
ating the British economy through a greater input from science and
technology. This was tactically shrewd in that it detached Labour from
its associations with nationalisation and the unions, tapped into the
'National Efficiency' tradition, and captured the enthusiasm of the journalists who heard the speech. However, the journalists were doubly
misled by Wilson's scientific revolution. The general public, for whom
science was not an issue, remained largely unmoved by the rhetoric.
Moreover, beyond proposing to appoint a Minister for Technology and
grant more subsidies to support science, the initiative had little substance.
However, Wilson undoubtedly made an impact on public opinion. He
had already done this in his first broadcast as leader in February where
he presented himself, quite authentically, as a suburbanite with a £5,000
mortgage in Hampstead Garden Suburb to a society obsessed with
home-ownership and housing costs. Immensely reassuring, Wilson was,
in effect, reviving Herbert Morrison's tactics of extending Labour's
appeal to middle- and lower-middle-class voters, professionals, admin-
istrators, managers and technicians, to win a popular majority.

During 1963 unemployment increased, Macmillan purged a third of
his Cabinet and by June Labour's lead in the polls had risen to 20 per
cent. Despite this, when the prime minister resigned at the Tory conference in September the prospects of victory began to look elusive.
Although Wilson had enormous fun mocking his successor, the aristocratic Sir Alec Douglas Home, who epitomised the failings already
identified in Macmillan, he was denied the early election Labour
needed. Home simply used his full term of office and by November
Labour's lead had diminished to 8 per cent; by late August 1964 it had
almost vanished. When the election eventually came in mid-October
it produced a 3.5 per cent swing to Labour, but with 44.1 per cent the

party's vote was only fractionally up on 1959, closely pressed by the Tories with 43.4. This produced 317 Labour members to 304 Conservatives and an overall majority of just five.

Why, after Wilson's brilliant work as Opposition leader and Labour's huge popular lead in 1963, did the party come so close to a fourth electoral defeat in 1964? In the first place the government bought time and the chancellor, Reginald Maudling, conciliated voters by engineering a pre-election boom through his spring Budget; as a result, although industrial output stagnated and the trade gap widened, people felt more comfortable and optimistic as the election approached. Moreover, Labour was reluctant to attack on the economy for fear of being accused of accelerating a crisis over sterling and because the strikes that occurred in this period gave the Conservatives the opportunity to blame Labour for poor economic performance. But were Labour's tactics well judged? In his concern to present Labour as moderate, Wilson played down economic radicalism; he proposed to renationalise steel but not otherwise to usher in socialism. As a result Labour neglected unemployment and its campaign lacked any strong intellectual or ideological theme; essentially it claimed to be able to manage the economy more competently by promoting efficiency and modernity. This approach was certainly reflected in constituency campaigns. Anthony Crosland, a politician well endowed with ideas on economics, defended his marginal Grimsby seat by arguing, 'Britain today needs a Government not of amiable aristocrats, but of men equipped to deal with a scientific, technological, and rapidly changing age.'[23]

Two further short-term factors help to explain the close result. The prospect of a Labour government during 1963–4 helped the Conservatives to regain some, if not all, of the support they had lost to the Liberals; some CLPs noticed this process in the May 1964 local elections.[24] The recovery was assisted by the change of prime minister. Having lost confidence in Macmillan many voters warmed to Home and in mocking him as a fourteenth earl who used matchsticks to work out economic problems Labour's attack may have misfired.

However, the question arises whether there were more fundamental, underlying factors at work. How far had Wilson's efforts at modernisation really changed the party by 1964? In some ways the answer is positive. His leadership marked a departure from the old-fashioned style of Attlee, who frankly disapproved of television, and Bevan who thought advertising would 'take all the poetry out of politics'. Wilson, who was especially interested in opinion polls, used Mark Abrams to identify groups of target voters to be contacted by the party. With the advice of Tony Benn, a former television producer, he had adapted himself to television, wielding his pipe and adopting the relaxed manner of Stanley Baldwin. As leader Wilson used Benn and an informal group of public relations and advertising men to devise party broadcasts and advertisements partly because he wanted to bypass the right-wingers who controlled Transport House. Labour's election fund amounted to an impressive £757,000, of which £740,000 was contributed by the unions, compared with just £186,000 in 1959. This enabled Labour to spend £150,000 on public relations and to launch an advertising campaign in the national press in May 1963. However, by the summer of 1964 this money had been exhausted before the election had properly begun.[25]

These improvements suggest that at national level Labour's machine was better equipped to take on the Conservatives than previously. But how far was this true at constituency level? Despite a national swing of 3.5 per cent, the results varied quite widely between regions and individual constituencies. This suggests that, although local activism was largely discounted by scholars at the time, the close result in 1964 owed something to the condition of the movement in the country. Sara Barker, the national agent, noted that with sixty-four gains and four losses Labour had come close to a decisive victory and that a few hundred votes in marginal seats would have made all the difference.[26] For example, Labour lost Reading by ten votes where 2,013 postal votes were cast, and Slough by eleven where 1,618 postal votes were recorded. Even where Labour improved its share of postal votes, as in Birmingham, it conceded that the Tories took most of them, and it seems likely that they won sixteen seats on the strength of their organisation of postal voters alone.[27]

Such work required money and manpower in the constituencies. Yet by 1962 Labour Party membership was officially down to 767,000 and continued its long-term decline to 734,000 in 1967 and 659,000 in 1977, though the true number was far lower. In several marginal constituencies, where the pressure to improve the organisation seemed obvious, progress was patchy. In Grimsby, for example, Labour had scraped home by a hundred votes in 1959 but the CLP was unable to run an effective membership campaign and continued to be dogged by financial problems. In 1966 it signed a formal agreement committing it to finding at least £600 towards election costs while the MP, Anthony Crosland, contributed £75 annually and £150 for the election.[28] But in 1962 Grimsby's organisation was so poor that Transport House paid for a part-time canvasser and for some student canvassers to build up a marked electoral register. This, combined with regular work by Crosland, enabled the party to achieve a 68 per cent canvass in the 1964 election and an above-average swing of 4.2 per cent.[29]

Derby had returned two Labour members in 1959 but on dwindling majorities of 2,000 and 3,500. Although the party claimed a membership of 2,220 for the two seats in 1960, the £200 yielded by their subscriptions suggests this was a sleeping membership.[30] The Derby party employed an agent but he was a local alderman who had occupied the role since 1936 and was not very effective. The East Midlands regional organiser, Jim Cattermole, tried to promote membership drives in 1961 and 1962 which failed to arrest the decline up to 1963. Despite the imminence of an election only a few wards participated and one of the MPs, Philip Noel-Baker, was absent as usual during the summer despite Cattermole's request for sitting members to assist the campaign.[31] Of the forty-one constituencies in the East Midlands, twenty-one recorded a membership of 800, a purely nominal total unrelated to live membership, and in 1967 the majority reported exactly 1,000 on the same basis.[32]

Another telling case was Swansea where one constituency was safely Labour but the other a marginal lost to the Conservatives by 400 votes in 1959. Yet despite being a key target for the next election Swansea West had just 490 members in 1962 and an old-fashioned organisation dependent on union funds and elderly activists.[33] Complaints by younger supporters and external pressure exerted by the Welsh Regional Council of Labour made little impression. Though the seat was recovered in 1964 with a below-average swing of 3.2 per cent, the decline had not really been arrested, for the party had imported paid canvassers from other Welsh constituencies – even the safe Swansea East was unable to supply them.[34] This lack of voluntary co-operation between parties continued to hamper election campaigns. In Poplar, a safe Labour seat, Ian Mikardo complained about the reluctance of party workers to assist marginal seats: 'What! you expect us to go to the other side of the river?'[35]

As in the 1930s Labour found it more difficult to develop efficient machines in the industrial constituencies than in the socially mixed, suburban ones in and around London. South Lewisham maintained a formidable organisation, claiming 8,000 members in 1964 and was still capable of canvassing 85 per cent of the electors in 1966.[36] The residential constituency of Putney, where Labour overturned a Conservative majority of 5,000 in 1964, offers an instructive example of improvement. Previously the Putney CLP struggled with a low level of activity and modest funding; its 1964 income of £1,525 relied heavily on £508 from social events, £319 from a tote and £476 from subscriptions, but only £52 from trade unions.[37] Its main resource lay in the individual members who numbered 2,025 by 1964 and 2,208 in 1966 when they paid £873.[38] Labour's candidate in 1964, Hugh Jenkins, managed to combine a national appeal with close attention to local issues including housing and aircraft noise. In this he was helped by his wife, a GLC councillor and chairwoman of the housing committee; they acted as a team by holding weekly advice sessions together. It may also be significant, in view of the assumptions routinely made about the handicap of the Labour left, that Hugh Jenkins was a consistently left-wing MP who not only achieved an above-average swing in 1964 but also retained his seat in 1970 against the trend and in defiance of the national leadership. Jenkins argued that it was a mistake for Labour to obscure the differences between the parties by employing bland national propaganda: 'for a party like Labour it is necessary for the candidate to offend the Tory right not conciliate it'.[39] This approach enabled Jenkins to mobilise the activists and thereby to sustain Labour's machine over the long term.

As the examples of Putney and Grimsby suggest, in the 1960s funding posed a major problem for many local parties many of which found the answer in forms of gambling. Putney charged members of its tote a shilling a week for prizes of £25, raised £464 from its tote by 1966, and thus managed to pay a full-time agent.[40] In Poplar Mikardo complained that his party boasted few members, no agent, little organisation and minimal political awareness, but raised a lot of money from bingo.[41] Yet most Labour MPs disapproved of gambling in general and the Conservatives' 1960 Gaming and Betting Act in particular. Noel-Baker complained that due to the Act 'my neighbourhood is being degraded by the opening of large and expensive-looking betting shops'.[42] He may not have realised that by participating in the East

Midlands Regional Football Pool his Derby party made £958, without which their finances would have collapsed.[43]

The high swing scored by Labour in places such as Putney, which would have given Labour a comfortable majority if achieved nationally, contrasted sharply with seats in Birmingham and the West Midlands where the turnover of votes in 1964 was minimal and the party made hard work of what appeared easy gains. In Birmingham All Saints a Tory majority of twenty votes was converted to a Labour one of just 470; in Yardley the Conservatives' 1,385 became a Labour majority of 169; in Sparkbrook Roy Hattersley turned a slender 886 Tory lead into an equally slender Labour one of 1,254; in Birmingham Perry Bar, retained by Labour by 183 in 1959, the Conservatives *won* by 327; there was virtually no movement of votes in Ladywood, and in Aston Labour increased its majority from 2,500 to just 3,300. Despite the trend towards a uniform national form of politics and the assumption that local candidates and campaigns scarcely mattered any more, it is clear that the traditional, regional political culture had survived in places like Birmingham and the West Midlands. There Conservatism was still capable of taking a populist stance, using local councillors and businessmen as candidates, and appealing across class lines.

The relative buoyancy of the West Midlands economy and the affluence it engendered may have consolidated this appeal, but since the late 1950s an additional factor had been at work in the shape of reactions to Commonwealth immigration. This was a crucial element in at least three Labour losses in 1964 at Perry Barr, Smethwick and Slough. In its post-mortem the Birmingham party commented that while Labour's support increased in owner-occupation areas, it fell in the traditional Labour wards.[44] This was corroborated by a comparison of the voting in the West Midlands in 1950 and 1964 which showed that there had been a swing in the Conservatives' favour of 4.2 per cent. Throughout the 1950s the attrition of the working-class vote had been a growing problem as Labour found itself trapped between the liberal instincts of many MPs and the trade unions who regarded immigration as a threat to employment and wages as they had done since the late Victorian period. In his Poplar constituency Ian Mikardo noted that racism built on an older tradition of anti-Semitism, and that in the docks the closed shop effectively excluded black men from employment.[45] Once the Commonwealth Immigration Act came into

force in 1962 the issue inevitably made an impact locally even though
the national party leaders largely avoided it. The Birmingham party
identified several wards where immigration had affected the result to
its disadvantage in the 1962 municipal elections.[46] At the same time
Patrick Gordon-Walker, the sitting member for Smethwick, where
Labour was also losing municipal elections, privately warned Gaitskell
about 'the difficulties in my constituency owing to colour and that I
might lose the seat'.[47] In Slough the majority of the veteran Labour
member, Fenner Brockway, was steadily whittled away, partly because
the booming economy attracted thousands of immigrants and
because he was regarded as unduly sympathetic towards the immi-
grant community, leading to his narrow defeat in 1964. In Birmingham
the local Conservative leaders deliberately exploited the issue. Geoffrey
Lloyd MP decided to make immigration a plank in the party's
campaign, thereby making it respectable for other Conservative candidates.[48] In nearby Smethwick a classic contest occurred between an
approachable, local Tory of working-class origin, Peter Griffiths, who
was an alderman and exponent of traditional West Midlands Tory
populism, and Labour's Gordon-Walker who, though the MP since
1945, was posh and distant and had neglected the organisation during
his long tenure. Although Gordon-Walker criticised Conservative legislation on immigration, he repeatedly shifted his ground, sometimes
opposing control and sometimes supporting it. Moreover, several
Smethwick Labour councillors publicly opposed immigration and the
Labour Club operated a colour bar. Thus Labour was not well placed
to resist Griffiths when he exploited the backlash against the 6,000
local immigrants, assisted by the local newspaper, the *Smethwick
Telephone.*[49] Griffiths' comfortable victory in 1964 came as no surprise;
though shocking at the time it signified that Labour's rise to power
had never displaced the continuity of regional political culture.

As a result of these losses, Harold Wilson faced the awkward task
of governing on a tiny majority; however, in contrast to Attlee in 1950
he was a vigorous premier leading a PLP with a keen appetite for
office after its years in opposition. Unfortunately, on taking office
Wilson rapidly became a victim of his own undoubted skills in party
management. With an average age of fifty-seven his new Cabinet was
weighed down with elderly and inadequate ministers including Frank
Soskice, Tom Fraser and Jim Griffiths. Wilson's personal insecurity

and desire to keep control also manifested itself in several odd appointments. He suddenly switched Richard Crossman from Education, for which he was well prepared, to Housing 'because he knows nothing about it and so has no preconceived ideas', making the housing expert, Michael Stewart, responsible for education.[50] Still anxious to appease the Labour right, he tried to rescue the defeated Gordon-Walker by appointing him Foreign Secretary which meant persuading the member for Leyton, Reginald Sorensen, to accept a peerage. In the ensuing by-election the Leyton voters resented being used as a convenience and rejected Gordon-Walker, thus cutting Labour's majority to three. Wilson then declined to make the foreign affairs expert, Denis Healey, Foreign Secretary, preferring Stewart who did not represent a threat. Worst of all, he deliberately provoked 'creative tension' between his two leading rivals, George Brown and Jim Callaghan, by making the latter chancellor, for which he was ill-equipped, and the former head of a new Department of Economic Affairs, an arrangement that proved a complete failure culminating in the abolition of the DEA in 1969.

As Callaghan settled into his first day at the Treasury the outgoing chancellor, Reginald Maudling, put his head round the door: 'Sorry to leave such a mess, old cock.' It transpired that the balance of payments deficit for 1964 was £800 million, raising the prospect of a run on the pound. Callaghan thus faced an immediate economic-cum-political dilemma that he was ill-prepared to resolve. Like so many of his Labour predecessors he succumbed to the advice generously bestowed on him by the Treasury – that he should defend the currency at all costs – regardless of the fact this implied a deflationary policy, expenditure cuts and low economic growth that would largely under-mine the expectations with which Labour had come to office. Yet the new Cabinet was not short of the economic expertise and experience required to challenge Treasury orthodoxy. It was the 'intellectuals' – Crosland, Jenkins and Crossman – who argued for tackling the problem by a quick devaluation on the grounds that Britain lacked the reserves necessary to defend the pound, and this would boost exports and help to avoid becoming trapped in another cycle of low growth. Wilson himself was better equipped by training and by experience than any modern prime minister to handle the economic situation. However, 'he had been a back-room boy . . . so he had a natural appreciation of the work that civil servants do', as Barbara Castle observed. Although Wilson had direct experience of the 1949 devaluation he misunderstood its significance; he regarded it as a policy that would be seen as unpatriotic – despite the beneficial effects it had actually had – and he desperately wanted Labour to avoid being associated with it again. In effect, he allowed conventional political considerations priority over rational economic judgements. As a result in July 1965 the Cabinet voted seventeen to six against devaluation, thereby trapping itself in a doomed deflationary strategy that it was forced to abandon in 1967.

Meanwhile the decision made nonsense of Brown's National Plan based on the assumption of economic growth amounting to 25 per cent by 1970. It was Callaghan, not Brown, who enjoyed power over economic policy, with the result that by 1967 Brown had become so frustrated that he had to be moved. Admittedly, the Wilson government was unlucky not only in inheriting a weak economy, but also in taking office at a time when it was being appreciated that neither full employment nor the welfare state had eradicated poverty in Britain. A 1965 study by Peter Townsend and Brian Abel-Smith identified an underclass of people who had been bypassed by 1950s affluence and found that since the mid-1950s poverty had increased from 8 per cent to 14 per cent, much of which was attributable to the low level of pensions and the failure of three million elderly people to claim means-tested benefits. Labour was keen to address such flaws and, despite the financial problems, the government initially made some progress by raising pensions and widows' benefits, abolishing prescription charges, repealing the 1957 Rent Act and restoring rent controls. However, after 1965 further progress proved financially difficult. As in the 1950s Labour found itself caught between a desire to redistribute income to help the poor and low-paid while also appeasing the unions and more affluent workers who paid for benefits through the tax system. As inflation and higher income tax eroded pay rises for the low-paid, Callaghan saw one answer by the introduction of VAT, in effect a way of avoiding income tax by returning to indirect taxes on consumption.

The division between the reforming minority and the conservative majority also manifested itself in the new government's approach to constitutional questions. Crosland had upbraided Gaitskell for being more conservative than the Liberals: 'It is Grimond, and not any of our own leaders, who make speeches about the public schools, the House of Lords and social privilege generally.'[51] Wilson's emphasis on modernism had aroused expectations about an extensive overhaul of Britain's antiquated system of government, but Tony Benn found 'he simply had no ideas as to how Parliament could usefully be modernised or developed when we were in government'.[52] The combination of his civil-servant mentality and tactical caution proved inhibiting. Wilson created five new ministries of which two, the Welsh Office and Science and Technology, survived, two, the DEA and Land, were abolished, and Overseas Development was downgraded. Wilson might have been expected to appreciate the recommendations of the report on the Civil Service by the Fulton Committee in 1968 for replacing the traditional reliance on classes staffed by generalists with a larger element of qual-ified accountants, economists and statisticians; but they were never implemented. Similarly the government ignored the Redcliffe-Maud Report which proposed to revive the declining local government system by creating eight provincial authorities. For the new Labour MPs the absence of a constructive role proved frustrating. The only minister keen to reform the parliamentary system was Richard Crossman in his capacity as Leader of the House after 1966; but his proposals for select committees designed to scrutinise government departments were largely sidelined and in 1969 his attempt to reform the House of Lords was scuppered by lack of enthusiasm among the MPs and a collapse of control by the whips in the face of obstruction by Michael Foot working in combination with Enoch Powell. Few ministers regarded constitu-tional reform as a priority; Wilson's colleagues were content with greater central control, while in municipal councils where Labour had been the ruling party for decades it was positively opposed to any reform calcu-lated to disturb the status quo. However, by 1966 their conservatism began to prove a handicap especially in Scotland and Wales where indus-trial decline and ineffective central government was undermining faith in the Westminster system. 1966 brought a harbinger of this shift when Labour lost a by-election at Carmarthen to Plaid Cymru.

In effect, Wilson's tactics during the early years of his administration closely resembled those of Ramsay MacDonald: to win a reputation for respectability and competence by conforming to existing practice and avoiding controversy. In this spirit orthodoxy on the economic front was complemented in external affairs by continuity with previous policies, notably in maintaining the special relationship with the United

States and retreating from the election pledge to abandon attempts to maintain an independent British nuclear deterrent. Wilson showed no interest in finding a new role for Britain by resuming the attempt to join the Common Market, concentrating instead on retaining the imperial role by means of bases east of Suez. Faced with an illegal rebellion by the white settlers in Rhodesia he misplayed his hand by announcing he would never use force, engaged in protracted negotiations and adopted economic sanctions against the regime. This antagonised Labour members who thought it a humiliating appeasement of a racist coup, but Wilson was playing safe with the general public who felt much less interested. More divisive was the backing he consistently gave from December 1964 onwards to the United States over its war in Vietnam. It emerged later that he and President Lyndon Johnson privately agreed a deal whereby America would support sterling in return for backing in Vietnam. Wilson drew the line at involvement by British troops, but he had tied Britain to a losing American war and eventually alienated Labour from a generation of politically aware youth. The government failed to recognise that it had entered a trap of its own making, for by opting to strike out independently by winding down Britain's costly imperial role they would have reduced the need for support for sterling.

However, while the government became bogged down in economic and external problems, it successfully promoted a notable series of social reforms. Several were accomplished through backbench legislation including Sydney Silverman's bill to abolish capital punishment, Leo Abse's bill to lift the penalties on homosexuality and David Steel's bill to legalise abortion. All received vital support from Roy Jenkins as Home Secretary. More in tune with social trends than his colleagues, Jenkins was also instrumental in promoting measures to relax the law on Sunday Observance, end the censorship of the theatre and establish the Race Relations Board. In his second tenure of the Home Office he enacted the 1968 Race Relations Act, making racial discrimination illegal, and a reform of the divorce law in 1969. However, this impressive record owed everything to Jenkins's personal liberalism and little to the party which was far from happy about the 'permissive society' of the 1960s. To be fair, few of these reforms would have been accomplished at all if left to a popular vote, but Labour showed no desire to offend traditional opinion in the movement; abortion continued to trouble Catholic supporters throughout the 1960s and 1970s.[53] The older Labour MPs, who still reflected the authoritarian and illiberal attitudes of their working-class supporters, felt happier with the conservative Callaghan as Home Secretary than with Jenkins. Callaghan admitted to being scarcely aware of the idea of homosexuality, while Brown opposed any liberalisation partly because he found the whole thing embarrassing: 'I don't regard any sex as pleasant,' he told Barbara Castle. 'It's pretty undignified.'[54]Authoritarinism resurfaced strongly in 1968 when a notorious anti-immigration speech by Enoch Powell put racism into mainstream politics and evoked a huge response from working-class communities. Fortunately for Labour the Conservative leader, Edward Heath, considered Powell's language calculated to stir up racial hatred and sacked him from his front bench, thereby reducing the party political relevance of the issue.

Labour also experienced difficulty in coming to terms with female emancipation in the 1960s. Labour's share of the female vote had actually fallen in 1964 from 43 per cent to 39.5 per cent though this was partly a reflection of extra Liberal candidates. Wilson, who was more relaxed about women's role than his colleagues, appointed four women, Barbara Castle, Judith Hart, Jennie Lee and Shirley Williams, to Cabinet posts, a distinct advance. But Brown, unnerved by the whole question of sexuality, adopted the classic masculinist approach towards women, becoming notorious for kissing women with whom he was not familiar and patting their bottoms; on marriage he had forced his wife, who had been a Labour activist, to give up her own work to be a house-wife and support his career.[55] These old-fashioned attitudes left Labour ill-equipped to respond to the upsurge of radical feminism in the shape of the Women's Liberation Movement. As 1968 marked the fiftieth anniversary of the winning of the parliamentary vote, it focused attention on how little had actually changed since 1918. The number of women MPs had remained stagnant since 1945, increasing only slightly to twenty-eight in 1964, before falling to twenty-six in 1966 and in 1970. Although Barbara Castle emerged as a front-rank politician in the 1960s, she continued to regard women's politics as a backwater as she had done since the 1930s, and so, along with her colleagues, was largely outflanked by the new generation of young, university-educated feminists who emerged at this time.

In view of his precarious parliamentary position Wilson was

constantly looking for an opportunity to win a working majority, but he refused to be rushed into an election in October 1965 despite the fact that his personal ratings were consistently high and Labour led in the polls. Eventually a by-election at Hull North in January 1966, a marginal seat which Labour retained with a 4.5 per cent swing, encouraged him to go in March. Although it lacked the excitement of 1964, Wilson found this election easier because he ran his campaign from Downing Street, ignored Transport House, which he regarded as a centre of left-wing opposition, and felt confident of victory. Since 1964 Transport House resented its exclusion from policy development and Wilson made no attempt to consult it or the NEC about the timing of the election.

Labour's success was chiefly due to the government's ability to convince the public that it had started clearing up the economic mess left by the Tories and had proved its competence in office. 'At last, after the drift and aimlessness of the Tory years, we have a government at Westminster capable of governing,' as Crosland put it.[56] Labour's bid for further time to complete the task seemed eminently reasonable and posed no awkward ideological issues. For the time being the Conservatives' appeal to affluence had lost credibility and their warnings about inflation and devaluation were ignored. Wilson himself enjoyed much greater personal popularity than Edward Heath. 'I have never seen so many middle-class people in Coventry so anxious to vote for us,' commented Richard Crossman. 'Harold's personality has been a great help . . . they think that they've got a p.m. like them.'[57] The third factor was shrewd timing. After seventeen months voters had had enough time to appreciate their new government, but ministers anticipated losses in the municipal elections in May; had they waited they would not have been able to risk a general election in June and would have delayed until October by which time the economy was expected to deteriorate again.[58]

With a fairly uniform swing of 3.5 per cent Labour polled 48.7 per cent to 41.4 for the Conservatives, winning with 363 seats to 253 and enjoying a majority of ninety-seven. The victory accentuated the gradual shift in the social composition of the parliamentary party. Now 51 per cent of Labour MPs had a university education and 43 per cent were professionals, compared with 35 per cent in 1951, while manual workers had diminished to 30 per cent compared with 37 per cent in 1951.[59] Among the electorate the usual class bias had not changed, but

Labour had improved its position at all social levels so that among upper- and middle-class people it polled 15.5 per cent compared with 8.9 per cent in 1964, and among lower-middle-class people 29.9 compared with 24.8. While the lead among men remained very high – 52 to 37 – Labour made a breakthrough in the female electorate, leading the Conservatives by 45–44, the first time since 1945. It looked as though Wilson had effectively recreated Labour's national appeal.

Yet however impressive at the time, the 1966 victory was soon forgotten as the new government quickly began to fall apart, in the process opening up the gap between Parliament and the movement in the country which had been suppressed since 1964. Paradoxically, though the prime minister was at the pinnacle of his success, he showed himself increasingly obsessed by the emergence of heirs and rivals and contrived to keep Callaghan, Jenkins and Crosland, all right-wing challengers, on an equal footing. Wilson's tactical skills became obvious in his sudden adoption of Europe, a cause he had previously neglected, in November 1966 when he made a new application for Common Market membership. This had the advantage of being a fresh initiative which was difficult for Edward Heath to criticise as an ardent Europeanist. In any case novelty was badly needed as the economy deteriorated in the summer and ministers increasingly supported devaluation. Eventually in November they agreed reluctantly to devalue the pound from $2.80 to $2.40 and Callaghan resigned. After being blown off course for three years the Cabinet now found itself trapped in five successive instalments of deflationary measures under the new chancellor, Roy Jenkins.

Another by-product of the economic crisis was to discredit the talk of planning and modernity with which Labour had come to power in 1964 and to make the DEA appear irrelevant. As the Labour MP Jeremy Bray later put it, 'Harold Wilson's talk of the white hot technological revolution and George Brown on the National Plan were largely presentational. They lacked substance, method and commitment.'[60] However, the collapse of the plan led Brown to resign thereby fuelling Wilson's paranoia about plots against him. In 1967 he successfully shunted Brown into the Foreign Office but made sure to use George Wigg to collect accounts from British diplomats about his embarrassing performances under the influence of alcohol. While at the DEA Brown had taken to dosing his morning coffee and tea with whisky, enjoying a liquid lunch and imbibing immoderately at evening receptions and parties.[61] At a

Marlborough House dinner for the Australian high commissioner, Lord Casey, Brown arrived intoxicated from a previous party and shouted across the table as he expatiated on the benefits of the Common Market. At length Lord Casey felt moved to say one should not forget 'the grand conception of the Commonwealth', at which Brown grabbed Lady Casey's arm and enquired: 'Have *you* ever had a grand conception?'[62] From Wilson's position the worst aspect of Brown's behaviour was his habit of revealing government business; at an Argentine embassy dinner he was 'rude and euphoric at times, morose and silent at others' and embarrassed his hosts 'towards the end of the meal [when] he began to make loud and critical remarks about the prime minister and announced that he had had enough of this Government and intended to get out as soon as possible'.[63] Eventually Wigg's damaging dossier was not needed as Brown finally quit in 1968 after offering his resignation seventeen times!

While relations deteriorated at Cabinet level, the movement in the country became demoralised amid ominous evidence of a collapse of public support. In 1967 Labour almost lost a safe seat at Rhondda West to Plaid Cymru, while the Scottish Nationalists won the Hamilton by-election and the Conservatives gained Glasgow Pollock, Cambridge, Walthamstow West and Leicester South-West, followed by Meriden, Acton and Dudley in 1968. In the Greater London Council elections the Conservatives swept the board with eighty-two seats to eighteen, the first time Labour had been out of power since 1934. The party also lost several thousand seats in successive local government elections in 1967, 1968 and 1969. Although commonly dismissed by the conventional wisdom, these municipal losses were significant because they hollowed out Labour's local machine so that when the general election came in 1970 the councillors who had an interest in maintaining ward membership and organisation were no longer there. By 1970 membership officially stood at 680,000, a loss of 150,000 since 1964, though live membership was far lower. Although the leadership took comfort from the continuing growth of trade unionism, the unions closest to Labour were now in decline: the NUM falling from 586.000 to 279,000 in 1960–70, and the NUR from 334,000 to 198,000. Combined with the alienation of union members by the government's incomes policy this was to have fatal effects.

The significance of the devaluation of 1967 as a turning point in relations between the government and Labour Movement is evident in the reactions of a loyalist CLP at Newcastle West. The MP, Bob Brown, freely admitted devaluation was a 'shock' and appeared unable to defend it before his constituency party.[64] Up to the mid-1950s his CLP had maintained a membership between 1,400 and 1,700; but from 1965 it went into decline, falling to under half the previous level by 1971; one result was that in the 1970 election only three wards even attempted to canvass.[65] As the Cabinet struggled to reduce expenditure, curb wage settlements and restrict strikes, CLPs began to blame Wilson for their electoral and organisational setbacks, while beleaguered ministers regarded party activists as a nuisance. The Birmingham party demanded drastic changes in economic policy and expressed 'its deep concern at the growing numbers of unemployed . . . we feel this is solely due to the Labour Government's Incomes Policy'.[66] In a damning attack on Wilson, Hugh Jenkins admitted '1967 was a very bad year for the Labour Party', arguing that 'pragmatism has been exposed as mere drifting and a prime minister without a philosophy is to be seen as an Emperor without clothes'.[67] He noted that after 1965 Putney members began to register their disapproval by withdrawing from activity and letting membership lapse. Jenkins retained his marginal seat in 1970 because he was already running as an anti-government candidate – an indication that left-wing MPs, far from being an electoral handicap, were sometimes more effective by keeping in touch with rank-and-file opinion.

Local activists also reflected the influence of the wider protest movements of this decade. Although CND was in decline, by the late 1960s its support fed into new campaigns provoked by Wilson's failure to dissociate Britain from the war in Vietnam which was increasingly seen as both immoral and futile. Vietnam greatly accentuated Labour's existing problems with youth. The Young Socialists were disbanded in 1965, but their replacement, the Labour Party Young Socialists, resented being used for donkey work at elections but excluded from influence in the party. Another by-product of the student radicalism and Vietnam War protests of the 1960s was the emergence of Women's Liberation. Sceptical about political organisations because they invariably turned into male-dominated hierarchies, young feminists explicitly rejected Labour Party activity in favour of decentralised, informal groups and single-issue campaigns. Although the protests by the young and students represented small minorities and their demonstrations never attained the size of student movements on the Continent, they were significant in the long term because they involved disproportionate numbers of left-wing, politically aware people who might have become Labour activists had they not been alienated from the party. Consequently, although the government's decision to extend the parliamentary vote to eighteen-year-olds in 1969 may have been calculated to tap fresh support, few of the three million new electors bothered to vote.

As the case of Hugh Jenkins suggests, the protesters did not lack support in Parliament. In March 1965 49 Labour members called on the Cabinet to withhold support for the Vietnam War and in February 1966 a hundred members protested against the American bombing of North Vietnam. The veteran MP Philip Noel-Baker, who was under pressure in his Derby South constituency, confided to his agent: 'I confess that I am much frustrated by my inability to make the present ministers who control Foreign Policy take any notice of what is being said by a large number of people in the House of Commons who agree with my views.'[68] In Derby dissent over policy was aggravated by a growing clash of generations during 1967–9 involving a split between an old guard of municipal councillors and a younger group who won a majority on the executive committee and denied the veterans nomination to the borough council.[69] Elected MP in 1936 Noel-Baker adopted a traditional approach, visiting the constituency once in three weeks and not at all during the summer recess when he went abroad to conferences. But the recently elected member for Derby North held regular surgeries which he advertised, thereby attracting some of Noel-Baker's constituents. The new Labour agent wanted Noel-Baker to adopt the same practice because it proved awkward for him to refuse interviews to constituents. 'Though [surgeries] perhaps achieve little,' he suggested, 'they are like a lot of other things in politics, something we cannot afford not to do.'[70]

The Derby case illustrates how a combination of national issues, generational conflict and personal tensions played havoc with party morale in the run-up to the general election of 1970. It is also a caution against the assumption that dissension among Labour activists in the 1970s was a product of entryism rather than genuine dismay among loyal party members. If Noel-Baker attracted criticism as a back-bencher, the position of a more patrician figure such as Roy Jenkins was much more precarious. Jenkins' justifiably high reputation as a parliamentarian and administrator was completely at odds with his standing among the rank and file who resented his policies as Chancellor of the Exchequer. Despite enjoying impeccable roots in the movement through his father, Arthur, who had been a Labour MP, Jenkins had entered Parliament as a young man soon after leaving Oxford without ever having worked for the party. By his own admission an 'old-style member' uninterested in cultivating local support, he spent the 1950s writing history books and caballing with the Gaitskellites while noticeably neglecting his Stechford constituency; the organisation deteriorated and the Labour majority dwindled under Jenkins' tenure from 12,300 in 1950 to 2,900 by 1959. In this context the criticisms levelled against such politicians on the grounds that they used the movement as a platform for personal advancement were not without foundation; this resentment helps to explain why, by the early 1970s, major Labour figures like Jenkins commanded little influence outside Parliament.

At Westminster, however, Labour ministers felt they could afford to ignore the criticism because they were making headway in converting the trade deficit into a surplus. This calculation was disastrously upset by the trade unions who had begun to lose patience with incomes policies, so much so that when the chancellor announced a 3.5 per cent limit on wage rises in 1968, both the TUC and the party conference rejected it by a five-to-one margin. As a result Jenkins abandoned a statutory incomes policy in 1969 so that by December wages were getting out of control and inflation rising fast. Meanwhile a near-fatal breakdown developed in relations between Parliament and the movement when the Secretary of State for Employment, Barbara Castle, attempted an alternative means of restraining wage rises by tackling trade union reform. 'I am under no illusion that I may be committing political suicide,' she admitted.[71] Castle proposed a twenty-eight-day period for conciliation on unofficial strikes and a secret ballot before official strikes could be held; in return employers were required to recognise unions and workers to enjoy a statutory right to join. Castle and Wilson felt that this would enable them to draw the sting from Conservative attacks without forcing the unions to sacrifice anything material. Initially Castle enjoyed support from George Woodcock, the TUC general secretary, but she was blown off course by rank-and-file hostility to all forms of legal regulation. One AEU branch in Birmingham accused Castle of trying 'to exterminate democracy' and warned 'should this legislation be enacted, this branch will reconsider its affiliation to the Labour Party'.[72] Castle's task became harder when Woodcock suffered a heart attack and was replaced by the hard-line Vic Feather. The TUC mobilised opposition in the NEC and in parliament where 113 Labour members opposed the unhappily named White Paper, 'In Place of Strife'; many felt it was as though the government had declared war on the founders of their movement. At this point the deterioration of relations between the prime minister and his colleagues had a fatal impact, for, when Callaghan opposed the reforms, Wilson interpreted it as a challenge to his leadership and rapidly backed away from what Castle described as 'a policy which three-quarters of the cabinet no longer believes in'. Wilson accepted the humiliation as the price for his survival.

Against this background the optimism with which the prime minister embarked upon a general election in June 1970 seems extraordinary. Part of the explanation is that ministers believed they had come through the worst. By December 1969 the Conservative lead in the polls, which reached 28 per cent in May 1968, had shrunk to a mere 11 per cent; and by the spring of 1970 Labour enjoyed a small lead for the first time since 1967. Nor were Wilson and his colleagues unduly upset by the demoralisation of the movement in the country. Aware that Heath remained an unpopular figure, they believed they could appeal over the heads of the party organisation and grass-roots critics to the mass of voters. As Wilson regarded Transport House as more trouble than it was worth, he did not consider its inefficiency as a problem, and he kept its officials in the dark about his thinking on the date of the election. From this perspective the thirty-six conference motions put forward by CLPs demanding reform of the national organisation were welcome as a reflection of dissatisfaction with Len Williams, the general secretary, and Sara Barker, the national agent. For Wilson it was enough that the unions, having got their way over Castle's bill, had agreed to increase affiliation fees from one shilling per member to one shilling and sixpence, boosting party income by 50 per cent.

However, by 1970 Wilson had become so out of touch that he was easily misled by the opinion polls. The Cabinet envisaged Roy Jenkins' 1970 Budget as the key to victory, but as he felt reluctant to throw away the gains of the last three years in a pre-election boom they were disappointed. Indeed, Jenkins himself had become so detached by this time that he had ceased to care much about winning another election; speculation had it that he actually hoped for a defeat as this would drive Wilson into resignation leaving the way clear for him to become leader.

Uncertain how to appeal to the electorate, Labour candidates rehearsed the arguments used in 1966 about rescuing the economy and the dangers of Tory extremism, but in 1970 they carried less credibility.[73] It was difficult to reconcile the opinion polls, which predicted a Labour lead of anything from 6 to 12 per cent, and thus a majority of up to a hundred, with the state of the campaign in the country. Constituency organisers noticed that after an early Labour surge, based on the erroneous polls, momentum fell away.[74] Yet even in the later stages the polls gave Labour an advantage of between 2 and 7 per cent. Consequently, on election night Wilson retired as usual to Liverpool's Adelphi Hotel to await the results with confidence. However, a swing of 4.7 per cent to the Conservatives gave them 46.4 to Labour's 43 per cent and a net Labour loss of fifty-eight seats. Among manual workers Labour support fell from 69.6 per cent to 57.1, reflecting a reaction against unemployment and incomes policy and a pragmatic calculation that they might do better under the Conservatives. Significantly the turnout dropped to 72 per cent, the lowest for thirty-five years, the clearest indication that many Labour sympathisers had become apathetic or alienated and resorted to abstention.[75] Long-term demoralisation combined with short-term disappointment over the Budget simply left them with no strong reason to vote.

The 1970 defeat was the signal to release the accumulated resentment over the government's record since 1964 and the prime minister in particular. 'His very presence in Labour's leadership pollutes the atmosphere of politics', as the New Statesman later put it.[76] Yet there was no challenge to Wilson's leadership. This was largely because the leading alternatives were all right-wingers who felt inhibited by their close association with Wilson's policies and their resulting weakness in the wider movement. With economic revisionism discredited and Wilson's endless pragmatism at a discount, the Labour right looked increasingly to entry into the European Economic Community as the best way forward. Symptomatic of the advance of the left in both

CLPs, the trade unions and the PLP was the election of Michael Foot to the shadow Cabinet in 1970 and the emergence of Tony Benn, formerly a right-winger, pro-European and an ally of Wilson, as spokesman for the left and an opponent of the EEC; by 1971 he had won second place in the constituency section of the NEC elections. Behind Benn stood the Campaign for Labour Party Democracy which aimed to ease out the unrepresentative MPs who had backed Wilson, move policy leftwards and ultimately to challenge the leadership. These objectives gained strength in March 1972 from the appointment of a new general secretary, Ron Hayward, who was not prepared to settle for a passive role and asserted the rights of Transport House as custodian of conference decisions against the parliamentary leaders.

To some extent, however, these internal tensions were mitigated by the provocation offered by the incoming government. Edward Heath appeared keen to tear up the consensus and to offer a principled alternative to Wilsonian opportunism, a change symbolised by the 1971 Industrial Relations Act which imposed a legal framework on the unions. On the other hand Heath's determination to press ahead with Britain's third application to join the Common Market accentuated the left–right debate within the Labour Party. Wilson's handling of the issue became the hallmark of his political style. 'I know perfectly well what I am doing,' he assured Barbara Castle. 'My one job is to keep the party united.'[77] Despite having made Britain's second application for membership in 1967, he now retreated under pressure from Labour MPs, 119 of whom signed an early-day motion opposing entry in January 1971, and the role played by the mischievous Callaghan who hoped to profit by the anti-European trend. Conscious that he could not afford to lose the support of the left, which was largely hostile to Europe, Wilson manoeuvred nimbly, posing as sympathetic to Europe but rejecting the government's terms; this sufficed to save his leadership, keep the party more or less together and allowed him to attack the Conservatives. But it was a close-run thing. In October 1972, when Parliament voted on British entry, sixty-nine Labour members defied the whips to support the government and twenty more abstained. Party conference had already rejected the terms and the NEC voted against by thirteen to eleven. Although the position of the right appeared to have been consolidated when its leading figure, Roy Jenkins, was re-elected deputy leader, his colleagues increasingly felt under pressure in their constituencies especially when Wilson bowed to opinion by adopting an idea, first advanced by Tony Benn, that the electorate should be invited to participate in a referendum on entry into Europe after the terms had been renegotiated by a Labour government. This infuriated Jenkins who dismissed the referendum: 'it is a splendid weapon for demagogues and dictators' he told Wilson.[78] In April 1972 he resigned the deputy leadership in protest against what he saw as Wilson's corrupting leadership. Several other frontbenchers also quit including David Owen, Harold Lever, George Thomson and Dick Taverne. This proved to be an error for Jenkins who had relinquished a position of influence and increasingly marginalised himself. Wilson contrived to hold things together by persuading the 1973 party conference not to vote for withdrawal from Europe but to stick to the renegotiation option. But this did not prevent Jenkins leaving the shadow Cabinet in November. Nor did it avert a crisis at Lincoln where the CLP had voted to drop its MP, Dick Taverne, because he backed the EEC. Denied support by the NEC, Taverne resigned to fight a by-election as an Independent Social Democrat in which he defeated the Labour candidate by 13,000 votes.

Lincoln was a harbinger of a greater split in 1981, and, more immediately, a warning that support for Labour in the country was now disintegrating. The divisions over Europe and economic policy were preventing Labour from benefiting from the unpopularity of Heath's government. Although the party won one by-election, the Liberals gained a succession of Tory seats and seized power from Labour in Liverpool in 1973. In Scotland, where Labour organisation was now in an advanced state of decay, a hitherto safe seat at Glasgow Govan fell to the SNP; an internal study in 1969 found that the average party membership in the fifteen Glasgow constituencies was a mere 120.[79] After polling 11 per cent of the vote at the 1970 election the Nationalists began to pose a dire long-term threat, for without a large majority of the Scottish and Welsh seats it was almost impossible for Labour to win an overall majority at Westminster. Despite this, it went against the grain to compromise with Scottish devolution or even to recognise the force of Scots nationalism. In its evidence to the Kilbrandon Commission Labour had opposed devolution; the Scottish Party Executive voted six to five against it, and the reactionary former Secretary of State, Willie Ross, remained a bitter opponent. However, the conversion of Heath to devolution and the favourable report of the Kilbrandon Commission in 1973 threatened to leave Labour isolated, so much so that in 1974 two Labour MPs, Jim Sillars and John Robertson, defected to form the Scottish Labour Party. Although the SNP made its immediate gains from the Conservatives, it had eclipsed Labour in Scotland by its livelier campaigning and boosted its vote to 22 per cent in February 1974 and to 30 per cent in the October election. It now posed a greater threat than the Tories because of its ability to attract working-class Protestants and to appeal to Scots pride by proposing to utilise oil wealth for investment in Scotland.

Despite this growing threat, Labour's attention was focused more on the need to conciliate the unions now moving leftwards under the leadership of Jack Jones of the TGWU and Hugh Scanlon of the AEU. Their willingness to co-operate with the constituency parties marked a new, dangerous phase, for previously leaders like Attlee and Gaitskell had usually been able to rely on the unions to help them resist pressure from CLPs. In February 1973 the TUC and the NEC adopted a social contract under which the unions agreed to accept wage restraint in return for social reforms. But the NEC also adopted some radical policies including the repeal of the Industrial Relations Act, a return to free collective bargaining, the establishment of a National Enterprise Board to extend state control by buying into private companies, and the nationalisation of twenty-five major industries. Wilson vetoed the proposals for nationalisation.

Meanwhile, by 1973 the travails of Heath's government were edging Labour towards an election it did not want. After promising an end to flabby consensus politics, Heath had returned to economic interventionism by saving inefficient companies rather than letting them go to the wall; mortgage rates rose to a punitive 11 per cent, public expenditure increased and the balance of payments deteriorated. Above all, the Industrial Relations Act was not working. Coal strikes and the resulting shortage of energy led to the introduction of a three-day working week in December 1973 and the declaration of a state of emergency. With the authority of the government now in question the press began to speculate about an early general election to resolve the deadlock, effectively recreating the situation that had prevailed before the General Strike. As in 1926 the Labour leaders found this prospect alarming, feared that additional disputes involving the NUR and ASLEF were making the unions very unpopular, and wanted the miners to settle quickly. In any case the party was not ready to fight an election. By January 1974 opinion among the Conservatives had moved towards an election on the basis that things would only get worse for the government during the next two years.[80] Enjoying a 4 per cent lead in the polls, they could expect to win a campaign fought on 'Who rules Britain?' However, Heath, who wanted to reach a settlement with the miners, delayed and looked indecisive in the face of mounting speculation. Yet by the start of February, when it emerged that 81 per cent of miners had voted for a strike, there was still no settlement in sight. 'The miners have had their ballot,' commented James Prior, 'perhaps we ought to have ours.' Heath, looking reluctant, but cornered between his party and the unions, called an election for 28 February.

Although Labour fought a better campaign than in 1970 the party expected to lose partly because the polls consistently gave the Conservatives a lead of between 2 and 5 per cent and partly because Wilson was now seen as a liability by Labour candidates.[81] During the campaign Labour lost votes heavily. The commitment in the manifesto to 'a fundamental and irreversible shift in the balance of power and wealth in favour of working people and their families' only corroborated fears among many voters that both main parties were lurching to the extremes.[82] 1974 appeared to mark the end of the long post-war consensus and a polarisation of politics, but the immediate effect was to make the Liberals much more attractive, thereby boosting their poll to over 19 per cent.

Despite this, Labour was saved because the voters reacted even less favourably to the Conservatives. 'Mr Heath has called this election in a fit of panic,' argued Crosland. 'He could easily have reached a fair and honourable settlement with the miners months ago.'[83] Such charges were corroborated when Heath himself announced that the miners' claim would be examined by the Pay Board which would report quickly, thereby apparently destroying the rationale for the election. Labour also derived advantage by tapping voters' anti-Europeanism; the timing of British entry proved unfortunate in that it coincided with the end of rising economic growth due to increasing oil prices. Hugh Jenkins, for example, blamed Europe for the higher cost of living, VAT, and the deteriorating balance of payments.[84] The Conservatives' own reservations about Europe were exploited by Enoch Powell who delivered several speeches at Birmingham urging a vote for Labour, contributing thereby to a high Labour swing in the West Midlands. For the first time the Birmingham party succeeded in transferring resources into marginal seats, thus gaining Perry Barr (helped by Sutton Coldfield), Yardley (helped by Solihull) and Handsworth (helped by Edgbaston).[85] A reconstituted Trade Union Liaison Committee also involved the unions more directly in constituency work, mobilising the vote in factories and organising the best factory gate meetings for twenty years.[86] In this way Labour made the most of its dwindling support.

Nonetheless the 1974 victory represented another stage in the party's long-term decline. Its vote fell nearly 6 per cent to 37.2 per cent – a figure last achieved in 1929. 'It was not a result to crow about,' as one Transport House official put it.[87] However, Labour was saved by the electoral system which gave it 301 seats to 296 for the Conservatives who won 230,000 *more* votes or 37.9 per cent. On the other hand, it was not clear how long Labour would retain this advantage, for 1974 marked an abrupt return to conditions of multi-party politics in which the Liberals had won 19 per cent and the SNP 22 per cent in Scotland. The electorate had become markedly volatile leaving voters more susceptible to issues and less influenced by traditional class loyalties. On the one hand, the expansion of state employment boosted middle-class Labour support among teachers and social workers, but on the other hand, manual workers, increasingly influenced by home-ownership, immigration and law and order, were moving towards the Conservatives. As a result only just over half the electorate voted with its 'natural' class party in 1974. The parliamentary party was also assuming middle-class characteristics despite the 155 union-sponsored members. Among the newly elected members 161 had a university education and forty-nine had attended public schools; there were 138 professionals and twenty-nine businessmen compared with only eighty-four manual workers.[88]

With no popular mandate and no parliamentary majority Wilson was once again obliged to manoeuvre until he could safely risk holding a second election. In this situation his tactical skills were at a premium. He immediately conciliated the left by appointing Michael Foot as Secretary of State for Employment. After nearly twenty years as a backbench rebel Foot proved to be a fine ministerial debater and an effective legislator, though his success rested largely on giving the unions what they wanted. In a matter of days the miners' dispute had been settled, the state of emergency ended, and politics became calm again. As the unions agreed to behave themselves by avoiding large wage demands, the social contract appeared to have been vindicated. Suddenly Heath's troubled three-year reign looked like a mere blip between periods of Labour rule and the idea that under Wilson Labour was evolving into a natural ruling party like the Social Democrats in Sweden gained credibility. Admittedly, the outward calm was deceptive, for behind the scenes the prime minister was under great strain caused by Marcia Williams in his personal staff and by Tony Benn who undermined him by mobilising support against his policies in the NEC. Although Wilson considered Benn 'completely mad', he dared not sack him for fear of the reaction in the party.[89] Instead he demoted him, perhaps hoping he might resign office, but Benn frustrated Wilson by swallowing the humiliation and staying on.

The question was when to seek a new mandate? June, though tempting, was rejected in favour of October for fear that the electorate might resent another election so soon. The second election proved straightforward for Labour in that no original or controversial policies seemed necessary; the government simply claimed to have resolved the crisis that had brought it to power.[90] Yet behind the scenes Wilson fought the election under enormous personal strain, reflected in his increasing resort to the brandy bottle. He was constantly embroiled in attempts by Marcia Williams to outmanoeuvre other Downing Street staff, including Joe Haines and Bernard Donoughue, whose influence she resented. She demanded the removal and sacking of Wilson's staff and interfered with the election arrangements. Yet, though exasperated by her tantrums, Wilson invariably attempted to placate her; he awarded her a CBE and even a peerage. 'What is her hold over him?' wondered Donoughue.[91] But the question was never answered and Wilson continued to be diverted from his work by problems of office management.

Publicly, however, there appeared no cause for concern for the opinion polls indicated a Labour majority of up to thirty. However, for a third time the polls proved wildly inaccurate. The election was another unpopularity contest between Heath and Wilson, and the electorate refused to return to two-party politics, giving the Liberals over 18 per cent and the SNP an alarming 30 per cent. A 2.2 per cent swing gave Labour 39.2 per cent of the vote but only eighteen net gains and thus 319 seats – a bare majority of three. In the Tory marginals the swing had been only 1.2 per cent reflecting Labour's continuing problems among its traditional supporters. Among trade unionists the proportion voting Labour had dwindled from 73 per cent in 1964, to 66 by 1970, and now to 55 per cent – a remarkable drop considering the extent to which Foot had conciliated the unions.[92] The figure declined further to 53 per cent in 1979.

Yet the small majority enhanced the importance of Wilson's skills in keeping party and government together and produced one final triumph. By March 1975 when the renegotiation of the terms of Britain's membership of the European Union was complete, the promised referendum was set for June. In April a special party conference rejected the terms by two to one, and no fewer than 145 Labour MPs, including seven Cabinet ministers, voted against them. In normal circumstances such a split would have destroyed a government, but the prime minister resurrected the historic 'agreement to differ' of 1932 when the National government allowed its component parties to disagree over tariff reform. Even so, the situation appeared risky for in the October 1974 campaign one minister, Shirley Williams, backed by Jenkins, had stated publicly that she would leave politics if the referendum went against British membership. In the event, the electorate voted to accept the renegotiated terms by a two-to-one margin.

This final vindication of Wilsonian statesmanship proved, however, to be an ephemeral one. The referendum campaign had led Jenkins, Williams and Owen into a close relationship with the Liberals, David Steel and Jeremy Thorpe, effectively preparing the way for more lasting collaboration. Demoted to Home Secretary, Jenkins now found himself isolated and regularly subjected to heckling at Labour meetings. In 1975 the first ministerial rebel, Reg Prentice, left the party. Admittedly Wilson felt strong enough to contain the left by restricting Benn to minor office. However, Benn still declined to resign, perhaps calculating that the attempt to marginalise him was of purely nominal significance in view of wider trends in the movement which made his succession to the leadership appear to be inevitable. It was symptomatic of the mood that in 1975 Reg Underhill, the national agent, conducted an investigation into the role of a left-wing group, the Militant Tendency, concluding that it was operating as a party within a party. Yet the NEC decided to take no action and not even to publish his report. As Wilson contemplated his final exit under cover of his fourth election success, he was leaving all Labour's problems unresolved.

13

'Forward march halted': Labour in Decline, 1976–1994

Although it was not obvious at the time, the resignation of Harold Wilson in March 1976 was a turning-point in party fortunes for it triggered a leadership contest that proved to be a disaster and inaugurated an acute phase of electoral decline. It was the signal for the divisions and discontents that Wilson had contained for so long to ignite an open conflict that three leaders struggled to extinguish. Though expected in his inner circle, Wilson's resignation took the movement by surprise. 'People were stunned but in a curious way, without emotion,' noted Tony Benn. 'Harold is not a man who arouses affection in most people.'[1]

All the diverse elements in the party were represented in the large field of candidates: Jim Callaghan, Denis Healey, Roy Jenkins, Tony Benn, Michael Foot and Anthony Crosland. The announcement of the first ballot on 25 March signalled the shift to the left as Foot, with ninety votes, did better than expected and Callaghan, with eighty-four, did worse; in third place was Jenkins with fifty-six, followed by Benn with thirty-seven, Healey with thirty and Crosland with seventeen. Jenkins' poor showing demonstrated that he had failed to mobilise even the pro-European element and it was interpreted as proof that he had become too detached ever to be leader. One Yorkshire member, when canvassed on Jenkins' behalf in the Tea Room, reportedly responded: 'No lad, we're all Labour here.'[2] After serving briefly in the new government he abandoned the party to serve as president of the European Commission, a prelude to his return as leader of the breakaway Social Democrats. Jenkins, Benn and Crosland withdrew and in the second ballot Callaghan won 141, Foot 133 and Healey thirty-eight, followed by a final round which Callaghan won with 176 to Foot's 137.

The result was a triple setback for Labour. Jenkins was on course for splitting the party; Foot had been elevated as leader-in-waiting when he might otherwise have retired; and more immediately Callaghan took over. Born in 1912 Jim Callaghan was as tired and bereft of ideas as the man he had replaced – and five years older. To a movement accustomed to the idea of 'buggins' turn' his succession seemed a deserved reward for long and loyal service. But the reality was that Callaghan had held the three highest offices in government without making a success of any of them. Moreover, though emollient and reassuring in manner, he was scarcely equipped to handle the divisions now afflicting the party. His politics had been moulded by the 1920s: pride in the Royal Navy, belief in the empire and service in the war; with no interest in Labour's intellectual rationale and no experience of higher education, he had advanced through the movement via the trade unions whose interests he had stoutly defended in Cabinet. Influenced by Baptism Callaghan held puritanical views on social and moral questions; as Home Secretary he had been instrumental in imposing drastic but disastrous laws on drugs; he admitted that until well into adult life he had been unaware of homosexuality or of homosexuals in Parliament and his own government: 'It all puzzles me,' he said, 'there have always been so many pretty girls.'[3] Callaghan, in short, was a classic working-class conservative in the tradition of Jimmy Thomas and Ernest Bevin who found himself in the Labour Movement because of his original class and poverty, not for intellectual reasons. Though such figures had once been an asset to Labour, by the 1970s this was no longer so obvious; for in a movement seething with discontent over the betrayal of socialism since 1964, antagonised by government foreign policy, and pervaded by feminism and the social thinking of a younger generation, he was a wildly unsuitable leader.

On the other hand, in a society in which the post-war consensus was palpably giving ground to a right-wing agenda, Callaghan's conservatism seemed, albeit briefly, in tune with the public mood, and, with better luck, he might have prospered. His fate, however, was sealed largely by external events compounded by his own errors. He had inherited a party steadily succumbing to the influence of the 'hard left'; by 1977–8 80 per cent of the constituency votes cast for members of the NEC went to left-wing candidates, for example. The NEC endorsed the appointment of a well-known Trotskyist, Andy Bevan, as the party's youth officer in 1976 and suppressed a report on entryism by Ron Hayward and Reg Underhill, the national agent. Admittedly Callaghan had no difficulty containing the left's leading figure, Tony Benn, by shunting him into a post as Secretary of State for Energy when he asked for Employment; 'Jim is much tougher on the left than Harold', commented Bernard Donoughue, 'and they soon cave in.'[4] However, he found the wider task of controlling the Labour Movement beyond him. The left now aspired to give control of election mani-festoes to the NEC, to impose a mandatory reselection procedure on all MPs, and to broaden the electorate for choosing the party leader to include general committees of CLPs – but not individual members. This agenda enjoyed wide support on the basis that the parliamen-tary leaders had betrayed their principles during the 1960s and 1970s, were out of touch, and should be more accountable to the movement.

Even before the adoption of reselection, the NEC appeared content to allow things to take their course in constituencies where sitting members were under threat from the left. In Hammersmith North, for example, the sixty-nine-year-old Frank Tomney, a right-winger and pro-European who had been MP since 1950, was replaced by his local party, but, as the correct procedure had been followed the NEC saw no grounds for intervention. However, the member for Newham North-East, Reg Prentice, was not so easily disposed of. An MP since 1957 and a minister, Prentice had been sponsored by the TGWU for sixteen years, but by 1974 union branches openly condemned him for calling on Labour members to resist the spread of socialism – 'we regard his statements as propaganda gifts to the Tories' – and demanded the with-drawal of his sponsorship.[5] In January 1975 Prentice resigned from the TGWU, condemned workers for engaging in picketing, and criticised the unions for not supporting the government's social contract.[6]

The constituency was targeted by Andy Bevan, the national youth officer who became vice-chairman of Newham. As relations between Prentice and his local party deteriorated, his colleagues became afraid of the damage to the party generally if so senior a figure were to be rejected, and in July 1975 no fewer than 150 MPs put their names to a letter of support including Robin Cook, Betty Boothroyd, Tam Dalyell, Brian Walden, Roy Hattersley and Jack Cunningham.[7] However, the Newham CLP voted by twenty-nine to nineteen to deselect Prentice who thereupon appealed to the NEC and to the party leader. But although Wilson agreed that Newham had no right to dismiss a sitting

member, he advised Prentice that he would be better off concentrating
on his constituency than waging a general campaign in the country
and making too many appearances on television. Angered by this
response, Prentice replied that he was entitled to more support from
his leader: 'rather than the kind of nagging letter you have just sent
me'.[8] By this stage, however, he evidently felt he had nothing to lose,
and in an angry letter to Ron Todd of the TGWU he extended his
grievance to a wider canvass: 'For some time now I have been actively
campaigning for a Labour Party which is social democratic, rather
than Marxist, and for policies based on the national interest rather
than on class-war dogma.' He concluded that this was obstructed by
the outdated relationship between the party and the unions. 'If the
Labour Party is to govern successfully, it must do so without any
special favours to the unions . . . we should abandon the whole rigma-
role of affiliated membership, block votes at conference and Trade
Union sponsored MPs.'[9] In this mood Prentice resigned from the
Cabinet in December 1976, left the party in October 1977, and took
the Conservative whip in 1979 before being elected as a Conservative
in the general election. Although the dispute centred on one trucu-
lent individual, it heralded a wider discontent on the Labour right that
eventually culminated in the SDP breakaway in 1981.

The Newham controversy also formed the backdrop to the unrav-
elling of Labour's relations with the trade unions. For Callaghan this
proved critical as his claims to competence rested largely on his ability
to handle the unions. However, with inflation running at 21 per cent
in 1976, workers inevitably sought high wage settlements. In this situation the chancellor, Denis Healey, had already abandoned the
Keynesian strategy on which Labour had relied since 1945 in favour
of a severe dose of deflation involving lower spending and higher taxation. Since July 1975 he and Foot had been working for an agreement
with key union leaders, Jack Jones and Hugh Scanlon, on maximum
wage increases of £6 a week; tax cuts made in the 1976 Budget were
conditional on a further agreement with the unions to extend the
incomes policy. This was both constitutionally dubious and politically
risky for it put government policy effectively in the hands of unelected
union leaders. Yet when the existing agreement expired in August 1976
it was replaced with a new £4 a week or 5 per cent ceiling on wages.
This had some success for average wage settlements were at 10 per

cent by 1977 compared with 26 per cent in 1975, and inflation dropped from 27 per cent in 1975 to 13 per cent in 1976. However, unemployment increased and the pound came under pressure from international financiers. As a result, by September Healey concluded he must seek a loan from the International Monetary Fund which implied reductions in government borrowing of £3 billion in 1977–8 and £4 billion in 1978–9. Such a drastic deflationary strategy provoked a prolonged and agonised debate within the Cabinet. Callaghan backed Healey in a speech to the annual conference in which he insisted Britain could no longer 'spend her way out of recession', repudiated Keynesianism and warned that industry's labour costs must be reduced – a line of argument dangerously close to that used prior to the General Strike of 1926. In December, when the Cabinet debated the terms of the loan, Tony Benn warned 'there is an eerie parallel with 1931' and characteristically he circulated the Cabinet minutes from 1931 when spending cuts had culminated in the collapse of MacDonald's government.[10] Callaghan's Cabinet did indeed come close to breaking up over the terms of the IMF's loan as several ministers contemplated resignation. Crosland rejected Healey's proposals, correctly arguing that the extent of the crisis was being exaggerated and that cuts on the scale suggested were not necessary. However, he acquiesced on purely political grounds so as to keep the government intact.

The decision proved fateful in both the immediate situation and the longer term. Labour's repudiation of Keynesianism and full employment effectively legitimised the adoption of full-blown monetarism by the Conservatives after 1979 and inaugurated a thirty-year period in which the party found itself unable to offer any coherent intellectual resistance to Tory policies. It also meant the abandonment of the kind of social policies desired by most Labour supporters and the end of the social contract with the unions. On the other hand, in the short term Healey's economic strategy enjoyed a measure of success and appeared to strengthen Callaghan's administration. The loan, which turned out to be larger than required, was repaid by 1979. By the autumn of 1978 inflation had fallen to 7 per cent and the unions had accepted a wage agreement of 10 per cent.

Meanwhile, the government's precarious parliamentary majority had dwindled through by-election losses and the defection of two MPs to the Scottish Labour Party in July 1976. Initially Callaghan bought

off the Ulster Unionist members and then agreed a pact with the
Liberals in March 1977 based on a mutual desire to avoid an early election. However, as the Liberals derived little benefit from the pact, by
August 1978 David Steel had been forced by his members to abandon
it. It was this that drove Callaghan to a deal with the eleven Scottish
and three Welsh Nationalists to retain a working majority. However,
the price was the creation of devolved assemblies. This was still repugnant to Labour members, twenty-two of whom had voted against a
devolution bill as recently as December 1976 while another fifteen had
abstained. Devolution enjoyed almost no strong support among ministers, including Callaghan himself, although Foot was sympathetic.
However, the immediate parliamentary crisis, combined with the
undermining of Labour's electoral position in Scotland, forced
Callaghan to impose the legislation on his reluctant party. Accordingly
a new devolution bill was enacted in July 1978 but it was sabotaged
by Labour amendments requiring the holding of referenda in Wales
and Scotland including a fatal condition, introduced by Tam Dalyell,
that 40 per cent of the total electorate must vote for devolution before
it would be implemented. Although it seemed likely that this would
sink the chances of devolution, in Wales at least, the Nationalists
judged it worth their while to humour Labour for the time being.

This left Callaghan's Cabinet at the mercy of the Nationalists and
the unions. In August it adopted a modified incomes policy based on
a 5 per cent maximum wage rise with the promise that the unions
could return to free collective bargaining early in 1979. However, as the
TUC rejected the limit, 5 per cent proved impossible to defend, and
before long the unions were demanding increases of 30 and even 40
per cent. Yet the dangers did not become apparent to a government
that had been gaining confidence. Callaghan's advisers were lulled by
his assured parliamentary performances where he patronised the new,
wooden Tory leader, Margaret Thatcher, failing to appreciate the depth
of demoralisation in the party outside Westminster.[11] Labour had lost
only one by-election in 1978 and it edged ahead of the Conservatives
in the polls after being 20 per cent behind in 1977. Buoyed by economic
improvements and successful parliamentary manoeuvring, the prime
minister began to contemplate holding an autumn election. One
MP, Joan Lester, actually organised a farewell party for retiring MPs,
and during September each party began to plan an election campaign

and draft manifestoes. Callaghan apparently consulted four ministers, Healey, Foot, David Owen and Merlyn Rees, all of whom advised against an autumn election; older colleagues simply wanted to make the most of their last period of office.[12] Callaghan did not consult the party but he spoke to Ian Mikardo, a shrewd electioneer who considered an autumn election a dubious prospect, 'but I can't see anything better for us during the winter, and I can see it getting a lot worse'.[13] This was not what the prime minister wanted to hear. He and Foot felt tempted to push ahead with their legislation, use their full term and thus demonstrate to the voters that they had tamed wage inflation and controlled the unions. As a result Callaghan prevaricated until 7 September when the polls showed a small Conservative lead; concluding that he could not win a clear victory he astounded the political world by announcing that the much-anticipated election would not take place.

It rapidly transpired that this was a major error of judgement. Strikes broke out in defiance of the incomes policy leading to what became known as the 'winter of discontent', thereby undermining the credibility of Callaghan as the one politician capable of handling the unions. By the spring the rationale that had sustained Labour since it took over from Heath in 1974 had been destroyed and most ministers were too demoralised to resist wage demands; several, including Tony Benn and Peter Shore, were manoeuvring to retain union sympathy at the expected leadership election following electoral defeat; 'watching this happen, it strikes me how governments are beaten', observed Donoughue, 'from *within* and not without'.[14]

Eventually the dramatic collapse of Callaghan's parliamentary strategy terminated his government. When the devolution referenda took place in March 1979 much of the Labour Party remained hostile or unenthusiastic, indeed for some months the anti-devolutionists had been campaigning in the constituencies for a 'No' vote in defiance of the official line.[15] Callaghan's declining popularity meant that Labour supporters felt no great encouragement to turn out. As a result devolution was roundly rejected in Wales and approved in Scotland by only 32.8 to 30.8 per cent; however as the 'Yes' vote represented less than 40 per cent of the electorate the scheme could not be implemented. When the Conservatives put down a motion of no confidence on 28 March the Nationalists, angry at the frustration of their hopes, refused to back the government which was defeated by a single vote.

Although Callaghan cheerfully described his critics as 'turkeys voting for an early Christmas', he was obliged to call an election on a date not of his choosing when morale was low and voters expected the economy to deteriorate. There were just seventy-seven Labour agents in the constituencies, and the national party machine under Ron Hayward – 'the worst general secretary in history', according to Bernard Donoughue – was in a poor condition.[16] In addition Labour entered the election still dogged by disputes between MPs and activists. The day after the parliamentary defeat Labour faced a by-election in a safe seat at Liverpool Edge Hill which had been represented for thirty years by Sir Arthur Irvine, another right-winger who had neglected the constituency. The local party had voted thirty-seven to three to reject Irvine as candidate, but his sudden death precipitated a by-election in which the Liberals, who had been increasingly active locally, won with a massive 32 per cent swing. Meanwhile the successor to Reginald Prentice, the former member for Newham now standing as a Conservative, resigned because the local party considered his election address insufficiently left wing.[17] The last-minute reselection played into Conservative hands by reminding voters of Labour's internal problems with left-wing extremism. Although Callaghan remained personally more popular than Mrs Thatcher, he was tired and defeatist, regarding the outcome as beyond control. 'I suspect there is now . . . a sea-change', he said, 'and it is for Mrs Thatcher.'[18] 1979 certainly appeared to mark the end of the post-war consensus as the Conservatives adopted monetarism and the Bennites advocated full-blooded socialism. The outgoing Cabinet had effectively acquiesced in the new monetarist ideology and tacitly accepted that full employment had ceased to be a realistic aim.[19]

A swing of 5 per cent to the Conservatives gave Thatcher a modest 44 per cent to 37 per cent for Labour, a 2 per cent fall in its share reflecting disillusionment rather than an endorsement of Thatcherism; among the non-voters 52 per cent said they would have voted Labour.[20] At the time no one expected Mrs Thatcher's rule to last as long as it did or to go to the extremes that it did in dismantling the institutional bases of the Labour Movement. Yet the symptoms of Labour's underlying decline were already apparent. In his Marx Memorial Lecture in 1978 entitled 'The Forward March of Labour Halted?' Eric Hobsbawm had renewed the 1950s debate about the long-term contraction of traditional working-class political culture and the structural changes in employment that gradually eliminated manual labour from the workforce. In fact trade union membership was still growing, reaching 13.4 million by 1979, some 55 per cent of the labour force. The real problem was that even union members had become reluctant to vote Labour, and among skilled workers only 42 per cent did so in 1979 compared with 49 per cent as recently as October 1974. The party was steadily coming adrift from its roots in the working-class community.

Callaghan compounded his error over the 1979 election by remaining as leader for a further seventeen months, ostensibly to prepare the way for Denis Healey. This meant enduring a bad-tempered party conference in October where he was attacked by defeated MPs and even by the general secretary, Hayward, who drew applause by proclaiming: 'I come not to praise Callaghan but to bury him'! In this angry mood the conference approved three crucial reforms: the introduction of mandatory reselection for MPs, empowerment of the NEC to draft the party's manifesto, and a new system for electing the leader by three electoral colleges of MPs, unions and constituency parties, though the details were not settled as yet. Michael Foot's supporters were anxious that as deputy leader he should continue as acting leader until the new system came into operation – fearing that Healey might win if the vote was confined to MPs.[21] However, the election went ahead under the old rules, contested by Healey and three left-wing candidates, Foot, John Silkin and Peter Shore. Healey had so antagonised members by his bullying that several right-wingers voted for Foot, though some reportedly did so as a wrecking tactic because they expected him to destroy the party; others succumbed to pressure from their CLPs to back Foot. Healey led on the first ballot with 112 to eighty-three for Foot, thirty-eight for Silkin and thirty-two for Shore; but when the latter two withdrew in Foot's favour he triumphed by 139 to 129.

Michael Foot's election surprised many and alarmed those who noted that Healey was more popular among the electorate. Right-wing members were appalled by the result. Giles Radice described it as 'the last fling of a vain old Bollinger Bolshevik' and David Owen as 'something only for nightmares'.[22] However, such reactions were not typical. Foot had been chosen on the assumption that he was the ideal candidate to unite the party, especially by contrast with Healey whose abrasive style seemed certain to provoke a complete breakdown

with the left. The son of Isaac Foot, an interwar Liberal MP, Michael
Foot had himself been an active Liberal until the late 1930s, keen on
promoting peace and the League of Nations – priorities that dominated his entire career. After a lifetime as a backbench rebel he had
scored an unexpected success as a minister in 1974–9, winning the co-
operation of the unions and reassuring the rank and file.

Despite these attributes, however, Foot was less well equipped to handle
Labour's internal problems than appeared to most contemporaries.
Despite his left-wing credentials, his opposition to the reforms advocated
by the Campaign for Labour Party Democracy was an indication that
his approach to politics remained rather traditionalist. Aged sixty-seven,
he believed MPs should be independent-minded figures rather than delegates called to account by unrepresentative management committees.
He also had reservations about choosing leaders through electoral colleges
because of the danger of foisting unsuitable figures on the PLP. Above
all, reverence for parliamentary tradition lay at the heart of Foot's politics. This made him shy away from reform of the House of Lords lest
it became a credible rival to the Commons. He rejected calls for a Bill
of Rights for fear of 'tipping the British Constitution into the Channel',
claiming it was 'a plan for destroying the sovereignty of the British
Parliament'.[23] He even rejected proposals to give MPs a more constructive role through specialist committees on the grounds that this would
reduce the authority of the Commons itself and 'help to breed a bipar-
tisan approach to politics'.[24] This devotion to parliamentary tradition also
made Foot a consistent opponent of British entry into the EEC.

His age and conservatism meant that, although popular among
party members, Foot's left-wing credentials were greatly exaggerated.
His politics had hardly developed from the romantic Liberalism of the
1920s and, though converted to socialism through the influence of
Cripps in the 1930s, he never grew much beyond his original interest
in peace and defence. In particular he never acquired an interest in
economics and championed a vague moralistic socialism redolent of
an earlier era that did not show up well in the scrutiny of the television age. In effect Foot was a throwback to Keir Hardie and George
Lansbury. Moreover, although he had received the support of Tony
Benn, the two men represented quite different expressions of socialism.
Benn, who had begun as a Gaitskellite, a pro-European, a supporter
of NATO and an ally of Wilson, had taken an abrupt turn to the left

after 1970. Now he regarded Foot as a temporary leader who would have to give way because he was too compromising and conservative over issues of party democracy. By contrast, Foot believed in parliamentary socialism and could never accept the subordination of MPs to regulation by rank-and-file members.

A conciliator rather than a natural leader, Michael Foot had the misfortune to assume the leadership at a time when much of the party, both left and right, was no longer susceptible to conciliation. By 1981 a phalanx of senior figures on the right including George Brown, Reg Prentice, Ray Gunter, Richard Marsh, Christopher Mayhew, Dick Taverne, Alun Chalfont and Woodrow Wyatt, had left, several joining the Liberals and others the Conservatives. Their remaining colleagues were reluctant to be pushed any further; they especially disliked the lurch to the left on policy towards defence, Europe, nationalisation and economic planning. Shirley Williams, who had lost her seat in 1979, had already told her Stevenage party that she would not stand again on the left-wing programme adopted by conference. Foot found it difficult to conciliate her colleagues, notably William Rodgers, a former Gaitskellite who had been elected to the shadow Cabinet but refused all offers of a post. Rodgers deliberately frustrated Foot's efforts to hold the balance between left and right by resigning from the shadow Cabinet to be replaced by the runner-up – Tony Benn.

During 1980–1 these right-wing members felt increasingly beleaguered as the reselection process took its course without any effective intervention by Foot. Things culminated in January 1981 when a special conference at Wembley settled the new method for electing the leader. Foot failed to put his weight behind a TGWU proposal to give the MPs 50 per cent of the votes and the unions and CLPs 25 per cent each. Instead conference awarded 40 per cent to the unions and 30 to MPs and CLPs. Some observers saw this as marking an early end of Foot's authority as leader; 'he looked like someone who wished he had stuck to book reviewing' as one journalist scathingly put it.[25] The right-wing minority felt let down by senior colleagues who shared their dislike of the reforms, and they were angered by Callaghan who appeared to have given up the fight by this time.[26] In effect, Wembley precipitated the decision by Shirley Williams, Roy Jenkins, William Rodgers and David Owen to issue the 'Declaration for Social Democracy', often known as the 'Limehouse Declaration', on 26

January. Claiming that recent events were the culmination of a long pattern in which Labour had steadily detached itself from its roots and from parliamentary government, the 'Gang of Four' insisted 'the calamitous outcome of the Labour Party Wembley Conference demands a new start in British politics'.

The four rebels had calculated that a breakaway party would make a greater impact than a decision to join the Liberals, a view apparently endorsed by David Steel.[27] By 1982 this view appeared to have been vindicated as twenty-eight Labour MPs and one Conservative had joined the new Social Democratic Party and other members were evidently waiting to see how the venture fared. Yet despite the seriousness of this split in the party, Labour found it hard to decide how to respond to the SDP except by employing ridicule. Official papers produced by the party took refuge in witticisms including Nye Bevan's 1951 remark: 'We know what happens to people who sit in the middle of the road. They get run over.'[28] In a way this was understandable as the rebels enjoyed limited support among their local parties and only four managed to retain their seats in the 1983 election. However, it was a mistake to ignore or belittle the SDP rather than to consider seriously how to deal with the issues raised by the split, not least because many voters took it as proof that Labour had lurched into extremism. By March 1981 the party's comfortable lead in the opinion polls had given way to a Conservative one. The breakaway effectively reinstated three-party politics on a scale not seen since the 1920s, thereby hugely complicating Labour's revival and even raising the possibility of its eclipse as a party of government.

These events exploded the theory that Michael Foot would be a unifying leader. It seems probable that the alternative, Healey, would have fought the left and thus retained the SDP rebels, but at the price of provoking a left-wing breakaway instead. As it was, the uncongenial task of managing the left remained with Foot. From the outset he was undermined by Benn who refused to abide by the principle of Cabinet responsibility though he declined to leave the shadow Cabinet. Foot saw Benn largely in terms of the Bevanite revolts of the 1950s in which he had been involved, but this was mistaken for Benn was far more ruthless, focused and organised than the Bevanites had ever been. As a result Foot attempted conciliation by allowing Benn to become chairman of the Home Policy Committee in 1980-1, for example. The nadir came with the election for deputy leadership in 1981 when Healey scraped home with 50.4 per cent to 49.6 for Benn who had won 78 per cent of the constituency votes on the first ballot but the support of only fifty-five MPs – clear evidence of the polarisation taking place in the movement.[29] The vote greatly overstated Benn's support, for left-wing union leaders had ignored the views of their members; in the TGWU for example, 52 per cent of branches backed Healey and only 24 per cent Benn, but all the union's votes had gone to Benn. Benn would have won but for several 'soft left' MPs who refused to vote for him. Foot's critics, who thought he should have backed Healey instead of abstaining, argued that the episode finally exposed his leadership as 'a warning against the follies of age and the seductions of ambitious wives'.[30]

Though it was not evident at the time the 1981 election marked the high-water mark of the Bennites' challenge for control of the party. At this stage they held fifteen of twenty-nine places on the NEC, leaving eight to the 'soft left' and six to the right. The left's influence could not easily be shaken because the party had been open to 'entryism' since 1973 when conference voted to abolish the list of proscribed organisations. In 1975 Wilson, always alive to left-wing influence, had condemned 'action by small and certainly not necessarily representative groups who have secured a degree of power within a constituency'.[31] However, right-wing complaints about entryism ignored how easy it was in a party in long-term organisational decline. By 1987 membership had dwindled to 288,000. What remained of the traditional individual membership was largely drawn from a narrow section of society – male, white and elderly – and was inevitably vulnerable to new recruitment.

Much of the controversy during the 1970s and 1980s focused on the activities of one small part of this phenomenon, the Militant Tendency, which had been founded as far back as 1964 and was little known except through a few prominent members including Ted Grant and Peter Taaffe. Militant aimed to capture the Labour Movement for revolutionary socialism. However, thanks to the press, the influence of Militant was greatly exaggerated. In 1970 it had only 200 members and its main strength was concentrated in Liverpool, Lambeth and Bradford. By 1982 there were 3,500 members, an impressive increase but nowhere near enough to control the constituency parties.

Consequently Militant never captured the party, nor did it even manage to get its candidates elected to the NEC.

Moreover, Labour MPs who suffered from Militant's attacks failed to recognise that it was essentially a symptom of a wider mood of disillusionment in the movement generated by the reaction against the Wilson–Callaghan governments of 1964–70 and 1974–9 which were seen as having ignored members' views and betrayed the policies agreed at conferences. This interpretation carried all the more credibility by the mid-1970s as Labour's parliamentary leaders' own confidence in Keynesianism collapsed, leaving them bereft of an economic strategy and marooned on the shores of monetarism. Consequently the rebellion sweeping the constituency parties in the 1980s was by no means simply the work of newcomers or infiltrators. One member in Islington, a notable scene of friction, contacted Michael Foot to point out that the challenge to the sitting MPs was not the work of Militant but was the result of extreme dissatisfaction among existing members caused partly by neglect by sitting MPs and partly by policy disagreements.[32] Militant was essentially a symptom of the party's problem, not the cause.

Moreover, the constituency infighting during the 1970s and 1980s was more than narrowly ideological in character for it reflected a genuine cultural clash over social and moral issues between older and younger generations of activists, the latter being more liberal and more highly educated than their predecessors. During the controversy in Bermondsey, for example, one supporter who objected to the new candidate, Peter Tatchell, angrily told Foot: 'Our Labour Party was in enough trouble without a known "PUFF" becoming an MP.'[33] Similar reactions had been provoked by Victor Grayson in the Edwardian period. By the 1970s many local Labour organisations, especially in the safe seats, had ossified into closed autocracies whose power was sustained by control of municipal and parliamentary election procedure. To the party Establishment almost any new members appeared to represent a threat to their control, but they also offered an influx of talent and energy to organisations that had been shrinking for several decades.

The significance of 'entryism' has also to be understood in the context of the challenges presented by Thatcherite policies in forcing local authorities to sell council houses and curtail expenditure; this provoked some socialists into defying central government even to the extent of ignoring their legal responsibilities. Labour councillors in Liverpool, for example, saw themselves as resisting Toryism just as the elected councillors of Poplar had done in the 1920s. The triumph of Militant in that city was also a reaction to the long period of dominance by right-wing Labour figures, notably Jack Braddock and his wife, Bessie, the MP for Liverpool Exchange, since 1945. By the 1970s Liverpool organisation had entered a severe decline leaving it open to a takeover.

However, Liverpool was not typical. While authorities such as Liverpool and Lambeth adopted radical responses to Thatcherism, other constituency parties avoided ideological tensions. In Salford, for example, where the two MPs, Frank Allaun and Stan Orme, gave a lead to the local activists, the party held together and avoided traumatic splits and disputes over entryism.[34] By contrast, in neighbouring Manchester seventeen Labour councillors rebelled against the city council's cuts and were suspended. Initially the NEC upheld the action of the city Labour Party but then reversed itself and criticised the Labour Group on the basis that 'it did not regard itself as a part of the Labour Party in the city' and that councillors were 'ignorant of Party views and insensitive to the reasonable desires of Party members'.[35] In 1982, when twenty-eight councillors were suspended, civil war broke out between the CLPs and the Labour Group on the council backed by right-wing MPs including Gerald Kaufman. The faction-fight lasted for two years until the dissidents, led by Graham Stringer, eventually triumphed. But the Manchester controversy was further evidence of genuine grass-roots dissent aggravated by national policies and remote party officials rather than mere entryism.

The chief focus of disputes in constituency parties was the mandatory reselection of parliamentary candidates, a procedure explained to CLPs in a manual by Chris Mullin MP – *How To Select or Reselect Your MP*. Despite the controversy only eight sitting MPs were actually deselected in 1980–1, though others decided to quit before reaching that stage. However, the impact of these local struggles proved to be damaging for Michael Foot and the party generally. Fred Mulley, an ex-Cabinet minister and member for Sheffield Park since 1950, was the most prominent victim. Known Militants were chosen in several seats, notably Terry Fields at Liverpool Broadgreen, twenty-nine-year-old Dave Nellist in Coventry South-East, and Pat Wall who replaced Ben Ford at Bradford North following a two-year period of what one member called intimidation and abuse of ordinary members by the hard left.[36] At Islington North the sitting member, Michael O'Halloran, was evicted when the left increased the size of the management committee, a comparatively easy coup in a constituency taken over by a few hundred new, young members.[37] More surprisingly the centre-left member for Hackney Central, Stanley Clinton-Davies, who supported unilateral disarmament and withdrawal from the European Union, was forced to appeal to Foot to save him from deselection.[38] He survived the challenge. One of the most shocking cases occurred in Hemel Hempstead where Robin Corbett was excluded from the shortlist, though nominated by sixteen branches, and replaced by Paul Boateng, a GLC councillor who was backed by just two branches. Despite Corbett's popularity the left managed to defeat him through its control of the small constituency management committee.[39]

Inevitably, rejected members felt aggrieved at receiving inadequate support from the party leader. Stanley Cohen complained that he sought reselection in Leeds South-East on an assurance from Foot that the infiltrators would be dealt with, but, 'I feel that both I myself and my supporters are being treated as sacrificial lambs because you and the NEC are not prepared to recognise and deal with the problems facing the Party.'[40] Cohen paid the price for voting loyally with Labour governments for twelve years. However, Foot's reaction to this pressure was coloured by his familiarity with the Popular Front expulsions in the 1930s and his experience of the Bevanite infighting of the 1950s, as well as his instinctive tolerance towards dissent. This made him very reluctant to intervene against infiltrators. 'I am against witch-hunts, whether conducted by the right, the left or any other section of the Party,' he told Frank Field.[41] In March 1981 he attended a meeting of members of the Manifesto Group where evidence about Militant's activities was presented by Arthur Palmer, Bryan Magee, Betty Boothroyd, Ben Ford, Willie Hamilton, John Golding, Dickson Mabon and Phillip Whitehead. In a comment that captured the cultural clash between traditional working-class respectability and the younger generation, Palmer protested: 'In the last couple of years the Party has been infiltrated by members of Militant, many of them young, male, unemployed, rootless, coming from various parts of Britain, many of them living in communes.'[42] But Palmer admitted that the small membership in his Bristol North-East constituency enabled Militant to gain a majority on its GMC and eject centre-right representatives with long service to the party; as a result the older members were refusing to pay subscriptions, thereby exacerbating the problem. Foot continued to insist that 'expulsions and prescriptions are not the answer'.

Eventually, however, even Foot felt obliged to intervene. In December 1981 the NEC agreed to investigate the activities of Militant Tendency. Conducted by Ron Hayward and David Hughes, the national agent, the report concluded that it was in breach of Clause 2, Section 3 of the party's constitution. 'It is clear that the Militant Tendency is a well-organised caucus[,] centrally controlled[,] operation within the Labour Party and it is equally clear that supporters of the Tendency are in control of the Labour Party Young Socialists at National and Regional level.'[43] However, things were complicated because, as Ted Grant, Peter Taaffe and others argued, Militant had no central list of members who might be expelled. It existed chiefly in the form of its newspaper, *Militant*, and any meetings and activities were ostensibly designed to promote the paper; what opponents described as a central committee was held to be no more than an editorial board. Militant did, however, hold a national conference and employed sixty full-time staff.[44] Consequently the NEC concluded that the best way of dealing with it lay in establishing a register of non-affiliated groups and giving them three months to come into line, a decision that was approved by five million to 1.8 million votes by party conference. By backing the report Michael Foot attracted vociferous support for what was seen as belated action against entryism.[45] Yet despite these efforts the immediate results were minimal. Militant simply refused to register and took legal action to resist expulsions. In December 1982 the NEC declared Militant ineligible for affiliation, but only five people were actually expelled from the party and nine Militants stood as Labour candidates in the 1983 election, largely because the responsibility for identifying and expelling them lay with constituency parties who often felt reluctant to intervene.

In any case, the controversy over Militant was put into perspective by the protracted dispute that occurred in the South London constituency of Bermondsey. Since 1945 Bermondsey had been represented by a sixty-nine-year-old, right-wing Labour MP and former chief whip, Bob Mellish, who commonly received three-quarters of the poll. 'Mr Mellish has no time for the new breed of young left-wingers,' as the local newspaper put it.[46] This was an understatement. In the autumn of 1981 Mellish threatened to respond to attacks in the local party by resigning and forcing a by-election, but the CLP, undeterred, adopted a new candidate, Peter Tatchell, a young Australian whose selection symbolised discontent with Establishment figures like Mellish. Tatchell was also symptomatic of the frustration aroused by the policies imposed by Mrs Thatcher without a mandate. He openly advocated direct action against the poll tax even if this led to a prison sentence, tactics that were anathema to most Labour parliamentarians including Foot.[47] But by way of justification Tatchell pointed to the Labour tradition of resistance to reactionary governments, citing Dr Alfred Salter, who had represented Bermondsey in the 1920s and 1930s. Though young and Australian, Tatchell was, to this extent, as authentic a part of the Labour tradition as Mellish. In any case, with the Scottish Labour Party openly encouraging local authorities not to collect the poll tax which was 'designed to destroy local democracy', a revolt in Bermondsey was by no means out of line with opinion in the movement.[48]

However, Foot, ever sensitive to anti-parliamentary tactics, belatedly chose to make a stand over Bermondsey by stating in the House of Commons that Peter Tatchell would never be endorsed as the Labour candidate. This was another error on his part, for although Tatchell was not an obvious candidate for a seat like Bermondsey with its large Catholic population, he was not a Militant and there had been no irregularities in his selection. Despite this, the NEC voted by twelve to seven not to endorse him and Mellish indicated that he would not, after all, resign the seat. In this way Foot and the NEC had put themselves in the wrong legally and morally as several appalled colleagues pointed out. 'You can't be seen to be censoring a guy like Tatchell,' complained Joan Lestor. 'It will be seen as sacrificing someone that the Movement will one day need in order to placate those that many feel we can do without.'[49] Meanwhile in Bermondsey the continuing split in the party led Mellish himself to rebel; expelled for opposing local Labour candidates he eventually decided to resign his seat. Faced with a by-election the CLP met and overwhelmingly re-adopted Tatchell, a decision humiliatingly accepted by Foot and the NEC. In a disastrous campaign Labour suffered a record 44 per cent swing to the Liberal–SDP Alliance.

These events formed the immediate background to the general election called for 9 June 1983. Bermondsey and the general issue of entryism had fatally undermined Foot's leadership as weak and inept, and kept the party's reputation for extremism and internal division before the public. The 1983 election should have been a difficult one for the Conservatives as their experiment with monetarism had resulted in a severe depression and three million unemployed. On the other hand, after Mrs Thatcher's patriotic triumph in the Falklands War in April–May 1982 the opinion polls registered a steady fall in support for both Opposition parties.

Yet although left-wing entryism continued to attract publicity, the influence of the Bennites on the NEC had been checked by 1983. Under an energetic right-winger, John Golding, who became chair of the Home Policy Committee, the soft left and the right began to co-operate with the leadership to purge the hard left from its commit-tees. However, the leadership had not yet succeeded in recovering control of the party manifesto partly because of the lingering resent-ment over Callaghan's role in 1979. The new general secretary, Jim Mortimer, who replaced Hayward in July 1982, shared Foot's willing-ness to fight on a left-wing manifesto. Golding was reportedly content for Labour to enter the forthcoming election with an extreme left-wing programme in the belief that, as the election was lost anyway, this would foist the responsibility firmly on the left.

Despite changes of personnel Labour was far from being well prepared for the 1983 election. Headquarters retained its traditional suspicion of public relations and opinion pollsters, especially the left-wingers, perhaps because pollsters' findings corroborated claims about the unpopularity of their policies. Eventually in May Foot, who showed no interest in polls, agreed to appoint Robert Worcester of MORI, who had worked for the party before, but it was not until October that Mortimer offered him a contract and he was then ignored until February 1983.[50] The pollsters advised Labour to focus on unemploy-ment and the welfare state and to avoid defence, but Foot proved reluctant to accept this. They also identified Foot's weakness as one who lacked credibility as a prime minister. Even his supporters appre-ciated his tendency to address himself to the party rather than to the country at large, but he was too old and fixed in his approach to change his style. Although attempts were made to persuade him to stand down in favour of Healey, a successful by-election at Darlington boosted his standing and consolidated his position.

As a result, when the shadow Cabinet met on 10 May, following Thatcher's announcement of the election, to consider a very left-wing campaign document entitled *New Hope For Britain*, 'there was considerable uproar' according to Peter Shore's account. Foot, who 'handled the whole thing appallingly', simply proposed to adopt the document as the election manifesto with a short introduction by himself.[51] Denis Healey, Roy Hattersley and Gerald Kaufman objected that as it was too long and detailed, lacking appeal, and addressed to the party rather than the electorate, the document was unsuitable as a manifesto.[52] It included proposals to withdraw from the EEC, scrap nuclear weapons unilaterally, remove American bases, and introduce further nationalisation. However, when Foot reconvened the meeting next day, he ignored the objectors. Tony Benn moved the adoption of the campaign document as Foot had suggested, arguing that it represented ten years of policymaking by the party. Foot claimed that it enjoyed the support of the NEC and the shadow Cabinet; it was adopted with the backing of John Silkin, Stan Orme, Tom Sawyer, Shirley Summerskill, Audrey Wise and Jim Mortimer who insisted it would be too difficult to alter it.[53] As a result Labour entered the 1983 election with a manifesto memorably denounced by Kaufman as 'the longest suicide note in history' and on a programme many candidates simply refused to accept; during the campaign Callaghan, for example, publicly repudiated its commitments on defence.

The election began with Labour trailing the Conservatives by 19 per cent, and the Liberal–SDP Alliance bidding strongly for the centre ground between the extremes of Thatcherite Conservatism and Bennite socialism. On 26 May Shore reported that 'the campaign is now in crisis'; in the course of four weeks Labour lost an unprecedented 8 per cent, falling from 36 to 28 per cent.[54] Reports from doorstep canvassing suggested that the party was damaged by defence and Foot's leadership. At one point Mortimer informed an astonished press conference that the campaign committee had unanimously acclaimed Foot as leader – an extraordinary blunder that invited journalists to enquire whether his leadership had been questioned, thus making re-endorsement necessary.[55] 'In all seriousness', commented one Labour candidate, 'I think it would have been better if we had not had a national campaign.'[56]

The Conservatives were vulnerable over unemployment which, according to the polls, was Labour's strongest suit. Yet, paradoxically, the party proved unable to capitalise on it. Why was this? To some extent Thatcher had succeeded in lowering expectations and creating a mood of defeatism on the basis that full employment had become an impossibility – in which the Labour leaders acquiesced. Also, Labour's own commitment to withdrawing from Europe was widely seen as likely to exacerbate unemployment even further. Nor was Foot competent to exploit the issue. 'Michael on the economy . . . is so unconvincing, so uninformed,' complained Peter Shore.[57] Under pressure from colleagues, who thought unemployment was not being pushed hard enough, Foot proved stubborn, insisting 'it was quite impossible for him – nor did he wish – to disengage from the great issue of defence and disarmament'.[58]

The outcome was almost a disaster. Labour lost sixty seats, ending up with 209 to 396 for the Conservatives and twenty-six for the Alliance. The party's share of the poll sank to 28.3 per cent, only slightly ahead of the Alliance on 26 per cent. This was lower than the party's poll at any time since 1922 and lower even than the 31 per cent in the 1931 election. In the post-mortem Gwyneth Dunwoody observed that the situation was similar to that in the 1920s when Labour had destroyed the Liberals: 'That process can be repeated if we do not take hold of our destiny.'[59] In effect Labour had been reduced to the status of a *regional* party as in the Edwardian period, with its strength concentrated in Scotland and the North, whereas in the South of England it polled 17 per cent to 29 for the Alliance.

There were few mysteries or disagreements about the reasons for the fiasco. The new electoral boundaries had disadvantaged Labour, and only forty-three constituencies now enjoyed full-time agents.[60] Yet these weaknesses were really symptoms. Despite criticism of the poor organisation, the incompetent national campaign and inept management of the media, the election, as Denis Healey noted, had not been lost in three weeks but in the three years preceding the election when Labour had acquired a reputation for extremism, division and unfitness for government.[61] It proved easy to blame the SDP for splitting the anti-Tory vote, indeed one adviser claimed the Alliance had lost Labour sixty-seven seats.[62] This was a misconception, however, for the SDP proved better at attracting Conservative votes, and in its absence many ex-Labour voters would actually have gone Conservative. According to some MPs the canvass underlined the extent to which Labour's manifesto appealed to party activists but was unconvincing to the majority of voters. This helps to account for the high morale reported to headquarters from several regions where the activists disbelieved the evidence of the opinion polls about the party's dwindling support.[63] Canvassers who claimed the national polls did not square with their own canvass were simply out of touch, not appreciating that some people remained loyal to Labour without agreeing with its policies. In particular regional reports confirmed the damage done by voters' concerns about leadership, withdrawal from Europe, the sale of council houses and defence. 'The Party failed to convince the mass of the electorate that we are fully committed to the defence of this country,' according to the East Midlands report.[64] The party's traditional base had crumbled most dramatically among manual workers; from a peak of 69 per cent in 1966, Labour support had fallen to 57 per cent in 1970, remaining almost unchanged in the 1974 elections, and had dropped again to 42 per cent. A fatal divide had also opened within the working-class community over housing in that whereas council-house tenants split 49–29 in Labour's favour, working-class homeowners split 47–29 in favour of the Conservatives.[65]

Long before polling day Foot's obituary as leader had been written. He had appeared to voters as out of touch, rambling on television and reluctant to address the key issues. At home as a stump orator, he had conducted the campaign almost as though back in the interwar era; on a visit to Oxford he allowed himself to be diverted into an attack on Lord Hailsham for his role as a defender of the Munich Settlement in the 1938 Oxford by-election, a sally that left his listeners bewildered. The original rationale for his leadership – that he could unite the party – had now collapsed amid evidence of his inability to reach out to the wider public. Consequently, despite the affection in which he was held, his departure was inevitable. Within two days of the election, two union leaders, Clive Jenkins and Moss Evans, pragmatic as ever, had manoeuvred him into a speedy resignation before his own office staff had been consulted.

Once again Labour plunged into an election fought between left- and right-wing candidates, Neil Kinnock and Roy Hattersley, but this time it was not divisive. Some derived comfort from the fact that as Tony Benn had lost his seat he could not be a candidate, and in any case his prospects had significantly diminished. Benefiting from the new electoral college system, Kinnock scored an overwhelming victory with 71 per cent of the vote including 73 among the unions, 91 in the

CLPs and 47 among MPs, and could thus claim a mandate to modernise the party. The member for Bedwellty in Monmouthshire since 1970, the forty-one-year-old Kinnock had no experience of office but had risen as a popular left-winger and as an ally of Foot. Yet it was a measure of his pragmatism that he had already moved closer to the soft left, and of his courage that he defied the hard left by refusing to support Benn for deputy leader in 1981. It was, he insisted, more important to 'put principles into effect than to enjoy powerless perfection in opposition'. Although Kinnock's critics complained that he travelled lightly ideologically, this enabled him to mobilise both the soft left and the right in order to outmanoeuvre the hard left in a way that Foot had never managed to do.

Yet he faced the formidable task of resolving party controversies and instituting reforms while somehow avoiding Foot's mistake of becoming too absorbed with internal affairs and failing to reassure the general public about Labour's fitness to govern. Kinnock appointed Charles Clarke, Patricia Hewitt, Dick Clements, Henry Neuberger, John Eatwell and John Reid as his personal staff and created a Campaign Strategy Committee to plan broadcasts, polling and campaigns independently from the NEC and party headquarters. Admittedly, headquarters functioned more effectively from 1985 onwards when Larry Whitty replaced Jim Mortimer as general secretary and Peter Mandelson became director of communications. The modernisers rapidly refurbished the party's image by adopting the red rose as its symbol and employing Barbara Follett to advise Labour candidates on dress, grooming and presentation – a process known as 'Folletting'.

Beyond these presentational novelties Kinnock's three main weapons were his oratorical performances at conferences, the revival of the traditional alliance between the leader and the unions, and the harnessing of the soft left with the right so as to outnumber the hard left on the NEC. To this end he won the backing of David Blunkett, a popular figure as leader of Sheffield council, Tom Sawyer of the NUPE and a former Bennite, and Michael Meacher, another ex-Bennite disillusioned by the miners' strike. Kinnock's other advantage was simply that the extent of the 1983 defeat had sobered the party sufficiently to make it receptive to proposals for modernisation and more sceptical about the Bennite left.

Even so, the limitations of Kinnock's influence quickly became apparent when he attempted to introduce the principle of 'one member, one vote' into the selection of candidates. OMOV, as it became known, signalled to the wider public that Labour was ceasing to be the union-dominated movement it had previously been. Also, for a party desperately in need of more individual members it offered a way of raising their status. Pressure for reform was underpinned by academic research suggesting that a high level of activism among members played a key role in mobilising Labour's vote; in 1987 constituencies with a high membership achieved above-average swings.[66] Despite this, OMOV was not widely supported in the 1980s and continued to be resisted by the Bennite left, presumably for fear that it would expose the limitations of their popularity. It was rejected by 3.9 million to three million at the 1984 conference, a disappointment to Kinnock which reflected the inexperience of his personal staff and a failure to mobilise sufficient union votes. As OMOV was not adopted until 1993 it seriously hampered efforts to recreate Labour's image in the country.

More immediately the defeat damaged Kinnock's standing and made it all the more important to assert himself as leader. In this he was handicapped by the coal strike during 1984–5. The miners' president, Arthur Scargill, had defeated Edward Heath in 1973–4 but was to find Mrs Thatcher a more wily and determined opponent. For some time Thatcher avoided a confrontation while building up coal stocks and waiting for the mood among miners to change; ballots in October 1982 and March 1983 showed that over 60 per cent opposed a strike. When the strike eventually broke out in March 1984 in opposition to pit closures, Scargill refused to risk a vote among his members, tactics that appalled Kinnock who told him 'that was what the Tories most wanted'. Kinnock distanced himself from Scargill by publicly endorsing a strike ballot and condemning the violence during the strike, but he was still exposed to attack from the Conservatives. Nor could he prevent the 1984 party conference backing the miners' cause. On the other hand, the eventual collapse of the strike discredited Scargill by setting the industry on the path to terminal decline, and fortified Kinnock in his refusal to be railroaded; he flatly refused demands for a future Labour government to reinstate the miners' jobs that had been lost or repay the union's fines as this would have been to approve incitement to breaking the law.

It was in this context that Kinnock delivered a sustained attack on the NUM's tactics at party conference in the autumn of 1985, electrifying his audience with a denunciation of the Militant regime in Liverpool in the presence of the council leader, Derek Hatton. Liverpool council had defied the government by spending more than it raised and refusing to set a new rate with the result that in August, with bankruptcy threatening, redundancy notices were issued to 30,000 employees. Denouncing their ideas as 'pickled into a rigid dogma', Kinnock condemned 'the grotesque chaos of a Labour council . . . hiring taxis to scuttle round a city handing out redundancy notices to its own workers'. One Liverpool MP, Eric Heffer, walked out in protest which earned him praise from some members. 'I got the feeling', wrote one, 'that Kinnock was going over our heads to the general public for his justification.'[67] This was true, and the speech proved to be a turning-point for Kinnock's leadership. After the conference the opinion polls moved in Labour's favour and the public increasingly recognised him as a strong leader.

Kinnock's confrontation with Militant also had a useful knock-on effect in fortifying members of the soft left, hitherto vulnerable to intimidation, to co-operate with the leadership on the NEC. He managed this without making any significant concessions to them.[68] This was possible because the soft left had no co-ordination or leadership, and they realised that as the Bennites became marginalised Kinnock's chances of winning an election were improving. His task became easier in 1986 when Eric Heffer and Margaret Beckett were voted off the NEC. During 1986–7 a Policy Review, packed with Kinnock's supporters, was established to eliminate the proposals that had damaged Labour in 1983. In 1987 the NEC backed Kinnock over the withdrawal of the candidature in Nottingham East and over the ousting of Militant from Liverpool, despite a walkout by Tony Benn, Dennis Skinner and other members.

However, the significance of Kinnock's sporadic victories over the hard left is easily exaggerated, for beyond the confines of the NEC his writ did not always run. One insider noted that investigations into breaches of the party's rules and constitution often 'flounder at the door of Joyce Gould's [deputy general secretary] office. Her view of what is prima facie evidence is too restrictive and she blocks investigations which should go ahead.'[69] In any case, final decisions remained with the NEC which was reluctant to enforce expulsions in the face of complaints that punishing Militants amounted to the appeasement of Thatcherism. In 1982 an NEC inquiry into the Liverpool District Labour Party concluded that it had interfered with the management and the appointments of the city council, used 'aggregate meetings' of visitors and delegates to assume decision-making powers, intimidated opponents, and changed meeting times without giving notice; Militant Tendency had a structure 'which shadows the Labour Party and trade union structure in the city at all levels'. [70] The inquiry identified sixteen individuals for expulsion including Derek Hatton, the chairman, Tony Mulhearn, the secretary, and the vice-chairman. However, as the DLP refused to change its tactics it was suspended. The rebels defended themselves by printing *Witch-Hunt News* in which Eric Heffer argued that the NEC had merely identified minor infringements of rules; though not himself a Militant, Heffer defended their right to party membership. [71] As late as 1986 the general secretary, Larry Whitty, was still issuing the final expulsion letters on the basis that Militants had been ineligible for membership since 1982. [72] Although the NEC suspended fourteen Liverpool councillors, Militant still had twenty-one councillors in Liverpool in 1990 and it remained active in the local branches, reportedly intimidating party members and plotting further deselections. [73] Faced with legal challenges that slowed the process down, proving that Militant activities were inconsistent with membership of the party was a laborious task. [74] Kinnock himself could do little more than reiterate his condemnation of the non-payment of poll tax, arguing that as a democratic party Labour could not 'seek power to use the law in office, but in Opposition show contempt for the law'.

Meanwhile the continuing influence of the left at constituency level resulted in deselection for six more sitting MPs, notably the former chief whip, Michael Cocks, at Bristol South. Of these, four were unpopular right-wingers, but two became victims of demands to represent a high black or Asian population – Hackney South and Stoke Newington – where Bernie Grant and Diane Abbott were the beneficiaries. In addition several MPs stood down rather than face a reselection struggle, including Renee Short (Wolverhampton North-East) and John Silkin (Deptford) who was punished for opposing Benn in the deputy leadership election. Other senior members, including Peter Shore and Gerald Kaufman, held on in the face of stiff local opposition. In effect, the problems that had dogged Foot's period as leader continued to trouble Kinnock, though now the leadership was fighting back to some effect.

Like his predecessor, Kinnock encountered difficulty establishing himself as a credible prime minister in the face of hostile press comment depicting him as a lightweight. His refusal of office under Callaghan in 1976 now appeared a serious error. His informality, unpretentiousness and sense of humour offered a refreshing contrast to Mrs Thatcher, but having initially given full rein to his humorous side Kinnock then felt obliged to compensate by appearing over-serious. Although a first-rate platform performer, his tendency to verbosity proved to be a flaw on television and in the House of Commons. Only on rare occasions when he delivered a succinct question or answer was he effective. In fact, since becoming an MP Kinnock had neglected Parliament in favour of campaigning in the country where he felt happier. His weakness was most evident in 1986 when he was felt to have mishandled the controversy over the Westland Helicopter Company. In the crucial debate, which could have forced Thatcher's resignation, Kinnock failed to focus on Thatcher's role and wandered into his usual rhetorical questions and generalisations, in effect letting her off the hook.[75]

Nonetheless, by 1987 the party had partially recovered from the 1983 debacle. In 1986, when forty-one trade unions conducted ballots on the continuation of their political funds, as required by the new law, every one recorded a heavy vote in favour; this was reassuring for Labour and embarrassing for the Conservatives.[76] As a result union contributions increased from £3.9 million in 1982 to £6.1 million. Under pressure from the Thatcher government the unions also became more amenable to policy changes, including the acceptance of pre-strike ballots designed to defuse the reputation Labour had inherited from the 'winter of discontent'. Meanwhile, by 1987 the Policy Review had agreed several modifications to the party's programme including abandoning the pledge to withdraw from the EEC, ditching commitments to restore denationalised industries to public ownership, and proposing no overall increase in taxation. By retreating from Keynesianism Labour also tacitly accepted that full employment could no longer be a serious goal. All this reflected the intellectual demoralisation that had set in under the combined pressure of the failures of the 1974–9 governments and the electoral successes of Mrs Thatcher. The most signal evidence of demoralisation was Labour's readiness to allow the Conservatives to portray themselves as the low-tax party, a bogus claim since heavy increases in indirect taxes outweighed limited cuts in direct taxes for the majority of people; whereas 35 per cent of GDP had gone to taxation before 1979, it rose to 38 per cent by 1984 and remained consistently above the 1970s level.

Consequently, despite the improvements in organisation and leadership, Labour approached the election of May 1987 without real hope of victory. Although the polls had given the party 38–40 per cent in early 1986, from August onwards this fell to 35 per cent, accelerated by the loss of a by-election at Greenwich to the Alliance in February 1987. Starting from a base of only 209 MPs, Kinnock's strategists compiled a huge and unrealistic list of target seats including Pembroke (Conservative majority 9,300), Vale of Glamorgan (Conservative majority 10,400) and Crawley, number 135 on the list, where the Conservative majority was 11,800.[77]

Admittedly campaigning was Kinnock's great strength, albeit with an old-fashioned, revivalist approach like Foot's, and it was the general verdict that Labour fought the best campaign in 1987. By mobilising stars of stage and screen, including Glenda Jackson, Julie Christie, Bill Owen and Billy Bragg, the party shook off its traditionalist image. In a moving speech Kinnock drew on his own experience to underline the necessity for the state to eradicate inequality and poverty when he told his audience he was 'the first Kinnock in a thousand years to go to university'. Labour also scored a triumph with a professional television broadcast produced by Colin Welland and Hugh Hudson, well known for the film *Chariots of Fire*, which focused almost entirely on the leader's rise from humble origins. This sharply improved his poll ratings and noticeably raised party morale. On the other hand, although Kinnock posed an effective moral challenge to Thatcherism, he, and the party generally, found it difficult to offer a credible intellectual challenge to Tory economics. Having surrendered Keynesianism and socialism in favour of an expedient monetarism in the late 1970s, Labour had not recovered a distinctive programme.

Consequently, although Labour had the best of the campaign it made only a modest impression on the poll, raising its vote share by three points to 31.5 per cent and gaining just twenty seats. This left the party 11 per cent behind the Conservatives, a huge gap by post-1945 standards; a future victory would require an 8 per cent swing and ninety-seven gains. Surveys suggested that around 36 per cent of voters identified with Labour but, as not all of them had actually voted Labour, the party was still failing to mobilise its potential, hampered by continuing perceptions about its extremism, divisions and dubious economic credentials.[78] 1987 was thus only the first step in what would be a two-stage recovery at best.

On the other hand, there were three positive aspects to the 1987 defeat. Tactically, the main achievement was to have avoided being overtaken by the Alliance and widened the gap from 3 per cent to nearly 9 per cent, thereby consolidating Labour's status as the main alternative to the Conservatives. There was an element of luck in this, however, for the Alliance had handicapped itself by continuing under two leaders – owing to the stubborn refusal of David Owen to merge the SDP with the Liberal Party – a cumbersome arrangement that voters found difficult to understand. The merger was achieved belatedly in 1988. The second encouraging sign for Labour, perhaps surprisingly, was a further decline in class-based voting among the middle classes. Although 54 per cent of middle-class voters had backed the Conservatives, they were increasingly split, with 65 per cent of those working in the private sector being Conservative, but only 44 per cent of those in public-sector occupations. Such trends heralded the eclipse of Tory representation in Scotland and a more gradual decline in England. Conversely, among the manual working class Labour's vote had barely risen from 42 to 43 per cent.[79] Thirdly, despite, or because of, the controversies over candidates, the social composition of the PLP changed significantly. Four new Labour MPs came from the black and Asian communities. Labour had nominated ninety-two women candidates of whom twenty-one were elected in the context of forty-one female MPs. The PLP was also losing its traditional bias towards elderly working-class men. Whereas in 1959 twenty-one Labour MPs had been aged seventy or over, now only Michael Foot remained in that group. The election of more teachers, lecturers and local government employees raised the professionals to 40 per cent of the PLP. Conversely, only 29 per cent came from manual occupations including only twelve of the sixty-nine new MPs.[80] Superficially the unions appeared to have retained their role in the PLP with 114 sponsored members elected in 1983 and 129 in 1987;

however two-thirds of them were actually white-collar employees not manual workers.[81] As these trends accelerated the PLP became more diverse and socially representative than it had ever been.

Nonetheless, the 1987 defeat demonstrated how little could be achieved by improvements in organisation and presentation. Kinnock's staff listed the 'essential conditions for victory' including presenting Labour as 'demonstrably economically competent', showing 'how each individual will be better off under Labour' and 'the projection of Neil Kinnock as potential prime minister'.[82] Accepting that he 'has to behave and perform more like a PM at all times' they hoped to neutralise his deficiencies by emphasising his effective management of the party. Meanwhile the modernisers continued to marginalise the hard left. In 1988 when Tony Benn stood in the leadership election he won only 12 per cent and the next year party conference finally endorsed the recommendations of the Policy Review. The chief shortcoming of the review to date was the failure to wean the party away from unilateralism, an issue vigorously exploited by Conservatives in 1987. Nearly all the sixty-four resolutions on defence submitted to the October 1989 conference reaffirmed unilateral nuclear disarmament, while only three commended multilateral disarmament.[83] This made it risky for Kinnock but he managed to persuade conference to adopt multilateralism largely by capitalising on the changing climate created by the willingness of Mikhail Gorbachev to engage in multilateral disarmament. On the economic front Kinnock relied on a team of modernisers, John Smith, Gordon Brown, Margaret Beckett and Tony Blair, who killed off all hopes of renationalising industry, persuaded the unions to abandon the closed shop, cultivated the City of London and embraced the EEC on the basis of the European Social Charter. Proposals to raise pensions and child benefits required a new top tax rate of 50 per cent and higher National Insurance contributions, but as the latter exposed employees earning as little as £21,000 to extra tax, Labour was left vulnerable at the election. The leadership also continued to be cautious about introducing OMOV after its defeat in 1984, but consultations during 1990–1 obtained responses from 265 CLPs, 827 branches, twelve unions and two socialist societies, and found overwhelming support for the reform.[84]

One further awkward policy readjustment remained to be made involving devolution and electoral reform. The repeated Conservative victories on the basis of a minority, and diminishing, share of the vote had reawakened enthusiasm for proportional representation, especially among the pragmatic unions who saw no prospect of ending Tory rule without reform. The long-term decline of Labour's vote since 1970 made the case for proportionality look compelling especially as Labour supporters were now permanently denied representation in much of Britain. Even in local government Labour was becoming the victim of the first-past-the-post system; in 1981 the party lost Tower Hamlets to the Alliance despite polling more votes, while in Southwark it raised its poll from 44 to 51 per cent and lost thirteen seats![85] Accordingly a Labour Campaign for Electoral Reform was launched under Austin Mitchell MP. Jack Straw, a leading opponent of PR, resorted to tired historical accusations to the effect that PR was responsible for bringing the Nazis to power and for forty governments in Italy since 1945.[86] But beneath these claims lay the real fear that a proportional system would boost the Liberal Democrats, destroy Labour's chances of winning a majority and force it to reconcile itself to governing under coalitions.

Consequently the argument would not have advanced beyond this point but for the dire electoral situation in Scotland where the deterioration of Labour's organisation had been underlined by the loss of the Glasgow Govan by-election to the SNP in December 1988. Privately Labour conceded that, like the rest of Glasgow, 'Govan CLP is a hollow shell' whose members did not expect to work at elections.[87] 'We could not command the streets with numbers of workers, because nobody bothered. We could not consolidate our votes in the district elections because local branches were too feeble.' Labour's dilemma had been exacerbated by Mrs Thatcher whose militant Englishness had stimulated Scottish nationalism and boosted the SNP. Hoping to puncture SNP popularity, Labour felt obliged to co-operate with the other non-Conservative parties in a Constitutional Convention in March 1990 to seek a consensus on devolution. However, Labour was now trapped, for the convention could not progress without agreement about the method of election and the other parties refused to accept first-past-the-post for fear of giving Labour a permanent majority in Scotland. Labour's leading devolutionist, Donald Dewar, who recognised that electoral reform was 'generally regarded as the key to the participation of the Social and Liberal Democrats', was happy to accept PR.[88]

Meanwhile, Labour established its own working party on electoral reform under Raymond Plant. Its main arguments focused on the Alternative Vote system which was favoured by Labour anti-reformers simply because it represented the least change from the status quo.[89] Eventually the working party agreed on a hybrid system, AMS, which retained single-member seats but produced proportionate results by topping up each party's representation to reflect its share of the total vote. Members had been forced to recognise that if this was not conceded the Scottish Liberal Democrats would withdraw from the convention. This agreement enabled Labour to go ahead with positive proposals for devolution, thereby giving itself some protection from the Nationalists and isolating the Tories as a beleaguered English minority. On the other hand, the implications were imponderable, for Labour had implicitly committed itself to coalition government, at least in Scotland, and struck another blow at the traditional system used for Westminster elections.

In the short term, however, all Labour's plans to make itself more electable were upset by the dramatic developments on the Conservative side. By 1990 the economy had descended into a second economic depression involving a huge trade deficit, mortgage repossessions and growing unemployment. Revolts against the poll tax were spreading and the Conservative Party became acutely divided over Europe. As a result many Conservative MPs concluded that Thatcher was unlikely to lead them to a fourth victory. With Labour leading in the polls there was a growing sense that opinion had decisively turned away from Thatcherite thinking. Finally the issue was forced in October 1990 by the resignation speech of Sir Geoffrey Howe, the former Foreign Secretary, who denounced the prime minister for sabotaging Britain's influence in Europe. Challenged by Michael Heseltine, Thatcher failed to win enough votes to save her leadership; she resigned and was replaced by John Major in November. Labour's fox had been shot. Despite his responsibility for the economic depression, Major managed to escape blame largely because he was so different a personality from Thatcher and because he repudiated her policies on the poll tax and Europe.

When the election eventually came in April 1992 Labour was well prepared and offered a fresh programme of reforms including a Freedom of Information Act, an elected second chamber, Scottish and Welsh devolution and fixed-term parliaments, even if the leadership was less than enthusiastic about them. During the campaign Labour activists were optimistic, buoyed by the opinion polls which consistently put them in the lead. On 1 April the lead stood at between 4 and 7 per cent, and the next evening a huge rally at Sheffield turned into a victory celebration. Kinnock entered, punching the air and shouting exuberantly 'You're all ri', you're all ri'' to the audience.[90] Shrewd tactics, however, dictated that Labour should have run from behind; by forcing doubting voters to contemplate the near-certainty of a Labour government and to wonder whether Kinnock was a suitable prime minister the rally undermined the party's chances. In fact, the Labour lead was already slipping, though on polling day four polls still gave the party a lead of 0.9 per cent and even the exit polls indicated a small Labour majority. In the event the Conservatives won with a stunning 7.5 per cent advantage and an overall majority of twenty-one seats.

The explanation for this shattering result was threefold. First, a million voters had fallen off the electoral register due to non-payment of their poll tax – by definition an anti-Conservative group who had been picked up by the pollsters though they were not voters. Second, the pollsters failed to identify the reluctance of some electors to admit to being Conservatives and they had thus underestimated the determination of Conservatives to vote. Thirdly, many voters switched in the last week and even the last twenty-four hours of the campaign, a trend only partly identified at the time. Admittedly Labour had increased its poll by 3.6 per cent and tactical voting had narrowed Major's majority drastically; however a poll of just under 35 per cent and 271 seats left the party a long way from victory. The result was interpreted more as a rejection of Labour than as an endorsement of the Conservatives, provoking the question that if the party could not win when the economy was, again, suffering from a depression, how would it ever win? After extensively redrawing its policies and improving its image since 1983 was there any further room for compromise and reform?

In the short term Neil Kinnock, who had been relentlessly damned by the newspapers as an inadequate leader, accepted responsibility by resigning. In fact, he had faced a far harder task than acclaimed leaders such as Attlee, Gaitskell and Wilson and achieved much more than they had done. As a moderniser he had proved how far the party could change without completely repudiating its traditional values, but, as he had not quite managed to make it electable again, he effectively paved the way for an even more drastic *bouleversement* under Tony Blair. Yet his immediate successor refused to accept that the reform of the party had not gone far enough. Born in 1938 to a Glasgow schoolteacher, John Smith had joined the Labour Party at sixteen and entered Parliament in 1970; a devout Christian and centre-right figure, he was a natural part of the Scots Establishment and never felt tempted to become a rebel. Although Smith had no base in the movement beyond Parliament, where his forensic skills were greatly appreciated, his five years as shadow chancellor spent reassuring the City of London by what was derided as the 'prawn-cocktail offensive' had made him a crucial figure. In contrast to Kinnock, Smith had proven competence as a legislator, a capacity for handling detail and ministerial experience. His lawyerly command and unflappable Scottishness seemed to inspire confidence with the public and although he had never cultivated the unions or the rank and file he won 90 per cent of the votes in all three electoral colleges.

During his twenty-two months as leader Smith's innate caution and even complacency became obvious. 'John Smith hasn't changed his mind on anything since he was seven,' complained Roy Hattersley.[91] Confident that Labour had done enough to make itself electable he appeared, to his critics, prepared to wait for the prize to fall into his lap. He had some reason for this, as by 1993 Labour was recording 48 per cent in the polls, a lead of 20 per cent, and claiming 37 per cent of the middle-class vote; the party won 44 per cent in the European elections in 1994. Smith did, however, take one risk, to promote OMOV for the selection of candidates which was endorsed in 1993. By the spring of 1994 the collapse of confidence in Major's government as a result of its economic misjudgements made Smith appear the inevitable prime minister. Tragically, after suffering a massive heart attack in October 1993, he recovered only to experience a repeat in May 1994 which proved fatal.

14

'She's changed it all': Tony Blair, Lady Thatcher and New Labour, 1994–2007

In July 1982 Michael Foot received a sycophantic twenty-two-page letter from an engaging young Labour candidate who had recently come a poor third in the Beaconsfield by-election. Trying to ingratiate himself with the leader, Tony Blair praised Foot's books and explained, rather implausibly, 'I came to Socialism through Marxism.'[1] Anxious to distance himself from both the Labour right and the Trotskyite left, his aim was to locate himself as close to Foot as possible. Just twelve years later Blair, with a minimal record in the Labour Movement, almost no knowledge of its history, and even less respect for its values and traditions, became party leader, winning the support of 60 per cent of MPs, 58 per cent of party members and 52 per cent of trade unionists. The immediate explanation for his triumph was fairly obvious. Labour had been severely traumatised by four successive election defeats, especially by the dashed expectations in 1992 when the party's vote remained stubbornly below that won in 1979. As an articulate, young professional Blair appeared more likely to restore the party's appeal to the southern, middle-class voters who had never really warmed to Foot and Kinnock. Labour's emasculation left it vulnerable to a new, autocratic leader, effectively ensuring that there would be comparatively little resistance to the 'New Labour' strategy he brought with him.

More fundamentally Blair's emergence was symptomatic of the extent to which the Labour Party had been shredded by Thatcherism ideologically and institutionally. Mrs Thatcher had gone a considerable way to destroying the institutional bases that sustained the party in the shape of the trade unions, heavy industry, council housing and local government. Thatcherism had also left Labour intellectually demoralised, unable to attack the logic of her economic policies but fearful about going further in revising its own policies. Perhaps the one positive influence was that whereas Thatcherism had made almost no impact on Conservative women, it energised Labour women, many of whom had abandoned the party hierarchy as irretrievably male-dominated. The fruits of this shift became apparent in 1997 when Labour outvoted the Tories amongst women, and in the adoption of female-only candidate lists in some constituencies which contributed to the election of 101 female Labour MPs.

However, if the immediate explanation for the emergence of Tony Blair and 'New Labour' presents few difficulties, its underlying significance in the party's historical evolution is more problematical. This is reflected in the methodological complications faced by Blair's biographers. Authors commonly feel an obligation to excavate a politician's intellectually formative forces thoroughly and explain how he came to adopt his creed and his values; but, as few British and American politicians are driven predominantly by ideas, it is all too easy to discover intellectual depths where there are only shallows. If we take Tony Blair's biographers at their word he was a man influenced by an extraordinary variety of ideas ranging from Christian socialism, to Clintonism and Thatcherism, the liberalism of Roy Jenkins and the illiberalism of George W. Bush. Such an approach is simply implausible. His devotees, Peter Mandelson and Rod Liddle, claimed, absurdly, that he was driven by certain 'core beliefs' reflecting his left-wing values. Jon Sopel put him in the tradition of Christian socialism, a movement that had been influential from the mid-Victorian era to the 1920s. However, the idea that Christ's teachings led to socialism and that Christians had a duty to promote state social welfare was hardly central to Blair's politics; for him it was part of the problem rather than the solution. The journalist John Rentoul saw his politics as moulded at Oxford by Peter Thomson who put him in touch with the writing of the philosopher John Murray about community and co-operation, concepts that scarcely seem consistent with Blair's pronounced belief in individualism and competition and were thus not discernible in his politics. Anthony Seldon, perhaps sensing the implausibility of Rentoul's approach, adopted an insurance policy by casting his account in the form of no fewer than twenty individuals who had influenced Blair's politics.[2] Seldon's unusual methodology was an implicit recognition of the problems his subject presented, and he himself admitted that in many cases Blair had *not* been much influenced! Shirley Williams got closer to the conundrum when she admitted to being confused by Blair: she 'doesn't know what he stands for'.[3]

Any realistic explanation must start by recognising that Tony Blair entered politics as an impressionable and largely *non-political* young man, with little political knowledge and superficial views, hence his susceptibility to strong personalities with firm opinions or successful track records including Bill Clinton, Margaret Thatcher, George W. Bush, Rupert Murdoch, Cherie Booth and Alastair Campbell. In the absence of any successful role models on the left – Wilson, Callaghan, Foot, Kinnock, Healey were all failures – he found himself drawn to a string of fairly extreme right-wingers including Thatcher, Bush, Silvio Berlusconi, Jose Maria Aznar and Nicolas Sarkozy. So persistent a feature of his career can hardly have been accidental, though journalists sympathetic to Blair have attempted to dismiss it and to argue that it is glib to see him as essentially a Conservative.

At first sight it does indeed seem extraordinary that the Labour Party was led for twelve years by someone whose views were basically those of a Conservative. However, if one places Tony Blair in historical perspective his career is far less remarkable than it initially appears. For, as we have seen, men and women from Conservative family backgrounds actually played a central role in the development of the Labour Party; and when Blair became adopted in County Durham he was following earlier middle-class outsiders including Sidney Webb and Hugh Dalton in that county. To this extent there was nothing eccentric about his rise in the movement. What, however, distinguished Blair from predecessors like Dalton, Cripps, Strachey or Lawrence was that he showed little of their intellectual grasp and never underwent a *conversion* to the principles and values of the movement he was joining; crucially they approached Labour from the perspective of a failed *Conservatism* rather than a failed socialism.

This is not to deny that Blair's politics had roots, only to recognise that they were of a rather limited kind. Although it is well known that his father, Leo, had been an active Conservative, the significance of his upbringing has not generally been appreciated. Leo Blair emerged from a working-class, socialist, Glaswegian background, but on service during the Second World War he converted to Conservatism. At a time when many young men were moving emphatically in the opposite direction this was an extraordinary step. The explanation is that Leo was ambitious, a social climber, and immensely impressed by the vision of the higher social classes that wartime experience gave him, a trait that was later to be reflected in his son's reactions to fresh experiences and contacts. It is, in fact, common to be drawn into the Conservative orbit in this way for those who recognise the importance of the money, influence and status attaching to the party, and Leo's behaviour resurfaced in his son's fondness for successful entrepreneurs, celebrities and power brokers. Consequently, after 1945 Leo abandoned manual work, became a tax inspector, took a law degree, worked as a barrister and became a law lecturer at Durham University. By the 1960s he had become chairman of Durham Conservative Association and was seeking a parliamentary seat. His son frankly described him as 'a gut Conservative . . . he was totally self-made. The sort of Tory represented by Norman Tebbit.'[4]

This background proved to be significant in several ways. Tony Blair strongly sympathised with his father as a self-made man and individualist even to the extent of sharing his admiration for Thatcherism. He never repudiated the values and aspirations that led Leo to opt out of the local schools and have his sons privately educated at the Durham Choristers School and then at Fettes College, known as 'the Eton of Scotland'; this was simply what any aspiring, affluent parent did. He frankly admitted that while disadvantaged people like his father had been helped by collectivist policies, they now believed they were 'holding people back, and in some ways they were right'.[5]

Conservative values, acquired in youth, were to persist. John Rentoul assumed that the young Blair 'could not have avoided absorbing something of County Durham socialism'.[6] This, however, is a misunderstanding. To become an active Conservative in North-East England in the 1960s, especially for one of working-class origin like Leo Blair, took some determination; it meant aligning oneself with an alien and beleaguered minority, and involved a most explicit repudiation of the values and achievements of the Labour Movement. The Blair household must have resounded to Leo's denunciations of the Durham Labour mafia on his doorstep that had dominated local politics since 1919. At the time the young Blair took little interest, but he never distanced himself from the ideas he had grown up with, and it is scarcely surprising that later in life he never managed to see the virtues in the Labour tradition. He was simply a non-political Conservative, implicitly accepting the assumptions and values of a typical middle-class English Conservative. He endorsed free enterprise, competition and individual success. He regarded taxation as a deterrent to enterprise and placed a high value on individuals who showed themselves good at acquiring money. He blamed the 'permissive society' of the 1960s for having undermined personal responsibility and saw crime as essentially the product of moral or personal failings, as the Victorians had done, rather than as caused by poverty or unemployment. And he instinctively gave precedence to the state over individual rights and liberties.

However, for some years Blair's assumptions remained dormant, so much so that his friends and teachers expressed surprise when he eventually opted for a political career. Though nominated as a Conservative candidate in a school mock election in 1966, aged twelve, he seems to have ignored politics until 1975 when he voted in the referendum on membership of the European Community. He became involved in no political causes, never joined the Labour Club at university where he enjoyed a relaxed undergraduate life, and only visited the Oxford Union once when dragged in by a girlfriend to hear Michael Heseltine speak. Yet during the late 1960s and early 1970s thousands of educated young people were stirred by the American war in Vietnam, by the threat of nuclear weapons, by the emergence of Women's Liberation, and by the clash between the miners and Edward Heath that led to the three-day week and the general elections of 1974. It all passed Tony Blair by.

It was only after leaving Oxford in 1975 that Blair gravitated to London where he was taken on by the pro-Labour barrister, Derry Irvine, along with Cherie Booth. It was at this stage that he joined the Labour Party, initially in Chelsea. Few contemporaries regarded this new commitment as indicative of serious intent. 'Oh, he'll soon grow out of it,' commented Leo Blair. When he announced his intention of becoming an MP friends laughed and asked: 'Really, which party?'[7] Completely ignorant of the Labour Party's ways, he was 'very impatient with the silly rules and routines you had to go through to be part of the party which were so off-putting to ordinary people'.[8] But

Blair was now a young man in a hurry. He quickly became a ward secretary and tried unsuccessfully to get adopted as a municipal candidate. Although his frustration with Labour made him a natural candidate for the SDP, any inclinations in that direction were now challenged by his relationship with Cherie Booth who had joined Labour at the age of sixteen. As always, the impressionable Blair found it difficult to resist such influence. In any case he was shrewd enough to see that even in its shrunken state Labour offered a more secure route to Parliament for an ambitious candidate.

After tackling the hopeless Beaconsfield at a 1982 by-election he was lucky to win the nomination at Sedgefield just before the 1983 election where he stood on a manifesto that included leaving the EEC, nuclear disarmament and ending the sale of council houses – policies he did not in the least support. But although Labour's manifesto was for Blair unmistakable evidence of the extent to which the party had become detached from working-class voters and their aspirations, in Sedgefield he found a Labour Party more compatible than the sophisticated, left-wing liberals of the metropolitan ward branches he had initially encountered. Here were working-class communities with right-wing instincts and middle-class aspirations to home-ownership like his own and a similar concern about crime and criminals: 'Tony Blair knew from Sedgefield that law and order was a working-class issue!'[9] The experience proved deeply reassuring, for in effect his constituents validated his own beliefs, thereby rendering it unnecessary to undergo any conversion to accommodate himself to the party he had so hastily joined.

Labour's defeats in 1983, 1987 and 1992 left Blair an uncompromising moderniser who felt the party had failed to change sufficiently and was therefore frustrated under John Smith's complacent leadership. He helped to accelerate the process of change as shadow employment secretary, committing Labour to abandoning the closed shop, and later redefining the relationship with the trade unions by warning: 'There'll be no special favours [for the unions] . . . there'll be no inside track . . . no sectional interest has any particular purchase on a Labour government.' As shadow Home Secretary he significantly repositioned the party simply by pushing crime much further up the agenda and by indicating a tougher line. In 1993 he wrote in the *Sun*: 'It's a bargain – we give opportunity, we demand responsibility. There can be no excuse for crime. None.'[10] This emphasis on social moralism was enhanced by what Blair learned about Bill Clinton's 'New Democrats' on visiting the United States in 1994. 'The guy's a winner and he's going to do really well,' he enthused.[11] Clinton's 1992 campaign appeared to demonstrate how a failing left-wing, tax-and-spend party could be transformed into a movement capable of capturing middle-ground voters. John Smith, by contrast, saw nothing of relevance for Labour in 'all this Clintonisation business'.

As leader Blair lost no time in trying to reassure the electorate that Labour really had changed, initially by removing the famous Clause IV from the party's constitution. In view of Gaitskell's failure in 1959 several colleagues thought this foolhardy, but 65 per cent of delegates endorsed it at a special conference at the Methodist Central Hall, where Clause IV had originally been adopted, in April 1995. Blair took the precaution of securing the backing of his deputy, John Prescott, as insurance against attack from the trade union leaders. Not since Ramsay MacDonald had a Labour leader been more contemptuous of the unions. A visit from Rodney Bickerstaffe of Unison left him seething: 'TB said they can just fuck off. We will never get elected if every little change produces this kind of nonsense.' When he told the Transport and General Workers of his intention to maintain an arm's-length relationship he was surprised by their response which left him 'speechless with rage . . . "these people are stupid and they are malevolent"'.[12] Blair also worried his advisers by his personal decision to reject local schools in Islington to send his eldest son to the Oratory, a Catholic grant-maintained school miles from home. His press secretary, strategist and confidant, Alastair Campbell, who felt offended by 'a Labour leader shipping his kids out of a Labour area because he thought the schools weren't good enough', repeatedly warned him this was offensive to Labour principles; but Blair instinctively understood that it was a sound way of reassuring middle-class parents that their aspirations were safe with him.[13] At the same time he endeavoured to cement links with the traditional working-class by cultivating the right-wing press, notably the *Daily Mail* and the *Sun*. He embarrassed his advisers by eagerly accepting an invitation from Rupert Murdoch to fly to Australia in July 1995 to address a News International conference. Subsequently he wrote articles on crime for the *Sun*, turned up for discreet *Daily Mail* lunches and fed the paper with attacks on unmarried mothers in an effort to reassure readers that he shared their conservative values. David Blunkett, an authentic working-class author-itarian, also cultivated the right-wing tabloids, arguing that 'great tranches of Labour voters – or potential Labour voters – read these papers. We need to know where they're coming from and how to get there.'[14] But others felt less happy. In July 1995 the former leader, Neil Kinnock, exploded with anger over Blair's attitude towards education and other issues: 'He's sold out before he's even got there . . . Tax, health, education, unions, full employment, race, immigration . . . It won't matter if we win, the bankers and stockbrokers have got us already, by the fucking balls, laughing their heads off.'[15]

Labour's rapprochement with the right-wing tabloid proprietors gained credibility from the mutually flattering relationship between Tony Blair and Mrs Thatcher. The Labour leader's admiration for Thatcher was no aberration but part of a pattern, central to his person-ality and politics. Just twenty-five when she became prime minister, he 'would talk wide-eyed of Thatcher's success in reworking the geom-etry of politics'.[16] Though she did not create his Conservative values, she undoubtedly *validated* them by offering the impressionable young politician the example of success and strength he wanted. As a result, on 22 May 1997, three weeks after becoming premier, he presented himself at her Mayfair office for an hour's advice on the single currency, Europe, Russia and the United States. This was risky as Thatcher remained a hate figure in the Labour Movement, but the knowledge that she held him in high esteem boosted his credibility as a strong, patriotic leader with former Tory voters. He offered them continuity by endorsing her uncompromising moral outlook, her middle-class aspirations and values, her dislike of the state, and her hostility to income tax. 'I've not got a reverse gear,' Blair liked to say, reminding voters of her famous boast: 'The lady's not for turning.' He never lost his conviction that this was his real strength. He once told Alastair Campbell 'it was important I understood why parts of Thatcherism were right'; when a policy adviser tried to persuade him to be more progressive he responded, 'What gives me real edge is that I'm not as Labour as you lot.'[17]

However, Blair could not have effected the programmatic shift to what became 'New Labour' single-handed. On his trip to America he had been accompanied by Gordon Brown, a man with genuine roots in the Labour Movement but equally intent on revising the party's traditions in economic affairs. 'Both Tony and Gordon were like excited schoolchildren going over to the States,' as one aide put it.[18] Brown was just as impressed by America generally and Clinton in particular. He was instrumental in getting Labour to become a party of free enterprise, competition and individualism, tacitly abandoning its commitment to full employment in favour of a 'high and stable' level of employment, adopting low inflation as the overriding priority for a Labour government, recognising that income tax had been too high and deterred enterprise, acquiescing in the deregulation of the labour market regardless of the cost to workers, downgrading the role of manufacturing industry as Thatcher had done, and accepting, or even extending, the privatisations implemented under the Conservatives. This catalogue itself indicated that Brown, though widely regarded as more of a Labour traditionalist, had become as intellectually demoralised as his colleagues and that, because of his greater intellectual grasp, his adoption of Thatcherism was more deliberate and fundamental than Blair's; as a result when Labour returned to office there was to be no attempt to challenge the assumptions or reverse the policies of the Thatcherite revolution in economic and social affairs; even acknowledged failures such as railway privatisation would be implemented, not reversed.

Nonetheless, continuity with Thatcherism posed a delicate problem for the architects of New Labour, Peter Mandelson and Roger Liddle, who sought to extend Labour's appeal to the right without alienating traditional support. They argued that New Labour gave 'renewed expression to the party's founding beliefs' while also embracing the free market, competition, inequality of wealth and income, restrictions on the unions and the irrelevance of public ownership.[19] The language Mandelson and Liddle employed has largely escaped notice. For example, in discussing the social moralism that became a hallmark of New Labour, they argued that 'rights carry with them obligations', perhaps unaware that in the debates over the enfranchisement of workingmen and women in the pre-1914 era this was the distinctive rationale adopted by Conservatives.[20] Whereas Liberals and socialists argued from basic human rights, Conservatives believed that anyone claiming rights or privileges must fulfil his obligations towards the state first. Mandelson and Liddle also depicted expenditure on welfare and unemployment as inherently wasteful and 'not socially productive', precisely the view taken by Victorian and Edwardian Tories when resisting state-financed welfare reforms by the Liberal governments. Whereas Conservatives assumed that the funds available were limited and anything spent on welfare automatically reduced productive investment, Liberals and socialists increasingly argued along under-consumptionist lines that the economy was hindered by inadequate demand and that a redistribution of income stimulated it by boosting the demand for goods and services. Ignorant of political history, Mandelson and Liddle strikingly drew on the language and the traditions of British Conservatism in the era of Lord Salisbury and A. J. Balfour in their exposition of New Labour thinking. Their rationale was symptomatic of the extent to which Labour had lost its intellectual and moral compass during the 1980s and 1990s.

However, the more Blair and his colleagues adopted the thinking of their opponents the less they appreciated that by 1997 the electorate had revolted against Thatcherism. Two severe economic depressions, the demise of British manufacturing and mass unemployment had seen the abandonment of monetarism except by a few eccentrics on the margins of the economics profession. Moreover, the bracing climate of free markets and deregulation had introduced an unwelcome element of insecurity into the lives of thousands of *middle-class* families who now found themselves facing redundancy, house repossession and the need to rely upon the welfare state. Voters increasingly understood that most of them were actually paying more of their income in taxes under Thatcher and Major than they had previously, because cuts in income tax affecting a small minority had been paid for by huge increases in indirect taxes on spending paid by the majority on average and below-average incomes. The resulting disillusionment was compounded by the incompetence of the Major government in handling British entry into the Exchange Rate Mechanism at an unduly high rate, leading to desperate attempts by the Bank of England to support the currency by using national reserves and by raising interest rates to 15 per cent. The disintegration of the Major government's reputation for competence as a result of 'Black Wednesday' left the electorate determined, as they had not been in 1992, to change their government. Consequently, by 1997 the detailed menu offered by the Opposition scarcely mattered – voters simply assumed that everything would be different. However, the New Labour enthusiasts had so lost their nerve that they never felt confident of winning a general election and they remained fearful of challenging Thatcherism head-on. As a result, although the Labour victory proved to be far more sweeping than expected, the reversal of his predecessor's policies was never on the agenda as Labour supporters and many voters undoubtedly expected. New Labour was to be the extension of Thatcherism by other means.

In the 1997 election Labour's vote rose from 35 to 43 per cent, producing 419 MPs and an overall majority of 179, while the Conservatives sank to an historical low point of 31 per cent and 165 members. The election seemed to have reconstructed Labour in such a way as to complement the party's new agenda and ideology. A third of Labour's 1997 voters had not supported the party in 1992 and the composition of the vote had changed in terms of gender and class. Among men Labour's share had risen by 6 per cent but among women by 10 per cent, thereby eliminating the usual advantage enjoyed by the Conservatives. Labour had also drastically narrowed the Conservative advantage among middle-class voters, winning 31 per cent in AB social class, a gain of nine points, and 47 per cent in C1 class, a gain of nineteen points. No fewer than 41 per cent of homeowners voted Labour.[21] Hence some remarkable Labour victories in such constituencies as Southgate, Wimbledon, Bristol West, Harrow West, Hove, Crosby, Hendon, Hemel Hempstead, Shipley and Upminster, dominated by middle-class owner-occupiers and with little or no obvious Labour base. In this sense Labour re-emerged as a national party on a scale comparable to that in 1945. Before and after the 1997 election a succession of former Tory MPs defected to Labour including Alan Howarth, Alan Amos, Shaun Woodward, Peter Temple-Morris and Quentin Davies.

What were the implications of this advance for the party itself? In one sense Labour had practically ceased to be the party founded in 1900, for just 13 per cent of the parliamentary party now came from a background in manual occupations. Blair had made no secret of his ambition to expand the individual membership as a means of altering the balance and emancipating Labour from its traditional reliance on the unions. Following the example of his Sedgefield constituency, where membership had increased from 400 to 2,000, the total party membership stood at an impressive 420,000 by 1997. About two-thirds of the newly recruited members came from salaried and professional backgrounds. However, the downside was some neglect of traditional supporters. Before the election Robin Cook confessed to feeling 'very fed up because he believes [Labour] no longer offer anything to their people, the working class, the poor unfortunates, the Ds and Es'.[22] Their detachment was to be reflected in the dwindling turnout at elections, reflecting a sharper class differentiation; by 2005 whereas 71 per cent in the higher social categories voted, only 54 per cent of those in the lowest did so. However, as many former Conservative voters were willing to sustain New Labour in office, this diminishing enthusiasm among traditional supporters seemed not to matter.

For several years Labour appeared to have effected a fundamental transformation extending to voters, members and even funding. As recently as 1986 75 per cent of the party's money had been donated by the unions, but the proportion had dwindled to 40 per cent by 1997. Blair, who made no secret of his admiration for successful entrepreneurs, cultivated prominent businessmen like Richard Branson. His Lord Chancellor, Lord Irvine, organised fund-raising dinners for Labour lawyers, and Lord Levy used his extensive contacts to win donations from wealthy people. Major donors up to 2001 included Lord Sainsbury, Lord Hamlyn, the publisher, and Christopher Ondaatje, the businessman and philanthropist, who were understood to have given £2 million each.

On the other hand, these new resources fortified the prime minister in his attitude towards the unions. Although grateful for the introduction of the minimum wage, the unions failed to win the repeal of Conservative union legislation and several became so antagonised by most government policies that they reduced their financial contributions. In 2004 Kevin Curran, leader of the GMB, warned that, failing some improvement, 'we would have to look for a political partner that would advance the interests of people we represent'. Bob Crowe of the RMT insisted that 'any hope of the Labour Party working for the workers is dead, finished, over. I think all of you who are staying in the Labour Party are just giving credibility to it.'[23] While fear of a Conservative revival remained alive, few unions were yet prepared to disaffiliate. But it was an indication of the extent of the antagonism that in 2004 the government negotiated the so-called 'Warwick Agreement' with the unions, which included a promise not to privatise the Post

Office, in order to stem withdrawals from the party. For their part the New Labourites argued that however much they grumbled the unions had nowhere else to go, and that reductions in their contributions were more than balanced by business donations. With the Conservatives losing money because big business felt nervous about Tory anti-Europeanism, this was a source of immense gratification for New Labour.

For the Labour Party itself the 1997 victory involved an uncomfortable adjustment to the pronounced *presidential* style of Blair's premiership that left it as marginalised as it had been under Harold Wilson. Along with Lloyd George and Margaret Thatcher, Blair operated more like an American president than a conventional British prime minister, and for similar underlying reasons: his basic detachment from his own party. For all three premiers the characteristic manifestations of presidentialism were the habit of drawing on ideas and personnel from outside the party and a fondness for bypassing the normal institutions of government. Since 1993 Blair had engaged in a prolonged courtship of the Liberal Democrat leaders, Paddy Ashdown and Roy Jenkins, that seemed inconsistent with his unapologetic admiration for Thatcherism. However, the Liberal Democrat link was essentially tactical. 'He is scared to death of being squashed between the unions and the left wing,' reported Ashdown in July 1993.[24] Lacking confidence in Labour's ability to win an election outright until the last moment, he continued to toy with some realignment of parties that would give him a majority in the event of a tight result and at the same time reduce his dependence on a rebellious Labour left. To this end Blair apparently went as far as to offer Ashdown two or three Cabinet posts. Yet he remained nervous about Labour reactions; during the 1997 campaign he sprang the idea on Alastair Campbell: 'How would people feel if I gave Paddy a place in the Cabinet and started merger talks?'[25] He also engaged in seminars with Jenkins who felt flattered to be treated as a father figure, especially as he realised that Blair and his colleagues had little idea how to run a government. Correctly sensing the shallowness of the Labour leader's grasp of political history, Jenkins equipped him with a summer-vacation reading list in 1996 focusing on the Edwardian era and including the speeches of Keir Hardie and Lloyd George and a biography of Sir Henry Campbell-Bannerman. As usual the impressionable Blair was apparently enthused

with the smattering of new knowledge he acquired, especially the
success of the two parties in excluding the Tories from power by
means of their electoral co-operation. But how deeply it penetrated
remains doubtful. Blair's knowledge of the politics of the previous
generation was so slight that he failed to appreciate that Jenkins had
been the only genuinely liberal Home Secretary of the twentieth
century. Amid the authoritarianism and social moralism of the New
Labour government he would have formed a subversive minority and
the Liberal Democrats generally would have exacerbated Blair's problems of party management rather than mitigated them. But he
pandered to Ashdown's pressure for electoral reform by promising a
referendum, regularly insisting: 'You can trust me in this.' However,
Blair, who had little sympathy for constitutional reforms of any kind
and regretted the commitments Labour had already given, never
backed electoral reform; he simply expressed interest in it as an insurance against a tight election result. In the event Labour's huge majority
in 1997 made both coalition and electoral reform unnecessary. Although
Labour had given a promise of electoral reform in its manifesto, it
was supported by a small minority led by Robin Cook. When the electoral reform commission that Blair had persuaded Jenkins to chair
reported in October 1998, he simply reneged on his promises, saying,
'I'll have huge problems getting my lot to agree to it.'[26] Moreover, as
Labour shifted to the right, self-interest for the Liberal Democrats
dictated distancing themselves so as to benefit from the government's
alienation of its traditional supporters, and under a new leader, Charles
Kennedy, they wisely backed away from Blair.

Another presidential feature of Blair's system was the extravagant
resort to honours and rewards to the party's financial supporters, something that genuinely surprised observers in view of his promise to set
higher standards in public life after the damage suffered by the
Conservatives by association with sleaze. However, as early as 1997 it
emerged that the prime minister was ready to drop a policy commitment to ban tobacco advertising in motor-racing under pressure from
the motor-racing tycoon, Bernie Ecclestone, who had given the party
£1 million. Blair also emulated Thatcher and Lloyd George in expanding
his personal patronage by the dubious award of titles and bypassing
the normal vetting process to advance personal friends and donors.
In 1970–4 Edward Heath had largely ceased to distribute political

honours, but the practice was revived by Thatcher who felt the need to bolster her position by patronage. Blair's similar concerns were reflected in his refusal to concede a fully elected House of Lords; he agreed to reduce the hereditary element to ninety-two peers but insisted on retaining life peers as a vital element in his powers of patronage; it emerged that all but one of those who had donated £1 million to the Labour Party had received peerages. In order to evade criticism, while continuing to attract wealthy backers, both Labour and the Conservatives obtained huge secret loans before the 2005 election, hoping to turn them discreetly into gifts later. Four businessmen who were nominated for peerages loaned £5 million to Labour, but several of the nominees were subsequently ruled out because of the loans they had given the party. Yet despite the obvious dangers, Blair was so dazzled by the world of wealth, and so eager for funding, that he never learned to be careful. Eventually his nemesis came during 2006 when a major police inquiry into political loans and honours culminated in the humiliating experience of subjecting him to questioning no fewer than three times. The widespread public belief in government corruption engendered by these events went a long way to discrediting Blair personally, but also highlighted the extent to which Labour had adopted Conservative attitudes and practice; the blatant distribution of honours was another symptom of the presidential form of government and the usurpation of the role of the party by its leader.

Amid the electoral success of New Labour it was not initially obvious that by comparison with the reforming governments of 1906–14 or 1945–51 Blair was achieving little. The explanation lay partly in the inexperience and inability of ministers in the arts of management and administration; only David Blunkett, formerly leader of Sheffield council, had actually run a large organisation. Ill-equipped ministers were further handicapped in running departments by being moved frequently; John Reid, for example, occupied nine jobs in ten years, being promoted for his presentational rather than administrative skills. In this situation the government was largely saved by the one minister who retained his job throughout, Gordon Brown as Chancellor of the Exchequer. The weakness was compounded by the prime minister himself who had neither experience nor understanding of the system of government and became notoriously impatient whenever confronted with details or practical problems of implementing policy. According to Alastair Campbell, 'whenever he was challenged or under attack he just curled up into a foetal position'.[27] Susceptible to the aura surrounding American presidents, Blair easily became diverted into foreign affairs and media management.

The other explanation for the meagre achievement was that before 1997 Blair and his colleagues had been so focused on winning power that they had devoted little thought to what to do with it. Moreover, during the first term crucial problems, notably housing, pensions, railways and council tax, were largely neglected as Blair devoted himself to winning a second term. Like an American president he spent a high proportion of his time on the press, public appearances and the polls, so much so that during much of his premiership he appeared to be conducting a continuous election campaign.

This approach had major implications for the party which found itself marginalised and regarded by Downing Street as an obstacle to the continuing success of New Labour. Like Lloyd George and Mrs Thatcher, Blair made few speeches in the House of Commons, appearing largely for brief exchanges of well-rehearsed remarks at question time. His Cabinets made few decisions as the prime minister preferred to make policy in small informal groups. Uncomfortable with his party, Blair relied heavily on close, almost feminine, relationships with a handful of advisers, notably Peter Mandelson and Alastair Campbell, a man who emerged from his diaries as a manic-depressive who exacerbated the prime minister's obsession with the press and the BBC, his intolerance of criticism and his tendency to ignore civil servants. Blair also made extensive, informal use of men drawn from outside the party including Lord Levy, who became his representative in the Middle East as well as his fund-raiser, Lord Adonis, who ran his educational policy, and Lord Birt who, among other things, tried to devise a transport strategy. Like Lloyd George, he used such figures to bypass both the Civil Service and the party when making policy.

Yet despite its resentment both about the substance of government policy and its effective exclusion from policymaking, the party was slow to challenge or complain, partly due to the emasculation of the left and partly because of the dazzling electoral success enjoyed by the New Labour strategy. Labour was the beneficiary of underlying social changes as well as Blair's tactical manoeuvres as the Conservatives had become the victims not just of short-term unpopularity but of long-term trends. Since the 1880s their huge organisational superiority in the country had rested on the voluntary work of thousands of middle-class women, but the spread of higher education, career-mindedness and employment among women had steadily reduced the number of women available. Thatcher's dismissive attitude towards female aspirations only accentuated their alienation from the party. In addition, the dramatic increase in the proportion of people attending universities during the 1980s and 1990s, an experience already known for reducing Conservative support, drastically weakened Conservatism among the younger generation of voters. As British society became inexorably more liberal in its attitude towards marriage, sexuality, single-parenthood, drugs and race, the Conservatives became increasingly marginal and uncomfortable, especially by comparison with the Liberal Democrats who were more in tune with social change. However, adjustment was hindered by rank-and-file members who resisted attempts to repudiate Thatcherism or embrace the more consensual politics offered by Michael Portillo. In successive elections in 1997, 2001 and 2005 the Conservative vote remained almost static at an historically low 31–33 per cent; even in historic defeats such as 1906, 1923, 1945 or 1966 Conservatives had usually polled at least 38 per cent and often well over 40 per cent. The Tory dilemma gave Blair an easy ride; but he exploited it effectively by comprehensively occupying natural Conservative territory. His pursuit of continuity with Conservative policy made it more difficult for the Opposition to attack Labour governments, at least until 2008 when the economy unravelled. This phenomenon had not been witnessed in British politics since the mid-Victorian era when the Liberals under Lord Palmerston had offered safe, patriotic, conservative government combined with economic growth, free trade and low taxes designed to satisfy a middle-class electorate; as a result, after winning in 1841 the Victorian Conservatives failed to win another general election until 1874.

Blair's success in outmanoeuvring the Tories also generated unintended consequences for Labour by consolidating the reversion to multi-party politics. After their foundation in 1988 from a union of the Liberal Party and the Social Democrats, The Liberal Democrats had achieved a distinctive appeal under Paddy Ashdown's leadership.

In 1997 they had lost votes but had dramatically increased their seats to forty-six, the largest total since 1929. Ever since the late 1950s the Liberals had enjoyed a series of revivals, largely at Tory expense, but each had been short-lived and always fell short of expectations, even in areas like the West Country, largely because Conservative unpopularity led to the return of Labour governments that became mired in economic problems and consequently sank in popularity. In the process Labour failures generated Conservative revivals that swept away the Liberal advance. However, after 1997 this familiar pattern failed to materialise both because New Labour proved to be reassuringly right wing and because Gordon Brown managed to keep the economy buoyant, leaving little scope to generate a Tory recovery. As a result the Liberal Democrats managed to retain their gains and, contrary to the predictions of pundits and pollsters, even extended them in subsequent elections, returning fifty-four MPs in 2001 and sixty-one in 2005. Moreover, at the same time New Labour became so right wing that it alienated traditional support to the benefit of Liberal Democrats and Scottish Nationalists. As a result the electoral map of Britain changed significantly. In a third of the constituencies the traditional battle between Labour and Tory continued; but in another third the battle was between Liberal Democrats and Conservatives, and in the other third between Liberal Democrats or Nationalists and Labour. In the process Britain reverted to a pattern of three-party politics last seen in the 1920s. In the short term this appeared to be very much to the disadvantage of the Conservatives especially as their marginalisation in Scotland, Wales and the North left them looking like a regional rather than a national party, but in the long term it exposed Labour to losses on two or three fronts simultaneously.

Moreover, although at the time the government appeared to have judged its policies shrewdly with a view to outmanoeuvring the Conservatives, it was not easy to appreciate the extent to which their success gradually undermined the Labour Party. One of the most damaging trends was the continuing retreat from the municipal tradition that had sustained the movement since the 1920s. The process had begun under Thatcher's premiership when the role of elective local government had been curtailed by removing housing from municipal control, by allowing Westminster to dictate local spending, and by encouraging schools to opt out of council control. The immediate effect had been to weaken the Conservatives by alienating Tory activists, undermining membership, and accelerating the defeat of councillors. However, Blair, who shared Thatcher's bias against municipal authorities, extended the process by removing education via the City Academies and by allowing planning decisions to be taken away from elected councillors and delegated to council officers. For him the municipalities, where 'Old Labour' was so strongly entrenched, represented part of the problem; they were too independent and left wing to be part of the New Labour project. However, the effect, in combination with unpopular national policies, was to undermine local Labour parties and play into the hands of their rivals. The Liberal Democrats, who usually made extensive gains at Conservative expense, increasingly advanced into urban territory that had formed the Labour heartlands for decades. They overtook Labour in the number of elected councillors and won control of traditional Labour cities including Liverpool, Newcastle, Sheffield and Hull. This represented an extraordinary throwback to the period before 1914 when such places had been Liberal, and Labour merely a marginal force at best. Municipal advances also fostered the local machine the Liberal Democrats needed in order to win parliamentary elections, such that by 2005 Liberal Democrats held parliamentary seats in major cities including Bristol, Birmingham, Leeds, Sheffield, Manchester and Edinburgh, as well as London, from which they had been largely absent since the 1920s. Though widely ignored by pundits at the time, these were symptoms of a shift of historic proportions.

Another momentous change in the underlying pattern of British politics was more obvious: the creation of a 129-member Parliament in Edinburgh and a sixty-member Assembly in Cardiff. Ironically, devolution was another expression of the continuity between Blair and Thatcher, for Blair damaged his party in Scotland as she had hers, he fully shared her distaste for the aspirations of the Welsh and Scots, positively disliked Scottish politicians and privately disparaged the 'whingeing Jock journos'.[28] Labour had been driven to promise devolution because it could no longer risk being undermined by the Scottish Nationalists and, though it went against the grain, Blair felt unable to renege on the commitment. He betrayed his feelings by devoting much fruitless and counterproductive effort to attempts to control regional power centres by excluding Rhodri Morgan as chief minister for Wales and by preventing Ken Livingstone gaining the Labour nomination as mayor of London.

In the event devolution proved to have major long-term ramifications for the party. It immediately involved Labour in coalitions in Edinburgh and Cardiff, displacing an historic aversion for such relationships because of the implications for Labour's status as an independent party of government. It also meant that with proportional systems operating in elections for the European Parliament, Northern Ireland, Scotland, Wales and, later, in Scottish local elections, the first-past-the-post system at Westminster looked increasingly anomalous. Moreover, the Scottish government, partly influenced by partnership with the Liberal Democrats, adopted a markedly more left-wing programme than that pursued by Labour at Westminster. Among other things Labour gave free care for the elderly in Edinburgh but refused it in London, free prescriptions in Cardiff while putting up the charges in London, imposed tuition fees in England and refused to implement them in Scotland, and defended the rights of property in England while allowing communities to buy out the landowners in Scotland. All this was more than merely embarrassing for it kept alive the New Labour/Old Labour dichotomy that was destructive of the party's integrity in the long run.

Above all, it remained uncertain whether the political calculation that underpinned devolution – that it offered the best means of blunting the Nationalist challenge and thus burying the case for Scottish independence – would be vindicated. In 2007 it became evident that Labour's expectations about permanently weakening Scots Nationalism had been optimistic. Under Blair support for Labour gradually dwindled in Wales and Scotland to the benefit of Liberal Democrats and Nationalists, thereby entrenching the three-to-four-party pattern of politics. In the elections of 2007 Labour retained only twenty-six of the sixty seats in Wales and forty-five of the 129 seats in Scotland, losing power to the SNP as a result. This implied that the party would increasingly struggle to win a majority of parliamentary seats in Wales and Scotland, a dire scenario since historically the party had only occasionally, as in 1945, 1966, and 1997, managed to win an overall majority in the *English* constituencies in Westminster elections.

During the ten years of his premiership Blair also repositioned his party in a way that heralded significant long-term consequences by polarising politics in terms of an authoritarian Labour-Conservative ideology against a liberal-libertarian one. This manifested itself in many ways, notably by the enactment of a huge amount of legislation on crime, a prison population exceeding 80,000, and a severe, if counterproductive, policy towards drugs. The strategy was consolidated by encouraging a continuing sense of moral panic about crime, pandering to the agenda of the tabloid press, and appointing working-class authoritarians, David Blunkett and John Reid, to the Home Office. New Labour's illiberal credentials were underlined by expressions of contempt by Labour ministers towards the sophisticated, liberal, lawyerly Establishment, who in effect adopted the tactics of the Republican right in America by using 'liberal' as a term of abuse. The assumption was that a tough approach would enable Labour to retain traditional working class support and generally outflank the Conservatives at all social levels. However, the bid for the authoritarian vote carried the danger of leaving Labour out of kilter with an increasingly liberal society. By 2005 eleven million people freely admitted to taking drugs at some time, 70,000 were being arrested each year for possession of cannabis, and some 60 per cent of cannabis was actually home-grown, a sign that it had become an indelible part of British cultural life. In trying to compete with the Conservatives to be tough New Labour began to isolate itself from the mainstream.

This pattern of polarising politics reached its climax in the years following the attack on the World Trade Center in New York in September 2001, as a result of which Blair committed Britain to President Bush's war against Islamic terrorism in Iraq. This involved British troops in what ultimately led to a military defeat in Basra and withdrawal from the country on the advice of the British commanders; but it also helped to spread terrorists to other parts of the world, turned Iraq, which had posed no threat, into a centre for terrorism, made Britain the target of terrorism, and hugely complicated domestic relations with the Muslim community by embroiling Britain in what appeared to be a crusade against Islam. The policy was misconceived from the start as it targeted what was a secular state that had no involvement with Islamic terrorism. Perversely, Bush and Blair preferred to treat the two states that *did* harbour Islamic terrorism, Saudi Arabia and Pakistan, as allies. In order to justify the invasion of

Iraq in 2003 Blair claimed that Saddam Hussein possessed 'weapons of mass destruction' by which he meant chemical and biological weapons, and that he could inflict them on Britain in forty-five minutes. It transpired that there was no basis for these absurd claims and that Blair had misused the intelligence reports on Iraq to lend credibility to an ill-conceived policy. By 2004 even he admitted that no such weapons would ever be found.

By the end of Blair's premiership the Iraq War was widely recognised as the worst foreign policy blunder since Munich in 1938, not least because it involved sacrificing British national interests for those of the United States and because it turned Britain into a target for terrorist attack. In the process the war largely destroyed the prime minister's reputation for competence and for integrity, and would have ended his premiership but for two factors. First was the loyalty shown by Labour MPs and the feebleness of the Cabinet, nearly all of whom entertained serious doubts about the policy but swallowed them. The second factor was the support for the Iraq War by the Conservative leaders whose wits deserted them in the initial patriotic euphoria. Had the Conservatives acted as an Opposition and seized their opportunity they would probably have defeated the government at the election of 2005. Instead the prime minister survived, but the war accentuated his reliance on Conservative votes to survive on crucial parliamentary divisions, notably on the Iraq War itself in 2003, on the establishment of school trusts in 2006 and on the replacement of the Trident nuclear weapon system in 2007.

The Iraq and Afghan wars also had damaging ramifications for domestic politics in that they destabilised the support Labour had previously enjoyed in the British Muslim community and led ministers into a wider and more dangerous phase of authoritarianism. Once the public realised that it had been deceived about the need for the war it became increasingly sceptical about subsequent official warnings about domestic terrorism. To counter this the government and the security services became drawn into a series of attempts to manipulate opinion by launching reports about threats to national security and about the number of terrorists operating in Britain.[29] However unreliable, these claims helped to fuel a wider attack on civil liberties. They led the government to enact a mass of legislation on terrorism which was abused by the police who used it as an excuse for stopping legitimate, peaceful protests on unrelated questions and arresting thousands of innocent British Muslims; ministers put pressure on universities to report on Muslim students and fought hard for the detention of suspects without trial, with the result that whereas in 1997 no one could be detained without charge for longer than forty-eight hours, the period was extended by stages to twenty-eight days, a practice unknown to other western democracies.[30] The policy also resulted in a gradual politicisation of the police force. One sign of the trend was the conduct of the chief of the Metropolitan Police, Sir Ian Blair, who intervened quite improperly in the 2005 election campaign to give public backing to the government's controversial proposals to introduce national identity cards; later he was sacked by the Conservative mayor of London, Boris Johnson. Although these trends did not turn Britain into a police state, cumulatively they carried her halfway down the road to a police state. Not since the rule of Lord Liverpool, who served as prime minister between 1812 and 1827, had there been so comprehensive an attack on civil liberties; significantly, the circumstances were similar, for Liverpool's colleagues had overreacted to fears about subversion generated by the French and Napoleonic wars.

The prolonged wars in Iraq and Afghanistan dragged the Labour Party into a situation whose ultimate consequences are still difficult to evaluate. On the one hand, war was consistent with Blair's strategic aim of depriving the Conservatives of the patriotic high ground and consolidating the party's links with its working-class base. On the other hand, it convinced many voters of the prime minister's duplicity, antagonised the Muslim community, and alienated Labour from a generation of young, educated people and much of the liberal intelligentsia. Historically, wars have been major formative forces in the party's character and fortunes. The effects – negative and positive – tend to reflect the party-political configuration during and after each conflict. For example, the Boer War left the Liberal Party horribly divided but capable of recovering once the anti-war backlash began because as yet there was no major alternative. However, after the 1914–18 war Liberalism could not repeat the recovery because by that time the Labour Party was able to articulate anti-war sentiment, claim the moral high ground and capitalise on the dilemmas and divisions of its rival during the 1920s.

This historical perspective is more relevant to the impact of the wars in Iraq and Afghanistan than appears at first sight. Although not on the scale of the First World War in terms of their impact on society and the economy, the timescale was increasingly ominous for Labour. By 2009 the war on terrorism had lasted eight years, twice as long as the First World War, and the government sanctioned an indefinite extension of the conflict in Afghanistan in the face of military advice that nothing was being achieved. As the 2005 election had demonstrated, opponents of the war now had alternatives in the shape of the Liberal Democrats, Scottish Nationalists, Respect and assorted socialists. Their stance over Iraq and civil liberties had gone a long way to giving the Liberal Democrats a distinctive role in the public mind that distinguished them from the New Labour–Conservative consensus. The effect was to consolidate multi-party politics, and thus made it more difficult for either of the main parties, but for Labour in particular, to win outright majorities.

For several years, however, this underlying reality was obscured by Blair's third victory at the 2005 general election which returned him with a diminished majority of sixty-six. However, Labour's vote had fallen steeply from 42 per cent to barely 36 per cent, an historically low vote. The parliamentary majority was thus a fluke, the result of the temporary advantage of a favourable distribution of constituencies and the Conservatives' ineptness over the war. Beneath the surface the pillars that had sustained New Labour's electoral dominance were now crumbling. Party membership had dwindled to 215,000, about half the peak in 1997. In Scotland, where Labour won only 39 per cent of the vote, redistribution reduced the representation from seventy-two to fifty-nine, all the losses but one being Labour seats, giving a foretaste of what would happen across England under new boundaries in 2009–10. Labour paid a price for antagonising liberal, middle-class opinion and university students, helping Liberal Democrats to make gains in such places as Cambridge, Bristol West, Manchester Withington, Leeds North-West and Hornsey with huge swings. And despite Blair's efforts to conciliate former Tory voters, the party's advantage over the Tories among homeowners had shrunk dramatically, producing heavy anti-government swings in the London suburbs as prosperous residential constituencies including Southgate, Wimbledon, Hemel Hempstead, Shipley and Upminster returned to their usual allegiance.

*   *   *

Only a year after his third electoral victory Tony Blair was forced to announce his intention of retiring before the next election. Although he prevaricated over the exact timing, he eventually quit in May 2007. In the interim he had exerted himself to ensure that his successor was fully committed to continuing his policies. However, the relief that greeted Blair's departure reflected assumptions that the New Labour project had run out of credibility and that under his successor, Gordon Brown, there would be at least a partial return to the party's traditions; conference had visibly warmed to Brown's assurance that 'we are best when we are Labour'. Symbolically the 'New' Labour tag had been dropped from party membership cards in 2003.

However, the party struggled to find a coherent alternative narrative. Although two candidates attempted to challenge Brown for the leadership, neither managed to obtain the forty-five nominations required, thereby depriving the party of a much-needed debate about its future and purpose. The failure to run a heavyweight candidate was a signal indication of the emasculation of the Labour left in Parliament. Conversely, the one candidate for deputy leadership who comprehensively attacked Blair's record, John Cruddas, came within a whisker of victory, an outcome that would have exposed the acute divisions between him and Gordon Brown. All the candidates distanced themselves from the outgoing prime minister to some extent, except for Hazel Blears who came bottom of the poll as a result.

The new prime minister took one or two eye-catching initiatives, including scrapping the plans to build huge new casinos, which suggested that a break with Blair's policies was imminent. However, the opportunity to build a fresh agenda was largely thrown away as it transpired that Brown intended to maintain continuity in almost all respects. In the face of widespread feeling that the special relationship with America had damaged Britain's national interests he emphasised that it would continue to be the foundation of foreign policy. He envisaged extending the war on terrorism almost indefinitely and returned to archetypal Blairite policies including attempts to extend the imprisonment of suspected terrorists without trial, the implementation of the identity cards scheme, privatisation of the Post Office and the NHS, the Private Finance Initiative, the employment of private companies to remove people from the unemployment register, curtailment of the local authorities' role in education, and a stricter approach to drugs. In 2009 when a number of Muslims were arrested in connection with a supposed new terrorist plot, Brown rashly endorsed police claims only to find that there was no evidence that a plot existed.

Above all Brown became trapped by his enthusiasm for unregulated free-market economic policies which shredded his reputation for economic competence. In June 2007, just before becoming prime minister, he had used his Mansion House speech as chancellor to lavish praise on the City of London, only to be overtaken by the collapse of the banks leading to a major recession, mass unemployment and a bill for £1.3 trillion in taxpayers' support for financial institutions. The origins of the disaster lay in a period in which the economy had been fuelled by consumer indebtedness, and the deregulation of financial institutions under Mrs Thatcher had led to reckless lending by banks with a view to reaping short-term profits. However, as chancellor, Brown had gone out of his way to associate Labour with the behaviour of the banks and he rejoiced in their success. Having faithfully followed Conservative thinking since 1997 he was consequently hampered from attacking Conservatism as the cause of the crisis. He had become so completely trapped by his earlier failure to mount an intellectual challenge to Thatcherism that, even as the financial collapse led to a major economic depression and to public disillusionment with unrestrained market forces, he proved unable to articulate a coherent alternative. Brown's belief in continuity with his predecessor was also underlined by the recruitment of entrepreneurs and bankers, including Digby Jones, David Freud and Alan Sugar, as government advisers and even ministers, only to be embarrassed when they refused to join Labour and later quit to work for the Conservative Party; their appointments underlined the extent to which New Labour and the Conservatives were still drawing on a common body of ideas.

Signs of disintegration within the party comparable to 1970 and 1983 now manifested themselves. Individual membership continued to dwindle to 176,000 in 2007, from 405,000 in 1997, and was understood to be around 160,000 in 2009.[31] In the face of Brown's determination to undertake a part-privatisation of the Post Office, in apparent contravention of assurances given to the unions in the Warwick Agreement, several trade unions threatened to disaffiliate, in the process bringing Labour closer to finally breaking the alliance that had brought it into being in 1900. By 2009 the pillars on which the movement stood were tottering. In addition to union disaffection, the steady demise of Labour's municipal base, as powers were removed by Blair and Brown, diminished the organisation with which to fight parliamentary campaigns. In the county council elections in 2009 Labour returned just 176 councillors to 473 Liberal Democrats and 1,476 Conservatives; Labour came third with 23 per cent of the vote to 28 per cent for Liberal Democrats and 38 per cent for the Conservatives. In the European elections the party was also third overall, but actually came fifth in several regions.

These disasters were exacerbated by profound disillusionment over revelations about claims for expenses made by Labour MPs immediately before the elections and the disgrace and enforced resignation of the Labour Speaker, Michael Martin, who had spent four years fighting the release of the details under the Freedom of Information Act. These events triggered a long-growing crisis of confidence within the government itself culminating in the resignation of seven ministers in the space of a week. It was widely accepted in the party that Brown suffered from poor judgement, lacked presentational skills, was hopelessly indecisive, and was unable to manage his government; in effect he was still the student politician he had been forty years earlier. As a result, during 2009 many Labour MPs and ministers became fatalistic in the face of what seemed inevitable electoral defeat. By August 2009 sixty-three Labour MPs had decided to stand down at the election, and the total was expected to reach 129, marking the demise of an entire generation.[32] In this situation the Conservative MPs would have lost little time in effecting a coup. But despite scattered signs of rebellion the party's traditional timidity when faced with an unelectable leader frustrated these efforts.

Admittedly Gordon Brown had inherited a precarious political situation in that Labour support was already down to 32 per cent in the polls when Blair retired, indicating a heavy defeat at a general election. Brown's failings only exacerbated things. The election of 2005 had left Labour much more vulnerable than the parliamentary majority suggested, for almost any fall below the existing 36 per cent level threatened to be disastrous in terms of seats. Labour occupied a position alarmingly similar to that faced by Asquith's Liberal Party at the end of the First World War in the sense that the party had become vulnerable to losses on two fronts simultaneously as both middle-class and working-class voters saw alternatives; alienated left-wing voters could back the Liberal Democrats and Nationalists while disillusioned right-wingers returned to their Conservative allegiance. A prolonged war had left the Edwardian Liberals demoralised, losing membership and local organisation, acutely divided at the parliamentary level, and generally lacking a clear sense of purpose. In this dilemma they had become victims of the electoral system which accelerated the decline and made recovery difficult despite the fact that the party retained 29 per cent of the popular vote in the early 1920s; after returning 275 MPs in 1910 the Liberals were down to forty by 1924. Following the disastrous election of 1983 Labour had appeared for a time to be entering a similar spiral of decline, but by a combination of internal reorganisation and luck in the errors of its opponents it managed to escape from this fate. This experience is a caution against assumptions about Labour's inevitable demise as an independent party of government. However, by 2009 the party's tactical and organisational weakness was more acute than in the 1980s in the face of stronger rivals. Between 2007 and 2009 Brown's government had the chance of grasping the opportunity that Asquith's Liberals had narrowly let slip in 1917–18 by introducing a form of proportional representation and thus fore-stalling a new era of Conservative rule initially based on a minority vote but consolidated by a redistribution of seats favourable to the Conservatives. Such an initiative, however, would have required historical perspective, clarity of purpose and a willingness to surrender the determination to govern as an independent majority party that had been central to Labour's strategy since the days of Ramsay MacDonald. Despite new expressions of sympathy for reform few leading politicians were ready for so drastic a reassessment of Labour's future.

Notes

1 'The votes of the football crowds': Explaining the Rise of the Labour Party

1. *Clarion*, 10 March 1900. • 2. *Report of the Conference on Labour Representation* (LRC, 1900). • 3. Quoted in M. Sissons and P. French, *The Age of Austerity* (1963), pp. 18–19. • 4. See H. C. G. Matthew, R. I. McKibbin and J. A. Kay, 'The Franchise factor in the rise of the Labour Party', *English Historical Review*, 91, 1976; Duncan Tanner, 'The Parliamentary Electoral System, the "Fourth" Reform Act and the Rise of Labour in England and Wales', *Bulletin of the Institute of Historical Research*, 56, 1983; David Howell, *British Workers and the Independent Labour Party 1888–1906* (1983); R. I. McKibbin, *The Evolution of the Labour Party 1910–1924* (1974); Duncan Tanner, *Political Change and the Labour Party 1900–1918* (1990). • 5. See Martin Pugh, *The Tories and the People 1880–1935* (1985); and more generally the essays in Jon Lawrence and Miles Taylor (eds.), *Party, State and Society* (1997). • 6. See Martin Pugh, 'The *Daily Mirror* and the Revival of Labour, 1935–1945', *Twentieth Century British History*, 9, 1998. • 7. Gregory Blaxland, *J. H. Thomas: A Life for Unity* (1964); but see important studies by two modern scholars: Andrew Thorpe, 'J. H. Thomas and the rise of the Labour Party in Derby 1880–1945', *Midland History*, 15, 1990; and David Howell, '"I Loved my Union and my Country": Jimmy Thomas and the Politics of Railway Trade Unionism', *Twentieth Century British History*, 6, 1995. • 8. B. Donoughue and G. W. Jones, *Herbert Morrison: Portrait of a Politician* (1973); Morrison's papers are available in the British Library of Political and Economic Science (BLPES), the Labour History Archives in Manchester and at Nuffield College, Oxford. • 9. See Martin Pugh, '"Class Traitors": Conservative Recruits to Labour, 1900–30', *English Historical Review*, 113, 1998. • 10. Eric Estorik, *Stafford Cripps* (1949), Colin Cooke, *The Life of Richard Stafford Cripps* (1957), Chris Bryant, *Stafford Cripps* (1997), p. 78, Peter Clarke, *The Cripps Version* (2002).

2 'Lily-livered Methodists':
The Origins of the Labour Party

1. *New York Daily Tribune*, 25 August 1852. • **2**. Ramsay MacDonald, *The Socialist Movement* (1911), p. 93. • **3**. Quoted in Howell, *British Workers*, p. 358. • **4**. *Reynolds News*, 23 November 1941; *Daily Express*, 22 November 1941. • **5**. H. R. S. Phillpott, *The Right Honourable J. H. Thomas* (1932), p. 5. • **6**. Robert Roberts, *The Classic Slum* (1971), p. 17; James Sexton, *Sir James Sexton, Agitator: The Life of The Dockers' MP* (1936), p. 111. • **7**. Robert Moore, *Pitmen, Preachers and Politics* (1974), p. 184. • **8**. David Clark, *Labour's Lost Leader: Victor Grayson* (1985), p. 33. • **9**. Harry Gosling, *Up and Down Stream* (1927), p. 82. • **10**. Ben Tillett, *Socialism* (1897). • **11**. George Lansbury, election address, 1894, Lansbury Papers vol. 30; John Shepherd, *George Lansbury: At the Heart of Old Labour* (2002), pp. 29–30. • **12**. George Lansbury, election address, 1894, Lansbury Papers vol. 30. • **13**. K. D. Brown, *John Burns* (1977), p. 17. • **14**. *Derby Daily Telegraph*, 5 December 1918. • **15**. See Stephen Reynolds and Bob and Tom Wolley, *Seems So! A Working-Class View of Politics* (1911), p. 6. • **16**. Martin Pugh, 'Working-Class Experience and State Social Welfare, 1908–1914: Old-Age Pensions Reconsidered', *Historical Journal*, 45, 2002, p. 789. • **17**. Frances, Countess of Warwick, *Life's Ebb and Flow* (1929), pp. 90–2. • **18**. *Clarion*, 26 March and 7 May 1892. • **19**. ibid., 9 July 1892. • **20**. ibid., 23 January and 2 July 1892. • **21**. Robert Blatchford, *Merrie England* (1894), p. 199. • **22**. ibid., p. 201. • **23**. ibid., p. 22. • **24**. *Clarion*, 12 March 1892; Blatchford, *Merrie England*, p. 105. • **25**. Blatchford, *Merrie England*, p. 34. • **26**. ibid., p. 59. • **27**. Quoted in Laurence Thompson, *The Enthusiasts: A biography of John and Katharine Bruce Glasier* (1971), p. 30. • **28**. Quoted in David Marquand, *Ramsay MacDonald* (1977), p. 18. • **29**. Hyndman quoted in Paul Ward, *Red Flag and Union Jack: Englishness, Patriotism and the British Left, 1881–1924* (1998), p. 38. • **30**. *The Times*, 23 January 1888. • **31**. Sidney Webb, *Socialism in England* (1889), pp. 116–17. • **32**. Keir Hardie and Ramsay MacDonald, 'The Independent Labour Party', *Nineteenth Century*, January 1899, p. 33. • **33**. Marquand, *Ramsay MacDonald*, p. 42. • **34**. E. H. Phelps Brown, *The Growth of British Industrial Relations* (1965), pp. 222, 224. • **35**. TUC Parliamentary Committee, minutes, 20 June 1889; Caroline Benn, *Keir Hardie* (1997), p. 49.

3 'No bigger than a man's hand':
The Foundation of the Labour Party

1. *Bradford Observer*, 14 January 1893. • **2**. ibid. • **3**. ibid. • **4**. Central Finsbury ILP minutes of the inaugural meeting, 1898. • **5**. Ben Turner, *About Myself* (1928), pp. 163–4. • **6**. Gosling, *Up and Down Stream*, pp. 84–5. • **7**. *Manchester City News*, 9 February and 9 March 1895. • **8**. Benn, *Keir Hardie*, p. 102. • **9**. ibid., pp.

121–3. • **10**. Colne Valley Labour League, minutes, 21 July 1891, 23 January 1892.
• **11**. ibid., 23 January 1892. • **12**. Meltham and District Labour Club minutes, 22
September and 6 October 1893. • **13**. David Clark, *Colne Valley: Radicalism to
Socialism* (1981), pp. 74–9. • **14**. Colne Valley Labour League minutes, 6 October
1891. • **15**. ibid., 1 January 1893. • **16**. Clark, *Colne Valley*, pp. 110–11. • **17**. Annual
Reports, 1912–1914, Colne Valley Socialist League. • **18**. Colne Valley Labour
League minutes, 16 April and 24 September 1904, 5 September 1908. • **19**. Clark,
Colne Valley, p. 85. • **20**. Quoted in Howell, *British Workers*, p. 387. • **21**. Martin
Pugh, *The Pankhursts* (2000), pp. 70–2. • **22**. Report of the First General Conference
of the ILP (1893), p. 3. • **23**. J. R. Clynes, *Memoirs 1869–1924* (1937), p. 72.
• **24**. Howell, *British Workers*, p. 178. • **25**. Quoted in K. Laybourn and J. Reynolds,
Liberalism and the Rise of Labour 1890–1918 (1984), p. 49. • **26**. Quoted in Howell,
British Workers, p. 117. • **27**. *Halifax Courier*, 10 July 1895, in Henry Pelling, *Social
Geography of British Elections 1885–1910* (1967), p. 300. • **28**. Howell, *British Workers*,
p. 269. • **29**. Marquand, *Ramsay MacDonald*, pp. 36–7. • **30**. Central Finsbury ILP
minutes, 17 January 1902. • **31**. *Nineteenth Century*, January 1899, pp. 21, 25.
• **32**. ibid., p. 35. • **33**. Jonathan Schneer, *Ben Tillett: Portrait of a Labour Leader*
(1982), p. 75. • **34**. TUC Parliamentary Committee minutes, 5 November 1889;
Philip Snowden, *An Autobiography*, Vol. 1 (1934), p. 101. • **35**. *Labour Organiser*,
January 1924. • **36**. E. A. and G. H. Radice, *Will Thorne: Constructive Militant*
(1974), p. 34. • **37**. *Report of the Conference on Labour Representation* (1900),
p. 11. • **38**. ibid., p. 12. • **39**. ibid., p. 13. • **40**. *Clarion*, 10 March 1900. • **41**. ibid.,
21 October 1899. • **42**. See George Lansbury election material for 1900,
Lansbury Papers vol. 30. • **43**. Quoted in Howell, *British Workers*, p. 217. • **44**.
Pelling, *Social Geography*, p. 261. • **45**. *Preston Guardian*, 6 October 1900. • **46**.
See Benn, *Keir Hardie*, pp. 13, 84.

4 'Not a single Socialist speech': Labour's Edwardian Breakthrough

1. Quoted in Marquand, *Ramsay MacDonald*, p. 70. • **2**. Bethnal Green Labour
Party minutes, 16 September 1909. • **3**. *Annual Conference Reports*, LRC, 1900–
1906. • **4**. Marquand, *Ramsay MacDonald*. p. 51. • **5**. Quoted in Howell, *British
Workers*, p. 195. • **6**. Will Thorne, *My Life's Battles* (1925), pp. 26, 44–5, 54, 59;
Howell, *British Workers*, p. 264. • **7**. Howell, *British Workers*, p. 216. • **8**. *Preston
Guardian*, 9 May 1903. • **9**. ibid., 16 May 1903. • **10**. Memorandum by Jesse
Herbert, 6 March 1903, British Library: Herbert Gladstone Papers 46025. • **11**. See
memorandum, 6 September 1903, Herbert Gladstone Papers 46106. • **12**. Winston
Churchill to Alexander Murray, 23 September 1906, Elibank Papers 8801.
• **13**. 'Memorandum on the Socialist and Labour Movement in Scotland', February
1908, Elibank Papers 8801. • **14**. *Preston Guardian*, 6 January 1906; Philip Snowden,

An Autobiography, Vol. 1 (1934), p. 117. • **15**. *Manchester Guardian*, 13 January 1906. • **16**. ibid., 22 December 1905. • **17**. ibid., 5 January 1906. • **18**. ibid., 29 December 1905. • **19**. *Jarrow Labour Herald*, 4 May 1906. • **20**. *Justice*, 15 December 1906. • **21**. *Nation*, 24 August 1907. • **22**. *Speaker*, 1 September 1906. • **23**. Ramsay MacDonald, 'The Labour Party and Electoral Reform', 1913. • **24**. *Jarrow Labour Herald*, May 1905. • **25**. Colne Valley Socialist League minutes, 19 January 1907. • **26**. Ramsay MacDonald to E. Whiteley, 8 July 1907 (copy), LP/PA/07. • **27**. Clark, *Labour's Lost Leader*, p. 21. • **28**. ibid., pp. 22–3. • **29**. *Daily Mirror*, 20 July 1907; Clark, *Labour's Lost Leader*, p. 33. • **30**. LP/PA/07. • **31**. *Huddersfield Examiner*, 20 July 1907. • **32**. *Pall Mall Gazette*, 20 July 1907; *Labour Leader*, 26 July 1907. • **33**. *Jarrow Labour Herald*, 1 June 1906. • **34**. See report in LP/EL/08. • **35**. See Tanner, *Political Change*, pp. 144–5, 157. • **36**. ibid., pp. 141–3. • **37**. Labour Party, *Annual Conference Report*, 1906. • **38**. Quoted in Schneer, *Ben Tillett*, p. 135. • **39**. Philip Snowden, *Socialism and the Drink Question* (1908), pp. 165–6. • **40**. Jon Lawrence, *Speaking for the people: Party, Language and Popular Politics in England 1867–1914* (1998), pp. 124–5, 140–1. • **41**. *Jarrow Labour Herald*, 14 December 1906. • **42**. Schneer, *Ben Tillett*, p. 178. • **43**. *Labour Leader*, 4 September 1908. • **44**. Colne Valley Socialist League minutes, 28 August and 22 September 1907. • **45**. Clark, *Labour's Lost Leader*, p. 63. • **46**. ibid., p. 61. • **47**. Victor Grayson, election address, 1910, Wilfrid Whiteley Papers 6/5. • **48**. NEC minutes, 1 December 1909. • **49**. ibid., 9 March 1910. • **50**. East Ham ILP minutes, 10 March and 21 April 1910. • **51**. Ramsay MacDonald to Alexander Murray, 4 October 1911, Elibank Papers 8802. • **52**. Ramsay MacDonald to Alexander Murray, 9 October 1911, Elibank Papers 8802. • **53**. *Labour Leader*, 10 May 1907. • **54**. *PR From a Labour Standpoint*, 1913, PR Pamphlet No. 24. • **55**. G. H. Roberts and W. C. Anderson, 'The Labour Party and Electoral Reform', 1913. • **56**. *Labour Leader*, 9 January 1913. • **57**. Labour Party, *Annual Conference Report*, 27 January 1914, p. 105. • **58**. Ramsay MacDonald, 'The Labour Party and Electoral Reform', 1913. • **59**. NEC minutes, 9 October 1913. • **60**. Labour Party, *Annual Conference Report*, 27 January 1914, pp. 104–8. • **61**. In 1907 ASS had just £49 of income: National Library of Scotland: Roland Muirhead Papers Box 153/10. • **62**. Figures from 'The Trade Union Act, 1913', LP/TUA/11. • **63**. LP/TUA/11. • **64**. *Labour Leader*, 9 January 1913. • **65**. LP/EL/08. • **66**. *Labour Leader*, 18 July 1912. • **67**. M. G. Shepherd and J. L. Halstead, 'Labour's Municipal Electoral Performance in England and Wales 1901–1913', *Bulletin of the Society for the Study of Labour History*, 39, 1979, p. 49. • **68**. LP/EL/08. • **69**. ibid. • **70**. ibid. • **71**. ibid.; *Daily Telegraph*, 3 November 1908. • **72**. LP/EL/08. • **73**. Quoted in L. Thompson, *The Enthusiasts* (1971), p. 136. • **74**. Martin Pugh, *The March of the Women: A Revisionist Analysis of the Campaign for Women's Suffrage 1866–1914* (2000), p. 233. • **75**. Marquand, *Ramsay MacDonald*, p. 148. • **76**. Alice Everett to George Lansbury, 26 June 1912, Lansbury Papers vol. 5. • **77**. NEC minutes, 15 October 1912. • **78**. G. Saunders Jacobs to George Lansbury, 27 November 1912, and J. Scotney to George Lansbury,

17 November 1912, Lansbury Papers vol. 5. • **79**. Eleanor Acland to Catherine Marshall, 1 April 1912, Cumbria Record Office: Marshall Papers. • **80**. P. Snowden to Maud Arncliffe-Sennett, 31 March 1912, British Library: Arncliffe-Sennett Papers C10.245. • **81**. Kate Courtney to Arthur Henderson, 23 April 1912, LP/WOM/12/4. • **82**. Report on Barrow-in-Furness, LP/WOM/1/46. • **83**. LP/WLL/2/164. • **84**. LP/WLL/1/93. • **85**. H. Brailsford to Ramsay MacDonald, 23 April 1912, PRO: MacDonald Papers 30/69/5. • **86**. *Common Cause*, 27 June 1912. • **87**. Arthur Henderson to Catherine Marshall, 6 August 1912; *Bolton Evening News*, 12 and 18 November 1912. • **88**. W. S. Holmes to J. S. Middleton, 14 June 1914, LP/ORG/10/29. • **89**. J. S. Middleton to W. S. Holmes, 17 June 1914, LP/ORG/10/29. • **90**. NEC minutes, 27, 28, 31 January 1913. • **91**. ibid., 16 September 1913. • **92**. ibid., 23 June 1914; Marquand, *Ramsay MacDonald*, pp. 155–6. • **93**. Marquand, *Ramsay MacDonald*, pp. 159–60. • **94**. *Labour Leader*, 30 January and 6 February 1913. • **95**. Beatrice Webb Diary, 6 February 1914. • **96**. Tanner, *Political Change*, pp. 321–4. • **97**. East Ham ILP minutes, 21 March 1914.

5 *'Come to your country's aid':* Labour and the Great War

1. *Hansard*, House of Commons Debates, 3 August 1914, cols 1829–31. • **2**. *Labour Leader*, 6 August 1914. • **3**. A. Fenner Brockway, *Inside the Left* (1942), p. 48. • **4**. NEC, minutes, 5 August 1914; Clynes, *Memoirs*, p. 172; MacDonald Diary, 23 September 1914. • **5**. Clynes, *Memoirs*, p. 186; East Ham ILP Minutes, 27 August 1914. • **6**. Brockway, *Inside the Left*, p. 46. • **7**. *The Times*, 1 October 1914; Marquand, *Ramsay MacDonald*, pp. 186–93. • **8**. Richard Denman to C. P. Trevelyan, 28 May 1915, Newcastle University: Trevelyan Papers vol. 63. • **9**. Clark, *Labour's Lost Leader*, pp. 103–4. • **10**. Quoted in Phillpott, *J. H. Thomas*, p. 150. • **11**. *Daily Telegraph*, 16 August 1918; *Christian Commonwealth*, 14 April 1915. • **12**. *Leeds Weekly Citizen*, 7 January 1916. • **13**. *Portsmouth Evening News*, 22 May 1923. • **14**. *Preston Guardian*, 23 September 1918. • **15**. See Alan Clinton, 'Trades Councils During the First World War', *International Review of Social History*, 15, 1970, pp. 206–7, 212, 219. • **16**. NEC minutes, 19 May 1915. • **17**. MacDonald Diary, quoted in Marquand, *Ramsay MacDonald*, p. 201. • **18**. Clynes, *Memoirs*, p. 215. • **19**. ibid., p. 234. • **20**. Phillpott, *J. H. Thomas*, p. 160. • **21**. ibid., p. 161. • **22**. ibid., p. 152. • **23**. D. B. Foster, 'My Life's Story', West Yorkshire Archives: Leeds Labour Party MSS 2102 (LP178); John Beckett, MSS autobiography. • **24**. *Leeds Weekly Citizen*, 21 January 1916. • **25**. ibid., 11 February 1916. • **26**. Clynes, *Memoirs*, p. 243. • **27**. Arthur Steel-Maitland to Andrew Bonar Law, 13 June 1916, House of Lords Record Office: Bonar Law Papers 64/G/8; Milner, speech at Leeds, *Leeds Weekly Citizen*, 28 January 1919. • **28**. Selborne to Salisbury, 12 September 1916, House of Lords Record Office: Selborne Papers vol. 6. • **29**. Memorandum n.d., Memorandum, 5 November 1917, Steel-Maitland Papers GD193/92/2/11–17 and 104. • **30**. *The Times*, 15 May 1916. • **31**. ibid., 26 January 1918. • **32**. Victor Fisher to Arthur Steel-Maitland, 27 April 1917, Steel-Maitland Papers GD193/99/2/4. • **33**. NEC minutes, 7 January and 26 April 1915. • **34**. Assistant Secretary to W. Holmes, 21 January 1915, LP ORG/14/1 and 2. • **35**. NEC minutes, 28 March 1916. • **36**. PRO CAB 37/147/31, 12 March 1916. • **37**. Martin Pugh, *Electoral Reform in War and Peace, 1906–1918* (1978), pp. 75–86. • **38**. 'Memorandum on Electoral Reform and Redistribution', attached to NEC minutes, 27 January 1917. • **39**. NEC minutes, 18 April 1917. • **40**. MacDonald Diary, 9 May 1917. • **41**. Phillpott, *J. H. Thomas*, p. 167. • **42**. MacDonald Diary, 7 October 1917. • **43**. Conference Report, January 1918, Women's Labour League, pp. 43–6. • **44**. Conference Report, June 1919, Women's Labour League, p. 80. • **45**. LPA/ORG 14/1 and 2. • **46**. Pugh, *Electoral Reform*, pp. 83, 116. • **47**. C. P. Scott Diary, 11 and 12 December 1917. • **48**. Pugh, *Electoral Reform*, pp. 165–7. • **49**. NEC minutes, 13 and 27 February 1918. • **50**. *Birmingham Post*, 25 November 1918. • **51**. ibid., 2, 3, 6 December 1918. • **52**. *The Boro' of West Ham, East Ham and Stratford Express*, 2 November 1918. • **53**. John Turner, 'The Labour Vote and the Franchise After 1918', P. R. Denley and D. Hopkin (eds.), *History and Computing* (1987), pp. 139–40. • **54**. *Derby Daily Telegraph*, 22 November and 5 December 1918. • **55**. ibid., 19 November 1918. • **56**. *Birmingham Post*, 3 December 1918. • **57**. *The Boro' of West Ham, East Ham and Stratford Express*, 30 November 1918. • **58**. *Preston Guardian*, 30 November and 7 December 1918. • **59**. *Weekly News for West Bromwich*, 1 November 1918. • **60**. *Smethwick Telephone*, 30 November, 7 and 14 December 1918. • **61**. *The Boro' of West Ham, East Ham and Stratford Express*, 20 November 1918. • **62**. ibid., 30 November 1918.

6 'Dollar Princess':
The Emergence of a National Party in the 1920s

1. MacDonald Diary, 7 January 1919. • **2**. Birmingham Trades Council and Boro' Labour Party, annual report, 1920. • **3**. Speech, 2 November 1918. • **4**. Labour Party, *Annual Conference Report*, 1919, p. 27. • **5**. Arthur Horner, *Incorrigible Rebel* (1960), p. 38. • **6**. Report, 30 April 1919, PRO CAB24/78/7128. • **7**. PRO CAB24/71/6425. • **8**. Report, 5 August 1920, PRO CAB24/110/1743. • **9**. Speeches 10 and 16 August 1919, Steel-Maitland Papers GD113/1/80. • **10**. Parliamentary Labour Party minutes, 5 December 1922, 16 December 1924. • **11**. Donoughue and Jones, *Herbert Morrison*, pp. 98, 102. • **12**. *Seaham Harbour Labour News*, April 1929. • **13**. Daniel Weinbren, 'Sociable Capital: London's Labour Parties 1918–45', in Matthew Worley (ed.), *Labour's Grass Roots* (2005), p.197; Shepherd, *George Lansbury*, p. 243. • **14**. Barrow-in-Furness CLP minutes, 15 February 1921; Salford Labour Party minutes, 3 February

1926; Morden Labour Party minutes, 3 January, 7 February and 11 April 1927. • **15**. Tottenham South Labour Party minutes, 1925. • **16**. Shepherd, *George Lansbury*, p. 243. • **17**. Clynes, *Memoirs*, p. 52. • **18**. See 'Labour In Power and Labour Not In Power', Morrison Papers 8/8. • **19**. John Beckett, MSS autobiography; Donoughue and Jones, *Herbert Morrison*, p. 68. • **20**. Quoted in McKibbin, *The Evolution of the Labour Party*, p. 145. • **21**. *Hackney Gazette and North London Advertiser*, 13 and 20 February 1929. • **22**. *Hansard*, House of Commons Debates, 20 March 1923, vol. 161, col. 2472 • **23**. 'London Threatened by Electrical Supply', London Labour Party, Morrison Papers 8/8. • **24**. Shepherd, *George Lansbury*. p. 201. • **25**. Donoughue and Jones, *Herbert Morrison*, p. 47. • **26**. ibid., p. 53. • **27**. Ben Pimlott, *Hugh Dalton* (1985), pp. 176–7; Celia Minoughan, 'The Rise of Labour in Northumberland: the Wansbeck DLP 1918–1932', Leeds University BA dissertation, 1980, Appendix 3. • **28**. Barrow-in-Furness CLP minutes, 28 June 1921. • **29**. Wansbeck DLP minutes, 31 March 1936. • **30**. ibid., 22 June 1918; Barrow-in-Furness CLP minutes, 28 June 1921. • **31**. Barrow-in-Furness CLP minutes, 28 September 1921. • **32**. Tottenham South Labour Party minutes, 20 March 1919. • **33**. ibid., December 1925. • **34**. *Gateshead Labour Herald*, 5 December 1924. • **35**. John Beckett, MSS autobiography. • **36**. ibid. • **37**. ibid. • **38**. ibid. • **39**. ibid. • **40**. *Labour Organiser*, January 1924. • **41**. A relationship ignored by Lansbury's biographer but confirmed by the Hon. Tom Sackville (private information); D. G. Pole, *War Letters And Autobiography*, pp. 177–8, Pole Papers 5/8: York University, Borthwick Institute. • **42**. *Daily Herald*, 4 February 1925. • **43**. Martin Pugh, *Women and the Women's Movement in Britain 1914–1959* (1992), p. 231. • **44**. *Daily Herald*, 27 February 1932; Roy Hattersley, *Who Goes Home?* (1995), p. 3; John Tilley, *Churchill's Favourite Socialist: A life of A. V. Alexander*, pp. 8–16. • **45**. Women's Co-operative Guild committee minutes, 14 December 1923, 20 September 1929, 11 April 1933. • **46**. Women's Labour League, *Conference Report*, June 1919, p. 88; Karen Hunt, 'Making Politics in Local Communities: Labour Women in Interwar Manchester', in Worley (ed.), *Labour's Grass Roots*, pp. 87–8. • **47**. *Labour Woman*, 1 March 1926, p. 88. • **48**. Bishop Auckland Women's Section minutes, 20 July 1932, 3 March and 10 April 1934. • **49**. ibid., 9 February, 5 April and 3 May 1939. • **50**. Labour Party Women's Organisation, *Annual Conference Report*, 1918, p. 41. • **51**. *Labour Woman*, 7 October 1918, p. 82. • **52**. See Pugh, *Women and the Women's Movement*, p. 160. • **53**. Labour Party Women's Organisation, *Annual Conference Report*, 1925, p. 84. • **54**. *Manchester Dispatch*, 3 February 1925. • **55**. *Liverpool Echo*, 13 January 1927. • **56**. John Beckett, MSS autobiography. • **57**. G. Morgan to Arthur Ponsonby, 20 December 1917, Ponsonby Papers 666; MacDonald Papers PRO 30/69/7/51. • **58**. John Beckett, MSS autobiography. • **59**. See Jim Simmons Papers vol. 2. • **60**. D. Englander and J. Osborne, 'Jack, Tommy and Henry Dubb: The Armed Forces and the Working Class', *Historical Journal*, 21, 1978, p. 620. • **61**. Draft autobiography, Attlee Papers 1 /2; Weinbren, 'Sociable Capital', in Worley (ed.), *Labour's Grass Roots*, pp. 195, 209; *Gateshead Labour Herald*, 15 June,

15 July and 15 September 1919. • **62**. Neil Riddell, 'The Catholic Church and the Labour Party 1918–1931', *Twentieth Century British History*, 8, 1997, p. 170. • **63**. See Ivan Gibbons, 'The Irish Policy of the First Labour Government', *Labour History Review*, 72, 2008. • **64**. Sam Davies, *Liverpool Labour* (1996), pp. 144–7. • **65**. ibid., pp. 214–26. • **66**. David Butler and Donald Stokes, *Political Change in Britain* (1969), pp. 166–7. • **67**. Gregg McClymont, 'Socialism, Puritanism, Hedonism: the Parliamentary Labour Party's Attitude to Gambling, 1923–31', *Twentieth Century British History*, 19, 2008, p. 299. • **68**. ibid., p. 307. • **69**. *Sunderland Daily Echo*, 22 August 1924, Durham CRO press cuttings DX 1268/26–30. • **70**. Brockway, *Inside the Left*, p. 137. • **71**. C. P. Trevelyan, *From Liberalism to Labour* (1921). • **72**. Egerton Wake to Christopher Addison, 11 August 1925, Addison Papers 81. • **73**. For a discussion see Martin Pugh, 'Class Traitors: Conservative Recruits to Labour, 1900–30', *English Historical Review*, 113, 1998, pp. 38–64. • **74**. *Manchester Guardian*, 25 October 1947. • **75**. Lord Listowel to Martin Pugh, 14 September 1994. • **76**. Godfrey Elton, *Among Others* (1938), p. 158. • **77**. *Daily Herald*, 1 April 1924; Egon Wertheimer, *Portrait of the Labour Party* (1929), pp. vii–x. • **78**. Lord Listowel interview (Martin Pugh), 2 May 1996. • **79**. Hugh Thomas, *John Strachey* (1973), pp. 16–17; Pimlott, *Hugh Dalton*, pp. 29–33. • **80**. L. S. Amery to Stanley Baldwin, 21 December 1923, Baldwin Papers 42, fol. 153–4. • **81**. Stafford Cripps to Hugh Macmillan, 26 October 1930, Macmillan Papers 25261. • **82**. Oliver Baldwin, *The Questing Beast* (1932), p. 214. • **83**. *Birmingham Mail*, 22 October 1924; *Daily Express*, 24 October 1937. • **84**. *Birmingham Mail*, 24 October 1924. • **85**. *Staffordshire Sentinel*, 22 April and 25 May 1929. • **86**. Pugh, *Women and the Women's Movement*, pp. 175–6. • **87**. *Daily Herald*, 13 July 1929; on financial contributions see Pole Papers 5/7; Constituency Reports 1929–31, Pole Papers 5/9. • **88**. NEC minutes, 29 November, 1 and 22 December 1926. • **89**. 'The Oswald Mosley/Wilfrid Whiteley Account for 1926', Whiteley Papers 6/4. • **90**. Wilfrid Whiteley to Oswald Mosley (copy), 21 August 1926, Whiteley to Mosley (copy), 23 June 1926, Mosley to Whiteley, 9 November 1926, Whiteley to Mosley (copy), 21 January 1927, Whiteley Papers 6/3 and 6/4. • **91**. Oswald Mosley to Wilfrid Whiteley, 2 April 1928, Whiteley Papers 6/4. • **92**. Oswald Mosley to Wilfrid Whiteley, 25 January 1928, Whiteley Papers 6/4; NEC minutes, 23 March 1927. • **93**. Sidney Webb, 'The First Labour Government', *Political Quarterly*, 32, 1961, p. 13. • **94**. See Trevelyan Papers 88. • **95**. William Wedgwood Benn to A. Munro, 25 January 1927, Stansgate Papers 85/1.

7 *'Aristocratic embrace': Labour in Power*

1. John McNair, *James Maxton: The Beloved Rebel* (1955), p. 99. • 2. MacDonald Papers PRO 30/69/7/56. • 3. PLP minutes, 21 December 1922. • 4. David

Kirkwood, *My Life of Revolt* (1935), p. 195. • **5**. ibid., p. 87; John Beckett, MSS autobiography. • **6**. John Sankey to Godfrey Elton (copy), 6 April 1932, Sankey Papers vol. 509. • **7**. Kirkwood, *My Life of Revolt*, p. 193; McNair, *James Maxton*, p. 109. • **8**. Beatrice Webb to Mrs Alexander, 29 January 1924, Alexander Papers 5/1. • **9**. Quoted in Nicholas Owen, 'MacDonald's Parties: The Labour Party and the "Aristocratic Embrace", 1922–1931', *Twentieth Century British History*, 18, 2007, p. 11. • **10**. Clynes, *Memoirs*, p. 326. • **11**. *The Times*, 17 and 19 March 1923. • **12**. PLP minutes, 21 and 27 February 1923. • **13**. ibid., 20 June 1923. • **14**. J. H. Thomas, *My Story* (1937), p. 154. • **15**. *Daily Telegraph*, 19 March 1923. • **16**. Robert Self (ed.), *The Neville Chamberlain Diary Letters* (2001), vol. 2, pp. 405, 412. • **17**. Quoted in Estorik, *Stafford Cripps*, p. 70; Philip Snowden, *Autobiography*, vol. 2, pp. 595–6. • **18**. *New Vote*, 4 February 1924. • **19**. Martin Pugh, *'Hurrah for the Blackshirts!': Fascists and Fascism in Britain between the Wars* (2005), pp. 58–9. • **20**. *Daily Herald*, 2 and 4 January 1924. • **21**. Earl De La Warr to Ramsay MacDonald, 27 December 1923, MacDonald Papers PRO 30/69/2. • **22**. Lord Bledisloe to Ramsay MacDonald, 14 January 1924, MacDonald Papers PRO 30/69/1168. • **23**. Hugh Macmillan to Ramsay MacDonald (copy), 7 February 1924, Macmillan Papers 25261. • **24**. Richard Haldane to Elizabeth Haldane, 15 January 1924, Haldane Papers 6013. • **25**. Richard Haldane to Elizabeth Haldane, 11 January 1924, Haldane Papers 6013; Ramsay MacDonald to Richard Haldane, 23 December 1923 and 12 January 1924, Haldane Papers 5916. • **26**. Ramsay MacDonald to Arthur Henderson (copy), 22 December 1923, MacDonald Papers PRO 30/69/5/33. • **27**. *Daily Herald*, 24 January 1924. • **28**. Sidney Webb, 'The First Labour Government', *Political Quarterly*, 32, 1961, p. 13. • **29**. PLP minutes, 11 February 1924. • **30**. ibid., 26 February 1924. • **31**. Lord Lytton to Richard Haldane, 6 February 1924, Haldane Papers 5916. • **32**. William Wedgwood Benn Diary, 19 March 1924, Stansgate Papers 66. • **33**. MacDonald Diary, 1 May 1923. • **34**. ibid., 21 January 1924. • **35**. ibid., 22 January 1924. • **36**. Clynes, *Memoirs*, pp. 343–4. • **37**. Ramsay MacDonald to Alexander Grant, 27 April 1924, MacDonald Papers 25274; Marquand, *Ramsay MacDonald*, p. 314. • **38**. Marquand, *Ramsay MacDonald*, p. 314. • **39**. *The Times*, 12 March 1924. • **40**. *Daily Herald*, 16 February 1924. • **41**. George Lansbury, *My Life* (1928), p. 268; *Hansard*, House of Commons Debates, 29 May 1924, vol. 174, col. 713; *Daily Herald*, 9 and 13 February 1924. • **42**. Quoted in Horner, *Incorrigible Rebel*, p. 68. • **43**. MacDonald Diary, 26 September 1924. • **44**. ibid., 1 October 1924. • **45**. Gosling, *Up and Down Stream*, pp. 232–3. • **46**. Herbert Morrison, Hackney South election address, 1924, Morrison Papers 8/24. • **47**. Press cuttings 1924, Sorensen Papers 3/B. • **48**. Philip Snowden, *Autobiography*, p. 710. • **49**. *Daily Mail* editorial, 25 October 1924. • **50**. 191 seats in 1923, plus one Liberal defector after the election, plus one by-election gain gave 193 at the dissolution; hence after forty-two net losses – 151. • **51**. National agent's report, MacDonald Papers PRO 30/69/5/129.

8 'Further from Socialism': The General Strike and
Mass Unemployment, 1925–1931

1. Quoted in Matthew Worley, *Labour Inside the Gate: A History of the British Labour Party between the Wars* (2005), p. 100; Kirkwood, *My Life of Revolt*, p. 228; McNair, *James Maxton*, p. 157; John Boughton, 'Working-Class Politics in Birmingham and Sheffield, 1918–1931', Warwick University PhD thesis, p. 272. • **2.** Harold Bellman, *The Building Society Movement* (1927), p. 53; *National Association of Building Societies Yearbook*, 1927, pp. 262–3. • **3.** Thomas, *John Strachey*, pp. 50–1; Michael Newman, *John Strachey* (1989), pp. 10–14. • **4.** Quoted in Harold Nicolson, *King George V* (1952), p. 415. • **5.** Notes by Walter Citrine, 9 March 1926, p. 127: Citrine Papers 1/7. • **6.** Marquand, *Ramsay MacDonald*, p. 483. • **7.** David Howell, *MacDonald's Party: Labour Identities and Crisis, 1922–31* (2002), pp. 103–4. • **8.** MacDonald Diary, 2 May 1926. • **9.** *National Review*, 86, September 1925, pp. 54–6. • **10.** 'General Strike: Russian Gold', memorandum, n.d., Baldwin Papers vol. 12. • **11.** John Beckett, Mss autobiography. • **12.** *Birmingham Post*, 21 May 1926; 'Statement of the General Secretary to Area Secretaries' Conference', 27 May 1926, Bevin Papers II 7/7. • **13.** Oliver Baldwin to Ramsay MacDonald, May 1926, MacDonald Papers PRO 30/69/1171/1 • **14.** Salford CLP minutes, 27 May, 2 June and 11 August 1926; Sheffield Labour Party, minutes of the Disputes Committee, 26 May and 2 June 1926, and Tom Garrett, circular letter, 23 September 1926. • **15.** *Sunderland Echo*, 17 November 1926, Durham CRO press cuttings, DX 1268/31. • **16.** NEC minutes, 31 August 1926. • **17.** *Seaham Harbour Labour News*, December 1927. • **18.** Quoted in Howell, *MacDonald's Party*, p. 187. • **19.** Quoted in ibid., p. 137. • **20.** H. H. Little to Sir L. Maclachlan, 3 June 1927; E. L. Spears to J. C. C. Davidson, 2 June 1927, Baldwin Papers vol. 51. • **21.** C. J. Richardson to A. Ponsonby, Ponsonby Papers col. 670, in Boughton, 'Working-Class Politics', p. 207. • **22.** Birmingham Ladywood Ward Women's Unionist Association minutes, 14 July 1926. • **23.** Boughton, 'Working-Class Politics', p. 204; *Labour Woman*, December 1928. • **24.** *Birmingham Post*, 17 May 1926. • **25.** Boughton, 'Working-Class Politics', p. 151. • **26.** ibid., p. 164. • **27.** ibid., p. 156. • **28.** ibid., p. 196. • **29.** *Smethwick Telephone*, 27 November 1927. • **30.** ibid., 18 December 1926. • **31.** *Birmingham Post*, 17 May 1926. • **32.** *Dudley Chronicle*, 9 May 1929. • **33.** *Birmingham Post*, 30 May 1929. • **34.** J. Johnson in *Labour Organiser*, April 1931. • **35.** *Daily Mail*, 20, 23, 28 April 1927. • **36.** See J. S. Rasmussen, 'Women in Labour: the Flapper Vote and Party System Transformation in Britain', *Electoral Studies*, 3, 1, 1984, p. 57; Butler and Stokes, *Political Change in Britain*, pp. 105–15. • **37.** Pugh, *Women and the Women's Movement*, pp. 151–2. • **38.** Quoted in Pamela Graves, *Labour Women: Women in British Working-Class Politics, 1918–1939* (1994), pp. 62–3. • **39.** Michael Savage, *The Dynamics of Working-Class Politics: The Labour Movement in Preston, 1880–1940* (1987), p. 166. • **40.** ibid., p. 167. • **41.** Labour Women's Organisation, *Annual Conference Report*, 1935, p. 97. • **42.** Quoted in

Graves, *Labour Women*, p. 29. • **43**. Martin Francis, 'Labour and Gender', in D. Tanner, P. Thane and N. Tiratsoo (eds.), *Labour's First Century* (2000), p. 203. • **44**. Pugh, *Women and the Women's Movement*, pp. 309–11. • **45**. Quoted in Graves, *Labour Women*, p.107. • **46**. *Labour Woman*, March 1924, p. 34; Women's Labour League, *Annual Conference Report*, May 1925, p. 123, May 1927, p. 47, May 1928, p. 27. • **47**. Graves, *Labour Women*, pp. 160–1. • **48**. Pugh, *Women and the Women's Movement*, p. 126. • **49**. Leah Manning, *A Life for Education* (1970), p. 79. • **50**. Jennie Lee, *My Life With Nye* (1980), p. 63. • **51**. Jill Liddington, *The Life and Times of a Respectable Radical: Selina Cooper, 1864–1946* (1984), pp. 295–7, 325–9. • **52**. Pugh, *Women and the Women's Movement*, pp. 175–6. • **53**. Edith Picton-Turbervill, *Life Is Good* (1939), p. 173. • **54**. See Pugh, *Women and the Women's Movement*, pp. 184–90. • **55**. Mary Agnes Hamilton, *Remembering My Good Friends* (1944), p. 176. • **56**. Women's Labour League, *Annual Conference Report*, May 1928, p. 11, April 1929, p. 24. • **57**. *Birmingham Post*, 14 May 1929. • **58**. Vernon Hartshorn to Ramsay MacDonald 2 March 1930; MacDonald to Tom Johnston (copy), 4 April 1931; Johnston to MacDonald, 1 January 1931; MacDonald to David Lloyd George (copy), 12 September 1930, MacDonald Papers PRO 30/69/5/174–5. • **59**. See MacDonald Papers PRO 30/69/5/166. • **60**. Fred Pethick-Lawrence to Ramsay MacDonald, 2 June 1929, MacDonald Papers PRO 30/60/5/166. • **61**. Memorandum on the Ullswater Conference, PRO 30/69/5/166. • **62**. Herbert Morrison to J. H. Thomas (copy), 2 February 1930, Morrison Papers 8/1. • **63**. *Labour Organiser*, June 1930. • **64**. Sam Davies and Bob Morley, 'The Reactions of Voters in Yorkshire to the Second Labour Government, 1929–32', in Worley (ed.), *Labour's Grass Roots*, pp. 125, 132. • **65**. Meeting of the TUC General Council subcommittee with the Cabinet subcommittee, 20 August 1931, Bevin Papers II 7/8. • **66**. Kirkwood, *My Life of Revolt*, p. 248. • **67**. Ramsay MacDonald to Emmanuel Shinwell, 24 August 1931, Shinwell Papers 3/1. • **68**. Marquand, *Ramsay MacDonald*, p. 644. • **69**. Reginald Sorensen, election address, 1931, Sorensen Papers 14/A.

9 'Reversal of parts':
From Crisis to Popular Front, 1932–1939

1. Andrew Thorpe, 'The Membership of the Communist Party of Great Britain, 1920–1945', *Historical Journal*, 43, 2000, p. 781. • **2**. William Woodruff, *The Road to Nab End: An Extraordinary Northern Childhood* (1993), pp. 382–3. • **3**. *News Chronicle*, 11 October 1936. • **4**. See Pugh, 'Hurrah for the Blackshirts!', pp. 198–202; Philip M. Coupland, 'Left-Wing Fascism in Theory and Practice: the Case of the British Union of Fascists', *Twentieth Century British History*, 13, 2002. • **5**. Nellie Driver, 'From the Shadows of Exile', unpublished MSS, n.d., p. 30, J. B. Priestley Library, Bradford University. • **6**. Quoted in Thomas Linehan, *East*

London for Mosley (1996), p. 262. • **7**. Speech notes, 30 June 1932, Citrine Papers 4/4. • **8**. Memorandum, 27 January 1932, Citrine Papers 4/4. • **9**. Ernest Bevin to G. D. H. Cole, 31 December 1935, in Alan Bullock, *The Life and Times of Ernest Bevin*, vol. 1, (1960), p. 532; Pimlott, *Hugh Dalton*, p. 251. • **10**. See Miles Taylor, 'Labour and the Constitution', in Duncan Tanner et al. (eds), *Labour's First Century* (2000), pp. 151–80. • **11**. *Financial Times*, 29 January 1924. • **12**. K. O. Morgan, *Wales: Rebirth of a Nation 1880–1980* (1982), p. 298. • **13**. *Labour Magazine*, August 1930. • **14**. Labour Party, *Annual Conference Report*, 1935, pp. 238–40. • **15**. Philip Williamson, 'The Labour Party and the House of Lords 1918–31', *Parliamentary History*, 10, 1991, pp. 326–7; D. C. Sutherland, 'Peeresses, Parliament and Prejudice: The Admission of Women to the House of Lords 1900–1963', Cambridge University PhD thesis, 2000, pp. 271–2. • **16**. Kenneth Harris, *Attlee* (1982), pp. 132–3. • **17**. For a recent expression of this view see Bernard Porter, *The Absent-Minded Imperialists* (2004). • **18**. *Fabian Tract No. 83* (1903) and *No. 128* (1906). • **19**. *Daily News*, 7 September 1926. • **20**. *Socialist* (Seaham CLP), October 1937; *Gateshead Labour Herald*, January, July and August 1938. • **21**. Labour Party, *Annual Conference Report*, 1921, p. 208. • **22**. *Lansbury's Labour Weekly*, 23 May 1925. • **23**. *The Colonial Empire*, Labour Party Report adopted by the annual conference October 1933: Stansgate Papers ST/91. • **24**. *Labour Organiser*, February 1931. • **25**. *Gateshead Labour Herald*, April and May 1920. • **26**. Robert Millward and John Singleton (eds.), *The Political Economy of Nationalisation in Britain 1920–1950* (1995), pp. 212–29. • **27**. ibid., pp. 88–112. • **28**. Kevin Manton, 'Playing Both Sides Against the Middle: The Labour Party and the Wholesaling Industry 1919–1951', *Twentieth Century British History*, 18, 2007, pp. 306–33. • **29**. Richard Toye, 'The Labour Party and Keynes' in E. H. H. Green and D. M. Tanners (eds.), *The Strange Survival of Liberal England* (2007), p. 159. • **30**. Bullock, *Bevin*, pp. 425–6. • **31**. Barbara Castle, *Fighting All the Way* (1993), pp. 55–6. • **32**. Wrexham Trades Council and CLP minutes, 9 February and 16 August 1932, quoted in Duncan Tanner, 'Labour and its membership', in Tanner, *Labour's First Century*, p. 253. • **33**. London Labour Party executive minutes, 9 April, 9 July and 13 September 1931. • **34**. London Labour Party executive minutes, 17 September 1931. • **35**. Figures in London Labour Party Papers, London Metropolitan Archives 2417/B155; Scottish Labour Party, annual report, May 1935. • **36**. Merton and Morden Labour Party, 3/1a, note by Dorothy Lidhall. • **37**. *London News*, August 1939. • **38**. Ben Pimlott, *Labour and the Left in the 1930s* (1977), pp. 111–38. • **39**. Pugh, *Women and the Women's Movement*, p. 131. • **40**. ibid., p. 126. • **41**. See *Labour Woman*, August 1931, p. 114. • **42**. Lewis Mates, *The Spanish Civil War and the British Left* (2007), pp. 96–104. • **43**. Sam Davies, *Liverpool Labour* (1996), p. 178; Leah Manning, *A Life for Education*, p. 104; Edith Summerskill, *A Woman's World* (1967), pp. 50–3. • **44**. North Lambeth Labour Party minutes 27 February and 7 September 1930. • **45**. ibid., 15 November 1929, 16 May 1930. • **46**. *Hansard*: House of Commons Debates, 1934, vol. 291, cols.

1192–3. • **47**. Keith Laybourn, '"There ought not to be one law for the rich and another for the poor which is the case today": The Labour Party, Lotteries, Gaming, Gambling and Bingo, c.1900–1960s', *History*, 93, 2008, p. 212. • **48**. John Wilmot, Fulham East election address, in North Lambeth Labour Party Papers 1/12. • **49**. *East Fulham Elector*, 25 October 1933. • **50**. 'A Call to the People of London', Labour Party manifesto, LCC elections 1934, Morrison Papers 8/10. • **51**. Labour Party, *Annual Conference Report*, 1935, p. 178. • **52**. Butler and Stokes, *Political Change in Britain*, p. 77. • **53**. Tom Stannage, *Baldwin Thwarts the Opposition* (1980), pp. 272, 287–99. • **54**. *Daily Mirror*, 2 June 1939. • **55**. Hugh Cudlipp, *Publish and Be Damned!* (1953), p. 229. • **56**. ibid., p. 192. • **57**. Mass Observation file report 126, May 1940, section 2, p. 8. • **58**. Mass Observation file report 1420, September 1942, pp. 33–4. • **59**. Mass Observation file report A11, December 1938, pp. 7–12. • **60**. *Gateshead Labour Herald*, March 1936. • **61**. ibid., June 1936. • **62**. *Daily Herald*, 4 September 1937. • **63**. Mates, *Spanish Civil War*, pp. 145–53, 165–73. • **64**. See Cole in *Political Quarterly*, 7, 1936, pp. 490–7, and Dalton, ibid., p. 485. • **65**. A. L. Rowse, 'The Present and Immediate Future of the Labour Party', *Political Quarterly*, 9, 1938, p. 28. • **66**. Frome DLP minutes, 23 January and 8 May 1937, 14 May 1938. • **67**. Hendon CLP minutes, 15 March 1936, 7 September 1940. • **68**. Merton and Morden Labour Party minutes, 17 May 1938, 21 February 1939. • **69**. North Lambeth Labour Party Papers 1/4, BLPES. • **70**. R. P. Hastings, 'The Birmingham Labour Movement 1918–1945', *Midland History*, 5, 1979–80. • **71**. Bishop Auckland Labour Party minutes, 9 February, 13 April and 13 July 1939, 11 January 1940. • **72**. Scottish Executive minutes, 3 June 1936, 10 March and 19 April 1937, 3 July 1939, Mitchell Library, Glasgow: Scottish Labour Party Papers TD 1384/1/1. • **73**. *Gateshead Labour Herald*, May 1936, August 1936. • **74**. ibid., April 1937. • **75**. Mates, *Spanish Civil War*, pp. 40–1. • **76**. *News Chronicle*, 17 July 1936; *Unity: True Or Sham?*, Labour Party pamphlet, February 1939, p. 3. • **77**. Martin Pugh, 'The Liberal Party and the Popular Front', *English Historical Review*, 121, 2006. pp. 1331–3. • **78**. *News Chronicle*, 11 and 28 May, and 16, 18, 21 and 25 July 1936; *Town Crier*, 17 June 1938. • **79**. *News Chronicle*, 8 July 1936; *Derby Daily Telegraph*, 22 June and 4 July 1936; Wilfrid Roberts to Philip Noel-Baker, 26 June 1936; Noel-Baker to Roberts (copy), 29 June 1936; F. Beaufort-Palmer to Philip Noel-Baker, 6 July 1936, Noel-Baker Papers 1/65. • **80**. Pugh, 'The Liberal Party and the Popular Front', p. 1337. • **81**. *Manchester Guardian*, 25 and 26 June 1937. • **82**. *News Chronicle*, 1, 2, 4, 5 and 6 April 1938. • **83**. ibid., 18 and 21 March, 11, 28 and 29 April, and 5 May 1938. • **84**. ibid., 14 and 23 April 1938. • **85**. ibid., 7, 9 and 10 May 1938. • **86**. ibid., 14 May 1938. • **87**. Merton and Morden Labour Party minutes, 18 April 1938. • **88**. Quoted in Graves, *Labour Women*, p. 205. • **89**. Graves, *Labour Women*, pp. 205–6. • **90**. Labour Party, *Annual Conference Report*, 1937, p. 161. • **91**. Wilfrid Roberts to Clement Attlee (copy), 1 October 1938, Roberts Papers 308/3/PF/5. • **92**. Gordon-Walker Diary, 12 October 1938, Gordon-Walker Papers

2/1. • **93**. ibid., 13 October 1938. • **94**. ibid., 13 and 15 October 1938. • **95**. *News Chronicle*, 17 October 1938; Patrick Gordon-Walker to *Reynolds News*, 16 October 1938. • **96**. National agent (copy), 19 December, 1938, Gordon-Walker Papers 2/1. • **97**. W. G. Bayley (copy), 5 December 1938, Gordon-Walker Papers 2/1. • **98**. Ben Pimlott, *Labour and the Left in the 1930s*, pp. 157–8. • **99**. Harold Macmillan to Hugh Dalton, 13 October 1938 and Dalton's reply (copy), 20 October 1938, Dalton Papers 5/2; Pimlott, *Hugh Dalton* pp. 258–61. • **100**. *Unity: True or Sham?*, Labour Party pamphlet, February 1939, p. 3. • **101**. *Manchester Guardian*, 13 December 1938; Scottish Executive minutes 19 December 1938, Scottish Labour Party Papers TD 1384/1/1. • **102**. C. P. Trevelyan to the Duchess of Atholl, 28 September 1938, Trevelyan Papers 153. • **103**. Note by Dalton, 23 January 1939, Dalton Papers 3/1. • **104**. Note by Dalton, 19 January 1939, Dalton Papers 3/1. • **105**. Labour Party, *Annual Conference Report*, 1939, pp. 44–53. • **106**. ibid., pp. 234–5. • **107**. 'File on Holderness', Sinclair Papers II 66/6. • **108**. *London News*, March 1939. • **109**. Philip Noel-Baker to Hugh Dalton (copy), 20 January 1939, Noel-Baker Papers 2/41. • **110**. Note by Dalton, 23 January 1939, Dalton Papers 3/1. • **111**. Birmingham Trades Council and Boro' Labour Party Report, 1937–8, p. 62, 1938, p. 6. • **112**. *Daily Mirror*, 10 March 1938.

10 *'Speak for England':*
Labour and the Second World War

1. Clement Attlee, *As It Happened* (1954), p. 111. • **2**. Pimlott, *Hugh Dalton*, p. 268. • **3**. ibid., pp. 269–70. • **4**. Quoted in Donoughue and Jones, *Herbert Morrison*, pp. 271–2. • **5**. Quoted in Francis Williams, *A Prime Minister Remembers* (1961), p. 33. • **6**. Attlee, *As It Happened*, p. 113. • **7**. Labour Party, *Annual Conference Report* (1940), p. 141. • **8**. Labour Party, *Annual Conference Report* (1941), pp. 3–4. • **9**. Broadcast MSS, 2 November 1940, Alexander Papers 13/6. • **10**. Faversham Labour Party minutes, 26 July 1938; Frome DLP minutes, 9 September 1939; Gloucester Labour Party minutes, 20 April 1939. • **11**. Morden Ward Labour Party minutes, 4 and 21 April 1944. • **12**. Birmingham Trades Council and Boro' Labour Party, *Annual Reports 1939–40*, p. 8. • **13**. London Labour Party minutes, 20 June 1940, London Metropolitan Archives 24/7/A/003; Sheffield Labour Party minutes, 30 November 1941. • **14**. Hendon CLP minutes, 7 September 1940; Frome DLP minutes, 30 April 1940. • **15**. London Labour Party minutes, 27 November 1941; Faversham Labour Party minutes, 24 September 1942. • **16**. Bishop Auckland Labour Party minutes, 17 November 1941; Ian Mikardo, *Backbencher* (1988), p. 60. • **17**. Bishop Auckland Labour Party minutes, 5 February and 18 March 1943. • **18**. Labour Party, *Annual Conference Report*, 1942, p. 95. • **19**. London Labour Party minutes, 14 March 1940. • **20**. Merton and Morden Labour Party minutes, 13 May 1944. • **21**. *London News*, May 1942. • **22**. Bishop

Auckland Labour Party minutes, 31 August 1944. • **23**. Andrew Thorpe, 'Conservative Party Agents in Second World War Britain', *Twentieth Century British History*, 18, 2007, pp. 334–64. • **24**. Frome DLP minutes, 23 September and 2 December 1939, 31 August 1940. • **25**. Thorpe, 'Conservative Party Agents', pp. 361–2. • **26**. Quoted in John Campbell, *Nye Bevan: A Biography* (1987), p. 112. • **27**. Quoted in ibid., p. 128. • **28**. Quoted in Stephen Brooke, *Labour's War: The Labour Party During the Second World War* (1992), pp. 67–8. • **29**. R. P. Hastings, 'The Birmingham Labour Movement 1918–1945', *Midland History*, 5, 1979–80, p. 88; Birmingham Borough Labour Party (BBLP) executive minutes, 21 February 1944. • **30**. *Gloucester Labour News*, March and July 1943, June 1944. • **31**. London Labour Party minutes, 15 June and 26 October 1944. • **32**. Frome DLP minutes, 29 May 1945. • **33**. Pimlott, *High Dalton*, p. 346. • **34**. Chuter Ede Diary, 26 October 1942, in Kevin Jefferys (ed.), *Labour and the Wartime Coalition: From the Diary of James Chuter Ede 1941–45*, (1987), p. 103. • **35**. Quoted in Campbell, *Nye Bevan*, p. 96. • **36**. Dalton Diary, 15 June 1943. • **37**. Quoted in Trevor Burridge, *Clement Attlee: A Political Biography* (1985), p. 150. • **38**. Pugh, *Women and the Women's Movement*, p. 279. • **39**. Quoted in Thorpe, '"In a Rather Emotional State?": The Labour Party and British Intervention in Greece, 1944–45', *English Historical Review*, 121, 2006, p. 1082. • **40**. Pimlott, *Hugh Dalton*, p. 366. • **41**. Chuter Ede Diary, 7 August 1942, in Jefferys (ed.), *Labour and the Wartime Coalition*, p. 92. • **42**. Chuter Ede Diary, 1 April 1943, in Jefferys (ed.), *Labour and the Wartime Coalition*, p. 132. • **43**. *Political Quarterly*, 14, 1943, p. 246. • **44**. Paul Addison, *The Road to 1945* (1975), pp. 144–5. • **45**. Hugh Dalton, *The Fateful Years 1931–1945* (1957), p. 465. • **46**. Mikardo, *Backbencher*, p. 59. • **47**. Jeremy A. Crang, *The British Army and the People's War 1939–1945* (2000), pp. 114–17, 119. • **48**. ibid., p. 127. • **49**. Butler and Stokes, *Political Change in Britain*, p. 77. • **50**. Harold Nicolson, *Diaries and Letters 1939–45*, vol. 2 (1967), p. 467. • **51**. *Daily Mirror*, 6 January 1945. • **52**. *Gateshead Labour Herald*, August 1943. • **53**. Pimlott, *Hugh Dalton*, pp. 361–2; Ina Zweiniger-Bargielowska, *Austerity in Britain: Rationing, Controls and Consumption 1939–1955* (2000), pp. 487–90. • **54**. Quoted in Campbell, *Nye Bevan*, p. 94. • **55**. Pugh, *'Hurrah for the Blackshirts!'*, pp. 294–7. • **56**. *Gateshead Labour Herald*, December 1943. • **57**. ibid., April 1945. • **58**. Broadcast MSS, 11 June 1945, Alexander Papers 13/32. • **59**. *Gateshead Labour Herald*, December 1942 and January 1943; *Tribune*, 4 December 1942; *Gloucester Labour News*, January 1943. • **60**. Mikardo, *Backbencher*, p. 77. • **61**. ibid. • **62**. See S. Fielding, 'What did "The People" want? The meaning of the 1945 General Election', *Historical Journal*, 35, 1992; S. Fielding, P. Thompson and N. Tiratsoo, 'England Arise', in *The Labour Party and Popular Politics in 1940s Britain* (1995). • **63**. Fielding, 'What did "The People" want?, p. 67. • **64**. *Daily Mirror*, 4 May 1940. • **65**. ibid., 9 May 1940. • **66**. ibid., 18 January 1945. • **67**. ibid., 1 April 1945. • **68**. ibid., 21 April 1945. • **69**. Dalton Diary, 26 February 1944, quoted in Pimlott, *Hugh Dalton*, p. 365. • **70**. Addison, *Road to 1945*, p. 252; Clement Attlee to Ernest Bevin, 1 March

1944, Attlee Papers Box 7; Attlee to Hugh Dalton, 13 July 1945, Dalton Papers 8/1. • **71**. Mass Observation Report 2268, 'The General Election', October 1945, p. 10; E. M. Simmonds to Morgan Phillips, 3 July 1945, 'General Election 1945', Phillips Papers. • **72**. Mikardo, *Backbencher*, p. 84. • **73**. Broadcast MSS, 11 June 1945, Alexander Papers 13/32. • **74**. Morgan Phillips to Long Maddox 26 June 1945, and reply 27 June 1945, 'General Election 1945', Phillips Papers. • **75**. Harold Macmillan, *Tides of Fortune 1945–55* (1979), p. 32. • **76**. Broadcast MSS 29 June 1945, Morrison Papers 2/2. • **77**. *The Times*, 9 April 1945. • **78**. Agnes Smith to Morgan Phillips, 5 June 1945, 'General Election 1945', Phillips Papers. • **79**. Hattersley, *Who Goes Home?*, p. 2. • **80**. *Daily Mirror*, 28 and 30 May 1945. • **81**. Quoted in Burridge, *Attlee*, p. 156. • **82**. Frome DLP minutes, 11 August 1945. • **83**. Morgan Phillips, circular letter to agents and candidates, 2 June 1945, 'General Election 1945', Phillips Papers. • **84**. BLPES, election addresses, 1945, 723/2. • **85**. BLPES, 723/5; Sorensen Papers 14c/66. • **86**. LP/ELEC/1945/1 'Biographies of Labour Candidates'; BLPES 723/3. • **87**. BLPES 723/5 and 22. • **88**. Michael Foot Papers M1; 'General Election 1945', Phillips Papers. • **89**. BLPES 723/17. • **90**. BLPES 723/15. • **91**. BLPES 723/3. • **92**. BLPES 723/8. • **93**. BLPES 723/2 and 4. • **94**. *London News*, February–March 1945; 'For Lewisham and the Nation', Morrison Papers 2/2.

11 *'We are the masters now': Labour, Consensus and Affluence, 1945–1959*

1. Chuter Ede Diary, 28 July 1945, in Jefferys (ed.), *Labour and the Wartime Coalition*, p. 229; draft autobiography, Attlee Papers 1/17. • **2**. Jean Mann, *Woman in Parliament* (1962), p. 13. • **3**. Richard Toye, 'The Labour Party and Keynes', in E. H. H. Green and D. M. Tanner (eds.), *The Strange Survival of Liberal England* (2007), pp. 172–3. • **4**. Anthony Crosland, *The Future of Socialism* (1956), p. 115. • **5**. Draft autobiography, Attlee Papers 1/20. • **6**. Mikardo, *Backbencher*, pp. 93–4. • **7**. Gordon-Walker Diary, 8 August 1945, Gordon-Walker Papers 1/6. • **8**. Pontypridd Labour Party minutes, 16 January 1950. • **9**. Dinah B. M. Evans, 'The Dynamics of Labour Party Politics in Swansea 1941–1964', University of Wales Bangor PhD thesis, 2008, pp. 51–67. • **10**. South Lewisham CLP, annual report, 1952. • **11**. Agent's report, South Lewisham, 30 September 1948. • **12**. Agent's report, South Lewisham, 30 June 1952. • **13**. Agent's report, South Lewisham, 30 September 1948. • **14**. South Lewisham CLP, report, 22 February 1952. • **15**. BBLP, annual report, 1947. • **16**. BBLP minutes, 5 June and 10 July 1946, 7 March 1948. • **17**. BBLP minutes, 9 November 1949. • **18**. BBLP annual report, 1955; BBLP executive minutes, 25 February 1955. • **19**. Clarke, *The Cripps Version*, pp. 518–21. • **20**. NEC minutes, 24 January 1950. • **21**. George Wigg, election address, 1950, Wigg Papers 6/5.

• **22**. Labour Party RD350, April 1950, p. 15. • **23**. *Daily Mail*, 3 July 1947. • **24**. NEC minutes, 20 March 1950. • **25**. General secretary's report, NEC minutes, 20 March 1950. • **26**. NEC minutes, 22 March 1950; *Tribune*, 10 March 1950. • **27**. Labour Party, RD350, April 1950, 'General Election 1950'. • **28**. Labour Party, RD350, p. 5. • **29**. ibid., p. 6. • **30**. Campbell, *Nye Bevan*, p. 233; Hugh Dalton to Nye Bevan, 7 April 1951, Dalton Papers 9/18. • **31**. BBLP executive minutes, 25 May 1951 and 'Secretary's Report on Municipal Elections, 1951'. • **32**. BBLP executive minutes, 25 May 1951. • **33**. Harris, *Attlee*, p. 485. • **34**. ibid., p. 486. • **35**. BBLP, annual report, 1951. • **36**. ibid. • **37**. See Foot's election addresses for 1950 and 1951, Foot Papers M1. • **38**. Quoted in Harris, *Attlee*, p. 491. • **39**. Ina Zweiniger-Bargielowska, 'Explaining the Gender Gap', in Martin Francis and Ina Zweiniger-Bargielowska (eds.), *The Conservatives and British Society, 1880–1990* (1996), p. 198. • **40**. 'General Secretary's Report on the General Election Campaign', NEC minutes, 7 November 1951. • **41**. Labour Party Women's Organisation, *Annual Conference Report* (1952), pp. 12–13. • **42**. Mikardo, *Backbencher*, pp. 111–13. • **43**. *News Chronicle*, 6 October 1952; *Daily Herald*, 15 October 1952; Noel-Baker Papers 2/99. • **44**. *Daily Herald*, 14 October 1952. • **45**. PLP minutes, 16 March 1955. • **46**. Mikardo, *Backbencher*, p. 130. • **47**. ibid., p. 123. • **48**. BBLP minutes, 11 March 1955. • **49**. *News Chronicle*, 1 October 1952. • **50**. Mikardo, *Backbencher*, p. 126. • **51**. Andrew Walling, 'Modernisation, Policy Debate and Organisation in the Labour Party, 1951–1964', University of Wales Bangor PhD thesis, 2001, pp. 273–9; Andrew L. Flinn, Gidon Cohen and Lewis Mates, 'Herbert Morrison and the South Lewisham Labour Party', *Lewisham History Journal*, 13, 2005, p. 51. • **52**. Richard Whiting, *The Labour Party and Taxation* (2000), p. 91. • **53**. Lord Birkenhead, *Walter Monckton* (1969), p. 274. • **54**. Martin Pugh, *ODNB* (2004), vol. 38, pp. 599–602. • **55**. Interim Report of the Subcommittee on Party Organisation, 1955, p. 6, General Secretary's Papers GS/HW/1–22. • **56**. BBLP executive minutes, 25 May 1955, 'Secretary's Report of the General Election, 26 May 1955'. • **57**. BBLP minutes, 11 March 1955. • **58**. Sorensen Papers 14C/94; Foot Papers M1. • **59**. David Butler, *The British General Election of 1955* (1955), p. 80. • **60**. Quoted in Kevin Jefferys, *Anthony Crosland* (1999), p. 59. • **61**. Interim Report of the Subcommittee on Party Organisation, pp. 6–7 GS/HW/1–22. • **62**. Walling, 'Modernisation', p. 163; quoted in D. Tanner and S. Fielding, 'The Rise of the Left Revisited: Labour Party Culture in Post-war Manchester and Salford', *Labour History Review*, 71, 3, 2006, p. 215. • **63**. Tilley, *Churchill's Favourite Socialist*, p. 25; Hattersley, *Who Goes Home?*, pp. 11 and 17. • **64**. Interim Report of the Subcommittee on Party Organisation, pp. 6 and 23, GS/HW/1–22. • **65**. Newcastle West Labour Party minutes, 25 August 1956, 7 February 1957. • **66**. Interim Report of the Subcommittee on Party Organisation, p. 7, GS/HW/1–22. • **67**. Pugh, *Women and the Women's Movement*, p. 303. • **68**. ibid., pp. 303–4. • **69**. Monica Whately to F. Pethick-Lawrence, (copy), n.d.,

The Women's Library: Six Point Group Papers Box 526. • **70**. Quoted Melanie Phillips, *The Divided House* (1980), pp. 159–60. • **71**. Labour Party Women's Organisation, *Annual Conference Report*, 1946, p. 16. • **72**. Equal Pay Campaign Committee minutes, 5 March 1948: The Women's Library Box 157. • **73**. Mikardo, *Backbencher*, p. 78. • **74**. Agent's report, South Lewisham, 30 September 1958. • **75**. Agent's report, South Lewisham, 30 June 1953. • **76**. Agent's report, South Lewisham, 31 December 1954; annual report, South Lewisham, 1957. • **77**. Mark Abrams, 'Class and Politics', *Encounter*, October 1961. • **78**. J. Goldthorpe and Lockwood, 'The Affluent Worker and the Thesis of *Embourgeoisement*', *Sociology*, October 1962. • **79**. Quoted in Lawrence Black, *The Political Culture of the Left in Affluent Britain 1951–1964* (2003), pp. 15, 125. • **80**. Quoted in Jefferys, *Anthony Crosland*, p. 30. • **81**. Patricia Hollis, *Jennie Lee: A Life* (1997), p. 223; Campbell, *Nye Bevan*, pp. 63–4, 69–70.

12 'A grand conception': Labour in the Wilson Era, 1960–1976

1. Quoted in Philip M. Williams, *Hugh Gaitskell* (1979), p. 293. • **2**. Richard Crossman, *The Backbench Diaries of Richard Crossman* (1981), 23 October 1959, p. 796. • **3**. Ben Pimlott, *Harold Wilson* (1992), p. 227. • **4**. Gordon-Walker Diary, 12 May 1960, Gordon-Walker Papers 1/14. • **5**. Anthony Crosland to Hugh Gaitskell (copy), 4 May 1960, Crosland Papers 6/1. • **6**. Hugh Gaitskell to Anthony Crosland, 4 September 1960, Crosland Papers 6/1. • **7**. Gordon-Walker Diary, 12 May 1960, Gordon-Walker Papers 1/14. • **8**. Gordon-Walker Diary, 2 October 1960, Gordon-Walker Papers 1/14. • **9**. Quoted in John Campbell, *Roy Jenkins: A Biography* (1983), p. 66. • **10**. 'A Manifesto Addressed to the Labour Movement', n.d., copy in Shinwell Papers 31/1 and Crosland Papers 6/1. • **11**. Memorandum, July 1961, Crosland Papers 6/1. • **12**. ibid. • **13**. Pimlott, *Harold Wilson*, p. 195. • **14**. Anthony Wedgwood Benn to Anthony Crosland, 31 October 1960, Crosland Papers 6/1. • **15**. ibid. • **16**. Campbell, *Roy Jenkins*, pp. 50–2. • **17**. Gordon-Walker Diary, 19 May 1960, Gordon-Walker Papers 1/14. • **18**. Quoted in Pimlott, *Harold Wilson*, p. 255. • **19**. Quoted in Gordon-Walker Diary, 2 June 1960, Gordon-Walker Papers 1/14. • **20**. Pimlott, *Harold Wilson*, p. 264. • **21**. Crossman Diary, *Backbench Diaries*, 31 January 1965, pp. 118–19. • **22**. See file 'Profumo Fan Mail', Wigg Papers 3/85. • **23**. Anthony Crosland Grimsby election address, 1964, Crosland Papers 7/5. • **24**. BBLP executive minutes, 7 May 1964. • **25**. David Butler and Anthony King, *The British General Election of 1964* (1965), pp. 369–70. • **26**. Sara Barker, circular letter to CLPs, 6 January 1965. • **27**. BBLP executive minutes, 'Report on the General Election of October 15 1964'; Butler and King, *The British General Election of 1964*, p. 226. • **28**. 'Financial Agreement', Crosland Papers 7/5. • **29**. 'Report of the Agent',

Crosland Papers 7/5. • **30**. Derby Labour Party, annual reports, 1960 and 1961.
• **31**. Jim Cattermole to Philip Noel-Baker, 5 July 1961, Noel-Baker Papers 1/187;
Derby Labour Party, annual report, 1962. • **32**. East Midlands Regional Council,
AGM, June 1962 and 1967. • **33**. Evans, 'The dynamics of Labour Party Politics
in Swansea', pp. 65–7. • **34**. K. O. Morgan in Butler and King, *The British General
Election of 1964*, p. 268. • **35**. Mikardo, *Backbencher*, p. 174. • **36**. 'General Election
Report 1966', South Lewisham Labour Party Papers 14/21. • **37**. Putney Labour
Party, annual report, 1964, Jenkins Papers 5/1. • **38**. Putney Labour Party, annual
report, 1966, Jenkins Papers 5/1. • **39**. Questionnaire, Jenkins Papers 5/1.
• **40**. *Putney Labour News*, February 1965, Jenkins Papers 5/2. • **41**. Mikardo,
Backbencher, p. 171. • **42**. Philip Noel-Baker to T. B. Richardson (copy), 22 April
1966, Noel-Baker Papers 3/104. • **43**. Derby Labour Party, annual report, 1967,
Noel-Baker Papers 1/210. • **44**. 'Report on the General Election of October 15
1964', BBLP executive minutes. • **45**. Mikardo, *Backbencher*, p. 173. • **46**. BBLP
minutes, 13 June 1962. • **47**. Gordon-Walker Diary, 11 September 1962, Gordon-
Walker Papers 1/14. • **48**. Butler and King, *The British General Election of 1964*,
pp. 362–3. • **49**. *Birmingham Post*, 21 and 24 September 1964. • **50**. Quoted in
Pimlott, *Harold Wilson*, p. 328. • **51**. Anthony Crosland to Hugh Gaitskell,
November 1960, Crosland Papers 6/1. • **52**. Tony Benn, *Out of the Wilderness:
Diaries 1963–1967* (1987), 5 May 1964, p. 110. • **53**. Reports to the secretary of the
Scottish Labour Party, 14 and 26 October 1977, Mitchell Library, Glasgow:
Scottish Labour Party Papers TD1384/1/1. • **54**. Quoted in Peter Paterson, *Tired
and Emotional: The Life of Lord George-Brown* (1993), pp. 31–2. • **55**. ibid., pp. 29–
33. • **56**. Anthony Crosland, Grimsby election address, 1966, Crosland Papers
7/6. • **57**. Crossman Diary, *Backbench Diaries*, 1 April 1966, pp. 488–9. • **58**. ibid.
• **59**. David Butler and Anthony King, *The British General Election of 1966* (1966),
p. 211. • **60**. Jeremy Bray to Michael Foot, 20 November 1980, Foot Papers L10.
• **61**. Paterson, *Tired and Emotional*, pp. 38–9. • **62**. George Thomson, secret
memorandum, 11 May 1967, Wigg Papers 4/147. • **63**. Memorandum, 19
December 1967, Wigg Papers 4/147. • **64**. Newcastle West Labour Party minutes,
25 November 1967. • **65**. Newcastle West Labour Party, secretary's reports, 31
December 1953, 31 December 1954, 31 December 1955; minutes, 27 February
1965, 2 August 1970, 14 October 1971. • **66**. BBLP minutes, 8 February 1967.
• **67**. Putney Labour Party, annual report, 1967, Jenkins Papers 5/1. • **68**. Philip
Noel-Baker to Gordon Parker (copy), 30 April 1969, Noel-Baker Papers 1/228.
• **69**. Philip Noel-Baker to Sara Barker (copy), 7 June 1968, Noel-Baker Papers
1/211. • **70**. Gordon Parker to Philip Noel-Baker, 28 October 1965; Noel-Baker
to Parker (copy), 8 July 1965; Parker to Noel-Baker, 6 July 1965, Noel-Baker
Papers 1/209. • **71**. Castle, *Fighting All the Way*, p. 412. • **72**. BBLP executive
minutes, 5 February 1969. • **73**. Anthony Crosland, Grimsby election address,
1970, Crosland Papers 7/7. • **74**. BBLP minutes, 26 August 1970. • **75**. Ivor Crewe,
Neil Day and Anthony Fox, *The British Electorate 1963–1987* (1991), p. 19; David

Butler and Michael Pinto-Duschinsky, *The British General Election of 1970* (1971), p. 386. • **76**. *New Statesman*, 26 May 1972. • **77**. Castle, *Fighting All the* Way, p. 448. • **78**. Quoted in Jefferys, *Anthony Crosland*, p. 143. • **79**. David Butler and Dennis Kavanagh, *The British General Election of February 1974* (1974), p. 202. • **80**. ibid., pp. 34–5. • **81**. ibid., p. 237. • **82**. ibid., p. 64. • **83**. Anthony Crosland, Grimsby election address, 1974, Crosland Papers 77/8. • **84**. Hugh Jenkins, Putney election address, 1974, Jenkins Papers 5/3. • **85**. BBLP executive minutes, 27 January and 6 March 1974. • **86**. ibid. • **87**. Butler and Kavanagh, *The British General Election of February 1974*, p. 271. • **88**. ibid., pp. 214–15. • **89**. Bernard Donoughue, *Downing Street Diary: With Harold Wilson in No. 10* (2005), 12 June 1974, p. 138. • **90**. Anthony Crosland, Grimsby election address, 1974, Crosland Papers 7/9. • **91**. Donoughue, *Downing Street Diary*, pp. 138, 140–1, 154–6, 185, 189, 191, 193. • **92**. David Butler and Dennis Kavanagh, *The British General Election of October 1974* (1975), p. 252.

13 *'Forward march halted':*
Labour in Decline, 1976–1994

1. Tony Benn, *Against the Tide: Diaries 1973–76* (1989), 16 March 1976, p. 535. • **2**. Quoted in Jefferys, *Anthony Crosland*, p. 193. • **3**. Quoted in Bernard Donoughue, *Downing Street Diary Volume Two: With James Callaghan in No. 10* (2008), p. 435. • **4**. ibid., p. 18. • **5**. Memorandum, n.d., Prentice Papers 2/4. • **6**. Reginald Prentice letter (copy), 12 January 1975, Prentice Papers 2/5. • **7**. Letter dated 16 July 1975, Prentice Papers 2/6. • **8**. Harold Wilson to Reginald Prentice, 30 October 1975; Prentice to Wilson (copy), 27 October 1975, Prentice Papers 3/3. • **9**. Reginald Prentice to Ron Todd (copy), 30 November 1976, Prentice Papers 2/4. • **10**. Benn Diary, *Against the Tide*, 23 November to 2 December 1976, pp. 670–9. • **11**. Donoughue, *Downing Street Diary Volume Two*, p. 59. • **12**. ibid., pp. 357–8, 362. • **13**. Mikardo, *Backbencher*, p. 200. • **14**. Donoughue, *Downing Street Diary, Volume Two*, pp. 432–3. • **15**. Scottish Executive minutes, 11 November 1978, Mitchell Library, Glasgow: Scottish Labour Party papers TD1384. • **16**. Donoughue, *Downing Street Diary Volume Two*, p. 371. • **17**. David Butler and Dennis Kavanagh, *The British General Election of 1979* (1980), p. 180. • **18**. Bernard Donoughue, *Prime Minister* (1987), p. 191. • **19**. Butler and Kavanagh, *The British General Election of 1979*, pp. 130–1. • **20**. ibid., p. 313. • **21**. See correspondence file in Foot Papers 6/1. • **22**. K. O. Morgan, *Michael Foot: A Life* (2007), pp. 379–80. • **23**. *Guardian*, 18 October 1976. • **24**. Memorandum, 23 March 1976, Foot Papers C13. • **25**. Quoted in Morgan, *Michael Foot*, p. 393. • **26**. 'Declaration For Social Democracy', 25 January 1981, Foot Papers L27/13; Denis Healey, *The Time of My Life* (1989), pp. 479–80. • **27**. Roy Jenkins, *A Life at the Centre* (1991), pp. 514, 526. • **28**. 'The

Gang Show', Labour Party Information Paper, n.d., Foot Papers L27/13.
• **29**. See Peter Shore Papers III/23. • **30**. *Guardian*, 18 November 1981. • **31**. Harold
Wilson to Neville Sandelson (copy), 21 July 1975, Prentice Papers 3/3. • **32**. Mrs
Shirley Torode, note from telephone message, n.d., Foot Papers L5. • **33**. Jim
Cusick to Michael Foot, 6 December 1981, Foot Papers L5. • **34**. Duncan Tanner
and Stephen Fielding. 'The Rise of the Left Revisited', pp. 226–7. • **35**. ibid.,
p. 224. • **36**. Michael Stanley to Michael Foot, n.d., Foot Papers L4. • **37**. See
Foot Papers L5. • **38**. Stanley Clinton-Davies to Michael Foot, 13 November
1981, Foot Papers L4. • **39**. *The Times*, 20 December 1982. • **40**. Stanley Cohen
to Michael Foot, 10 July 1981, Foot Papers L4. • **41**. Michael Foot to Frank
Field (copy), 15 April 1981, Foot Papers L4. • **42**. Synopsis of Manifesto Group
meeting, 18 March 1981, Foot Papers L4. • **43**. 'Militant Tendency Report',
NEC, 23 June 1982. • **44**. Peter Taaffe to Ron Hayward, 8 February 1982, Foot
Papers L25/7; *Labour Solidarity Campaign*, 12 May 1982, Foot Papers L25/7.
• **45**. Statement by Foot, 19 June 1982, Foot Papers L25/7. • **46**. *South London
Press*, 20 April 1982. • **47**. *Standard*, 16 November 1981. • **48**. Scottish Executive
minutes, 10 October 1987, Scottish Labour Party Papers TD 1384. • **49**. Quoted
in Morgan, *Michael Foot*, p. 423. • **50**. David Butler and Dennis Kavanagh, *The
British General Election of 1983* (1984), p. 57. • **51**. Shore Diary, 10 May 1983, Shore
Papers 1/22. • **52**. Shore Diary, 11 May 1983, Shore Papers 1/22. • **53**. ibid. • **54**.
Butler and Kavanagh, *The British General Election of 1983*, p. 275. • **55**. Shore
Diary, 26 May 1983, Shore Papers 1/22. • **56**. Quoted in Butler and Kavanagh,
The British General Election of 1983, p. 253. • **57**. Shore Diary, 26 May 1983, Shore
Papers 1/22. • **58**. ibid., 30 May 1983, Shore Papers 1/22. • **59**. 'Analysis of the
1983 Election', Foot Papers L26/18. • **60**. General Secretary's Report, 9 June
1983, Foot Papers L 26/18. • **61**. 'Analysis of the 1983 Election', Foot Papers
L26/18. • **62**. Henry Neuburger, 'What Went Wrong?', 24 June 1983, Kinnock
Papers Box 89. • **63**. 'General Secretary's Report', 9 June 1983, Foot Papers
L26/18. • **64**. ibid. • **65**. Crewe, Day and Fox, *The British Electorate*, p. 19; Butler
and Kavanagh, *The British General Election of 1983*, p. 296–7. • **66**. Patrick Seyd
and Paul Whiteley, *Labour's Grass Roots: The Politics of Party Membership* (1992),
pp. 196–8. • **67**. G. MacGill to Eric Heffer, 7 October 1985, Heffer Papers 10/81.
• **68**. J. J. G. Burke, 'Leading the Labour Party 1983–1992', Cambridge University
PhD thesis, 2004, p. 142. • **69**. John Evans to Neil Kinnock, 15 December 1989,
Kinnock Papers Box 83. • **70**. *Findings of the Independent Investigation Into the
Liverpool District Labour Party*, Heffer Papers 9/9. • **71**. *Witch-Hunt News*, 2,
March 1986. • **72**. J. L. Whitty to Terry Harrison, 6 March 1986, Heffer Papers
9/7. • **73**. Letter by a Liverpool councillor to Neil Kinnock (copy), 16 March
1990, Kinnock Papers Box 83. • **74**. John Evans, note, 30 July 1990, Kinnock
Papers Box 83. • **75**. Speech 'She is on trial', 1986, Kinnock Papers Box 326B.
• **76**. See Kinnock Papers Box 326B. • **77**. See file in Kinnock Papers Box 412.
• **78**. David Butler and Dennis Kavanagh, *The British General Election of 1987*

(1988), p. 271. • **79**. ibid., p. 274; Crewe, Day and Fox, *The British Electorate*, p. 19. • **80**. Butler and Kavanagh, *The British General Election of 1987*, p. 203. • **81**. 'General Secretary's Report', 9 June 1983, Foot Papers L26/18. • **82**. 'Strategy in 1990 for the General Election', Kinnock Papers Box 14. • **83**. Kinnock Papers Box 95. • **84**. 'Note on Levy Payers' Participation in OMOV Reselections', Kinnock Papers Box 240. • **85**. File on electoral reform, Foot Papers L10. • **86**. Jack Straw, press notice, 23 March 1981, Foot Papers L10. • **87**. Peter Russell, 'Govan By Election', Scottish Labour Party Papers, TD 1384/11/7. • **88**. 'Briefing Note', Donald Dewar, n.d., and 'Note on meeting with Donald Dewar and Murray Elder', John Reid, 10 January 1990, Kinnock Papers Box 83. • **89**. Minutes of the working party, 4 December 1991; Iain Maclean letter, 3 October 1991, Kinnock Papers Box 60. • **90**. 'The 1992 Election and the Sheffield Rally', Kinnock Papers Box 13/3. • **91**. Jon Sopel, *Tony Blair: The Moderniser* (1995), p. 152.

14 *'She's changed it all': Tony Blair, Lady Thatcher and New Labour, 1994– 2007*

1. Tony Blair to Michael Foot, 28 July 1982, Foot Papers MF/L/31. • **2**. Peter Mandelson and Roger Liddle, *The Blair Revolution* (1996); Sopel, *Tony Blair: The Moderniser* (1995); John Rentoul, *Tony Blair* (1995); Anthony Seldon, *Blair* (2004). • **3**. Paddy Ashdown, *Diaries 1988–1997* (2000), p. 462. • **4**. Quoted in Sopel, *Tony Blair*, p. 7. • **5**. ibid. • **6**. Rentoul, *Tony Blair*, p. 20. • **7**. Quoted in Rentoul, *Tony Blair*, p. 53; quoted in Seldon, *Blair*, pp. 53–4. • **8**. Seldon, *Blair*, p. 52. • **9**. Quoted in ibid., p. 88. • **10**. *Sun*, 3 March 1993. • **11**. Quoted in Seldon, *Blair*, p. 124. • **12**. Alastair Campbell, *The Blair Years* (2007), pp. 58, 70–2. • **13**. ibid., pp. 25, 28–9, 35. • **14**. Stephen Pollard, *David Blunkett* (2005), p. 318. • **15**. Campbell, *The Blair Years*, 31 July 1995, p. 78. • **16**. Quoted in James Naughtie, *The Rivals: Blair and Brown* (2002), p. 265. • **17**. Campbell, *The Blair Years*, 30 August 2000, pp. 467–8. • **18**. Seldon, *Blair*, p. 121. • **19**. Mandelson and Liddle, *The Blair Revolution*, pp. vii, 20. • **20**. ibid., pp. 20, 27. • **21**. David Butler and Dennis Kavanagh, *The British General Election of 2001* (2001), p. 257; Stephen Fielding, *Labour: Decline and Renewal* (1999), p. 2. • **22**. Ashdown, *Diaries*, 17 July 1996, pp. 453–4. • **23**. *Guardian*, 10 July 2007. • **24**. Ashdown, *Diaries*, 14 July 1993, p. 228. • **25**. Campbell, *The Blair Years*, 26 April 1997, p. 179. • **26**. Ashdown, *Diaries*, 3 July 1998, p. 233. • **27**. Campbell, *The Blair Years*, p. 611. • **28**. ibid., 2 March 1995, p. 50, 7 March 1996, p. 105, 5 December 1996, p. 140. • **29**. *Guardian*, 26 April 2007. • **30**. *Observer*, 14 May 2006, 15 July 2007; *Guardian*, 16 October 2006. • **31**. *Guardian*, 17 March 2009. • **32**. *Observer*, 9 August 2009.

Bibliography

Primary sources

PRIVATE PAPERS

Christopher Addison Papers (Bodleian Library, Oxford)
A. V. Alexander Papers (Churchill College, Cambridge)
Clement Attlee Papers (Churchill College, Cambridge)
Austen Albu Papers (Churchill College, Cambridge)
Stanley Baldwin Papers (Cambridge University Library)
John Beckett MSS autobiography (Labour History Archive, Manchester)
Ernest Bevin Papers (Churchill College, Cambridge)
Andrew Bonar Law Papers (House of Lord RO)
Walter Citrine Papers (BLPES)
Stafford Cripps Papers (Nuffield College, Oxford)
Anthony Crosland Papers (BLPES)
Hugh Dalton Papers (BLPES)
Lord Murray of Elibank Papers (National Library of Scotland)
Michael Foot Papers (Labour History Archive, Manchester)
Herbert Gladstone Papers (British Library)
Patrick Gordon-Walker Papers (Churchill College Cambridge)
Richard Haldane Papers (National Library of Scotland)
Judith Hart Papers (Labour History Archive, Manchester)
Eric Heffer Papers (Labour History Archive, Manchester)
Hugh Jenkins Papers (BLPES)
Neil Kinnock Papers (Churchill College, Cambridge)
George Lansbury Papers (BLPES)
Ramsay MacDonald Papers (National Archives)
Ramsay MacDonald Papers (National Library of Scotland)
Hugh Macmillan Papers (National Library of Scotland)
Marshall Papers (Cumbria record office)
Herbert Morrison Papers (BLPES)

Sir Oswald Mosley Papers (Birmingham University Library)
Philip Noel-Baker Papers (Churchill College, Cambridge)
Morgan Phillips Papers (Labour History Archive, Manchester)
David Graham Pole Papers (Borthwick Institute, York University)
Arthur Ponsonby Papers (Bodleian Library, Oxford)
Reginald Prentice Papers (BLPES)
Jo Richardson/Ian Mikardo Papers (Labour History Archive,
    Manchester)
Wilfrid Roberts Papers (Modern Records Centre, Warwick University)
Lord Sankey Papers (Bodleian Library, Oxford)
Lord Selborne Papers (House of Lords RO)
Peter Shore Papers (BLPES)
Emmanuel Shinwell Papers (BLPES)
Jim Simmons Papers (Birmingham Central Library)
Sir Archibald Sinclair Papers (Churchill College, Cambridge)
Lord Sorensen Papers (House of Lords RO)
Viscount Stansgate Papers (House of Lords RO)
Arthur Steel-Maitland Papers (National Library of Scotland)
J. H. Thomas Papers (Kent CRO)
Ben Tillett Papers (Labour History Archive, Manchester)
Charles Trevelyan Papers (Newcastle University Library)
Wilfrid Whiteley Papers (Borthwick Institute, York University)
George Wigg Papers (BLPES)
Ellen Wilkinson Papers (Labour History Archive, Manchester)

PAPERS OF ORGANISATIONS

Barrow-in-Furness CLP
Bethnal Green Labour Party
Birmingham Borough Labour Party
Bishop Auckland Labour Party
Bishop Auckland Women's Section
Central Finsbury ILP
Colne Valley Labour League / Labour Party
Coventry Trades Council
Derby Labour Party (Noel-Baker Papers)
East Ham ILP
Fabian Society Women's Group
Faversham Labour Party
Feltham Labour Women's Section
Frome Labour Party
Gloucester Labour Party

Hendon CLP
Labour Party Archives:
  NEC minutes
  Parliamentary Labour Party minutes
  War Emergency: Workers National Committee minutes
  Subject files
  Morgan Phillips files
  Annual Conference Reports
  Press cuttings files
  Women's Labour League/Labour Party Women's Organisation
  Research Department
  Elections
Leeds LRC
London Labour Party
Merton and Morden Labour Party
Newcastle West Labour Party
North Lambeth Labour Party
Pontypridd Labour Party
Putney Labour Party (Hugh Jenkins Papers)
Salford Labour Party
Scottish Labour Party
Sheffield Labour Party
South Lewisham CLP
South Paddington Division Labour Party
Southwark ILP
Stockport Labour Party
Tottenham Labour Party
Women's Co-operative Guild Papers

ELECTION MATERIAL

'The General Election of 1945' (BLPES collection)
Mass Observation Files
Election Addresses – National Liberal Club Collection (Bristol University)
Election Addresses – Morgan Phillips files (Labour History Archive, Manchester)

JOURNALS AND NEWSPAPERS

Birmingham Mail
Birmingham Evening Dispatch
Birmingham Post
Boro' of West Ham, East Ham and Stratford Express

Bradford Observer
Clarion
Daily Herald
Daily Mail
Derby Daily Telegraph
Dudley Chronicle
East Ham Echo
Hackney Gazette and North London Advertiser
John Bull
Manchester Guardian
Midland Advertiser and Wednesbury Herald
News Chronicle
Political Quarterly
Preston Guardian
Sheffield Mail
Smethwick Telephone
The Times
Weekly News for West Bromwich
Wellingborough News

LABOUR PARTY JOURNALS

Argus (Merton and Morden)
Gateshead Labour News / *Gateshead Labour Herald*
Gloucester Labour News
Jarrow Labour Herald
Labour's Northern Voice (Manchester)
Labour Leader
Labour Magazine
Labour Organiser
Labour Sentinel (Sedgefield)
Labour Woman
Leeds Weekly Citizen
Leyton and Leytonstone Pioneer
London News
North Lambeth Citizen
Seaham Harbour Labour News
Socialist (Seaham)
Town Crier (Birmingham)
Witch-Hunt News

CONTEMPORARY WORKS

Norman Angell, *The Great Illusion* (1910)

Oliver Baldwin and Roger Chance, *Conservatism and Wealth: A Radical Indictment* (1929)

Aneurin Bevan, *In Place of Fear* (1952)

Robert Blatchford, *Merrie England* (1894)

A. Fenner Brockway and Frederick Mullally, *Death Pays A Dividend* (1944)

'Cato', *Guilty Men* (1940)

G. D. H. Cole, *The People's Front* (1937); 'A British People's Front: Why and How?', *Political Quarterly*, 7, 1936

Hugh Cudlipp, *Publish and Be Damned!* (1953)

Hugh Dalton, *Practical Socialism for Britain* (1935); 'The Popular Front', *Political Quarterly*, 7, 1936

Godfrey Elton, *Towards the New Labour Party* (1932)

Fabian Society, *Fabian Tracts*, Nos. 1–129 (1884–1906)

Wilfred Fienburgh and Richard Evely, *Steel Is Power: The Case for Nationalisation* (1948)

Wal Hannington, *The Problem of the Distressed Areas* (1937)

Keir Hardie and Ramsay MacDonald, 'The Independent Labour Party', *Nineteenth Century*, January 1899

Ramsay MacDonald, *The Socialist Movement* (1911)

The Labour Party and Electoral Reform (1913)

Herbert Morrison, *Government and Parliament* (1954)

Marion Phillips, *Women and the Labour Party* (1927)

Stephen Reynolds and Bob & Tom Wooley, *Seems So! A Working Class View of Politics* (1911)

A. L. Rowse, 'The Present and Immediate Future of the Labour Party', *Political Quarterly*, 9, 1938

Emmanuel Shinwell, *When the Men Come Home* (1944)

Philip Snowden, *Socialism and the Drink Question* (1908)

John Strachey, *Revolution by Reason* (1925); *The Theory and Practice of Socialism* (1936); *What Are We To Do?* (1938); *A Programme for Progress* (1940)

J. H. Thomas, 'What Holding Office Has Taught Me', *Pearson's Magazine*, March 1925

Ben Tillett, *Socialism* (1897); *The Prosecution of Ben Tillett* (1893)

Robert Tressell, *The Ragged Trousered Philanthropists* (1911)

Charles Trevelyan, *From Liberalism to Labour* (1921)

Sidney Webb, *Socialism in England* (1889)

Ellen Wilkinson, *The Town That Was Murdered* (1939)

Konni Zilliacus, *The Mirror of the Past* (1944)

Secondary sources

DIARIES, MEMOIRS AND AUTOBIOGRAPHIES

Paddy Ashdown, *The Ashdown Diaries*, 2 vols. (2000)

Clement Attlee, *As It Happened* (1954)

Oliver Baldwin, *The Questing Beast* (1932)

M. Bondfield, *A Life's Work* (1948)

A. Fenner Brockway, *Inside the Left* (1942)

Maureen Callcott, *A Pilgrimage of Grace: The Diaries of Ruth Dodds* (1995)

Barbara Castle, *Fighting All the Way* (1993)

Lord Citrine, *Men and Work* (1964)

J. R. Clynes, *Memoirs 1869–1924*, 2 vols. (1937)

Richard Crossman, *The Diaries of a Cabinet Minister* vol. I (1975)

Hugh Dalton, *Call Back Yesterday* (1953)

Bernard Donoughue, *Downing Street Diary: With Harold Wilson in No. 10*
    (2005); *Downing Street Diary Volume Two: With James Callaghan in No. 10* (2008)

Godfrey Elton, *Among Others* (1938)

Harry Gosling, *Up and Down Stream* (1927)

Mary Agnes Hamilton, *Remembering My Good Friends* (1944)

Roy Hattersley, *A Yorkshire Boyhood* (1983); *Who Goes Home?* (1995)

Denis Healey, *The Time of My Life* (1989)

Arthur Horner, *Incorrigible Rebel* (1960)

Kevin Jefferys (ed.), *Labour and the Wartime Coalition: From the Diary of James*
    Chuter Ede 1941–45 (1987)

Roy Jenkins, *A Life at the Centre* (1991)

Jack Jones, *My Lively Life* (1928)

David Kirkwood, *My Life of Revolt* (1935)

George Lansbury, *My Life* (1928)

Jennie Lee, *My Life With Nye* (1980)

Hugh P. Macmillan, *A Man of Law's Tale* (1952)

Jean Mann, *Woman in Parliament* (1962)

Leah Manning, *A Life For Education* (1970)

Ian Mikardo, *Backbencher* (1988)

Geoffrey Mitched (ed.), *The Hard Way Up: The Autobiography of Hannah Mitchell,*
    Suffragette and Rebel (1968)

Lord Parmoor, *A Retrospect* (1936)

F. W. Pethick-Lawrence, *Fate Has Been Kind* (1942)

Edith Picton-Turbervill, *Life Is Good* (1939)

Ben Pimlott (ed). *The Second World War Diary of Hugh Dalton 1940–45* (1986)

C. P. Scott, *Diary* (1970)

James Sexton, *The Life of Sir James Sexton: Agitator* (1936)

Philip Snowden, *An Autobiography* (1934)

Edith Summerskill, *A Woman's World* (1967)

J. H. Thomas, *My Story* (1937)

Will Thorne, *My Life's Battles* (1925)

Ben Turner, *Memories and Reflections* (1931)

Countess of Warwick, *Life's Ebb and Flow* (1929); *Afterthoughts* (1931)

John Wilson, *Memories of a Labour Leader* (1910)

Biographies

J. A. D. Adams, *Tony Benn* (1992)

Francis Beckett, *The Rebel Who Lost His Cause: The Tragedy of John Beckett, MP* (1999)

Caroline Benn, *Keir Hardie* (1992)

Gregory Blaxland, *J. H. Thomas, A Life for Unity* (1964)

K. D. Brown, *John Burns* (1977)

Chris Bryant, *Stafford Cripps* (1997)

Alan Bullock, *The Life and Times of Ernest Bevin* (1960)

Trevor Burridge, *Clement Attlee: A Political Biography* (1985)

John Campbell, *Nye Bevan: A Biography* (1987); *Roy Jenkins: A Biography* (1983)

Doris Nield Chew, *Ada Nield Chew* (1982)

David Clark, *Labour's Lost Leader: Victor Grayson* (1985)

Peter Clarke, *The Cripps Version: The Life of Sir Stafford Cripps* (2002)

Colin Cooke, *The Life of Richard Stafford Cripps* (1957)

B. Donoughue and G. W. Jones, *Herbert Morrison: Portrait of a Politician* (1973)

Ruth Dudley Edwards, *Victor Gollancz: A Biography* (1987)

Eric Estorik, *Stafford Cripps* (1949)

Trevor Evans, *Bevin* (1946)

Sheila Fletcher, *Maude Royden* (1989)

Reg Groves, *The Strange Case of Victor Grayson* (1975)

June Hannam, *Isabella Ford* (1989)

Kenneth Harris, *Attlee* (1982)

Brian Harrison, *Prudent Revolutionaries: Portraits of British Feminists Between the Wars* (1987)

Royden Harrison, *The Life and Times of Sidney and Beatrice Webb 1858–1905: The Formative Years* (2000)

Patricia Hollis, *Jennie Lee: A Life* (1997)

Kevin Jefferys, *Antony Crosland* (1999)

Mervyn Jones, *Michael Foot* (1994)

Raymond Jones, *Arthur Ponsonby* (1989)

Andro Linklater, *An Unhusbanded Life: Charlotte Despard, Suffragette, Socialist and Sinn Feiner* (1980)

Iain McLean, *Keir Hardie* (1975)

John McNair, *James Maxton: The Beloved Rebel* (1955)

David Marquand, *Ramsay MacDonald* (1977)

Arthur Marwick, *Clifford Allen: The Open Conspirator* (1996)

Kenneth Morgan, *Keir Hardie: Radical and Socialist* (1975); *Michael Foot: A Life* (2007)

Jane and Kenneth Morgan, *Portrait of a Progressive: The Political Career of Viscount Addison* (1980)

A. J. A. Morris, *C. P. Trevelyan 1870–1959: Portrait of a Radical* (1977)

Michael Newman, *John Strachey* (1989)

Charles W. Ould, *William Stapleton Royce: A Memoir* (1925)

Peter Paterson, *Tired and Emotional: The Life of Lord George-Brown* (1993)

Edward Pearce, *Denis Healey* (2002)

Robert Pearce, *Attlee* (1997)

Anne Perkins, *Red Queen: The Authorised Biography of Barbara Castle* (2003)

H. R. S. Phillpott, *The Right Honourable J. H. Thomas* (1932)

Ben Pimlott, *Hugh Dalton* (1985); *Harold Wilson* (1992)

Martin Pugh, *The Pankhursts* (2000)

E. A. and G. H. Radice, *Will Thorne: Constructive Militant* (1974)

Fred Reid, *Keir Hardie: The Making of a Socialist* (1978)

John Rentaul, *Tony Blair* (1995)

Jonathan Schneer, *Ben Tillett* (1982); *George Lansbury* (1990)

Antony Seldon, *Blair* (2004)

Carole Seymour-Jones, *Beatrice Webb* (1992)

John Shepherd, *George Lansbury: At the Heart of Old Labour* (2002)

Robert Skidelsky, *Oswald Mosley* (1975)

Jon Sopel, *Tony Blair: The Moderniser* (1995)

Hugh Thomas, *John Strachey* (1973)

Laurence Thompson, *The Enthusiasts: A Biography of John and Katharine Bruce Glasier* (1971)

John Tilley, *Churchill's Favourite Socialist: A Life of A. V. Alexander* (1995)

Millie Toole, *Mrs Bessie Braddock MP* (1957)

Betty Vernon, *Ellen Wilkinson 1891–1947* (1982)

Ian Wood, *John Wheatley* (1990)

Philip M. Williams, *Hugh Gaitskell* (1979)

Chris Wrigley, *Arthur Henderson* (1990)

OTHER SECONDARY WORKS

M. Abrams and R. Rose, *Must Labour Lose?* (1960)

Paul Addison, *The Road to 1945* (1975)

David Blaazer, *The Popular Front and the Progressive Tradition* (1992)

Lawrence Black, *The Political Culture of the Left in Affluent Britain, 1951–64* (2003)

Neal Blewett, *The Peers, the Parties and the People: The General Elections of 1910* (1972)

Marc Brodie, *The Politics of the Poor: The East End of London 1885–1914* (2004)

Stephen Brooke, *Labour's War: The Labour Party During the Second World War* (1992)

Kenneth D. Brown, *Labour and Unemployment 1900–1914* (1971)

Kenneth D. Brown (ed.), *The First Labour Party 1906–1914* (1985)

Tom Buchanan, *The Spanish Civil War and the British Labour Movement* (1991)

Trevor Burridge, *British Labour and Hitler's War* (1976)

Julia Bush, *Behind the Lines: East London Labour 1914–1919* (1984)

David Butler, *The British General Election of 1955* (1955)

David Butler and Richard Rose, *The British General Election of 1959* (1960)

David Butler and Anthony King, *The British General Election of 1964* (1965); *The British General Election of 1966* (1966)

David Butler and Michael Pinto-Duschinsky, *The British General Election of 1970* (1971)

David Butler and Dennis Kavanagh, *The British General Election of 1979* (1980); *The British General Election of 1983* (1984); *The British General Election of 1987* (1988); *The British General Election of 1992* (1992); *The British General Election of 1997* (1997); *The British General Election of 2001* (2001)

David Butler and Donald Stokes, *Political Change in Britain* (1969)

John Callaghan, *Socialism in Britain Since 1884* (1990)

Alastair Campbell, *The Blair Years* (2007)

Martin Ceadel, *Pacifism in Britain 1914–1945* (1980)

Lewis Chester, Stephen Fay and Hugo Young, *The Zinoviev Letter* (1967)

David Clark, *Colne Valley: Radicalism to Socialism* (1981)

C. Cline, *Recruits to Labour* (1963)

Michael Cocks, *Labour and the Benn Factor* (1989)

Margaret Cole, *The Story of Fabian Socialism* (1961)

Nigel Copsey, *Anti-Fascism in Britain* (2000)

Jeremy A. Crang, *The British Army and the People's War 1939–1945* (2000)

Ivor Crew, Neil Day and Antony Fox, *The British Electorate 1953–1987* (1991)

James E. Cronin, *New Labour's Pasts* (2004)

Sam Davies, *Liverpool Labour* (1996)

R. E. Dowse, *Left in the Centre* (1966)

Roger Eatwell, *The 1945–1951 Labour Governments* (1979)

Maurice Edelman, *The Daily Mirror: A Political History* (1966)

Matthew Engel, *Tickle the Public: One Hundred Years of the Popular Press* (1996)

S. Fielding, *Labour: Decline and Renewal* (1999)

S. Fielding, P. Thompson and N. Tiratsoo, *England Arise: The Labour Party and Popular Politics in the 1940s* (1995)

Michael Foley, *The British Presidency* (2000)

Paul Foot, *Immigration and Race in British Politics* (1965)

Martin Francis, *Ideas and Policies under Labour 1945–1951* (1997)

Martin Francis and Ina Zweiniger-Bargielowska, *The Conservatives and British Society 1880–1990* (1996)

Jim Fyrth (ed.), *Britain, Fascism and the Popular Front* (1985)

A. Geddes and J. Tonge (eds.), *Britain Decides: The UK General Election of 2005* (2005)

Pamela M. Graves, *Labour Women: Women in British Working-Class Politics 1918–1939* (1994)

Trevor Griffiths, *The Lancashire Working Classes 1880–1930* (2001)

James Hinton, *Labour and Socialism: A History of the British Labour Movement 1867–1974* (1983)

Sandra Stanley Holton, *Feminism and Democracy: Women's Suffrage and Reform Politics in Britain 1900–1918* (1986)

David Howell, *British Workers and the Independent Labour Party 1888–1906* (1983); *MacDonald's Party: Labour Identities and Crisis 1922–1931* (2002)

D. James, A. Jowitt and K. Laybourn (eds.), *The Centennial History of the Independent Labour Party* (1992)

Oliver James, *Affluenza* (2007)

Kevin Jefferys, *War and Reform: British Politics During the Second World War* (1994)

J. Jupp, *The Radical Left in Britain 1931–1941* (1982)

Dennis Kavanagh and Peter Morris, *Consensus Politics from Attlee to Thatcher* (1989)

Jon Lawrence, *Speaking for the People: Party, Language and Popular Politics in England 1867–1914* (1998)

Jon Lawrence and Miles Taylor, *Party, State and Society* (1997)

A. M. McBriar, *Fabian Socialism and English Politics 1884–1918* (1962)

R. B. McCallum and A. Readman, *The British General Election of 1945* (1947)

J. M. MacKenzie, *Propaganda and Empire: The Manipulation of British Public Opinion 1880–1960* (1984)

R. I. McKibbin, *The Evolution of the Labour Party 1910–24* (1974); *Ideologies of Class: Social Relations in Britain 1880–1970* (1990)

Andy McSmith, *John Smith: A Life 1938–1994* (1994)

Peter Mandelson and Roger Liddle, *The Blair Revolution* (1996)

John Marriott, *The Culture of Labourism: The East End Between the Wars* (1991)

Lewis Mates, *The Spanish Civil War and the British Left* (2007)

Lucy Middleton (ed.), *Women in the Labour Movement* (1977)

Ralph Miliband, *Parliamentary Socialism* (1972)

Robert Millward and John Singleton (eds.), *The Political Economy of Nationalisation in Britain 1920–50* (1995)

Lewis Minkin, *The Contentious Alliance: Trade Unions and the Labour Party* (1991)

Robert Moore, *Pitmen, Preachers and Politics* (1974)

Roger Moore, *The Emergence of the Labour Party 1880–1924* (1978)

Kenneth Morgan, *Labour in Power 1945–1951* (1984)

John F. Naylor, *Labour's International Policy: the Labour Party in the 1930s* (1969)

Henry Pelling, *The Origins of the Labour Party* (1965); *A History of British Trade Unionism* (1987); *Social Geography of British Elections 1885–1910* (1967)

Ben Pimlott, *Labour and the Left in the 1930s* (1977)

David Powell, *British Politics and the Labour Question 1868–1990* (1992)

Martin Pugh, *The Making of Modern British Politics 1867–1945* (2002); *Women and the Women's Movement in Britain 1914–1959* (1992)

Andrew Rawnsley, *Servants of the People: The Inside Story of New Labour* (2000)

A. K. Russell, *Liberal Landslide: The General Election of 1906* (1973)

Michael Savage, *The Dynamics of Working-Class Politics: The Labour Movement in Preston, 1880–1940* (1987)

Patrick Seyd and Paul Whiteley, *Labour's Grass Roots: The Politics of Party Membership* (1992)

Eric Shaw, *The Labour Party Since 1979* (1994)

Robert Skidelsky, *Politicians and the Slump: the Labour Government of 1929–1931* (1967)

N. C. Solden, *Women in British Trade Unions 1874–1976* (1978)

C. T. Stannage, *Baldwin Thwarts the Opposition: The General Election of 1935* (1988)

M. Swartz, *The Union of Democratic control in British Politics during the First World War* (1971)

Duncan Tanner, *Political Change and the Labour Party 1900–1918* (1990)

Duncan Tanner, Pat Thane and Nick Tiratsoo (eds.), *Labour's First Century* (2000)

Duncan Tanner, Chris Williams and Deian Hopkin (eds.), *The Labour Party in Wales 1900–2000* (2000)

Noel Thompson, *Political Economy and the Labour Party* (1996)

Nick Tiratsoo (ed.), *The Attlee Years* (1991)

Andrew Thorpe, *A History of the British Labour Party* (1997); *The British General Election of 1931* (1991)

Paul Ward, *Red Flag and Union Jack: Englishness, Patriotism and the British Left, 1881–1924* (1998)

Richard Whiting, *The Labour Party and Taxation* (2000)

G. L. and A. L. Williams, *Labour's Decline and the Social Democrats' Fall* (1989)

Philip Williamson, *National Crisis and National Government: British Politics, the Economy and Empire, 1926–1932* (1992)

J. M. Winter, *Socialism and the Challenge of War* (1974)

Matthew Worley, *Inside the Gate: A History of the British Labour Party between the Wars* (2005)

Matthew Worley (ed.), *Labour's Grass Roots: Essays on the Activities of Local Labour Parties and Members, 1918–45* (2005)

Ina Zweiniger-Bargielowska, *Austerity in Britain: rationing, controls and consumption, 1939–1955* (2000)

THESES

John Boughton, 'Working-Class Politics in Birmingham and Sheffield, 1918–1931', Warwick University PhD thesis, 1985.

J. J. G. Burke, 'Leading the Labour Party, 1983–1992', Cambridge University PhD thesis, 2004.

Dennis Dean, 'The Contrasting Attitudes of the Conservative and Labour Parties to Problems of Empire, 1922–1936', University of London PhD thesis, 1974.

Dinah B. M. Evans, 'The Dynamics of Labour Party Politics in Swansea 1941–1964', University of Wales Bangor PhD thesis, 2008.

Lewis H. Mates, 'The United Front and the Popular Front in the North-East of England 1936–1939', Newcastle University PhD thesis, 2002.

A. W. Purdue, 'Parliamentary Elections in North-East England 1900–1906: The Advent of Labour', Northumberland Polytechnic MLitt thesis, 1974.

Huw Richards, 'Construction, Conformity and Control: The Taming of the *Daily Herald*, 1921–1930', Open University PhD thesis, 1992.

D. C. Sutherland, 'Peeresses, Parliament and Prejudice: The admission of Women to the House of Lords 1900–1963', Cambridge University PhD thesis, 2000.

Andrew Walling. 'Modernisation, Policy Debate and Organisation in the Labour Party, 1951–1964', University of Wales Bangor PhD thesis, 2001.

ARTICLES AND CHAPTERS

Mark Abrams, 'Class and Politics', *Encounter*, October 1961

Tony Adams, 'Labour Vanguard, Tory Bastion or the Triumph of New Liberalism? Manchester Politics 1900–1914 in Comparative Perspective', *Manchester Region History Review*, 14, 2000.

Amy Black and Stephen Brooke, 'The Labour Party, Women and the Problem of Gender, 1951–1966', *Journal of British Studies*, 36, 1997.

Alan Booth, 'How Long are Light Years in British Politics? The Labour Party's Economic Ideas in the 1930s', *Twentieth Century British History*, 7, 1996.

John Boughton, 'Working Class Conservatism and the Rise of Labour: A Case Study of Birmingham in the 1920s', *Historian*, 59, 1998.

Tom Buchanan, 'Britain's Popular Front? Aid Spain and the British Labour Movement', *History Workshop Journal*, 31, 1991.

Martin Ceadel, 'Interpreting East Fulham', in Chris Cook and John Ramsden (eds.), *By-elections in British Politics* (1997).

M. Childs, 'Labour Grows Up: The Electoral System, Political Generations and British Politics 1890–1929', *Twentieth Century British History*, 6, 1995.

Alan Clinton 'Trades councils during the First World War, *International Review of Social History*, 15, 1970.

Chris Cook, 'By-elections of the First Labour Government', in Chris Cook and John Ramsden (eds.), *By-elections in British Politics* (1997).

J. Davis, 'Slums and the Vote', *Historical Journal*, 14, 1991.

Sam Davies and Bob Morley, 'The Politics of Place: A Comparative Analysis of Electoral Politics in Blackburn, Bolton, Burnley and Bury', *Manchester Region History Review*, 14, 2000.

Michael Dawson, 'Money and the Real Impact of the Fourth Reform Act', *Historical Journal*, 35, 2, 1992.

Roy Douglas, 'The National Democratic Party and the British Workers' League', *Historical Journal*, 15, 3, 1972.

R. Eatwell, 'Munich, Public Opinion and the Popular Front', *Journal of Contemporary History*, 6, 4, 1971.

David Englander and James Osborne, 'Jack, Tommy and Henry Dubb: The Armed Forces and the Working Class', *Historical Journal*, 21, 2, 1978.

S. Fielding, 'What did "the People" want?: The meaning of the 1945 general election', *Historical Journal*, 35, 3, 1992.

Ivan Gibbons, 'The Irish policy of the first Labour Government, *Labour History Review*, 72, 2008.

J. Goldthorpe and D. Lockwood, 'The Affluent Worker and the Thesis of Embourgeoisement', *Sociology*, October 1962.

Brian Harrison, 'Traditions of Respectability in British Labour History', in *Peaceable Kingdom* (1982).

R. P. Hastings, 'The Birmingham Labour Movement 1918–1945', *Midland History*, 5, 1979–80.

C. Howard, 'MacDonald, Henderson and the Outbreak of War', *Historical Journal*, 20, 4, 1977.

R. Heller, 'East Fulham Revisited', *Journal of Contemporary History*, 1971.

David Howell, '"I loved my union and my country": Jimmy Thomas and the Politics of Railway Trade Unionism', *Twentieth Century British History*, 6, 1995.

Keith Laybourn, '"There ought not to be one law for the rich and another for the poor which is the case today": The Labour Party, Lotteries, Gaming, Gambling and Bingo, *c*.1900–1960s', *History*, 93, 2008.

Gregg McClymont, 'Socialism, Puritanism, Hedonism: The Parliamentary Labour Party's Attitude to Gambling, 1923–31', *Twentieth Century British History*, 19, 2008.

David McKie, 'By-elections of the Wilson Government', in Chris Cook and John Ramsden (eds.), *By-elections in British Politics* (1997).

Iain McLean, 'Red Clydeside, 1915–1919', in J. Stevenson and R. Quinault,

Popular Protest and Public Order (1974); 'Oxford and Bridgwater', in Chris
   Cook and John Ramsden (eds.), *By-elections in British Politics* (1997).
Barbara Malament, 'British Labour and Roosevelt's New Deal: The Response
   of the Left and the Unions', *Journal of British Studies*, 1978.
Lewis Mates, 'Britain's Popular Front? The Case of the Tyneside Foodship
   Campaign, 1938–39', *Labour History Review*, 69, 2004.
H. C. G. Matthews, R. I. McKibbin and J. A. Kay, 'The Franchise Factor in
   the Rise of the Labour Party', *English Historical Review*, 91, 1976.
Adrian Oldfield, 'The Labour Party and Planning – 1934 or 1918?', *Bulletin of
   the Society for the study of Labour History*, 25, 1972.
Nicholas Owen, 'MacDonald's Parties: The Labour Party and the "Aristocratic
   Embrace", 1922–1931', *Twentieth Century British History*, 18, 2007.
Henry Pelling, 'The 1945 General Election Reconsidered', *Historical Journal*,
   23, 1980; 'The Impact of the war on the Labour Party', in H. L. Smith
   (ed.), *War and Social Change* (1986); 'British Labour and British Imperialism',
   'Labour and the Downfall of Liberalism' and 'The Story of the ILP', in
   Popular Politics and Society in Late Victorian Britain (1968).
Martin Pugh, '"Class Traitors": Conservative Recruits to Labour 1900–1930',
   English Historical Review, 113, 1998; 'The Rise of Labour and the Political
   Culture of Conservatism, 1890–1945', *History*, 87, 288, 2002; 'The *Daily Mirror*
   and the Revival of Labour 1935–1945', *Twentieth Century British History*, 9, 1998;
   'The Liberal Party and the Popular Front', *English Historical Review*, 121, 2006.
A. W. Purdue, 'Arthur Henderson and Liberal, Liberal–Labour and Labour
   Politics in the North-East of England 1892–1903', *Northern History*, 11, 1976.
J. S. Rasmussen, 'Women in Labour: the Flapper Vote and Party System
   Transformation in Britain', *British Electoral Studies*, 3, 1984.
Alastair Reid, 'Glasgow Socialism', *Social History*, 2, 1986.
Neil Riddell, 'The Catholic Church and the Labour Party, 1918–1931', *Twentieth
   Century British History*, 8, 1997.
Peter Rose, 'The Wilson–Callaghan Government of 1974–79: by-elections
   (eventually) bring down a Government', in Chris Cook and John Ramsden
   (eds.), *By-elections in British Politics* (1997).
M. G. Shepherd and John L. Halstead, 'Labour's Municipal Election
   Performance in England and Wales, 1901–13', *Bulletin of the Society for the
   Study of Labour History*, 39, 1979.
Richard Sibley, 'The swing to Labour during the Second World War: When
   and why?', *Labour History Review*, 55, 1, 1990.
C. T. Stannage, 'The East Fulham By-election, 25 October 1933', *Historical
   Journal*, 14, 1971.
J. O. Stubbs, 'Lord Milner and Patriotic Labour', *English Historical Review*, 77,
   1972.

Duncan Tanner, 'The Parliamentary Electoral System, the "Fourth" Reform Act and the Rise of Labour in England and Wales', *BIHR*, 56, 1983; 'Class Voting and Radical Politics: The Liberal and Labour Parties, 1910–31', in Jon Lawrence and Miles Taylor (eds.), *Party, State and Society* (1997).

Miles Taylor, 'Labour and the Constitution', in Duncan Tanner (ed.), *Labour's First Century* (2000).

Nick Thomas-Symonds, 'A Reinterpretation of Michael Foot's Handling of the Militant Tendency', *Contemporary British History*, 19, 2005.

J. A. Thompson, 'Labour and the Modern British Monarchy', *South Atlantic Quarterly*, 70, 1971.

Andrew Thorpe, 'J. H. Thomas and the Rise of Labour in Derby, 1880–1945', *Midland History*, 15, 1990; 'Stalinism and British Politics', *History*, 83, 1998; 'The Membership of the British Communist Party', *Historical Journal* 43, 3, 2000; 'Conservative Party Agents in Second World War Britain', *Twentieth Century British History*, 18, 2007.

Richard Toye, 'The Labour Party and the Economics of Rearmament, 1935–39', *Twentieth Century British History*, 12, 2001; 'The Labour Party and Keynes', in E. H. H. Green and D. M. Tanner (eds.), *The Strange Survival of Liberal England* (2007).

John Turner, 'The Labour Vote and the Franchise after 1918', in P. Denley and D. Hopkin (eds.), *History and Computing* (1987).

R. C. Whiting, 'Income Tax, the Working Class and Party Politics 1948–1952', *Twentieth Century British History*, 8, 1997.

Philip Williamson, 'The Labour Party and the House of Lords', *Parliamentary History*, 10, 1991.

J. M. Winter, 'Arthur Henderson, the Russian Revolution and the Reconstruction of the Labour Party', *Historical Journal*, 15, 1972.

Anthony Wright, 'British Socialists and the British Constitution', *Parliamentary Affairs*, 43, 1990.

Index

Abraham, William 36, 79, 115
Abrams, Mark 315, 328
Abse, Leo 336
Abyssinia 242, 244, 265
Adamson, William 128, 174
Addison, Christopher 108, 156, 289
Adonis, Lord 402
Alden, Percy 156
Alexander, A. V. 145, 209, 221, 260, 274, 279, 310; and imperialism 227, 260–1
Allaun, Frank 304, 321, 367
Allen, Clifford 144
Allighan, Gary 272, 281
Amery, L. S. xiii, 114, 158, 258
Anderson, W. C. 82, 107
Angel, Norman 103
Arnold-Forster, William 157, 159, 251
Ashdown, Paddy 399, 404
Asquith, H. H. 78, 95, 104, 153, 171
Astor, Nancy 149, 160, 272
Atholl, Duchess of 254
Attlee, Clement x, 73, 134, 150, 242; becomes MP 142–3, 165; and Abdication crisis 225; as leader 220, 224–5, 240–1, 250, 252–4, 261–2, 264–5, 277–9, 281–2, 289–90, 295, 298, 300–1, 308–9; and Coalition 259–60, 267, 268; as prime minister 286–7, 293–4, 298

Australia 226
Ayrton-Gould, Barbara 201, 313

Bacon, Alice 304, 311, 312
Baldwin, Oliver 157, 158, 159–60, 194, 197, 213
Baldwin, Stanley 158, 194; attitude to Labour 170–1, 179; and Abdication crisis 225–6
Banbury, Sir Frederick 169, 172
Barker, Sara 344
Barnes, George 54–5, 66, 81, 109, 112, 116, 119, 123, 150
Barrow-in-Furness 132, 139–41
Bartlett, Vernon 250, 252, 253
Barton, Eleanor 146
Beckett, John 113, 141–2, 193
Bell, Richard 57, 59, 60, 76
Benn, Tony 9, 322, 328, 335, 352, 353, 355, 359; and socialism 362–3; and Campaign for Labour Party Democracy 346–7, 351, 364, 372; and deputy leadership 365; and declining influence 371, 376–7, 382
Bentham, Ethel 147, 205
Bermondsey 366, 369–70
Betts, Barbara see Castle, Barbara
Bevan, Andy 354–5
Bevan, Aneurin 204, 223, 221, 242, 248, 280, 309, 314, 364; as war-time rebel 261, 266–8, 273–4; and

Bevanites 302–5; resignation of 298–9; and affluence 317–18

Beveridge, Sir William 206, 262, 267–8, 274, 275

Bevin, Ernest 7, 102, 133, 179, 184, 189, 190, 213, 222, 252; and economic policy 229, 232–3; and defence policy 240, 244; in Second World War 260, 264, 268; as foreign secretary 293–4

Birmingham 9, 72–3, 91, 129, 134, 146, 160–2, 196–8, 248, 256, 261, 265, 285, 292–3, 300, 304, 307, 331–2, 341, 349–50

birth control 146, 148, 153, 202, 237

Birt, Lord 402

Bishop Aukland 139, 147–8, 248, 262, 263

Blackburn 25–6, 44, 57, 66, 72, 123, 205–6

Blair, Cherie 389, 391, 382

Blair, Leo 389–90

Blair, Tony 382, 386; and Conservative background 8, 13, 389–91; joins Labour 391–2; and New Labour 388–9, 395–6; and Thatcher 394–6; and Clinton 388–9, 393, 395; as leader 387, 392–7; and presidential style 399–402; as prime minister 401–3, 411; and terrorism 407–10; and police state 409

Blatchford, Robert 1, 18, 26–30, 37, 55–7, 105, 115

Blears, Hazel 7, 411

Blunkett, David x, 7, 375, 394, 401, 407

Boer War 56–7, 60, 65, 67

Bolshevik Revolution 118, 129–30, 152, 182

Bolton 87

Bondfield, Margaret 84, 146, 148–9, 190, 200, 203–4, 236

Bow and Bromley 89, 93–4

Bowerman, Charles 73, 107, 112, 127, 154, 168

Braddock, Bessie 275, 304, 311, 367

Bradford 37, 46–8, 62, 91, 207, 367

Brailsford, Henry 95, 188, 229

Bridgwater 253–4

Bristol 45, 160, 207, 264, 405

British Broadcasting Corporation 270–1

British Legion 150, 219

British Socialist Party 78, 99

British Workers League 115–16

British Union of Fascists 219–20, 273

Broadhurst, Henry 35–6

Brockway, A. Fenner 77, 101, 155, 226

Brown, George 7, 19, 255, 286, 289, 323–4, 333–4, 339–40

Brown, Gordon 382, 394–5, 401, 404, 411–13

Buchanan, George 154, 169, 218

Burns, John 23–4, 25, 30, 32, 37, 40, 55

Burt, Thomas 35, 79

Burton, Elaine 264, 311, 313

Butler, R. A. 266, 268, 306, 307

Buxton, Charles 156

Buxton, Noel 156, 161, 165, 174, 205

Callaghan, James 7, 286, 324, 333–4, 337, 339, 344, 353–4, 361, 372; as prime minister 356–60

Campaign for Nuclear Disarmament 319, 341

Campbell, Alastair 393, 394, 402

Campbell case 180–1

Canada 227

Castle, Barbara 234, 268, 272, 286, 293, 302, 311, 313, 343–4; and anti-feminism x, 201, 312, 337

Catholics 44, 58, 64, 66, 71–2, 148,
151–4, 202, 236–7, 312, 337
Cattermole, Jim 329
Chamberlain, Joseph 12, 14, 33, 56,
60
Chamberlain, Neville xiii, 138, 160,
161, 170, 242, 248, 251, 257–9
Champion, H. H. 30, 31, 41
Chartism 15, 26, 46
Chelmsford, Viscount 159, 174–5, 227
Churchill, W. L. S. 12, 88, 130, 190;
opinion of Labour 172; in
wartime coalition 259–60, 268,
271; and Bevan 266; in 1945 elect-
ion 277–80; adopts consensus
305–7
Citrine, Walter 169, 192, 213, 221, 229
Clarion 1, 27
Clinton-Davies, Stanley 368
Clitheroe 62–3
Clydesiders 164–5, 167, 169
Clynes, J. R. 47, 119, 168; pro-war
views 101–2, 109–10, 122; as food
minister 113–14; as leader 128,
132, 133, 165
Cocks, Michael 378
Cohen, Stanley 368
Cole, G. D .H. 3, 106, 110–11, 159,
186, 222, 229, 246, 253
Colman, Grace 159
Colne Valley 6, 21, 41–3, 44, 67–70, 79
Common Wealth Party 264
Communist Party and Communists
5, 131–3, 152, 180–1, 193, 218–19,
229, 246–7, 249, 321
Conservative Party and
Conservatism 2, 9, 20, 22, 25, 44,
50, 80, 91, 106, 165, 187, 195, 228,
254, 260, 263, 295–6, 305–7, 313,
331, 350, 380, 384, 403–4
Cook, A. J. 18, 188, 190–1, 192
Cook, Robin 355, 398, 400

Co-operative Societies 135, 145–6,
237
Corbett, Robin 368
Creech-Jones, Arthur 188, 226
Cripps, C. A. *see* Parmoor, Lord
Cripps, Sir Stafford 6, 8, 157, 159,
220, 232; and anti-parliamentary
views 221–2; and Popular Front
247–8, 253; and expulsion 248,
254–5; return to favour 262, 267;
as chancellor 288, 295, 297, 333
Crittall, Valentine 157, 160
Crooks, Will 51, 63, 73, 101, 104
Crossman, Richard 253, 283, 293,
302, 308, 317, 319, 335
Cummings, A. J. 250
Curran, Pete 48, 68–9
Curzon, Lord 33, 71, 158
Crosland, Anthony 286, 297, 318,
320, 324, 327, 329, 334–5, 339, 349,
353; views on economics 288,
308–9, 333, 357

Daily Citizen 144
Daily Express 160, 225
Daily Herald 6, 130, 144–5, 158, 173,
225, 242–3, 254
Daily Mail 160, 182, 191, 199, 225,
296, 393
Daily Mirror 127, 225, 241–3, 256,
270, 272, 275, 281
Dalton, Hugh 3, 7, 139, 154, 222,
225, 248, 254–5, 259, 260, 266, 273;
as ex-Tory 157–9, 205; and
economic policy 229, 231; and
foreign policy 244, 246; under-
mines Chamberlain 258–9; as
chancellor 287–8, 297
Dalyell, Tam 355, 358
Davison, J. E. 126
Deakin, Arthur 303, 304
Denman, Richard 104, 156

Deptford 44, 73, 127, 236
Derby 59, 125, 250, 329, 342
devolution *see* Labour Party
Dewar, Donald 383
Driberg, Tom 264, 302, 321
Duncan, Charles 140–1
Dunstan, Robert 133
Dunwoody, Gwyneth 373
Durbin, Evan 229, 230
Dyson, Will 144

East Ham 80, 99, 102, 127, 149, 204, 283
Eden, Sir Anthony 254, 258, 306, 307, 314
Ede, James Chuter 266, 269, 286
Edward VIII 225
elections: 1892 39–41; 1895 41, 43; 1900 56–7; 1906 65–6; 1910 78–9; 1918 116–27, 122–7, 133, 277; 1922 164–5; 1923 170–1; 1924 181–3; 1929 189, 195, 199, 205–8; 1931 215–16; 1935 240–1, 246, 249–50; 1945 256, 263, 270, 272–3, 275–6, 277–85, 293; 1950 293–4, 295–8; 1951 299–302; 1955 307–8; 1959 291, 314–15; 1964 326–32; 1966 338–9; 1970 342, 344–5; February 1974 348–50; October 1974 351–2; 1979 358–61; 1983 370–4; 1987 380–1; 1992 384–5; 1997 396–8; 2001 404; 2005 410
Elton, Godfrey 158
Ensor, Sir Robert 73

Fabian Society 9, 14, 27, 32–4, 56, 159, 229, 234
family allowances 201
fascism 172, 219–20, 269, 273, 280, 283
Fawcett, Millicent 94
Fels, Joseph 144
Fenwick, Charles 36, 79
Fields, Terry 367

Fisher, Victor 115–16
Follett, Barbara 375
Foot, Isaac 9, 251, 361
Foot, Michael 9, 270, 283, 286, 293, 300, 302, 304, 304, 307–8, 356, 359, 381; opposes constitutional reform 335, 362; rise to leadership 346, 350, 361–2; as leader 363–74
Fraser, J. Lovat 159, 198
Freedom of Information Act 384
Friendly Societies 34–5
Frome 207, 247, 263, 265, 282
Fulham 235, 238, 251

Gaitskell, Hugh 8, 159, 229, 258, 286, 294, 299, 303, 306–7; as chancellor 298–9; as leader 309, 311, 314–15, 319–23
Gallagher, Willie 18
gambling 42, 154–5, 237–8, 292–3, 330–1
Gateshead 79, 95, 141–2, 151–2, 245, 248–9
General Strike 5, 153, 190–7
George V 155, 168, 169–70, 173, 176–7, 239
George VI 300
George, Henry 24
Gladstone, Herbert 63–4
Gladstone, W. E. 12, 15, 16–17, 82
Glasgow 129, 152–3, 164, 347, 383
Glasier, John Bruce 17, 25, 92–3
Gloucester 265
Golding, John 371
Gollancz, Victor 252
Goodman, Arnold 325
Gordon-Walker, Patrick 253, 290, 303, 320, 332–3
Gosling, Harry 22–3, 181
Gould, Joyce 377
Grant, Alexander 180

Grant, Ted 365, 369

Grayson, Victor 6–7, 19, 21, 69–70, 74, 77–8, 91, 104–5

Greater London Council *see* London County Council

Greene, Ben 236

Greenwood, Arthur xiii, 19, 136, 202, 221, 241, 245, 258, 260, 267, 274, 285

Grey, Sir Edward 100

Griffiths, Jim, 221, 223, 258, 332

Grimond, Jo 314, 323, 334

Grimsby 328–9

Guilty Men 270

Haldane, Richard 156, 174, 176–7

Halifax 46, 48, 62, 65

Hamilton, Mary Agnes 205–6

Harben, Henry 144

Hardie, James Keir 25, 27, 31, 36, 37, 48, 50, 226; and working-class hedonism 18, 57–8; and socialism 21, 24–5; and women's suffrage 18, 93; in Parliament 40–1, 43, 51, 55, 57–8, 60, 68, 81, 98; opposes First World War 100–2

Hastings, Sir Patrick 180–1

Hattersley, Roy 281, 331, 355, 372, 374, 386

Hatton, Derek 377–8

Hayward, Ron 346, 355, 360, 361, 369

Healey, Denis 286, 333, 353, 356–7, 361, 364, 365, 372

Heath, Edward 337–9, 344, 346, 348–9, 499–501

Heffer, Eric 377, 378

Henderson, Arthur 63, 81, 84, 97, 148, 174, 179, 202, 221; and Liberalism 52, 63; attacks Communists 130–1; and electoral organisation 51, 89, 140, 143–4; in First World War 101, 106, 108–9, 118–19, 122–3, 127; visits Russia 118–19, 121; promotes Party unity 192, 213–15

Herbison, Margaret 311

Hewitt, Patricia 375

Hobson, J. A. 104, 188

Hodge, John 63–4, 66–7, 105, 107, 109, 112, 115, 123, 125

Home, Sir Alec Douglas 326–7

Houghton, Douglas 313

House of Lords 14, 24, 74, 76, 78, 168, 173, 224, 289, 335, 384, 401

Huddersfield 46, 79

Hyndman, Henry 28, 30–1, 67, 105, 115

Independent Labour Party 5, 18,39, 43, 56, 77, 92, 165; foundation of 37–8; membership 38, 49, 72, 185; methods 38, 51, 142; weaknesses 44, 46, 48–9, 50–1; and socialism 38–9, 184–5, 188; seeks new strategy 49, 52; criticises Labour 68, 70–1, 80, 167; and First World War 101–2, 124; leaves Labour Party 78, 99, 218, 230

India 226, 227–8

Irish Home Rule 14, 31, 43, 50, 52, 80, 152

Irish Nationalists 25, 46, 69, 151–3

Irvine, Sir Arthur 360

Irvine, Lord 398

Islington 366, 368

Jarrow 68–9, 71, 75, 79, 219

Jay, Douglas 229, 230, 233, 294, 319

Jenkins, Hugh 330, 341, 349

Jenkins, Roy 8, 283, 286, 303, 319, 322, 333, 336, 339, 388, 399–400; detachment from Labour 342–3, 345–7, 352–4

Jews 72

Jewson, Dorothy 149, 201, 205–6
Jones, Jack (MP) 19, 54, 125, 127, 154, 226, 238
Jones, Jack (TGWU) 348, 356
Jobling, Wilf 249
Jowett, Fred 62, 107, 174

Kaufman, Gerald 367, 372, 378
Keep Left Group 293
Keynes and Keynesianism 187, 189, 206, 228, 230–4, 287–8, 315, 356–7, 366, 379
Kinnock, Neil 6, 374–7, 378–9, 380, 382, 385–6, 394
Kinnoull, Earl of 157
Kirkwood, David 164, 165, 167, 171, 184, 214, 218

Labour Party: **historiography:** ix-xi, 1–5, 10–11, 315; **chronological development:** foundation of 1, 54–5; recruits Conservatives 8–9, 12–13, 156–63, 175, 397; agrees Edwardian pact with Liberals 62–6, 68–70, 79–82, 89–90, 95–7, 116–17; recruits Liberals 155–6, 162; joins cabinet 108–10; and War Emergency Workers National Committee 107; adopts new strategy in 1918 116–20; adopts new constitution in 1918 120–22; and Clause IV 111, 120, 319, 322, 393; adapts to political system 76–7, 108–9, 155, 158–9, 167–9, 174–6, 289; accepts honours 169, 177–8, 180, 224, 400–01; forms first government in 1924 152, 162, 171–81, 192; forms second government 1929 208–14; reactions to 1931 crisis 217–18, 221–3, 228, 229; revises economic policy in 1930s 228–34; disapproves of hunger marches 219; and Liberal collaboration in 1930s 246–56; opposes Popular Front 218, 246–56; adopts collective security 239–40, 243–6; joins Churchill coalition 259–62, 264–9; manages wartime divisions 260, 264–5, 266–70; forms 1945–51 government 287–9, 290, 293–5, 298–9; and Cold War 293, 302–3, 305, 314; and Bevanite disputes 302–5; and consensus politics 305–7; and nuclear disarmament 319–20, 372, 374, 382; and Campaign for Democratic Socialism 320–3; forms 1964–70 governments 332–7, 339–40, 343–4; and Vietnam War 336, 341, 391; forms 1974–79 governments 356–60; and 1977 Liberal pact 358; and Campaign for Labour Party Democracy 346, 361; and rise of the left 342–3, 346, 352, 354–5, 360, 365–71, 376–7; and Militant 352, 365–9, 377–8; and New Labour 388–9, 395–6, 404, 406, 409, 411; forms 1997–2005 governments 401–3, 407–9; **organisation:** federal structure 8, 55, 217–18; membership 55, 62, 79, 85, 89, 95, 97–8, 120, 139–49, 146–7, 234–5, 262–3, 290, 310–11, 328, 340–1, 347, 376, 397–8, 410, 412; agents 51–2, 140, 143, 263–4, 311, 329; income 55, 62, 86–7, 98, 121, 140, 161–2, 195, 290, 311, 328, 344, 379, 398; constituency organisation 78, 89, 96, 121, 138–40, 161–2, 200, 203, 218, 235–8, 261–2, 265, 290–3, 309–11, 316, 328–32, 341, 347, 367–8; candidates 65, 78–9, 89–90, 97, 116, 121–2, 141–3, 282; composition of PLP 71, 139, 154, 155, 207, 286, 338, 350, 378, 381–2, 397; canvassing 51, 144, 329; public rallies 143–4, 181, 281, 300–1; 1918 Constitution 120–22; municipal dimension 89–90, 107, 133–4, 203, 239, 289, 335, 340, 404–5, 413; Constituency Parties Movement 236; view of polls and advertising 327–8, 371; new system for leadership elections 361, 363; and OMOV 376. 382, 386; de-selection of MPs 355–6, 367–9, 378–9; **ideological stance:** constitutional reform 2, 137 8, 168, 222–5, 288–9, 334–5; electoral reform 82–4, 118, 121–2, 210–11, 382–4, 400, 406; direct action 128–31, 370, 378; religion 2, 20–1, 25, 42, 71–2, 151–2, 159, 199; alcohol 17–19, 73–5, 113–14, 154, 231; free trade 9, 24, 29, 60, 165, 178, 216; socialism 9, 23–9, 43, 55, 65, 67, 70, 74, 91, 98–9, 110–12, 137, 145, 162–3, 166, 185–6, 188–90, 272–6, 308–9, 327, 348; planning 230–1, 274–5, 278, 283, 287–8; devaluation 294–5, 327, 333–4, 339, 340–1, 358–9, 382–4, 385, 405–6; income tax 297, 306, 379, 382; Tory-socialism 7, 12–13, 22, 28–30, 44–5, 47–8, 56–9, 63–4, 66–7, 72–5, 112–16, 125–7, 162–3, 226–7; Liberalism 9, 11, 24–5, 42, 44, 46–7, 49, 52, 57–8, 63, 76–7, 79, 104, 156, 162, 166, 172, 179–80, 210–11, 238–9; imperialism 56–7, 75, 225–8; monarchy 41, 168, 169–70, 176, 225; patriotism 13, 67, 75, 105–6, 124–5, 150, 198, 269, 280, 282; attitudes to First World War 100–7; pacifism 238, 243–4,

245; affluence 186, 302, 309, 315–17, 331; housing and home-ownership 10, 108, 136, 179, 186–7, 317–18, 374, 410; European Union 294, 322–3, 336, 339, 345–7, 349, 352, 362, 373, 379, 382; immigration 331–2, 337; conscription 75, 112–13; illiberalism 336–8, 354, 366, 391, 406–7, 408–9; devolution 335, 347–8, 358, 383, 405–6; Scottish nationalism 223–4, 340, 347–8, 358–9, 383, 405–6; Welsh nationalism 223, 340, 406; impact of Thatcherism 357, 366–7, 370, 379–80, 387–8, 395, 397, 412; **links with social groups**: women 4–5, 95, 120–1, 146–9, 198–203, 236, 252, 284, 297, 301, 311–13, 316–17, 337, 339, 341, 388, 397; women's suffrage 82, 92–6, 117–18; women MPs 148–9, 203–6, 221, 236–7, 311–13, 388; trade unions 7, 22–3, 27, 47–9, 53–4, 70–1, 86–7, 98–9, 120–1, 139–41, 179, 191–2, 195–9, 203–6, 213, 221, 235, 321, 328, 343–4, 348–9, 352, 355–8, 361, 365, 379, 381–2, 393, 398–9, 412; middle-class vote 284, 285, 297, 381, 393, 397, 410; troops 124, 150–1, 271–2, 282; youth 69, 241, 284, 298, 317, 341, 342, 366, 369; *see also* British Workers League, Catholics, Communist Party, Co-operative Societies, *Daily Mirror*, elections, General Strike, Independent Labour Party, nationalisation, Nonconformists, parliamentary reform, Popular Front, Social Democratic Party
Lambeth 237, 238, 247–8, 365
Lancashire 9, 10, 38, 44–5, 59, 66–7, 72, 125

land reform 24, 76, 156

Lansbury, George 18, 23, 25, 44, 52, 126–7, 130, 134, 136–7, 171, 174, 177, 209, 220, 226, 237; and women's suffrage 89–90, 93–4; resigns leadership 240

Laski, Harold 145, 159, 186, 223–4, 266, 277, 281–2

Lawrence, Susan 137, 149, 155, 157, 159, 161, 200, 203–4, 236

Lawther, Will 302–3, 304

League of Nations Union 146, 245

Lee, Jennie 200, 201, 204, 264, 312, 313, 318, 337

Leeds 71–2

Lees-Smith, H. B. 156

Left Book Club 229, 247, 251–2, 253

Leicester 65, 96–7

Lestor, Joan 358, 370

Levy, Lord 398, 402

Lewisham 284, 291–2, 304, 316, 330

Lib-Labs 35–6, 38, 52

Liberal Democrats 372–3, 380–1, 383–4, 399–400, 403–5, 410

Liberal Party and Liberalism 2, 9, 10, 12, 16–17, 24, 27–8, 32, 35–6, 48, 50, 52, 64–5, 106, 112, 145, 208, 234, 301, 363–4; and Liberal revivals 314, 323, 347, 349, 351, 360

Listowel, Earl of 157, 158

Liverpool 9, 20, 45, 71, 72, 153, 207, 237, 238, 365, 367, 377–8

Lloyd George, David 12, 76, 81, 104, 109, 116–17, 119, 122, 131, 133, 152, 180, 206–7

local government 15, 23, 38–9, 74, 108

Logan, David 153, 237

London 6, 21–3, 43, 45, 73, 116, 126–7, 134–5, 151, 207, 235–6, 237, 261, 285

London County Council 39, 239, 330, 340

Londonderry, Edith 167

Luton 316

Macarthur, Mary 146–8

MacLean, John 18

MacDonald, J. Ramsay x, 17, 25, 31, 34, 48–9, 52, 93, 95, 187, 205; and Labour's evolution 9, 34, 49, 68, 80–3, 90, 96–7, 104, 119–20, 156, 172; and socialism 60–1, 166, 188–9; as Secretary 55, 60–2; as MP 65, 81; and 1903 Pact 62–5, 68–70, 78, 90; and aristocracy 61, 167; as leader 81, 101, 165–6, 169; opposes First World War 100–1, 103–4, 109; recovers reputation 128, 164–5; as orator 143, 165–6, 181; and first Labour Government 171–81; and trade unions 166, 179, 192, 213, 221; forms second Labour Government 208–14; leads National Government 214–15

Macmillan, Harold 254, 258, 280, 284, 306, 314, 322–3, 325–6

Macmillan, Hugh 159, 173

Magee, Bryan 320, 368

Major, John 384–5, 396

Manchester 39, 44, 66–7, 72, 102, 284–5, 367

Mandelson, Peter 375, 388, 395–6

Mann, Jean 286, 304

Mann, Tom 36, 42, 44, 53, 88 130

Manning, Leah 204, 237, 313

Marx, Karl 16, 20, 24, 26

Maxton, Jimmy 164, 169, 171, 184, 188, 212, 218

Mayhew, Christopher 319, 363

Meacher, Michael 375

Mead, James 229, 230

Mellish, Bob 369–70

Merton and Morden 235, 247, 261, 262–3

Middleton, Jim 107

Mikado, Ian 262, 275, 279, 286, 290, 293, 302, 315, 329, 331, 359

Miliband, Ralph 5

Milner, Viscount 33, 56, 114

Money, Sir Leo 156

Monckton, Walter 306–7

Morel, E. D. 103, 156, 165

Morris, William 28, 30

Morrison, Herbert 2, 7, 18, 29, 101, 134, 167, 211, 255–6; and Party organisation 6, 116, 134–5, 235, 239, 261; and the Constitution 138, 222; and anti-Communism 132, 247–8, 249; and national-isation 232; bids for leadership 241, 277, 309; in Second World War 258, 260, 268, 269, 274–5, 277, 280, 284; in Attlee Government 286, 288–9, 295, 300

Mortimer, Jim 371, 372

Mosley, Lady Cynthia 157–8, 160, 197, 205

Mosley, Sir Oswald 8, 157–8, 160–3, 187–8, 196–7, 211–13, 220, 268

Mullin, Chris 367

Murray, Alexander 80–1

Mussolini, Benito 244, 265

National Democratic Party 116, 122

National Government 214–15, 228, 234, 239, 240, 243, 257

National Unemployed Workers Movement 219

National Union of Societies for Equal Citizenship 202

National Union of Women's Suffrage Societies 92, 94–6

nationalisation 46, 111, 113–14, 185–6, 230–2, 287–8, 295–6, 348, 379

Nellist, Dave 367

New Zealand 226–7

Newbold, Walter 132, 212

Newcastle-upon-Tyne 15, 52, 70, 92, 142, 311, 341

News Chronicle 225, 250, 251, 253, 257, 270, 281

newsreels 279–80

Noel-Baker, Philip 156, 250, 256, 329, 330, 342

Nonconformists 11, 17, 18, 19–21, 71, 154–5, 237

O'Grady, James 71, 105, 107, 112–13, 115

O'Halloran, Michael 368

Oldham 89

Orange Order 45, 153

Osborne, W. V. 86

Owen, David 8, 347, 352, 359, 361, 381

Oxford 252–3, 374

Palmer, Arthur 368–9

Pankhurst, Christabel 92–3, 126

Pankhurst, Emmeline 39, 46, 92

Pankhurst, Richard 39, 45–6, 92

Parker, James 62, 65, 102, 109

parliamentary reform 3–4, 14–15, 51–2, 84–5, 117–18, 198, 342

Parmoor, Lord 8, 157, 159, 174, 209

Plaid Cymru 335, 340, 358

Peace Ballot 245

Peters, Arthur 89

Phillips, Marion 120–1, 147, 202, 205–6

Phillips, Morgan 279–80, 295, 296, 303, 311, 315

Pickard, Ben 36

Picton-Turbervil, Edith 2–1, 205

Pole, Major Graham 144, 150, 159, 161, 168, 227–8

Pollitt, Harry 130, 132, 247

Ponsonby, Arthur 103, 156, 165
Pontypridd 291
Poor Law 15, 23, 26, 39, 136–7
Popular Front 5–6, 238–9, 242, 246–56
Powell, Enoch 335, 337, 349
Prentice, Reg 352, 355–6, 363
Prescott, John 393
Preston 44–5, 58, 63–4, 106, 125, 200, 298
Priestley, J. B. 270–1
proportional representation see Labour Party
protectionism 9, 12, 26, 29, 48, 60, 171
Profumo scandal 325–6
Putney 330, 341

Ramsay, A. H. M. 273
Rathbone, Eleanor 201
Reid, John 7, 375, 401, 407
Roberts, G. H. 82, 108, 115
Roberts, Robert 20, 97, 109
Roberts, Wilfrid 250, 252
Rodgers, William 320, 324, 363
Rowse, A. L. 222, 246, 253
Royce, W. Stapleton 157, 160, 227

St Helens 45, 66
Saklatvala, Shapurgi 132
Salford 20, 37, 44, 72, 132, 304, 310, 367
Salter, Dr Alfred 73, 370
Sankey, John 157, 159, 166, 209, 214–15
Scargill, Arthur 376
Scotland 24–5, 223–4, 248, 254, 370, 410
Scottish National Party 223, 340, 347–8, 350–1, 383–4
Seddon, J. A. 107, 115, 123
Sexton, James 20, 71, 72, 154, 168, 169
Shackleton, David 18, 62–3, 77, 169
Shaw, George Bernard 32, 37, 56, 144, 155

Shaw, Tom 106, 125, 174–5
Sheffield 48–9, 145, 195, 207, 310, 367
Shinwell, Emmanuel 165, 240, 266–7, 274, 302, 308
Silkin, John 361, 372, 378
Silverman, Sydney 336
Simmons, Jim 150
Sinclair, Sir Archibald 234, 250, 252, 253
Skelton, Noel 187
Smethwick 73, 123, 161, 197, 332
Smith, Herbert 190–1, 192, 195
Smith, John 382, 386, 392, 393
Snowden, Ethel 147, 167
Snowden, Philip 19, 20–1, 51, 57, 66, 82, 95, 123, 154, 213, 215; views on economics 136, 189, 233; as chancellor 174, 178, 209–10
Social Democratic Federation 14, 23–4, 30–2, 49, 61, 70, 75
Social Democratic Party 347, 356, 363–4
socialism 10, 17, 23–9, 33–4, 80, 145, 162–3, 110–12, 185–6, 272–5; see also Labour Party
Socialist National Defence Committee 115
Society for Socialist Inquiry and Propaganda 229
Sorensen, Reginald 182, 215, 226, 282, 307, 333
Southampton 48–9, 182
Spanish Civil War 237, 245–6
Stanton, C. B. 102, 115
Steel, David 336, 352, 358, 363
Steel-Maitland, Sir Arthur 113–14, 198
Strachey, John 157, 158, 160, 163, 187, 197–8, 213; and economic policy 228–9, 233
Strauss, Arthur 157, 160

Strauss, George 157, 161, 237, 247–8, 252, 255, 262
Straw, Jack 383
Summerskill, Edith 221, 237, 251, 304, 311, 313
Sunderland 89, 205–6, 237
Sutherland, Mary 313
Swansea 291, 329
syndicalism 87–8, 190

Taaffe, Peter 365, 369
Taff Vale 61–2, 65, 77, 86
Tatchell, Peter 366, 370
Taverne, Dick 320, 347, 363
temperance 18, 43, 74–5, 113
Temple, William 159
Thatcher, Margaret 358, 360, 371–3, 376, 379, 384, 403; see also Blair, Tony
Thomas, Jimmy 2, 7, 19, 21–2, 26, 111, 133, 154, 167–8, 174, 187, 209, 227; and the Constitution 170, 222; supports First World War 105, 109, 112–13, 119, 125
Thomson, C. B. 150, 174
Thorne, Will 29, 53–4, 75, 107, 127
Thurtle, Ernest 154, 202
Tillett, Ben 7, 19, 21, 23, 37–8, 46–7, 50, 53, 70, 74–5, 88, 102, 115
Todd, Ron 356
Trade Union Act (1913) 86–7,121
trade unions 10, 34–6, 52–3, 85–8, 106–7, 121, 129–301, 179, 194, 220, 234, 262, 306, 340, 361; see also General Strike, Labour Party, Trades Union Congress, Triple Alliance
Trades Disputes and Trade Union Act (1927) 194–5, 290
Trades Union Congress 36, 51, 82, 116, 130, 145, 190–1, 213, 229, 233, 343–4

Tressell, Robert 9, 26
Trevelyan, Sir Charles 103, 142, 156, 161, 165, 174, 228, 244, 247, 255, 262
Tribune 247, 304
Triple Alliance 88, 129, 133, 190
Turner, Ben 38, 169

Underhill, Reg 352, 355
Union of Democratic Control 103–4, 157

Wake, Egerton 138, 156
Walden, Brian 320, 355
Wales 223–4, 359
Wall, Pat 367
Walsh, Stephen 109, 115, 117, 174
Wansbeck 139
Wardle, G. H. 77, 117
Warr, Countess de la 144
Warr, Earl de la 157, 173
Warwick, Countess of 27, 61, 161
Webb, Beatrice 32, 34, 92, 98, 110, 167, 233
Webb, Sidney 32, 33, 106, 111, 155, 162, 165, 174, 186, 227, 232
Wedgwood Benn, William 9, 156, 209, 228
West Ham 39, 51, 73, 127, 138
Whately, Monica 201, 312
White, Eirene 311, 312, 313
Whiteley, William 161–2
Whitty, Larry 375, 378
Wigan 45, 72, 125
Wigg, George 264, 295, 325–6, 339–40
Wilkinson, Ellen 148–9, 204, 221, 311
Williams, Len 311, 344
Williams, Marcia 324–5, 351
Williams, Shirley 337, 352, 363, 389
Wilmot, John 238, 283

Wilson, Harold 286, 288, 294, 299, 302, 319, 355–6; and report on organisation 309–11; rise to leadership 321–2; as Leader of the Opposition 324–7; as prime minister (1964–70) 332–7, 339–40, 343–4; as prime minister (1974–76) 350–2; declining reputation 339, 341, 344–5, 347, 349; resignation 352–3
Wilson, J. Havelock 37, 39, 107
Wilson, John 36, 79
Women's Co-operative Guild 146, 202
Women's Institutes 148
Women's Liberation Movement 337, 341–2

Woodcock, George 343–4
Woolwich 44, 63, 73, 127, 164, 236, 263
Wootton, Barbara 229
working class 2–4, 10–11, 15–17, 19–20, 22–3, 84–5, 114, 154–5, 187, 220, 315, 361, 374, 392, 398
Wyatt, Woodrow 271, 363

XYZ Club 229

Yorkshire 44, 46–8

Zilliacus, Koni 273, 274, 304, 321
Zinoviev Letter 6, 182–3, 193